Fifth Edition

FAMILIES, SCHOOLS, AND COMMUNITIES

BUILDING PARTNERSHIPS FOR EDUCATING CHILDREN

Chandler Barbour
Towson University, Emeritus

Nita H. Barbour
University of Maryland, Baltimore County, Emerita

Patricia A. Scully
University of Maryland, Baltimore County

Boston Columbus Indianapolis New York San Francisco Upper Saddle River
Amsterdam Cape Town Dubai London Madrid Milan Munich Paris Montreal Toronto
Delhi Mexico City Sao Paulo Sydney Hong Kong Seoul Singapore Taipei Tokyo

Vice President and Editor in Chief: Jeffery W. Johnston
Senior Acquisitions Editor: Julie Peters
Editorial Assistant: Tiffany Bitzel
Vice President, Director of Marketing: Quinn Perkson
Marketing Manager: Erica DeLuca
Senior Managing Editor: Pamela D. Bennett
Production Editor: Kerry Rubadue
Project Manager: Susan Hannahs

Senior Art Director: Jayne Conte
Cover Designer: Suzanne Duda
Photo Coordinator: Carol Sykes
Cover Art: Getty Images
Composition: Aptara®, Inc.
Full-Service Project Management: Ravi Bhatt/ Aptara®, Inc.
Printer/Bindery: Hamilton Printing Co.
Cover Printer: Lehigh-Phoenix Color
Text Font: Palatino

Every effort has been made to provide accurate and current Internet information in this book. However, the Internet and information posted on it are constantly changing, so it is inevitable that some of the Internet addresses listed in this textbook will change.

Photo Credits: Bettmann/Corbis, p. 49; Anne Vega/Merrill, pp. 53, 93, 127; Anthony Magnacca/Merrill, pp. 64, 272, 279, 323; Belle Kuhn, p. 240; Chad Turgeon, p. 108; Chandler Barbour, p. 43; Corbis—NY, p. 35; David Kuhn, p. 31; David Mager/Pearson Learning Photo Studio, pp. 103, 143, 168; George Dodson/ PH College, p. 207; Getty Images, Inc.—PhotoDisc, p. 331; Greg Mekras, pp. 28, 246, 318; iStockphoto.com, pp. 5, 9, 20, 67, 80, 97, 175, 215, 222, 262, 292; James D. Caldwell, p. 123; Jennifer Turgeon, pp. 7, 72, 138, 210; Karen Turner, pp. 15, 228, 248; Ken Karp/PH College, p. 115; Kevin Bennett/Bangor Daily News, p. 299; Krista Greco/Merrill, p. 140; Laima Druskis/PH College, p. 310; Larry Hamill/Merrill, p. 267; Lewis W. Hine/Getty Images Inc.—Hulton Archive Photos, p. 38; Lori Whitley/Merrill, p. 306; Marian Fowler, pp. 83, 100, 182, 202, 232; Merrill, p. 152; Patricia A. Scully, pp. 1, 23, 56, 109, 117, 120, 146, 149, 154, 157, 162, 194, 289; Photos to Go, pp. 86, 197, 221, 250, 256, 260, 302, 327; Scott Cunningham/Merrill, pp. 25, 46, 284, 296; Stephen M. Katz/Bangor Daily News, p. 237; Steven Barbour, pp. 132, 170; SW Productions/Getty Images, Inc.—PhotoDisc/Royalty Free, p. 188; Teri Stratford/PH College, p. 59; Tony Freeman/PhotoEdit, Inc., p. 76; Travis Caldwell, p. 173.

Library of Congress Cataloging-in-Publication Data

Barbour, Chandler
 Families, schools, and communities : building partnerships for educating children / Chandler Barbour, Nita H. Barbour, Patricia A. Scully. —5th ed.
  p. cm.
 ISBN-13: 978-0-13-703546-5
 ISBN-10: 0-13-703546-2
  1. Community and school—United States. 2. School environment—United States. 3. Students—United States—Social conditions. 4. Education—Curricula—United States. 5. Child development—United States. I. Barbour, Nita. II. Scully, Patricia A. III. Title.
 LC225.3.B27 2011
 371.19—dc22
                                                                      2009050186

10 9 8 7 6 5

PEARSON

www.pearsonhighered.com

ISBN 10:   0-13-703546-2
ISBN 13: 978-0-13-703546-5

We dedicate this edition to Valerie Mekras and to Steven Barbour, our children, and to their wonderful partners, Greg Mekras and Tom Ponti.—CB/NHB

I dedicate this edition to the children, parents, teachers, and staff of W. T. Page Elementary School in Silver Spring, Maryland. Through hard work and collaboration, they have created a wonderful community of learners.—PS

PREFACE

This fifth edition of *Families, Schools, and Communities: Building Partnerships for Educating Children* provides teachers and teacher candidates with a comprehensive guide to establishing effective collaboration with parents and the larger community. This book will help future teachers develop the understanding and tools they need to work with others to give children a better education. The underlying message of this book is that all persons involved in early childhood education or child advocacy should join hands in promoting the highest quality of education for young children in America.

All readers know that education of children is one of the biggest concerns in our country. Political figures at all levels, the general public, and many social agencies wonder if our schools are going in the best direction. This concern is not new, of course. Questions about educational reform have existed for generations, but today's challenges include funding, evaluation, and management issues as well as curricular matters.

Our book presents the argument that strong educational programs are best achieved when school personnel work carefully with children's families and the surrounding community. Too often the social settings of school, home, and community pull in different directions when successful collaboration on an agreed-upon objective is the most effective answer.

The notion of agency collaboration in many ventures has moved to the forefront in the last two decades. We now find partnerships emerging in welfare and health programs, in environmental and urban development programs, and in courts and incarceration programs. President Barack Obama's administration has moved the issue of cooperative and collaborative action to center stage. It is a good time to forge new relationships between schools, families, and communities.

The authors have witnessed and participated in joint educational ventures that rested on collaborative actions. We are convinced of the merit of partnerships and have seen its positive outcomes. We also are aware of the challenges and the hard work required of teachers as they take the lead in establishing relationships with parents and the community. Educators must get to know their colleagues and school administrators as well as the families and community members related to their school. They must be open to learning about different cultures, economic situations, and the problems of everyday life that families face. To that end, this book presents a lot of information on parents' circumstances and the challenges they face in raising children and earning a living in the United States today.

In this book, we make sure that the reader is well acquainted with the many influences focused on young children from all sides, because these affect the child's interests and readiness to learn. We also present a case for the beyond-the-school curriculum that so often gets lost in our concerns for school objectives. With good planning, teachers can make education more effective for children by uniting and using the reservoir of outside help in homes and community. In other words, this book makes a case for a "school and beyond" curriculum for young children.

A basic tenet of *Families, Schools, and Communities: Building Partnerships for Educating Children* is that schools will always be a primary setting for educating the young child. We also believe that educators must be in the forefront of any endeavor to bring about change. The authors stress that to meet the significant new responsibilities of 21st-century schools, all child care programs and educational districts must develop vibrant partnerships—uniting parents and community members with teachers in educating tomorrow's citizens. Schools are where the action will bloom, but respectful collaboration is the key to success.

Significant steps for improving children's education through collaboration and partnership are already being taken in schools and communities across the United States. A growing number of research studies, controlled assessments, and personal accounts support new partnership approaches. The authors salute all these efforts. We maintain that most schools do not need to reconceptualize curricula or most of their current teaching practices. The big job now is to study and adapt the amazing examples that already exist to fit the needs of individual programs, schools and communities. This book aims to help readers learn how to do just that.

NEW TO THE FIFTH EDITION

Overall Changes

- The new feature *Implications for Teachers* highlights strategies and bridges theory and practical application. This feature appears several times in each chapter and conveys, in an informal way, practical suggestions and examples of how the content applies to real-world situations.
- We have omitted the chapter on school curriculum and integrated suitable parts of that chapter into other chapters.
- There is greater focus on children in the first 5 years: infants, toddlers, and preschoolers.
- We have rearranged topics to give this book greater coherence and usability.
- We have updated references and resources throughout the book, as well as streamlined research citations, to provide smoother reading.
- New vignettes and figures have been provided throughout the book, and many existing figures and tables have been updated. We have renamed some chapters to reflect changes in content, and in the references section we have grouped references by chapter.

Specific Changes

Particular additions and modifications for the individual chapters are as follows:

Chapter 1. This chapter has been streamlined to provide a clear introduction to the three social settings—home, school, and community—and makes the case for the importance of collaboration. The section on media has been expanded to include a focus on the new media and their influence on children.

Chapter 2. Family systems theory and the work of Murray Bowen are introduced in this chapter and further developed in Chapter 4. We have updated information on understanding infants and preschool children, and we have presented Orfield's concerns with resegregation in American schools.

Chapter 3. The figures and tables on demographic material have been updated to reflect the increasing diversity of families in the United States. We have also added coverage of single-parent families, especially those headed by single mothers by choice. Particular attention has been given throughout the chapter to helping prospective teachers understand the dimensions of diversity and how to work successfully with the various types of families they'll encounter in their work.

Chapter 4. This chapter features Family Systems Theory as a way to help teachers understand how families function. We have also expanded the section on family features in various cultures in regard to infant care, physical contact, and family roles. Additional content has been added to help readers appreciate the uniqueness of each family and the way culture, economics, and family roles contribute to family diversity.

Chapter 5. This chapter has been expanded to include more detailed information on infant and toddler care. A table on age group categories and recommended group size and staff-child ratios has been added. Particular emphasis has been placed on how teachers can help families recognize and obtain quality child care.

Chapter 6. The focus of this chapter has shifted to working with the families of children with disabilities as well as with the children themselves. To that end, new sections have been added on sustaining parents of children with disabilities and helping parents find support and respite services. A new table has been included that provides regular education teachers with strategies for working with children with disabilities. A new figure features ideas for parents on helping children complete their homework.

Chapter 7. We have added content on protecting children's health and information on substance abuse and sexual abuse. There is also coverage of social issues that involve prejudice, bullying, and media exploitation of children.

Chapter 8. This chapter includes added information on sibling relationships and gender identification, as well as new concerns that families have about Internet use and other media. We have introduced new content on economics and money issues for children, as well as a focus on conservation and recycling as part of education.

Chapter 9. The idea of different environments in a child's community and the impact of children's play in natural settings have been expanded in this chapter. Information has also been added on human structures in a community's physical makeup. We have introduced ideas on using community newspapers in education, and we show the values of using community mentors with young children.

Chapter 10. A new title emphasizing how to establish and maintain collaborative relationships makes this chapter even more practical and useful to students. We have introduced new information on understanding cultural differences and possible barriers to involvement. We also have provided strategies to use with units on diversity. A survey to help teachers make contact with outside helpers and collaborators and information about the National Parent–Teacher Association have also been added.

Chapter 11. We have included one additional model program and streamlined coverage of other collaborative programs that are still being used successfully in the United States.

The Appendix. We updated the children's books in this substantial list of books for use with children on specific issues. New sections on bullying, intolerance, sexuality, child health, and child care issues have been added as well.

ORGANIZATION OF THIS BOOK

We begin this book with an overview of the powerful influences surrounding all young children in America. Together with this, we identify the three primary contexts of home life, school life, and community life and discuss how these social settings interplay to affect children's lives. Society does change, of course, and some forces influencing children have intensified in recent years. We categorize these influence patterns so that readers will gain a better perspective of the situation in the United States today.

Chapter 2 focuses on (a) how responsibilities for children's education emerged over time, (b) the range of philosophies and perspectives that have appeared in American education, and (c) how different ethnic groups in the United States have been affected educationally for more than three centuries. We look particularly at the uneven progress of collaborations associated with schoolwork.

Chapters 3 and 4 present information on U.S. family life, and we review various family patterns and clarify the different ways in which families function. This information helps prospective teachers grasp the range of situations that professionals encounter as they work with children in a diverse society. Our hope is that readers will appreciate our urging of more collaborations in light of this diversity.

Chapter 5 is devoted to the expansion of out-of-home care programs for the millions of preschool-age children as well as young school-age children. Far more mothers have joined the American workforce and must now find adequate care for their preschool-age children and their in-school children who need care during after-school hours. We discuss the various child-care arrangements and practices as well as the agency-directed preschool programs that a growing number of young children encounter.

Chapter 6 focuses on the need in both schools and communities for an inclusive program for children with disabilities. Ensuring the optimal growth and development of children with disabilities is a responsibility shared by their families, schools, and community agencies, and in this chapter, we examine the issues from the perspectives of parents, teachers, and other professionals.

Chapter 7 examines the responsibilities and expectations society maintains for parents and professionals in protecting and enhancing the education of children in the three social settings. In this chapter, we point out the various educational assignments and expectations that each setting places on the others.

Chapters 8 and 9 deal with the extensive but informal curriculum in homes and communities. Curriculum surrounds children, and although we do not always take notice of it, much of what children learn comes from the world outside the classroom. The reader must recognize that all citizens are educators and that when teachers acknowledge this, an even greater potential for learning exists.

The last two chapters focus on the possibilities for collaboration among the three social settings. In Chapter 10, we offer many practical suggestions for ways teachers, parents, and others can work together. Chapter 11 examines the demanding and often difficult process of merging the efforts of people interested in collaboration. In this final chapter, we present eight successful models that demonstrate collaboration. We believe that these time-tested programs can provide helpful examples for agencies and communities seeking to establish healthy partnerships.

The Appendix presents an extensive bibliography of children's books to help make the family, school, and community diversity presented in this book more realistic.

SPECIAL FEATURES

To assist instructors and students using this book, we have included several pedagogical aids.

Chapter Objectives, Summaries, and Questions

Concise statements of each chapter's main ideas serve as advance organizers for the content that follows. A chapter summary reviews the highlights of the content in each chapter. Each chapter ends with questions and activities that give instructors another means to make the text applicable to their course outlines and to students' lives. For students, the activities will help apply concepts presented and will stimulate reflection and discussion on the reading as well as on their own experiences.

Vignettes

Stories of real-life events that we have encountered clarify many concepts presented throughout the chapters. The children in the vignettes represent families from a wide range of ethnic and socioeconomic groups who live in a variety of geographic areas. These personal stories (except the names used) are all from our experiences and give a human connection to the chapter's information and purpose.

Reflections

Each chapter contains several reflections that ask readers to pause and connect particular content to their own life experiences.

Implications for Teachers

This new feature provides connections between the ideas related in the chapter and their application in classrooms and schools.

Resources

No book can give comprehensive coverage of the diverse topics included here for either community workers or teacher candidates. All instructors will supplement this content with their specialized knowledge, particular readings, and projects. We provide a small list of key organizations and agencies that relate to our profession, as well as Web sites that give current information and status reports for our chapter features.

Figures and Tables

Throughout the book, we have encapsulated text content in a table or a figure for review or, in some cases, to translate pieces of information.

Bibliography of Children's Literature

The selections in the Appendix present valuable examples of children in different family arrangements learning in a variety of settings. This updated bibliography provides instructors, as well as in-service teachers and other professionals, with curriculum material to illuminate the chapter content. It will be particularly valuable for Chapters 3 to 9.

Glossary

Because the book draws from sociology, psychology, human development, and anthropology as well as from pedagogy and curriculum content, we include a glossary to help readers with specialized terms.

SUPPLEMENTS

The following instructor tools supplement support and reinforce the content presented throughout the book. All supplements are available for download for instructors who adopt this book. Go to www.pearsonhighered.com, click on Educators, register for access, and download files. For more information, contact your Pearson representative.

Online Instructor's Manual

The Instructor's Manual extends the activities, questions, and overviews from each chapter to provide professors with additional practical application.

Online Test Bank

The Test Bank includes essay, multiple-choice, and true/false test questions to assess student understanding of chapter concepts. An Answer Key is provided.

Online PowerPoint Slides

The PowerPoint slides can work in conjunction with the Instructor's Manual to summarize key chapter concepts.

Pearson MyTest

Pearson MyTest is a powerful assessment generation program that helps instructors easily create and print quizzes and exams. Questions and tests are written online, allowing ultimate flexibility and the ability to efficiently create and print assessments anytime, anywhere!

To access Pearson MyTest and your test bank files, simply go to www.pearsonmytest. com to log in, register, or request access.

Features of Pearson MyTest include:

Premium Assessment Content

- Draw from a rich library of assessments that complement your Pearson textbook and your course's learning objectives.
- Edit questions or tests to fit your specific teaching needs.

Instructor-Friendly Resources

- Easily create and store your own questions, including images, diagrams, and charts, using simple drag-and-drop and Word-like controls.
- Use additional information provided by Pearson, such as the question's difficulty level or learning objective, to help you quickly build your test.

Time-Saving Enhancements

- Add headers or footers and easily scramble questions and answer choices—all from one simple toolbar.
- Quickly create multiple versions of your test or answer key and, when ready, simply save them in MS Word or PDF format and print them.
- Export your exams for import to Blackboard 6.0, CE (WebCT), or Vista (WebCT).

ACKNOWLEDGMENTS

We would like to thank the following individuals who reviewed the previous edition for their valuable input, which helped make this fifth edition a success: Angelo Alcala, North Lake College; Gail A. Guss, The Pennsylvania State University; Susan Johnson, Northern Virginia Community College; Christy Lleras, University of Illinois, Urbana-Champaign; Nicole Ramirez, The University of Texas at San Antonio; and Cheryl Williams-Jackson, Modesto Junior College.

BRIEF CONTENTS

CONTENTS

Chapter 5   **Meeting Child-Care Needs from Infancy Through School Age   120**

Chapter 9   **Curriculum of the Community   237**

CHAPTER 1

Home, School, and Community Influences on Children's Lives

*Getting to know children, their families, and communities in new ways
allows us to uncover funds of knowledge and networks of support so
we can honor and build from what children know.*

(LONG, ANDERSON, CLARK, & MCCRAW, 2008, P. 253)

After reading this chapter, you will be able to do the following:

- Discuss how the three social settings—home, school, and community—affect children's perceptions and attitudes about learning and their success at school.
- Explain how these three social settings have greater or lesser impact, depending on the child's age, the child's stage of development, and the social context.
- Identify some of the key issues facing children today and discuss how collaboration among the social settings is helping to address them.
- Describe the impact of professional development standards on preparing teachers and other professionals to work with families and the community more effectively.
- Give examples of the impact that special interest groups can have on children's perceptions of their world and on their behavior.
- Explain why collaboration between the social settings is essential for children's optimal learning and development.

As a beginning professional in the field of early care and education, you have undoubtedly studied child psychology, curriculum, and teaching methods to enable you to work successfully with the children in your future classroom. To succeed as a teacher, however, you also must develop skills in working with families and discover how to connect with the larger community. Although teachers and schools influence children's growth and development in significant ways, their learning, behaviors, and viewpoints are also affected by their families, members of the immediate community, and forces in the larger society. It is important for you to understand these other influences so that you can provide the most appropriate education for the children you will teach.

At one point in time, the family was the main socializing agent for children. Home and school were one and children learned from their parents, siblings, and others within the context of work at home and in the surrounding community. Over the years, however, school and community influences have increased dramatically. The purpose of this book is to help you understand how the social settings of the family, school, and community influence children in the 21st century and how you, as an educator, can help promote **collaboration** among the three settings. Today, strong collaboration is needed to resolve the challenging issues facing children in our increasingly diverse country.

This chapter provides an overview of the three social settings and their influences on children's development. It also serves as an introduction to topics that will be covered in more depth in the succeeding chapters.

Zach was waiting impatiently at the child-care center for his mother to pick him up. He looked in his "cubbie" for the transformer toy—a gift from his father during last week's visit. Zach picked up the red and blue semitruck from his backpack, where he had left it on arriving at the center, and approached Kelsey, who was also waiting for her mother. He grinned, and in his deepest voice he said, "I'm warning you, if you don't tell me where you planted the Decepticons, I'm going to transform you into Optimus Prime," and he lunged at Kelsey. "No, I won't tell. We'll all blow up," giggled Kelsey, entering into the play and holding up her fists to Zach as he deftly changed the truck into a monster. The children jabbed at each other, growling and hissing, until Zach accidentally struck Kelsey's head, and Kelsey began to cry. At that moment, Zach's mother and the teacher entered the room. The teacher, calming Kelsey, said to Zach's mother, "We don't allow aggressive play here at the center. I really wish you wouldn't let Zach bring toys like that."

In spite of Zach's attempt to explain what had happened, his tired mother, while she got ready to go out, informed him that he couldn't watch television that evening. When they reached home, she let Zach select The Three Billy Goats Gruff and Max's Dragon Shirt to read while he waited for his father to pick him up. When Tom, Zach's mother's boyfriend, arrived, Zach asked him to read. As Tom got to the first little goat crossing the bridge, Zach exclaimed, "Oh, let me read the troll part," and pulling the book closer, asked, "Is this where the troll speaks?"

"Yeah, how did you know?" Tom exclaimed.

Zach replied, "Dad told me," and then, in a gruff "pretend read" voice, demanded, "Who's that tramping on my bridge?" At each goat's passing, his voice got gruffer, and he clenched his fist as he told the goats he was going to eat them up. When the third goat passed, Tom, in character, gave Zach a gentle push, hugging and tickling him as the "goat" pushed the troll into the river. Zach giggled and said, "Let's read it again, and I'll be the goats this time." When Zach got to the third goat part, he butted Tom, who pulled Zach off the couch with him, "falling into the river." A bit of horseplay ensued. Zach then got up and said, "Now, let's read Max's Dragon Shirt. You know, I'm gonna ask my dad to buy me a dragon shirt like that. Isn't it wild?"

The messages children receive from their surroundings are not always consistent, but they still influence attitudes and values. One can't be sure, for example, exactly what Zach is internalizing. His father bought him a transformer toy that represents aggression, but the child-care center bans violent toys. In spite of the ban, his friend Kelsey seems to share in his "aggressive-acting behavior," at least until she is hurt. Zach's mother attempts to reinforce the school's non-aggression policy by forbidding him to watch television temporarily and by suggesting a more passive activity. Still, Zach finds acceptance of his need to express aggression by reenacting a story with his mother's friend and engaging in horseplay.

Children like Zach, who are being raised by parents who are separated or divorced, may receive very different messages about issues such as violence. The media also play a role in the development of toys for young children, but these toys are based on movies with PG-13 ratings. Perhaps Zach even attended the transformer movie with his dad, a movie that his mother might not be comfortable having him see. Conflicting messages from family members, teachers, peers, and the larger society underscore the complexity of influences on children as they grow and develop.

It appears that Zach has gotten a more consistent message about reading from those close to him. Reading appears to be fun for Zach. People answer his questions about the text and respond to his reactions to the story. Though his mother denied him television that day, she allowed him to select books to entertain himself.

As a teacher, you cannot ensure that all the influences impacting children are positive or consistent, so you must be sensitive to the idea that children's learning will be affected both positively and negatively by many factors beyond your control. You must also be attuned to your own feelings and reactions, as these, too, affect children's growth. As you identify the strengths of **family**, media, and community influences, you should strive to build on these qualities. Figure 1-1 shows you the influence of home, school, and community experiences on the typical young child today.

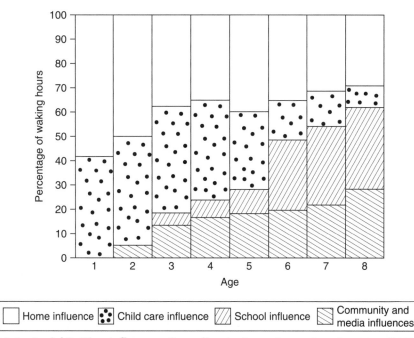

FIGURE 1-1   Social Setting Influences According to Age   *Source:* Based on Berns (2009), Douville-Watson and Watson (2002), and Woolfolk (2009).

Note: Percentages show the waking-hours experience of composite American children. The increasing influence of school and community relates to other factors in addition to age—for example, stage of development, location, family socioeconomic status, and extent of contact.

CHILDREN'S PERCEPTIONS AND ATTITUDES

Parents, teachers, and community members all play an essential role in helping to socialize children to the values and customs of the larger society (Vygotsky, 1978). For example, at early ages, children are aware of their family's and community's attitudes regarding education, other cultures, racial or religious groups, and roles that males and females play in society (Ramsey, 2004). As you will learn in Chapter 3, the cultural background, family configuration, and economic situation of the family are all important factors in determining a child's perceptions and attitudes.

Attitudes determine what individuals attend to in a situation, how they perceive the situation, and even their response to the event. Therefore, children acquire certain attitudes by hearing words, observing actions, and surmising the feelings of significant others in their environment. These attitudes then become more firm when children are encouraged to express such beliefs. However, as children become aware of different values and beliefs, they may modify their attitudes and can even help to change those of adults. Through social interaction, both adults and children can influence each other's perceptions and attitudes.

Home Influence on Attitudes and Perceptions

Children's attitudes and perceptions emerging from home influences develop early. Family members communicate verbally and nonverbally to their young children how they feel about themselves and their neighbors and about their schools and community.

Mrs. Kohl was astonished when her 3-year-old, Brittany, spat at Mrs. Foster, an older woman living upstairs in their building. Mrs. Kohl didn't remember that the day before, when Mrs. Foster knocked at the apartment door, she had told her husband not to answer, saying, "I'm tired of the old hag coming around, nosing in our business, and always borrowing something. I feel like spitting, she annoys me so." When Brittany's mother took her to her room as punishment, the child said defiantly, "I spit. She old hag."

At this point, it may be just Mrs. Foster that Brittany has antipathy for, but continued negative attitudes expressed by her parents and others toward older persons will affect the child's acceptance of and attitude toward the presence and the authority of older persons. If Mrs. Foster displays friendliness and kindness toward Brittany, however, she may modify the child's perception of her and perhaps influence Brittany's mother to feel differently, as well.

Parents' attitudes and feelings toward school will influence their children's feelings in a similar way. The annual Phi Delta Kappa/Gallup polls (Rose & Gallup, 2008) over the past 30 years show that on the whole, Americans value their local schools and have confidence in them. On the other hand, we find vast differences throughout the country in individuals' faith in schooling in general. Parents communicate this faith, or lack thereof, to their children and thus influence how their children react to their teachers, their learning experiences, and even attending school.

A few years later, Mrs. Kohl and her neighbor, Mrs. Reed, received letters stating that their daughters would be in Mrs. Owens's kindergarten class. Reactions in the two households differed, and each affected the children's feelings about school. Mrs. Reed was delighted. Turning to her daughter, she said, "Oh, Sammie, you're going to love school! Mrs. Owens was my teacher, and you'll just love all the fun things you'll do in class."

Mrs. Kohl, on the other hand, felt quite different. She expressed her thoughts to her husband in her daughter's presence: "Rats, Brittany has that old Mrs. Owens. I was hoping she'd get the new young teacher." It was no wonder that the two children reacted differently when they met at the bus stop on the first day of school. Samantha jumped up and down and grabbed

Brittany's hand as she ran toward the stopped bus, saying, "Oh, we're going to have so much fun." Brittany, however, pushed her away and refused to get on the bus. No amount of cajoling from the adults could convince her to get on. Mrs. Kohl was forced to drive Brittany to school for several days before the child would take the bus with her friend. ⎯⌒

Initially, both children appear to be responding to their parents' attitudes as they viewed and responded to schooling. It is also difficult to determine what caused the change in Brittany. School may have been fun, and she may have started to enjoy her teacher. Or, perhaps her peers influenced her thinking on "how one ought to go to school."

Coleman (1991) pointed out that children whose parents stress the impor-

Even very young children respond positively to books when significant adults engage them in literacy interactions.

tance of good work habits, punctuality, and task completion carry these traits over into their schoolwork and have greater academic success. In another classic study, Durkin (1966) noted the commonality of influences on early readers relating to the effect of home environment and parental perceptions of **literacy development**. Her work and later studies indicate that parents' attitudes toward reading and their modeling of reading with their children are critical factors in children's development. Readers will find a fuller examination of parenting and its influence on children's development and learning in Chapter 4.

IMPLICATIONS FOR TEACHERS

Challenges of Differing Home Values

When children's attitudes and perceptions are in sync with the values of the school, it tends to be easier for teachers to establish relationships with the family and consider them cooperative parents. For example, in the Coleman (1991) study cited in the previous section, children whose parents stress good work habits, punctuality, and task completion tend to do better in school. But these middle-class values may not be stressed in families who are struggling economically or whose cultural backgrounds may lead them to regard time as more fluid and relationships as more essential than completion of a particular job. Not all parents read to their children at bedtime. Perhaps they are unable to read English, are working the night shift, or tell their children stories instead. So, a big challenge for you as a teacher is trying to understand and appreciate attitudes and perceptions that are different from those you have experienced.

As a teacher, you will need to develop interpersonal competence as you work with families who seem different and have attitudes that are new to you. Teachers who have interpersonal competence cope effectively with the unfamiliar, quickly establish rapport with others, sense other people's feelings, connect effectively with people from various backgrounds, and work to clear up miscommunication (Heilman, 2008). As you think about yourself as a developing professional, keep these qualities in mind and work to cultivate them in yourself. They will prove invaluable to you as a teacher in our diverse society. As the next section indicates, the attitude of school personel toward families can have a great impact on children's perceptions of school and success in that setting.

School Influence on Attitudes and Perceptions

Although the thesis is questioned by some (Harris, 2002), most developmental psychologists agree that parents' attitudes have a major effect on children's learning and acceptance of school (Borkowski, Ramey, & Stile, 2002). The attitudes of school personnel also affect how children learn. Research by the Institute for Responsive Education on educators' attitudes toward low-income parents shows that many educators didn't expect low-income parents to be productive participants in their children's education, and sometimes these parents didn't recognize how important their participation was to their children's learning. Children internalize these attitudes of mutual disrespect. Children's self-worth is diminished or enhanced as they sense how school personnel view the lifestyle and culture of their families, and these attitudes can breed tolerance or intolerance for others.

In the following vignette, Camille and Helen reacted differently to a bus driver's careless words, but both were distressed.

Camille and Helen arrived at their homes upset over a comment their bus driver had made. There were empty cans on the bus, and the driver said, "Don't touch them cans. I just drove a bunch of Black kids on a trip, and they aren't clean." Camille exclaimed to her mother, "But I ride the bus every day. Does he think I'm not clean 'cause I'm Black?"

Helen's distress was similar, but from a different perspective. "We had to ride the bus after a bunch of Black kids today, and they left it dirty. Ugh!" Both Camille and Helen could have misinterpreted the bus driver's words, but their attitudes about self and others were affected by the driver's careless speech.

Teachers can't prevent what happened to Camille or Helen. They can only be alert to problems and provide an emotional climate that accepts all children regardless of their ethnic or social class standing. They must be cognizant of how their own words and actions can bring to pass the **self-fulfilling prophecies** noted long ago by Rosenthal and Jacobson (1968).

Rosenthal and Jacobson's study indicates that teachers' expectations of children result in self-fulfilling prophecies. For example, the children whom teachers perceive to be capable and intelligent will do much better than will those children whom teachers do not perceive to be capable and intelligent. Studies conducted in the 1970s, 1980s, and 1990s continue to show that children are affected by their teachers' perceptions of them and react both behaviorally and academically according to their teachers' expectations.

GENDER ISSUES   In elementary school, girls are likely to do better academically than boys, but by the time students graduate from high school, boys score higher in math on the **Scholastic Aptitude Test** (College Board, 2009). Some researchers suggest that this happens because teachers treat boys and girls differently. Researchers have noted that as early as preschool, girls are inclined to select activities with more rules, guidelines, and suggestions for accomplishing the task, whereas boys tend to select activities that allow for more open-ended behavior. Because they are rewarded for such behavior, girls tend to become more compliant and boys become more assertive (Eccles, Wigfield, Harold, & Blumenfeld, 1993). As children progress through school, these reinforced behaviors get boys more attention, more opportunities for classroom discussion, and more specific guidelines as to the correctness of their responses. Girls are called on less often than boys, are given less feedback on their responses, and are encouraged to listen rather than to participate. Girls tend to be praised for their neatness, whereas boys receive praise for their academic contributions.

Consequently, some girls get the message that their academic responses are not as important as those of boys. Because achievement in elementary school is often measured on tasks that require mastery skills, girls, who are reinforced for obeying the rules, can be expected to do better than boys, but as children progress and school success depends more on problem solving and assertiveness, boys, who have been reinforced for more aggressive behavior, can be expected to outperform girls (Harris, 2004; Sadker & Sadker, 2005). Teachers who recognize that boys and girls may have different strengths and learning styles will avoid gender stereotyping, which shortchanges both girls and boys.

ETHNICITY ISSUES   Because of their ethnically based preconceived expectations of performance, teachers also may discriminate against children of different ethnic and ability groups by treating them differently (Teacher Expectations and Student Achievement, 2004). Teachers are likely to give high achievers and majority-culture children more opportunities to respond, more praise, and more time to formulate a response. Teachers who perceive minority children to be low achievers do not expect them to know answers and do not give them as many opportunities or as much encouragement to respond. Such differential treatment over time lowers children's involvement in school and may prevent them from developing confidence in their abilities (Dilworth & Brown, 2001; Hrabowski, Maton, Greene, & Greif, 2002). A particularly troublesome outcome of this discrimination is the low number of men of color who attend postsecondary programs.

Community programs that involve families in growing their own food broaden children's perceptions of economics and nutrition.

IMPLICATIONS FOR TEACHERS

Bridging Home and School Outlooks

Recognizing that your own attitudes and perceptions can be a powerful force in helping children succeed in school is an important step in your professional development. During your teaching career, you will undoubtedly work with children who are very different from you. Their family situations may be much more complex than the one you experienced as a child. Their religious or cultural beliefs may be unfamiliar to you. The amount of money available in their homes may be much greater or much less than in that of your family. It is essential that you accept children and their families as they are and not use your own experiences as the norm, with other situations considered as deviations. Work on becoming a teacher who believes that all children are capable of success and actively try to make connections with their families (Chavkin, 2005). Not only will you be making a great contribution to the lives of the children you teach, you may also be creating connections between the family and school that might not have been made without your efforts toward understanding and acceptance. It only takes one person to create the bridge between school and home.

Many schools offer the community the use of their buildings for recreational, athletic, and social activities. Schools can become places of sanctuary for children and families both during the school day and in later hours. When the school building becomes a focal point of the community and school personnel act as intermediaries between families and the community, the school can strengthen the ties between the two social settings.

Community Influence on Attitudes and Perceptions

Both **formal** and **informal community structures** (Bronfenbrenner, 1986, 1993) influence children's attitudes toward learning and schooling. Formal structures include political and social systems, health and recreational services, business enterprises, entertainment, and educational services. Informal structures are the social networks that each family establishes with people outside the home. The range of influence in these structures can be complex because of the different perspectives held by the organizations within a community and the interactions of individual citizens. Nevertheless, members of many communities hold common positive attitudes toward their local schools. This is shown by the communitywide political support for school activities, linkages established with other community organizations, and news coverage by local media.

It is difficult to measure the actual effect of community attitudes on student achievement, but we know that children quickly assimilate attitudes expressed by adults around them. Research suggests that a community's **social climate** and the personal relationships that children form within the community influence their attitudes about learning (Maeroff, 1998). For example, if school sports activities are highlighted in media coverage and the teams get money for trips but the school librarian can't buy children's literature for the library, children soon get the message that being a good athlete is more important than being a good reader. When a community paper publishes the poems, stories, and artwork of local primary-school children, children understand that the community values their academic achievements. Primary-school children are less likely to make such direct connections to community attitudes toward their schools, but they get excited about winning a pizza for reading a certain number of books. Eventually, they get the message that reading is important.

Businesspeople often provide support for various school programs. The support may be given as money, contributions of goods, or volunteer activities. When children witness that support, they learn that important people value learning. When children hear the local grocer, businessperson, or politician comment on the positive qualities of teachers, they learn that others value the learning experiences these teachers provide.

IMPLICATIONS FOR TEACHERS

Focus on the "Community Orchard"

There are many ways to connect with both the informal and formal communities to support your work with children and their families. At the beginning of the school year, get to know each family and the important people who make up their community. At back-to-school night, for example, you could have each family make up a "community orchard" rather than a family tree. In their orchard, they might place neighbors, extended family members, close friends, a child-care center, a religious group, and/or other organizations with which they have important connections. This information will help you learn about the child and also give you sources for resources, volunteer help, or service opportunities for your class.

You can help influence community attitudes toward your school when you plan field trips to local businesses, invite workers to school to talk about their jobs and read to children, and include officeholders and other community workers in school-sponsored assemblies. Make certain that children write thank-you notes and offer children's work for display in public places and commercial spaces. One teacher's display of her first graders' artwork outside a department store led to a countywide art show in a large regional shopping mall the following year. When businesses are thanked by parents for their contributions to the school, the connections between home, school, and community are further strengthened.

Peer Group Influence

In ways similar to the community, the peer group becomes an agency of **enculturation** and learning. Even very young children develop a sense of self from their perceptions of important people in their surroundings, including relatives, teachers, and peers. Socioeconomic status, ethnic identity, and parents' occupations affect how families view themselves and the process by which they socialize their children (Bornstein, 2002). Later, as children leave the home setting, their self-perception and socializing skills become influenced by how their peers view them.

When children move from home to the child-care center, the school, and the community at large, they begin to form attachments, and friendships emerge through their play. These relationships will, of course, influence behavior. Even infants and toddlers are observed reacting to other infants and toddlers by touching them, by crying when they cry, and later by offering nurturance or comfort. By about age 3, early friendships begin to form and children's peers begin to have a more lasting influence.

We find that peer influence on any child's behavior gradually becomes more important. Harris (1998, 2002) and Rowe (1994) maintain that peer groups have an even stronger influence than parents, although that extreme position has been challenged by other researchers (Berk, 2005). Gradually, children discover that others can share their feelings or attitudes or have quite different ones. The perspectives they gain from other children can affect how some children feel about their own families.

It is often difficult for children to adjust to the idea that other families can function radically differently from their own and yet hold many of the same attitudes and beliefs and be equally nurturing and secure. Children usually have a "family" view of their own culture and that of others. So, when confronted with the perspectives of peers, they often need to rethink their own viewpoints. You can think of the peer group as a barometer for children when they examine themselves and their feelings about self and family.

The peer group will, of course, influence the development of children's socializing skills. These early friendships help children learn how to negotiate and relate to others, including their siblings and other family members. They learn from peers how to cooperate and socialize according to **group norms** and group-sanctioned modes of behavior. The peer group can influence what the child values, knows, wears, eats, and learns. We find that the extent of this influence, however, depends on other situational constraints, such as the age and personality of children and the nature of the group (Ladd, Herald, & Andrews, 2006). Socialization is particularly important for children with disabilities, and it is the reason many programs include peers who are typically developing in special education programs or include children with disabilities in general education classrooms.

In its most acceptable form, the peer group is a healthy coming-of-age arbiter in which children develop negotiating skills and learn to deal with hostility and to solve problems in a social context. In its most destructive mode, the peer group can demand blind obedience to a group norm, which can result in socially alienated gangs and experiments with addictive substances (see Chapter 7).

When parents use the computer with children, the children benefit more and adults learn more about their children.

Media Influence

Whereas print and the analog broadcast models of television and radio were the principal media until the 1980s, the new media of digital, computerized, or networked information technologies have revolutionized communication in the past 25 years. Increased speed, volume, and interactivity of communication are characteristics of media today, and the Internet can be accessed by computers as well as by hand-held devices like MP3 players or cell phones. Digital television, on-line publications, and satellite radio are transforming the older forms of media so that they, too, have many of the interactive characteristics of new media. Today, all members of our society are influenced, both directly and indirectly, by powerful media vehicles.

Even the youngest children in America are surrounded by media, spending many hours a day watching TV, viewing videos, using computers, and playing video games. On average, children under the age of 6 are reported to spend about 2 hours a day using screen media (Rideout & Hamel, 2006). Older children, those between 8 and 18 years of age, spend considerably more time doing so—about 45 hours per week. A new trend in this age group is the amount of time youngsters are spending using more than one medium simultaneously. Consequently, they are exposed to even more media in the same amount of time.

Because parents generally view television watching and computer use positively, it is unlikely that media usage will diminish in the coming years. Despite the American Academy of Pediatrics' recommendation that children under 2 have no screen time, television shows and other media are being developed and promoted for this age group. A comprehensive analysis of 170 research studies (Common Sense Media, 2008) tracking the impact of media on children's health indicated that heavy media exposure was associated with negative health outcomes for children and adolescents. In 80% of the studies, childhood obesity, tobacco use, sexual behavior, drug and alcohol use, low academic achievement, and attention deficit hyperactivity disorder were all positively related to greater media exposure. Other long-term consequences of heavy media involvement are being studied extensively, but findings are inconclusive at this point.

PRINT MATERIALS   Despite the prevalence of new media, reading continues to be an important part of young children's lives. The kinds of books and other print media that children read and have read to them influence and support their emotional, social, and intellectual development both directly and indirectly. Books, magazines, and newspapers reach the child indirectly, through parents, caregivers, and teachers, and directly, such as when children participate in a library presentation or select particular publications to buy or borrow. Increasingly, printed material is based on television shows, computer games, and movies, with children seeking out the printed material after experiencing the characters in another format. Print media are also highlighted in Web sites such as http://www.starfall.com that make reading an interactive experience for children.

Print media also affect children's development indirectly through the publications their parents read. Books, magazines, and Web sites inform adults how to lead healthy, productive lives and proclaim the dangers of unhealthy practices. Advertising affects the types of clothing, food, and (especially) toys bought for children. Some toys engage children's imagination and are designed for groups of children playing together. Other toys are more suitable for children playing alone. Children's potential for social and intellectual development is affected by which type of toy adults are motivated to buy.

Studies on early literacy indicate that the amount and types of printed materials that adults have in the home, as well as how adults interact with these materials in the presence of children, affect the children's interest and literacy achievement (Desmond,

2001). From the books that adults read to children, children internalize attitudes, feelings, and biases about their own and other cultures. Zach, in the chapter's opening vignette, had a chance to express aggression in acceptable ways through *Three Billy Goats Gruff*. He was influenced in the kinds of clothes he wanted by the story *Max's Dragon Shirt*. Books, like peers, provide children with a vision of their world that sometimes reaffirms their own lives and sometimes challenges their perspectives.

When Meringoff (1980) compared children's reactions to stories presented through television, books, and radio, children seemed to view television events as something not directly associated with themselves, but they appeared to personalize the events in books. Berns (2009) and Singer and Singer (2007) stress that because the reader is more intimately involved in the book, it is a stronger socializing agent. However, the stronger personal influence of printed materials compared to television or the Internet could also reflect the manner in which the two are presented to children. Young children first know about books because someone reads to them and interacts with them about the story, whereas more often than not, children are left to watch television and movies and use the computer by themselves. We know that children are socialized on how to react to books; thus, they get more personal meaning from them as they become readers themselves. Some researchers (Desmond, 2001; Neuman, 1997) suggest that when parents or other adults interact with children viewing television or using the computer, those children develop better interactive and processing skills.

TELEVISION   Television's substantial impact on all growing children began in the 1950s with the proliferation of TV sets. Three generations of children have been raised with TV, and very different role models, interaction modes, and experiences are now visited on American youth. Today, more than 99% of American households contain at least one television set, and children start the viewing process early—even before they reach 2 years of age. In the 21st century, however, television viewing is declining somewhat because of increased use of computer games and the Internet, and also because children now spend more time in child care, school, and **after-school care** programs.

Television influences children in direct proportion to both the time spent viewing and the overall effect of what is viewed. Certainly, eating habits, family interactions, and use of leisure time are considerably influenced by television. Commercials take up 12 to 14 minutes of every hour of television, and in that time, advertisers try to influence viewers with all types of consumerism. Not all TV advertising is negative, of course. There have been efforts through TV to modify behaviors such as smoking, drunken driving, and poor nutritional habits (Van Evra, 2004). How children are affected by both positive and negative advertisements also depends on such factors as parent–child interactions, how children are disciplined, and even to some degree, socioeconomic factors (Strasburger, Wilson, & Jordan, 2008).

Children are especially susceptible to electronic media, and televised advertising has a huge effect. Heavy viewers are drawn to the advertised products, including unhealthy food products, and they tend to eat more snack foods and to be overweight. Social interactions are also affected. Heavy television viewers hold more traditional sex-role attitudes, behave more aggressively, are less socially competent, and perform more poorly in school when compared to light viewers or nonviewers (Pecora, Murray, & Wartella, 2004). Two additional concerns about the effects of television are the amount of violence, in both commercials and programs, and the amount of time children's television watching takes away from more creative, active, and intellectual pursuits. Research has shown that those children who have television in their bedrooms spend more time watching it and interacting with other media than other children. Heavy TV viewing means that children spend less time reading or playing outdoors.

REFLECTION

Consider how much TV you watched while growing up and reflect on the positive and negative influences that it had on how you worked, how you dressed, and what you ate. Are these influences on children more potent now?

Research on the impact of television viewing on academic achievement indicates that this influence is complex in nature (Gunter, Harrison, & Wykes, 2003). Television viewing takes time away from important social interactions, such as conversation, storytelling, imaginative play, and, for primary-school children, the leisure reading that promotes literacy. We must remember, however, that the amount of viewing, the kinds of programs watched, IQ, and socioeconomic status are all factors that affect children's attitudes and achievement.

NEW MEDIA   Almost all young children in the United States are exposed, on a daily basis, to entertainment and education delivered through media other than print and television. Films (in theaters or on DVDs), sound recordings on compact disc and MP3 players, games on hand-held devices, game systems, and the computer, and the Internet are the main sources.

The Internet is now the world's largest source of information; it completely dwarfs even the world's renowned libraries. In 2009, 77% of families with minor children in the home had high-speed Internet access from their homes (Horrigan, 2009). In addition, 97% of American elementary and secondary schools have broadband Internet access (Organization for Economic Co-Operation and Development, 2008). Using the Internet at home and at school is the norm for a large majority of American children.

The amount of information available to today's young people is extraordinary; it also carries great potential for misuse. For example, many primary-school children regularly use social networking sites and chat rooms to connect with others. Predators are inherent dangers in such use, especially if children misrepresent their age on these sites. Children may also unwittingly encounter pornography, hate-group Web sites, and other inappropriate material as they search the Internet.

Some help arrived with the Children's Online Protection Act of 1998 and the availability of filtering software designed to protect children from dangerous and unsavory information. These systems are used to monitor, filter, and control inappropriate use of the Internet and to make its use by children at school and at home safer. WebBlocker or other software is installed in many schools, and a 2003 Supreme Court decision permits such programs to be used by public libraries as well. Net Nanny® and Cybersitter® are just two examples of the many filters for home computers. A filtering system is a resource that must be harnessed successfully by families, schools, and communities if its potential is to be productive.

Despite the dangers, electronic media provide children with opportunities to practice skills, solve problems, use their creativity, connect with others with similar interests, and expand their knowledge base. For example, some primary-school children use the Internet to practice chess, to communicate with faraway relatives and friends with webcams, to post photos and creative writing for others to view, and to retrieve information. When children's Internet access is closely monitored by parents, it can be a rich resource for children's lives. It is generally recommended that computer use be in a common area of the household so that parents can be aware of the information the child is accessing.

THE ENTERTAINMENT INDUSTRY   The entire entertainment industry now has a tremendous influence on American society. Whereas a few movie stars, musicians, and sports figures were the entertainment models for generations during the 20th century, today the visual and auditory stimuli of the new media vibrate in most homes and communities. Some of this exposure is educational, positive, and directed at an appropriate level for young children. A considerable amount of current fare, however, is violent in nature, is provocative, and is presented in ways unsuitable for children's level of maturity. With the rapid expansion of electronic transmission devices, young people are exposed more than ever to both good and bad influences.

Producers and advertisers expand successful films and television shows by producing associated toys, clothing, and DVDs. Similar marketing comes from developers of video and computer games. These games influence individuals' values, compete for children's attention, and certainly reduce the amount of reflection and interaction time children have with both adults and peers (Singer & Singer, 2007).

When parents and other adults watch DVDs or television or use the computer with children, the children benefit more from the programs and the adults learn more about the children. Adults discover what children know and what interests or bores them. The adults may then act to enhance their children's learning. Adults may introduce children to the original stories from which the TV programs were adapted, helping them to learn to make comparisons and develop better discrimination skills about stories and presentations.

REFLECTION

Think of films or other media you have found that focus on other cultures; then compare these to aspects of your own life. How much do the living habits, music, dress, and work styles of these other cultures resemble your own?

For children to be engaged in positive learning, it seems urgent that schools, parents, teachers, and other concerned individuals develop partnerships for interpreting and dealing with the products of currently available media sources and those soon to appear in their communities. Helping children develop skills as critical consumers of media can help to reverse the negative influences of the media industry.

One desirable outcome of our highly mediated world is that all people see and sense the diversity of individuals living in modern American communities. As we view televised images of children playing in the streets of Guatemala, Canada, or Kazakhstan, we see them delighting in the same things that children in Seattle or Pittsburgh find desirable. Cultures across the world are borrowing steadily from each other, and far more rapidly, than in previous generations. In *American Skin* (Wynter, 2002), a hopeful thesis on diversity is advanced for the **transracial** effect now found throughout the United States. Wynter makes a persuasive case about most Americans no longer reacting to racial and ethnic differences but adopting wholeheartedly the interesting and beneficial features of other cultural groups. This appears to be a positive departure from our society's background of **ethnocentrism**.

IMPLICATIONS FOR TEACHERS

Entertainment Sources and Children's Learning

The entertainment industry influences the actions, dress codes, and values of many adults. It also captures and holds children's interests for a large part of each day (see Figure 1-2). As a teacher or community worker, you must understand that this influence on children both enhances and inhibits their growth as human beings. You should not underestimate the effect of this influence but rather try to incorporate it into your teaching so that children assimilate

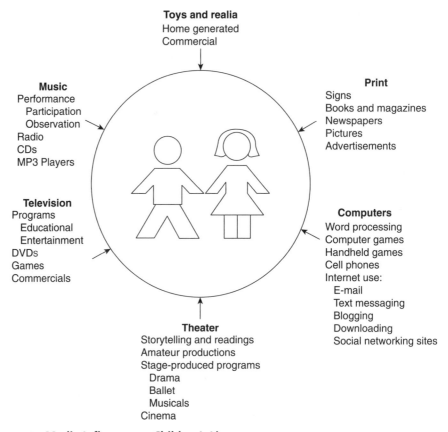

FIGURE 1-2   Media Influence on Children's Lives

it in a healthy context with the rest of their education. For example, knowledge that children pick up from TV can be startling but relevant, and schools, communities, and families can reinforce the unexpected learning in positive ways. Consider the following vignette:

 The teacher in Amanda's kindergarten class was introducing the letter–sound relationship of J. When soliciting words children could recall, Mrs. Pineo got *judge* from Juan. So, she asked if anyone knew what judge meant. Children responded, "It's someone who would send you to jail if you did something wrong . . . especially if you murdered someone, he'd be sure to send you to jail!" When asked how they knew this, the class as a whole replied, "It was on television!" That evening during dinner, Amanda announced to her family, "A judge would put you in jail if you did something really bad—like murder." The give-and-take of the subsequent table conversation between Amanda and her parents provided further clarification on how Amanda was assimilating information from school, the media, and home.

AGE LEVELS AND INFLUENCE

The community, home, school, peers, and media exert a greater or lesser influence on children's learning, depending on the age of the children concerned (note again Figure 1-1). You will learn in the next chapter how theorists have described the stages in children's development from dependency to independence and how children learn (see Table 2-1). In practice, parents, teachers, and community members rarely subscribe to one particular theory, but the decisions they make about children's learning reflect a stronger belief in one viewpoint. As you develop strategies to promote **partnerships** for children's education, it is helpful to keep in mind that the perspective others have on development may differ from your own.

The Early Years—Strong Home Influence

Early researchers such as Maslow (1970), Erikson (1963), and Piaget (1967) all emphasize the strong need for attachment and environmental support of infants and toddlers. Developing children require a physically and emotionally supportive home in which their basic needs can be met. Infants must first develop trust in others so that they can explore their surroundings. According to Piaget, it is this exploration that enables them to construct knowledge about themselves and their world (Piaget, 1967).

Neuroscientists have discovered links between brain structure and brain activity, and brain research substantiates the notion that a child's knowledge develops because of an interactive process, beginning even as the brain develops before birth. Heredity may determine the framework of a developing child's brain, but researchers point out the many ways in which genes, environment, and infant responses interact to develop the connections between the brain cells that account for learning (Brynes, 2001; Pinker, 2002).

Because of this brain–environment interactive development, we can see that myriad events will affect growth, some positively and some negatively. Type of housing, presence of caregivers, and lifestyles associated with different homes will influence children's lives in profound and dramatic ways. Some environments are extremely supportive and nurturing, whereas others are dominating, negligent, and even dysfunctional. For example, in a landmark report released by the Carnegie Corporation (1994), affectionate interactions, consistent practices, organized schedules, and high-quality nourishment bring support and security to young children. Such nurturing environments have secure caregivers who respond to their children by touching, cuddling, talking to, telling stories, and reading with them. Most authorities agree that emotional support and interactions with the child provide building blocks for intellectual competence and language comprehension.

On the other hand, the trials of homelessness, highly mobile families, absentee parents, and poverty often mean that parents are unable to provide positive and secure environments. The lack of a responsive environment, which stems from the parents' own life experience, will affect a child's intellectual, social, and emotional competence. The young brain is quite resilient, however, and later stimulation or strong emotional bonds can help many children overcome some of the negative results of early deprivation (Bruer, 2002).

Regardless of family configuration, American society expects all families to provide economic and emotional support for infants and toddlers. With more single-parent and dual-income families and fewer extended family members available to support them, families face many challenges in providing optimal care for their children. The roles of caregivers and teachers have become even more important in children's lives. These issues will be discussed further in Chapters 4 and 5.

Children reenact behaviors of significant others as they move toward autonomy and independence.

Preschool and Kindergarten Years—Increasing School Influence

As children develop a sense of autonomy, they need to learn the boundaries within which they can operate, and they must learn to identify new ones they will encounter as they separate from home. Bronfenbrenner's (1979, 1993) bioecological model accurately explains the transitions from the intimate **microsystem** of home to the **mesosystem** of outer linkages that come to bear on the developing child's perceptions and behavior. As parents give their children necessary support, they must also give them freedom to try things on their own.

As we noted, one's sense of self first develops in the home and then extends into the neighborhood, child-care center, and larger community. At school, the teacher and the children's peers begin to alter or reinforce this sense. Children modify their behavior in school in response to various rules and regulations and to perceived teacher and peer expectations. At the same time, significant others in the home setting continue to influence development as the early schoolers move from basic trust to **autonomy** and independence.

Many children have school-like experiences in their preschool years. For other children, school as a culture first comes into focus when they enter formal public or private elementary school. In the preschool years, children may encounter several different types of school-like experiences. Head Start programs, child-care centers, and nursery schools all demonstrate somewhat different philosophical orientations. Some programs seek to introduce children to school through a more structured curriculum, others try to extend the nurturance of the home, and still others combine facets of both. The current movement toward universal preschool for children is an indication of the growing awareness of the importance of this developmental stage. Although it is difficult to conduct rigorous studies to determine the influence of different programs on developing children, we have evidence that quality preschool programs do have a lasting, positive effect on children's academic growth and on subsequent life-skill development (Weikart, 2004).

Primary Years—Growing Community Influence

Community influence appears early in children's lives and progresses steadily as children mature; refer again to Figure 1-1 to see that by the time a child turns 8, community impact is high. The effect of the community depends, however, on how families use neighborhood resources. The nature of that effect is not simple; it derives from the many subsystems within the community. For example, the family may live in a neighborhood that provides positive social and physical support or in an area where parents are afraid to take their children outdoors.

As children expand their horizons, the living conditions of the neighborhood and community provide experiences on which to build their linguistic, kinesthetic, artistic, spatial, and interpersonal skills. Children who can visit zoos, museums, libraries, business establishments, parks, and other natural settings are better equipped to deal with the many mathematical, scientific, social, and language concepts discussed in schools than are children who can't. Recent decades have produced a rich mix of cultural and ethnic diversity in many American communities—which contrasts starkly with the situation that existed in the mid-20th century. Inclusive schools, ethnically diverse neighborhoods, and **transcultural** events all produce a positive effect on young children.

Traditions, cultural values, community **mores**, opportunities for recreation, and other social and cultural activities all play a part in children's development. Experiences in interacting with adults in clubs, sports, and art and music activities open up children to differences in communication styles and offer them a range of experiences. Coleman (1991) called this type of involvement with adults a child's **social capital** and stressed that this capital is as important as financial capital in determining school performance. Maeroff (1998) pointed out that children living in poverty may have fewer opportunities to participate in interactive incidents with different adults than children who do not. Although socialization practices are learned at home, children who participate in community activities have greater opportunities to practice their negotiating, problem-solving, and intellectual skills. Steven, in the following vignette, begins to learn some of these important lessons.

Steven, in third grade, signed up for tae kwon do sessions but was unhappy because the instructor was "always criticizing" what he did. "I don't even know what I do wrong," he told his mother.

"And what do you do when he tells you something" she asked.

"Oh, I get so mad, I just grit my teeth."

"Are you sure he never compliments you?"

"Uh, uh, hardly ever," pouted Steven.

"Well, want to try an experiment?" his mother suggested. "The next time he even suggests something is good, smile at him and say, 'Oh, that really helps me know what I should be doing,' and just ignore the criticisms." Steven reluctantly agreed to give it a try.

Two weeks later, a jubilant Steven returned from a practice session saying, "Hey, Mom, he really does tell me lots about what I'm doing right!" Whether Steven or the instructor changed behavior patterns isn't clear, but certainly Steven was learning new ways of working with adults so that he could profit from their instruction.

Positive interactions between community and family give a sense of security and well-being to all. This situation helps families provide the kind of nurturing that children need. Regrettably, not all communities provide healthy conditions for children. Community tolerance for gangs, illicit activities, or establishments with erotic content will have unhealthy and negative influences on children's growth and the experiences they have. Violence in the streets limits everyone's sense of security. Yet, even in neighborhoods besieged by poverty, the extended family, the churches, the social and service organizations, and neighborhood groups will make a positive difference in children's lives and extend the work of families and schools (Ramsey, 2004).

REFLECTION

Think of the neighbors and workers in your childhood community and reflect on how they influenced your growth. Did they influence how you saw school when you were in the primary grades? Did they make you feel safe in your area? How? Now compare this situation to that of the school community that you last visited. Are there any differences?

INFLUENCE OF SPECIAL-INTEREST GROUPS

In recent years, the United States has witnessed a steady increase in the number and potency of **special-interest groups** with agendas focused on political, environmental, gender equity, or school curriculum issues. Groups such as the Family Research Council, Common Cause, Children's Defense Fund, Action for Children's Television, and the various pro-choice and anti-abortion groups are all organized to affect everything from legislative matters to informal controls on school procedures. These groups can have both direct and indirect influence on children's learning, depending on family, school, and community reactions to their efforts and objectives.

Although a number of special-interest groups have a broadly conceived objective and have existed for many years, other citizen groups have a single objective and are short-lived. The single-issue group is frequently very successful in its endeavors because it focuses on an emotional issue that is newsworthy: One example is "Let's stop the building of more 'big box' stores in Newton." These groups disband quickly after a mission is accomplished.

Some groups have been formed by parents concerned about a particular educational issue affecting children. For instance, in 1968, Peggy Charren, concerned about the amount of violence in children's programs, organized a group of parents to form Action for Children's Television (ACT). The group lobbied for improved television programming and advertising during children's viewing time and worked to educate the public regarding television's positive and negative influences. The action resulted in the Children's Television Act of 1990.

Grassroots efforts by special-interest groups resulted in the special education legislation of the 1960s that improved education for all children. As children with disabilities were first mainstreamed into regular classrooms, curricula, classroom environments, and learning for all children expanded. Continued pressure by these special-interest groups has led to an examination of the effects of the laws and to the passing of additional legislation to better serve children with special needs.

The influence of special-interest groups is not always viewed as positive, however. Some conservative interest groups seek legislation that would permit censoring of library books and dictating particular elements in curricula. In many communities, both schools and libraries have been forced to remove from their shelves certain books, deemed quality literature by literary critics, because of the views of special-interest groups. One teacher was dismissed for focusing on Langston Hughes's poems, which a special-interest group found racially inflammatory (Kozol, 1991).

At the local level, some religious groups have succeeded in banning Halloween activities and even traditional fairy tales that include supernatural events and characters. Other groups have successfully changed units of study in schools about Christmas and Hanukkah and banned community displays of the Nativity. Special-interest groups have a positive influence when they act to initiate dialogue among parents and teachers concerning the appropriateness of materials in schools. Their influence is negative when they seek to restrict children's access to humanity's best artistic, philosophical, and intellectual efforts and attempt to deny children the opportunity to learn about different ethnic and cultural groups and other historical periods.

Federal Agencies as Special-Interest Groups

Although it is difficult to describe our federal government as a special-interest group, it does work that way at times. For more than one and a half centuries, our national leaders left education entirely to the individual states, and only Supreme Court action, on occasion, visited the school arena. In recent times, however, political administrations have become increasingly concerned about educational policy and practice because these have affected political goals and objectives.

During the 1960s, President Lyndon Johnson began the federal incursion into education with the very ambitious **War on Poverty** program, which carried many implications for schools. Since that time, most administrations have deliberated about school problems, and they have developed mandates and regulations and have used federal funding to stimulate action for one procedure or another. Enhancing legislation for science study is one example; promoting a voucher plan for selected groups is another; Goals 2000 (Educate America Act) is still another, as is the **No Child Left Behind (NCLB) Act**.

Federal mandates have expanded and are often fitted to different political agendas that bear little relationship to the needs, cultural expectations, and developmental levels of children in various parts of the country. The danger of such an approach is that the broad sweep of a mandate limits the diversity and uniqueness of individuals and groups. When schools reflect the political agendas of national leaders rather than focus on teaching children to develop inquiring minds, our children are in danger of becoming docile followers.

Standardized tests have become common in our schools, and in recent years we have seen even greater use of tests because of the mandates of the NCLB Act. Overreliance on tests, however, detracts from teacher oversight and reduces the opportunity to develop curricula keyed to the needs of particular children. Despite child development and brain development research that emphasizes the need for choice and the value of play and active learning in all aspects of children's growth (Olfman, 2005), many schools have moved toward tightly focused, direct instruction to prepare children for the high-stakes standardized tests required by NCLB (Hatch, 2005).

We need federal oversight and influence to promote certain programs that make life more productive and fair for children. Quality education is often cited as a dominant interest of the U.S. public, and most educators like to see our national government showing interest in schools, providing funds for programs, and acting as a partner in the huge task of educating young people. If these preferences are valid, the government has a reason to be involved in supporting our schools and community efforts. Increasingly, however, critics are raising concerns about the narrow definitions of school accountability and academic success that have resulted from the increased federal involvement in education (Sacks, 2005).

Professional Associations as Special-Interest Groups

In recent years, the **National Association for the Education of Young Children (NAEYC)** and the Association for Childhood Education International (ACEI), two long-established and well-respected organizations devoted to children's education and well-being, have partnered with the National Council for the Accreditation of Teacher Education (NCATE) to develop professional standards for the initial licensure of early childhoood and elementary teachers. Although these standards (which can be viewed in their entirety at http://www.naeyc.org and http://www.acei.org) emphasize the importance of prospective teachers understanding child development and curriculum, a key element in both sets of standards is the equal importance of teacher collaboration with families and communities.

For example, NAEYC Standard 2, Building Family and Community Relationships, underscores the importance of teachers developing respectful, reciprocal relationships with families and the communities in which the families reside. Standard 3, Observing, Documenting, and Assessing to Support Young Children and Families, stresses the need for a partnership between professionals and parents as essential for children's optimal development and learning. Standard 4a, Connecting with Children and Families, highlights the importance of teachers establishing positive relationships with parents as the foundation for their work with children. The last standard, Standard 5, Growing as a Professional, puts emphasis on the teacher as a continuous, collaborative learner who serves as an advocate for children. The standard also accentuates the teacher's use of ethical guidelines (see above Web site for NAEYC for the NAEYC Code of Ethical Conduct).

Like NAEYC, ACEI has several standards that relate directly to the importance of the relationship among elementary teachers, families, and communities. ACEI Standard 5.3, Collaboration with Families, affirms the significance of teachers establishing and maintaining partnerships with families to promote the intellectual, social, emotional,

Community groups influence children's education, so teachers need to collaborate with organizations to maximize the opportunities and resources.

and physical growth of children. The standard urges teachers to use multiple strategies to engage families who may have diverse beliefs, traditions, values, and practices.

ACEI Standard 5.4, Collaboration with Colleagues and the Community, concerns the teacher's need to be aware of the influence of the larger community environment on students' lives and learning and recommends that teachers collaborate with community organizations and utilize community resources to support children's learning.

Although not all colleges and universities may participate in the NCATE accreditation process, the standards set by NAEYC and ACEI resonate with teacher and parent educators. The ideas reflected in these standards are also echoed in the professional standards of other groups, such as social workers, curriculum specialists, and health workers in school settings. There is broad agreement that it is through partnerships between professionals, families, and communities that the best outcome for children can be achieved.

UNDERSTANDING AND COLLABORATION

Why is it important for you as beginning teachers, caregivers, or community workers to be knowledgeable about these influences that affect children's development? First, by understanding these influences, you will be able to recognize situations in which children appear to be strongly affected. Then you can reinforce or support those events that exert positive influences on children. It is equally important to recognize and then offset the harmful influences. As suggested throughout this chapter and in subsequent chapters, teachers and community workers have used particular strategies effectively to improve children's experiences.

IMPLICATIONS FOR TEACHERS

Collaboration Is Part of Teaching

As you work with children, you will use various media, engage children in group processes, and take children into the community to learn important concepts. Often children will express very different responses to a learning situation that you provide. For example, Zach's teacher attempted to counter some of the influence of the home and peers by "not allow-ing" aggressive play in the school. The strategy may work well for this teacher but other so-lutions may be useful as well, such as having a discussion with both children and parents, noting where electronic toys may be acceptable. Such a discussion might have been produc-tive in this situation. Professionals try to be attuned to children's and parents' responses. If you follow this course, you will become more sensitive and adept at responding to children's development and needs.

As children enter the primary-school years, peers will exert greater influence. When this influence is problematic and harmful, professionals will want to modify it. Counteract-ing negative peer influences is very difficult, however. Still, becoming aware of these influ-ences gives you some background while you continue to show an accepting attitude and model positive interactions with all persons.

Your job is to provide the foundation for children's thinking skills, plus the develop-ment of competency in reading, writing, math, science, and social science concepts. Under-standing the impact of both negative and positive influences on a child's learning makes your objectives and goals clearer as you plan for each student's learning.

At the present time, there are a number of issues related to children that particularly require collaboration between families, schools, and communities in order to affect positive change. We discuss some of these issues in the following sections.

Diversity

One of the challenges facing American schools today is educating the diverse child pop-ulation with a teaching force that remains largely White, middle-class, and female. Beginning teachers and community workers, regardless of their race or ethnic back-ground, have a responsibility to increase their awareness of the beliefs and values of the families they serve. By continuously examining your own background and perspec-tives, you will become aware of your assumptions about families and children from various ethnic, social, and racial groups. As mentioned earlier in this chapter, your atti-tude toward and expectations of your students have a profound effect on their learning and school success. As a member of a school community, you will have the opportunity to get to know families as individuals. For some families, perhaps newly arrived in the United States, the school will be an important link to the larger society, and as a profes-sional in a school setting, you will have an essential role to play in helping children and families adjust to life in the United States.

REFLECTION

Become aware of your own attitudes toward the different families you find in schools and neighborhoods where you are involved. Increase your objectivity and professional-ism by doing the following:

- Listen to their family stories about themselves.
- Help them interpret school policies and regulations.
- Put yourself in their shoes when considering complaints.
- Be willing to reassess children's work when you find new information.

Continued discrimination against certain groups and increased social stratification in the United States seem to fly in the face of the values of equality and justice that have been foundations of our democracy. You as an individual can only do so much to help overcome the inequities that exist as a result of poverty, race, and cultural differences, but you do have an obligation to provide the best education and support that you can to the children and families you serve. Chapters 3, 4, and 10 will address the issues of diversity and suggest ways to work successfully with families and communities of all kinds.

Childhood Obesity

The increasing concern about adult and childhood obesity reflects a worldwide health issue in many of the developed countries. Nowhere in the world, however, is the problem as grave as in the United States, where nearly one-third of adults are classified as obese and almost two-thirds are overweight, an increase of more than 20% since 1994. Childhood obesity is increasing at an even more alarming rate.

Although many approaches to fighting childhood obesity have focused on weight loss, increasing attention is being paid to the societal influences that seem to be leading children to gain weight in the first place. Television commercials for sugared cereals, candy, fast food, soft drinks, and snack foods dominate children's programming. Internet sites use fast food and candy products as part of the plot or reward system. Administrators allow vending machines filled with soda and sugary and salty snacks in school buildings. Children are being targeted by food industries that use media figures, pop stars, and athletes to promote their products in ways that are difficult to avoid.

Changes in school curricula fostered by the increasing reliance on high-stakes standardized tests have significantly decreased the amount of time for recess, physical education, and other opportunities for children to move about in school. This may be one factor in the rise in obesity. Another may be the changes in communities where children cannot play outdoors because of safety and supervision concerns, and still another factor could be the increased time spent on the Internet and watching television.

Obesity has strong negative effects on children's health, but there are also serious social, psychological, and economic ramifications. At present, however, there is no national program to combat the obesity epidemic in the United States. Until there is, individual parents, professionals, schools, and communities will continue their grassroots efforts to increase exercise time and restrict unhealthy foods in schools. Advocates suggest that regulating advertising directed at children, prohibiting advertising in school, and promoting media literacy among children are necessary steps in the long-term solution of this difficult issue. You will find more information on nutrition, obesity and wellness in Chapter 7.

Bullying

Like childhood obesity, school bullying is a serious public health problem that can have long-term implications for all of those involved. Bullying is not new, but the school shooting tragedy at Columbine and other similar situations have focused attention on the consequences of bullying behavior. And although most children who are bullied do not resort to deadly violence, the effects of being bullied can influence children's physical and mental health and prevent them from achieving their full potential.

Bullying is a greater problem among boys, where it often involves physical aggression, but girls engage in bullying behavior as well. Typically, girls use more subtle forms of bullying such as exclusion, spreading rumors, and manipulating friendships. Another alarming kind of bullying has emerged: cyber-bullying. Through the anonymity of technology, bullies can harass others using Web pages on social-networking sites, text messages, phone calls, and e-mails.

One of the difficulties in dealing with bullying is that much of it goes on out of sight of adults, and many victims are reluctant to report their abuse. As a teacher, you will need to be alert to any subtle signs of bullying and try to create a classroom community in which children work together to eliminate the problem. Like the other issues discussed in this section, bullying is a problem that will benefit most from strong collaboration among the three social settings. You will find more statistics and discussion about bullying in Chapter 7.

Other Home and Community Issues

There are many educational issues affecting young children's lives that are best handled through collaborative and shared action by families, schools, and communities. In subsequent chapters, we examine these issues more fully and suggest strategies for addressing them. You will find that most of them—even though they are treated in a particular chapter as a home or a school or a community issue—normally have implications for the other two settings as well. For example, substance abuse by children is discussed as a family issue in Chapter 9, but clearly this requires substantial attention by schools and community officials. Economic education and recycling principles are featured as part of the home curriculum in Chapter 9, but these involve collaboration with schools and communities to be successful.

Brain research emphasizes the need for choice and the value of play and experimentation in all aspects of children's growth.

Summary and Review

As a teacher or community worker acting alone, you have minimal opportunity to change the attitudes, feelings, and biases of others that impinge on local classrooms. In collaboration with families and community members, however, you can make a greater impact on children's lives. As anthropologist Margaret Mead famously stated, "Never doubt that a small group of thoughtful, committed citizens can change the world; indeed, it's the only thing that ever has."

Children are well or poorly educated, depending on many factors that both directly and indirectly influence what they learn and how they learn it. The attitudes, values, and interests of families, schools, and communities regarding children's learning can be in concert or in conflict. Young children are usually more strongly influenced by the attitudes of immediate or extended family members, and primary-school children begin to be influenced by peer groups, media, and community mores and traditions. Teachers in many instances have no control over these factors, and must study and be alert to their influence in order to provide appropriate education for the children in their classrooms.

According to Coleman (1991), children need many types of support systems to grow into functioning adults.

They need what he called human, financial, and social capital, which provide the nurturing and physical environment in which children learn to cope with their world. Children with little financial capital may still succeed if sufficient social and human resources are available to them. We find that families can compensate somewhat for lack of effective community and school influences on their children, and community and school personnel can exert influence and extend resources to compensate for missing family social resources. Schools, however, are far more effective in educating children when families, schools, and communities unite their efforts. When these three social settings recognize the influences on children's experience and work together to resolve conflicting issues undermining child development, the best possible circumstances result.

This chapter has provided a brief introduction to the three social settings and some of the ways they influence children's attitudes and perceptions. In later chapters, you will explore many of these concepts in more depth. In the next chapter, you will learn about the history of collaboration between home, school, and community. You will also delve deeper into family diversity and parenting in

Chapters 3 and 4 to help you understand the parental perspective more fully. Issues related to child care, working with families with children with disabilities, and protecting children will also be covered in detail in the forthcoming chapters. The curriculum of the home and community will be explored as well. Throughout the book, you will have many opportunities to reflect on what you are learning and to examine the implications of these concepts for you as a teacher. The final two chapters will provide extensive examples about how to work effectively with families and the community.

Suggested Activities and Questions

1. List what you consider the major influences that guided your education. Are they different from those we have noted in this chapter? What influences did your classmates list? Discuss.
2. Watch a half hour of commercial children's television or of a sporting event that children might watch. Make note of all the commercials and the nature of each, and determine how much of the half hour is devoted to them. Identify what you believe could be the effect of these ads on young children. Discuss your conclusions with your classmates.
3. Interview a teacher in a local primary school and determine whether any special-interest group influences the decisions this person makes with regard to curricula. Do some groups exert positive pressure? If so, how does the teacher view the groups' effects on children's learning? Do some groups exert negative pressures? If so, how does the teacher view these pressures as limitations on children's learning?
4. Discuss with a primary-school child a list of favorite books, movies, television shows, computer games, Web sites, and entertainers. Find out what the child likes or finds important about these choices. Ask whether the child wants to be like any of the people or characters, and why. How do you think the media to which the child is exposed has influenced these choices?

Resources

Organizations

American Obesity Association *http://www.obesity.org*
Parents Television Council *http://www.parentstv.org*
Children Now *http://www.childrennow.org*
National Institute on Media and the Family *http://www.mediafamily.org*

Web Sites

http://www.learntobehealthy.org A science learning site for educators that includes games and activities related to fitness and nutrition for children K–6.
http://www.kidshealth.org A site devoted to information about health, development, and behavior from before birth through the teen years.
http://www.bullying.org A site dedicated to increasing the awareness of bullying and to preventing, resolving, and eliminating bullying in society.
http://www.screentime.org The Center for Screen-Time Awareness aims to help families and communities reduce screen time through Turn-off Week and other activities.
http://www.commonsensemedia.org Reviews movies, games, Web sites, TV programs, books, and music for children ages 2–18 and provides media guidance for parents and educators.

CHAPTER 2

Historical and Philosophical Perspectives

> *History is the witness of the times, the light of truth,*
> *the life of memory, the mistress of life.*
>
> (CICERO, DE ORATORE)

After reading this chapter, you will be able to do the following:

- Discuss the various beliefs about child development and the modes of instruction stemming from philosophical convictions that go back centuries.
- Explain that historically the family and the community have played significant roles in children's education but that, at different periods, each setting has had a more dominant position, with the school assuming leadership at the beginning of the 20th century.
- Describe how parents, teachers, and community members have always worked together to some degree for children's benefit, although the idea of partnerships is relatively new.
- Identify how, in recent decades, the federal government has encouraged new procedures for parental involvement in children's education.
- Discuss how, since the 1960s, programs for poor children, children with special needs, and children of differing ethnic backgrounds have focused on the importance of parents as an educating force.
- Explain the growing importance of a curriculum emphasis on diversity in American schools as our society becomes more multicultural and global engagements bring greater requirements to American life.

In this chapter, we examine the underlying beliefs of and the evolution of roles played by persons in the home, in the school, and in the community. Then we point out how these past and present views have impacted children's education.

OVERVIEW OF PHILOSOPHICAL VIEWPOINTS

Over the years, the philosophical ideas present in society, together with political, socio-logical, and global events, have influenced educators' ideas about children's development and the purpose of education. Further, these ideas, which range from a conservative academic approach to liberal progressivism, have influenced the ways in which children are taught. As ideology and the social, political, and global circumstances change, the type of relationship and the dominant role that each of the three social settings (home, school, community) has in the lives of children also change. New technologies in today's society enable children (as well as adults) to access burgeoning knowledge bases. The following overview of philosophical theories presents the forces that influence how families, schools, and communities play their roles (see Table 2-1).

The 20th century brought rapid changes to our world society and altered not only our views about how children learn best, but also our views of who is responsible for their education. We also see changes today in ideas about what the content of their education should be. Rapid changes in technology have resulted in changes in how people, even in the most isolated and rural areas, view the world. Events that happen in Africa can affect what students in a small American community study as they acquire the knowledge and skills they need to cope with their own world in the 21st century.

Our views and philosophies today have roots in early philosophical teachings. For example, we find in early Chinese society Confucius (552–479 B.C.) proclaiming that the basic aim of education was to teach individuals to become good and productive citizens and even to make good use of leisure time. These are important goals even today. For instance, Goal 3 of Goals 2000 (U.S.D.O.E., 1993) states that schools should provide an education "so that all children learn to use their minds so they may be prepared for responsible citizenship."

At present, some educators insist, as did Confucius, that there be a **predetermined curriculum** that all children learn and are tested on periodically to show mastery. This is the academic or traditional program, and No Child Left Behind (NCLB) legislation supports this view. Others believe that educators should build on children's prior knowledge and interests to stimulate further learning.

Early Greek philosophers, like Plato (470–347 B.C.), believed that children were the hope of the future. He stated that education must train the spirit through music, the body through gymnastics, and the mind through philosophy, a notion not unlike today's view that education must encompass the whole child (physical, social, emotional, and intellectual). Aristotle (384–322 B.C.) insisted that the teacher must take into consideration the successive stages and rates of child development when considering what to teach individual children. Advocates of an **age-appropriate curriculum** and **individualized teaching** find commonality with some of Aristotle's precepts.

The early-20th-century theories on development tended to cluster around two contrasting views, known today as the **nature–nurture** (or genetics–environment) **controversy**. Brain research findings have added new information on how genetics influence brain functioning and also on how development results as infants and toddlers respond to their world. Some theorists (e.g., Piaget) propose that neither nature nor nurture fully explains child development but rather an interactive–constructive perspective. Other authorities (e.g., Bronfenbrenner, 1979) maintain that although both environmental and biological factors influence development, one cannot understand the development of particular children without considering the cultural, historical, and ecological evidence around them. The family, of course, is an important part of that environment. Murray Bowen takes this concept one step further (Bowen, 1987). His theory of human behavior perceives the family in a holistic way and the family as one emotional unit.

The development of the Internet and the prospect of world cultures moving to a global society have precipitated different outlooks on educational needs. Political perspectives now affect how we perceive education. Traditionally, America has been a society that supports individual accomplishments, but students in the 21st century need new skills and outlooks to relate to persons whose culture and language are very different from their own. By considering the values of the social rituals, the communal orientation, and the different responsibilities found in many cultures worldwide, young people will have a better global understanding in the 21st century and, hopefully, develop the skills to cope with an ever-changing world.

Evolution of Philosophical Perspectives

In the following section, we examine the evolution and status of the constrasting views that influence how we educate our children. Understanding how we change our views of what children need as times change should help you recognize that the political, social, economic, and even global factors at any given time influence how schools and educational practices swing from one perspective to another.

John Locke (1632–1704) was an early advocate of the importance of environmental influences on children's behavior. He believed that a child's mind was a blank slate and that stimuli from others and from the environment controlled the child's development and learning. Following this, the behaviorists, such as John Watson (1878–1958) and B. F. Skinner (1904–1990), believed that children learned as a result of conditioning by adults, who provided stimuli and then rewarded correct responses. Children learned because their needs were satisfied (or not satisfied) by another person or because of environmental factors.

In contrast, Jean-Jacques Rousseau (1712–1778) viewed children as unfolding and developing according to an innate plan—the result of systematic and natural internal forces. Johann Pestalozzi (1746–1827) and Friedrich Froebel (1782–1852) formed schools and developed materials for children based on this naturalistic philosophy. They believed that children learned through play and sensory experiences during the unfolding stages of development. They also maintained that children learned best when homes, schools, and communities were involved. The first kindergartens of the 19th century in America followed these models, using specific materials designed to stimulate this sensory learning. These early Froebelian kindergarten materials changed when John Dewey (1859–1952) introduced his precepts on how children's thinking develops.

Dewey maintained that children develop concepts using their natural environment as they organize and manipulate the world around them. They form and test hypotheses of how things happen and then evaluate and interpret the evidence they have discovered. Dewey proposed that children constantly test and hypothesize as they play and entertain themselves. A playful attitude, he maintained, keeps children motivated, and this motivation is what allows them to grow and learn (Dewey, 1910, 1944). Thus, the development of a child-initiated or play-oriented curriculum in early childhood settings stems from Rousseauian and Deweyian ideas. In a related way, Arnold Gesell (1880–1961) documented children's growth, finding general developmental similarities and trends among children. He concluded that development is a result of laws and a sequence of maturation that is a continuous spiral. Gesell and his associates maintained that parents and teachers must permit the child's natural unfolding before learning can take place (see Table 2-1).

In the mid-1800s, Charles Darwin's (1809–1882) work on evolution and natural selection provided enormous momentum for the scientific study of children, and his theory supports principles in both the nature and nurture positions. Darwin's studies of his own children, as well as studies of different species in the Galapagos Islands, challenged

TABLE 2-1   Perspectives of Major Theories of Child Development

Orientation	Nativism	Behaviorism	Interactionism
Basic premise	Based on Darwinian theory, *On the Origin of Species* (1859), that all organisms seek to enhance their chances of survival. Genetics or internal mechanisms are primary focus in children's development.	Environment as a primary force in children's development.	Both internal mechanisms and environment are forces in children's development.
Major contributors	G. Stanley Hall (1844–1924) Arnold Gesell (1880–1961)	J. B. Watson (1878–1958) B. F. Skinner (1904–1990)	Jean Piaget (1896–1980)
Stages of development	Developed sequences of characteristic behavior. *Maturational readiness* means that a child must develop to an appropriate point before training or teaching has an effect.	No stages. Learning happens as a result of conditioning. *Classical conditioning* and *unconditional stimuli* result in a reflex response, which later becomes a learned response. *Operant conditioning* means that a child learns as a result of receiving positive reinforcers or rewards.	Children develop by assimilating external stimuli and accommodating new stimuli to already existing structures. Sensorimotor stage (birth–2 years): use of senses. Preoperational stage (2–7 years): use of mental imagery. Concrete operations stage (7–11 years): logical thinking occurs.
Meaning for parents and educators	Adult supports development and observes outward behaviors that indicate readiness of learning.	Adult determines desired behavior and sets up strategies for reinforcing children when behaviors occur.	Adults provide a rich and stimulating environment that assists children in interacting with that environment as they construct their own knowledge.

Children develop concepts using their natural environment as they organize and manipulate the world around them.

the idea of a fixed nature for species. Development, he insisted, unfolds in a natural, dynamic way, and all species adapt to their particular environments in order to enhance their chance of survival.

A third view, often labeled the **interactionist–constructivist theory**, has emerged in recent decades. Theorists with this orientation insist that both biological and environmental factors affect development in a reciprocal manner. As different theorists expanded this perspective throughout the 20th century, they focused on specific aspects of development. Jean Piaget (1896–1980), a cognitive theorist, proposed that children develop by assimilating and acting on stimuli, or information, from the environment and by

TABLE 2-1 *(Continued)*

Psychoanalytical (Psychological)		Social-cultural Context
Sexual energy within humans as a force for personality development		Environmental and biological factors affect human development, but cultural, sociological, and historical factors play an important part. Individual development depends on the relationship and interactions of all these elements.
Sigmund Freud (1856–1939)	Erik Erikson (1902–1994)	Urie Bronfenbrenner (1917–2005) Lev Vygotsky (1896–1934)
Three structures: Id—instructive Ego—rational Superego—moral	Expanded on Freud's theories.	Multiple and distinct ecological systems affect development. The systems and all institutions within the systems interact and affect each other.
Oral stage (birth–1 year): need for gratification from the mouth. *Anal stage* (2–3 years): need for gratification from the anal area. *Phallic stage* (4–5 years): need for gratification from the genitals. *Latency stage* (middle years of repression of sexuality).	*Basic trust* (birth–1 year): development of sense of inner goodness. *Autonomy* (2–3 years): development of sense of self and pride in achievement. *Initiative* (3–5 years): takes charge of activities. *Industry* (6 years–puberty): becomes a producer and user of things.	*Microsystems*: experiences and influences from school, family, peers, church, etc. *Ecosystems*: institutions that do not directly affect the child but indirectly affect the child's experiences— extended family, neighbors, mass media, etc. *Macrosystem*: overarching values, laws, and customs of a particular culture or society. *Metrosystem*: the interconnections between these systems.
Adults provide the needed support so that children's instincts are satisfied, but not so much that children fail to move appropriately from one stage to the next.		Adults are only one part of the influences that affect learning. Adults who are aware of influences can to some degree control them.
Family Systems Theory.	Murray Bowen (1927–)	Interdependence of members within the group. Dynamic nature of the family: as one member changes, others change to develop an equilibrium within the unit.

accommodating new stimuli to already existing structures. He held that children construct their own understanding and knowledge, which change only as they find inconsistencies in their environment and incorporate the new information to produce new insights or knowledge.

Another view recognizing both internal and environmental influences was advanced by Sigmund Freud (1856–1939) and his followers. Freud was the first psychologist to view human nature as all-encompassing. He formed his views by studying his dreams and recollections of his childhood experiences and those of his patients. His psychoanalytical theory was mainly concerned with human emotional, motivational, and personality development, even though he recognized the biological, social, and intellectual aspects of development. He believed that both the positive and negative aspects of sexual energy are the driving forces of human behavior. Freud viewed sexual energy as biologically determined, but allowed that environmental factors do determine how this energy is invested and thus how children grow.

Erik Erikson (1902–1994), a follower of Freud, felt that sexual energy as the driving force of development was too limiting an explanation. Erikson identified eight stages of development, each with positive and negative attributes, and he insisted that cultural and social values affected how one progresses from one stage to another. For Erikson, there are **critical periods of development,** and for a person to develop normal patterns of behavior, the positive attributes at each stage need to be satisfied before the next stage can truly develop.

Theorists, of social–cultural context such as Lev Vygotsky (1896–1934) and Urie Bronfenbrenner (1917–2005) also regarded development as being influenced in a reciprocal manner by both biological and environmental factors. They believed, however, that to understand development, it is necessary to take into account the cultural and historical contexts in which development occurs. These theorists contended that there are many social systems with which a child interacts (e.g., family, school, neighborhood, community, and dominant beliefs in society), and it is a combination of these interactions that affects development. The theorists of social–cultural context have steered educators to a greater understanding and acceptance of the complexities of development.

Vygotsky stressed the importance of recognizing both the biological–physiological and cultural factors that influence a child's development. He insisted that it is the social interactions that children experience within their unique cultural and historical context that determine each child's unique developmental pattern.

In earliest development, Vygotosky believed that biological and maturational factors influence a child's physical and intellectual development to a large degree. Later learning, he felt, was a result of children's independently acting on and interpreting their environment, and his theory shows that at that point, the varying social factors better explain the physical and mental changes in children's growth. For example, in one significant Russian study, Vygotsky (1978) shows that children interact in different ways with various adults, and how these interactions progress over time determines the whats and the hows of a child's learning.

As children's development approaches the problem-solving stage, Vygotsky believed that two spheres of operation are present. One is the ability to problem-solve independently when concepts are already mastered; the other is the potential learning and problem-solving ability. The space or variation between these two levels was labeled the **zone of proximal development** (Vygotsky, 1978) and is the area where teachers can be most effective by controlling the amount of guidance they provide (see Figure 2-1).

In a similar fashion, Bronfenbrenner's theory examines the ecological systems that affect children's development. According to Bronfenbrenner, these interacting, interdependent social–ecological systems are the primary elements that differentiate and actualize the biological potential of children (Bronfenbrenner, 1979). In other words, the interplay between biology and ecology causes changes in the child, which in turn produce other changes. In addition, the theory holds that these cascading changes have ever-increasing effects, both positive and negative, on a child's development.

Murray Bowen (1927–) describes the complex interaction of the family unit (Gilbert, 2006). There is an interdependence among family members that provides solidarity and mutual cooperation. Individual members within the family system demand support, approval, and attention from each other. They also respond to other family members' needs or expectations. The ambitions and goals of one member can alter those of other members, or the first member may be pressured to change his or her goals. For

FIGURE 2-1 **Vygotsky's Proposition on the Process of Children's Intellectual Development** *Source:* Based on Vygotsky (1978).

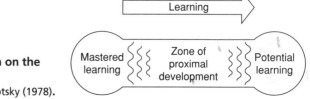

example, in one patient's family (Gilbert, 2006), children were expected to attend college, but Holly was involved with an interesting young man. However, he was unsuited for her, according to her family (i.e., "He wasn't college material"), and family members began to exert pressure on Holly until she stopped dating him. As family goals and ambitions can cause changes in one member's behavior, the theory indicates that stress on one member will cause anxiety among the other members. Bowen's theory requires teachers to view children's social, emotional, and intellectual development in the context of the family unit, because the family's functioning affects the child's functioning.

Children have two spheres of operation. One is their ability to problem-solve independently. The other is their problem-solving ability under the guidance of a more skilled adult.

Cognitive ability, or intelligence, is normally associated with theories of child development. It is impossible to present even a summary of the extensive literature dealing with human intelligence, but we urge readers to seek this information in educational psychology and child development books such as Puckett and Black (2005) or McDevitt and Ormrod (2009). Readers will find the traditional early-20th-century views of Spearman, Terman, and Thorndike on the innate and unchanging nature of IQ (intelligence quotient) still supported in contemporary research and writing. For example, Herrnstein and Murray (1994) and Jensen (1998) argue for this viewpoint. For a contrasting position, readers should look at Nisbett's (2009) recent analysis of studies that concludes firmly that environment accounts for most of children's intellectual development.

Most educators and child development authorities, however, find the work of Howard Gardner (1993) and Robert Sternberg (1997), who present convincing evidence of multiple intelligences, to be very useful. These two authorities and their associates provide convincing evidence that IQ does move beyond a single, static reasoning ability and does change with time and experience.

It should be clear that throughout history, theorists and researchers have stressed specific but different elements and aspects of development. All these theories, together with political and social events, have influenced how families, schools, and communities envisioned their roles in educating children throughout the generations. We believe students should maintain a perspective on human development that recognizes the contributions of various theorists, thus providing a richer understanding of human growth and development, as well as a platform for decision making.

IMPLICATIONS FOR TEACHERS

Theories and Schooling

Pause for a moment and see how the following vignette connects with some of the perspectives on learning described in this section.

⌒◝⎯ Mr. Bozeman, the new principal at Edwards Elementary School, is pleased with his faculty's response to the recent workshop on Using a Project Approach in Classrooms. And during a teachers' meeting focused on meeting state standards, he was delighted to hear the librarian's comment on the fourth and fifth graders' interest in and questions about Somalia. Apparently, a newspaper article about hungry children in the African nation had piqued the children's interest. They asked where Somalia is located and what life is like in that country. The question "Why do children starve there?" began the search for more information.

The librarian then asked the teachers if any children had expressed an interest in pursuing those questions as they looked for projects to work on in their classes. She wanted to know if she should gather more materials and displays on Somalia and on the causes of hunger around the world. "Is this something that would lend itself to a class project?" she wondered.

Several teachers felt that this particular focus could be very productive for their groups because it contained the ingredients for a term project to research, write about, pursue artistic work, and even dramatize. One teacher objected: "Heavens, I have my outline already set for next term. And I can't afford to have the students go off on a tangent just because there's a tragedy in some other part of the world."

HISTORICAL PATTERNS

Partnerships among homes, schools, and communities for children's education is a concept of the 1980s, 1990s, and 2000s, yet throughout the history of the United States, we find connections among the functions of these three vital social settings. At different times, each, as an institution, has occupied a dominant role in children's education, at the same time acknowledging the others as important forces in helping children to succeed in society.

In colonial times, the family was the major force for educating children, although the community exerted pressure on families that did not conform to local codes of conduct. Later, as towns and villages developed, community leaders recognized that some families were not willing or able to educate their children successfully. Taking command in the later colonial period, community leaders gave needed support to families, developed laws concerning education, and eventually formed public schools to ensure that children met the community's objectives. Still, infants and toddlers were to remain at home with their mothers, and there was no distinction in programs for children according to age. A classroom would include children 3 or 4 to 16 years old. The primary purpose of their education was to teach reading so that they could learn to read the Bible and become moral persons.

In the late 1800s, as public schools developed into bureaucracies, professional educators moved to the forefront and took responsibility for overseeing schools and curricula. At the same time, the public mandated a more diverse curriculum, so teachers were required not only to teach academic skills but also to provide programs that would help children develop socially, physically, morally, and emotionally. At this time, when blue-collar jobs required increased technical skills, schools also became responsible for teaching vocational skills. In the later 20th century, when only part of the school population succeeded in these extended schools, questions began to arise. Parents and communities became perplexed and displeased about the low success rates, and alienation often set in.

In the late 1930s and early 1940s, mothers were expected to be home with their infants and toddlers. But during the 1940s, the time of the Second World War, women were needed to work in the munitions factories, and programs for infants and toddlers were needed as these women went to work. In the 1950s, these programs ended as men came home from war and women returned to their homes, becoming once again responsible for the upbringing of the young. In the 1960s, women became interested in careers outside the home and children were in need of care. Another concern in the 1960s focused on children raised in poverty. Many of these children lacked the skills to succeed in school, and this meant care and programs for preschoolers to overcome deprivation. Parent education plans were also needed. In the 1980s, there were more single parents and more women in the workforce, so infant and toddlers programs expanded again.

Beginning in the 1990s, a new trend for developing collaborations (stimulated by researchers, by educators, and more recently by federal agencies) became a focus for parents, community leaders, and teachers. In this way, many people came to appreciate the truth of the African proverb, "It takes an entire village to educate a child." As you consider the following historical overview of relationships among parents, communities, and schools, consider what happens to children as society changes.

In this section, we trace the changes and forces that have shaped our present educational condition in the United States with respect to the roles played in childhood education by families, communities, and schools from the dominant culture. We also consider attitude changes over three centuries toward the children from minority cultures and other special populations. Naturally, all changes have affected the roles and responsibilities of the three institutions for the education of all children. Table 2-2 lists major American events affecting family–community–school relationships.

TABLE 2-2   Events Affecting Family–Community–School Relationships

1600s	**Families Responsible for Children's Education**
1642	Massachusetts Bay School Law requires all families to teach children to read the Bible and the laws of the land.
1647	Old Deluder Satan Law requires every community of 100 or more to establish schools.
1700s	**Communities Responsible for Children's Education (national influence—state responsibility)**
1800s	**Educational Establishment Responsible for Children's Education**
1815	First Parent Program established in Portland, Maine.
1835	Massachusetts establishes first state board of education.
1852	Massachusetts establishes the first mandatory school attendance law.
1867	U.S. Office of Education established.
1873	First public school kindergarten founded in St. Louis.
1888	Federation for Child Study founded.
1889	G. Stanley Hall establishes the first child study center at Clark University for studying children and disseminating information to parents about child-rearing practices.
1896	*Plessy v. Ferguson* Supreme Court decision supports segregation.
1897	National Congress of Mothers founded (later became the Parent–Teacher Association).
Early 1900s	**Educational Establishment Responsible for Educating Parents as Well as Children**
1909	White House holds first conference on care of dependent children.
1912	Children's Bureau established in Washington, DC.
1916	First parents' cooperative founded at the University of Chicago.
1920	Rehabilitation Act assists veterans of World War I to get job training.
1924	Immigration Act establishes the national origins quota system.
1942–1945	Japanese American internment program.
Mid-1900s	**Parent and Community Involvement in School Policies**
1954	*Brown v. Board of Education* Supreme Court decision opens the way for desegregation of schools.
1956	Ford Foundation offers a grant to New York City to train volunteers to work with teachers.
1964	Civil Rights Act mandating desegregation of schools paves the way for compensatory education acts, which require parental involvement in schools.
1965	Elementary and Secondary Education Act/Title I Head Start and Chapter 1 programs begin.
1965	First Bilingual Education Act passed.

(continued)

TABLE 2-2 *(Continued)*	
1967	Economic Opportunity Act follow-through programs begin.
1972	Home Start programs established.
1975	Public Law 94-142, Education for All Handicapped Children Act (amended in 1990 to the Individuals with Disabilities Education Act [IDEA]) passed.
1975	Rehabilitation Act, Section 504, amended to prevent discrimination against persons with disabilities in programs using federal funds.
1984	First national symposium on partnerships in education sponsored by the President's Advisory Council.
1986	Federal Preschool and Early Intervention Program Act, Public Law 99-457, extends Public Law 94-142, mandating services for preschoolers.
1986	Handicapped Children's Protection Act (Public Law 99-472) is passed.
Late 1900s	**Parent and Community Involvement in School Policies**
1988	National Association of Partners in Education is formed.
1988	Educational Partnerships Act, Title VI, is passed.
1988	Family Support Act is passed.
1990	Americans with Disabilities Act extends Section 504 of the Disabilities Act to prohibit discrimination against any person with disabilities in private or public employment.
1992	Head Start Improvement Act passed, extending services to infants and toddlers.
1994	Goals 2000: Educate America Act signed into law.
1996	Personal Responsibility and Work Opportunity Reconciliation Act (Welfare Reform Act) passed.
1997	IDEA reauthorized.
1999	Twenty-First-Century Community Learning Act introduced as part of the Educational Excellence for All Children Act (Title X, *Chapter 1*—a reauthorization of the Elementary and Secondary Act).
Early 2000s	
2001	USA Patriot Act passed.
2002	Education Sciences Reform Act—In Title I schools, the instructional strategies for any new projects are to be based on scientific research.
2002	No Child Left Behind Act (Title I, Section A)—Families in Title I schools have a right to select a "preferred" school if their child is in a "chronically underachieving school."

FAMILY AS A SIGNIFICANT EDUCATIONAL FORCE

From prehistoric cultures to modern society, the family has been the most important social setting for educating the child. In all societies, children must learn skills of survival, the rules and regulations of the society in which they live, and the values by which their society functions (Eitzen & Zinn, 2005). We all know that children learn by imitating the actions of others and repeating these actions, especially if they are rewarded in some way. Children also learn by imitating movements, sounds, and actions in their environment.

The education that children received in the colonial period depended on economic status, ethnic background, the child's gender, and to some extent the section of the country in which the child lived. Early settlers, for the most part, were able to form cohesive family units that depended on one another for survival. Towns and villages, particularly in New England, were initially established around particular religious groups migrating from Europe. With their religious heritage, early colonists believed that children needed to learn not only the vocational skills necessary for survival but also particular codes of behavior and moral integrity. The more economically advantaged also valued reading and writing for their own children. It was a patriarchal society, and in most cases teaching was the responsibility of the home, with the father the dominant force. Parents, grandparents, and older siblings were the primary instructors. Fathers taught their sons the skills needed to carry on the family vocation; mothers taught their daughters homemaking skills. In the intact homes, children had a profound appreciation for and sense of family. They tended to understand their social roles in the family and the role their family played in the larger community.

Puritans in New England were adamant about the need to learn to read and write and stressed the importance of reading the Bible. Parents assumed this responsibility. In addition, certain women who became more skilled in teaching gathered in their homes children whose parents were unable to teach reading and writing. The practice resulted in the creation of *dame schools,* precursors of our current primary schools.

The education that children received in colonial times depended on their economic status and needed vocational skills.

In the southern colonies, wealthy settlers hired tutors to teach their children academic skills, in addition to the behaviors befitting the children of a plantation owner; poor parents were responsible for educating their children as best they could. For the most part, African Americans were forbidden an education, and because of slavery, Black families were often torn apart, so that even parental teaching of basics was hampered.

When colonial children needed to learn skills the family was unable to provide, apprenticeships were sought, and boys as young as 7 years old were sent to live with a master craftsman. Apprenticeships were the precursors of our later grammar schools, for in many colonies the masters were expected to teach reading and writing as well as the skills of their trade.

In the colonies, basic formal education was available to established families, but children of slaves and Native Americans were considered unworthy of this basic education (Davis, 2006). There were, however, notable exceptions to this trend. The Church of England in the South and Quakers in the middle colonies provided educational opportunities for a few African Americans, some Native Americans, and some poor European colonists.

REFLECTION

Think of your own family's influence on your education and compare it to the types of education your parents and grandparents received. Share stories with your classmates to see how the historical patterns of families are similar or different.

COMMUNITY AS A SIGNIFICANT EDUCATIONAL FORCE

As townships in the colonies became more established in the late 1600s and the early 1700s, religious leaders began to dominate the determination of children's education within the community. Thus began the American tradition, extant today, that a community oversees its schools and determines school policy and curriculum.

The Puritans are credited with establishing the foundation of public education in this country because of their belief that all children, whatever their economic status, need to be educated. They believed that every child in the land should learn the rigid codes of behavior for a religious society and the "meaning of salvation" from Bible reading. As early as 1642, a Massachusetts law required all parents and master craftsmen to teach reading and writing to children in their care to ensure that children attained "religious understanding and civic responsibility" (Pulliam & Van Patten, 2007). However, it was difficult to enforce such a mandate because of widespread illiteracy in the adult population. Consequently, in 1647, the Old Deluder Satan Law was passed; this required townships with 50 or more households to provide a teacher of reading and writing for young children in the community. Townships that had more than 100 households were also to provide a Latin grammar school to prepare boys for university study.

These laws were not easy to enforce, but they were important in establishing a precedent for education as the young nation expanded. First and foremost, the family had primary responsibility for educating a child, but the laws also laid a foundation for community responsibility in assisting families in educating the young. Because communities hired the teachers, they also taxed families on their property so as to have funds to pay them.

In the late 1700s and early 1800s, political and economic factors in the United States again affected the relationship of families and communities in educating children. The advent of the Industrial Revolution meant that families moved from an agrarian-based economy to one increasingly dependent on manufacturing. Now fathers, and sometimes mothers, left home to earn a living, and there was little opportunity to teach children vocational skills or reading and writing in the home. As urban populations began to rise, many families became isolated from their kin. Thus, the changed circumstances demanded a new response to the country's needs.

The Republic came into being at the end of the 18th century, and as it unified, the strong influence of religious communities was replaced by the notion of nonsectarian education. Political leaders such as Benjamin Franklin and Thomas Jefferson believed that the new nation needed a literate populace and that it was not sufficient to educate only the wealthy and the strongly religious. Education, they felt, needed to be available to children from different social and economic classes and should be more functional. Merchants added their voice to that of politicians, for business interests realized that the nation needed workers with more than rudimentary literacy skills and more practical skills than those provided in Latin grammar schools (Sadker & Sadker, 2005).

If wider schooling opportunities were to be available, something needed to be done to help communities establish schools. The new government responded, and significant pieces of legislation, such as the Land Ordinance Act of 1785 and the Northwest Ordinance Act of 1787, were passed by the Continental Congress. These acts encouraged settlers to move to the Midwest and to set aside land to support schools. Such acts indicated the new nation's faith in education, even though, in writing the Constitution, the founding fathers left the responsibility for education to the individual states.

The ideas and practices of European philosophers and educators also influenced educational thought in the United States. These new ideas regarding who was to be educated, as well as where and how, did not immediately change American children's education, however (Pulliam & Van Patten, 2007). Community sentiment first had to endorse any practice. Even today, in a general sense, community standards, mores, and expectations are among the strongest determinants of social behavior and participation. Community validation continues to be necessary for any substantial change or redirection to take place in children's educational opportunities.

IMPLICATION FOR TEACHERS

Historical Periods and Expectations

Pictures can show very different educational requirements. To check for differences, look at the photo at the beginning of this chapter, where 19th-century children are doing their lessons. Then look at a modern photo—for example, that of the child at a computer (the third photo in Chapter 1). The children in both photos are observing a process important to their lives. The adults in the photos most likely realize the important educative process demonstrated too, but how adults handle the learning depends on the times and the culture. So, considering the generational values, what effect do you think these events would have on the school's expectations for the children pictured?

SCHOOL AS A SIGNIFICANT EDUCATIONAL FORCE

The mission of formal schools and support for public education have increased gradually over the more than two centuries the United States has existed as a nation. Our founding fathers expressed the need for universal, free, and secular education, but it has taken a long time to achieve this goal for all children.

Even in the early 1800s, the prevailing view was that education was a family responsibility; any education beyond a family's immediate capacity to give it was a luxury. Some communities at that time maintained public schools for their children, and some charity schools existed for the poor. In addition, religious sects continued to provide schooling in some areas for all children, and, of course, there were private schools for the wealthy. In the early 1800s, though, universal education was not yet supported in the United States.

It was not until the mid-1800s that the political and economic climate provided fertile ground for the establishment of free, open, and secular schools in the United States. On one front, new immigrants were voicing dissatisfaction about being barred from the political process. Trade unions were forming, and unionists believed that the path to success was by educating their children. Also, humanists and educators, such as Horace Mann (1796–1859) and Henry Barnard (1811–1900), wrote and lectured about the benefits of universal and secular education (Pulliam & Van Patten, 2007). In addition, the movement of the population from rural to urban areas meant that many families lacked the resources to educate their children at home. The time for public education had arrived.

States at this time urged local communities to begin taxing themselves to provide public schools for their citizenry. States also started the practice of giving aid to communities needing support. In 1852, Massachusetts began to require compulsory attendance, but it wasn't until 1918 that the last state in the union to do so—Mississippi—enacted legislation requiring children to attend school. With such enactments, parents began to relinquish to schools the responsibility for educating their children; however, home and community continued to influence many educational trends.

As schools became the major force in educating American children, a professional education establishment emerged that influenced parents as well as local and state governments on curriculum. Some collaborations between schools and homes resulted, but often parents and communities were at odds regarding the specifics of children's education.

As compulsory education took hold in the late 1800s, it became apparent that many children in the United States were not being reared in the manner that the dominant culture felt necessary. Poor children in urban communities were often viewed as neglected, and new immigrants from southern and eastern Europe, unable to speak English, had different values and views on child rearing (Davis, 2006). It became clear

With new immigrants and a growing urban society, a movement emerged in the 1920s and 1930s for more openness in education.

that schools with a prevalent Puritan ethic did not meet the needs of many children. Something needed to be done, and parent organizations with strong female advocates were formed to press for action on more comprehensive schools. Schools were urged to provide hot lunches for needy children, and the children of immigrants were taught English so that they could be assimilated into American society (Fass & Mason, 2000).

Newer Trends

Philosophical swings in education, from conservative and academic to more liberal and progressive, have resulted from what the American public has perceived was needed in different periods. For example, with new immigrants and a growing urban, industrialized society, a movement emerged in the 1920s and 1930s for more openness in education, with schooling tailored to the needs, interests, and abilities of children. The methods used reflected the view that if children's innate abilities differed, then the type of teaching should differ, and the materials and time allowed for learning should also differ. Then, in the 1950s, as the space race captured people's imaginations, U.S. citizens became concerned about the lack of an academic focus, and a swing to a more rigorous academic curriculum followed. This required that all children learn specific material or face failure.

Following the civil rights movement of the 1960s, social issues were of great concern, and again schools were pressured to change to a more responsive curriculum (Edwards, Derman-Sparks, & Ramsey, 2006; Schuman, 2004). Many recognized that a child's cultural setting had an influence on how he or she learned; therefore, it was important to use techniques that accommodated these differences. Then in the 1980s and 1990s, globalization of the economy and communications produced pressure from parent groups and communities to again promote greater academic achievements (Eitzen & Zinn, 2005).

In the 21st century, there is considerable interest in brain research, which has implications for schools and curricula. Researchers (Bruer, 1999; Dowling, 2004) emphasize the complexities of influences that affect how children grow and develop. Steven Pinker (2002) and others have pointed out that environmental, ecological, and contextual factors do make a difference: They affect genetic development of the embryo, and these effects extend through the prenatal stage. In spite of beliefs that the nature–nurture controversy would be resolved by now, political and social forces, as well as genetic studies, continue to challenge curriculum and how schools should operate. Families, schools, and communities are challenged to blend these new perspectives to provide the best learning environment for each child.

Parent Involvement in Schools

At the beginning of the 20th century, as society brought pressure on schools to change the ways in which they operated, similar forces were directed at parents. No longer were parents viewed as most knowledgeable on how to rear their children. Psychology as a science came into its own at this time, and young children quickly became a focus of study. A number of theories on child development and the best ways to rear children were advanced.

In 1815, the first parent education program was held in Portland, Maine, to instruct parents in proper child-rearing practices. Also, through the efforts of Elizabeth Peabody (1804–1894), a follower of Froebelian programs, kindergartens were established, first by church societies and settlement homes and later as part of public schools. Not only did kindergartens provide moral and religious training and a safe, healthy environment for children, they also provided a subtle and indirect way to reach immigrant families and influence them in rearing their children according to the beliefs of mainstream society (Fass & Mason, 2000).

In the late 1800s and early 1900s, interest in the plight of urban children became a focus for some early childhood educators. Armed with new knowledge of the importance of good nurturing and proper training in the early years, child-care centers and family child-care programs were established as extensions of kindergarten programs. Many of these programs were directed at poor families in which mothers worked outside the home.

Early parent involvement meant educating parents and encouraging them to support school activities. The National Association of Parents and Teachers, later to become the Parent–Teacher Association (PTA), was established in 1897 for this very purpose. Community involvement in parent education came in the form of women's organizations, such as the Society for the Study of Child Nature (1888), the American Association of University Women (1881), and the National Association of Colored Women (1896). These organizations sponsored conferences and published magazines promoting parent education and stressing the importance of parents taking an active role in children's education (Sadker & Sadker, 2005).

Child study in the late 1800s became a focus at colleges and universities as a result of the work of G. Stanley Hall (1844–1924), one of the first psychologists to use a scientific method for studying children. Many universities established laboratory schools for preschool-age children where educational theories and child-rearing practices could be tested. Supported by federal and private funds, these schools provided courses in child development and parent education, as well as courses in practice for teachers and researchers; then they disseminated information on their research.

Perhaps the zenith of early parent involvement came with the founding of parent cooperatives at the University of Chicago in 1916. These programs were modeled on the British nursery school program, founded by Margaret McMillan (1860–1931). Although McMillan founded her school for the poor, **nursery schools** and the first **parent cooperatives** were adopted in the United States by middle-class parents, and parent involvement became entrenched. An open **play-oriented curriculum** was emphasized in both nursery schools and parent cooperative programs as they developed. Not all of the newer nursery school programs were as committed to total parent involvement as were the parent cooperative programs, however. Parents of children in cooperative programs were decision makers within the schools. They hired teachers, approved the type of program, served as assistants in classrooms, and planned the parent education programs (Gutek, 2005; Taylor, 1981).

During the first half of the 1900s, parent education became viewed as vital to the welfare of society, and professional educators began to feel responsible for providing this service. Parents, even though no longer considered experts in child upbringing, were still viewed as essential components of children's success in school and later in life. Professionals felt that parents needed help in determining how they could support their children's learning and thus benefit society (Taylor, 1981). A rather popular belief of the time, at least among the middle class, was that the mother should stay at home to raise her children, and she should learn how to raise them from the experts. With ur-banization, however, more mothers worked outside the home, and they needed child-care services.

During some periods in history more than others, emphasis has been placed on the need for society to help provide child care. In the 1930s, the Works Progress Admin-istration (WPA) offered a program that provided full-day care for families in poverty. Then, during World War II, **child-care centers** were set up in factories so that mothers could support the war effort. Great attention was paid to training teachers in child de-velopment and to creating curricula. Parents, however, were seen not as collaborators, but rather as needing support and education.

Parent involvement in education was given a boost in the 1960s, when President Lyndon Johnson launched his War on Poverty. The legislation started the Head Start programs that not only provided educational and health services for children in low-income families, but also mandated parent involvement in these programs (Withers, 2006).

In the late 1990s, with large numbers of mothers again in the workforce and wel-fare mothers required to return to work, quality child-care services gained importance as a buttress for all parents. National child-care organizations such as the National As-sociation for the Education of Young Children had established guidelines for quality care in the late 1980s, and the Welfare Reform Act of 1996 stressed the need for such care if mothers were to leave the welfare rolls.

During this time, research on early brain development stressed the importance of home influences on children's cognitive, social, and emotional development (Kamerman, 2005). Equally important was the Head Start research that demonstrated positive long-term effects for children in programs with strong parental involvement. These programs led not only to academic success in later schooling but also to success in employment later in life (Stewart & Kagan, 2005).

REFLECTION

Now would be a good time for you to check with some neighbors who have children in school in order to find out what they expect to teach their children themselves and what they expect the school to do. As prospective teachers, do you and your classmates feel that the responses reflect current professional viewpoints?

Federal Involvement

Following the establishment of the U.S. Office of Education in 1867, the federal govern-ment took particular interest in families. The first White House Conference on Care of Dependent Children in 1909 sparked interest in child welfare throughout the nation, and in 1912, as a follow-up, the Children's Bureau was established. Following that pe-riod, educational opportunities abounded through university courses, lectures and con-ferences, school programs for parents, magazine articles, and books. Later, television programs instructing parents on how to educate their children were developed, even though TV was seen as both a positive and a negative influence on child learning. A proliferation of publications from various federal agencies has continued into the 21st century, with even more information available through the Internet.

As society has become increasingly urban, decision making regarding children's education has become more complex. The federal government influences educational issues by granting monies for projects or by withholding them from states not complying with federal mandates. State educational offices, in turn, have also developed curricula and issued mandates regarding what should be taught in schools. The federal government's focus has changed somewhat in recent years, however, and it now requires that the states take more responsibility. Still, by establishing goals and then financially supporting schools by block grants and special funding for specific goals, the federal government continues to play an active role in influencing educational issues.

New Federal Directions

The Goals 2000: Educate America Act of 1994 signaled a change in federal involvement in educational practice. Goals 2000 was presented as a new effort in which the federal government's role was to be one of support and facilitation to improve schools for all children. Provisions in the act established very general goals as incentives and then gave support to states and communities as they worked to meet those standards and objectives (Riley, 1995). The legislation, incorporating eight national education goals, emerged from 1990 legislation passed during the first Bush administration (U.S.D.O.E., 1993).

After the establishment of Goals 2000 in 1996, President Bill Clinton added the America Reads Challenge. Recognizing that reading is a skill developed not only in school but also in the home and community, the initiative called for schools to involve community organizations and homes to help ensure that all children could read by the end of third grade (Mitchell & Spencer, 1997).

In January 2002, President George W. Bush signed the No Child Left Behind Act (NCLB) and in November 2002, the Education Sciences Reform Act, as part of Title I, Section A. Under these acts, local, state, and federal agencies assume certain responsibilities for ensuring that parents are offered better and expanded opportunities for their children in Title I schools. Institutions must be evaluated on the basis of state standards, and failure produces sanctions. For example, if a child is in a chronically underachieving Title I school, his or her parents have the right to select another school and seek supplemental academic help from approved educational providers. Schools, private educational enterprises, and **faith-based** organizations are eligible to provide supplemental educational services to low-income students, students with limited English proficiency, and students with disabilities. The approved organizations provide help in teaching language arts, reading, and math before or after school, on weekends, and during the summer. Schools seeking funds to improve their programs must select strategies that have been demonstrated to be effective based on scientific research (Reyna, 2005).

FORCES AFFECTING EDUCATION IN THE 21ST CENTURY

As noted previously, practices regarding education in America have changed from one generation to the next. Our perceptions about child development and learning styles change as new studies and findings present evidence to confirm or modify one theory or another. Evolution is natural and ongoing as research and empirical studies continue.

In addition, social changes, political forces, and economic pressures, as well as beliefs and values, continue to develop in our country. These are bound to influence educational practices. Futurists study signals and societal trends and make sobering pronouncements about what will happen in future decades and generations. As writers of this book, we resist any urge to speculate on how new movements will fit into this overview of historical patterns of philosophical outlooks. As observers of current practices and new developments, however, we conclude that the following topics will likely have a significant impact on future school objectives.

Population Diversity

The rapidly expanding mix of culture and ethnicity in America will continue, and the changing demographics will affect U.S. education. Although some legislation and judicial decisions that affect amounts of immigration, employment practices, and educational opportunity in the United States exist, these guidelines will be revisited in the years ahead. American culture has changed rapidly since the civil rights legislation was passed in the 1960s, and most agree that minorities, recent English-language learners, and foreign-born residents meet greater acceptance in the majority culture and find more positive responses than before.

Ethnocentrism is less prominent than in previous generations, and most Americans are confident and positive about the "tossed salad" quality of American communities in the 21st century. Multicultural curricula and pointed attempts to foster antibias programs have made a positive impact on American schools and neighborhoods (Edwards et al., 2006). The election of Barack Obama as president in 2008 has given strong credence to the notion that America has entered a postracial era. We feel that this emphasis will continue and that partnerships formed by families, schools, and communities will continue to be the best possible ways to promote the advantages of diversity and demographic change.

Globalization

Interest in and concerns about global issues will affect our country's schools and our attitudes toward education for years to come. In the space of two decades, much of American cultural life has been influenced by connections to worldwide products, information on different values and beliefs, and shifting job markets.

Americans have been forced to shed their traditional insular stance and to focus on events taking place on all continents. We rarely think now of a self-sufficient "fortress America" that looks inward for inspiration and services. Each year, new electronic developments tie the U.S. economy and lifestyle to other parts of the world. The end of the Cold War and the beginning of new conflicts brought about a dramatic change in American influence and interest in other regions. A new feeling that what happens in Africa, Asia, Europe, and South America engages Americans as never before and is bound to affect all education. Major educational associations in the United States now have an international department, and the increase in international conferences highlights this trend. The achievements of American students have been compared to those of foreign students for more than 50 years, but in the last decade, the intensity of the scrutiny has increased and comparisons are now made yearly. All this comes from the question "Will Americans be able to compete in the **global marketplace**?"

New comparative education procedures are helpful in using global perspectives on education, and this practice provides a logical extension of our need to extend educational partnerships to another level. Already, many schools have established connections with "sister schools" in foreign lands to enhance the notions of worldwide common interests and concerns (Swiniarski & Breitborde, 2003). The Internet and other electronic communication devices make the thousands of miles of distance a trivial variable in worldwide communications.

Technology

Technological advances have always been viewed as support and enhancement for schools and other educational projects. During the 20th century, these advances were viewed much like new appliances that would make the home more efficient. Today, however, new technological developments (starting with networked personal computers) influence curriculum decisions, modes of instruction, and communication with families and communities.

The use of audiovisual devices to enhance curriculum grew rapidly during the second half of the 20th century. In the last decade, however, an explosion of technological equipment to enhance communication, entertainment, and retrieval of information has pushed young children's education and interests in very different directions (Wartella & Gray, 2004).

The emphasis on the ability to use a keyboard at an early age, the skill in flipping from one TV screen or browser window to another, and the location of information in vast databases scattered over the planet all show that education outside the classroom will only increase. Linear paths, chronologies of events, and local schedules have far less importance in

Changes in the world force Americans to realize that educational approaches in other countries will have an effect on American education.

a high-tech-mediated environment. The new overarching frame of reference affects our work with children and all that we do with families and communities.

Religious and Spiritual Variables

America, as well as other nations, is witnessing greater interest in spiritual concerns and the expansion of religious practices in local communities and abroad. Most teachers realize that studying different religious practices can be a beneficial and stimulating project that will enhance a multicultural classroom. In elementary schools, religious dogma must remain outside any curriculum. The science curriculum in American secondary schools, however, has been affected in recent years by the issue of **evolution** versus **creationism** and **intelligent design**. Statutes in several states and judicial decisions have come about as special-interest groups have contested the secular orientation typical of American public schools. As different religious groups become more visible and expand their influence in public education, questions about religious beliefs and principles are likely to receive more study and adjudication.

PARTNERSHIPS AND COLLABORATIONS

Partnerships in education is not a new concept if we consider the various groups that have worked with schools in this country over the years. As we have pointed out, families and community leaders have great input into the functioning of schools. The question arises as to how these would-be partners of the professional education establishment view their roles and how they assume responsibility and leadership.

In the 1950s and 1960s, the American public, for the most part, viewed all education as the responsibility of schools, and parents were expected to support teachers and their programs. The community school movement also developed at this time, though, and for those subscribing to the movement, the purpose of schools was more comprehensive. Community-school advocates felt that schools, in addition to serving young children, could serve the larger community by providing various resources for the public within the school facility.

Educators took an active and strong role at this time, often advising parents on their roles and responsibilities. There was prosperity in the United States and a belief that through education the United States could provide equal opportunities for all citizens. In supporting this goal, programs staffed by volunteers sprang up in New York City and elsewhere. In the beginning, these volunteers were primarily nonworking mothers, but as the programs expanded and spread to other areas, retirees, college students, and businesspeople also began providing volunteer services.

A new impetus for collaboration came in the 1980s as businesses became concerned with the quality of education in the United States. Some government officials recognized that educational problems could not be solved by the public sector alone. Thus, an Educational Partnerships Program was established under the Educational Partnerships Act of 1988. The purpose of the act was to encourage community organizations, including businesses, to form alliances to encourage excellence in education (Danzberger & Gruskin, 1993).

Partnerships no longer involved just the basics of establishing good relationships with parents and using community resources. Businesses became involved in schools in a variety of ways. Partnership arrangements grew to include such supports as volunteers for the classroom, internships for teachers, mentors and tutors for particular areas of study, visits to business establishments, special projects sponsored by businesses, provision of new technology for classrooms, and assistance in shaping school policy. The *businesses for education* notion continued to prosper in the 1990s, and the 21st Century Community Learning Centers provision was introduced as part of Title 20 of the NCLB Act. Under the act's provisions, communities acquired grants to establish safe places during after-school hours, homework centers, and tutorial services. In addition, special cultural, recreational, and nutritional opportunities were offered. Communities were encouraged to use public schools as a base for uniting the services within a community in order to deliver education and human resources to all members of the community.

REFLECTION

Make a brief checklist of parent, volunteer, and community persons involved in a primary classroom with which you have contact. Try to label their contributions and then check with the administrator about the philosophy behind this type of involvement.

CHILDREN WITH SPECIFIC NEEDS

Major social events in each generation result in social policy changes that affect persons with special needs. After World War I, Congress enacted the Rehabilitation Act to assist wounded veterans. The act enabled veterans to receive special training and therapy so that they could return to work. In the 1930s, the Great Depression resulted in Franklin Roosevelt's New Deal programs. As education was extended to persons with special needs, it soon became apparent that education alone was insufficient to provide opportunities necessary to use these skills in the workplace. In 1975, the Rehabilitation Act was amended (Section 504). The amendment was intended to prevent discrimination against persons with disabilities; thus, a program receiving federal funding could not refuse employment to individuals solely on the basis of a disability. In 1990, the Americans with Disabilities Act extended these same rights to persons seeking employment in any public or private venue (Turnbull, Turnbull, & Wehmeyer, 2007).

In a similar vein, political movements in the 1960s resulted in sweeping changes for American education and in the corresponding roles of parents, schools, and communities.

The civil rights movement resulted in the Civil Rights Act of 1964, which acknowledged that children in segregated schools received an inferior education. Whereas middle-class White parents have always felt themselves a part of their children's educational process, before the landmark legislation of the 1960s, many parents in minority and low socioeconomic groups felt disenfranchised. Parental involvement for all, regardless of heritage or economic status, became highlighted in this era and continues to be an important issue. In spite of all the progress, Orfield and Yun (1999) and their associates in the Harvard Civil Rights Project present sobering figures on resegregation patterns appearing in several regions of the United States.

Children in Poverty

In the 1930s, social welfare programs were seen as a way to help the poor. Aid to Families with Dependent Children was just such a program. It existed at first primarily to assist unmarried mothers in providing for their children. Even with a rising economy after World War II, large numbers of American children were still living in poverty and entered school with many problems that affected their ability to learn. In 1965, President Johnson launched his War on Poverty, which had a far-reaching impact on children raised in poverty.

The Elementary and Secondary Education Act of 1965 (Public Law 89-10) was the largest grant ever made by the federal government to aid education. Educational programs such as Title I/Chapter I, **Head Start, Home Start,** and **Project Follow Through** were designed under this act to compensate for the lack of early education for children living in poverty. In addition to receiving educational experiences, children and families were provided with health, nutritional, and psychological services. Parents also were to play important roles as volunteers, paid aides, and instructors in their children's education. Parents became part of Head Start advisory boards, thus acquiring decision-making powers both in selecting teachers and in making curriculum decisions. Teachers in these programs were expected to make home visits, and the curriculum used was expected to reflect both the experiences and the cultural heritage of the diverse population of children. By implementing the federal guidelines, these programs provided an early model for family–school–community involvement.

By the 1990s, Americans believed that although Head Start was deemed successful, the War on Poverty had somehow failed. In spite of many welfare programs, child poverty increased from the early 1970s to the 1990s. In an attempt to change this trend, the Family Support Act of 1988 stressed education and job training for welfare recipients. Mothers on welfare who returned to work or enrolled in education programs were guaranteed child-care assistance and coverage for health insurance through Medicaid.

After some degree of success, there were new proposals in the 1990s to considerably modify the act. The 1996 welfare reform act (titled the Personal Responsibility and Work Opportunity Reconciliation Act) replaced child-care entitlement programs with a single federal Child Care and Development Block Grant (CCDBG) and gave states responsibility and authority to administer and fund grants. The bill required all child-care funds to be administered from one lead agency, thus avoiding overlap of programs. Other aspects included the following: (a) A limit was placed on how long a family could receive welfare; (b) persons receiving welfare were required to get a part-time job or receive job training; and (c) mothers with a child less than 1 year old were exempt, but only for one child (Blank, 1997). The funding stressed improving the quality of care for children and providing education for the parents, although child care was not guaranteed.

In 1998, Congress reauthorized the Elementary and Secondary Education Act, with provision for appropriations to be made until fiscal year 2008 (Head Start Bureau, 2006). President Bush's reauthorization of Head Start in 2003 was to ensure that Head Start and

An important aspect of IDEA is that children with disabilities are to be included in the regular classroom setting.

other preschool-prepared children would have higher success rates in school. The reauthorization also stipulated that states receiving Head Start dollars would need to include in their plans certain accountability requirements. The proposal encourages states to develop plans for comprehensive and integrated preschool services within the local school systems.

Children with Disabilities

As federally supported programs developed over the years, parent groups realized that they had the power to determine educational opportunities for their children. A group of parents in Missouri, concerned about how their children with disabilities were being treated, united with a civil rights organization to focus on rights for children with disabilities. Thus, the Education for All Handicapped Children Act (Public Law 94-142) emerged in 1975. This legislation ensured a free and appropriate education to all children with disabilities; in 1986, amendments to that act (Public Law 99-457) extended rights and services to 3-year-olds. In the 1990 amendment, the title of the act was changed to the **Individuals with Disabilities Education Act (IDEA)**, and the term *handicapped* was changed to *disabled*. In keeping with this legislation, the Head Start Act was amended in 1992 by the Head Start Improvement Act, and services were extended to infants and toddlers. In 1997, the act was reauthorized, with modifications in the delivery systems, requirements for placement of students with discipline problems, and provisions for professional development. IDEA became such a comprehensive law that it was divided into three parts: Part A describes the extent and policies of the law; Part B describes the rights and benefits for 3- to 21-year-olds; and Part C (formerly Part H) addresses infants and toddlers (Turnbull et al., 2007).

Under the preceding acts, parents have the right to be involved in the entire process of their child's evaluation, placement, and educational objectives; and if there are differences of opinion, they have a right to the services of a mediator. Children placed in special education programs now must receive an **individualized education program (IEP)** prepared by a school team, including the parents, and an **individualized family service plan (IFSP)** for families with infants or toddlers with disabilities. Readers will find more specifics on these regulations in Chapter 6.

Since the laws have been enacted, the number of children classified as having disabling conditions has risen steadily. And in many instances, parents and educators have collaborated successfully in educating children with special needs. They have also used the resources of the community in different ways, including having volunteers work one-on-one with children.

Implications for Minority Populations

The history of parent–community–school involvement has taken a different course for minority families. In the early years of immigration, many families saw their ethnic, cultural, religious, and social traditions blended into a homogenized "American ethic" (Edwards et al., 2006). Greater educational opportunities and material benefits were afforded to those immigrants who lived by the dominant code of values. For many families, however, assimilation was more difficult or less desirable. Poverty and racial distinctions also caused many families to be denied opportunities for equal access to quality education or job opportunities (Davis, 2006). Today such access continues to be a problem, though in more subtle ways. In spite of antidiscrimination laws throughout the United States, many families, though assimilated, still feel the sting of subtle discrimination. Poverty and racial distinctions mean that certain persons have to work much harder to gain access to the rights and privileges assumed by White, middle-class Americans.

Marcus, whose Mexican immigrant father was a struggling tenant farmer in a small midwestern community during the 1960s, confronted poverty and daily discrimination at school and in his community. He was advised to take technical and agricultural courses at his small high school. His adviser pointed out, "After all, your father is a tenant farmer, so your hope for college is pretty slim, isn't it?" In spite of lack of school support, Marcus persisted in following the college preparatory curriculum and surmounted other challenges—social and financial—as he coped in his small community in rural America. He succeeded, and today he has a doctorate from a prestigious university and is a candidate for a college presidency in the Midwest.

Although he achieved his goals, Marcus had to overcome bias toward his ethnic heritage and prejudice about the abilities of migrant farm families in America. The determination of minority students like Marcus, supportive legislation, and attitude changes in America have produced greater acceptance and enhanced opportunity for persons from other cultures.

The history of the United States is a story of waves of immigration. In the 1600s and 1700s, western Europeans, bringing an Anglo-European culture and a Christian ethic, came to colonize different parts of the United States—crowding out Native Americans and bringing slaves from Africa. In the 1800s, more Roman Catholic groups moved to the United States as a result of European famines and the U.S. military acquisition of Mexican territories. Then, in the early 1900s, other groups from central and southern Europe and Asia came to the United States seeking new opportunities. In the later part of the 1900s, as other countries sustained internal strife, a large number of immigrants came from Latin America, Asia, the Caribbean, and Middle Eastern countries, seeking refuge from conflict and persecution. By the mid-1900s, three-fourths of the immigrants each year were from Asia and Latin America (DeVita, 1995). All these immigrant groups have had an impact on American culture, values, and traditions; however, the dominant culture in America has remained European American and the dominant religious traditions stem from Judeo-Christian beliefs (Gollnick & Chinn, 2006).

Since the early 1800s, concerns over the impact of immigration and the challenge to European American culture and values from immigrants with non-Western cultures resulted in a series of immigration acts, several of which were passed in the 1920s (Davis, 2006). The Immigration Act of 1924 was a major law that established a national origins quota system for the United States that narrowed immigration to persons coming mostly from European countries. The Immigration and Nationality Act of 1965 changed the policy again to one of "first come, first served." Finally, in the late 20th and early 21st centuries, issues concerning **undocumented immigrants** stirred controversy in political, economic, and educational settings.

In the 21st century, Americans witness national and global events that affect their lives and challenge their lifestyles. A War on Terrorism is being waged worldwide, causing concern about the safety of American borders and making citizens feel more vulnerable to attack. Because of problems in developing countries, an increasing number of immigrants are entering the United States, both legally and illegally. Some Americans feel the need for cheap labor, which new immigrants provide, whereas others argue that schools and social systems are not equipped to accommodate this influx of new residents. The U.S. Congress has long debated the need for new immigration statutes and procedures. Whatever the outcome, however, in the 21st century American educational institutions will be challenged to provide an appropriate curriculum to meet the needs of culturally diverse children and to prepare young people to face not only national but also global challenges.

The early minority groups were assimilated in accordance with their ability or willingness to adapt to the majority culture. This usually worked for Europeans but rarely for ethnically different populations. Today, Native Americans, African Americans, and Hispanics are large ethnic groups in the United States. In spite of civil rights legislation and affirmative action, however, they have higher poverty rates than Whites (Lichter & Crowley, 2002). Throughout the history of the United States, these particular groups have been denied easy and equal access to quality education, which means that their chances of moving out of poverty are less than those of their European American counterparts (Lichter & Crowley, 2002).

REFLECTION

An educator working in an ethnically diverse classroom with several children with special needs commented, "I do a lot of drill and practice with my students because I'm trying to get them caught up. But, you know, I wish I could do more art and music with them." Which philosophical and societal influences do you think cause this educator to hold this view?

MINORITY POPULATIONS AND FAMILIES   During the colonial period, the two major non-White ethnic groups were Native Americans and African Americans. For these two groups, the family, in conjunction with its ethnic community, was the primary means of educating children.

A communal ethic has always prevailed in Native American communities. Historically, community groups helped parents educate children and teach them economic skills, their cultural heritage, and spiritual awareness. The community expected all women to teach necessary homemaking skills, and boys, as they matured, were taught by various elders to hunt, survive, and fight. Through rituals, ceremonies, and oral traditions, the tribal elders passed on the religious beliefs and cultural heritage to young Native Americans (Szasz, 1988).

African Americans have lived in the United States since 1619, when the first individuals appeared as indentured servants at Jamestown. By the 1700s, most African Americans were slaves, and plantation owners exercised complete control over them. Although slaves had few opportunities for formal education, African Americans formed a distinct culture. It was the family and plantation that taught the children values, community behaviors, and as many of their native customs as possible. In some instances, the children learned to read and write as they played with their owners' children (Rich, 1997). During these early years, however, the sanctioned education for African American children was limited to the skills necessary for working and living within the plantation community (Davis, 2006).

MINORITIES AND THE COMMUNITY   As the American expansion began, conflicts arose among European American settlers regarding the education of non-Anglo persons. Some colonists believed that Native Americans should be segregated or even annihilated and that African Americans should be kept from getting an education so as to avoid revolts (Berlin, 1998; Davis, 2006). Others, whether from religious zeal or from practical considerations, maintained that it was necessary to acculturate minority children about European American culture through education. In different parts of the country, religious groups

In the South, despite laws forbidding education for African Americans, some plantation owners did teach the children of slaves to read and write.

established schools and missions to educate and convert Native Americans. In the Southwest, priests and nuns taught Native Americans farming practices, vocational skills, and the Spanish language. Still, the major emphasis at that time was that all groups should accept the Caucasian conquerors' religious teachings and codes of behavior.

In the South, despite laws forbidding education for African Americans, some plantation owners did teach the children of slaves to read and write so that they could become skilled workers and read the Bible. Later, some African Americans formed their own clandestine schools (Weinberg, 1977). In the early 20th century, a Black Muslim faith known as the Nation of Islam emerged to promote different views of Black history and culture (Gollnick & Chinn, 2006).

Despite these modest efforts to provide a better education, the majority community, up to the 1960s, made little effort to work with Native American and African American children and their families. The European American community dictated the rules of conduct, irrespective of the values and culture of other groups. For many minority groups, these early practices were the beginning of problems between schools and families. Such practices of disrespect have resulted in serious alienation problems and further discrimination against minority-group members.

IMPLICATIONS FOR TEACHERS

Textbooks Over the Years

To see some of the dramatic changes in social outlook over the last 50 years, examine a primary grade textbook from the 1950s. Check out the amount of material, references, and photos related to minorities. Now examine a current textbook to see how minorities are included. Are we doing enough? Are we planning well for a multiracial/multicultural society?

MINORITIES IN THE SCHOOLS   In the 1800s, as schools became the major force for educating children of the dominant culture, they were also seen as the way of melding the increasing number of immigrants into a common cultural ethic for American society. Mexican Americans and Asian Americans migrated to the United States in increasing numbers during the late 1800s, though, and these groups created more variety in ethnic grouping, and therefore, more controversy (Davis, 2006). Differences that existed in earlier periods in how society provided schools for minority groups compared to the dominant group reappeared in the late 1800s. The controversies continue in some areas today.

Native Americans.   To ensure better **acculturation** of Native Americans, boarding schools were established in the late 1800s, and children were removed from their families to attend them. Some schools were established on reservations, but the Bureau of Indian Affairs, not the tribe itself, was in charge of them. European American–style schools were established to teach Christianity, English, and basic skills and to provide some vocational training to young Native Americans. No sense of partnership in education existed, and each Native American community was expected to submit to the type of education provided by the majority culture (Szasz, 1988).

African Americans.   The aftermath of the Civil War offered greater chances for formal education for many African Americans. *Freedman schools* were established in the South, where former slaves and their children, together with some impoverished White children, were taught the curriculum of the New England common schools. Reading, writing, math, geography, moral development, and industrial education were taught so that these students would be ready for the labor force (Berlin, 1998; Gutek, 2005). There was, however, so much resistance to literacy for African Americans from southern Whites after Reconstruction that until 1954, African American children were educated in segregated schools. The landmark case *Brown v. Topeka Board of Education* (1954) precipitated action by African American leaders and many Whites that led to the Civil Rights Act of 1964, forcing school desegregation (Davis, 2006).

Although numerous writers describe the positive effects of integrated schools and point to evidence of racial harmony in the United States, Gary Orfield and associates (Boger & Orfield, 2009; Orfield & Yun, 1999) present disturbing evidence of trends toward resegregation in urban and southern schools. A postracial America appears to be a work in progress.

Hispanic Americans.   For the Hispanic American population, family, school, and community attempts at partnerships have had a history more of alienation than of cooperation. When America gained possession of the northern half of Mexico in 1848, the Spanish–Mexican–Indian population was expected to become American. Most Americans at that time believed that Mexican Americans were inferior and could be denied their rights (Rich, 1997). In spite of negative attitudes and unequal treatment throughout the era, however, migration of Mexican Americans to the United States has continued to the present.

Large numbers of other Hispanic groups from Central America and the Caribbean have migrated to the United States, especially since the 1960s. Some new émigrés were affluent and had few economic and educational hardships, but the great majority were poor. Presently, over 60% of Hispanic Americans are of Mexican origin and, together with Puerto Ricans, experience the most discrimination (Sadker & Sadker, 2005). It is projected that by 2010, Hispanic Americans will number 50 million (U.S. Bureau of the Census, 2008), making them America's largest minority group.

From the beginning, the concept of assimilation in American public schools created conflicts with Mexican American populations. English was the language of instruction, and newly enrolled children were expected to abandon Spanish as well as other aspects of their culture. Although no segregation policies or statutes existed for Hispanic Americans, de facto segregation did, and most Mexican Americans over the years attended separate and inferior schools or were placed in separate classes. Accounts (Sadker & Sadker, 2005) show Hispanic American classrooms over the years reflecting Anglo-American curricula and traditions, fewer well-prepared teachers, and less money spent on programs.

These circumstances often alienated Hispanic parents, who saw no purpose in education that destroyed their family lifestyles, even though early political leaders in the Hispanic community urged assimilation to avoid trouble. During the civil rights movement of the 1960s, new leadership appeared for Mexican Americans. Parents and political leaders joined forces in making demands for better schools and more equal treatment. Some gains came in a curriculum more responsive to their cultural heritage, instruction in Spanish, and "culture-free" IQ tests (Weinberg, 1977). The Bilingual Education Act of 1968 and subsequent acts provided non–English-speaking children with instruction in both their native language and English, but much controversy regarding the best way to teach non-English speakers persists. Presently, individual states determine the type of language instruction for their students.

In states with large Hispanic populations, bilingual programs were popular. In these programs, children received at least some academic instruction in their native language. But many believed that the programs delayed Hispanic children's progress in English and denied them academic opportunities. In 1998, California voters replaced their extensive bilingual programs with **Structured English Immersion (SEI)** programs. Children in these programs are immersed in English now—these are labeled **English Language Learner (ELL)** programs—and get assistance as needed. Shortly after the programs started, achievement scores went up, and opponents of bilingual education used this evidence as a reason to eliminate more programs. This has practically eliminated bilingual education in California. More recent studies (Gandara, Maxwell, Garcia, Asato, Gutierez, & Stritikus, 1999) challenge these findings, though, and indicate that factors other than SEI programs resulted in higher test scores. Most recent linguistic and sociocultural studies indicate that multilingual and multicultural experiences are very important for both majority and minority students in America (Trawick-Smith, 2009).

Asian Americans.   Asian Americans, an extremely varied group, are relatively late arrivals to this country. Chinese workers first came to the western United States in the 19th century to help build the railroads. The first Japanese came at the beginning of the 20th century, and Southeast Asians immigrated in the 1970s and 1980s as they fled their war-torn countries. Korean immigrants have steadily moved to American cities over the last half century. As with all immigrants, cultural and religious beliefs and practices vary, but Buddhism and Hinduism are two strong religious influences for Asians. Asians have been discriminated against and have experienced hardships in adjusting to life in the United States. Discrimination was most profoundly felt when Japanese American families (as well as some other Asians) living on the West Coast were forced into internment camps in 1942 and denied their civil liberties. In spite of the hardships, as a group, these immigrants have been more academically and economically successful (Turnbull et al., 2007).

However, like other émigrés, Asian Americans have been expected to put aside their languages, cultural mores, and customs and adjust to European American culture. Because there are many different Asian languages, schools struggle to find the best types of language instruction for Asian children. As with other minority groups, Asian American parents have often been alienated or confused by school expectations and by mainstream American culture. This problem often makes good parent–school–community relations in Asian communities difficult to maintain.

Arab Americans.   Immigrants from Middle Eastern and South Asian countries have come to the United States in relatively small numbers throughout American history. Many of them practice Islam, the Muslim faith, and individuals (though Caucasian in ancestry) have become a distinct minority community within the larger American culture. For a large number of Americans, a Muslim presence did not make an impact until the Al Qaeda attacks on the World Trade Center and in Washington, D.C., in 2001. This tragedy brought the Muslim culture into greater focus in America, and it highlighted the influence of minority religions in our country (Davis, 2006). Religious practices have changed and altered in form in America for generations, and they frequently have an impact on traditional Judao-Christian practices. In addition to Asian-based religions, a number of European Americans are beginning to seek non-Christian spiritual guidance (Gollnick & Chinn, 2006).

CURRICULUM EMPHASIS ON DIVERSITY

Adjustments in educational opportunity for minority groups have changed dramatically in recent decades. As federal legislation has guaranteed educational opportunities for all children, regardless of race, ethnicity, religious beliefs, ability, socioeconomic class, or sexual orientation, greater voice has been given to minority persons with different orientations. Many authorities believe that a multicultural and antibias curriculum is strengthening American educational standards, living conditions, and productivity (Edwards et al., 2006).

Increased migration to America in the 21st century has resulted in a more heterogeneous American society. This heterogeneity, Internet access to the world's different cultures, and globalization of the world's economy require teachers to develop new strategies to respond to children from various language, religious, and cultural backgrounds, and also to respond to the educational needs of the nonimmigrant population. Teachers need to help monocultural children learn how to function in a diverse America and in a world economy where knowledge of other languages and cultures will be a key to success (Stewart & Kagan, 2005). As education for diversity gains dominance, it will be incumbent on teachers to include parents and community members even more than they do now in shaping the curriculum, staffing the school, and providing appropriate and authentic materials. Education for diversity requires substantial change from the techniques of the **monocultural** curriculum that dominated education in the United States in the 19th and 20th centuries.

Changes in Attitude

At the beginning of the 20th century, the prevailing attitude in the United States was that minority groups and new immigrants should be assimilated. The children from different groups were to learn the behavior codes, values, and cultural expectations of the majority culture. This attitude of assimilation continued into the 1950s and 1960s, with the tacit assumption that "something was wrong with the other culture" that assimilation could fix. **Cultural deprivation** was the term used during the 1960s War on Poverty and in the initial bilingual programs to describe this practice. Officials believed that children needed compensatory programs to make up for this deprivation, and one healthy dimension in the legislation of this period was that parents became included as decision makers. This important step required teachers and parents to communicate and work together, thus affording all a chance to grow.

As parent–school–community partnerships became established in the 1980s and 1990s, attitudes toward ethnic groups and people of different heritages gradually changed. At first, different racial and ethnic groups were recognized; then steps were taken to incorporate and adjust to these differences. Children from diverse cultural and racial families, as well as those in gay and lesbian families, contribute important content to others in the classroom and the community when they share with classmates similiar yet different values, religious practices, and family culture. Acceptance of diverse cultural viewpoints and a sense of our pluralistic society are important curriculum goals if the United States is to remain a strong force in a globalized world (Mbugua, Wadas, Casey, & Finnerty, 2004).

Staff diversity is important in demonstrating positive role models for children from different ethnic groups.

Curriculum and Teaching Materials

Throughout most of the 20th century, all curriculum materials were based on a European American worldview. Caucasian children were the main characters in stories where people lived in pleasant homes surrounded by nice lawns. There were two parents: The father worked hard, and the mother lovingly tended the children. Extended families were rarely depicted. Individuals with different lifestyles were often portrayed as wrong, to be pitied, or quaint. Moral lessons, based on Puritan ethics, were often taught along with reading and writing. History and geography were taught from the Anglo-European viewpoint, and the contributions of other cultures to society's development were largely ignored.

A curriculum of diversity presents materials from several perspectives. People of all cultures and religious beliefs, and those with differing degrees of disabilities and varied sexual orientations, are viewed in a variety of situations, and children study the major contributions of numerous cultural groups (Derman-Sparks, 1989). Customs, rituals, and traditions of different cultures are explored so that students may appreciate both similarities and differences. Teachers can now begin to view minority-group parents as a vital link in communicating aspects of culture to all children.

Problems still exist, though. Textbook companies have, at times, yielded to "political correctness" pressure from ethnic groups and have distorted their presentations of both history and cultures in an effort to "be fair" (Stille, 1998). Alternatively, some school systems have banned textbooks or literary titles that expand on nonmainstream views. Teachers should preview materials to be used with children for their accuracy and currency. When pressure groups exert so much influence that a skewed view of history, different cultural expectations, literary quality, and the makeup of American society hinder children's educational development, teachers must enlist parents and community members to find authentic international, intercultural, and intergenerational materials (Mbugua et al., 2004).

REFLECTION

Consider the different cultures represented in an early childhood classroom with which you are connected. Does the curriculum you have observed relate to or reflect aspects of the cultural backgrounds of the children? Do you find any involvement of parents from the different cultures?

Patterns of Interaction

When minority-group children were first educated in public schools, teachers assumed that they learned in the same manner as children from the predominant culture. If they responded in an unfamiliar way, the teacher assumed that they were either impolite or not very bright. Majority-culture America had a "correct" way to rear children, and minority-group parents were expected to learn these ways or doom their children to failure. Competitive, individualistic, and aggressive learning styles have always been rewarded in traditional American schools, and cooperative learning, until recently, was seen as cheating.

In schools where education for diversity is part of the curriculum, different learning styles are recognized and staff employ different strategies to accommodate all children's learning styles (Banks, 2007). In diverse classrooms, children learn about these different patterns and learn to accept these differences. The family is important in providing a bridge from the family's cultural patterns to the more diverse patterns found in a multiethnic and multicultural society. Given proper opportunities, all children can become conversant with more than one culture (Gollnick & Chinn, 2006; Salend, 2001). In a global economy, this is an important goal for our country's schools.

Summary and Review

Parents, communities, and schools have always assumed significant roles and responsibilities for the education of children in any society. At different times in American history, each of the three social settings assumed greater leadership and responsibility than did the other two. And in most periods, we find some instances of parent–school–community cooperation and collaboration. At other times, conflicts appeared when one institution seemed to dominate the way children were educated.

Parents, communities, and schools have, of course, collaborated from time to time. Not until recently, however, have we seen any significant joining of forces. By the 1980s, it became clear that strong parent–school–community relationships were necessary if schools were to meet the challenge of educating all children. Various partnerships for educating children have been formed since then.

Although free and compulsory education has been a tenet of American educational theory for many years, some communities still have not extended equal opportunity to all cultural groups. From the 1800s to the mid-1900s, most minority-group children attended segregated schools or de facto segregated classrooms with fewer educational opportunities. As desegregation became more prevalent in the 1950s and 1960s, the federal government provided special programs for children living in poverty. Initiators of these programs recognized that to be successful, they must involve parents and the leaders of the communities where these children live. As a result, many minority-group parents acquired decision-making powers over their children's education—a situation that had been absent for generations.

In the 1980s, Americans began to realize the importance of multicultural education for all children. Attitudes continue to change, school staffs have become diverse, and curriculum materials now present topics from a multicultural viewpoint. Many educators have started to value differences and, in the process, to include parents as valuable partners in teaching the curriculum.

In the 21st century, in spite of many federal programs, the number of children living in poverty has remained quite constant for a generation. The federal initiatives to address poverty issues have varied but have included welfare reform, the establishment of national goals, and growing support for schools to develop home, school, and community partnerships.

Understanding the major issues in different historical periods helps you view current events in a broader light. In studying this chapter, you have seen that homes, schools, and communities have always affected how children learn, but recognition or use of this knowledge by educators has varied. In the 21st century, family structure and societal expectations are very different from those at the beginning of the 20th century. Some things have not changed, though, and the way parents, families, and communities were viewed in the past can act as a beginning in deciding how to work with parents and community members today.

Suggested Activities and Questions

1. As you review different philosophical beliefs concerning how children learn, reflect with some classmates on your own experiences in a third-grade classroom. Recognizing that teaching and learning are never linear, speculate on whether you think the teacher followed a more behaviorist perspective or a more developmental view. Justify your decision to the others.
2. Interview a senior citizen and determine whether he or she thinks that family influence patterns have changed since his or her childhood. Request some examples.
3. As you review the history of major legislation affecting education in this chapter, select laws from different time periods and discuss how, even now, you may have benefited (or not benefited) from that legislation.
4. As you review a community's involvement in children's education, develop a list of methods or actions that you and your classmates have actually seen taking place.

Resources

Organizations

American Anthropology Association   *http://www.aaanet.org*
Children's Defense Fund   *http://www.childrensdefense.org*
Civil Rights Project, Harvard University   *http://harvardcrcl.org*
Education Resources Information Center (ERIC)   *http://www.eric.ed.gov*
National Head Start Association   *http://www.nhsa.org*
National Association of Social Workers   *http://www.naswdc.org*

Web Sites

http://www.nap.edu   Site gives information on brain research from neurons to neighborhoods.

http://www.nclb.org   U.S. Department of Education—No Child Left Behind relates to No Child Left Behind legislation—discusses how government is actively involved in education.
http://www/ed/gov/pubs/goals/progrpt/index.html   Gives information on the national education goals and progress made in different areas.
http://www.globaled.org   Site gives resources for teaching about other cultures and countries.
http://www.headstartinfo.org   The federal office for statistics and information on the programs.
http://thomas.loc.gov   Site for Library of Congress that tracks the progress of bills in Congress.

CHAPTER 3

Viewing Family Diversity

*The vast diversity of families found in school and society today suggests an
urgent need for a reconsideration of the ways in which families are currently
and have come to be represented in school curriculum and culture.*

(TURNER-VORBECK & MARSH, 2008, P. III)

After reading this chapter, you will be able to do the following:

- Identify the many different types of family households within which American children are being raised today.
- Discuss the social and economic factors that affect family life.
- Explain how racial, ethnic, and language differences, as well as the marital status of parents, affect the structure and functioning of families.
- Describe how religious factors, cultural expectations, and conditions of disability have an impact on family life.
- Appreciate that families are always in the process of changing from one stage or condition to another.

This chapter will focus on the demographics and diverse nature of families in the United States today. American families vary greatly in makeup and reveal a complexity that has increased significantly during recent decades. Many students have parents who have come from foreign countries, speak native languages at home, and maintain customs, traditions, and celebrations of various religions and cultures. The majority of children do not live in what was once considered the traditional family structure led by a mother and father. Many children are now raised in single-parent families, stepparent families, gay/lesbian parent families, adoptive-parent families, foster-parent families, biracial families, and extended-family situations. Some children have more than one home; others are homeless. Economic resources, a child with special needs, a family member with a chronic illness, and other factors add to the differences among families.

Despite these diversities and differences, however, the American family remains a basic building block in our society. As you read this chapter, consider the complex ways in which families are formed, viewed, and function and how family units work with others and for themselves. The more we understand how families operate, endure, and connect, the better we are able to bring them into a positive connection with their schools and communities. As teachers, we need the support of all parents to promote the best outcomes for children.

DIVERSE HOUSEHOLDS ARE COMMON IN AMERICA

The following vignette points out some not uncommon changes that unfolded in one American family as its members progressed through several years of life:

Five-year-old Jana had just entered Mrs. Thompson's nursery school classroom. Mrs. Thompson found her to be a happy child who came from a "nice family." Like other neighborhood mothers, Jana mother drove her to school. At noon, her mother picked her up, and they often visited Jana's Gramma. In the evening, Jana bubbled away at the dinner table, telling her father and older brother all about her day. Jana was secure and snug in her world, where love abounded. Jana's world was about to change, however.

That winter, Jana's mother became very ill and was often hospitalized. Gramma came to take Jana to school and pick her up afterward. Jana's mother died within the year, and the following year, Jana's life was filled with adjustments. Gramma and Grampa came to live at her house and take care of her, and that helped. Jana missed her mother taking her to school, for now she had to go to the local elementary school with her older brother, who wanted to be with his friends, not with her. Her dad, always involved in his work, just didn't seem to be there every evening, as she would have liked. Jana, however, enjoyed school, worked hard, and made friends.

At age 8, Jana's world shifted again. Her father remarried, and now she had an extra older brother and an older sister. Her own older brother was a "pain" when he looked after her while her father and stepmother were out. Sometimes when that responsibility was shared by her brother and stepbrother, the two boys quarreled and the house got messy. When Jana tried to tell her side of the boys' squabbles, it seemed that her stepmother always became annoyed and then unresponsive. Jana's father tried to comfort her in her room after the quarrels, but he implied that Jana should cooperate more and help become a part of their new life. Gramma and Grandpa had moved away that year, and this seemed to delight Jana's stepmother, who felt they interfered, but Jana missed them.

When Jana was 10, a new baby was born into the family. At times, Jana enjoyed the delightful baby, but she also became jealous when the baby got a lot of attention. Eventually, Jana did begin to develop a more accepting, although shaky, relationship with her stepmother. They especially enjoyed cooking together and taking special packages to neighbors who were ill or in need.

What is a family? Family can mean different things at different times. Jana, in this opening vignette, was always part of a family, but the structure changed several times during her growing-up years.

The term *family* describes particular household groupings that occur in all human societies. According to the U.S. Bureau of the Census definition (2004), a family household has at least two members related by birth, marriage, or adoption. In today's world, however, sociologists argue that a family also includes clustered adults and children who have formed a unit based on mutual agreement (Casper & Bianchi, 2002). For some families, the cluster remains relatively constant; other families, like Jana's, evolve into different arrangements over the years. Whatever the cluster, the family is a dynamic and ever-changing force in a child's life that affects his or her well-being.

REFLECTION

Think back to your own family and how it has changed over the years. How did these changes affect you during your childhood? As you work with children, remember that they need to know you accept their family composition, and they need your support when changes occur within their families.

The term *family* in Western culture was traditionally based on heterosexual married adults raising their biological children. Our definition in this textbook is broader, as we look beyond marriage and sexual orientation. Many stable and prospering family units involve unmarried adults, and although some partners have been married to others, they have reconstituted a family singly or with a new partner without the formality of marriage.

Cultural concepts of what constitutes a "proper" family and the percentages of different family clusters have altered considerably over the years. In the late 19th century, Victorian society in Britain and the United States idealized the family as consisting of two doting parents with several adoring and capable children at their knees. Well into the 20th century, the typical family was considered a father who worked full time and a stay-at-home mother who raised their children, who were born after their parents' only marriage. Of course, this arrangement was far from universal even then, but through literature and folklore, people accepted this picture of what "ought to be" the situation in their towns, cities, and neighborhoods.

Changes in family arrangement in the latter part of the 20th century certainly were dramatic, and we now find far more diversity in the structural aspects and processes of American families. The idealized family form of a married couple raising children has diminished in contemporary America as other arrangements have grown more common (Bianchi & Casper, 2000). Although from 1970 to 2003 the total number of households expanded, the nuclear family (with two parents plus their biological children) decreased from 40% of all household units in 1970 to only 24% in 2006. In the same period, single-parent families increased from 11% of all households to 16%. For families with children, this means that about 68% of children live with two parents, 26% with a single mother, and 6% with a single father (U.S. Bureau of the Census, 2008). The number of single-parent families is particularly noteworthy in the African American community, where more than 60% of families are headed by one parent.

There may be distinct advantages for children raised in a nuclear family, but labeling it as the "normal" family form is risky. Many other family arrangements provide children with a positive upbringing and secure surroundings. Human service professionals need to be aware of subtle and not-so-subtle prejudices toward families that differ from the nuclear model. It is all too easy for teachers to value or feel comfortable with only those configurations that approximate their ideal family unit. The important thing to remember is that many arrangements work quite well, and over time many young children will experience changes in their family structure.

At present, recognized family groups in the United States are very different and vary more from traditional arrangements than ever before (Hanson & Lynch, 2004). It is important to remember, however, that only 40% of all American households have children. Statistics on family makeup cited in this textbook are based on families with children in the household. See Figure 3-1 for the breakdown of household units and note that our categories include only the first two bars of that graph.

Most families, like Jana's in the chapter-opening vignette, are dynamic. Family structure is never permanent; members may form a particular configuration for only a

FIGURE 3-1   Types of American Households in 2008   *Source:* U.S. Bureau of the Census, Current Population Report P20-537, 2009.

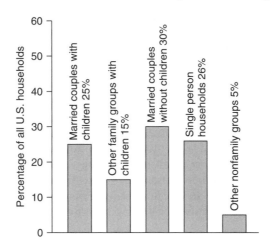

brief time before change comes about. For example, when Jana was in eighth grade, her teacher asked her to draw and label two pictures: one of her family when she was in kindergarten and another of her family now. Jana's explanation shows her grasp of family changes.

In her kindergarten picture, Jana drew and labeled "my real mom, my dad, my brother, and me." In her eighth-grade picture, she drew herself in the center, with other people in clusters around her. Closest to her were figures labeled "dad and my older brother." On the other side but distanced from her were four people labeled "my stepsister, my stepmom, my stepbrother, and my little sister." In the right corner, she had drawn a circle for four people and wrote "my aunt, my uncle, me, and my cousin." When her teacher asked her to explain her pictures, she said, "This first picture is me and my family before Mom died. Dad remarried, so now I have a stepmom and a brother and sister and a little sister. These people," she added, pointing to the encircled group, "aren't really my family, but I stay with them a lot, so sometimes they feel like my family."

Extended family arrangements provide extra care and nurturing for the young.

Public schools in the United States must accept all children in a community, with whatever conditions, orientations, and experiences they have. This means that as a teacher, you will relate to and interact with children from many different family types. You must learn to accept and value all families. Sensitive and responsive interactions are the only basis for healthy home–school–community relations.

As you start interacting with families, be sensitive to differences. Find out about the children's family household as soon as possible. Use inclusive language like *your grown-ups* and *caregivers* rather than *mother* and *father* when talking to children. It's good to find out what individual children call the adults who care for them; then you can use these terms when possible. Have children draw pictures of their family household, label the family members, and display the pictures. You can add family photos to the drawings to create a bulletin board labeled "We Love Our Families." Chapter 4 discusses family functioning in more detail.

DIFFERENT TYPES OF FAMILY GROUPINGS

Nuclear Families

The term nuclear family was coined in the 1940s to distinguish it from the extended family form, a grouping that included parents, children, aunts, uncles, grandparents, and others living in one household. *Nuclear family* originally referred to a family in which the parents are first-time married, the children living with them are their biological children, and no other adults or children live in the home. This form is sometimes referred to as an intact family. A minor variation is the home where the children are not biological offspring but are legally adopted.

From shortly after World War II through the early 1970s, media producers in the United States presented what they considered to be the typical American family. That image of the nuclear family with a father breadwinner and mother homemaker was viewed throughout the United States as the all-American *Leave It to Beaver* or *The Adventures of Ozzie and Harriet* model family. Both families appeared in film, on television shows such as the two mentioned here, in books and magazines, and in advertisements of all types.

This model two-parent home with children usually was presented as stable, thrifty, economically secure, and very happy. Of course, individual situations varied with regard to health, social status, and problems encountered for the sake of plot or to meet current marketing needs. From 1984 through 1992, an updated version of the idealized American nuclear family was portrayed on *The Cosby Show*. This television program featured a happily married African American couple raising their five children. In a nod to changing times, however, both parents were successful professionals. The nuclear family model, and particularly the version with the breadwinner father, is much less predominant today, although some still refer to it as the "normal" family. In reality, this family form was widespread only in the 1940s, 1950s, and early 1960s (Coontz, 2005).

Role redefinitions for men and women, social pressures, changing economic conditions, relaxation of marriage mores, and shifting family functions have all affected the nuclear family's dominance, and only 25% of children currently live with both their married biological mother and father (U.S. Bureau of the Census, 2008). Further, the arrangement with breadwinning father and homemaker mother is now true of only 7% of U.S. households, as women have increasingly entered the workforce while raising children (Hansen, 2005). This significant demographic change for the nuclear family household implies concurrent changes for other types. Figure 3-2 shows this demographic distribution as of 2008.

FIGURE 3-2 Types of Families Where American Children Lived in 2008

Source: Based on 2008 census projections: U.S. Bureau of the Census, Current Population Reports P20-506 & P20-509, 2008.

Note: Foster children are included in various categories.

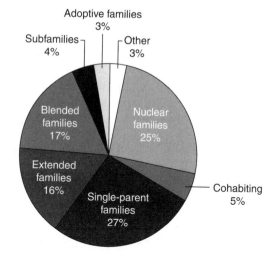

Children in American Families

Adoptive families 3%

Subfamilies 4%

Other 3%

Blended families 17%

Nuclear families 25%

Extended families 16%

Single-parent families 27%

Cohabiting 5%

Single-Parent Families

For a variety of reasons, the **single-parent family** is becoming one of the most common family groupings in the United States today. The *Kids Count Data Book* (Annie E. Casey Foundation, 2008) reported that approximately 32% of children lived in single-parent homes for part of 2007, in contrast to 1970, when 11% of children lived with one parent. Projections also show that about 60% of all children born in the last 18 years will spend part of their minor years in a single-parent family (Annie E. Casey Foundation, 2008). The large majority of single-parent families are led by mothers.

Single-parent families have always been a part of society. The death of a spouse was not an uncommon occurrence in the lives of our ancestors. In earlier periods, however, surviving spouses often remarried soon after the death of a partner—creating stepfamilies rather than remaining single parents. In recent years in the United States, divorce and separation, rather than death, have led to the increasingly large number of single-parent families, as well as the record number of births occurring outside of marriage. In 2005, over 1.5 million babies were born to unmarried women, accounting for almost 37% of all births (Child Trends Data Bank, 2009).

Interestingly, the number of single teenage mothers has steadily decreased from 50% in 1970 to about 24% of the total births to unmarried women, and it is women in their 20s, 30s, and 40s who account for the increase in births outside of marriage. Fueled by greater acceptance of unmarried motherhood and advances in reproductive technology, a small but growing group of single women are adopting children or becoming pregnant through alternative insemination using known or anonymous donors. These women define themselves as "single mothers by choice" and are generally well educated, financially secure, and reaching an age where they feel the need to pursue motherhood even if they have not formed a committed relationship with a man (Bock, 2000).

REFLECTION

Do you use the term *broken family* to refer to a family in which the parents have separated or divorced? Be aware that it implies that the resulting single-parent or blended family is wrong in some way. Do you recall hearing educators use gender-neutral, inclusive terms such as *parent* rather than *mother* or *father*?

Although many single parents achieve noteworthy results, a number of critical issues face the single-parent family, and poverty is foremost. About 42% of children who live with their single mother are poor (Side, 2006), and single-mother families are by far the most common one-parent families (87%). Father-led families make up a much lower percentage—about 7% (2.1 million) in 2007—but their number has doubled since 1990 (U.S. Bureau of the Census, 2008).

Recent census data indicate that even when children lived with only one parent, other adults were present in the home about 41% of the time when the parent was the mother and 60% of the time when the parent was the father (Turner-Vorbeck & Marsh, 2008). Although not counted as stepparents, these other adults might function as such in children's lives as an unmarried opposite-sex partner to their single parent. So, although the following variations in structure are accurate, they may not tell the full story of an individual child's experience in a single-parent household:

1. Single mothers—divorced, widowed, or never married—living alone with their biological children
2. Single fathers—divorced, widowed, or never married—living alone with their biological children
3. Single parents (male or female) divorced, widowed, or never married, living alone with adopted children
4. Male or female parent living alone with children, and spouse incarcerated, deserted, or moved away

As you work with children from single-parent families, remember the various ways these families may have been formed. Keep in mind, too, the difficulty a single, working parent may have in balancing the demands of raising children, maintaining a home, and earning a living. These parents may want to be involved in their child's schooling but find it difficult to manage. Try to provide small projects that can be completed at home for parents who may not be able to spend time in school but still want to help out and be involved.

Blended Families

Most divorced and widowed persons remarry, and **postnuclear family units** emerge from the remarriages. In some cases, a single adult joins an already existing single-parent family to form a stepfamily, and in others, an adult with his or her own children joins a partner with children to form a **blended or reconstituted family**. In any given year, 7% of children live with a legally married parent and stepparent and another 2.5% live with a parent who is cohabiting with a heterosexual partner (Penn & Crosbie-Burnett, 2005). Several studies conducted near the end of the 20th century (Bianchi & Casper, 2000) reported that soon this family form, when we include cohabiting couples with children, will be the most common in America. The following are typical arrangements in blended families:

1. A parent with children remarries a single adult to produce a stepfamily for the new partner.
2. Two parents, each with children, remarry to produce stepchildren for each other and stepsiblings for the children. At least one-half of such new marriages produce children who are half-siblings for the existing children.
3. Cohabiting or common-law couples with children or with children from previous relationships live together but without marrying.

Not all parents seek marriages when realigning their living arrangements. Blended families can easily be formed without marriage; these function exactly as married blends would. The Census Bureau in 2008 revealed that of 6.8 million unmarried couples sharing a household, more than one third have children under 15 years of age (U.S. Bureau of the Census, 2009). Figure 3-2 shows only blended families derived from marriages.

Extended Families

The multigenerational family unit is made up of a nuclear, single-parent, or blended family with additions, usually adult relatives. The identifying feature of an **extended family** is that the reference person, head of household, or wage earner is the adult with young children. Older relatives or other adults are appended to this nucleus. An extended family can occur in any of several combinations. The following are typical:

1. Mother and father with children, plus one or more grandparents
2. Mother and father with children, plus one or more unmarried siblings of the parents or other relatives
3. A divorced or separated mother or father with children, plus grandparents or siblings or other relatives

The extended family arrangement is typical for agrarian societies, and many farms in the 19th and early 20th centuries had three generations of a family living together. Intergenerational families have advantages over nuclear ones: The "extra" adults could provide care and nurturing for the young, to say nothing of helping with farm chores. The extended family was common in Europe in the 19th century and immigrants to the United States brought the practice with them when resettling, but increased mobility of families and other economic factors have led to a decline in this type of family.

Extended families survived in urban areas for different reasons than they did in rural areas. This family form fit the need to economize, to bolster cottage industries, and to stabilize the social situations of newcomers. Extended families became less common in American culture after industrialization, but the configuration has been retained in some immigrant and minority-group homes and sometimes temporarily in single-parent homes, as in the case of Jana in the chapter-opening vignette. Economics alone can dictate the need for sharing a dwelling when families are pressed. Heritage, a need for security, reverence for elders, and the sharing of materials all combine to make the extended family a logical arrangement for many groups.

Adoptive Families

We have seen in the last decade a substantial increase in the number of adopted children; as of 2007, over 2.5 million adopted children lived in American families (Herman, 2007). **Adoptive families** are a varied group and represent many of the kinds of diversity that characterize the American family today. For example, 17% of adopted children are a different race than their parents, 17% live with a single mother, and 5% live with a single father (Wegar, 2006). Many adoptive families also function as nuclear ones, except that some of the family's children are not the biological issue of either parent. Many families include both biological and adopted children. In addition, single-sex families (gay and lesbian partners) also adopt children. Over 3% of American children are adopted, and more than 3% of couples with children fall into the adopted family category.

Some adoptions are arranged through public agencies; others are handled privately by physicians, lawyers, or individuals. About half of all U.S. adoptions are classified as **kinship adoptions** by a stepparent or a biological family member (Geen, 2005). International adoptions make up over 15% of the total, with 48% of that number coming from Asia, 33% from Latin America, and 16% from Europe.

Seventeen percent of adopted children are a different race than their parents.

If you find yourself teaching or caring for children who have been adopted internationally, you will have an opportunity to explore their cultural background with your class. With the permission of the families, you can introduce children to the geography and culture of other countries, along with some of their foods, customs, and traditions. Adopted children can also help your students learn that parents and children don't have to look like each other to be a family. Sharing some of the adoptive family books listed in the Appendix, Bibliography of Children's Books, is another way to promote acceptance and understanding of adoption.

Subfamilies

Although certainly not a new phenomenon, some family groupings, referred to as **subfamilies**, reside in other households for economic or protective reasons. The most common situation is that of the young single mother who lives with her parents or other family members. Although this arrangement is much like that of the extended family, in this case the parent with young children is appended to and is not the central family figure in the household. For tax purposes, though, these units do qualify for head-of-household status. We also find communal arrangements in which two or more family groups choose to live together for economic and other support reasons (Gabe, 2003). New immigrants to the United States often find such communal arrangements helpful as they seek to gain their economic footing.

Foster Families

Families with **foster children** have been in existence for centuries. Charles Dickens and other novelists have alluded (frequently in poignant terms) to foster home arrangements. The arrangements, both legal and informal, exist today in the United States and are increasing in many urban areas as social welfare agencies try to find suitable living quarters for orphaned, unwanted, abused, and neglected children. Although sources vary concerning the numbers of foster children, the U.S. Department of Health and Human Services (2008) recorded 523,000 children, or slightly less than 1% of American children, in foster care. Two-thirds of all foster children are children of color, and although one-half of the total group is available for adoption, records show that only 18% of foster children are actually adopted. Many of these children are considered hard to adopt because of their age, race, or medical and other needs.

At times, childless couples elect to become foster parents for children, but more frequently it is a nuclear family that extends itself to accommodate additional children. The Child Welfare League of America (2003) advanced the argument that kinship must be considered in any foster care arrangement to preserve a child's culture and family heritage, so **kinship care**, care by close relatives, is often sought first for children needing a home. We also have to remember that children are frequently in foster care because of homelessness, abandonment, abusive situations, or medical involvement situations. This means that challenges are often present for families providing foster care.

Arrangements for foster care are most often financial contracts by which a family agrees with a state agency to accept one or more state wards for a stated remuneration. The time span varies from several weeks for newborns, who will be placed for adoption, up to 18 years for other children. In the 19th century, foster care often took place without remuneration, and families accepted children for humanitarian reasons as well as economic objectives, such as help for farms or households.

Families Headed by Gays and Lesbians

Gay and lesbian partnerships are becoming more mainstream in America, and this leads to greater acknowledgment of **gay and lesbian** family units. A child becomes part of a gay or lesbian family in several ways: as a product of a previous heterosexual relationship, through **alternative insemination,** through surrogacy, or via adoption. Working through the foster care system as a foster parent is another route that can lead to adoption by gay men and lesbians who are willing to consider older, harder-to-adopt children (Lewin, 2006).

Although single-sex partnerships comprise a very small percentage of total family units, they function much like other family configurations, have similar child-care needs, and have comparable numbers of separations. Gay and lesbian parents and their children can be subjected to prejudice, however, which can lead to loss of physical custody, restrictions on visitation, and prohibitions against adoption. Yet, an increasing body of research on the children of gay and lesbian parents indicates that their children do as well as other children across many measures (ACLU Lesbian and Gay rights Project, 2002; Cohler, 2006).

Some employers provide medical and employee benefits to partners of either gender, but few states at present recognize same-sex marriages. Currently, Massachusetts, Vermont, Iowa, and Connecticut allow such marriages, and seven other states grant status to gay and lesbian couples through civil unions or domestic partnership provisions, although the legal protections fall short of those provided by marriage. Other states, however, are working actively to prevent marriage between same-sex couples and to ban adoption of children by gay men and lesbians. In 2009, 30 states had constitutional amendments barring recognition of same-sex marriages.

Because of the current social climate, gay and lesbian families must work through the legal system to ensure inheritance and other financial benefits for partners and children. Without the protection of legal marriage, gay and lesbian couples and their children are also denied rights of hospital visitation, financial security, and other protections established by state and federal government. As the United States continues to debate the issue of gay and lesbian marriage, more than 20 countries around the world, including Canada, Spain, and South Africa, have legalized gay and lesbian family relationships through marriage or domestic partnership legislation.

Other Family Groupings

Parental abuse and neglect, substance abuse, HIV/AIDS, homicide, mental illness, incarceration, abandonment, death, and other circumstances (Hanson & Lynch, 2004) can cause children to be without parents able or willing to provide care for them. Some of these children, as Figure 3-2 shows, are living in institutions or boarding facilities that serve as a family substitute, but other runaway and abandoned children, who have escaped social agency notice, find informal living arrangements and temporary homes that provide the basics. These arrangements are always fragile and extralegal. Significant numbers of young children also live with grandparents, aunts, uncles, cousins, and even nonrelated adults. Census Bureau reports show that in 2008, more than 1% of American children were living in such arrangements (U.S. Bureau of the Census, 2009).

Children living with grandparents, with no parent present or involved, is one of the most common arrangements, and approximately 4 million children are part of such families (Hayslip & Patrick, 2006). Taking on the parental role is often an unexpected interruption in their lives, and many grandparents struggle to support their grandchildren and provide adequate housing, nutrition, and care while living on fixed incomes. Despite the difficulties, however, many grandparents find joy in raising their grandchildren and feel the satisfaction of providing a home for children whose lives have been disrupted. Working with this group of caregivers requires teachers and community workers to be sensitive to their needs and alert to social services that might be required.

IMPLICATIONS FOR TEACHERS

Working with Diverse Families

Working with diverse families can be a challenge but also constructive for working in 21st-century classrooms. As an educator, you must develop the knowledge, communication, and interaction skills required to work with all kinds of parents. Your ability to accept differences and celebrate families will help your students do the same.

We have given you a synopsis of family types because these all exist to some degree across the United States. And although the quality of child rearing may vary, any family structure can be effective if children receive love and nurturing. It is more than likely that you know people who fit into one or another of the previously noted patterns, as you do yourself. The economics and social pressures in our country will certainly ensure that diversity in family arrangements continues.

Here are some strategies for new teachers to begin with:

- *Display family photos on a bulletin board and ask willing parents, other family members, and children to explain them.*
- *Create a classroom book of family drawings that children made and present it to the class after practicing the "story" they have related.*
- *Read several stories from our list in the Appendix about the different types of families to show positive accounts of the variety that exists in our country.*
- *Work with your room parents to arrange a family night when all parents bring samples of one of their favorite foods and explain how they cook them. The same can be done with hobbies and crafts. These gatherings always produce marvelous ideas for projects and special exhibits at school.*
- *If you have special-needs children in your class, ask the parents and their case workers to do a presentation on "how Robbie does things and why" or what it means, for example, to take a child with hearing loss on a trip. Educating everyone on what a disability means creates a strong foundation for all persons who have contact with the child.*

SOCIAL FACTORS RELATING TO FAMILIES

Racial, Ethnic, and Cultural Factors

The U.S. Census Bureau has used four racial categories (plus "Other"), for a century, but in 1990, when respondents had an additional write-in blank for "race," they indicated nearly 300 different ethnic group labels. The 2000 census went one step further and provided citizens a place to indicate "more than one race." Although only 1% of the population used the multiple categorization, demographers predict much higher use of the category in future censuses. **Biracial families** are emerging rapidly, and the public in general attaches less importance to race and ethnicity, as evidenced by the election of

President Barack Obama, the biracial son of a white mother and an African father.

Physical characteristics, language, and cultural factors distinguish some families from mainstream culture in the United States and may give them a different identity. In addition, it is important to remember that *race, ethnicity,* and *culture* are terms about human variation that are used constantly in discussions, publications, and research studies. All of this means that students of social action or education must ponder the uses of the terms and the appropriateness of their use, because so much information is arbitrary and subjective.

Although racial awareness has a long history in our nation, race labels are often unproductive, inaccurate, and meaningless. The American Anthropological Association (2002) has labeled race categories as political and social constructions with no basis in human biology, clearly suggesting that current labels provide inadequate information. But a history of race-based policies in the United States has created social and economic differences that persist to this day. With continued reliance on census-based formulas for distributing aid, conducting demographic research, constructing election districts, and tracking racial discrimination, the United States seems destined to use the term for some time.

Biracial families are emerging rapidly in America, and the public in general attaches less importance than formerly to race and ethnicity.

In this textbook, we use the term **ethnic orientation** primarily to refer to the general complex of cultural and physical characteristics, and we use the term **cultural background** to refer specifically to the complex of created, linguistic, and societal—but nonphysical—characteristics that distinguish societies and groups. We do use *race* at times, because it is a social reality and communicates generally used demographic data.

Ethnic identification does, however, more accurately represent the wide demographic palette in the United States. Table 3-1 gives statistics on the major racial and ethnic groups in the United States.

Until the 1970s, American schools and communities operated mostly on the basis of assimilating different cultural and ethnic minorities and language groups into the mainstream European American culture. Since then, however, the concept of **cultural pluralism** (discussed in Chapter 2) has taken root. A large number of schools and communities currently subscribe to the idea of recognizing the positive contributions and qualities of the numerous ethnic and cultural groups in the United States and use them to build a stronger society. Most professionals accept the notion that diversity produces strength (Erickson, 2005).

TABLE 3-1 U.S. Population by Race and Ethnicity in July 2008	
Total U.S. population	308,936,000
Non-Hispanic White	201,112,000
African American	40,454,000
Asian/Pacific Islander	14,241,000
Native American and Eskimo	3,100,000
Hispanic	44,756,000
All Other and Multiple Race	3,007,000

Source: U.S. Bureau of the Census projections. Retrieved April 20, 2009, from *http://www.census.gov/population.*

Majority and Minority Status

The terms *majority and minority* denote the percentage of a population, with the former being more than 50% of the total and the latter being less than 50%. Although the majority in the United States remains predominantly of Western European, White derivation, the popluation has expanded swiftly in the past century to include numerous ethnic and cultural groups. At the beginning of the colonial era, the eastern seaboard colonists were mostly Europeans, with a tiny minority of African Americans. A large group of Native Americans, indigenous to the continent, existed as a separate and parallel cultural complex. Of course, vast changes have come about since that time.

The minority population in the United States reached 20% in 1980; it was 27% in 1995 and about 35% in 2008 (U.S. Bureau of the Census, 2009). Minority families are now common in all but a few of the 50 states. Figure 3-3 shows that African American, Asian, and Hispanic minorities will grow much faster than the White population in the decades ahead. Minority children currently account for almost 40% of our youth population (18 and under), and 22 of the 25 largest city school systems have more than 50% minority students (U.S. Bureau of the Census, 2009). By 2028, one-half of our school-age children will be minorities. It is further projected that by 2050, no single racial or ethnic group will constitute more than 50% of the population in the United States. We will soon need new descriptive terms to replace *minority* and *majority*.

Six states have already arrived at or are nearing a 50% minority population, which means that European Americans are approaching minority status in some parts of our country. These figures indicate a homogenizing of America, for, whereas a few decades ago minorities were concentrated in the West and South, the dispersal of minorities throughout the continental United States has grown rapidly in the last two decades. Of course, this trend has significant implications for our schools.

We have indicated that educational expectations and learning styles vary within all families, and many minority families have favored and even encouraged different learning strategies for their children. So, we must all recognize that people have different ways of knowing and expressing. Then we can acknowledge that differences can be beneficial for schools and our communities.

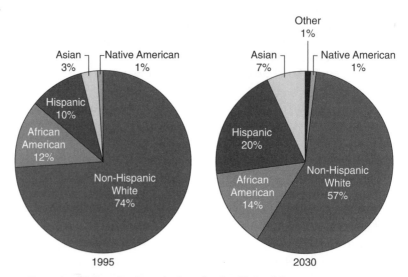

FIGURE 3-3   **Growth of Minority Populations in the United States**   *Source:* U.S. Bureau of the Census, Current Population Report P25-1104 and Projections, 2009.

English-Language Learners

The number of English-language learners in school is increasing rapidly, and language-minority children are the fastest-growing group in American schools (Ovando, 2005). Although Spanish-speaking households account for the largest percentage of this population and are continuing to increase at the greatest rate, a huge array of other languages are represented in schools and communities throughout the United States. In fact, more than one-fifth of the American population over 5 years of age speaks a language other than English at home, and of these 50 million people, more than 11 million speak English either not well or not at all. The school-age members of this group may be foreign-born children of voluntary immigrants, **involuntary refugees**, or undocumented immigrants. They may also be U.S.-born children of earlier immigrants or of Native Americans who have maintained a heritage language in the home. Children may come to school monolingual in the home language, bilingual with that language and English, or with only rudimentary skills in the ancestral language. The diversity of languages and backgrounds is remarkable.

Consequently, about 3.6 million students in the United States need special linguistic assistance in order to participate in a public school curriculum. Less than 10% of these students are now in such programs (Webb, Metha, & Jordan, 2007), however. These statistics are significant for communities and schools where concentrations of non–English-speaking families live and work. Particular problems in communication and general acceptance do appear, and because English is the language of instruction in most schools, children with less than full fluency are at a distinct disadvantage. In fact, a disproportionate number of English-language learners do not achieve well in schools (Ovando, 2005).

English as a Second Language (ESL) or English for Speakers of Other Languages (ESOL) programs focus on **immersion and submersion** with all instruction in English. Some programs provide some follow-up work in a child's native language, but the diversity of languages and the shortage of teachers who speak them make this problematic in many locales. You may wish to refer to the HABLA program, outlined in Chapter 11, that seeks to address this issue.

One of your challenges in community and school programs will be to support children and families with different language backgrounds in seeking language instruction. This challenge forms another basis for school–home–community discussion and action. Teachers of English to Speakers of Other Languages (TESOL) provides publications, training, and conferences aimed at ensuring excellence in English-language teaching.

Here are some techniques that teachers have found helpful in multilanguage school districts:

1. Learn a few key words in the other languages you are likely encounter in your work with children and families. Knowing how to greet, thank, and say good-bye in these languages helps you establish rapport with families and ease children's transition to school.
2. Use visual cues like photos, charts, and objects in your presentations.
3. Use repetition of terms and slower (not louder) speech to help English-language learners.
4. Set up a buddy system so that children with more language skill can help those with less fluent in English.

Biracial and Interethnic Families

Because interethnic and interracial marriages are becoming more common, more children with parents of different backgrounds attend American schools today. When given a chance in the 2000 census to indicate more than one race, more than 4 million (one half were minors) indicated more than one racial identity. Demographers predict that this figure will rise dramatically in the next census, because the actual numbers are much higher and sensitivity will be less.

In the popular press, one frequently finds descriptions of the changing racial diversity in the United States, and this indicates a gradual homogenizing of our population. The notion is supported when we find 5% of all births nationally classified as "mixed race" or as having two or more racial heritages (U.S. Bureau of the Census, 2008). Higher proportions of interracial and interethnic marriages occur in Asian and Hispanic groups. More than anyone else in recent years, Tiger Woods, the professional golfer, drew attention to multiracial backgrounds by labeling himself "Cablinasian." *Interracial Voice*, an independent, information-oriented on-line journal, is marketed to this increasing group of Americans with combined heritages.

Because different ethnic groups generally hold differing cultural expectations, interethnic families will have varying perceptions about culture and about their child's participation in school and the community. There is also the pressure that biracial children feel for acceptance. Although living in two worlds has advantages, Coles (2006) noted that some feel rejection by one or both parents' cultural groups.

Through adoption, some families are rearing children from a culture or race different from that of the adoptive parents, and many of those parents are interested in preserving features of the adopted child's heritage. In the United States, interracial adoptions almost always involve White families adopting children of color (National Adoption Information Clearinghouse, 2004). Over the past decades, in response to various wars and political changes, children from Europe, Japan, Korea, Vietnam, and South and Central America have been adopted in America. Currently, the largest number of children are being adopted from China and Russia. The topic of transracial adoption has been debated over the years, but research indicates that ~~children adopted interracially do as well as other children~~ (Coles, 2006). Still other families have a multiethnic makeup as a result of remarriage or combinations of parent and child ethnicity.

Race has been and continues to be an issue in America, and while great strides have been made in merging the interests, opportunities, and talents of all members on the racial palette, the job of educators, community leaders, and families themselves is to work to ~~celebrate racial differences~~. Race should not be avoided but instead validated in our community lives.

∽— Annie is an adopted Asian child living in a totally European American small town. She brings no Asian culture to the community, as she would if her biological family resided there, but her race is evident and she constantly brings up the fact of her physical difference. Her fourth-grade teacher works hard to feature photos of minority persons, particularly Chinese. The objective is to validate the accomplishments, heritage, and history of this particular ethnic group. One new project that has started well, and is exciting for all of Annie's classmates, is the e-mail writing exchange with children in a Chinese sister-city school. —∽

Wynter (2002) expressed encouraging thoughts on ~~racial acceptance~~. He indicated that America is moving into a "postracial" period and that multiculturalism will soon be irrelevant. He uses examples of the crossover phenomenon in the music, toy, sports, entertainment, and advertising businesses to show how the race of featured persons becomes irrelevant in mainstream America. Madison, a doll in the Barbie line, is typical of the new forms we find in toy manufacture showing an ambiguous race. However, this acceptance is still far from total. For some time yet, race will undoubtedly be in focus in American schools and neighborhoods.

IMPLICATIONS FOR TEACHERS

Working with Children and Families with Racial and Cultural Differences

As a teacher, a good starting point for exploring the traditions of various cultural and ethnic groups is the families represented in your classroom. Some teachers send home a simple survey asking the names and ages of everyone in the child's household, the family's ethnic heritage and/or the places they are from, and information about holidays celebrated, beliefs/traditions practiced, and special times the family spends together (Rieger, 2008). With this information, you can invite families to visit and share any of this information with the class. Once parents recognize that you are defining family broadly to include all the people in the children's homes who love and care for them, they will feel more comfortable sharing their family characteristics.

Another good strategy is to take advantage of President Obama's fascinating racial and cultural heritage to help children. His election has produced a huge leap in eliminating racial stereotyping, so use the extensive mix of ethnic and cultural backgrounds now represented in the cabinet. Make a bulletin board with photos of these national leaders and then show, using strings, how each is attached to places around the world.

The history of race relations in the United States has seldom been positive, and most minority-group children have felt the stings of racism and ethnocentrism. If children from our various ethnic groups are to succeed, they need to know and feel that schools and communities want them to succeed. As a teacher, you will assure families that they are welcome in your classroom when you establish open communication, acceptance, and interest in their lives and experiences.

SOCIOECONOMIC STATUS OF FAMILIES

During the 1950s and 1960s, American writers, educators, and politicians tried to downplay social class, but class levels have become more obvious in recent decades and are now more openly acknowledged. There is growing polarization between the wealthy and the poor in America. One need not look far to find vast differences in buying power, access, and vocational opportunity for citizens at different economic levels, and this is closely related to **socioeconomic status (SES)**.

Social classes are not easily portrayed because there are overlaps, but in general, class standing is based on the occupation, income, education, and values of the parents in a family. Figure 3-4 diagrams the social classes generally used to show the organization of American society.

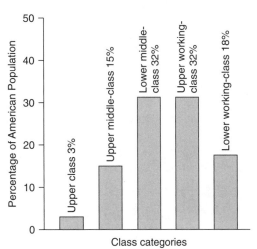

FIGURE 3-4   Social Class in America
Source: Based on Thompson and Hickey (2005).

Historic Class Descriptions

The ~~upper class~~ in the United States parallels the aristocracy in other societies. These families have inherited wealth and a close-knit circle of friends, family, and colleagues. Children from upper-class families normally attend exclusive private schools and prepare for careers in a family enterprise or in public service, such as in politics or with social help organizations. ~~Family heritage~~ and "proper rearing" are very important in this class, and children are expected to ~~conform to established standards of behavior, etiquette, and education.~~

~~Middle-class~~ families are characterized by their pursuit ~~of higher education~~ and ~~occupational productiveness~~. Upper-middle-class families are generally hardworking and achievement oriented. They are often the community's leaders, physicians, lawyers, and successful businesspersons. A defining quality of these families is the practice of cultivating their children's attrributes through leisure activities that foster development of their cognitive and social skills (Thompson & Hickey, 2005). Middle- and lower-middle-class families closely resemble the upper middle class in their expectations and desires. Less highly paid professionals are in this category, as are many successful businesspersons. This is "middle America," enjoying many social advantages and high-quality living standards.

~~Upper-working-class~~ families consist of skilled tradespersons, factory workers, and other hourly wage earners, many of whom have ~~benefited from membership in unions to bolster their wages and benefit~~s. Members of this class emphasize high school graduation and hard work but hold ~~higher education to be less important~~ than do members of the middle and upper classes. Working-class children are encouraged to expect a life of wage earning. Economic ups and downs often affect working-class families, who are more likely to suffer in the coming decades with the decline of union jobs.

~~Lower-working-class~~ families are distinguished by their ~~lack of education and skills and their low-paying jobs~~. Many adults in the lower working class have ~~not completed high school,~~ and because salaries have declined significantly in the last 30 years for those who have not graduated, they ~~can be below, at, or just above the poverty leve~~l, ~~despite working full time~~. A parent earning the minimum wage and receiving ~~food stamps,~~ for example, will live below the poverty level and is considered poor. Other families in the lower working class are sometimes termed the *working poor*, and earn above the minimum wage but are still near the poverty line. Families in this class often live in substandard housing but still spend a significant amount of their income on rent. They often have inadequate benefits or none at all.

Even though a large part of American wealth, capital, and general services is due to working-class labor, 20% of all jobs in the United States pay wages below the poverty level. The minimum wage is not a living wage, and those in the working class are most at risk for depleting their available resources for unexpected expenses, such as illness. See Figure 3-5 for a graphic portrayal of American incomes. Members of the the upper and lower working class will face continued economic difficulties in the emerging high-tech global labor market.

High school graduation is a critical educational outcome in American society. But too many young people from the working class drop out or feel "pushed out" of high school (Orfield, 2004), leading to a crisis in high school completion in many areas.

Middle-class families enculturate their children through activities that foster their cognitive and social skills.

Like middle-class parents, working-class parents provide care, food, shelter, and other basic support for their children, but they are unable to provide the enriched leisure-time activities that many middle-class parents fund for their children. Instead, working-class children often have more autonomy in their free time, but they are also expected at an early age to be responsible for taking care of their younger siblings and doing chores around the house.

The Urban Underclass—A New Dimension

Sociologists and demographers now recognize a subgroup (although it is not represented in the classic diagram), previously merged with the lower working class, that occupies the lower margin of our economic and social scales (Rainwater & Smeeding, 2004). The **urban underclass** comprises individuals and families locked into a debilitating cycle of poverty and despair from which they can find little escape. The combination of **welfare-to-work programs** and economic boom times in the late 1990s reduced the size of this group, but by 2009, with recession and high unemployment figures, it had expanded once again (Urban Institute, 2009). In the current economic downturn, the numbers in this group could swell greatly.

Underclass families subsist primarily on welfare, other government assistance, and an underground economy. They live in inferior housing or on the streets and face lives frequently racked by crime, deprivation, chemical dependency, and abuse. Most individuals in this class possess little education and limited work experience, so they are locked into the culture of poverty. This perpetuation of economic and social dislocation gives individuals and families little chance for working out of the chain of burdens. There is now renewed concern for the children in this group, because many underclass families have exhausted the social benefits of the welfare-to-work programs and must depend again on charitable institutions.

Many children in the underclass are at risk; nutrition and health care are minimal, and illness, disease, and neglect are common. Minority families are also highly represented in this once more expanding group. How to help the underclass is perhaps the greatest challenge we face in our efforts to eradicate poverty.

We have considerable evidence that in the past, Americans moved from one socioeconomic or social class group to another via education and successful personal improvement efforts. Evidence is mounting, however, that differences in the way children are raised in their respective classes make it difficult for them to move up to another class (Lareau, 2003). Although upward movement for middle-class Americans seems assured, future options for the working class and underclass seem far more limited. Low education levels and minimal experiences, as well as neglect by mainstream America, represent a fixed ceiling for this group. With welfare reform having spread across America since the mid-1990s, many families suffer even more hardship (Lichter, Qian, & Crowley, 2007).

Economics and American Families

A family's economic base is extremely important. It determines the family's quality of life, health care, nutrition, and living conditions, the level of self-worth of its members, and their ability to function in a community. A majority of U.S. families maintain a high standard of living compared with families in the rest of the world, but we find increasing numbers living in poverty. Industrial jobs are rapidly being eliminated in America and are being replaced with lower-paying service employment. The effect is that real wages for most families fell 19% between 1973 and 2003 (Lichter et al., 2007), and the buying power of a majority of households was reduced even further throughout the 1990s. Downward rather than upward mobility has become the pattern for more Americans

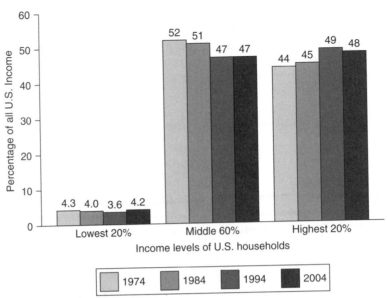

FIGURE 3-5   Distribution of American Household Income, 1974–2004   *Source:* U.S. Bureau of the Census, Current Population Report P60-213, 2005.

in the present generation. Note in Figure 3-5 that the lowest 20% and the middle 60% of households receive only about one-half of the total income distributed in our country. Discouraging as it appears, we seem destined for more bipolar economic situations in most U.S. regions.

REFLECTION

Be sensitive to the economic situation of the families and children with whom you work. Some families live from paycheck to paycheck, and others rely on a monthly assistance check. There may be times during the month when families have no money in the house. How could families contribute to your classroom in nonmonetary ways? How will you assist a child who may not be getting enough to eat at times?

In an attempt to guard against declining living standards, both parents in many nuclear families now work. **Dual incomes** may provide families with increased economic support, but child care, home maintenance, and time to participate in the school and community become real challenges. Economics correlates with risk factors; almost always, the lower the income, the higher the risk. However, we also find at-risk children in middle- and upper-income families struggling to balance the needs of home and family, and teachers and other helping professionals must be alert to such situations.

MIDDLE-INCOME FAMILIES   The American dream has been to achieve a middle-class lifestyle. Middle-class families are supposed to enjoy full employment and the esteem that society places on the engine that propels the nation. For many, this scenario is true. In 1996, more than 28 million families enjoyed an income above the median, one that permitted them to enjoy a better-than-average lifestyle. We must keep in mind, however, that real earnings slipped badly in the 1970s and 1980s, so to remain in the middle class, many of these families moved to the dual-income plan in order to maintain the features of suburban living, recreational opportunity, and college education for their children (Bianchi, Robinson, & Milkie, 2006). Unfortunately, public policies that would help parents balance their work and family responsibilities have lagged in the United States (Kamerman, 2005), and middle-income families struggle to manage the challenge of raising a family while pursuing demanding careers.

Middle-income families tend to follow professional advice with regard to child rearing and have shifted their behaviors as recommendations have changed over the past few decades (Lareau, 2003). Parenting practices tend to feature timeouts, discussion, and reasoning with children in lieu of physical punishment. Communication is valued. Middle-income families are comfortable participating in school and community activities, and the parents' educational level usually makes communication with schools and community agencies easier. Parents' volunteer work can be considerable, and because parents' participation has a long history, minimal instruction or organization is necessary. Members of this group can make valuable contributions to your school program in sharing talents, giving presentations, or managing projects. Time may be scarce for middle-income parents, though, and new demands—especially on dual-income families—do result in further family time constraints.

WORKING-CLASS FAMILIES   Values in working-class families may differ from those presented in schools. Although there are certainly exceptions, many parents in the working class tend to favor an authoritarian parenting style (see Chapter 4) and engage in far less discussion and reasoning with their children on behavior issues (Lareau, 2003). These families may also feel constrained in the school setting because of their own negative experiences during their years in school. They may even question the value of higher education for their children as preparation for the real world of wage earning.

Helping working-class families feel comfortable and welcome in the school is an essential first step in fostering their involvement. Once families feel respected and appreciated, they fit well into school and community programs where tasks are carefully defined and arranged. Family members here consider themselves "doers" and normally are willing to work avidly on specific projects or use other means to support a school or agency. Comer (1997) pointed out that many schools successfully arrange for participation by up to one-half of their working-class family members.

UNDERCLASS FAMILIES   As discussed, the United States has for generations contained an underclass of families with limited education, limited employment, and a history of subsisting on government and institutional assistance. In addition, financial reversals and economic deterioration in some locations have resulted in poverty for previous working-class families. At the beginning of the 21st century, the number of families in the United States at or below the subsistence level was growing again. According to the National Center for Children in Poverty (2006), the number of children under 6 years of age who were poor increased by 12% between 2000 and 2004. Currently, 22% of this age group live in low-income homes and 21% are members of families that are considered poor (an income of less than $20,000 for a family of four). Minority children under the age of 6 have the highest rate of poverty, with figures ranging up to 40%. Refer again to Figure 3-5.

Poverty is a risk factor associated with numerous negative outcomes—particularly for children. Poor children tend to have lower attendance in school and may change schools frequently because of the instability of their living situation. In the 1980s and 1990s, poverty became more permanent because individuals found it difficult to break out of menial jobs. The United States now appears to have a permanent underclass (poverty figures have remained almost static for nearly 25 years), and two expanding groups at this level are homeless and itinerant families.

Children from homeless families tend to suffer from poor health, anxiety, depression, and developmental delays.

HOMELESS FAMILIES The ~~main cause of homelessness is lack of affordable housing~~ for very-low-income families (Alexander, 2003). Some families suffering economic hardships must surrender their homes and spend increasing amounts of time in shelters, in automobiles, or on the street. Because poverty is increasing at the present time, more families will undoubtedly be pushed into homelessness in the future (Hanson & Lynch, 2004).

Although the typical media image of the homeless person is that of the unemployed male who abuses substances and wanders the streets, statistics show that more than 40% of the homeless in 2005 were families, and 58% of the family members were children (National Child Traumatic Stress Network, 2005). The numbers of homeless persons is difficult to ascertain, and estimates differ sharply. Some estimates indicate that more than 1 million American children experienced homelessness in 2006 (National Allliance to End Homelessness, 2006), and the younger the child, the greater is the risk of homelessness. The Urban Institute (2009) estimates that 2.3 to more than 3 million Americans experience homelessness at some point in a given year. This represents about 1% of the population.

Many of the parents in homeless situations are employed but have low-end jobs that pay insufficiently for housing. A minimum-wage job is insufficient to pay rent on a very modest apartment in any state in the United States. Homelessness is also related to seasons and seasonal work. Winter figures for homelessness (in most states) are almost 50% higher than those for the summer and early fall.

Children who are homeless tend to suffer from poor health, anxiety, depression, and developmental delays. Some manage to attend school, but they often have poor attendance, behavior problems, and lower academic achievement than children who are housed. Although shelters can provide a basic refuge from the streets, living in one is often very stressful for families, as parents may be separated from each other and older male children may have to relocate to another facility. Although housing assistance is available from the U.S. Department of Housing and Urban Development, only 12% of those eligible receive help because of insufficient funding (Ispa, Thornburg, & Fine, 2006).

Clearly, such circumstances offer a challenge to communities and schools working together to produce basic health and nutrition services for our neediest children (Thoennes, 2008). One example of success is the U.S. Office of Education's validating the efforts of Sandra McBrayer by naming her 1994 Teacher of the Year for her work with homeless students on the streets of San Diego, California. Increasingly, school systems such as the Seattle Public Schools provide transportation to children who are homeless and must move to a shelter outside of the district where they have been attending school so that they can continue at that school if they wish. Providing such continuity for children is an important aspect of support.

MIGRANT AND ITINERANT FAMILIES Some families are highly mobile because of erratic work availability and the unsettled lifestyles of the parents. These families experience poor living conditions, and their members often suffer from serious health problems.

Migrant workers constitute a significant proportion of both U.S. citizens and resident aliens who move up and down the continent during harvesting seasons. The United States has more than 1 million migrant workers in any one year (Waller & Crawford, 2001). Many families are without a permanent home; children live in one location for several weeks and then move to another. Life for these children has little security, health care, or stability, and this group is more likely to suffer from infant mortality, disabilities, and chronic illness than any other in the nation (Werts, Culatta, & Tompkins, 2007).

Migrant-worker and itinerant families pose a particular challenge for schools and teachers. Children are forced into new situations every few weeks and thus have little continuity in school or community experiences. Cognitive growth for migrant children is often minimal, and such children frequently become socially alienated simply because they cannot feel a part of any school or community. Even Start programs are attempts to bolster educational opportunities for the young children of at-risk families, and 5% of Even Start funds are earmarked for migrant families (Dimidijian, 2001).

Low-SES families have been a constant in American society for generations. Large amounts of federal funds have been spent, but positive results are few. Community action teams, school program developers, and others need to continue to identify realistic educational initiatives that will produce better opportunities for the economically beset. On the positive side, we do have programs that work (see the models outlined in Chapter 11). Selected plans across the country show that low-SES children need not be trapped in the spiral of agony and misery so frequently associated with a disadvantaged life.

Ansel's parents are migrant farm workers; they follow employment opportunities from Florida to Maine each year, harvesting crops. Their life is filled with needs for food, clothes, car repairs, and medical treatment. Still, 4-year-old Ansel has many happy days exploring farms and playing with pet animals and other migrant children.

The parents work daily in the fields, and the children help with small tasks during the harvest. At one Georgia site, a child-care worker visited the workers' quarters, and in spite of their exhausting day, Ansel's parents learned how to enroll him in the local Even Start program. His experience was a success, and after his first week, Ansel showed off his favorite picture books, an art project, and the three games he had learned. Now, in the few hours at the end of each day, Ansel shares material with his tired but willing parents.

In Maine a farmer's wife gave Ansel a box of paperback picture books, and Ansel enjoys "reading" the pictures to his parents. In another community in early fall, a child-care worker started a portfolio of Ansel's artwork and his writings—from scribbles to forming numbers and letters. She encouraged Ansel and his parents to share these "recordings" at their next several stops on the way to Florida. Gradually, the parents are learning to ask the right questions to find preschool programs in other communities.

Ansel will start kindergarten in the fall and will follow a similar intermittent pattern of schooling. Ansel's parents, however, are beginning to develop skills in reaching out to the community for help and in sharing his portfolio with others. Educating migrant children is never an easy task, but caring parents, interested community workers, and receptive schools provide great help for the resilient migrant child.

Effects of Economics

The economic foundation of a society largely governs the SES of individuals within that society. The financial resources of families become the most important variable in determining class status and opportunity; money governs diet, place of residence, access to health care, and chances for the future. Naturally, children's achievement in school is greatly affected by these factors.

Early studies by Coleman (1966) showed a strong correlation between family SES and children's cognitive development and achievement. More recent studies qualify those findings. Mayer (1997) pointed out the importance of the psychological environment in the home for child learning. Hrabowski, Maton, Greene, and Greif (2002) found a similar pattern, noting that parents' behaviors toward children are more strongly predictive of cognitive growth than are SES variables. We may thus hope to keep alive the chance for upward mobility and improvement for economically disadvantaged populations if we can provide intervention for these families in the form of educational programs. If parents' attitudes and behaviors can be affected by education and training, schools and communities have the best chance for engaging parents in the process of educating their children.

IMPLICATIONS FOR TEACHERS

Family Economics Impact Schools

We have given you a lot of information on class structure and family economics because, as a teacher, you need to know the economic realities of the children you teach. Be especially careful about not judging middle-class families as the "good" families just because their values tend to match the school culture most closely. Getting to know families is the way to understand and appreciate what they provide for their children and their hopes for them.

You may need to adjust your way of thinking about the reasons for poverty and the complex issues surrounding many families. Find out which children are in the economic risk category. Ask former teachers, and observe children's habits and who they associate with for clues. This will give you a chance to recommend support for certain children when social agencies inquire or when private sponsors and foundations provide funding.

Some teachers have formed after-school clubs focusing on art, chess, sports, or other resources that they make available for low-income children at minimal or no cost. Libraries are another source of extracurricular activities that are generally free. However, although you may want to help poor families connect with enrichment activities for their children, be mindful that these families are under great stress to maintain their lives and may view such activities as needless frills. On the other hand, allowing children to celebrate their birthdays in school with a simple party, for example, may be much appreciated by families. Often the school counselor will have information about families that can help you determine how to relate sensitively to their children.

FAMILIES WITH CHILDREN WITH DISABILITIES

The education of children with disabilities involves a large number of diverse families with children who have learning disabilities, speech and language impairments, autism, mental retardation, emotional disturbance, physical impairments, or other conditions. Although all parents raising children face challenges, those raising a child with a disability have additional responsibilities and may vary greatly in their ability to cope with the demands placed upon them.

During the 2003–2004 school year, more than 6.3 million children and youth from ages 3 to 21 were served under federal programs for children with disabilities (U.S. Department of Education, 2004). In addition, about 951,294 infants, toddlers, and preschool children received **early intervention services** in that same year (Heward, 2006). This is a significant population (more than 12% of children in that age bracket, according to U.S. Census Bureau statistics), and it places considerable pressure on available assistive time and resources. When professionals work with schools and communities, they need to understand not only particular disabilities but also the problems and pressures that affect both the family and the child. They must be sensitive and support-ive when working with families of children with disabilities. (See Chapter 6 for more detailed information on children with disabilities and their families.)

Families raising children with special needs are a part of all communities, and be-cause disabilities cut across all socioeconomic groups, affected children will be present in most schools. Diversity is always a challenge for education professionals, but often special-needs families require more school–home–community planning to achieve the most positive outcomes. Although major physical disabilities are evenly distributed across SES groups, milder disabilities (called **school-identified disabilities**) occur much more frequently in poor and disadvantaged families (Lichter et al., 2007). Poverty, lack of health care, and particularly lack of prenatal care are responsible in large part for the dispropor-tionate number of disabilities in minority families. Programs for children with special needs are thriving throughout the United States (Turnbull, Turnbull, & Wehmeyer, 2007).

RELIGIOUS ORIENTATION

A family's religious affiliation can be an important aspect of its uniqueness, and teach-ers and other community professionals need to be knowledgeable about different spiri-tual practices. Yet, in their attempt to adhere to the constitutional requirement for separation of church and state, schools often try to ignore or deliberately overlook the religious affiliation of children and their families. We must realize, however, that reli-gious affiliation and commitment affect how children feel about school activities, rules, and the behavior of others.

Religion helps many persons find purpose and meaning in their lives. Socioeco-nomic success does not seem to be linked with any particular faith, but some re-searchers indicate a correlation between religious commitment and moral behavior (Hoge, 1996). This finding should be comforting, considering that 85% of Americans profess to have a religious attachment. However, attendance at religious services rarely exceeds 20% of the population in any one community.

Religious practices affect interaction and participation, holiday observances, foods eaten, and gender roles, so it is important that you know and respect the tenets of the different religions represented in your school's families. A school's ability to accom-modate different religious practices directly affects whether teachers' work with chil-dren, their families, and particular communities will be successful.

REFLECTION

Consider the various religious traditions in the United States and think about ways to present information about different religious holidays. Imagine how you could get dif-ferent family members to share their traditions with your class.

Religious diversity has increased dramatically in the United States since the mid-20th century (Goff, 2004) because of changes in immigration patterns, intermarriage, ur-banization, and the global economy. You will find inquiry about America's religious groups highly educational, and the information you get will be valuable for the groups with whom you work. For all of our ethnic and religious diversity, most American chil-dren and adults are ill-informed about Judaism, Buddhism, and Islam, to say nothing of Native American religious practices. References that provide help in reflecting on reli-gious practice include *Melton's Encyclopedia of American Religions* (Melton, 2009) and the Gollnick and Chinn (2006) textbook on multicultural education.

Religious application may affect how children feel about school activities, rules, and the behavior of others.

The religious landscape in the United States is in constant flux, as one would expect in a country where religious tolerance abides. New faith traditions emerge frequently, and membership in established congregations moves up and down (Lindner, 2009). The major faiths represented in the United States are Christianity, which includes Protestants and Catholics; Judaism; and Islam. Much smaller representations of Hinduism, Buddhism, and other Eastern religions are found in major U.S. cities as well. All major faiths are divided into smaller sects and denominations, which vary considerably. For example, within the Protestant Christian faith there are dozens of denominations, ranging socially and politically from liberal to conservative. Catholic subgroups include Roman Catholic and Eastern Orthodox. Jewish groups range from conservative Hasidic sects to liberal Reform groups. The rapidly expanding Islamic affiliations in the United States include Black Muslim groups and Near Eastern aggregations, as well as immigrants from East Asia. Mosques are now becoming common in U.S. urban landscapes.

The *Yearbook of American and Canadian Churches, 2009* (Lindner, 2009) catalogs the religious affiliation of approximately 248 million persons in the United States indicating a religious connection. Of that figure, the membership percentage for the predominant groups in 2006 was as follows: Protestant Christians, 57%; Catholic Christians, 26%; Muslims, 3%; Jews, 3%; no religion, 11%; and other, 2%. These figures affirm a dominant Protestant religious heritage in many areas of the United States that stems from a strong Protestant affiliation during the colonial era.

Religion directly influences how families rear children, as well as how they conduct their affairs and relate to a community. Even though federal and state court decisions (case law) have traditionally separated church work and state regulations, one finds a great deal in legal codes and the common law of the United States resting firmly on a Protestant ethic (Gollnick & Chinn, 2006). The administration of George W. Bush supported more connections between religious institutions and government programs. Some of the faith-based social support groups and school **voucher plans** that include religious schools are taking new steps to involve federal and state governments in indirect support for religious organizations. Court decisions in 2003 upheld these new connections.

Applications of Religion

All religions have sacred ideas, objects, and practices, and these have implications for observance within those groups. Even though many children are only casually acquainted with the practice of their family religion, it is still a background feature in their lives, and their behaviors and reactions will demonstrate this fact. The following are points you should consider as you collaborate with parents and community members in educating children.

OBSERVANCE OF HOLIDAYS Most religions have selected faith-specific holidays. Christians celebrate Easter and Christmas; Jews celebrate Passover, Yom Kippur, and other holidays; Muslims observe Ramadan, Bayrami, and other holidays.

CODES   Religious groups have codes relating to sexual behavior as well as to the observance of marriages, births, and deaths. Many religions have dietary laws, and children will seek or avoid specific foods at certain times or on particular occasions.

All religions have a moral code, and when we compare religious practices around the world, we find that many aspects of the different codes resemble one another. Differences are found in such features as locus of control. For example, Protestant groups hold that humans are individually responsible for determining their behavior, but other groups teach that it is loyalty to the group that counts and that individuals must adhere to acceptable practices as defined by the religion or its authorities.

IMPLICATIONS FOR TEACHERS

Acknowledge Religions in Your Community

As a teacher, you need to be knowledgeable and respectful of the religious beliefs of the children in your classroom and their families. Following are some helpful points regarding instruction about religion or comments and questions about religion:

1. *Know the religious affiliations of your associates, the children you teach, and community members.*
2. *Have the students study what all people believe, but do not teach them what to believe.*
3. *Learn to value all religious practices and encourage people to share information about their faiths.*
4. *Learn about the larger community endeavors that focus on religion or feature religious holidays.*
5. *Learn how to use the various religious links in the school and community to help you teach the children and help them develop tolerance for others.*

Some practices may be hard for you to accept, especially when they require particular accommodations for a child who has specific religious observations. A child who is a Jehovah's Witness, for example, should not participate in celebrations of holidays and birthdays. Working with the child's parents, however, may reveal some creative forms of celebration that would not require the child to leave the room (Rieger, 2008).

CHANGES IN CONTEMPORARY FAMILIES

Even though the concept of family has existed since Paleolithic times, we still find gradual changes in the form and function of this basic unit. In recent decades, America has seen new family forms and the public acceptance of one-parent households, cohabiting couples, families headed by gay and lesbian parents, and multiracial families. The focus of this book is on families in the United States at the beginning of the 21st century, but in this section we consider family evolution over the past two centuries. The comparisons will help explain how we arrived at our present situation.

From its birth to the mid-1800s the United States was primarily an agrarian country, and its population was mainly rural. This meant a farming family structure across the United States. These early families were typically extended and often included three generations. Children were considered valuable assets, because farmwork involved numerous tasks calling for extra hands.

With the advent of the Industrial Revolution in the late 1700s and early 1800s, the American economy and social structure started to change. Urban centers expanded and whole new classes of jobs in manufacturing and commerce became available. Changes in the economic situation brought changes to families. A large working class emerged, and a new ethic was injected into family life. Roles in the home changed. The need for many hands at home diminished, because children of factory workers could not participate in the work of parents. Homes changed from places where child rearing was linked to acquiring adult skills to environments where only child rearing took place. Education was no longer passed from older to younger family members but became something taught in schools as children's need for literacy and calculation skills moved beyond parental expertise.

By the end of the 19th century, the urbanization of the United States was well underway. Industrial and commercial development continued to make rapid strides until World War II. Following the westward expansion in the 1880s and the availability of railroad transport, relocation became common for American families, especially after the early 1900s. This meant that some families became isolated from their relatives as they established roots in other communities and regions. It is during this period that the extended family diminished and the classic model of the nuclear family, consisting of children living with their parents in an individual house with the mother as homemaker and the father as breadwinner, became more prominent. After World War II, mobility intensified as large groups moved to different parts of the country to find better living conditions. Such activity and reorganization increased the prevalence of nuclear family features.

Of course, there were many exceptions to these norms in early-20th-century households. Death often left in its wake single-parent families. Single parents clearly had a difficult task, so remarriages and, consequently, the formation of stepfamilies occurred frequently. Divorce was rare during this time, but foster care was not.

With World War II, new shifts in economics, a rise in minority populations, and changes in social habits had a great impact on families in the United States. These changes included an increasing number of women in the workforce, instability in marriage, a rise in divorce rates, increased mobility for families, and the rise of an influential peer group culture (Gollnick & Chinn, 2006).

Women joining the workforce became more independent, redefined family roles, and changed attitudes for both men and women. Many couples chose divorce, remarriage, and different styles of living when they found that they now held different expectations of family life. Female heads of households became more common, and there were fewer adults in a family unit. Figure 3-6 shows the dramatic changes in family

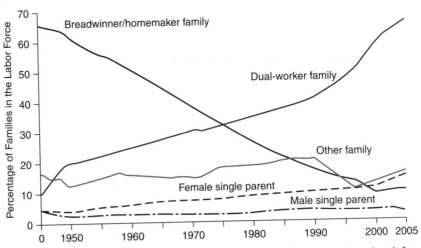

FIGURE 3-6 **American Families in the Labor Force, 1940–2005** *Source:* Based on information from U.S. Bureau of Labor Statistics. (2001). Bulletins 2217, 2340, and 2307; plus U.S. Bureau of Labor Statistics. (2002–2007). *News*, USDL97-195.

support in the last part of the 20th century. (Remember that this is not the total workforce, but only the workers supporting families.) The proportion of traditional breadwinning fathers and homemaking mothers is now below 10%, and dual-worker families now represent over 60% of the population. One drawback to this shift in family structure is the loss of what Coleman (1991) called "social capital" in families—meaning adults' attention to and involvement with children's learning at home and in community life.

American social behavior took an even greater turn in the 1960s and 1970s. Younger Americans challenged the older order and experimented with different types of living arrangements. The more informal relationships, more flexible marriage and living arrangements, and new lifestyles that emerged since the 1980s are outgrowths of this period.

Roles in contemporary homes differ from those of previous generations.

The postindustrial era arising in the United States at the beginning of the 21st century has brought new directions and implications for families. The rise of massive service and communications industries shows that the physical labor important to previous generations is now far less prominent. In lieu of high-energy occupations, more U.S. workers are now employed in the service of equipment, the service of living conditions, and the transmittal of information and processes. More and more employees work at home and in a variety of locations. Thus, the notion of a constant skill for employment or an established workplace has diminished.

The rise of the information age and the service economy has meant a growing gap between economic haves and have-nots. Blue-collar workers are finding physical labor less in demand. Automation and robotics increasingly replace manufacturing jobs, and large segments of our skilled labor force are witnessing the end of their vocations. Younger members of this force find themselves inheriting a decreasing number of jobs, and others have come to depend on welfare. Although the information age has brought acceptance of different lifestyles, it has also produced abrupt economic demands that leave Americans scurrying to find new ways to cope. Sociologists (DeVita & Mosher-Williams, 2001) have recently pointed out the need for recapturing viable communities and family traditions, for our new faster pace of life and our new emphasis on individual work push all Americans toward isolation.

All of these changes have important implications for family and home situations. Think about the needs of 21st-century persons and how your primary grade classroom connects with that future world:

- Is the ability to spell correctly as important as it was before the age of the word processor?
- Are projects on foreign lands helpful when children's parents are working for companies in Singapore or London?
- Will our group history keep pace with global communications?

In the 21st century, new attitudes concerning sexual behavior have also emerged, and cohabitation without marriage has become socially acceptable. Interethnic marriages are now common, and out-of-wedlock births are no longer controversial. Same-sex partners raising children are becoming more mainstream. Advances in reproductive technology and other factors are allowing increasing numbers of individuals to delay parenthood into their 30s and 40s, when they are more economically secure and emotionally mature. Although flexibility and tolerance are key requirements for these new lifestyles, educators must appreciate the need for a far more sophisticated education of all young people. The demand for literacy, problem-solving, and negotiating skills today is higher for youngsters, who as adults will be very mobile and less constrained in living arrangements, and who will face frequent job changes and must constantly learn new skills.

IMPLICATIONS FOR TEACHERS

Concepts to Remember

The information in this chapter forms a base for the strategies you will use in working with the diverse families you will contact in teaching. The essential elements for you are understanding and accepting the variety of family groupings in our towns and cities and figuring out how they connect with your school curriculum. So, think carefully about the following items:

- *Language tolerance. What is your attitude toward persons who are English-language learners or use nonstandard forms of English? We all need to develop a tolerant ear for the range of English forms spoken in the areas where we work. If possible, identify persons who use the local language and ask them to advise you on improving your communication and understanding of cultural differences.*
- *Lifestyles. How do you react to different lifestyles and different household configurations? Can you see quality in these relationships and how they work for the benefit of these families and their children? Now think of yourself talking to an unmarried couple or a same-sex couple about their first-grade child. What will your say first to show acceptance?*
- *Diversity. Some educators have found it beneficial for teachers to join the activities in a different community. For example, you could help plan a craft show for the neighborhood, attend different religious ceremonies, or volunteer for a booster club event or for work on a farm.*

Summary and Review

The family, though undergoing radical change in many communities, is still the primary social unit in the United States. Families vary in cultural, ethnic, religious, economic, and educational features, but all parents contribute in some way to their communities and to the schools where their children seek instruction and guidance.

The diversity of American families is said to be their strength. That fact can be generally interpreted to mean that different heritages, values, work styles, and habits give a character to the American landscape that is both stimulating and an incentive for production. Members of some of these diverse groups, however, are in dire need of help and special support services.

Families have changed over the history of the United States and will continue to change. Ethnic proportions are constantly shifting, mobility may increase, values will alter, and even SES will change. The reality is that children living in nontraditional families now represent a majority of the students in U.S. schools. This means that our schools and communities need a more sensitive and inclusive environment that supports children regardless of their family configuration. In the past, each generation had its special problems and its particular successes. With this dynamic base, schools and communities must shape programs that can involve all participants fully and productively.

Suggested Activities and Questions

1. Discuss the structure of your own family of origin with several colleagues. Has it changed over time, or has it remained constant?
2. Survey the cultural and ethnic makeup of your school or neighborhood. How does it compare with that of the overall U.S. population?
3. Have the children in your class draw pictures of their families and then tell you about the persons portrayed.

How much information do you receive about the types of families these children have?

4. Find out why children whom you meet in your fieldwork are identified as disabled. Was a school or center involved in referrals? Did the diagnosis come through a clinic, a family physician, or another source?

Resources

Organizations

Family Pride Coalition   *http://www.familypride.org*
National Alliance to End Homelessness   *http://www*
    .endhomelessness.org
National Council on Family Relations   *http://www.ncfr.org*
Stepfamily Foundation   *http://www.stepfamily.org*
Urban Institute   *http://www.urban.org*

Web Sites

http://www.parenting.adoption.com   Comprehensive Web
    site for general information on adoption, publications,
    adoption directories, statistics, laws, and other resources.

http://www.colage.org   A Web site supporting young
    people with gay, lesbian, bisexual, and transgender
    parents.
http://www.prb.org   Population Reference Bureau entry
    Web site for objective demographic statistics and analy-
    sis of U.S. and world population studies.
http://www.census.gov   The primary Web address for ex-
    tensive information about your own state, as well as
    national statistics.

CHAPTER **4**

Understanding Roles and Experiences of Parents

The single most important factor in an infant's life is the bond formed with a primary caretaker. All other needs begin with this one, the foundation of a primal awareness that needs can be met, comfort can be provided, pain can be alleviated, inner peace can be achieved.

(LEVINE & ION, 2002, P. 285)

After reading this chapter, you will be able to do the following:

- Explain how parents are key persons in providing the nurturance needs of young children.
- Describe parental roles in children's upbringing and how these roles have changed in recent years.
- Compare and contrast commonalities and differences in parenting practices and approaches to child rearing among different ethnic communities in the United States.
- Identify various parenting styles and how these styles affect children's participation in school and community life.
- Consider what motivates individuals to become parents, the rewards of parenting, and how new and intensified stressors have had a great impact on parenting in American families.

In this chapter, we turn our attention to the adults who care for children in their homes. As the previous chapter on diversity in families made clear, these adults may be biological, adoptive, step-, or foster mothers and fathers. They may be grandparents, aunts, uncles, older siblings, or close family friends. In this book, we use the term *parents* to refer to these primary caregivers, who have established a deep, potentially lifelong bond with their children. Although differences in family roles, cultural patterns, interaction styles, and outside influences affect the **nurturing practices** in all family situations, the importance of parenting in the lives of children is impossible to overestimate. This chapter discusses how these qualities and conditions affect the parent role and the outcomes of parent practices.

Alll families have dreams and aspirations for their children. Keep in mind that there is no "ideal" family form and that most families, no matter how they are constituted, provide appropriate care for their children. Although some household arrangements may be more vulnerable or sensitive than others, each family can and does make positive contributions to children's development.

When we consider how families function, we find different customs, different priorities, and even somewhat different values. Of course, the differences signal the uniqueness of our diverse society, but at the same time, those very different elements fuse in most families to provide coherence and stability for members in the household (Heilman, 2008).

In spite of the differences, we find some constants in all families with children. The first constant—the nurturance of children—precedes all others. Nurturance is followed by defined family roles, cultural patterns, interaction styles, and family experiences. Additional characteristics, such as child-care arrangements, poverty, and divorce, can emerge as stressors that have an impact on the parenting quality of some family units.

NURTURANCE IN FAMILIES

Generally, *nurturance* means providing the basic necessities of life for children, but in a wider sense, it denotes general support, love, and cultivation for the growing child. In other words, nurturance is parenting.

Few adults are actually trained for nurturing roles, but our society expects certain minimum levels of support and effectiveness from parents as they rear children. The assumption is that nurturance, in its general and wider sense, has been modeled by preceding generations and is refined by an individual's experience and participation in society. The range of nurturing competence in U.S. homes, however, is wide indeed.

Range of Child Rearing

The nurturer accepts responsibilities not only for giving children basic physiological care, guidance, and love, but also for stimulating a child's investigations of the world and monitoring the child's social relationships with others. The nurturing parent is one who is grounded in humane practice and who has a vision of what children can become. Traditionally, this role has been filled by mothers and fathers; however, other loving adults, such as grandparents, older siblings, foster parents, and others, can and do assume the responsibilities of parenting.

Some aspects of parenting may be instinctual, but the most effective nurturers have certain characteristics in common, such as motivation to be with children and knowledge about how to care for them. Health and a sense of well-being, empathy, predictability, responsiveness, and emotional availability have also been identified as traits that enhance parents' effectiveness. On the other hand, traits like self-centeredness, depression, and drug or alcohol abuse can affect parenting adversely and may lead to abuse or neglect of children.

Abusive behavior in families moves parenting toward the antithesis of nurturing. Although few parents are so disordered in outlook as to carry out destructive acts with children, a significant number suffer lapses in judgment and vision that result in psychological and physical abuse or indifferent care practices. As a teacher, you must learn to recognize the signs of abuse and neglect and follow the laws of your state in reporting suspected abuse. Chapter 7 covers this topic in greater detail. This book does not focus on the pathologies that accompany abuse and indifference; rather, we have chosen to consider the range of positive nurturance that is featured in the great majority of U.S. families.

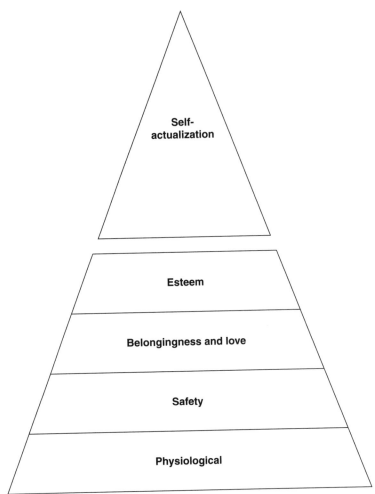

FIGURE 4-1   Maslow's Hierarchy of Needs   *Source:* Maslow (1968).

REFLECTION

Think back on your family of origin and the ways in which you were nurtured through-out your childhood. How have these early experiences shaped you as the person you are today?

Features of Positive Nurturance

Maslow (1968) provided a very useful **paradigm** (Figure 4-1) that shows, in ascending fashion, the scale of human needs. When related to the lives of young children, the levels of the pyramid clearly imply the need for nurturance. It is easy to associate the early nurturing practices of parents—and these are almost universal—with the hierarchy developed by Maslow.

ADDRESSING PHYSIOLOGICAL NEEDS   Food, warmth, and shelter are bare necessities for survival, and all parents provide them, except in rare cases, when families are caught in physical distress, dislocation, or mental illness. In spite of positive intentions, some financially stressed families find providing these basics difficult. Cold or hungry children cannot respond to any educational program. At the same time, unhealthy living climates can lead to reduced functioning, and improper food choices can lead to obesity and other nutritional problems.

ENSURING PHYSICAL SAFETY   The next level of Maslow's hierarchy involves safety. Ensuring a child's safety is almost instinctive with parents, and we expect this attention to be provided carefully and lovingly. Most parents are alert to dangers from natural disasters (such as earthquakes and storms), but it is all too easy to overlook hidden dangers, such as lead paint, polluted areas, and unsafe objects and locations.

PROVIDING LOVE   Giving emotional support and providing love are features of nurturance that occur naturally in typical families. Families express these feelings in different ways. Expressions of love range from nonverbal signals and understated expressions to effusive expressions of affection. Differences in discipline practices are linked to this area of nurturance as well. Some families use physical punishment, whereas others depend on verbal reprimand and discussion or explanation to rechannel behavior. All practices can be effective under particular circumstances. Occasionally, parents overdo their support role and encourage dependency and immaturity in their child. Overconcern and hovering often have undesirable consequences.

PROMOTING ESTEEM, SUCCESS, AND ACHIEVEMENT   Families vary greatly in how they foster esteem and support the achievements of their children. Some parents campaign vigorously with and for their children, whereas others gently encourage or deliberately withhold praise until the end of an activity or a task. Parents sometimes hold children to adult standards in playing games, conversing, or socializing. These expectations can be problematic if children do not succeed, for their aspirations may be deflated. Adult encouragement and delight in partial success normally provide a foundation for children to lift their levels of aspiration.

SELF-ACTUALIZATION   The final level in Maslow's hierarchy is an adult level of competence, but families foster readiness for self-actualization by supporting children's growing independence and sense of responsibility and by encouraging problem solving and decision making at children's appropriate levels of growth.

IMPLICATIONS FOR TEACHERS

Maslow's Hierarchy in Practice

As a teacher, you can do many things to support children's needs described in Maslow's hierarchy. Keep healthy snacks on hand for children who have missed breakfast or forgotten their lunch. Obtain a few extra jackets, mittens, and hats for children to use when needed. Provide a classroom with predictable routines and a sense of community so that all children feel they belong. Acknowledge children's accomplishments regularly. Let parents know of their children's small successes so that they are aware of their progress and can acknowledge it regularly. Help parents access parenting support classes and groups to increase their skills. And perhaps, most importantly, be alert to problems and deficiencies in nurturance and arrange referrals for assistance, if necessary.

Family Systems Theory

Just as children have their basic human needs met through the nurturing they receive from their families, they also learn how to interact with the larger world based on their experiences at home. Recognizing a family's communication and interaction patterns, separateness and connectedness, loyalty and independence, and adaptation to stress, for example, can help us understand better why members of a family act the way they do in certain circumstances. Family Systems Theory (Bowen, 1978) suggests that family members influence each other in predictable and recurring ways. Although this theory has been used in family counseling and therapy for some time, it can also be helpful for educators in their work with families (Christian, 2006).

Six characteristics of the family as a system are especially relevant for teachers: boundaries, roles, rules, hierarchy, climate, and equilibrium. Some of these characteristics occur on a continuum, and each family will have a unique profile determined by where it falls along each continuum. Thinking about families in this way can help you better serve children and families and give you insight into a family's perspective.

BOUNDARIES *Boundaries* refer to the range of a family's togetherness and separateness. On one end of the continuum are families who value autonomy and independence in their members. Such families tend to be open to new people and ideas. On the other end of the continuum are families who value belonging, conformity, and togetherness within the family group. In these families, an individual's behavior can be seen as a reflection on the whole family. Neither way is right or wrong, but it will influence how much different families participate in school events or the amount of independence families want for their children.

ROLES Members of families also have roles they play within the family that will be carried into the school setting. For example, one member may be considered the responsible one in the family, whereas another may be considered a jokester. Some individuals tend to be peacemakers; others take on the role of troublemaker or victim. A child who is a helper at home will carry these helping behaviors to school. Having insights into the role a child plays in the family can help a teacher broaden children's experiences while capitalizing on their strengths.

RULES All families have rules, spoken or unspoken, that determine how they live in relation to one another. Such rules may also overlap with the roles family members play, especially those related to gender, power, and how the family interacts. Some families have many rules and follow them closely; others have fewer rules and are inconsistent in following them. Teachers may have to help children make distinctions between home rules and school rules. They may also have to help families understand why certain expectations occur at school that may be different from those at home. For example, a teacher may wish to have children participate in a cooking activity that a family may consider inappropriate for a boy because males in the family do not cook. Being open to hearing about different expectations and providing alternatives that meet the goals of the activity can help keep lines of communication open when school and home rules collide.

HIERARCHY A family's hierarchy denotes who has the decision-making power. This hierarchy may be determined by gender or age and may be influenced by a family's culture, religion, or economic status. In some families, for example, the male head of the household is clearly in charge and controls much of what goes on in the family. In other cases, it may be less clear who is the leader; this may be the role of someone in the extended family who is considered the matriarch or patriarch of the family. Noticing who signs permission forms, who attends conferences, and who returns phone calls can give clues to the family hierarchy and can help smooth communication between school and home.

CLIMATE   The *climate* of a family refers to its emotional and physical environment. A child growing up in a family without a lot of money can still thrive when the family provides an encouraging and supportive atmosphere. Alternatively, a beautiful home and many possessions cannot compensate for a distant and cold emotional life. Teachers who create a warm, caring classroom climate help all children, especially those whose homes may be less supportive, develop feelings of security and safety.

EQUILIBRIUM   Stability and balance are two family characteristics that fall at one end of the continuum of equilibrium. At the other end are instability and imbalance. Most families will fall somewhere between these extremes most of the time, but circumstances can interfere with a family's equilibrium. Serious illness, death, separation, and divorce are family events that can cause destabilization, as can unemployment or other economic factors. Because children thrive on consistency and predictability, it is important for teachers to be aware of family circumstances that may cause the equilibrium to shift out of balance. Providing as much consistency in the school setting as possible can help a child feel more secure in times of turmoil at home.

IMPLICATIONS FOR TEACHERS

Family Nurturing Practices and You

The nurturing behaviors you have just read about will, of course, have an impact on the children with whom you work. Because there is a broad spectrum of parenting behavior and competence, you will find yourself dealing with a wide range of attitudes, behaviors, and skills coming from your students' homes. So, prepare yourself with a working knowledge of the above viewpoints.

Family Systems Theory and Maslow's hierarchy of needs help you understand families better and why children exhibit certain dispositions. Therefore, make a sincere effort to know the families of the children with whom you work. This is an essential first step in developing your awareness of the family dynamic. Try hard to avoid making judgments about families. Just try to find out how the parents interact with their children. Establishing relationships with families before problems arise will help you deal with conflicts in a climate of respect and caring.

FAMILY RESPONSIBILITIES

The family at the beginning of the 21st century has many crucial functions to perform. Because society evolves, these familial roles vary from those of a century ago. Lifestyles are different now, circumstances have changed, and new expectations have emerged. The family, however, continues to serve an essential role in the lives of adults and children who are tied to each other by bonds of love and obligation (Bianchi, Robinson, & Milkie, 2006). Responsibilities such as providing economic and emotional support, socialization, and education for children remain essential aspects of parenting.

How these functions are fulfilled varies from family to family, depending on circumstances. When parents are unable to carry out their responsibilities, other persons and agencies may assume parental capacities and duties. In all cases, the family roles are complemented by the efforts of teachers and various community agencies.

REFLECTION

Continue to reflect on your own childhood and the roles the adults who raised you played in your life. Compare this situation to those of the families and children with whom you work. Do you note changes in roles?

Economic Support

We recognized in Chapter 3 that some families in the United States live on a few thousand dollars per year, whereas others enjoy extraordinarily high incomes. This variable determines the differences in the type of shelter and the quality of food and clothing families acquire, as well as other family living conditions.

Even though one or more family members are employed, some families cannot meet economic minimums and must depend on government assistance and private charities to supplement the basics. Because women in general earn only 80% of men's annual incomes, and because African American and Hispanic men earn 78% and 63% of White men's salaries (Haddock, Zimmerman, & Lyness, 2003), respectively, the families most likely to struggle economically are single-parent families headed by women and families of color. Although the United States is one of the wealthiest nations in the world, 18% of American children under the age of 18 live in families with incomes below the federal poverty level of $22,050 for a family of four (National Center for Children in Poverty, 2009). On average, a family needs an income of about twice that amount to cover basic expenses, which would leave about 39% of children living in low-income families.

Most families do manage their economic situation marginal as it may be at times. Although many U.S. families are subsidized, most do have adequate shelter, food, and clothing. Most families also have reasonable choices in allotting their finances. Poverty is exacerbated for families struggling to make appropriate choices, though, and those with meager resources may need support and education to learn how to make sound financial decisions. More desperate circumstances characterize the underclass, where the basic levels of Maslow's hierarchy are often threatened. At the present time, 5.8 million children have been identified as living in extreme poverty, with household income below $10,600 for a family of four (Children's Defense Fund, 2008). Poverty overshadows all other factors as the largest threat to children's well-being.

Social agencies are established in communities to guarantee economic basics for all families. Their success rate is reasonable, but communities must pursue even more aggressively the task of monitoring and guiding basic economic practices. Although **welfare reform measures** have helped former recipients obtain jobs, adequate resources for housing, health-care benefits, and child care are often not available. Extended training and education for parents are the real needs to lift families out of poverty for good. Parent education that focuses on the economics of family life as well as on parenting skills can be an important step in improving the lives of poor families. It is a focus that integrates well with collaborations among communities, schools, and families.

The economic downturn that began in 2008 has brought even more families into difficult economic circumstances. Job loss has been particularly significant in manufacturing and construction, industries that typically employ many more men than women. For the first time in U.S. history, women now make up the majority of the workforce because layoffs have affected men more than women. All of these changes have led to a volatile economic climate characterized by high unemployment, home foreclosures, and loss of savings earmarked for college tuition and retirement. The changes in the economic circumstances of many families may have far-reaching, yet presently unknowable, implications for children. One thing we do know, however, is that the rate of child poverty rises in times of recession (Children's Defense Fund, 2008).

Emotional Support

Even though most parents have little training or instruction in psychological support roles, emotional nurturance for their children appears to be a natural response. In addition, although most new parents use the parenting skills they observed and experienced in their own childhood, others make a conscious decision to parent their children differently than the way they were raised.

Parents who are sensitive to an infant's needs, responsive to the infant's cues, and both supportive and stimulating enhance their child's secure attachment to them. That bond between parent and child lays the foundation for children's later loving relationships (Sclafani, 2004). Physical affection, appreciation of the child as an individual, and acknowledgment of a child's competence all contribute to the development of self-esteem in children, the basis of sound emotional health. Research on "strong families" (Westman, 2001) suggests that emotional development in children benefits from parenting practices that emphasize mutual respect for family members, open communication, and parental authority.

Parenting classes and support groups are available (and needed) for parents who are uncertain about the ways to nurture their new children most effectively. A growing problem with the present generation is that smaller families, dual-income families, and especially single-parent families provide noticeably less modeling of parenting behavior (Casper & Bianchi, 2002). Again, community policies must ensure availability and use of resources to support parents who need guidance in providing emotional support for their children.

Socialization

Many agents, such as the school, the peer group, the church, and the media, are involved in socializing children, but the family has the primary responsibility for beginning the process. Socialization of young children involves learning to relate to a variety of people in varying circumstances and modifying behavior in different environments. Strong social skills, specifically the ability to get along with other children, are the best childhood predictors of adult competence. Emotional and social development are closely linked, and children with high self-esteem are better able to face the challenges of social interaction.

As children enter school and community life today, other forces begin to exert increasing influence on their socialization. You found in Chapter 2 that parents' impact on children's socialization was more significant in earlier periods of history. More isolated communities, less mobility, and the virtual dominance of parental figures ensured that values and attitudes were quickly inculcated in children through example and statement. In addition, communities in the early United States were highly idealistic in orientation, and **role expectations** were similar for everyone in those areas.

Patterns differ today. There is less general agreement in the United States on

Strong social skills, specifically the ability to get along with other children, are the best childhood predictor of adult competence.

social mores as a result of the heterogeneous communities in which we live. But schools still have certain expectations for children, and those who enter without the rudimentary social skills of sharing, cooperating, and respecting rules find themselves at a disadvantage. Families must work hard today to prepare their children for the social expectations of the school and the community while maintaining their own values, beliefs, family ethnic and religious identity, and gender roles.

VALUES, BELIEFS, AND ATTITUDES   Parents rarely plan to teach their children values and beliefs. They do, however, model via their behavior what they value and prize and what they are willing to accept. This practice has both positive and negative implications. If a parent rushes to help a neighbor in need, the idea is passed on to children; if a parent models lying, that habit is passed on. Recall that one part of Jana's story in the opening vignette in Chapter 3 was the way Jana's stepmother modeled "helping neighbors." Today, Jana is raising her own children and responds to neighborhood difficulties by preparing and donating food.

Just as children learn from their parents' examples, they also learn values as they interact with family members. Daily conversations, struggles, and explanations of the world all help to build children's attitudes and beliefs about the world and other people. Spending time as a family playing games, watching a movie, hiking, or just talking conveys to children the priority their parents place on the family.

If we consider that children average nearly 30 hours a week watching TV or playing video games, it is no surprise that they gain many beliefs and values from participating in these activities (Van Evra, 2004). Of particular concern is the increasing amount and level of violence (DeGaetano, 2005) and sexualized gender roles in media for children (Levin, 2005). The culture of violence and sexualization created by the media teaches children lessons that do not fit into the value systems of most parents. Parents, of course, can monitor and watch programs to discuss actions and make comments, but the problem of media violence and other aspects of media culture is being increasingly viewed as a public health issue, and schools and community agencies are beginning to get involved in protecting children from unhealthy and undesirable images.

GENDER ROLES   Although both gender and parenting roles today appear quite different from those of earlier generations, and although gender-related expectations are less rigid in many U.S. homes, most parents do try to steer their children toward **gender-appropriate behaviors**. The process of gender socialization often begins even before a child is born, as parents use information about their coming child's gender in order to choose a name, clothing, and nursery decorations. Parents also tend to give children gender-stereotyped toys and to interact with their children differently, depending on their gender. Some gendering in family life is inevitable, but rigid expectations perpetuate the inequities of power between men and women in our society. Many quality children's books, listed in the Appendix, now portray more flexibility in gender roles.

In the past, fathers were the primary economic mainstay, but that role is changing. Today, 62% of mothers with children under 6 years of age are in the labor force and 78% of mothers with children between ages 6 and 17 are employed (U.S. Department of Labor, Bureau of Labor Statistics, 2008). In many dual-career homes, mothers and fathers now contribute equally to the family's economic support. In addition, mothers are the breadwinners in the majority of single-parent homes. Thus, the notion of associating economic support with one particular parent does not fit many children's life experiences.

Beyond economic dimensions is the changing character of family duties in the household. Historically, roles determined that the mother was cook and general homemaker, whereas the father was in the field or away at work. In the modern home, duties are not so clearly defined. Some fathers, although still a small percentage, now have major responsibilities for meal preparation and cleaning, in addition to child monitoring. Husbands now attend childbirth and parenting classes together with their wives and take responsibility for infant care. Research also indicates that men born between 1965 and 1979 spend, on average, an hour or more per workday caring for and doing things with their children than men born between 1946 and 1964 (Piburn, 2006).

The vast majority of married couples, however, still adhere to traditional family roles, and even women who are employed do about 80% of the household chores and child care. In addition, although fathers are increasingly assisting with the tasks of raising children and running a household, mothers still have the major responsibility of organizing child care, meal planning, cleaning, and so on (Bookman, 2004).

Attempts to eliminate gender-specific tasks in the family have been slowed by the lack of changes in the workforce. The persisting lag in women's incomes compared to men's, traditional full-time work schedules that don't allow flexibility or part-time options, and work that spills over into family life make it very challenging for families to balance the needs of employment and raising children.

Over the course of their lives, children may live in various family configurations because of separation, divorce, death, remarriage, and other family changes. These reconfigured family structures expose children to more flexible gender roles. Single-parent households and families led by gay or lesbian parents also provide a less rigid idea of what roles men and women can play in family life and society (Ramsey, 2004).

REFLECTION

Were there gender-specific tasks that certain family members took on in your own family? Were the expectations different for boys and girls? How do children with whom you work now see their responsibilities for certain tasks? How do you feel about fairness and equity in modern society?

RACIAL AND ETHNIC IDENTITY Defining race and ethnicity in the United States is a complex and sometimes contested endeavor. As our society grows more diverse physically (Figure 4-2), it is becoming increasingly difficult to categorize by race, as discussed

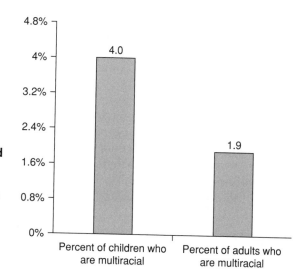

FIGURE 4-2 Multiracial* Children and Adults in the 2000 Census *Source:* Population Reference Bureau, analysis of data from U.S. Bureau of the Census, 2000 redistricting data (Tables PL1 and PL12), 2003.

*Multiracial refers to people who chose more than one race on the 2000 census.

in Chapter 3. In 1998, for example, 5% of Black Americans were foreign born (Banks, 2002). Many of these individuals are far more likely to identify with their ethnic heritage (Jamaican American, for example) than with their racial identity.

Children begin to become aware of racial differences in skin color and other physical characteristics at around age 3 or 4, but their understanding of the social and political implications of race develops much later (Wright, 1998).

꙾—— When Catherine, an African American 3-year-old adopted by a White family, asked what color her mother was, her mother replied, "Well, I am peach color, but most people would call me White." She went on to say that people would call Catherine Black, to which Catherine replied incredulously, "I'm not Black, I'm silver!" By age 5, Catherine was coloring her skin brown in self-portraits and referring to herself as brown. ——꙾

Typically, Black children become aware of their race at younger ages than do White children (Wright, 1998), perhaps because of the continued salience of race as an issue for African Americans. Ethnic identity and validation are clearly in the province of the family, and feelings about self depend on accurate information and sensitive guidance (Ramsey, 2004). Some minority homes provide support and foster pride in the family culture and give training on how to overcome derogatory messages. Responsibility for enhancing a heritage goes beyond family efforts, though; it must be supported throughout the community.

Much of a family's cultural history comes in the form of stories shared and passed down through generations. In many African American, Latino, Hawaiian, and Southeast Asian families, storytelling is also a way of passing on life lessons and values. Parents who have come to the United States from other countries often seek to preserve their heritage by maintaining their native language in the home and sharing stories of their homeland with their children. Children who maintain and develop a home language while learning English at school and other places outside the home preserve their sense of belonging to their families and become biliterate as well as bicultural, an increasing advantage in our diverse world (Giambo & Szecsi, 2005).

Education

As we noted in Chapter 2, parents in previous centuries assumed a major role in all aspects of educating their children. Even in the 1800s, many families still taught basic lessons for living and vocational preparation to their children. In the 1900s, however, schools expanded rapidly in scope and assumed most of the role of educating children in literary skills, calculation, and sciences. They even acquired the job of developing work habits; moral training and health education were added quickly thereafter. Today's schools have expanded to include sex education, health and recreation training, vocational training, and other educational aspects that were formerly a family's responsibility.

One regrettable outcome of this transfer of educative roles is that many parents have become much less involved in teaching their children essential responsibilities. The importance of parents in educating their children remains, however, and schools need to help families understand their significance as their children's first and most important teachers. Parents who have high academic expectations for their children, monitor their schoolwork, and reward their accomplishments in school find that their children have more successful academic outcomes (Sclafani, 2004).

Families can provide the support, critical demonstrations, and follow-up for a child's learning opportunities if they are mindful of (a) the parents' logical status as guides, (b) their intimate knowledge of the learner, (c) the influence parental status provides, and (d) the many chances for applying text material to everyday life. Most parents do much of their teaching in informal ways; they share their skills, hobbies, and other interests during everyday events and conversations. In fact, the importance of the shared family meal as a socializing and educational factor in children's lives is increasingly recognized, even as such gatherings occur less and less often in many families (Noddings, 2005). Other parents, however, have assumed responsibility for educating their children in a more direct and formal way by home schooling. Chapter 8 provides more detail on home learning and home schooling.

Family mealtime is an important socializing and educational factor in children's growth.

Changes in Functions in the 21st Century

As we have noted, U.S. families are diverse and will continue to become more diverse in the foreseeable future. Roles for family members in the information age are still evolving, and certainly changes will continue to appear. Although one can only guess how different the typical family roles will be in another few decades, the family has shown itself to be a social form that is strong and adaptable.

Some changes in recent decades show increased momentum: (a) fathers are more involved in early education, and this benefits children; (b) mothers are more involved in sports and recreational activities, and this benefits children; and (c) extended families continue to decrease in contact and impact, and this does not benefit children (Bookman, 2004). Single parenting, which can be less advantageous for children, is likely to continue at a similar pace, particularly as single women become mothers by choice. School responsibilities are still increasing, but efforts to share and exchange responsibilities are more in evidence. (See Chapter 11 for particular models of cooperation.)

IMPLICATIONS FOR TEACHERS

Understanding Parenthood Challenges

Children of the 21st century face a very different socializing environment than did children of previous generations. Less constancy is found in family matters, and more adults from outside the family are involved with children's experiences. Peer-group influences have expanded, to say nothing of the explosion in influence of the media and entertainment industries. As a teacher, you will need to work for more joint efforts among homes, schools, and communities, where well-reasoned decisions about roles will enable families to provide quality experiences and opportunities for their children. Chapters 10 and 11 will explore this topic in detail.

You will also be at the forefront of experiencing all the dimensions of diversity that families reveal today. Initially, you will have to educate yourself about the differences and unique contributions of the families you work with who come from ethnic, racial, and language backgrounds that are different than your own. Your sincere interest in each family will reward you with a rich understanding of various cultures and lifestyles. Remember that diversity includes race, ethnicity, language, special needs, gender, sexual orientation, religious beliefs, educational background, and other qualities that are manifested in individuals.

*You will also be involved in making sure that the curriculum you implement in your classroom reflects the diversity of the families and communities you serve. Including children's books in different languages on your shelves, lining your bulletin boards with traditional fabrics of the ethnic groups you serve, and having photos of the children's families prominently displayed in the classroom are examples of ways to visibly show families that you are aware of their languages, cultures, and lifestyles. You have heard of or studied **multicultural education** in other courses. This approach refers to the curricular changes made in schools and other social institutions to respond to our diverse society. It has also come to mean a broader school reform effort designed to increase educational equity for various cultural, ethnic, and economic groups.*

CULTURAL PATTERNS AND FAMILY FUNCTIONS

The United States is a diverse country that encompasses an array of ethnic minority groups, and we find differences in the ways groups perform tasks, establish values, and relate to one another (McGoldrick, 2003). Different ethnic groups frequently have varying cultural features, but we also find multiple cultures within the larger groups. Professionals must be knowledgeable about and reflect upon this interesting cultural mix.

Ethnic background refers to the shared history and culture, common values, behaviors, and/or other characteristics of a group that create a sense of identity among its members (Banks & Banks, 2005). Although some ethnic groups, such as African Americans, can have distinguishing racial characteristics, other ethnic groups, such as Puerto Ricans, include people who belong to several different racial groups. In the case of Jewish Americans, their shared religious and cultural background, rather than their racial identities, creates a common bond.

Culture refers to the attitudes, traditions, beliefs, symbols, and customs held by a group of people. In the United States, there is an overarching core culture shared to a greater or lesser extent by all individuals and groups within the nation. Ideas related to equality, individualism, and opportunities for social mobility are examples of the core ideals of the culture of the United States. Within our country, there are also many smaller subcultures that reflect the components important to particular groups.

Ethnicity and culture frequently overlap; for example, many Native Americans continue to identify themselves by ethnic background and hold cultural beliefs separate from those of mainstream U.S. culture. We also find groups of people with similar ethnic backgrounds who differ culturally. For example, in English-speaking regions, Appalachian Americans are very different from Oregonian ranchers or Connecticut commuters, even though they have similar roots. Their traditions, values, and attitudes place them in different cultural groups.

For simplification, we differentiate in this book between the European American (White), English-speaking majority and non–European American minorities in the United States, even though each of these delineations contains more than one ethnic group. Table 4-1 presents the proportions of these primary minority groups as of 2008.

Ethnic and cultural groups may have lifestyles, ways of communicating, and parenting practices that differ from those of the mainstream in the United States. Gender roles, social class, socioeconomic status, and parents' occupations are variables that may further impact a group's parenting style in unique ways, depending on the culture. Because of increasing diversity and overlap of cultures, it is essential for professionals to examine their own behavior and increase their awareness of other ways of living and communicating so that discussions with parents are carried out with respect. Professionals must keep in mind that individuals also vary greatly in their identification with their ethnic group, so they must take care not to stereotype people on the basis of their ethnic background.

TABLE 4-1   Major Ethnic Groups in the United States in 2008

Ethnic Group	Percentage of the U.S. Population
African American	13
American Indian/Alaskan Native	1
Asian/Pacific Islanders	5
European Americans	64
Hispanic Americans	14
Other and multiple ethnicity	3

Source: U.S. Bureau of the Census, Population Division Estimates, May 1, 2009.

Note: Persons of Hispanic ancestry may be of any race but are separated from other groups in this table.

Despite the differences in parenting practices that families from various cultures may employ, it is important to be aware that most parents do have similar goals for their children. Families want their offspring to live healthy lives, achieve economic stability, and adhere to certain cultural values (Greenfield & Suzuki, 2001). Parents from different cultures may, however, vary in their expectations about development of competencies at different ages.

REFLECTION

Consider the different cultural groups you have encountered in your life. Then reflect on the underlying beliefs and values that families in the different groups demonstrated. Can you describe how those beliefs and values were manifested? List some of the similarities and differences that you have noted.

The values of a culture are transmitted primarily through adult modeling, storytelling, directions and instructions given to children, pressures from the cultural group, and reinforcements for certain serendipitous actions that each child displays. So, although the goals for children's development are similar, various cultural groups may rear their children quite differently. You must also bear in mind, however, that today many children's values and attitudes are influenced more and more by the media, schools, and peers.

Parenting Features in Various Cultures

Child-raising practices in the United States changed considerably during the 20th century. We now find great variation from one cultural group to another within the society as a whole. The **socioeconomic status (SES)** of different families within one cultural group indicates that other differences exist as well.

For European American groups, **behaviorism** was valued in the early years of the 20th century, and many parents at that time valued the principles of reinforcement and extinction, popularized by psychologists. A child-centered phase bloomed in the middle years of the century, but in recent decades the swing has been toward a middle ground. Overall, contemporary European Americans are quite susceptible to current theories and depend less on folklore and tradition than did prior generations. Although most minority cultures in the United States have retained their traditional child-raising practices to a greater extent than have European American families, the proliferation of ideas in the mass media has altered some of their practices as well.

Keeping all the complexity about approaches to parenting in mind, certain practices do tend to differ among various ethnic groups. It is essential to remember, however, that these are broad generalizations meant to suggest the range in approaches to caring for children. Although it is possible to find general characteristics of a group, individuals within the group may not conform to the generalizations. Further, socioeconomic level, education, and parental occupation are all important factors in determining an individual's child-rearing practices.

INFANT CARE The European American way of socializing children has been characterized as geared toward the goal of **technological intelligence**, whereas other groups have a goal of social intelligence (Greenfield & Suzuki, 2001). The emphasis in many European American families is on babies' manipulation and labeling of objects, whereas recent immigrants from Africa and Asia seem to value positive interactions between babies and other people. These different goals, although vastly oversimplified, can help to explain various infant-care practices.

In the European American tradition, where the development of autonomy and separate, individual existence is an important parental goal, babies tend to be held less than they are in many other cultures and to be left to cry after all obvious physical needs have been met. In Native American society, by contrast, babies and mothers have traditionally had continuous contact, and other groups, such as African Americans, Hispanic Americans, and various Asian American cultures, tend to feed infants on demand and maintain very close physical connections between mothers and infants.

Although most babies sleep alone in a room separate from their parents in the European American family, bed sharing between parents and infants is the norm in about two-thirds of the world's cultures. Many minority and immigrant groups continue this practice after they come to this country. Other parents use cosleeping as a way to maintain closeness with an infant from whom they have been separated during the day. Cosleeping remains controversial in the United States, however, with proponents believing that it has many benefits and detractors warning of risks to the infant.

Bed sharing is the norm in two-thirds of the world's families.

Cosleeping is most common in cultures that emphasize interdependence and family bonding above independence. Immigrants from many African countries, as well as Japanese Americans, Korean Americans, and other Asian groups, may cosleep or keep children in the same room with them through early childhood. Although the American Academy of Pediatrics (2009) has stated that cosleeping puts babies at risk for suffocation, that organization does encourage parents to keep their infants in the same room with them in a separate crib or a sleeping device attached to the adult bed.

PHYSICAL CONTACT Different cultural groups vary greatly in the amount and kind of physical contact that takes place between parents and their children. Affection is displayed in different ways, and physical punishment is used to a greater or lesser extent among various groups.

In many Asian American homes, the physical closeness common between infants and parents is reduced as children grow. In African American families, however, body contact is expected and encouraged throughout childhood. Less physical intimacy is found between parents and children in many European American homes, although playful interaction is encouraged. Some physical punishment is accepted in many Hispanic families, but these families also tend to be physically affectionate with their children. African American families are more likely to use physical punishment than Native American families, who avoid its use.

FAMILY ROLE   In many cultures, the solidarity and importance of the family are primary; however, in others, children are encouraged to be more independent. In some groups, the nuclear family is paramount, whereas in others the extended family and the kinship network are essential aspects of child rearing. **Patriarchal, matriarchal,** and shared leadership can be found in different cultures.

Interaction styles within the family reflect the roles expected of children. In many Hispanic families, for example, children are encouraged and expected to play with siblings rather than peers. European American families, on the other hand, may encourage their children to move beyond the family to establish other relationships. In most Asian American families, children are expected to be family oriented and to work hard for the support of the family. Much value is placed on respect for elders within the family in most Asian cultures. Many African American families also place great emphasis on children being part of an extended family of relatives and other adults who function as part of a large kinship network and who all participate in raising the children. Clearly, differences exist among ethnic groups in parenting practices, although we restate that these are general characteristics only. One can easily find homes displaying few of the practices noted in the preceding sections.

The numerous decisions parents must make regarding the conflicting forces that surround all homes in busy America—media, entertainment, peer culture, and other attractions—can make it very challenging for parents to meet their responsibilities. Parenting is complex, and often factors other than a family's culture or ethnic background can influence child-rearing behaviors. Birth order of children; the child's age, temperament, or gender; parental experiences; and parent temperament will all have an impact on how a parent raises a particular child. All parents, we find, use a mixture of child-rearing practices, and the impressions and the information from other sources will influence their behavior.

IMPLICATIONS FOR TEACHERS

Cultural Aspects of Parenting

As you advance in your professional preparation, remain open to parenting that may be very different than the way you were raised or intend to raise your children. Parenting practices generally make sense in the context of the culture the parent is trying to preserve. Therefore, become familiar with different cultural practices on parenting so that you do not become flustered by the nursing mother at your PTA meeting. Learn to speak openly and listen respectfully to all of your students' parents from a variety of interesting backgrounds. This will help you understand how parenting fits in with the larger cultural goals of different groups.

INTERACTION STYLES WITHIN FAMILIES

Another major feature of child rearing is the interaction and communication between children and significant family adults. Researchers confirm the effect of parents' verbalizations and actions on their children's interactions, and this effect relates to all other elements of parenting. The studies we present in this section demonstrate connections between parenting and child behavior, and will give you some background on this aspect of parenting behavior that you will find once you are in a classroom.

Baumrind's Classification

Baumrind, in her classic study of parent–child interactions, showed that very different styles of parenting exist and that those styles affect children's skills and attitudes. Baumrind (1966, 1968) placed parenting styles along the following three-part continuum:

1. *Authoritative (democratic).* Controlling and demanding but warm; rational and receptive to the child's communication.
2. *Permissive (child-centered).* Noncontrolling, nondemanding, and relatively warm.
3. *Authoritarian (autocratic).* Detached, controlling, and somewhat less warm. than the authoritative or permissive style.

Later work by Baumrind and others (Sclafani, 2004) resulted in the addition of a fourth parenting style as a refinement of the permissive style. See Figure 4-3 to find the undemanding but unresponsive permissive style that indicates neglect.

Baumrind found that most children of authoritative parents showed independence and were socially responsible. They were also better able to regulate their emotions and behaviors, and they tended to have good tolerance for frustration as well as the ability to delay gratification. These traits translated into competence and resistance to substance abuse during adolescence, according to a later study. Baumrind found that authoritative parents took into account their children's needs as well as their own before dealing with situations. The parents respected children's need to make their own decisions, yet they exerted control. They reasoned with their children and explained things more often than did other parents.

On the other hand, Baumrind found that the children of permissive parents frequently lacked social responsibility and often were not independent. She concluded that parents who considered all behavior to be natural and refreshing had unrealistic beliefs about young children's growth and socialization.

Baumrind found that children of authoritarian parents also showed little independence and were less socially responsible. Such parents feel that children require restraint and need to develop respect for authority, work, and traditional structure.

The authoritative style requires parents to guide, share activities, and talk and listen to their children. The following summary illustrates the adult behaviors that

	Accepting, Responsive	Rejecting, Unresponsive
Demanding, controlling	AUTHORITATIVE	AUTHORITARIAN
Undemanding, uncontrolling	PERMISSIVE-INDULGENT	PERMISSIVE-NEGLECTFUL

FIGURE 4-3 Four Parenting Types

produce Baumrind's authoritative style. To foster socially responsible and independent behavior in children, parents

- Serve as responsible and self-assertive models.
- Set standards whereby responsible behavior is rewarded and unacceptable behavior is punished.
- Are committed to the child in a way that is neither overprotective nor rejecting.
- Have high demands for achievement and conformity but are receptive to the child's rational demands.
- Provide secure but challenging and stimulating environments for creative and rational thinking.

Maccoby and Martin (1983) supported the findings of Baumrind. And Clark (1983) produced similar findings showing his **sponsored independence style** to be consistent with Baumrind's authoritative style. Later studies measuring the long-term effects of the authoritative style produced even more evidence that it engenders positive adolescent behavior.

One caveat is needed concerning this research. Baumrind used White, middle-class parents in her study, whereas later, in their replication studies, Maccoby and Martin (1983) found that Baumrind's conclusions did not always translate directly to poor, minority, and single-parent families. Cross-cultural research (Harris, 1998) suggests that although the authoritative style works well with middle-class Americans, Asian American children, who are raised in an authoritarian style, perform well in school and have success in later life. Clark (1983), however, found that the authoritative or sponsored independence behaviors in Mexican American and African American homes often made the difference between success and failure for minority children in school. As far as parenting in a contemporay society is concerned, the authoritative style seems to be most effective in preparing children for school expectations as well for later positive outcomes (Noddings, 2005).

Bernstein's Work

Language is a primary means by which a child learns to understand and function in the world. Children tend to develop language on a predictable developmental scale, but different parental language styles and interactions do affect children's socialization and literacy development. Bernstein's (1972) classic study of family language patterns produced two general linguistic codes used in many homes. He termed these very different patterns *restricted* and *elaborated*. The codes reflect two quite different styles: those of the **position-oriented family** and the **person-oriented family**.

Position-oriented families use a restricted code, and the family role system is positional, or object oriented and present oriented. In contrast, person-oriented families use an elaborated code, and the family role system is personal, or person oriented and future oriented. The following vignette illustrates the two codes.

In the space of 3 minutes, two attractive family groups approached a traffic light–controlled crosswalk at a busy intersection. One mother and her preschool son

Person-oriented families allow children to make decisions as they engage in family activities.

approached hand in hand, talking freely. Within a few feet of the crosswalk, the mother leaned down toward her son and said, "See the light there? It's red, and we have to stop. See the cars still coming this way? We need to stay right back here, 'til we get the flashing walk light, okay? You watch and tell me when to go." When the boy continued to advance into the crosswalk, his mother tightened her grip on his hand and said more firmly, "Stop here. It's not safe yet."

The second family, a mother, father, and little girl, approached the crosswalk and stopped. Suddenly, the mother noticed the child, who was slightly ahead, start toward the crosswalk and yelled, "Stay here!" The girl continued to advance, and the mother screamed again, "Stay here, I said!" The father leaped and yanked the girl back beside him. "Just stand!" the mother said, and the family waited silently for the signal to change—bodies rigid, the parents holding tightly to the child.

The second family here appears to be more position oriented and has a prescribed role system. Members have little choice, and roles are assigned according to family position. According to Bernstein, their communication is object oriented and present orisiented. Aspects of a **restricted language code** appear, characterized by syntactically simple sentences and concrete meanings. The parents communicate one thing only to the daughter—to obey a single command. There is no explanation, and sentences are simple and direct.

The open quality of the mother and son in the person-oriented family, on the other hand, permits discretion in learner performance. Communication in the open system includes judgments and reasons, and children learn to cope with abstractions and ambiguity. The **elaborated language code** accommodates this type of content. The mother chats with her son about the crosswalk, explaining what is happening. She engages the child in the decision making. Yet, when it appears that he may advance into the crosswalk too soon, she, too, physically restrains the child for his safety.

Teachers must know that children from a closed or position-oriented family must depend on the school and the larger community to help them acquire elaborated language. As a teacher, you can become a vital communication model for children from families using restricted codes, as can other children. Older children may often help their teacher communicate with new children who are not familiar with school language and culture. We find this situation in the following vignette.

Ms. Dansky, a White teacher, wasn't successful in getting Philip, an African American 5-year-old just entering school, to join other children in a circle. She had used a polite invitation to call all the children. When Philip didn't move, she gave a sterner and more specific command to Philip. Then Greg, a seasoned African American 8-year-old, raised his hand and asked quietly, "You want me to get him for you, Ms. D?" Upon receiving a polite "Yes, thank you," he yelled to Philip, "Get over here right now!" When Philip came immediately to sit beside Greg, Greg leaned [over] to him and continued, "When she says, 'Boys and girls join me,' she means 'Come here.' And when she say, 'Philip, it's time for circle!' she means, 'Get over here right (pats a spot beside himself) NOW!' " (adapted from Seefeldt & Barbour, 1998, p. 340)

Greg had learned not only the correct language patterns of the school but also the politeness rules. Then he used language and tonal patterns familiar to Philip, and he skillfully switched between the two patterns to explain what their teacher's words meant. One can appreciate the advantages that elaborated codes have in the broadening requirements of the information age. Research has shown that preschool children who engaged in conversation with adults that went beyond the here and now to include past, future, and imagined events and abstract ideas had a larger vocabulary on school entry and performed better on comprehension tests up to sixth grade (Bardige, 2005). Clearly, the langue environment in which a child is brought up will have long-term consequences.

Hart and Risley's Studies

Hart and Risley (1995) also concentrated on language development and demonstrated that quality of parenting and richness of the linguistic environment are not necessarily linked to economic status or ethnicity. In their study of homes representing three SES levels, they discussed the linkages between young children's language development and meaningful experiences. The longitudinal study provides convincing evidence that the type and amount of interaction between parents and children result in significant differences, irrespective of SES.

According to the study, the quality of interactions in everyday parenting center on the following five variables:

1. *Amount and richness of vocabulary.*   Parents deliberately use various terms, labels, and expressions and model their use when talking. "Yes, these are all clothes—pants, shirts, socks."
2. *Sentence usage.*   Parents make a connection between objects and events when responding to children. "Yes, it is a doll, and it's Cindy's, so you need to give it back."
3. *Discourse function.*   The quality of utterances used is important when parents give choices or directions to prompt child behavior. "Did you remember to hang up your coat?"
4. *Adjacency condition.*   This variable centers on the relation between the parent's and child's behavior when the parent listens or initiates for the child. Child: "Soup's good!" Parent models by saying: "Yes, it's delicious, isn't it?"
5. *Valence of communication.*   The emotional tone given to interactions is important, whether the parent tries to be pleasant or not. Simply smiling and repeating a child's word: "That's right, juice!" has positive valence.

The positive dimension of this study shows us that parenting behaviors leading to increased child performance can be learned and practiced. Hart and Risley (1995) assert that parents who purposely concentrate on meaningful differences are being "social partners" with their children.

In a follow-up study, Hart and Risley (1999) suggested that the most important aspect of parent talk to young children is its amount. They learned from their study that parents who talk as they go about their daily activities expose their children to more than 1,000 words per hour. Even more important, however, is the way that conversation between parent and child during the first 3 years of the child's life contributes to their relationship and builds a foundation of analytic and symbolic competencies that will serve the child for a lifetime. Spending time talking together is the most important way parents can help their child learn to speak and listen, and, of course, speaking and listening are the foundations of literacy.

With parents' busy work schedules and the amount of television viewing by the entire family, substantive conversation—which does not include directions, commands, or reprimands—between parents and children is becoming rare in many homes. Ideally, adults would take time to talk to their young child, focusing on things that the child has done, seen, or heard and using experiences with picture books to move conversation beyond the here and now. Although teachers and community workers alone cannot compensate for the shortage of meaningful parent–child interactions, a quality childcare or school experience can help children develop larger vocabularies and strong functional language (Bardige, 2005).

No two families are exactly alike, and parents have diverse ways of managing. The various features of parenting make family behaviors very complex and difficult to understand. We can examine general patterns of parenting, though, and we can relate these patterns to children's behavior. The investigators previously noted—Baumrind, Clark, Maccoby, and Martin—found that neither extreme of the parenting pattern— referred to respectively as *permissive* and *authoritarian*—is ideal for children. In his conditional sequence model of disciplinary responses, Larzelere (2001) reaffirmed the need for combining reason and discipline in effective parenting. Clearly, a combination of love and limits appears to be most beneficial.

Always remember that parenting practices are influenced by more than cultural background and interaction styles. As professionals, you must also be alert to the influence of family size, family SES, levels of stress in the home, and different community characteristics surrounding the children with whom you work.

IMPLICATIONS FOR TEACHERS

Linking Home and School Talk

Athough most research indicates that the authoritative style of parenting provides the best outcome, some families you meet will be raising their children using other approaches. Remember that the authoritative method is more closely aligned with the interaction style we find in most schools today. So, you may have to help some of your children adapt to the differences between home and school. Use the following principles of the authoritative style to guide your interactions with children:

- *Maintain a warm and affectionate demeanor.*
- *Set clear guidelines and high expectations.*
- *Be willing to discuss the reasons for your decisions, and be prepared to negotiate at times.*
- *Show the students that you value and respect their opinions.*

Children who have been raised in more permissive or authoritarian homes may also need help developing appropriate autonomy. You can help them develop this skill by having the class determine class rules, classroom jobs, and other projects in which they can make choices and develop their own timelines for accomplishing tasks.

EXPERIENCES OF FAMILIES

The life experiences of children within their families establish a background for their performance and their contributions in their school and community. What children see, hear, smell, taste, and do creates a foundation for their communication patterns, perceptual styles, and modes of thinking. Within the context of learning about life, children begin to comprehend messages and understand their place in the world (Lareau, 2003; Ramsey, 2004). Likewise, children's understanding of encountered images frequently depends on explanations and connections made by nearby adults.

Culture, economic, and experiential backgrounds make a significant difference in the way a child learns, communicates, and participates. In addition to basic nurturing, family histories of interactions, experiences, and practices will enhance or reduce children's development potential. When stress or problems arise, some families are **resilient** and display an ability to deal with changes and modify problems; others are ill equipped and cannot cope (McKenry & Price, 2005). Some adults even lean on their own children for support. Such resilience or its absence derives from many aspects of family experience. The communication styles and parenting practices noted earlier have an effect, but we should also consider the skill levels of parents and the type and degree of family mobility.

REFLECTION

As you pursue your daily activities, be aware of how parents are interacting with their children in the grocery store, library, mall, and other locations. What are some differences in the way parents appear to be talking to their children? Are they mainly directing their children's behavior or is there some discussion about the activities?

Skill Levels and Experience

Most parents and caregivers have extensive knowledge of their world—how to operate within society and how to manage their everyday lives. Passing on wisdom and skills is one of the pleasures of parenting, and some parents impart this knowledge in particularly beneficial ways.

Homemakers know their living quarters and what it takes to live in a particular home. Parents have experiences with food shopping, preparation, and serving, and some have added knowledge of nutrition and skills with food presentation. Involving children in food management can be done easily in all homes and provides a foundation for healthy living.

Using tools to build or repair household objects is common in many homes. Some parents have woodworking or metal-finishing skills and perhaps have home workbenches. Almost all parents have interesting experiences involving tools, and many take pleasure in their use. Adults can easily transfer these skills to interested children through demonstration, home projects, or the classic children's book *The New How Things Work* (Macaulay, 1998).

Some families invest a great deal of time in gardening for relaxation or growing summer vegetables. The growing of green things fascinates most youngsters, and it is the beginning of a basic science that children encounter during their school years. A child's home is a nice place to learn about gardening, and any growing project provides a healthy venue for discussion and interaction between adult and child. An example of "gardening" learning was demonstrated when our neighbor Melissa involved her 3-year-old son, in a very natural way, in her regular gardening, singing, and reading activities:

Having just received Inch by Inch *(Mallett, 1995) from the community's* Growing Up Reading Project, *Melissa and her son, Adam, immediately opened the new treasure and looked at the end pages, which contained pictures of vegetables. Adam saw a picture of a carrot and exclaimed, "That's a carrot." "Yes," said Melissa, "we've just gathered those from our garden, haven't we? See any more vegetables we have?" Adam thumbed through and found a huge beet. "Beet, yum, yum!" He turned to the end pages again and with a scooping motion began to "pick up" the imaginary vegetables, named them, and pretended to stuff them into his mouth. In the next few months, Melissa and Adam often played the "Garden Song" tape that accompanied this new book and sang the song together. It was a delight to see Melissa and Adam in the garden together the next spring, weeding. Adam trotted along the rows singing, "Inch by inch . . . make my garden grow . . . inch by inch, make my garden grow." Then he stopped to pull a "weed" and exclaimed, "A carrot! No, a beet! Yum, yum."*

Many games feature family interactions, and by using games as entertainment, parents can provide children with involvement in group activities, experience in strategy development and planning, positive use of aggressiveness, and practice in cooperative activities. Games are fundamentally simulations of life experiences, and children who have extensive experience with various games internalize approaches for living

Games involve children in group activities and develop skills for interacting with other children.

and many strategies for facing interactive situations. Many families have instituted a family game night when they gather together to enjoy cards, board games, and time together.

Storytelling plays an important role in children's growth. A large part of language development comes through stories. In families where stories are used for re-creating family history, for entertainment, or as examples, listeners grow in appreciation of language, their culture, and their family's experiences and identity. In some cultures, life lessons are passed on through such stories and connect children with their cultural history. One very important manifestation is the story in book form. In a book, the story belongs to someone else, but it gives much the same satisfaction to the young child.

Parents' skills in these and other aspects of daily life can and should be passed on to children in the family. All community life and school programs must reinforce these practices. Given the right conditions, home management and repair, gardening projects, game playing, storytelling, and other family-oriented experiences represent important resources and a worthy heritage for parents to pass on to their children. Most parents are not skilled instructors, but they can be very successful in teaching home activities and projects informally. When a caregiver is engaged with a single child on a topic of mutual interest, most classroom "teaching" demands are not present. Instructor and student can go directly to the task of transferring a particular skill to the learner. Most parents are successful at this natural process, and most yearn to pass on their knowledge when an opportunity occurs.

REFLECTION

Reflect on some of the activities and special skills that your parents possessed and that you learned. Did they ever visit your school classroom to share their skills? If so, how did you react to that experience?

Mobility of Families

Another feature of experience that affects children's emotional and academic progress is the mobility that families have in and around their community and farther afield. Americans move more than people in other countries, and moves frequently place families farther from their kin and other members of their social network. On the average, between 16% and 20% of the U.S. population moves every year, but a great deal of that relocating occurs as young adults move out of the home for work, education, or marriage. We find, however, that 23% of the persons who moved in 2000 were children under age 5, and this has an impact. Studies of military families who move, on average, every 3 years indicated that many of the affected children gave up trying to form close friendships (Karpowitz, 2001).

High levels of residential mobility can intensify social problems for both adults and children—if the move is accompanied by significant change in the quality of home life. African Americans and Hispanic Americans move more often than Whites because their residences are often rented. For most relocating families, mobility comes in two forms: forced and voluntary.

FORCED MOBILITY   A number of families are forced to relocate because of migrant work, homelessness, coping with unemployment, or escaping hostile actions or trouble. Many children also move after a divorce and experience the difficulty of going back and forth between two homes. Forced mobility (apart from job-related transfers) is always a reaction to undesirable conditions and contributes to erratic lifestyles for parents and their children. Isolation is implied, for forced mobility signifies that a family lacks connections or community linkages that could provide help. During the economic downturn that began in 2007, increasing numbers of families were forced to move when their homes went to foreclosure. Whatever the conditions, a family's forced move to a new environment presents different but rarely positive learning experiences for children. Little pleasure comes with a transfer from one home to another under duress.

RECREATIONAL AND VOLUNTARY MOBILITY   On the other hand, voluntary travel and relocation frequently connotes vacation time or an improved socioeconomic situation for the family. Both local travel and long-distance travel involve the positive expectation of new encounters. Arranging for the travel is a learning experience. Getting to a destination involves a certain amount of investigation, map reading, negotiating transportation schedules or checking driving requirements, and anticipating difficulties. Family members learn together, and these social and educational values are important. Transnational or international travel brings a family in touch with other cultures, as travelers need to adapt to new conditions, different foods, and a different sense of space. Such travel is expansive, and families gain psychic income and social capital.

The ways that families exploit surroundings, relationships, agencies, and even challenges show facets of their child-rearing practices and socializing acumen. Some families use their experience with great facility; others do not. Such use of experience may be a function of SES, as economically privileged families have the means to provide the benefits of local and long-distance travel. We also find instances of modestly endowed families enriching their children's lives through carefully developed experiences (Lareau, 2003; Monroe, 1997), however, and some affluent families neglect the need for family interaction and experience and fill their children's lives with sports, cultural, and other activities in a concerted pattern of cultivation (Laureau, 2003).

OTHER INFLUENCES ON PARENTING

We have tried to show that parenting needs to be examined and analyzed in the context of culture and community. As noted earlier, numerous variables affect family life and may be external factors of community and environment as well as internal factors of cultural background,

Travel and new experiences can bring about positive new encounters.

family demographics, and economics. Following is a brief discussion of some of these other dimensions.

Child-Care Arrangements

With extended work schedules for most American families, a huge number of parents now must cope daily with requirements for temporary care of their children. At one time, when many mothers were homemakers, child care was merged with running the household. Mothers attended their preschool-age children, welcomed their older children home from school, and supervised most at-home activities.

Today, however, the situation is very different: Welfare reform has increased the number of parents in the workforce, single-parent and dual-income families grow every year, and fewer extended family members are available to care for children. More than 65% of mothers with children under 6 years of age are in the workforce (Children's Defense Fund, 2001). This means that a huge number of young children are in some type of child-care arrangement for part of every workday. These arrangements include center-based and family child care as well as less formal situations, such as babysitters or care by slightly older siblings.

Infant, toddler, and preschool child care and after-school care for older children are now facts of life for most communities. As more parents, formerly on welfare, enter the workforce, the demands for quality care for children will intensify. Many child-care programs have waiting lists for children who need this service, and added requests will intensify the problem. Although a number of schools now operate their own after-school care programs, the need for care outstrips availability. Furthermore, the quality and costs of care are quite variable—adding another dimension to the problem for parents seeking care for their children.

Good child care, once found, solves many problems for parents. Supportive caregivers become an extension of the family and often develop strong affectional ties to the child and parents. These caregivers know the child well and can offer parents advice and reassurance as issues and concerns arise. This can be especially helpful to single parents. Child care also fosters connections between parents and other families with children, allowing them to develop a larger support network. Knowing their child is well cared for relieves parents of stress and anxiety and allows them to do their jobs. We consider the topic of child care more fully in Chapter 5.

Life-Changing Events as Family Stressors

The circumstances of modern life have led to an increase in stress among children and their parents. Separation, divorce, chronic illness, and death of a parent can reduce children's feeling of security and subject them to new patterns of family life. Living in a blended family, in a single-parent household, or with parents who travel frequently also increases the stress level of all involved. These circumstances are difficult for all families, but children and parents who live in poverty or suffer economic setbacks face added challenges that can contribute to additional stress (Bartholomae & Fox, 2005).

Stressors resulting from changes in family life and economic difficulties can be challenging for every family; some families, though, with good coping skills and resources, are better able than others to handle problems. Although a few stressors are self-inflicted, many are unavoidable or are developed through conflicts and economic pressures and through racist, elitist, and sexist practices.

Accumulated stressors lead to risky situations, and policy makers, educators, and others must be mindful of this possibility. The effects of risk on the intelligence measurements of preschool children shown in a startling study of 4-year-olds by Sameroff, Seifer, Barocas, Zax, and Greenspan (1987) are instructive. These researchers found that most

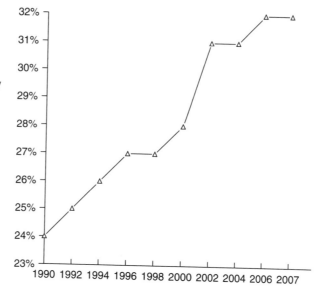

FIGURE 4-4 Children in Single-Parent Families, 1990–2007

Source: Annie E. Casey Foundation (2008). *Kids count data book: State profiles of child well-being.* Baltimore: Author. Also retrieved May 18, 2009, from *http://datacenter.kidscount.org/data/acrossstates/*

children seem able to cope with low levels of risk, but the presence of more than two risk factors jeopardizes their mental development. The message is clear: We must either prevent or compensate for accumulated risk factors (Stanford & Yamamoto, 2001).

Before ending our discussion of parenting and family functioning, we review in the following sections the concerns and risk factors that cause stress in families. Bear in mind, however, that strategies exist to deflect or accommodate stress arising from these factors. Helping children and their parents cope with stress is becoming an increasingly important role for teachers and community-service providers (Scully, 2003).

SEPARATION, DIVORCE, AND RECONFIGURED FAMILIES   As noted earlier, divorce has become common for U.S. families in recent decades, and although the divorce rate is no longer increasing, at the present time, first marriages in the United States have a 47% chance of breaking up and second marriages have a 49% chance of ending (Pann & Crosbie-Burnett, 2005). Consequently, more than 40% of American children will experience the effects of divorce, with nearly 90% placed in the physical custody of their mothers (although increasingly, legal custody tends to be shared between the parents). Of the children born in the 1990s, more than half will have spent some or all of their childhood in a single-parent household (Anderson, 2003). As Figure 4-4 indicates, about a third of all children are being raised by a single parent.

Liberalization of divorce laws in most states permits couples to separate more easily and more amicably, and although parents may adjust reasonably well to a divorce, many children of divorced parents tend to have long-term difficulties (Wallerstein, Lewis, & Blakeslee, 2000). Separation changes all roles in a family and alters the way a family functions. Responsibilities for the custodial parent increase dramatically, particularly with regard to child-care arrangements. There are more household tasks to perform, and financial obligations are heavier than before. Complicating the situation for children is the likelihood of one or both of their parents remarrying (65% of divorced women and 75% of divorced men remarry within 4 years). Even more likely are the nonmarital short-lived cohabitations of either parent. Finally, one-third of American children today will become part of a stepfamily.

Financial Aspects of Divorce.   Mothers are most often given custody of children in a divorce, but this can have dire consequences for the resulting single-parent family (Fine, Ganong, & Demo, 2005). Casper and Bianchi (2002) reported that the poverty rate for single-mother households was 38.7% compared to 6.9% for two-parent homes. In the United States, women in the workforce earn less than men, and even though child support judgments are made in divorce cases, fathers frequently do not pay, leaving mothers to assume full financial responsibility for their children. Casper and Bianchi (2002) stressed the financial inequities after divorce: Divorce improves the economic position of men but reduces that of women and children left with their mothers.

Other Consequences of Divorce. Increased work hours for **custodial parents** are typical after divorce, and decreased social interaction with children can result (Anderson, 2003). This means less parenting. Children in the home may face increased responsibilities, less time with either parent, and less emotional support after separation. A serious long-range effect of divorce is the removal of marriage models for affected children.

Behavioral changes in youngsters often result from divorce and separation. A considerable amount of research shows that the negative effects for children of divorce are sadness, anger, fear, aggressiveness, anxiety, and disobedience (Hetherington & Kelly, 2002; Schwartz & Kaslow, 1997). Children who have positive, nurturing relationships with both parents, low levels of parental and family conflict, and adequate economic resources, however, seem to adjust better to the diverse forms of family life that occur after a divorce.

For many children, these diverse family forms may include living in a single-parent home, moving between the homes of both parents as part of shared-custody arrangements, or becoming part of a stepfamily. All of these situations can pose challenges to children, but all can have strengths when compared to a predivorce situation: happier environments, better custodial parent–child relationships, more commitment to a wider community, and better-run households. Hetherington and Kelly (2002), in their review of hundreds of clients, found that most single-parent households do provide the nurturance that children need, despite the challenges. Negative stereotypes continue to affect single parents, stepparents, and their children, however. For example, teachers tend to assume that problems in school are related to the situation in the home. Research has shown that 80% of children from divorced homes eventually do adapt to their new lives and become reasonably well adjusted (Hetherington & Kelly, 2002).

IMPLICATIONS FOR TEACHERS

Working with Reconfigured Families

In the foreseeable future, many children will experience their parents' separation, divorce, and remarriage. As a teacher, you will be in a position to help families going through these life changes. For example, you may be able to connect parents with support groups to ease them through the initial period of adjustment during a divorce. Parents who learn not to criticize the other parent in front of their children, who seek help for their own emotional upheaval, and who shield their children from heated discussions tend to have healthier divorces and a better outcome for their children. Alerting your school counselor to changes in a family's configuration and enlisting her assistance in helping the children deal with the emotions that arise as they cope with the losses and changes associated with divorce and remarriage are other steps you can take to help families.

As a professional in early care and education, you are responsible for accommodating the extra needs that families and children may have during this time of transition. Make certain that you are communicating with all the significant adults in the child's life. It can be stressful for parents not to have information about homework, projects, and school events because the information was sent to only one of the child's homes. E-mail can simplify sending out needed information and ensure that everyone has it. Children's literature, sensitively read and discussed both at home and in school, can also be of great help to children who are caught in a family upheaval. See the Appendix for recommended titles.

Economics and Parenting

Financial resources underlie the quality of life in all communities and for all parents. Obtaining an adequate income to support housing, a good diet, and health care is a challenge in many areas of the world. This challenge also exists in many U.S. neighborhoods.

DUAL-INCOME FAMILIES Statistics show that 67% of children living with both parents have mothers and fathers in the workforce, and this trend increases each year. As parents try to balance the potentially competing demands of jobs and child rearing, many find the conflict between caring for children and employment physically and psychologically draining. The stress is particularly pronounced for women who, despite their increased participation in the workforce, still have primary responsibility for children in the majority of families. It appears, however, that it is the nature and intensity of the work and family responsibilities, rather than employment or parenthood per se, that determine the impact of parents working outside the home.

Although a double income enables a family to enjoy a higher standard of living, it has drawbacks, such as less time for family interaction, tighter schedules, increased dependence on child care, and fewer choices in recreation. Research has found, however, that working parents have increasingly developed a number of strategies to maximize the time they spend with their children. Through multitasking and incorporating their children in their own leisure activities, many working parents are able to spend as much quality time with their children as in past generations when women were not as highly represented in the workforce (Bianchi et al., 2006). Smaller families, less time spent on housework, and greater income are all factors that allow dual-income parents to devote time to their children. For the more than 7% of American working men and women who hold two or more jobs, however, time for family interactions is minimal.

POVERTY Poverty restricts many positive experiences for children and their families, because financial resources dictate the quality of education, housing, diet, clothing, and amount of health care, to say nothing of entertainment and recreation. Most of all, poverty lays a veil of despair on poor or near-poor families—a group disproportionately composed of single-parent families and families of color—and aspirations and a sense of self-worth become hard to elevate (Dodson & Bravo, 2005). Of all the stressors present in U.S. families, poverty is perhaps the greatest, and it is expanding in the lower-income brackets (refer again to Figure 3-5 in Chapter 3).

The Children's Defense Fund (2008) found that in 2008 more than 13.3 million, or almost 18% of U.S. children under age 18, were living below the poverty line. In addition, poverty in the United States has increased each year since 2000. This is a disturbing reversal of the gains made from 1992 to 2000, when close to 4 million children were lifted out of poverty. Even more disturbing is the growing number of children who live in extreme poverty, defined as an income of less than $10,600 per year for a family of four. Poverty rates among minority groups are disproportionate to their populations. Whereas the poverty rate for Whites was 14.4%, that for Hispanics was 28.9%, and for African Americans it was 33.2% (Children's Defense Fund, 2005). Figure 4-5 gives a picture of American children living in poverty.

Poor families are burdened with the challenges of survival, and their lives are punctuated with stress brought on by lack of money. Family members are frequently ill, they sustain injury more often, and they encounter hostility from numerous sources. Their lives become saturated with despair, and each new plight adds to family discouragement (Dodson & Bravo, 2005; Laureau, 2003). The buildup of stress in poor families is extensive. Housing that is affordable to families near or below the poverty line tends to be in crime- and drug-ridden areas, where children and many adults lead lives of

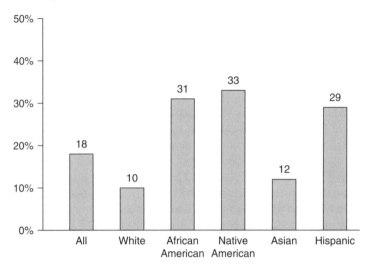

FIGURE 4-5 **Children Under Age 18 Living in Poverty in 2007** *Source:* U.S. Bureau of the Census. (2009). *Income, poverty and health insurance coverage in the United States, 2007.* Report P60, n. 235, p. 53.

sheer terror. Cramped living quarters and meager diets result in illnesses that precipitate even more stress. Not surprisingly, children raised in poverty are more likely to become teen parents, and as adults they earn less and have more unemployment than those raised in families with higher incomes. They are also more likely to raise their own children in poverty, continuing the cycle.

Homeless Families. One dire consequence of poverty can be the loss of housing for a family. And although we tend to associate homelessness with urban environments, it exists in suburban and rural areas as well. Rather than living on the streets or in shelters, families may live in their cars, camp in the woods, or double up with other family members or friends. Homelessness is a fluid state with frequent moves and many upheavals that reduce children's ability to attend school and to benefit from educational services. Because families with children under the age of 5 are the fastest-growing segment of the homeless population in the United States (Thoennes, 2008), increasing numbers of children in elementary schools will be homeless for periods of time.

Reversing poverty in the United States requires strong community action and large investments in federal, state, and private aid to provide job training, child care, adequate housing, and health facilities to help rebuild families in besieged areas of society. Recommendations outlined in *The State of America's Children* (Children's Defense Fund, 2005) serve as a good starting point.

IMPLICATIONS FOR TEACHERS

Working with Families Living in Poverty

The needs of children living in poverty can seem overwhelming. Although you may choose to work as an advocate for greater social change, you can also increase your awareness of ways to support these children on an everyday basis in your classroom. Berliner (2009) suggests principles for teaching homeless students that apply as well to children living in poverty. Among his suggestions are making schools safe havens for children, attending to the needs of the whole child, and working with parents and guardians to develop goals. In

TABLE 4-2 Areas of Critical Need That Teachers of Children Living in Poverty Must Consider

1. Develop meaningful relationships with children to facilitate classroom management.
2. Determine what motivates children and use motivation strategies to foster involvement and learning.
3. Cultivate family and community partnerships.
4. Connect families to health-related support services through school social workers and counselors.
5. Help build children's background knowledge.

Source: Based on recommendations from the Center of Excellence to Prepare Teachers of Children of Poverty. Retrieved June 20, 2009, from *http://www.fmucenterofexcellence.org.*

practical terms, this may mean keeping nutritious snacks and clean clothes on hand, helping connect families to the school counselor to help them access social services, and providing warmth and acceptance to children caught in circumstances beyond their control and understanding. Don't assume that children have a place to do homework or the needed materials. Simple things like providing a clipboard and an attached pencil for children or an after-school homework club can make a big difference in their ability to complete outside work. Most of all, however, don't stigmatize children living in poverty or in homelessness. Your loving care and acceptance can make a big difference in children's lives (see Table 4-2).

Health and Disabilities

Conditions of health and well-being impact the success of parenting. And although many families contend only with minor illnesses and accidents, others encounter major issues with long-term illness, obesity, or handicapping conditions.

ILLNESS The illness of any family member adds stress to parenting. When a family member becomes injured or ill, numerous interaction patterns must cease or be modified. Family communication can be limited, and attention to those who are not ill is lessened. Realignment of the priorities in family functioning is a consequence of long-term illness. Illness of a wage earner has even greater consequences for the family. Furthermore, if inadequate health care is the cause (which is the situation for one-seventh of the U.S. population), this particular stress gives rise to others. When a child becomes seriously injured or is chronically ill, parents must develop coping skills to adjust to the need for medical care and the other issues that arise.

CHILDREN WITH DISABILITIES Caring for a child with a disability presents unique challenges to families and often leads to an increase in families' stress levels.

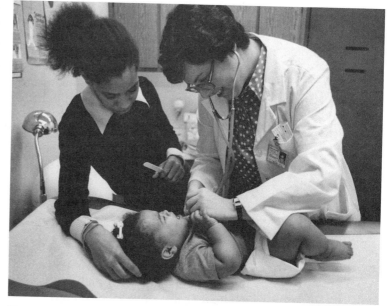

Illness is a stressor in families.

Although some disabilities are evident from birth or early infancy, others, such as learning disabilities and emotional problems, may not show up until the child attends school. Not only do parents have to struggle with their own acceptance of the disability and the attendant shattered expectations, guilt, anger, and parental conflict, but they must also expend great time and energy on the child. Just getting the child's disability identified can be a long process, and determining treatment, obtaining needed services, and following up on the child's progress are also time-consuming. Teachers and community-service personnel play an important support role for families parenting children with disabilities.

Everyday Stress

Although they are not life-changing events, the hassles of everyday life are another source of stress for families. These day-to-day common annoyances, although relatively minor, are a more frequent and continuous form of stress. Included in this category are the difficulties associated with commuting, balancing work and family life on a daily basis, minor childhood illnesses that require parents to make unexpected schedule changes and arrangements, and the myriad other stressors that occur as a part of daily life. Research indicates that these everyday hassles can be even more important determinants of family stress than the major life events discussed previously (Helms & Demo, 2005).

As expected, the way parents respond to these everyday stressors determines how much they contribute to the family stress level. Some parents are able to buffer their children from the everyday hassles of life, but others are not. Factors such as SES, perceptions of the severity of the hassles, parent temperament, and responses to the ongoing, relentless nature of caring for a family and home all influence the way a family will adapt to and cope with the stresses of everyday life.

MEETING THE CHALLENGES OF PARENTING

Despite the well-known stressors associated with parenting, most adults find that caring and providing for children is rewarding and pleasurable. In addition, although families may function in a variety of ways and possess different attributes, most families, given reasonable conditions, develop along healthy lines and rear children who respect the home culture and get ready to meet the world. Though most families are independent, others may at times need the help and support of friends, community, and other services.

At times, stresses are too great, and family dysfunction may result. If this occurs, professional aid via the community is the first level of response. It may be possible for school professionals to help by advocating for the family, talking with family members, counseling the family, and listening to family members to show support. Recall the dramatic study by Sameroff et al. (1987) that we referred to earlier. We can demonstrate the likelihood that problems will emerge if risk factors continue unresolved.

REFLECTION

Do you ever feel stress? Are you aware of any strategies you use to relieve it? Are these positive strategies for you? Are you familiar with community resources to help you and others understand and practice stress-reduction techniques such as deep breathing, meditation, and muscle relaxation?

Abuse and Neglect

Abuse and neglect of children can be one outcome of unrelieved stress. Because families in poverty are in dire straits and services are meager, abuse rises in concert with the frustrations and anxieties of needy families. And remember, physical and sexual abuse and neglect occur at all levels of society; they are not restricted to the poor. The Children's Defense Fund (2001) stated that between 2 and 3 million abuse cases are reported each year, about one-third of which are substantiated. Neglect is the most prevalent form of child abuse, with more than half of the children mistreated or suffering from neglect. More than one-third of the victims are physically or sexually abused, and one-fourth are mistreated in more than one way. Despite these large numbers, caseworkers assert that only a small fraction of abusive situations is ever reported (Osofsky, 1998).

Abuse is insidious and continues in the fabric of families for generations; many abused children become abusive adults or victims of other abusers later in their lives. Abuse is an infection that colors the feelings and attitudes of families, and it destroys normal relationships for the entire family. Research indicates that parent education can help to break the cycle of abuse and neglect. All interventions that help reduce parents' stress level, increase their understanding of child development and their social coping skills, and assist them in developing supportive networks are effective in reducing and preventing child maltreatment (Reppucci, Britner, & Woolard, 1997). See Chapter 7 for detailed information on how to partner with parents to protect children.

A Competent Family

What is a competent family? The competent family does not require affluence, extensive education, or a particular setting. It does, however, provide for what Brazelton and Greenspan (2000) described as "the irreducible needs of children." In order to help their children grow and flourish, competent parents meet the following six needs:

1. Ongoing nurturing relationships
2. Physical protection, safety, and regulation
3. Experiences tailored to individual differences
4. Developmentally appropriate experiences
5. Limited settings, structures, and expectations
6. Stable, supportive communities and cultural continuity

Children need unconditional love and affection from their parents. They also require the security that comes from a safe, familiar environment, a consistent daily routine, and the knowledge that adults expect certain behaviors from them. When planning experiences for their children, parents must consider their children's unique temperaments, learning styles, and interests. Further, parents who understand the stages of child development are better able to plan experiences that are compatible with their child's level. Children also need parents who will guide their behavior in ways that will help them make responsible choices, cooperate with others, and develop self-confidence. Both parents and children need the support of the larger community for optimal development.

Children need unconditional love and affection from their parents.

IMPLICATIONS FOR TEACHERS

Supporting Families

Children and families all are resilient to some degree. We find situations that appear depressing and even disastrous, but many children survive intact and view the traumatic events in their lives, such as death, divorce, and hardship, with objectivity (Levine & Ion, 2002) and, later, even with humor. This demonstrates that most children are not so fragile and impressionable that they must succumb to their problems. As a teacher or community service provider, you may be the person who helps a child overcome difficulties through your support and belief in the child. You must also remember that as long as reasonably positive experiences and interventions punctuate the lives of developing children, their outlook and perspective can be ultimately optimistic.

Teachers need to know their students' families as well as their situations, for teachers are in a unique position to explain the community to families, and vice versa. It is imperative for school personnel to take time to learn about family functioning in order to discover the values, ways of doing things, and methods of care that work for them. When you obtain this information, you may then find ways of integrating schoolwork with the home situation.

Summary and Review

The nurturance of a parent or another loving adult is the most significant factor in a child's healthy growth and development. Despite changes in the role of parents over the years, they continue to provide major economic and emotional support for their children, as well as experiences, education, and socialization.

Different styles of interaction exist within families, and various cultural groups may have parenting practices that differ from one another. Research shows that the authoritative parent style, characterized by a warm emotional tone coupled with high expectations and open communication, usually produces better results for most parents and their children than does either a permissive or an authoritarian pattern.

Experience defines a family's quality of life, and all families pass on their culture and attempt to instruct children in profitable ways. Some families have natural gifts for instructing the young about tasks, thereby giving them added command of their lives. Mobility is one avenue for enhancing experience; another is manual work skills.

Economic circumstances, life-changing events, and everyday stressors all impact family functioning. Handling such stressors is a mark of a family's ability to cope with the major and minor stressors that are a part of life. All families encounter stress, but processing and managing it appropriately are hallmarks of stable families. Competent families are those that are able to provide for children's physical and psychological health, promote their growth, and shape their behavior to meet socially accepted norms. Poverty can undermine parents' best efforts to provide for their children, and unfortunately, the rates of poverty for children are increasing in the 21st century.

Suggested Activities and Questions

1. Name three ways that families provide nurturance for their children. Speculate about how you see them manifested in one child with whom you work.
2. Consider the home environments of children appearing in the vignettes in the book to this point. Deduce the parenting style of each family and compare it to your own upbringing.
3. Select two families represented in your classroom or community. What appear to be the social and cultural influences affecting them? Are there differences? What do you infer about the parenting practices in these families?
4. Observe a parent interacting with his or her child in a library. Observe a similar situation in a supermarket. What circumstances do you think account for any differences you see?
5. Locate the social service agencies, tutoring options, after-school programs, and other community resources that support children and families and develop a Web-based directory for your future use.

Resources

Organizations

Stepfamily Foundation   *http://www.stepfamily.org*
Common Sense Media   *http://commonsensemedia.org*
National Parenting Center   *http://www.tnpc.com*
Zero to Three: National Center for Infants, Toddlers, and
   Families   *http://www.zerotothree.org*

Web Sites

http://www.lifematters.com   Life Matters: Tools for Stress-
   less Living offers a compilation of articles from various
authors that promote education, information, and support for those wishing to learn more about democratic
styles of parenting.
http://www.parentsworld.com   A Web site with articles and
   resources for single parents.
http://www.familyeducation.com   A Web site with parenting
   articles, a message board, and activities for children.

CHAPTER 5

Meeting Child-Care Needs from Infancy Through School Age

Establishing a network of high quality early learning and parent support programs in a community may not be as glamorous or dramatic as building a sports stadium or convention center but it is likely to have a more immediate and powerful payoff and make a stronger lasting contribution to the public welfare.

(BARDIGE, 2005, P. 201)

After reading this chapter, you will be able to do the following:

- Identify the societal changes in family structures and workforce participation that have led to an increased need for child care from infancy through the school-age years.

- List the benefits of quality child care for families and children.

- Assist families in recognizing the characteristics of quality care from infancy through the school-age years.

- Define the following child-care arrangements: **in-home care**, family child care, **center-based care**, and before- and after-school care.

- Contrast licensing regulations and minimum standards with voluntary accreditation systems.

- Explain why collaboration among parents, schools, communities, and caregivers is needed to develop social policies to enhance the accessibility, affordability, and quality of child care.

With about 65% of the mothers of children under the age of 6 in the workforce and over 76% of the mothers of older children working (Children's Defense Fund, 2009), affordable, accessible, quality child care has become an increasingly important issue for families and communities. Parents may turn to you for advice about locating good care for their young children. You may even find yourself teaching or directing a child-care center at some point in your career as the lines between education of and care for young children become increasingly blurred. This chapter will help you develop greater knowledge about the issues related to child care.

⌒◟— In about 3 weeks, Renata and her partner, Gregg, anticipate the birth of their third child. They are excited about the prospect of having another child and have been preparing for the new arrival. Yet, they are feeling anxious, too, because they wonder how they will cope with the additional financial burden. Renata currently works as an office manager for a legal firm. When she is working, her 18-month-old daughter, Evelyn, is cared for by a grandmotherly neighbor, Mrs. Carlson, at a cost of $110 per week. Her 4-four-year-old son, Josh, attends a nearby church-affiliated child-care center at a cost of $125 per week. Neither facility is licensed, but both are in the neighborhood and are supervised by caring personnel.

Renata and Gregg have carefully considered their options. "If we have to pay out another $110 a week for child care," says Renata, "it'll hardly be worth my while to keep my job. I'm not sure Mrs. Carlson will want to take both the new baby and Evelyn, and, you know, the center at church won't take Evelyn until she's potty trained."

"Yeah, but we need the extra money, and you really like what you do," replies Gregg. Renata is unsure, though. She ponders for a while and thinks to herself, what with paying out almost $350 a week for child care, we're going to have only a little bit left over. I may as well stay at home and look after the children myself. Finally, she muses aloud, "Boy, we really do have some tough decisions to make." —⌒◞

Renata and Gregg are part of the growing and changing child-care dilemma that many American families are facing. The number of American children needing care outside the home has increased dramatically over the past decades. Over 11.3 million children under age 5 need care while their mothers work, and an even greater number of children need before- and after-school care (National Association of Child Care Resource and Referral Agencies, 2009). Currently, about 57% of women with infants younger than 1 year old are employed, compared to 31% in 1976. The percentage of children from ages 5 to 11 whose mothers work outside the home is even greater than that of younger children. Clearly, the need for child care is a concern, not only for families like Gregg and Renata's, but for many others as well.

In addition to the increased number of dual-earner families, many low-income single mothers have entered the workforce as required by welfare reforms. All of these changes put more demands on communities and agencies to identify **out-of-home care** facilities. Affordable and accessible child care is increasingly seen as an issue not just for families but for society as a whole. Without child care, families cannot work, and without quality care, children will not succeed.

Child care includes a wide array of arrangements that reflect the age of the child, the setting where care is provided, and the purpose for care, such as infant–toddler centers, family child-care homes, and before- and after-school care. In this chapter, we will focus on the various child-care arrangements made by parents who are working, in training, or unable to care for their children. Remember that although the primary purpose of these arrangements is the provision of substitute care, child care should also support children's growth and development.

Increasingly, as parents become more aware of the importance of early learning, they are seeking care arrangements that offer appropriate cognitive stimulation and socialization experiences. For this reason, there are more and more overlaps among the various programs. For example, nursery schools have begun to offer extended-day options, and child-care centers are strengthening their instructional programs. It is difficult to divide these arrangements into neat categories, but the term *early care and education* is increasingly used to describe child-care programs.

In this chapter, we trace the history of child care in the United States and provide an overview of the current state of affairs. A description of each type of child-care arrangement and factors to consider when assessing the quality of particular programs will also be included to help you advise parents on choosing care. We will pay particular attention to the costs of care and how this relates to staff quality and turnover. Finally, we will address the effects of child care on children's development and the well-being of families, concluding with some of the policy issues that relate to raising the quantity, affordability, and quality of child-care services.

HISTORY OF CHILD CARE

At earlier times in the United States, **extended family** tended to live with the nuclear family or nearby. When a mother found it necessary to work outside the home or a father lost his wife, the child was usually cared for by a female relative. Because most of these caregivers were assumed to have some commitment to the well-being of their relative's child, quality of care was rarely a concern. Industrialization, which started in the early 19th century, changed these informal family arrangements. As increasing numbers of families moved from rural areas to the cities and as immigrants entered the country, women found work in factories to help support their families. Child-care centers were opened in Boston, New York, and Philadelphia to provide care for children during the hours their parents worked. Most of these centers provided custodial care to meet the basic needs for food, shelter, rest, and supervision, but some also provided instruction for both children and families. The care was provided in large part for reasons of social support, to help needy families in those urban areas.

During World War II, large numbers of women, many with children, went to work in factories to support the war effort by taking the place of men who were fighting. Under the 1944 Lanham Act, the country intensified its mobilization on behalf of the defense industry and increased many services. Under provisions of the act, many communities were able to build excellent child-care centers to serve the children whose mothers were working. When the war ended, however, and the men returned to the factories, many of the women lost their jobs, and eventually most of the child-care centers closed. The economic prosperity and sharp increase in the number of births during the postwar years led to an arrangement in most families whereby the father worked outside the home and the mother cared for the children.

The economic boom of the 1950s, however, increased consumer demands for goods and services, and in turn opened up new opportunities for women to work. Gradually, more women became employed outside the home. As changing attitudes concerning the roles of women that began in the 1960s continued, women increasingly combined motherhood with working, whether from need or preference. Divorce became more common during this era, and often single mothers needed to provide much of their family's income. During the 1960s and 1970s, as more families sought care for their children, there was little support from either the government or the private sector to increase the availability of child care. Concerns about the quality of the child-care centers that did exist began to develop. The concerns focused on health and safety standards, plus the lack of training and the low wages that led to high staff turnover. In the 1980s, additional concerns were raised regarding the consequences of child care for children's development (Casper & Bianchi, 2002).

After-school programs began in the United States in the 19th century. In addition, programs such as those of YMCAs and YWCAs, Scouts, 4-H, and other youth organizations emerged from programs initially started in storefronts, settlement houses, and churches. These were all designed to offer places where young people could safely gather to have fun and learn useful skills. Some, like the Y, have gone on to become major providers of care for school-age children during the hours before and after school.

CHILD-CARE ISSUES IN THE UNITED STATES TODAY

Although some form of informal, shared child care has always been practiced in the United States, the increased isolation and fragmentation of families,

Because of the increase in the number of working mothers, affordable child care has become an issue in many American families.

together with other changes in family structure and social expectations, have increased the need for more formal arrangements in recent decades. Today, nearly 21 million children need care while their parents are at work. In many families, both parents work outside the home in order to maintain or increase their standard of living. Other families are headed by a single parent. Welfare reform, which began in the late 20th century, requires many mothers of young children to work. In addition, other women, who have trained for a career, choose to combine work and motherhood in order to maintain their professional opportunities. One of the most dramatic changes in U.S. society over the past 40 years is the great increase in the number of working mothers. Consequently, the need for affordable, quality child care is a fact of life for many American families.

Availability of Child Care

For middle-class families, the emergence of a market-based system of child-care services in the late 1980s and 1990s increased the visibility and availability of options for caring for children. During this time, a number of for-profit child-care centers emerged to meet the needs of working families who could afford to pay for them. **Resource and referral programs** made it easier to locate child care, which became more visible as centers sprang up in public places, and family child-care homes become more formally organized as small businesses.

The trend over the past 40 years toward center-based care has been significant. In 1965, only 6% of U.S. preschool children were cared for in centers. By 2008 the percentage had tripled to 18%. Grandparents, other relatives, nonrelative care, or family child-care homes (NACCRRA, 2009) provided care for the remaining children. Figure 5-1 shows the distribution of primary care arrangements in 2008. Another interesting trend is that 25% of children under age 5 are in multiple child-care arrangements over the course of the week. Research is inconclusive at this point on the effects of multiple caregivers, but it is a situation that might be a result of too few high-quality child-care programs and the economic difficulty of paying for such care.

Over 40% of all school-age children are now in nonparental care before and/or after school. Like their preschool counterparts, many of these children are also in multiple

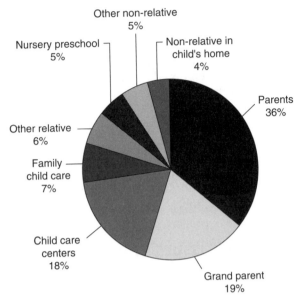

FIGURE 5-1 **Primary Child-Care Arrangements for Children Under Age 5 in 2008** *Source:* U.S. Bureau of the Census. *Who's minding the kids? Child care arrangements: Spring 2005: Detailed tables.* March 2008. Retrieved June 8, 2009, from *http://www.census.gov/population/www/socdemo/child/ppl2005.html*

child-care arrangements before and/or after the regular school day. Those in a single arrangement are most likely in center or school-based child-care programs, relative care, nonrelative care, or self-care. Figure 5-2 shows the distribution of care arrangements for school-age children. What the data cannot show is whether parents made the arrangements for their children by choice or by default due to costs, transportation, work schedules, or availability. The accuracy of the data on school-age child care can also be difficult to assess because some parents may not want to admit that their children are in self-care. The Afterschool Alliance (2009) has estimated that approximately 25% of children are on their own after school, including more than 40,000 kindergarten children. In a poll this group conducted in 2000, 60% of voters felt that it was difficult to find after-school programs in their communities, and 30% of families—not currently enrolled in an after-school program—said they would do so if one were available.

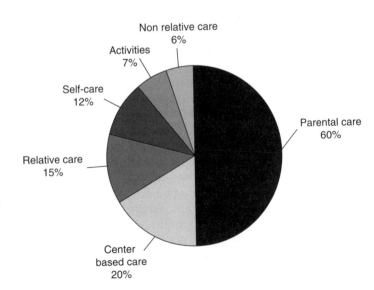

FIGURE 5-2 **Before- and After-School Child-Care Arrangements for School-Age Children** *Source:* Lawrence and Kreader (2006).

Low-income families face significant issues in finding child care and rely increasingly on juggling informal arrangements with relatives and babysitters. The number of **subsidized child care** slots is not adequate for the demands, and lengthy waiting lists exist in many communities. Higher-income families have more choice about the kinds of child-care arrangements they make and tend to use centers, generally the most expensive option, more than do low-income families. Parents who have nonstandard work schedules (Presser, 2003) are also unable to use centers and family child-care homes, which generally provide care only during the day. Like low-income families they must piece together care, often using multiple caregivers.

Financing Child Care

Most of the cost for out-of-home care is borne by individual families, and this cost can be prohibitive for many parents. Low-income families (with earnings up to 200% of the poverty level) spend approximately 16% of their incomes on out-of-home care, whereas higher-income families spend only 6% (Urban Institute, 2007). Therefore, cost in relation to family income is a major factor influencing many families' child-care arrangements. In the past, families on or transitioning off of welfare could receive subsidies for child care. As regulations have changed, these families may no longer receive assistance at the level or for the length of time needed. Middle- and low-income families are generally less able to afford high-quality child care than are high-income families. Consequently, a two-tier child-care system has emerged in which only certain families have access to the highest-quality care (Cryer & Clifford, 2003).

The child-care situation for low-income families varies greatly from state to state. Low-income families can be subsidized for child-care expenses through the Child Care and Development Block Grant provided to states by the federal government. In 2006, this provided $4.8 billion for child-care services for low-income families and other activities related to the provision of child care. Currently, no state serves all families eligible for child-care assistance under federal regulations, and only 12% of eligible children nationally are receiving help. The availability of subsidies and the accessibility of programs that accept subsidized children can be major issues in limiting choices. Full-day center-based child care can cost between $4,000 and $10,000 yearly, more than the annual tuition at a 4-year public university in most states (Children's Defense Fund, 2009). Child-care expenses are particularly significant when one considers that one out of four families with young children earns less than $25,000 a year. In half of the states, families with annual incomes above $25,000 are ineligible for aid and a large number of states are cutting assistance to families that are just above the poverty line but cannot afford the full cost of child care (Hartman, 2003). Forty states actually require copayments from families with incomes below the poverty level. Though Renata and Gregg in the chapter-opening vignette are above the $25,000 cutoff, their dual income is still not enough to pay for the rising cost of child care. They are ineligible for any government subsidy or assistance.

Although welfare reforms have resulted in dramatic increases in the number of working mothers, the lack of reliable child care and help in paying for it may end up undermining efforts to lift families out of poverty. The rates that states are willing to pay for child care for low-income families reflect the pressure they are under to get as many children as possible into child-care centers at the lowest cost. In 2008, only 1.8 million children of the 13 million eligible were receiving subsidized care. This is a reflection of the limited resources for care (particularly for school-age children), the inability of low-income families to pay the copayments, and their unawareness of eligibility for assistance (Hartman, 2003). Consequently, many families among the working poor are patching together informal child-care arrangements with relatives, friends, or neighbors.

REFLECTION

Think about a young family you know and write down how they are meeting their child-care needs. Then explore with your classmates the different situations you have all identified and compare these to the national norms you have just read about. Are the situations you have found typical?

Carla, in the following vignette, provides an example of the benefits that subsidized care can offer low-income families. Later, however, she becomes a victim of a system that gives few options and produces a dilemma.

Carla's sons, Tommy and Cody, both attended Head Start, and Carla became an active program participant. She gained skills and confidence in herself. As a result, 2 years ago, with Tommy in school and Cody in Head Start, she took a job as a part-time administrative assistant. Her employer was pleased with her work and urged her to continue her education and job training. With her salary added to her husband's part-time work, the family moved off welfare and even obtained medical insurance.

Suddenly, things changed. This year, Carla's husband left and provides no financial support. Carla's employer wants to help her and urges her to get more training and become a full-time employee. To continue her training, though, Carla must find partial child care for her boys. Such care is expensive and hard to find. Carla's salary increase is good, but it no longer covers her insurance payments and child care while still meeting basic needs.

Carla is eligible for child-care supplements, but when she applies, she is told that all new applicants are placed on a waiting list. As Carla seeks solutions, she is told that she could go back on welfare because she hasn't used up all of her allotted time. Presently working full-time, she makes too much money to receive any welfare support. If she works only part-time, she can get welfare benefits plus Medicaid, but her employer needs a full-time person. Her job, career training, and future employment are all in jeopardy. Carla is seriously considering going back on welfare until both children are a little older, but she's afraid that by then, the skills she has gained plus her employer's goodwill will have vanished.

One can see that those families whose income is above the poverty level but below $25,000 are less likely to be able to afford center-based care, as is the case with Carla in the preceding vignette. In short, these families have fewer options when it comes to selecting appropriate out-of-home care.

The federal government does offer a tax credit to help families pay for child care. The Child and Dependent Care (Tax) Credit reduces the income tax liability of families at all income levels with work-related care expenses. Because the credit is nonrefundable, however, its value to low-income families is limited, as the credit amount cannot exceed a family's tax liability. The maximum credit is $3,000 a year for one qualifying individual or $6,000 a year for two or more qualifying individuals. In 2002, it provided $2.7 billion to working families and is considered the second largest source of federal child-care assistance after the Child Care and Development Block Grant. There is a distinct possibility that the tax credit may become refundable in the future, increasing its value to low-income families.

Concerns About Quality

Advocates for children are increasingly concerned about the outcomes for low-income children. Substandard care, accidental injury or neglect, and an inadequate developmental environment can have devastating effects on children whose families lack adequate funds for quality child care. Even for families who can afford child care, concerns remain about the quality of these facilities for young children. The Children's Defense Fund (2001), reporting on various studies on quality in child-care centers, concluded that "much of the child care in the United States is poor to mediocre" (p. 2). In addition, a national study of family child-care programs reported that more than one-third of the programs were rated as inadequate. These studies, of course, raise concerns about children's safety as well as the harm to children's development. Research has confirmed that quality programs are linked to positive outcomes for children (Mardell, 2002). Conversely, children in poor-quality care are at risk when they do not receive the attention, nurturance, and educational enrichment that will help them succeed. Yet, we find considerable variation in the quality of both centers and family child-care homes.

Federal legislation has stimulated development of services and programs for infants and toddlers and their families.

The "Cost, Quality, and Child Outcomes in Child Care Centers" study conducted by Suzanne Helburn and colleagues examined more than 400 child-care centers and found that only 14% of preschool programs provide high-quality care (Helburn & Bergmann, 2002). The study also reported that 12% provided poor-quality child-care arrangements, and the majority of programs were mediocre. The situation for infants and toddlers is equally disturbing. Some studies suggest that only 9% of the child-care settings were excellent, 30% were good, 53% were fair, and 8% were poor (Vandell & Pierce, 2003). Research findings on family child-care programs and relative care are also troubling. Only 9% of such facilities were of sufficient quality to positively influence children's development, 56% were considered adequate, and 35% were deemed to be so poor that children's health and development were endangered. These are startling statistics for all families and professionals, and it seems that they will not change soon (Greenspan & Salmon, 2001).

The federal government requires states to spend at least 4% of the funds they receive from the Child Care and Development Block Grant to improve the quality of care in their jurisdictions. Congress also set aside $173 million of the discretionary funds for additional quality building activities: $100 million for increasing and improving infant- and toddler-care programs, $10 million for child-care research, and $18.1 million for school-age care and resource and referral programs. Despite these expeditures, the limited availability of affordable, quality child care remains a serious problem in the United States.

IMPLICATIONS FOR TEACHERS

Availability, Costs, and Quality of Child Care

Do you wonder why it is important for you to be aware of the issues surrounding child care today? As a teacher, you may find yourself helping families who are struggling to locate before- or after-school care for their elementary school-age child. Families may assume that you know some of the local child-care programs for younger children and may seek your advice about discovering care for their infants, toddlers, or preschoolers. As an education professional, inform yourself about the various child care options in your community. The National Association of Child Care Resource and Referral Agencies (NACCRA) is an excellent starting point to help families locate child care. Later in this chapter, we will present some guidelines to help you advise parents how to assesss the quality of this care as well.

It is also important to remember that finding and affording child care is a family stressor. Make sure that you know about subsidized care and can help families find local community agencies that will help them apply for such aid if they qualify.

Most importantly, you need to know what arrangements the children in your class have before and after school so that you can communicate with these other caregivers when needed. Often it is the staff of the after-school center or the family child-care provider who is helping the child with homework. Knowing who cares for the child in the absence of parents will also allow you to talk about these important people with the child and will help you understand the child's situation. Because more and more children are in multiple child-care arrangements due to economic constraints, availability, transportation, and other factors, you may find that the children are stressed and confused about what is going to happen after school. As their teacher, you can be the one who reminds them of the plans for each day and helps them to travel to these settings. Later in this chapter, we will suggest specific ways to develop communication systems with parents and care providers.

We will now turn to the various types of child-care arrangements and then describe the characteristics of quality programs for infants, toddlers, 2-year-olds, preschoolers, and school-age children. Table 5-1 provides a description of these age groups and the recommended group sizes and staff-to-child ratios. A discussion of the effects of child care on children's development and the policy issues that will help to ensure available, affordable, quality care for all who need it will conclude the chapter.

TABLE 5-1 Age Group Categories for Child-Care Programs and Recommended Maximum Group Sizes and Staff-to-Child Ratios

Developmental Stage	Approximate Age	Developmental Level	Maximum Group Size	Ratios for Maximum Group
Infant	0–15 months	Birth to mobility	8	1:4
Toddler	12–28 months	Mobility to accomplishment of self-care routines such as feeding self	12	1:4
2-Year-Old	21–36 months	Continuing development of self-care routines such as toileting	12	1:6
Preschooler	36–50 months	Achievement of self-care and entry into elementary school	20	1:10
School-Age Child	5–12 years	Entry into elementary school through sixth grade	26	1:13

CHILD-CARE ARRANGEMENTS

∽— *Mr. McGee, Tina's father, is a bit surprised not to see Mrs. Holden in her office as he enters the child-care center. The assistant smiles and says that Mrs. Holden is with the infants because an extra lap is needed. On the way to the 3-year-olds' room, Tina urges her father to stop and watch the fish in the tank. A mother watching the fish exclaims, "We've been stopping here lately, too. Just watching seems to help Janda relax before starting the day. Mrs. Holden did tell me what a boon this tank was, and I can see it."*

On entering the classroom, Tina notices that Billy is crying loudly. Martha, the aide, is holding him and saying, "Mama's coming to the phone, and she'll talk with you." Tina goes over to Billy, pats him, and says kindly, "It's okay!" She then puts her coat in her cubbie and hurries over to her friend Claire at the water table. Soon Billy's mother is on the phone, and her voice appears to be quieting Billy. As Mr. McGee waits to talk with Martha, he smiles at his neighbor Felicity, who is seated on the floor with two other children reading. Several children are working at the table while Miranda pours juice. Martha turns to Mr. McGee, who asks if everything is okay. "Oh, yes. Billy does take change hard. His dad brought him today for the first time, and now he seems uncertain about his mama. I got her on the phone, and she's reassuring him."

"Oh, that's good," replies Mr. McGee. "Well, I just need to remind someone that Tina's grandmother will pick her up this afternoon. Tina knows this, and I put it on her chart."

"Okay. Just remember to let them know at the office on your way out."

Mr. McGee kisses Tina goodbye, saying, "Remember, Grandma will pick you up this afternoon, 'cause Mommy has to work late."

As Mr. McGee leaves the building, he greets the toddlers' teacher, who is starting her first outing of the day. Five toddlers are happily seated in their cart for an excursion along the sidewalk to look in the shop windows. Mr. McGee thinks, "I remember how Tina enjoyed those cart rides. Boy, we were lucky to find such a great center so near home." —∽

Quality child care makes a difference for families, and the McGees reflect the changes now taking place within American families. Tina's parents are both professionals and believe it important that Mrs. McGee continue her career. They represent the **postmodern family**, in which most parenting for very young children is provided by the mother, sometimes with the father's assistance, and by other caregivers. Since Tina's arrival at this center, Tina's family has been pleased with the program. Although the cost of care is high, the center has provided a consistent staff of caregivers and a safe environment. Many families use the center even into the school years, because it has extended-day programs.

Parents like the McGees seeking child care are faced with many issues in determining the appropriate arrangement for their children. Aside from issues of affordability, location, and availability, families want to ensure that their children are in a safe, healthy environment where they will receive nurturing care. Figure 5-3 lists indicators of safe, healthy child-care arrangements. Later in this chapter, we will discuss indicators of quality that go beyond the minimal standards of health and safety.

Resource and referral agencies have been established in many communities to support parents in locating child-care centers and family child-care homes; other agencies assist in locating nannies and au pairs. These various options for child care are described in the following sections.

REFLECTION

Would you feel comfortable leaving your own children in the center described in the McGee vignette? List three features that appeal to you; then note anything that concerns you.

- *Supervision:* Children should be supervised at all times, even when sleeping.
- *Discipline:* Children should be guided positively, clearly, consistently, and fairly.
- *Sanitation:* Children and teachers should wash hands frequently. Diapering areas, restrooms, and places where children eat should be cleaned and disinfected regularly.
- *Director qualifications:* Directors should hold at least a bachelor's degree in a related field and have 2 or more years of experience with children.
- *Teacher qualifications:* Teachers should hold a degree in a related field, and assistants should have training about child development and appropriate activities that is ongoing.
- *Child–staff ratio and group size:* The younger the children's age, the smaller the group size should be and the lower the child–staff ratio.
- *Safety:* Toxic substances and medications should be kept out of reach of children and poison control information posted. Programs should have an emergency plan, first-aid kits, fire drills, and other safety measures in place. Staff should be trained in first aid and know how to administer medications.
- *Child abuse:* All staff should have been subject to a background check and should know how to recognize and report signs of suspected abuse.

FIGURE 5-3   Indicators of a Safe and Healthy Child-Care Arrangement

In-Home Child Care

Care that takes place in the child's home is an unregulated arrangement. In the case of a babysitter, the family determines the necessary qualifications, screens applicants, and makes an agreement with the individual of their choice. The advantage of this type of care for parents with long work days or erratic schedules is its flexibility. The caregiver, who may even live in the child's home, becomes an employee of the family, who then assumes certain financial responsibilities in terms of taxes and Social Security deductions (and some decide not to report the payments or income). Some families, knowingly or not, may hire undocumented immigrants to provide child care. Wage levels for these positions are low, and the supply of babysitters is limited to persons who may have no training in child care and few options for other work. For many families, however, this arrangement works out well.

Families can also hire a nanny to provide in-home care. Generally, nannies are registered with an agency and have had some training in the care of young children. Another option is an au pair, a young person from another country who performs child care and light housework in exchange for room and board and a small salary. The au pair system is organized by the U.S. Information Agency as a cultural exchange program to allow young and usually well-educated participants to take courses and enjoy living and traveling in the United States. Generally, the au pair has minimum training and experience in child care. Other families make arrangements with a babysitter to provide care in the sitter's own home. This is also unregulated care that, like the options for in-home care, can have considerable variation in quality, depending on the individual caregiver.

Family Child Care

In this arrangement, children are cared for in the home of the provider. A small family child-care home generally includes one provider and a small number of children, whereas a large or group family child-care home includes the provider and an assistant caring for a larger number of children. Individual state licensing regulations determine the number of children permitted in each type of family child-care setting. Care is generally offered all day, 5 days a week, year round, and can meet a family's need for flexibility more easily than a center-based program with fixed hours of operation.

Many providers begin this work initially as an extension of caring for their own children, but some continue it as a career choice and may even become part of the movement to professionalize this type of care (National Association for Family Child Care, 2009). In that case, caregivers will provide enriching educational and social experiences for the children in their care in the context of an appropriate daily schedule (see Table 5-1 and Figure 5-3 for preschool and school-age schedules that can be adapted for family child-care settings) and an environment organized to support children's development.

The number of family child-care programs has increased over the past 20 years as the demand for services has continued. The 2007 Family Child Care Licensing Study (National Association for Regulatory Administration, 2009) reported that there were 197,294 regulated family child-care homes in the United States. Of these programs, 49,967 are considered group or large-family child-care centers, serving up to 20 children, and the remaining 147,327 are small-family child-care homes usually limited to 6 or fewer children. The number of regulated child-care homes has more than doubled since 1984.

Family child care is generally a more affordable option because fees are substantially lower than those charged by child-care centers. Although some caregivers will only accept particular age groups, others care for the same children year after year as they grow older. A family child-care home can mirror a family, serving children from infancy through school age. Many families prefer this type of arrangement, particularly for children under age 2, because of its convenience, individualized relationships, and homelike environment. In fact, 6-year-old Travis expressed surprise upon seeing his mother give money to his child care provider. "You *pay* Mrs. Black?" he asked in shock. It had never occurred to him that her loving care for him was a job (Koralek, 2002).

All states have some type of licensing and regulation of family child care, but the requirements and oversight are generally minimal. (See *http://www.naralicensing.org* for information about the family child-care licensing regulations in your state.) The 2007 Child Care Licensing Study provides much information about this type of child-care arrangement. Unfortunately, with the pressing need for care for children of mothers returning to work because of changes in the welfare regulations that began in 1996, standards may become even less stringent. By contrast, military family child-care programs, which have high standards for training and requirements for safety, health, nutrition, and developmental care, are increasingly serving as models for states seeking ways to improve quality.

Child-Care Centers

Center-based child care can serve children from infancy through school age, although some programs limit themselves to a particular age group such as preschoolers. Infant and toddler care in centers is a relatively recent phenomenon, and it is a costly arrangement due to the labor-intensive nature of caring for such young children. A high teacher-to-child ratio, such as one caregiver for two or three babies, is recommended.

Typically, child-care centers, like the one the McGees selected, are open all day, 5 days per week, year round, and close only for major holidays and extreme weather conditions. Many centers provide multiple programs, including half-day nurserylike classes for 3-, 4-, and even 5-year-olds, and many offer extended-day programs for children in kindergarten and up to 12 years old. Child-care centers have long hours of operation and can serve children of various ages, which makes them a particularly convenient and appealing choice for families.

As noted before, the number of child-care centers increased dramatically between 1977 and the present, with the largest growth area in for-profit programs. For-profit centers include independent programs or those that are part of local or national chains. Child-care centers may also be run as nonprofit operations sponsored by organizations such as the YMCA, local churches and colleges, social service agencies, or state and federal government agencies. **Employer-sponsored child care** centers have also opened in recent decades, although their number is still quite small. The U.S. Military Child Development Program's extensive system of child-care centers, like their family child-care programs, are an example of large-scale, employer-sponsored child care and can serve as a model for other organizations (Neugebauer, 2005).

Child-care centers are housed in a variety of locations, including community centers, church basements, former school buildings, storefronts, industrial parks, or spaces built specifically for the center. Usually, a center will have multiple classrooms, each arranged for a particular age range. Increasingly, centers provide an educational curriculum appropriate for each age group. Although the requirements vary drastically from state to state (National Association for Regulatory Administration, 2009), there are generally some educational requirements for staff and an expectation that staff participate in continued training activities.

INFANT–TODDLER PROGRAMS The partnership between parents and caregivers is one of the most important aspects of out-of-home care for infants and toddlers. Daily communication about the baby is essential to ensure continuity of care, health, and well-being. Many programs have a care book that the caregiver and parent use to jot down important information to share with the other each day.

Center-based child care for infants requires particular materials, equipment, and room arrangements (Greenman, Stonehouse, & Schweikert, 2009). Many centers provide rooms designed for small groups of caregivers and infants in spaces comfortable for both. Rocking chairs, carpeting, mats, and duplicates of popular toys are basics. Ideally, a separate sleeping area is available with a designated crib for each child. A good infant–toddler room should look more like a home than a school.

Center care for infants and toddlers, like care for this age group in other settings, should be as individualized as possible. Infants and toddlers need much interaction with their primary caregivers, as well as opportunities to explore and learn in a more-opened ended way than older children require. Much of their learning will occur in the context of basic care activities such as eating, diapering, preparing for sleep, and nurturance. Although caregivers may provide some learning activities, like water play, much of the curriculum for infants and toddlers is based on the provision of a rich environment for them to explore both indoors and out. Both planned and spontaneous experiences in the context of routine care and

Quality programs for preschoolers provide opportunities for rest, outdoor play, and consistent interactions with caring adults.

play are recognized as essential for optimal growth. As our knowledge of early brain development has increased, infant–toddler programs are recognized as having great responsibility to contribute to the cognitive and social-emotional growth of the children in their care.

PRESCHOOL PROGRAMS Center-based care for 3- to 5-year-old children is the most popular option for American families. Young children cared for in centers can be there for up to 50 hours a week, so much of their basic needs must be met during that time. Centers make provisions for children to eat up to two meals and two snacks each day. Children also need opportunities to rest, play outdoors and inside, and interact consistently with caring adults.

Providing for children's physical safety and basic needs, however, is only the beginning of what a preschool child-care program should offer young children. Children need opportunities to participate in a program that enriches them emotionally, socially, and intellectually as well. There are a number of approaches to early education programs for this age group, but it is widely accepted that young children need to make choices and initiate their own activities for large blocks of time. Although teacher-directed activities, such as stories, songs, and arts and crafts projects, should be part of the daily routine, play and child-initiated experiences should predominate (Copple & Bredekamp, 2005). Table 5-2 illustrates an appropriate schedule for preschool child care.

SCHOOL-AGE CHILD CARE Although some centers offer care for school-age children in addition to their services for younger children, other programs limit themselves to the latter age group. In some cases, centers rent space in the public schools, but increasingly school districts are offering care directly. No matter how they are administered, however, school-age child-care programs provide a number of options for families who need care for the hours before and after school. In many programs, care is also available during weather emergencies, school holidays, and summer vacation.

School-age programs often provide breakfast for children who attend before school and offer a snack as children arrive at the end of the school day. Outdoor play is usually one of the first options for children as they transition from their academic program to the more relaxed setting of child care. Although before- and after-school care is offered mainly in elementary schools, some middle schools have also begun to offer

TABLE 5-2 Sample Schedule for a Preschool Day

6:30–8:00 A.M.	Arrival/breakfast/quiet free-choice play/transition to center
8:00–8:20 A.M.	Opening circle: stories/music/planning for the day
8:20–9:20 A.M.	Free-choice play in learning centers
9:20–9:40 A.M.	Cleanup time
9:40–10:00 A.M.	Toileting/hand washing/snack
10:00–10:20 A.M.	Small-group activities: art/science/literacy, etc.
10:20–11:30 A.M.	Outdoor play
11:30–11:50 A.M.	Circle: stories/music/movement/games/conversation
11:50–12:30 P.M.	Toileting/hand washing/lunch
12:30–3:00 P.M.	Rest and provisions for quiet play starting at around 1:15 for nonsleepers
3:00–3:15 P.M.	Transition from rest/toileting/hand washing/snack
3:15–4:00 P.M.	Outdoor play
4:00–4:15 P.M.	Story and songs
4:15–6:00 P.M.	Free play in center/special activities/classroom cleanup/transition to families

TABLE 5-3 Sample Schedule for Before- and After-School Child Care	
6:30–7:30 A.M.	Arrival/breakfast/quiet free-choice play/transition from home
7:30–8:00 A.M.	Special activities (art, crafts, cooking)
8:00–9:00 A.M.	Clubs/group games/gym/outdoor play
9:00–9:15 A.M.	Conversation/quick games/transition to school
3:15–4:00 P.M.	Transition from school/outside games and free play
4:00–4:20 P.M.	Conversation/snack
4:20–5:00 P.M.	Homework/quiet free-choice play when homework completed
5:00–6:30 P.M.	Choice time: clubs/sports/special events/outside games/gym, etc./transition to home

such care as an option. Middle school programs tend to be child-directed so that the youngsters can help to design a program that is very different from that for younger children. Both programs offer time and support for children to do homework, and many help facilitate children's involvement in extracurricular school options such as scouting, sports, and other activities. Table 5-3 is a sample schedule for before- and after-school child care for elementary school children.

Child Care for Children with Disabilities

Federal laws now prohibit both private and public child-care programs from discriminating against children with disabilities. Consequently, children with special needs are increasingly participating in child-care programs alongside their typically developing peers. Fortunately, many providers are discovering that including children with disabilities in their programs has advantages for all children. Typically developing children learn to understand and accept differences and serve as role models of age-appropriate communication and social behaviors. Children with disabilities enjoy the activities and materials provided and form friendships with their peers. Some adaptations may be needed to allow children at all physical, emotional, and academic ability levels to take part in the same learning environment. In Chapter 6, you will find a fuller treatment of the laws and issues concerning the inclusion of children with special needs.

Other Programs

To meet the needs of families for the informal and infrequent care that used to be provided by family members, friends, or neighbors, other programs have emerged.

MOTHER'S-DAY-OUT PROGRAMS   These programs are designed to offer a few hours of child care each week for stay-at-home parents who need time for activities like doctors' appointments, shopping, and respite from their children for a short period of time. Often sponsored by religious organizations or other community groups, **mother's-day-out programs** offer children a chance to play and socialize with other children.

DROP-IN CHILD CARE   Some child-care programs provide child-care services for parents with part-time jobs, flexible work schedules, and those who need a place to leave their children for short periods of time on occasion. Increasingly, centers designed only for **drop-in child care** are being offered in shopping centers, gyms, movie theaters, and other conveniently located places. These are casual programs that provide safe supervision in a play environment.

IMPLICATIONS FOR TEACHERS

Child-Care Options

As increasing numbers of children are placed in multiple settings during the course of their parents' work days, you will find that communication can be challenging among the adults charged with caring for and educating children. As a teacher, consider the following ideas to help you organize and communicate with parents and caregivers:

1. *Create a data sheet for individual children with their weekly schedule of before- and after-school placements. Include the e-mail addresses, telephone numbers, and physical addresses of all caregivers, including the parents. Provide a copy of this information for all involved persons and keep your copy updated.*
2. *Obtain a composition book from each family that will reside in the backpacks of individual children. Attach the above data sheet to the inside cover. Use this book to communicate with all caregivers about the child's day, homework, upcoming events, and whatever else will help the transition among those responsible for the child. Older children can take responsibility for recording some of this information.*
3. *Gather photos of all of the caregivers and make a "family and important people" bulletin board display a focal point of the classroom.*
4. *Provide time for children to share some of their out-of-school activities with each other. Children who are engaged in sports, arts, and other activities after school can share their accomplishments and upcoming events with their classmates, creating a stronger community bond.*

FEATURES OF QUALITY CHILD CARE

Despite the great diversity in child-care arrangements and the wide variations in state regulations governing center-based and family child-care homes, there is much agreement among professionals on the characteristics of quality child care needed to provide the safe, healthy, and nurturing environments that parents want and children deserve.

High-quality care is the result of a combination of a healthy and safe environment together with educational and social stimulation appropriate to the age and development of the children being served. These features of quality child care include both structural elements relating to the physical environment and staffing requirement and process elements relating to curricular practices, caregiver qualities, and parental involvement (Wortham, 2006). The McGee vignette suggests that the family has found a center with both structural and process elements that ensure quality.

Structural Elements

The structural elements of a child-care environment establish the foundation for optimal process conditions. Characteristics of the child-care space, for example, are structural elements. The square footage required for each child, the amount and kind of outdoor space, the requirements for furniture, sinks, toilets, windows, flooring material, and myriad other details related to the classroom, kitchen facilities, bathrooms, and diaper-changing areas are included in this category. The adult-child ratio, amount of initial and continuing staff training required, plus the salaries, benefits, and working requirements for staff are all structural elements of child care.

The individual licensing requirements of each state set minimum expectations for many of the structural elements, and a center or family child-care home can get licensed by meeting these requirements. Unfortunately, these minimum standards do not necessarily lead to a quality program, and professional organizations and individuals have established optimal structural elements that can have a large impact on program quality. For example, although the state may require only one adult for every eight 2-year-old children and have no limit on the total number of children in the group, the National Association for the Education of Young Children recommends a ratio of four children to one adult, with a maximum group size of 12. High adult-child ratios are considered one of the strongest structural elements in supporting the intellectual and social development of children in child care and are important indicators of quality.

Quality programs also set up inviting environments with an abundance of appropriate resources (furniture, equipment, materials, and toys), often far above the minimum requirements (Greenman, 2005). The requirements for staff education and continued training are also above minimum requirements in quality centers.

Process Elements

Process quality refers to the experiences children have in child care and includes such factors as adult–child interactions, children's exposure to and involvement with learning materials, and parent–caregiver relationships. These are critical components that directly affect children's behavior and learning experiences in the child-care setting.

TEACHER QUALITIES   The most important process element in quality child care is the human relationships between the teaching staff and children and their families. Teachers who interact with children in a nurturing manner help to create attachments between themselves and the children, the foundation for further social development. As they engage children in conversation, ask questions, and respond to them when they speak, they help children acquire cognitive and language skills. Not only do teachers need to be knowledgeable about the developmental characteristics of the children they serve, understand how to provide enriching experiences for them, and be able to communicate effectively with the children's parents about their shared concerns, they must also be warm and nurturing people.

Ideally, those who care for young children consider themselves professionals and have an educational background in child development and curriculum. Continuing professional education by attending conferences, participating in workshops, reading professional literature, and sharing ideas and information with colleagues are all indications of professional behavior. Partaking in activities like these builds commitment to the field, satisfaction with the work, and greater sensitivity to the needs of children.

Unfortunately, the low wages for working with children in child-care settings has had a very negative effect on the quality of care (Harrington, 2000). Salaries for nonprofessional entry-level personnel are rarely higher than the minimum wage, particularly at national for-profit chains. The median salary for child care workers was $17,630 in 2006 (U.S. Bureau of Labor Statistics, 2009), with a range between $12,910 and 27,050. The more education a person has, the higher the salary. Still, starting salaries for child-care center teachers with college degrees are often less than half of what many entry-level public school teachers receive. Low wages have kept the educational level of caregivers from rising and have led to an annual turnover rate of about 30% in the child-care field. Programs that manage to retain their caregivers are generally of higher quality than those that have a high turnover rate. The Center for the Child Care Workforce is an organization dedicated to improving the quality of early care and education by promoting policies and research that ensure that those who work in child-care settings receive higher compensation and a stronger voice in their workplace.

CURRICULUM   Although the relationship between caregiver and child is the most important process element, another mark of a quality program is the curriculum. Curriculum in child care is generally understood as an approach to learning that includes both planned and spontaneous experiences that occur within a predictable daily routine. Many child-care programs have faced the pressure of including direct academic instruction, and that leaves little time for child-initiated learning. Research has confirmed that a play-based curriculum is most appropriate for young children (Singer, Golinkoff, & Hirsh-Pasek, 2007). Given the importance of the early years for children's physical, social, emotional, and cognitive development, the curriculum should reflect all of these domains.

In high-quality child care programs, ample time is designated for outdoor and indoor play. Through their exploration and creative engagement with materials, children develop the skills they will need for later school success. The teaching staff facilitates children's play by providing an environment with materials that encourage learning and engaging with children responsively. Large-group gatherings are used for stories, music, movement, and more, as well as for routines like eating, toileting, and resting. Small groups provide for brief teacher-initiated experiences with science, cooking, and other opportunities to learn about the world. A well-planned curriculum will meet the needs of the children enrolled by considering their age, developmental levels, interests, special needs, and cultural backgrounds.

A quality curriculum in a program serving infants and toddlers requires that teachers be especially responsive to the rapid growth and change that is occurring during these years. Wortham (2006) summarized the characteristics of effective teachers for this age group; they must be able to

- Understand and appreciate children's unique temperaments and developmental stages.
- Meet children's needs for care while encouraging increasing independence.
- Frequently initiate physical, social, and verbal interactions.
- Be responsive to children's physical, social, and verbal behavior as much as possible.
- Be consistent and predictable.
- Plan experiences and interactions appropriate to the children's level of functioning.

Play and routine caregiving activities are the fundamentals of the curriculum for this age group. A quality caregiver follows the lead of the children in determining when they sleep, eat, and need to be changed. Between these times, they interact with the infants and toddlers in an environment that has been set up to enhance their physical, cognitive, social, and emotional development. Children's cultures and families are represented in various ways, highlighting child care as an extension of the home.

As children reach age 2 and move into the preschool years, the curriculum changes to meet their developing needs. The daily schedule includes opportunities for children to work individually and in small groups most of the time, with some short periods of whole-group gatherings for stories and music. The room is arranged in activity areas, such as blocks, dramatic play, art, science, math, computer, language, and others. Each area is well stocked with interesting materials, which allows the children to make choices about what to do when they are there. Indoor and outdoor play is respected as the best way for children to learn, and teachers facilitate their play to enhance the social, physical, and cognitive benefits for development (Wortham, 2006). See Table 5-2 for a sample of a preschool schedule that incorporates these aspects of a quality program for young children.

The curriculum in the quality before- and after-school age program tends to be more informal than that for younger children and will vary greatly, depending on the needs and interests of the group. Centers or family child-care homes of high quality provide many toys and materials appropriate to the children's ages and interests, as well as lots of free time for children to participate in self-directed activities. In a center, the room is divided into activity areas, with space set aside for computer use and

Play is an important element in children's learning. Child-care workers facilitate this play.

homework and other areas devoted to construction, games, music, art, and other interests. The best programs for this age group are seen by the children as clubs where individual interests can be pursued. Generally, the time before school is low-key, with breakfast available and time to participate in individual and small-group projects. After-school programs usually begin with a period of vigorous outdoor play followed by snacks, some time for homework, and individually chosen activities. Allowing children as much choice as possible and providing many opportunities for socializing and pursuing interests are hallmarks of the most successful programs for school-age children. Table 5-3 provides a sample school-age child-care schedule that incorporates these aspects of a quality program.

Full days in school-age care that occur during inclement weather, school holidays, and summers are characterized by a camplike atmosphere. School-age children are developing many interests, and the more the program can support their choices, the more eagerly the children participate. In the highest-quality programs, child-care staff and the children's school teachers confer regularly and communicate issues of mutual concern.

Although quality child-care programs may have somewhat different philosophical orientations, all of them will offer a curriculum that extends the cognitive and socialization processes that have begun in the children's families. For many children, child care is where they first learn to interact with children and adults outside their families, and this marks the beginning of community socialization.

PARENT INVOLVEMENT   Quality child-care programs recognize the importance of parental involvement and the strong need that families feel to be fully informed about their child's progress. In a quality program, parents are asked to share detailed information about their children as they come into care so that teachers can provide continuity with the home. A meeting prior to the child's beginning the program can help to build rapport between parents and teaching staff, which is essential to the success of the child-care experience. Continuing collaboration facilitates the continuity of experiences for the child and enhances the potential for meeting the child's needs.

Collaboration relies on communication, and it is the teacher's responsibility to establish many ways to keep families informed about their own child. Because most parents bring in and pick up their child at the child-care setting, every day presents an opportunity to establish a relationship between the parent and the teaching staff. Once such a relationship is established, information about what is going on with the child can be regularly shared. In infant–toddler programs, parents and teachers often record information about the child in a book that is passed back and forth between the child-care setting and the home. Quality programs also schedule formal parent conferences throughout the year.

Parents also welcome opportunities to become involved in the child-care program in ways that don't interfere with their work schedules. Making phone calls to other parents, donating recyclables, repairing toys, or washing the sheets used at nap time are all tasks parents may be willing to do. By becoming involved in these ways, parents feel more connected to the program and more committed to supporting it.

Potluck dinners, family breakfasts, workshops on parenting, and other events can also build family involvement. Chapter 10 offers additional strategies for establishing positive relationships between schools and families that are applicable to child-care settings as well.

Other Characteristics of Quality Child Care

In addition to the structural and process elements discussed above, exemplary child-care programs share certain characteristics that can serve as a model for others seeking to improve the quality of care for children. According to Kinch and Schweinhart (1999), a high-quality program includes the following features:

- *Financial resources.* Uses financial resources beyond fees from parents, such as subsidies for low-income families and donations from individuals and foundations.
- *Creation of alliances.* Forges a variety of alliances with organizations to bring in additional resources. For example, a center might collaborate with a community organization on fund-raising efforts.
- *Parent education.* Seeks ways to educate parents about the value of early childhood education. In doing so, parents become better consumers and are more likely to support programs.
- *Staff benefits.* Seeks higher salaries and other benefits for their staff. In addition, the program secures adequate planning time and arranges opportunities for professional development.
- *Establishment of advisory committees.* Strengthens relationships with the community by establishing a board of directors or a community advisory board.
- *Recognition of needs.* Recognizes family needs and stresses and works flexibly with families, making a program viable for parents.
- *Institutional structures.* Plans for future existence through structures that promote quality, compensation, and affordability.
- *High standards.* Has established policies and clearly written standards on the program's mission, philosophy, and educational approach.

High-quality child care is essential for children's everyday experiences and their later school achievement and social interactions. When every child receives the highest-quality care possible, the beneficial effects of child care will increase dramatically.

Effects of Quality Child Care

Research indicates that although the family remains the major influence on the child's outcomes, the quality and stability of the care that young children receive have important effects as well. The results of three recent longitudinal studies (Vandell & Pierce, 2003) confirm that high-quality child care can have positive effects on children's development in a number of areas. One of these studies reported that the cognitive and language development of children, as well as their social and emotional well-being, are enhanced by high-quality child care. Another study concluded that higher-quality child care was associated with better cognitive development, better receptive and expressive language skills, and better functional communication skills. The third study followed children through 2 years of child care and the first 3 years of school; its findings suggest that children from high-quality child-care programs demonstrated better receptive language and math skills. This study and other research indicate that these positive effects on children's development are especially significant for low-income children and those at risk for failure in school. Studies have also shown that quality programs for school-age children play an important role in children's school achievement and long-term success, as well as in their safety and well-being (Afterschool Alliance, 2009). As we have pointed out in other chapters, all those who care for and educate children make an important contribution to their lives.

IMPLICATIONS FOR TEACHERS

Helping Families Find Quality Child Care

As the need for quality care for infants and school-age children continues to increase, professionals in education like you have a responsibility to understand the issues related to child care. You can use your knowledge of child care to assist and guide parents in determining the quality of various care arrangements. Suggest that parents visit programs to determine the following:

1. *The experience and training of the caregivers*
2. *The safety, cleanliness, and appropriateness of the indoor and outdoor environments*
3. *The demeanor of the children and whether they appear to be happy and actively involved*
4. *The interaction among the caregivers and the children*
5. *The discipline policy of the program*
6. *The curriculum and if it provides many opportunities for child-initiated, teacher-facilitated play and active learning*

There are many resources in print and online to help parents determine if a particular child-care setting is appropriate for their children. As a trusted professional, you can help them to locate and use these materials. One unique resource you can suggest for parents and child caregivers is the television series A Place of Our Own. *This daily Public Broadcasting System program, offered in both Spanish and English, is designed for those who care for children. In addition to the television show, there is a Web site and an extensive outreach program that is designed to help those who care for children learn ways to help children learn and grow. These resources, found at http://www.aplaceofourown.org, can be a great support to families and caregivers.*

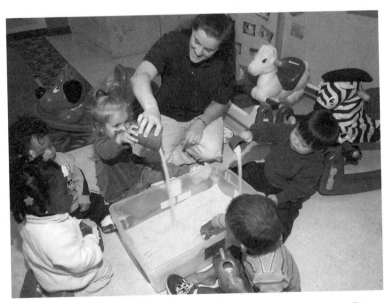

Quality child care is important for young children's development as well as for their safety and well-being.

LICENSING REQUIREMENTS AND VOLUNTARY ACCREDITATION

All 50 states and the District of Columbia have regulations concerning the operation of child-care centers, family child-care homes, and other programs that care for children. In most cases, a child-care center cannot operate unless it is licensed by the state. The regulations for family child care vary from registration to licensing, depending on particular state statutes. Licensing regulations, however, are usually only minimum standards designed to protect the safety and well-being of children. Generally, the procedure for licensing includes regular inspections to ensure that programs are operating according to the guidelines. As you would expect, licensing regulations cover a multitude of issues, such as the ratio of adults to children, health, safety issues, building codes, and staff qualifications. The National Resource Center for Health and Safety in Child Care has a Web site with links to each state detailing family child-care and center-based licensing regulations. The standards for child care vary greatly from state to state.

Some child-care centers and family child-care providers go beyond state licensing requirements by participating in voluntary accreditation programs. Accreditation is considered an indicator of child-care quality and is the result of a process of collaboration between the program and other professionals to determine whether it meets nationally recognized standards of excellence.

National Association of Family Child Care Accreditation

The **National Association of Family Child Care (NAFCC)** is a national membership organization that works with more than 400 state and local family **child-care provider** associations across the United States. It developed its first accreditation system in 1988, and by 1998 there were NAFCC-accredited family child-care providers in 44 states and the District of Columbia. In studies of accreditation, we find that accreditation increases providers' professionalism and self-esteem, improves the quality of care, and develops leadership skills. As of 2007, there were 2,048 accredited family child-care programs in the United States (NAFCC, 2009).

NAFCC's accreditation process includes an initial self-study by the provider, who then makes quality improvements, if necessary, and gathers required documentation. The candidate then submits an application, and if it is considered eligible, a representative of NAFCC observes the program and documents what has been seen. Annual renewals and reaccreditation are later parts of the process. The current standards for NAFCC accreditation are based on the following five areas:

Part 1: Relationships

Part 2: The Environment

Part 3: Developmental Learning Activities

Part 4: Safety and Health

Part 5: Professional and Business Practices

National Association for the Education of Young Children Accreditation

The National Association for the Education of Young Children's (NAEYC's) Academy for Early Childhood Program Accreditation administers the nation's largest voluntary accreditation system for all types of preschools, kindergartens, child-care centers, and school-age child-care programs. According to NAEYC's Position Statement on Developmentally Appropriate Practice (2009), a high-quality early childhood program meets the physical, social, emotional, and cognitive needs of children through developmentally appropriate practices that include both child-guided and teacher-guided experiences.

A major indicator of an appropriate program for children from birth through age 8 is the provision of sustained high-level play that is actively supported by the teaching staff.

NAEYC's accreditation process includes a four-step process that begins with an extensive self-study by the program directors and concludes with a site visit by a team of highly trained assessors who verify the accuracy of the self-study. There are currently about 8,000 NAEYC-accredited programs, which can be located through *http://www. naeyc.org*. In the fall of 2006, revised standards were established, and, as a result, the following areas are studied in the current accreditation process:

- *Relationships between children and adults:* The program promotes positive relationships among all children and adults to encourage the development of each child's sense of worth and belonging to a community and to foster each child's ability to contribute as a responsible community member.
- *Curriculum:* The program implements a curriculum that is consistent with its goals for children and promotes learning and development in the social, emotional, physical, language, and cognitive areas.
- *Teaching:* The program uses developmentally, culturally, and linguistically appropriate and effective teaching approaches.
- *Assessment of child progress:* The program is informed by ongoing, systematic, formal and informal assessment approaches, sensitive to the cultural contexts in which children develop and in reciprocal communication with families.
- *Health:* The program promotes the nutrition and health of children and protects children and staff from illness and injury.
- *Teachers:* The program employs and supports a teaching staff that has the educational qualifications, knowledge, and professional commitment necessary to promote children's learning and development and to support families' diverse needs and interests.
- *Families:* The program establishes and maintains collaborative relationships with each child's family to foster children's development in all settings. These relationships are sensitive to family composition, language, and culture.
- *Community relationships:* The program establishes relationships with and uses the resources of the children's communities to support the achievement of program goals.
- *Physical environment:* The program has a safe and healthy environment that provides appropriate and well-maintained indoor and outdoor physical environments.
- *Leadership and management:* The program effectively implements policies, procedures, and systems that support stable staff and strong personnel, fiscal, and program management.

The accreditation process represents a professional judgment as to whether a program demonstrates satisfactory performance in meeting the criteria for each standard. NAEYC accreditation is now given for a period of 5 years, during which time programs submit annual reports and are subject to unannounced visits by the accreditation agency.

Other Types of Accreditation

Although NAEYC sets the accreditation standard for center-based early childhood programs, other organizations also offer program accreditation. Among these are the National Early Childhood Program Accreditation (2009), which currently has over 300 programs accredited across the United States, and the National Accreditation Commission for Early and Education Programs of the National Association of Child Care Professionals (2009). The latter group also offers an optional faith-based component.

Good child care must be available for all working families irrespective of their income.

The Council on Accreditation (2009) recently launched its After School Initiative and is now accrediting school-age programs based on standards developed in partnership with the National Afterschool Association. One of the unique facets of this program is the three distinct recognition opportunities for school-age programs, which range from registration to certification to accreditation. Some states, such as Florida, Maryland, and Missouri, also have statewide systems for accrediting child-care and other early childhood programs.

MEETING THE CHALLENGES THROUGH COLLABORATION

The greatest concern in the 21st century is no longer that children will be cared for outside the home but that the quality of care they receive might be substandard. Fortunately, numerous groups are working to resolve what has come to be seen as a real crisis for American parents—finding affordable quality care for their children so that they can work. The National Association of Child Care Resource and Referral Agencies works with communities to improve the supply and quality of child care through its research, ongoing professional development opportunities, parent education component, and support of accreditation. Many other national groups, such as the NAEYC, the Children's Defense Fund, NAFCC, the National Afterschool Association, and the National Child Care Information Center, are committed to improving the quality of child care.

It is generally agreed that quality child care is directly related to the adults providing the care (Cohen, 2001). As noted earlier, however, the child-care workforce, which is 98% female and one-third women of color, is inadequately compensated. The average center-based teacher earns about $7 per hour, and many teachers receive only the minimum wage. Teachers with a college degree and some experience earn on average barely $10 per hour. Family child-care providers are even more poorly paid, and only one-third of all child-care staff has health benefits. Many providers must also contend with poor working conditions. Consequently, approximately one-third of those who work in child care leave the field each year. The shortage of public-school early childhood teachers—because of reductions in class size and increases in prekindergarten programs in elementary schools—has increased the job opportunities for well-trained early childhood teachers. Therefore, many are leaving the child-care field to pursue better-paid positions in the public schools. The mission of the Center for the Child Care Workforce, which merged with the American Federation of Teachers Educational Foundation, has been to improve the quality of child-care services by upgrading the wages, benefits, training opportunities, and working conditions for child-care teachers and family child-care providers.

School-age child care is receiving increased attention, and creative collaborations are developing to cultivate interesting and worthwhile programs for elementary and middle school children. Community-based organizations, schools, museums, universities, and other groups are also coming together to share resources and ideas for school-age care. The Children's Initiative (2009) of San Diego County, California, is a good example of a public–private partnership that has helped to develop effective policies, programs, and services that support the health and well-being of children. By taking leadership in the area of after-school programs, the Children's Initiative has helped San Diego develop the highest quality and capacity in school-age care in California.

REFLECTION

As you think and talk about the child-care options available to families in your home community, attempt to assess the following:

- Is there enough affordable child-care service available to families at all income levels?
- What part of the available service could be considered quality care?
- Are families satisfied with what they have, or are there unmet child-care needs?

Child-care policies in the United States lag behind those of most other modern industrialized countries (Cryer & Clifford, 2003). In France, for example, there is an excellent child-care system for children from birth to age 5 that is close to universal and moderately priced. Changes in federal policies in the United States are occurring, however, as the importance of early childhood care and education is being recognized. There are also some indications that businesses are beginning to recognize the importance of supporting the family life of their workers. The number of employer-sponsored child-care centers is very small, but a growing number of firms are providing child-care assistance through referral services, partnerships with local child-care programs, and the provision of **backup care** for the children of employees. Changes in benefit packages, including flexible spending accounts that allow employees to pay for child care in pretax dollars, offers some financial support as well.

In the changed political climate beginning in 2009, early education and care are receiving increased recognition at the federal level. The Obama administration is on record for supporting efforts to provide affordable, high-quality child care and has pledged to establish a Presidential Early Learning Council to increase collaboration and program coordination across federal, state, and local levels. It will be interesting to see the changes that occur as a result of this change in awareness of the need for quality child care from birth though elementary school and beyond. Extending tax credits, making parents' expenditures for child care refundable for poorer families, and other federal and state policies are needed to help working families. The reality of quality care is that providing the service cannot be based solely on what parents can afford to pay. Families and programs need additional community and government support in order to make quality care available to every child.

Summary and Review

Child care is essential to family life today. National surveys confirm that an increasing number of children are being cared for outside the home so that parents can work. Increasingly, as families recognize the importance of early experiences to children's later development, they are seeking care that goes beyond custodial to care that has an educational component as well.

Child-care arrangements include care that may be offered by a nanny, babysitter, or au pair in the child's home. Family child care occurs in the home of the provider and is offered for small groups of children, often of variable ages. Center-based child care can serve children from infancy through school age, generally in classrooms designed for children of a particular age range.

Considerable variation exists in the quality of child-care services. All states have regulations to govern family child care and center-based programs, but very little oversight is provided for families who use in-home care. State regulations, however, only provide minimum guidelines, and being licensed does not guarantee that a program is of high quality. Nationally accredited centers and family child-care homes, although still a small percentage of the total, serve as models of quality programs. Quality of care includes both process and structural components in the child-care setting.

The most important indicator of quality is the caregiver. The 30% annual turnover rate of those working with children because of poor compensation, lack of benefits, and poor working conditions is a serious issue facing child care. Improvement of the quality, affordability, and accessibility of child care is one of the biggest challenges facing families, schools, and communities today. But increased awareness at the national level signals exciting opportunities for improvement in child-care options for the future.

Suggested Activities and Questions

1. Interview several parents who use different kinds of child-care arrangements. Determine how they feel about the care their child is receiving and the challenges they face in navigating work and parenthood.
2. Obtain a copy of your state's child-care regulations. What is the ratio of adults to children at various ages? What are the qualifications required of caregivers? How do these compare to national recommendations?
3. Visit a child-care center and arrange to observe several classes. What elements of a quality curriculum can you see? What changes might you make?
4. In the McGee vignette, identify the incidents that would indicate to Mr. and Mrs. McGee that the center probably has high structural and process qualities.

Resources

Organizations

National After-School Association   *http://www.naaweb.yourmembership.com/*

National Association for Family Child Care   *http://www.nafcc.org*

National Child Care Association   *http://www.nccanet.org/*

National Association of Child Care Resource and Referral Agencies   *http://www.naccra.net/*

Web Sites

http://www.afterschoolalliance.org   The Afterschool Alliance provides information for establishing school-age programs as well as disseminating research to support after-school care.

http://www.ccw.org   The Center for the Child Care Workforce is committed to quality early care and education for all children by promoting policies and research and by organizing to improve the wages, benefits, training opportunities, and working conditions for those who work in child-care settings.

http://www.childcareexchange.com   Child Care Exchange offers support to child-care directors and others interested in promoting quality child care through its journal, Web site, and international conferences.

http://nccic.acf.hhs.gov   The National Child Care Information and Technical Assistance Center provides linkages with other agencies interested in enhancing and promoting child care.

http://www.nrckids.org   The National Resource Center for Health and Safety in Child Care and Early Education promotes health and safety in child-care settings and promotes standards guidelines for out-of-home care.

http://www.schoolagenotes.com   School-Age NOTES produces a monthly newsletter, offers on-site training, and provides a selection of resources related to school-age programs.

CHAPTER 6

Working with Families of Children with Disabilities

Parents are their child's first and best advocate. By knowing children's strengths and needs, understanding the basic special education process, and being able to work collaboratively with school people, parents can be instrumental in shaping a successful experience for their children in school, and help prepare them for life as full members of their communities.

(ANDERSON, CHITWOOD, & HAYDEN, 2008, P. X)

After reading this chapter, you will be able to do the following:

- Discuss the emotional impact that a child with disabilites can have on a family.
- Describe why the early identification of disabilities is desirable and how early intervention can help families ensure that their children achieve their maximum potential.
- Explain the importance of the Individuals with Disabilities Education Act (IDEA) for families and how IDEA's six principles governing the education of students with disabilities provides support for them and their children.
- Define individualized education plan (IEP), individualized family services plan (IFSP), and least restrictive environment (LRE) and describe how decisions are made through collaboration between families and professionals to determine the services necessary for a child with disabilities.
- Make a case for inclusion and its benefits to children with disabilities and to children who are typically developing.
- Assess the importance of community agencies in meeting the needs of persons with disabilities and the needs of their families.

The number of children identified as having special learning needs has increased dramatically over the past 30 years as federal laws mandating appropriate intervention and education have been developed. About 15% of all infants, toddlers, children, and adolescents have been recognized as having disabilities (Turnbull, Turnbull, & Wehmeyer, 2007), and increasingly, such children are being taught in general education classrooms, an approach referred to as **inclusion**. Other children with more pronounced disabilities need to be educated in special education classrooms and are included with groups of typically developing peers for certain parts of the daily routine, as appropriate. A small percentage of children with severe disabilities attend special schools or receive their education at home or in another kind of facility. Regardless of the setting, however, ensuring the optimal growth and development of children with disabilities is a responsibility shared by their families, schools, and community agencies.

⌒ — As Joan gave the final push and her new baby was born, she was thrilled to hear "It's a girl!" Josh, her 2-year-old son, now had a baby sister. A hush had fallen in the delivery room, however, and Joan, waiting for the baby to be lifted to her, noticed Rob, her husband, staring at the baby in disbelief. "What's wrong?" she cried. As the baby was gently laid on her breast, Joan's doctor quietly said, "I think the baby has Down syndrome. We'll have to run some tests to be sure." Joan looked at her husband in dismay as tears welled in her eyes, and her newborn was taken from her and rushed to the Neonatal Intensive Care Unit. — ⌒

R ob and Joan, like many parents who have a child with severe disabilities, were un- prepared for the birth of a child with special needs. As they awaited the test re- sults for the little girl they named Zoe, they clung to the hope that the doctor was wrong and that their child was normal. Some years later, as they played on the beach with Josh and Zoe, now age 7, they couldn't imagine life without their spirited little girl. True, she had had some difficult medical problems early on and now needed accommo- dations in school, but she had a sunny disposition and brought them all much joy. They didn't think of her as an abnormal child but as a child who in many ways was similar to her typically developing brother.

Zoe was fortunate to have been born during the era of the **Individuals with Disabilities Education Act (IDEA)**. Thanks to increasingly protective laws, she and her family had received early intervention services when she was an infant and a toddler (Lewis & Doorlag, 2006). Later, Zoe was able to participate in a community nursery school and was currently attending a second-grade class in a public school, where she also received speech and language services, physical therapy, and counseling.

Children with disabilities are a subgroup of the larger category of children with special needs. The special-needs group includes gifted and talented children, children who are linguistically or culturally different from the mainstream, and children who are at risk for school failure because of poverty or other social conditions. These groups may need special intervention to achieve their maximum potential in school, but they are not protected by the laws that have been enacted for children with disabilities.

Some children with attention deficit hyperactivity disorder (ADHD), for example, do not qualify for special education services but may require accommodations to func- tion well in general education classes. These students may need to take a test orally, need extra time for tests, have a peer note taker, or need a behavior plan. A **504 plan**, legally mandated by federal law, is put in place for such children to ensure that they re- ceive needed accommodations. When the student does not perform as expected even with the 504 plan, further evaluation may be done to determine if the child may be eli- gible for special education services.

Children who are gifted and talented may also benefit from accommodations to the general curriculum in order to achieve their full potential, but such help is not mandated by law at this time. Many school systems do attempt to identify gifted and talented students and provide differentiated instruction for them. Typically, these children are grouped together when possible, and the pace of instruction is accelerated and content is enriched with opportunities for creative and critical thinking.

Some parents, like Rob and Joan, learn about their child's disability at birth or soon afterward; others find out later. For example, a pediatrician might raise concerns when a child fails to meet developmental milestones for motor or language development and may recommend further screening. Other children are not identified as having a disability until they enter preschool, elementary school, or even middle or high school, when their learning differences become apparent.

Although it is impossible to calculate exactly how many children with disabilities are in the United States, the U.S. Department of Education's annual report to Congress on the education of children with disabilities provides the most accurate estimate (see Table 6-1). When all children from birth to age 21 are counted, the total number rises from the 6,109,569 children now served in elementary schools to over 6.7 million individuals with disabilities. But the majority of school-age children receiving special education services have mild disabilities, with slightly more then two-thirds of these children falling into two categories: specific learning disabilities and speech or language impairments.

This kind of labeling will alert you to the kinds of disabilities and the percentages of children within each category, but it is important to remember that these numbers refer to individual children, who, like Zoe, have strengths and weaknesses, like all children. When thinking about children with disabilities, be aware of the person first and avoid labeling that highlights the disability as an individual's most important characteristic. For example, referring to "the boy who is blind" is preferable to saying "the blind boy." Even better, call children by their names and refer to their disability only when it is relevant.

TABLE 6-1 Number of Students Ages 6 Through 21 Served Under IDEA in the 2005–2006 School Year

Disability	Number	Percentage
Specific learning disabilities	2,780,218	45.50
Speech or language impairments	1,157,215	18.94
Mental retardation	545,492	8.92
Emotional disturbance	472,384	7.73
Multiple disabilities	133,914	2.19
Hearing impairments	72,387	1.18
Orthopedic impairments	63,127	1.03
Other health impairments	561,028	9.18
Visual impairments	25,996	.42
Autism	193,637	3.16
Deaf-blindness	1,592	.02
Traumatic brain injury	23,509	.38
Developmental delay	79,070	1.29
All Disabilities	6,109,569	

Source: U.S. Department of Education (2007). *IDEA data.* Retrieved April 1, 2009, from *http://www.ideadata. org/PartBReport.asp.*

REFLECTION

You may have had limited experience with children with disabilities when you were growing up. In the past, children with disabilities were often kept separate from their typically developing peers. Think about how you will educate yourself about disabilities and help children understand the importance of treating all people with respect, regardless of their abilities.

After providing an overview of the federal legislation concerning individuals with disabilities, we will look at the issues associated with serving the needs of children with disabilities within the family, school, and community. Collaboration within these social settings is essential to achieve the most successful outcome for these children.

OVERVIEW OF FEDERAL SPECIAL EDUCATION LAWS

In Chapter 2, we discussed the beginnings of federal legislation that ushered in a new era for recognizing and ensuring educational opportunities for children with disabilities. In the subsequent 30 years, America has undergone considerable adjustment (not without difficulty) in providing special education facilities, restructuring buildings, reorganizing staff, and modifying curricula. Perhaps most of all, more educators have a new outlook on, appreciation for, and interest in accommodating children with special needs in regular classrooms.

Many adults today can remember a time when children with disabilities did not attend school. Many were cared for at home; some were institutionalized, but most of these children were marginalized and lived their lives outside of the mainstream of society (Hiatt-Michael, 2004). In some parts of the world, this remains the fate of persons with disabilities. But federal laws enacted over the past 30 years in the United States protect children from exclusion from school based on their disability. These laws also provide early intervention services for infants, toddlers, and preschoolers within their families and other appropriate settings that will help them achieve their potential.

As Table 2-2 in Chapter 2 indicates, several legislative endeavors since 1975 have expanded and clarified the provisions for special education. In 1986, legislation expanded school programs to cover preschoolers (ages 3 to 5 years) with disabilities. The notion driving this move was that early identification of disabilities meant that additional time and instruction would enhance the child's later schooling. It was only a matter of time until the first 3 years of a child's life were also considered for special services when needed. Therefore, in 1997, legislation brought services (though not through schools) to infants and toddlers. Specialists meet with parents of children in this group to help establish a better foundation for their later schooling.

Now known as the Individuals with Disabilities Education Act (IDEA), this legislation has been immensely important

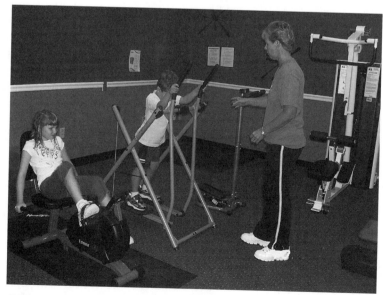

Children with physical disabilities can receive a therapist's services in a variety of places.

in making certain that children, adolescents, and young adults to age 21 have access to and benefit from special education services. The law is very specific about who is eligible for special education and how this education is individualized to meet the person's unique needs. Consequently, special education is seen as a service and not as a place. Instruction may take place at home, in a hospital, or in a regular classroom and may be supplemented with speech therapy, physical therapy, occupational therapy, and other services necessary for the child to benefit from special education.

Readers anticipating a career in early childhood education or related human services professions must be cognizant of several provisions in the legislation designed to protect the rights of children with disabilities. The following six principles undergirding special education reform (summarized from Turnbull et al., 2007) have become the specialized language of special education.

1. *Zero rejection.*   A provision against excluding any student from school because of behavior that violates school rules but is a manifestation of the student's disability.
2. *Nondiscriminatory and multidisciplinary evaluations.*   A rule that requires a nondiscriminatory evaluation to determine if, indeed, the student has a disability and, if so, the kinds of services the student should receive. This rule requires schools to assess children in their own language using a team of evaluators who avoid procedures that may be culturally or racially discriminatory.
3. *Appropriate education.*   A rule requiring educators to plan individually tailored education and related services for each student with a disability.
4. *Least restructed environment.*   A rule that requires schools to merge children with disabilities with typically developing peers in regular education classrooms to the maximum extent appropriate for the child.
5. *Procedural due process.*   A rule establishing the safeguards that make the school and parents accountable to each other for carrying out the student's IDEA rights, safeguards all students' right to privacy, and establishing procedures for legal redress if violations occur.
6. *Parent and student participation.*   A rule that requires schools to collaborate with parents and adolescent students in designing and carrying out special education programs.

Parents and special education leaders have been at the forefront of the movement to establish laws that guarantee children with disabilities an equal opportunity for education (Hiatt-Michael, 2004). It was because of the commitment and **advocacy** of these families and educators that legal actions in the courts and in the Congress have evolved to the present inclusion of children with disabilities in mainstream education. In some cases, parents continue to struggle for the appropriate educational services for their children in the courts. Ideally, of course, families, schools, and communities work together, sharing their expertise, support, and resources to provide the best outcome for all children.

IMPLICATIONS FOR TEACHERS

Build Relationships with Parents

The majority of children with disabilities are educated in public school settings side by side with their normally developing peers. And although you will work closely with all parents, it is particularly important to establish a close relationship with the parents of children with disabilities. The following suggestions will help you to begin building a partnership with these parents:

- *Make the parents feel welcome in your classroom, and respect their expert knowledge of their children and their needs.*

- *Use e-mail, telephone calls, and/or notes to introduce yourself to families.*
- *Contact families early in the year with positive comments about their child. Many parents of children with disabilities may have received mainly negative information from other teachers.*
- *Determine the best way for you and the parents to communicate with each other and then do so.*
- *Listen carefully to parents' concerns and perceptions even if they are different than yours.*
- *Realize that unless you yourself are raising a child with a disability, you really cannot know what it is like for these families, but show your willingness to learn from the parents.*

FAMILIES RAISING CHILDREN WITH DISABILITIES

Trish had been dreading the conference with Katie's preschool teacher at Grove Nursery School. Ms. Criner had been calling almost every day with concerns about 3-year-old Katie. "She wouldn't stay in circle, she grabbed things from other children, she hit and kicked them when they grabbed back, then she ran away from the teachers." As soon as Trish sat down, Ms. Criner smiled kindly but wasted no time getting to the point of the conference, stating, "I'm afraid we are not going to be able to continue having Katie here at Grove. We don't feel we can keep the other children safe from her aggressive behavior. We don't think this is the right place for her." Blinded by her tears, Trish rushed from the room and out to her car.

Emotional Impact

Having a child with special needs presents unique challenges to parents, and for some, the initial discovery can be an intense and traumatic event. Studies reported by Heward (2006) indicated that parents of children with disabilities go through an adjustment process similar to grieving in working through their feelings. Initially, parents may experience shock, denial, and disbelief. These feelings may be followed by periods of anger, guilt, depression, shame, rejection, or overprotection of their child. Eventually, most parents accept their child's disability, and some grow to appreciate the positive impact their child has had on their lives (Hanson & Lynch, 2004).

Although research indicates that some parents move through a grief cycle of confronting, adjusting, and adapting, it is inappropriate to believe that all families will react in similar ways. Parents are unique and should be supported sensitively in their adjustment process. Depending on the nature of the disability, parents and siblings may need to make many changes as they learn how to provide the appropriate care and accommodations for the child. Often the family's routines, resources, and activities will need to be modified, and this can cause resentment and stress. Families raising children with disabilities need teachers and community service personnel who are sensitive, tolerant, and helpful.

Early Identification and Intervention

When Katie, in the vignette above, was dismissed from Grove Nursery School, her mother was devastated. For several years, Trish had been ignoring the warning signs that Katie was developing differently than others. She walked and talked very late and seemed to have difficulty getting along with others. Now that the nursery school had confirmed her fear that something was wrong, Trish finally decided to have some testing done. Through the **child-find** process in her local school district, Trish was able to have her daughter evaluated. When Katie was identified as having a language processing disability, she became eligible to attend a prekindergarten program in a local elementary school that served children with developmental delays and other

Young children diagnosed with developmental delays, such as Down syndrome, are eligible for preschool programs that provide natural settings, such as a playground.

learning problems. By the time Katie was in first grade, she was progressing well in a general education class with support from the resource teacher of special education. Katie's success in school was largely the result of the **early identification** of her disability and the intervention services she received.

The benefits of early identification and intervention are well documented (Lerner, Lowenthal, & Egan, 2003). When children's learning problems are recognized early, behavior problems and school failure can be prevented or reduced. Early intervention is generally a family-centered approach, so the parents of children with disabilities also benefit as they learn ways to support their child's development at home. Society also profits from the early identification of children with disabilities because these children, like Katie, are often ready to participate in a general education classroom at significantly less cost than that of extensive special education services (Schweinhart & Weikart, 1997).

Early Intervention Program for Infants and Toddlers with Disabilities

The Early Intervention Program for Infants and Toddlers with Disabilities was established in 1997 as Part C of the IDEA—1997. To be eligible for services, children must be experiencing developmental delays in cognitive, physical, communication, social or emotional, or adaptive development, as measured by appropriate diagnostic instruments. Children whose diagnosed medical condition has a high probability of causing developmental delay (Lerner, Lowenthal, & Egan, 2003) are also eligible for services.

The evaluation of infants and toddlers requires a comprehensive multidisciplinary approach, which often results in a variety of needed services, such as family training and counseling, home visits, speech or language pathology and audiology therapy, occupational and physical therapy, and health services. By law, these intervention services need to be provided in the child's home, in a child-care facility, or in another setting that is natural for children in this age group. The law also requires that a service coordinator be provided to help guide the family and manage the efforts of the various agencies that provide services to the infant or toddler.

REFLECTION

Do you feel that you know enough about the early identification of children with disabilities? Your state department of education can provide information and materials related to services for children with special needs who live in your district.

Zoe, identified with Down syndrome soon after birth, began to receive services as an infant guided by the **individualized family service plan (IFSP)**, required for children from birth to 3 years of age. This plan, which is developed once a child has been deemed eligible for service, is based on the results of comprehensive assessments and is reviewed at least every 6 months. Parent participation in the development of the IFSP is essential, and parent input is sought for decisions related to evaluation, identification,

Section I:	**Enrollment Information** (name, contact information for parents and caregivers)
Section II-A:	**Family Considerations for the IFSP** (parents' perception of the child's and family's strengths and needs, including a checklist of concerns)
Section II-B:	**All About Our Family** (narrative of family members, what they do, neighborhood information, and other people important to the family)
Section II-C:	**All About My Child** (checklist of things the child likes to do or things parents would like the child to do, as well as a narrative section on who the child spends time with)
Section III:	**Summary of Child's Present Levels of Performance** (completed by the IFSP team as a summary of their observations and evaluations of the child's physical, communication, and social and emotional development, cognition, and motor and adaptive skills)
Section IV:	**Natural Settings/Environment** (includes a checklist of settings that could be considered as options, as well as those that have been selected and why they reflect the most natural settings for the child)
Section V:	**Major Outcomes** (a list of the major goals, current status, needed changes, and what will be done to accomplish these changes)
Section VI:	**Transition Planning Checklist** (information about the transition to community programs)
Section VII:	**Early Intervention Services** (a summary of the kinds, duration, and outcomes of the related services the child has received, including service coordination and assistive technology)
Section VIII:	**Other Services** (medical and other services that the child needs but that are not funded by the infant–toddler program and the funding source)
Section IX:	**IFSP Implementation and Distribution Authorization**
Section X:	**IFSP Team** (names, titles and roles, agencies, and signatures of all persons involved in the interdisciplinary team)
Section XI:	Progress Summary/Modifications/Revisions to Outcomes in the IFSP

FIGURE 6-1 Components of the IFSP

possible placements, and services. Although a detailed discussion of the IFSP is beyond the scope of this book, you may want to visit the following Web site for examples of IFSP forms used by various states: http://www.nectac.org/topics/families/stateifsp.asp. Figure 6-1 provides an overview of the categories addressed in this important document.

Multicultural Issues

A growing concern among educators and child advocates is the disproportionate number of minority children who receive special education services. Both African American and Hispanic students are more likely to be referred to special education than are European Americans. Although multiple factors may account for the overrepresentation of children of color in special education (Gorman, 2004), one possible explanation is the fact that children from minority backgrounds are also disproportionally from families with low incomes. There are strong connections between low income and exposure to

A school and family team works on an IFSP for a child with special needs and his family.

toxins, poor nutrition, lower birth weight, and less stimulating home and child-care environments. Other researchers (Heward, Cavanaugh, & Ernsbarger, 2005) suggest that there is evidence that some children's placement in special education is a result of culture, class, or gender influences. A study by the National Research Council (2002) addressed this issue and noted that the referral process for special education is subjective, and bias could be a factor in diagnosing more minority children as having disabilities than their percentage of the population seems to justify.

When working with families from minority ethnic or language groups, it is essential that professionals display respect for the parents' culture and provide the legally mandated translations of important documents and a translator during meetings about the child. Some families will have great difficulty acknowledging that their child has a disability. They may not agree with the diagnosis or not wish their child to participate in the services that are being suggested. These disagreements can occur with any family, but professionals working with families from diverse cultures must be especially sensitive to misunderstandings and miscommunications. The collaborative nature of developing an individualized plan for children with disabilities requires a high level of trust between professionals and parents, and this may need time to develop.

As an educator or community service professional, you will be part of the stronger efforts that are being made to provide early intervention for children at risk for educational failure because of poverty or lack of English language in the home. There is long-standing evidence that early intervention and quality early childhood experiences can significantly reduce children's need for special education services later (Schweinhart, 2004). To reach those children most in need of these services, professionals need to work hard at communicating well with families who may be struggling with anger and denial with regard to their child's possible disabilities and who may distrust the educational system.

Medication

The decision to give medication to a child with disabilities can be a difficult one for parents. Because this is a medical decision, they must work closely with their child's physician to determine if the use of drugs will be beneficial. Medication is most often recommended for children diagnosed with ADHD, who usually take a stimulant. The use of stimulant drugs is somewhat controversial. And although there are known side effects, such as loss of appetite, stomach pains, headaches, irritability, sleep problems, and mood changes, the long-term impact of these drugs has not been well researched. Children diagnosed with anxiety or mood disorders, such as depression or bipolar disorder, may also benefit from medication therapy.

Parents are cautious about having their children take a medication and worry about their growth, their health, and the long-term effects of drug therapy. On the other hand, many teachers have seen children's school performance improve with medication, and research indicates that children correctly diagnosed and appropriately medicated do demonstrate improved classroom performance (Anstine-Templeton & Johnson, 2004). Children who are medicated should have full-treatment plans that include behavior interventions and therapy as needed. When medication is given, parents and educators need to monitor the child closely to ensure that the right dosage is being given. Finally, teachers must respect and support the decision of parents who oppose medication for their children and disallow its use.

Respite and Support

Parenting a child with a disability can be demanding, and the more severe the child's disability, the more challenges the family faces. Programs, training, and support groups for families raising children with disabilities can sustain parents and provide much-needed information. These supports can also help families find others who are dealing with similar issues. Research indicates that families who participate in support groups are more likely to be involved in their children's schooling (Newman, 2004), and this involvement leads to higher achievement.

Respite care, which provides temporary relief from the caretaking responsibilities associated with parenting, is especially needed for families whose children have problem behaviors and severe disabilities. Parents of children with challenging behaviors may be harshly judged by strangers or family members, who may perceive the child's behavior as the result of poor parenting rather than as a reflection of a disability (Lee & Ostrowsky, 2004). Parenting such children can be very stressful, and if the parents do not have a network of extended family and friends to assist them, they can become burned out from trying to meet the demands of their responsibilies.

IMPLICATIONS FOR TEACHERS
Ways to Support Parents

As the teacher of a child with disabilities included in a regular education class, you will play an important role in the child's family. Once you have established a relationship with the parents and learned some of the family's aspirations for their child, you can help them connect with other families in the classroom community. Isolation can be a big problem for families with children with disabilities, and you will be in a good position to help the child form relationships with other children that can extend outside of school. You will also want to partner with other professionals such as social workers, school counselors, and psychologists to help families locate support groups, therapy, print and online resources, and sources for respite care. Don't assume that you know what families are going through, however; use your good communication skills and rapport to uncover their needs.

REFLECTION

What do you think about the increased use of medication for children with behavioral and emotional problems? Make a list of the pros and cons of medication therapy in order to understand the various perspectives on this issue.

CHILDREN WITH DISABILITIES IN SCHOOL

Although parent involvement and input remain essential as the child enters preschool, families who have been part of the infant–toddler program do experience a transition at this juncture. Children who are diagnosed with disabilities as infants and toddlers transition to the preschool program when they turn 3, which means that they shift from the IFSP to an **individualized education program** (IEP). This can be a significant passage for the child, as services at the preschool level are generally provided outside of the home. For some families, this can be a traumatic adjustment because they may be separated from their child for the first time. Other children are newly diagnosed as preschoolers, and still others may not be identified as having a disability until later in elementary school. In the following section, you will find out about the services provided by the preschool program of IDEA and the legal aspects that apply to children during the elementary school years.

Preschool Program

One aspect of IDEA mandates school districts to locate, identify and evaluate preschool children with disabilities within their communities through the child-find process. The goal of child find is to locate children who may need early intervention. As you work with parents of young children, you can help them determine if their child may need such screening. Working with the family to answer the following questions might be helpful (Lerner et al., 2003):

- Is the child developing typically and achieving developmental milestones?
- Does the child exhibit appropriate behaviors for his or her age level?
- Are there any factors in the child's developmental history that cause concern?
- Are there any situations in the home that might influence the cognitive, physical, linguistic, and emotional development of the child?
- Does the child require more stimulation and nurturance than the typical child?

Child-find efforts are enhanced by the work of pediatricians, early childhood educators from Head Start, child-care and nursery schools, personnel from community agencies such as public health and social services agencies, and others who come in contact with preschool children. These professionals can alert parents to the child-find process and can even refer the child for testing if the parent is reluctant.

After an initial screening, the child-find team will arrange for a full evaluation of the child's strengths and weaknesses for those children who require it. If the child is diagnosed with a disability, the next step is to develop an IEP for intervention, which will focus on the instruction goals for the child.

Another section of IDEA devoted to preschool mandates that 3- to 5-year-old children with a diagnosed disability receive a **free, appropriate public education (FAPE)** and the related services they require. Zoe, who had been receiving services under the early intervention program for infants and toddlers with disabilities, made a smooth transition to the preschool program. Because she had been helped in developing self-care skills and had had many opportunities to interact and play cooperatively with other young children, Zoe had developed the **adaptive behaviors** needed for social acceptance in a general education setting. Thus, when she turned 3, Zoe's parents decide to enroll her in the same neighborhood nursery school her older brother had attended, because they wanted her to have the same opportunities that he had experienced.

This nursery school had never had a child with an IEP before, but the staff was willing to work with Zoe's family and the related professionals who would help to meet her IEP goals. The early childhood special educator, speech pathologist, and

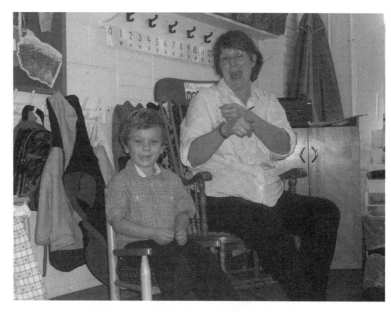

A speech therapist is to be provided for a child with a hearing impairment who is in a nursery school and involved with a group of peers.

occupational therapist came to the nursery school to work with Zoe and a small group of peers when appropriate. They also collaborated with the nursery school teachers and staff to make sure that Zoe was progressing. You may want to read the article by McCormick, Wong, and Yagi (2003) for a full description of how one nursery school planned for the successful inclusion of a child with Down syndrome.

Attending school with typically functioning children allowed Zoe to be in the **least restrictive environment (LRE)** based on her educational needs (another facet of the law, which requires children with disabilities to be in the most normalized settings possible). Zoe's strong social skills were a plus in her success at nursery school. She established friendships with some of her peers, which led to play dates and birthday invitations. Although she continued to need extra services and assistance with certain tasks, she was a well-liked child who was fully included in the school's program.

Katie, the child with a language disability who had been excluded from Grove Nursery School, was later placed in the preschool classroom at a nearby public elementary school. In this preschool program for children with developmental delays and diagnosed disabilities, typically developing peers are invited to participate in the program, allowing all children to benefit from the experience of learning together.

General Educators and Children with Disabilities

Children with disabilities receive a continuum of services provided by both general and special educators, as well as other specialists. Hence, there are a number of ways that general educators have responsibilities related to children with disabilities. Children with a diagnosed disability may be placed in their classroom full time, in what is often termed **full inclusion**. These children will also receive services from a special educator and other specialists but will spend the majority of their in-school time in a general education classroom. Other children may be placed in a self-contained special education classroom but be included in a general education class for lunch, recess, and special subjects like art and music so that they can benefit from social interaction with typically developing peers. The individual child's IEP will determine the extent of his or her participation in a general education classroom based on the child's needs and the LRE.

It is beyond the scope of this book to provide detailed information about each kind of exceptionality and the ways that teachers can work with students with particular disabilities. But we can say that teachers who appreciate individual differences and are prepared to differentiate instruction based on these differences will have the most success integrating children with disabilities into their classroom. With some disabilities, of course, the issues go beyond differentiation, and general educators will need guidance on how best to include specific children in their classrooms. It is essential that general education teachers and other professionals who work with children with disabilities recognize the importance of working as a team with parents, special education teachers, and other specialists. The most successful outcomes result from the collaborative efforts of a team working together for the child's optimum education.

THE REFERRAL PROCESS   As mentioned earlier in the chapter, some disabilities are diagnosed at birth, others during the preschool years, and still others during elementary school. General educators may be the first to suspect that a child has special learning needs and may require special education. General educators do not have the responsibility or training to diagnose disabilities, but they are often in a position to recognize learning and behavior difficulties that suggest that a child may need further evaluation. Well-developed observation skills, along with a strong knowledge of child development, typical patterns of behavior, and learning at various developmental stages, are essential for teachers and others working professionally with children. Their observations will assist the team in making a diagnosis of a disability.

Educators, together with doctors, nurses, other school personnel, or parents, can make a referral to determine if a child needs special education. Typically, a referral must be a written document sent to the school principal, special education director, or chair of the committee that oversees special education placements. The referral must include the date the request is being made, as well as the child's full name, date of birth, home school, and why the sender believes the child might need special education. The referral should specify what the child is currently not doing that peers are able to do. School personnel must then evaluate the child, and if it is determined that the child qualifies for special education, they will write an IEP for the child. All this must be done within 90 calendar days.

REFLECTION

As a future teacher or community service professional, your attitude toward children with disabilities will have a powerful effect on the children with whom you work. Take a few minutes to reflect on the following children and write a few words that come to mind when describing each of them: the girl who is blind and deaf, the blind man, the teenager with ADHD. Put your list aside for a moment and then do a similar activity using adjectives to describe the following people: Helen Keller, Stevie Wonder, Cher. If your descriptive words differ from list to list, you may want to think about some of your attitudes toward disabilities. Begin to educate yourself about the person-first approach mentioned in this chapter and about why individuals with disabilities prefer not to be termed *handicapped* or have their disability described as their primary characteristic.

THE ASSESSMENT PROCESS   Once a child has been referred for special education, an evaluation team will begin the assessment process. The evaluation team is made up of certain core members, such as the resource teachers, speech and language specialists, school psychologist, and school administrators. They will gather information from the

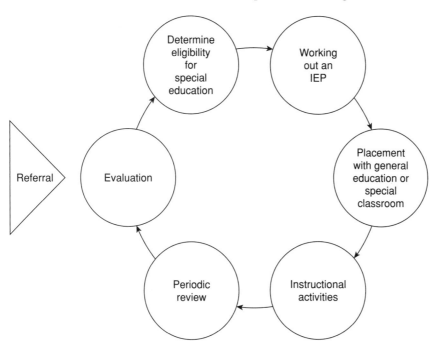

FIGURE 6-2 Processing a Referral for Special Education

School personnel follow a sequence of events and meetings after receiving a referral. The sequence may be repeated annually or modified.

child's parents and from former and present teachers who have worked with the child. They will determine the kinds of testing that need to be done and may call on the school psychologist, speech and language specialist, or resource teacher to evaluate the child using various assessment instruments. Parents, teachers, and other concerned individuals become equal partners with the core members on the team when they discuss the referral and the results of the evaluation for a specific child. See Figure 6-2 for a summary of the referral and placement process.

Ideally, parents will take the opportunity to become active partners in the evaluation and placement process and attend all meetings concerning their child. As the experts on their child, parents have much to contribute to the evaluation team, but they may find it intimidating to sit at a table with professionals who use terminology and abbreviations that may be unfamiliar to a layperson. It is essential that the core members of the team work hard to make the parents feel welcome and ensure that they understand everything said about their child. If the parents do not speak English, a translator must be made available and important written materials must be translated into the native language, if at all feasible.

Once the child has been evaluated, the evaluation team will meet to share the findings of the various professionals who have tested the child. Each professional will supply a written report that summarizes the results of his or her testing, together with the observations and insights of the child's parents and teachers. At this point, the team will determine if the child has one or more of the impairments that are considered disabilities and will decide if the child is eligible for speical education services.

Once eligiblity has been established, the team writes the IEP and determines what specific services the child needs. Parents will receive copies of the IEP; they will also receive reports on their child's progress in meeting IEP goals several times during the school year. If the child is not making adequate progress, the team will meet to revise the IEP. Parents may also request changes to the IEP based on their perceptions of their child's growth.

The protections of due process of the IDEA legislation determine the timing of the course of action on the referral and admission to special education service programs, as well as the written notices to parents that are required. Once the evaluation of the child is completed and it has been determined that the child is eligible for special education, the evaluation team has 30 days to write the IEP. Parents must be notified in writing before the team evaluates the child, before the school provides special education services to the child, and before the school changes the IEP. Parents must give their permission for the child to be evaluated and to receive special education services. Schools are also required to inform parents of their child's educational rights and to let them know how they can request a hearing if they disagree with the school's findings with regard to their child.

The IEP. The IEP is, in a sense, a contract setting out the goals and instruction for a student with a disability from ages 3 to 21. The term *individualized education program* has been in education practice for the past 30 years, and it means basically what the phrase implies, that is, a plan worked out by the team of general education teachers, specialists, parents, and sometimes the learner as well, to serve the learner's needs. (See Figure 6-3 for the general components of the IEP.) At least once a year, an IEP will be written for the child. Every 3 years, children who have an IEP will be reevaluated to ascertain if they still require special education services.

Part I:	**Identifying Information** (child's name, birth date, grade, current placement)
Part II:	**Meeting Information** (type of meeting, participants, and notice and permission information)
Part III:	**Current Assessment Information** (data source, scores, strengths, indicated areas of need)
Part IV:	**Eligibility** (educational impact of the disability, disability codes)
Part V:	**Parent Information**
Part VI:	**Progress on IEP Goals and Objectives on Benchmarks**
Part VII:	**Instructional Areas** (annual goals and short-term objectives for each instructional area)
Part VIII:	**Supplementary Aids and Services** (needed accommodations, modifications, and adaptations)
Part IX:	**Nonparticipation with Nondisabled Peers** (percentage of time the student will not participate with nondisabled peers in the general education environment)
Part X:	**Primary Special Education Services**
Part XI:	**Related Services to Support Instruction** (speech/language, occupational or physical therapy, counseling, or others)
Part XII:	**Least Restrictive Environment** (placement and rationale for the decision)
Part XIII:	**Placement Decision**
Part XIV:	**Referral for Consideration of Alternative Placement**
Part XV:	**Specialized Transportation**
Part XVI:	**Summary**

FIGURE 6-3 Components of the IEP

Assistive Technology.   **Assistive technology** is used by individuals with disabilities to perform tasks that otherwise might be difficult or impossible. Such devices can include items, pieces of equipment, or product systems, whether acquired commercially off the shelf, modified, or customized, that are used to increase, maintain, or improve the functional capabilities of individuals with disabilities. The term *technology* may conjure up images of computers and other hardware, but it actually refers to high-, mid-, and low-tech devices that help children with disabilities accomplish practical tasks.

The use of assistive technology, although not an actual IEP goal, can help children accomplish their tasks by increasing their independence and allowing them to participate more fully in classroom activities. For children unable to move freely from place to place, motorized scooter boards, wheeled go-carts, and wheelchairs are necessary assistive devices. Taped books, calculators, and timers are examples of mid-range technology that can help children participate more fully in the classroom. Other, more complex devices that read printed books aloud and talking computer programs are also available for children who have problems reading and writing. Keyboards with large keys, a specially designed mouse, and software that enlarges screen content are examples of modifications made to computers that allow them to be used by persons with various disabilities. Items that use no electronic components, such as pencil grips, nonslip placements, and study carrels, are examples of low-tech assistive technology devices.

The IEP team should carefully consider any assistive devices that may be necessary to help a child move, communicate, and learn most effectively. Choosing and modifying these technologies can be challenging, but the increasingly sophisticated computer and other assistive devices available are bringing individuals with disabilities into the mainstream.

One controversial form of technology is the cochlear implant device, which can restore hearing for people who are deaf. The implant bypasses the damaged part of the ear and transmits digitally processed sound directly into the cochlea; the surgery is best performed on very young children. Many members of the deaf community, however, feel that the cochlear implant device threatens the deaf way of life, which is based on American Sign Language. The debate continues on this issue, but other uses of technology are less controversial, and children with disabilities benefit from the advances being made in many areas of assistive technology.

Inclusion

As the IEP meeting came to an end, Pat and Joan, parents of third-grader Devin, said, "So the bottom line is, Devin has been diagnosed with a language impairment. And, instead of going to the school in our neighborhood, he'll be attending Page Elementary School, where they have a special class for children with learning disabilities. Because he will be receiving special education services, he'll get bus transportation from our home to the school, right?" One of the team members quickly assured them that this was the case and reminded them that Devin would be participating in many activities with one of the regular third-grade classes at Page Elementary based on his IEP goals. "Remember," said Mr. Robey, his current teacher, "he'll still have recess, specials, and lunch with the kids who are in general education." Pat and Joan sighed and signed the IEP, hoping that this was the best course of action for their struggling child. Now they had to tell him that he'd be changing schools and convince him that this was going to be a new adventure.

Although Pat and Joan reluctantly accepted the advice of the evaluation team that the best placement for Devin was in a self-contained special education classroom, other parents would push for full inclusion. In the full inclusion model, children with disabilities are educated in the general education classroom all day. In this model, children have a home base in a general education classroom, and any different instructional

Most Restrictive to Least Restrictive

Home or hospital placement

Full-time placement in a residential facility

Full-day placement in a special education school (public or private)

Full-day placement in a special education class

Full-day placement in a special education class with social integration with the general school population

Part-day general class placement and part-day special education class placement

Part-day general class placement and part-day resource or itinerant services

Full-day general class placement with instruction delivered in the regular class by a specialist

Full-day general class placement with consultation services for the teacher

FIGURE 6-4 **Continuum of Possible Placements for Children with Disabilities** *Source:* U.S. Department of Education (2002). *Twenty-fourth annual report to Congress on the implementation of the Individuals with Disabilities Education Act.* Washington, DC: Author.

approaches or services that they require are offered within its parameters. Proponents of this approach argue that placing children in as typical a setting as possible is essential for three reasons:

1. Separation is inherently stigmatizing to children with a disability.
2. Children with disabilities benefit from interaction with nondisabled peers.
3. Children placed in separate classrooms function at a lower level and with lowered expectations, and lower performance becomes a self-fulfilling prophecy (Simmons, 2004).

Others argue that not all children with disabilities benefit from full inclusion and state that the environment should be appropriate for the child. Some children really need the small group size, close monitoring, and individualized interactions that a separate classroom provides. Other children may require instruction in a special school or may need to be educated at home for a period of time. See Figure 6-4 for the continuum of possible placements meeting the criteria for the LRE.

Critics of full inclusion also consider the needs of nondisabled students, whose learning may be interrupted by the socially inappropriate or disruptive behavior of some children with disabilities. Although the issue of full versus partial inclusion continues to be debated in the professional literature and in the courts, general educators can expect to have children with disabilities in their classrooms

Assistive technology includes devices that help children with special needs, such as a child with hearing and speech impairments, to be more independent and more fully involved in classroom activities.

on a full- and part-time basis for the foreseeable future. The principle of the LRE always makes the general education classroom a desirable option or goal for the majority of children with disabilities.

Welcoming a Child with Disabilities into the General Education Classroom

The teacher's attitude is the single most important influence on the success of a child with disabilities placed in a general education classroom. Fortunately, research indicates (Wood, 2002) that teachers' attitudes about inclusion are becoming more positive. In addition to this positive attitude, however, teachers do need training and support in order to best meet the needs of the children with disabilities assigned to their classrooms. They also must learn how to work collaboratively with special educators and other specialists who will be part of the child's team.

Once assigned a child with a disability, general education teachers will need to find out as much information about the child as possible, and they may want to become educated about the specific disability. The child's IEP (see Figure 6-3 for the components of the IEP) is an important source of information. Teachers may also need to prepare typically developing children for the presence of a child with disabilities in their classroom, particularly if the child uses a wheelchair or other assistive devices. Helping the children recognize that everyone has strengths and weaknesses is an appropriate starting point to ensure that all learners will be welcomed. Through their positive attitude and warmth, teachers will model acceptance of all individuals and set a respectful tone. Some teachers find that children's literature is helpful in introducing different kinds of disabilities and opening up discussion. Others follow up this discussion with a conversation involving the child and his or her parents, as appropriate. For example, children who use a wheelchair or other assistive devices can demonstrate how the devices operate and how they help them to move and learn.

Although Georgie was more than 6 years old when he entered Ms. Williams's kindergarten class for the first time, he was very small for his age and very busy. Within minutes, he was running around the classroom, shrieking and laughing. As the days went by, it became clear that Georgie would have difficulty participating in the kindergarten curriculum. Ms. Williams began to have him sit on her lap during circle time, which calmed him down and helped him focus. When other children wanted to sit on her lap as well, Ms. Williams gently reminded them that they didn't need this assistance. Soon the other children were helping Georgie through the daily routines, and he began to sit in the circle with a friend on either side holding his hands and reminding him about the rules. Later in the year, Georgie was diagnosed with a disability and began receiving services from the special education teacher, Ms. Britt. She was delighted to see that Georgie was a fully accepted member of the kindergarten. What pleased her, too, was the empathy the other children showed for Georgie and how proud they were of his accomplishments.

Although the debate continues about the merits of full and partial inclusion, it is certain that all children benefit when children with and without disabilities attend school together. Special educators who work carefully with general educators in preparing for inclusion and offer support during its implementation can help to promote the positive attitudes essential for a successful experience. Together, the general educator and special educator will determine how to help the child understand and follow class rules and routines and to fit in socially with the other children. Depending on the nature of the disability, accommodations and modifications may need to be made in the physical environment and in academic expectations (see Figure 6-5).

The general education teacher will need to become very familiar with each child's IEP, particularly Part VIII, which spells out the accommodations children require in order to enable them to be educated with nondisabled children to the maximum extent appropriate.

- Set high but realistic expectations for each student.
- Get to know the students' strengths and needs.
- Anticipate difficulties before each lesson.
- Structure the learning environment to support all students.
- Make expectations clear.
- Use flexible grouping for differentiation.
- Hold students accountable for their learning.
- Model acceptance, respect, and patience.
- Don't just give instructions verbally; write, demonstrate, and model them.
- Give instructions in one or two steps at a time.
- Use visual aids such as posters, charts, word walls, key vocabulary, etc.
- Have incentive programs in place to encourage children to work hard and cooperate.
- Reduce the pace of instruction for those who need it.
- Use cooperative learning strategies, paired learning experiences, and buddies for support.
- Create a community of learners who care about and support each other.

FIGURE 6-5 **Strategies for Working with Children with Disabilities** *Source:* Based on Merz (2009).

The most common adaptations include providing children with shorter or different assignments, reading assignments and tests for them, and/or providing extra time for assignments and tests. Other supports include slower-paced instruction, more frequent feedback, books on tape, use of a computer for activities not allowed other children, and the ongoing support of a special education teacher, instructional assistant, and/or personal aide. A well-functioning team of skilled professionals can make all the difference in ensuring that the inclusion of children with disabilities is a positive experience for all concerned.

IMPLICATIONS FOR TEACHERS

Making Inclusion Work

Keep in mind that the instructional program in an inclusion classroom will not be exactly alike for all children but will be designed to help all children learn. Even in classrooms where no children have a diagnosed disability, you should think about differentiating your instruction for the various levels of ability and experiences that children bring with them. The suggestions for working with children with disabilities listed in Figure 6-5 are good teaching strategies for all children. Remember that the children you teach who have disabilities are more similar to their peers than different from them. And finally, recognize that fair is not necessarily equal in terms of the instructional program. Fairness means that every student gets what he or she needs.

Sustaining Parents of Children with Disabilities

Chapter 10 offers many general strategies for collaboration between schools, families, and communities. Professionals working with parents raising children with disabilites, however, have some unique challenges in establishing and maintaining positive relationships with these families. The importance of a trusting relationship between educators and parents in these situations can hardly be overstated. Families are an integral part of the educational process, from referral through evaluation, placement, and reevaluation. Parents are equal partners in decision making for their children.

Research conducted with parents of children with disabilites (Gorman, 2004) reports that families regard the following behaviors of school professionals as especially important in establishing collaborative relationships:

- Friendliness
- Optimism
- Patience
- Sincerity and honesty
- Tact
- Responsiveness
- Openness to suggestions

Other researchers (Hanson & Lynch, 2004) suggest that professionals need to have a family-centered approach in order to work successfully with children with disabilities. This includes acknowledgment of and respect for each family's strengths, culture, language, and ability to make decisions for their child, even if these decisions differ from those the professionals would choose. As mentioned earlier in the chapter, establishing a relationship with parents starts with getting to know them and allowing them to get to know you. Before attempting to communicate about sensitive topics, make a sincere attempt to establish rapport with the family through positive phone calls and general meetings.

One area that can be particularly challenging for parents of children with disabilities is getting their children to do homework. Without some good strategies and support, families may be faced with tantrums and meltdowns at homework time. Urge families to allow their children to have some vigorous play, a healthy snack, and a chance to relax before attempting homework. Make sure the family knows that you are willing to work with them as needed to get the homework done. Besides modifying homework as appropriate to the child's needs, share the suggestions in Figure 6-6 with parents so that they know that you are eager to support their efforts at home. Ongoing communication is particularly helpful concerning homework, so establish how the family would like to stay in touch. Telephone calls, e-mail, or a homework notebook that goes back and forth in the child's backpack all work to keep parent and teacher in touch.

IMPLICATIONS FOR TEACHERS

Ongoing Communication with Parents

Once you have established a positive relationship with parents, it is essential that you maintain ongoing communication through whatever means you have established. Just as you might share tips about successful homework strategies, you will also want to ask the parents what is going well at home and make certain that you are aware of their concerns. You will also want to make them aware of other ways that they can work with their child at home.

Most children with disabilities can clearly benefit from a reading routine at home. For example, you may want to suggest that parents put aside a short amount of time to read to or with their child on a regular basis. You can also suggest the value of board games for helping children build their math and reading skills. A family game night at school is a great way to introduce all families to the benefits of playing together. Remember, just as children with disabilities are much like their typically developing peers, so are their parents like all parents.

Share the following suggestions with parents to help them ease homework hassles, which can be particularly difficult for children with disabilities.

Find the Right Place and Keep It Consistent	Kitchen table, floor, desk, or any other location that works
Organize Technology	Use a word processor; allow music if it helps your child focus; use a paper with an opening so that your child sees only one math problem at a time
Stay Involved	Show your interest by being nearby; read or rephrase questions as needed; offer little rewards as small amounts of work get done
Make Adjustments	Work with your child's teacher if the work seems too easy or too hard and find out if you can scribe for your child or offer choices of assignments
Stay Connected	Develop a plan for making sure that your child brings home accurate homework assignments and all needed material by establishing a system with the teacher and a contact with a family memer of another student in the class to double-check assignments; make certain that your child's homework is returned to school in a systematic way

FIGURE 6-6   **Helping Parents Help Their Child with Homework**

COMMUNITY SUPPORT FOR CHILDREN WITH DISABILITIES

Although schools play an important role in educating children with disabilities and supporting their parents, the larger community also offers resources for these children and their families. Teachers and other professionals can be instrumental in helping to link families with needed services available in the community and also with online organizations and resources.

As Laverne and Reggie sat in the stands watching their 9-year-old daughter, Latisha, dribble the ball down the court and successfully sink a basket, they grabbed each others' hands and leaped to their feet, cheering. The idea of Latisha, diagnosed with autism during her second year of life, competing in a basketball tournament was something that they had never even considered a few years ago. Special Olympics had made it possible.

Fortunately for Latisha and her family, her special education teacher had informed them about the opportunity for Latisha to participate in Special Olympics. With 30 Olympic-like summer and winter sports available in more than 200 programs throughout the United States, Special Olympics has given individuals with intellectual disabilities the chance to be part of a team and to compete with others of similar ability. Besides this national organization, many local communities also provide sports and recreational activities geared to children with disabilities. These children may also need before- and after-school care, occasional evening babysitting, and chances to participate in community events and activities with typically developing peers.

Teachers and other school personnel who are knowledgeable about their community can help parents and children access these out-of-school opportunities. They can also help families connect with other parents raising children with the same disability in the local or online community. Finally, community agencies have a responsibility to reach out to families raising children with disabilities to alert them to the resources available for them and their children.

Helping to Find Support for Parents

As a warm and sympathetic person who genuinely cares about children with disabilities and their families, you may find yourself in an uncomfortable position when parents share personal information about family issues that are beyond the scope of their child's education. In these cases, it is particularly important for you to have resources for support to suggest to the parents. The school psychologist, social worker, or counselor can be a great help in generating a list of community services that can be accessed by families. Helping parents learn how to obtain needed help for themselves and their children will enable them to meet their ongoing needs.

REFLECTION

It is natural to be nervous about teaching children with disabilities and working with their parents if you have not had much experience or preparation for doing so. Arrange to visit some of the settings along the continuum of most to least restrictive educational settings for children with disabilities mentioned in Figure 6-4 and talk to the teachers about their experiences.

You may want to suggest resources and support to those parents who seem stressed and overburdened with the responsibilities of caring for their child with a disability. Other parents may seem to need guidance in providing the best parenting. Disability rights organizations, respite programs, parent networks, and family resource centers are found in many communities. Although you may have many ideas to share with families about parent-to-parent support groups and online communities that address issues related to parenting children with disabilities, remember that the family must decide whether or not they wish to participate in such organizations and activities. The role of the professional is to provide the information and to respect parents' decisions about how they choose to utilize it.

It is important to remember that families find support in many ways. Some will choose to participate in formal networks of parents, professionals, and helping agencies; others will rely on informal networks of extended family, friends, neighbors, and members of their spiritual congregation. Many families will utilize available support from both the formal and informal networks that they establish. Over time, their needs may change, and they will establish new connections and discontinue participation in some groups.

Darcie smiled at the group of nervous-looking women gathered in the meeting room of the family support center. When Becki, the social worker, arrived, she greeted Darcie warmly and then introduced herself to the other women. All were mothers of boys with complex social and behavioral disabilities, but Darcie was the only one who had been participating in such groups for many years. As the weeks went by, she realized that she was practically coleading the group with the social worker as she shared her experiences with her son, Abe. Although she was gratified to recognize how far she had come in meeting Abe's needs and was happy to help the others, she also realized that her need for this kind of support group had diminished, and she began to make plans to leave the group. Before she left, however, Becki invited Darcie to formally colead the group, and Darcie accepted this new challenge. ⟞Ꭷ

As Darcie's story indicates, parents raising children with disabilities often develop great expertise in working with other children with the same disability and with the parents of those children. Their input and perspectives are helpful both to other parents coping with the same issues and to professionals. So, although it is important to provide parents with resources for support, also remember that many parents can be support persons, as well.

Children with Disabilities in the Community

As the earlier vignette about Latisha and the Special Olympics basketball team indicates, children with disabilities can participate in community activities that are planned just for them. Various community organizations, spiritual groups, and family support networks often plan activities, field trips, recreational classes, dances, and other gatherings geared to children with particular disabilities. Some day and residential camps also offer summer programs that meet the needs of children with various physical, behavioral, and cognitive disabilities. All these activities help children with disabilities make friends and increase their social network.

As important as these opportunities are, however, it is also essential that children with disabilities are included in the general community activities provided for all children. Consequently, we are increasingly seeing children with disabilities participating in clubs, scout troops, before- and after-school child-care programs, sports teams, performing arts groups, and other activities alongside their typically developing peers. Building community connections foster children's sense of belonging, which helps them to develop friendships, social skills, and the support system necessary to partake fully of community life (Falvey, 2005).

Throughout their childhood years, children with disabilities will transition from one setting to another. Children diagnosed early in life transition from preschool and early intervention services to the elementary school. Later, they transition to middle and high schools, and finally they must make the transition to adult lives. For those children who have actively participated in the community, these transitions are less traumatic, because the children have other relationships and activities that continue even when their school setting changes.

Early intervention, inclusion, and the general change in society's attitude toward persons with disabilities that has occurred over the past 35 years have made a huge difference in the opportunities that children with disabilities have to participate in the mainstream life of childhood, both in and out of school. With advances in technology and increased awareness of the benefits of inclusion for all children, we expect that children with disabilities will have even greater chances of developing to their full potential within their families, schools, and communities.

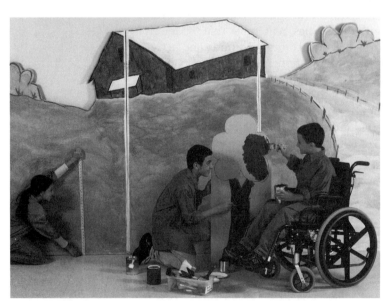

Children with disabilities participate successfully in community activities such as performing arts groups.

Summary and Review

Federal legislation over the past 35 years has had a profound effect on children with disabilities and their opportunities for education. Early identification of disabilities and developmental delays and the provision of intervention services for infants, toddlers, preschoolers, and their families have helped many young children acquire the skills and behaviors that allow them to participate in the activities typical for their age group.

One of the most important aspects of the Individuals with Disabilities Education Act (IDEA) is the principle that parent collaboration is essential in the process of determining the best educational setting for the child. Parents have expert knowledge of their child, and their perceptions of their child's strengths and needs are important to the process of evaluating and placing their child. Effective collaboration requires mutual trust and respect. Professionals must be especially sensitive in helping parents negotiate the complex process of identifying children with special needs and the legal procedures involved in making a placement. For parents, school meetings can be an alphabet soup of acronyms that they may not understand (e.g., IFSP, IEP, FAPE, LRE). The law requires a translator for those parents who do not speak English, but the sensitive teacher will find ways of making the complex process understandable for all parents.

Most children with disabilities benefit from being included with their typically developing peers for as much of the school day as possible, and their peers will also gain from their presence. Children with disabilities also profit from participation in community activities designed for all children, and teachers can play an important role in helping to connect families and children to resources and supports available in school, in the community, and online.

Suggested Activities and Questions

1. Make arrangements to visit an inclusion classroom. Prior to your visit, develop a list of questions about working with the families of children with disabilities and interview the teacher after your observation. Get together with peers who have visited other settings and compare what you have learned.

2. In an effort to understand the various perspectives on inclusion of children with disabilities in general education classrooms, arrange to interview a general education teacher, a special educator, and a parent of a child with a disability. What do you learn about the issues and challenges of this approach? What more do you need to learn?

3. In order to learn about specific disabilities, select one that you wish to learn more about and do an Internet search. Develop a one- to two-page fact sheet to share with your peers, detailing some of the characteristics of children with this disability, ways that the general educator can work successfully with such children, and supports that are available for their parents.

4. Do an Internet search for articles about inclusion from the perspective of the families of children with disabilities in the general education journals available in your chosen field. Write a brief review of one of the articles that you feel is most helpful to you.

Resources

Organizations

American Speech-Language-Hearing Association *http://www.asha.org*

Autism Society of America *http://www.autism-society.org*

Council for Exceptional Children *http://www.cec.sped.org*

National Center for Learning Disabilities *http://www.ncld.org*

Web Sites

http://www.familyvillage.wisc.edu Provides resources for persons with disabilities, their families, and professionals.

http://www.nichcy.org The U.S. Office of Special Education Programs sponsors this site, which provides information on IDEA and NCLB, as well as research-based information on effective educational practices.

http://www.ldonline.org A wide-ranging source of information about learning disabiliites and ADHD, offered as a community service of WETA, a public broadcasting system in Washington, DC.

http://www.thearc.org Offers information on mental retardation and related areas, with discussion boards and access links to related sites.

http://www.irsc.org Internet Resources for Special Children.

http://www.childfindidea.org Offers information and resources related to the earliest possible identification of young children and their families who may benefit from early intervention or education services.

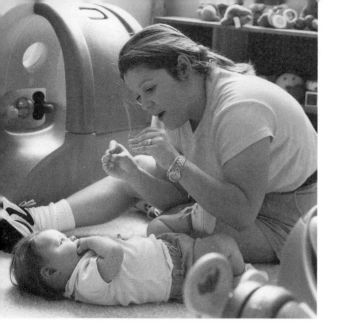

CHAPTER 7

Protecting Children While Fostering Learning

*Families, neighbors, community members, and educators together
create a web of support that contributes to the healthy and
meaningful growth of children.*

(ARCE, 1999, P. 136)

After reading this chapter, you will be able to do the following:

- Discuss the societal traditions that convey responsibilities to families, schools, and communities for protecting our young children.
- Outline the legal requirements that hold families, schools, and communities accountable for providing different aspects of education while safeguarding children.
- Describe the informal or nonacademic curriculum that society anticipates will be provided by families and communities.
- Discuss the broad areas in children's experiences where there is potential for physical, social, and emotional harm.
- Identify the agencies responsible for providing the various safeguards for children's experience and learning, and discuss the overlaps that can occur regarding these responsibilities.
- Describe how partnerships among homes, schools, and communities produce the best protection and the most meaningful experiences for children.

The central message of this book concerns building partnerships to enhance children's development and education. In the preceding chapters, you have become acquainted with the many situations and settings that affect and indeed dictate much of our educational practice. But before focusing in greater depth on curricula and educational strategies found in the social settings, we will acquaint you with the protections and safeguards that teachers, parents, and community members must keep in mind while considering children's cognitive growth and social development.

To some degree, risks are present in any child's growing years, ranging from victimization to overindulgence by family members. Therefore, because risks of one kind or another are part of learning, parents, teachers, and child-care workers must be aware of the pitfalls and hazards and guide children carefully. Our task here is to show how these potential problems affect growth and learning, and to seek ways to make a child's life space more normal, with minimal risks.

In Chapter 1, we stated that young children become what their world provides and that they learn concepts and skills to the degree that surroundings guide, entice, or motivate them. The influences and forces affecting children in the 21st century are numerous and constant, and children encounter them in all three of our fundamental social settings: family, school, and community. As you prepare for a career in teaching, child care, or community work, it is important for you to identify and understand where and how adults in each setting assume responsibility for children's learning and protection. You also need to understand that each institution can and should work cooperatively with the other two.

LEARNING REQUIRES SAFEGUARDS

All experience is educational in a general sense, of course, but some features of that experience can be harmful. Therefore, vigilance in recognizing the possible corrosive effects of experience is the duty of every parent, caregiver, community member, and teacher. A protective nature is required if a child's experience and practices are to be beneficial. Too much food, exercise, media exposure, and disruption can be harmful and must be monitored. Then, again, too little exercise, food, and entertainment can be harmful too for the young. Instincts help most of us, but careful observation and evaluation of children's habits and experience are needed as safeguards for proper development.

Much of what children learn in their formative years, however, actually comes from the experiences and interactions they have outside the home and beyond scheduled school activities. This is the unplanned or hidden curriculum that teachers and parents often overlook or don't recognize. This associated curriculum is a dominant part of any child's life, and it should be related to the formal curriculum as prepared and implemented by schools whenever possible (Apple, 1995).

Karen's popular day-care center has been tense this fall since Jason, an obese 4-year-old, joined the group in September. Jason's young parents have relinquished most of their home responsibilities, and Jason lives most of the time with his overweight grandmother.

Jason came to the center at the request of the Children's Health Services office, where it was felt that he could benefit from the program. But Jason has been a challenge from the first week, when he destroyed two projects at the center and shoved two boys into the swing set. Because of his aggressive behavior, most of the other 4-year-olds reject him and call him mean. This intensifies Jason's aggression, and he is disciplined frequently by being placed in the time-out chair.

One part- time helper at the center quit recently after Jason punched her when she tried to prevent him from flinging toys. When staff members do approach him after his bullying acts, Jason says that he didn't do anything and runs off.

Staff members have noticed that when Jason's grandmother picks him up, she negotiates almost all demands with candy bars. She often slaps his head if Jason resists her follow-up requests. But then, she says, "Oh, he'll outgrow it" when staff members request help in controlling his aggressive acts.

Karen is worried about Jason's effect on other children's behavior, on staff members' morale, and on Jason's worsening social skills. "I think we'll have to drop him at holiday time unless we get some help from Children's Health Services," she said at the end of a tiring week.

A worker from Children's Health Services did visit the next week and persuaded the staff to plot out with her ways of involving Jason's grandmother in their concerns. It is only a beginning, but they have started a conversation on the weight issue and its connection with the rejection that Jason feels. Protection for Jason and the other children has become a dominant concern for all participants at Karen's center; other program matters will take a back seat until this issue is resolved.

We all know that children's interests and stage of development determine what is meaningful for them. We also know that the stimuli and experiences that result in learning come from many forces within each child's life. And when we consider who is responsible for children's education, we have to take into account all the forces bombarding children with information and experience. For example, a definite curriculum in the home exists, although we do not label it as such. (This is considered fully in Chapter 8.) It starts at birth and continues to be dominated by primary caregivers during children's earliest years. The community begins to affect children by the time they are toddlers, and children identified with special needs may begin receiving intervention services from community agencies and school programs soon after birth.

Many families do not go to extremes, but they recognize that quality conversations, regular book-sharing sessions, and lots of hands-on experiences at home help to prepare their children for formal schooling. On the other hand, some families are unable to prepare their children adequately for school. Although low-income families and those who are linguistically and culturally different than the mainstream want their children to succeed in school just as much as their majority-culture counterparts do, they sometimes lack the necessary skills to prepare their children for typical schooling. Programs like Head Start and other publicly funded preschool and **family literacy programs** (Paratore, 2001) have been established to help minimize that problem by working with parents on routines and basic skills that help children make a more successful transition from home to formal schooling.

Communities do affect children's learning by (1) providing (or disallowing) opportunities in sports facilities, recreation arenas, libraries, museums and arts areas, plus clinics and other health facilities and by (2) supporting or challenging particular attitudes, lifestyles, and mobility patterns. The "way of doing things here" is the community ethos, and therefore, is part of children's informal curriculum. Children of color, for example, are still very young when they encounter the attitudes and mores, whether positive or negative, of the dominant racial group.

REFLECTION

Reflect on your growing-up years and the "way you did things" in your own family. For example, what was the Monday morning ritual for your family, for the school, and for the community? Now compare that to what you and what your friends do now. How have things changed for you and your classmates?

PARTNERING WITH PARENTS TO NURTURE CHILDREN AT HOME

Positive educational outcomes stem from homes that are nurturing and safe. So, parents and caregivers have a primary responsibility to take care of the basic physiological needs of their children and keep them safe. The areas of responsibility are numerous, and when we total them, we appreciate the vast responsibility and effect that the home has on the education and development of the growing child.

Nurturance spreads across large areas of human life and a large part of it is involved in sheltering children, which means teaching life skills that will protect them and prepare them for later life in the school and community. The broad areas that we discuss below are physical safety, healthy homes, stimulating homes, and socially productive homes.

Physical Safety in the Home

Most parents think of "childproofing" an area for their toddlers to avoid dangers and problems. But this same attitude must continue as parents and caregivers work with older children. Parents must consider childproofing the farm or the house lot for preschoolers and carefully size up the neighborhood for their beginning schoolers. Safety is a basic need, and all caregivers must ensure a physically safe environment. While protective measures are put in place, caregivers also need to use caution in educating the child; risk spots can be learning opportunities too. So, children must gradually learn to keep themselves safe.

Parents and caregivers need to be aware of danger zones in the home and do periodic childproofing.

Figure 7-1 is a general listing of potential dangers in and around the typical home and the source of most child injuries (Centers for Disease Control and Prevention, 2009). Although society expects parents to be the primary advocates, protectors, and supervisors of children in the family unit, most families regularly depend on others to alert them to danger—for example, to notify them when toxic substances or dangerous individuals are in the neighborhood. All caregivers must develop the habit of appraising situations and anticipating problems or dangers. They must also invest time in educating young children about keeping themselves safe.

Other home areas that require regulation, safeguards, and education for the child's physical safety are noted in Figure 7-2. Although parents and child-care workers are the primary guides in monitoring these danger zones, teachers and community agencies are necessary partners in following through with guidelines, screening, and programs.

• Heat Source	Burns from fires, stoves, appliances, and hot liquids
• Implements	Injuries from knives, scissors, tools, and appliances
• Machines	Injuries from anything with sharp, hot, or moving parts
• Electrical Power Sources	Burns and shocks from sockets, appliances, and faulty lines
• General	Wounds from glass, stairs, windows, plastic bags, and unexpected prisons (e.g., discarded refrigerators)
• Poisons	Sickness from cleaning fluids, insecticides, medicines, disinfectants, mislabeled items, solvents, and liquor

FIGURE 7-1   Hazards for the Young Child

1. Traffic Hazards	Needed are rules for streets and driveways, as well as skill in crossing and using bicycles.
2. Abduction and Sexual Assault	The number one terror for parents is abduction by strangers, but this is far less probable than molestation by neighbors, acquaintances, and family members. This concern calls for intensive and ongoing education of children on how to avoid dangerous situations and how to report suspicions. Child-care workers need to avoid the regulation "Don't talk to strangers" but enforce the regulation "Never go with strangers."
3. Water Safety	Bathtubs and wading pools need supervision when used by toddlers. Pools and swimming holes require adult supervision. Boating and use of inflatables require careful instruction.
4. Nonsexual Assaults	Teasing because of differences, tormenting verbally or physically, and discrimination cannot be tolerated. These hazards are common and require safeguards plus social education.

FIGURE 7-2 Danger Zones for Typical Families *Source:* Based on Leach (1996) and National Center for Missing and Exploited Children (2009).

Providing for Wellness in the Home

Health implies attention to complete personal well-being, not just the absence of disease or infirmities. Instruction in and attention to healthy practices are considered part of normal child rearing, and most parents readily accept responsibility for promoting the health of their young. Most health and safety concepts that parents focus on do grow out of situations associated with everyday living. Effective families attend to medical check-ups and immunizations, and they ensure that their children live and play in smoke-free buildings that are well ventilated and well lighted. They are attuned to mental health evaluations when symptoms appear. Schools and communities have the same objectives for the community's children and provide many support systems to enhance children's health. See the Community Schools model in Chapter 11 for more details.

On the other hand, marginalized families frequently suffer from chronic health problems, accidents, and inadequate nutrition. Smoke pollution, crowded buildings, poor sanitation, bad food choices, and minimal skill in managing resources engender unhealthy homes. Some problems stem from ignorance about basic home maintenance, some come from inadequate planning and substance abuse, and many come from the inability of persons to secure and follow through on available care and help from social agencies. Illness and health problems become all too often a function of income.

PHYSICAL EDUCATION Provision for physical activity, exercise, and movement skills is almost a given in most American homes. Parents readily encourage all types of informal as well as structured games and practice for their children. This can include everything from encouraging the toddler to take more steps to urging the primary-school-age child to sign up for Little League. In addition, healthy homes stress cleanliness, keeping rubbish cleared, and avoiding toxic substances. Guided activity and more concentrated practice can be found in homes where disabilities are present.

In spite of expectations, in recent decades educators and medical practitioners have registered concerns about diminishing physical activity in many children's lives. Busy family lifestyles and overly attractive media outlets are often blamed. So, ensuring adequate exposure to physical activity and arranging programs is another area that should become a common focus for homes, schools, and communities, to promote the use of playgrounds, gyms, and parks.

The number of overweight children in America has doubled in less than 20 years.

PROVIDING GOOD NUTRITION Competent families know about healthy food use and preparation, the basics of nutrition, and how to deal with allergies. They are alert to the need for regular mealtimes, good sanitation, and making mealtimes pleasant experiences. When health and nutrition standards are preserved, healthy families serve meals with food from the major food groups (see Figure 7-3) and do the following:

- Reduce the use of packaged, treated foods containing high levels of fat, salt, and additives
- Reduce the use of sweets and soft drinks
- Promote regular eating habits and provide sensible snacks

Lifelong eating habits are formed during the early years (Aronson, 2002), and families and child-care providers play an important role in introducing new foods and establishing a relaxed eating environment. Hand washing, teeth brushing, and caring for bodily functions are other expected home responsibilities. These are also practiced in child-care settings, where many young children spend a large part of the regular workweek.

OBESITY IN CHILDREN Alarming statistics in recent years point to the need for families, with help from schools and communities, to address problems of overeating and poor food choices. Obesity is recognized as a major problem for America's youth and has implications for the emotional health and the later physical health of children (Institute of Medicine, 2006). Liverman, Kraak, and Koplan (2005) state that 25% of American children ages 6 and up are now **obese** or **overweight**, and this figure has doubled in less than 20 years. These statistics concern many citizens and call for pointed action by parents, schools, and community agencies.

Paul was restacking shelves in the small rural grocery when he was approached by two huffing and excited young boys with large bags of potato chips under their arms. "Hey, mister," said the 8-year-old, "there's no big bottles of cola on the shelf over there. Mum's lettin' us pick out our lunch, and we want cola."

Paul smiled at the overweight youngsters and said, "Sure, I'll get some," and he went to the storeroom to get liter bottles of Coca-Cola. Upon returning, Paul noticed that an overweight mother has arrived with a grocery cart heavy with more soft drinks, stacks of bread, frozen dinners, and cold cuts. He handed bottles to the two boys, saying,"Is this what you needed?"

"Yep," replied the 7-year-old. "Okay, Mum, we got our lunch. Let's go!" Then the boys and their mother moved slowly along the aisle to the checkout counter.

FIGURE 7-3 Food Guide Pyramid *Source:* USDA Center for Nutrition Policy and Promotion (2009).

At that moment, Paul noticed the large sign showing healthy lunches that the Healthy Community Project volunteers had posted near the potato chip shelf. Neither potato chips nor cola is pictured on the poster. ⟶⌒

This vignette illustrates the weight problem already evidenced in these young children, and we surmise that it comes from a family that struggles to implement good nutrition practices. This problem could continue for years and will be costly not only for the family but for the community as well. Good food choices and nutrition make excellent topics for family, school, and community collaborations. Units on nutrition carry little controversy and, when initiated by a school, can easily extend to families and community agencies for support. Figure 7-3, which shows the USDA Food Guide Pyramid, provides a good starting point. And Table 7-1 provides some basic strategies for parents concerned about overweight children.

Good nutrition and a focus on obesity will continue to attract attention in our society. Our culture pays attention to weight issues; hence, many diet programs exist. But people who work with children must exercise care because children's nutrition is different than that of adults. For example, young children require more fat in their diet for proper energy and for brain development. A general rule for those monitoring a growing child's development is to aim for a steady weight while the child's height increases to correct the height/weight imbalance. "The right amount of food is the amount which keeps an individual's energy intake and expenditure balanced over time" (Leach, 1996, p. 276).

REFLECTION

Recall scenes in your family life that indicate your family's involvement in your learning to read, to make nutritionally wise decisions, and to get along with others. Have you moved away from these teachings, or do you still retain these habits?

PROVIDING FOR SEX EDUCATION   Health education is always part of a quality childcare experience, but sex education can be a controversial topic. Families have the initial responsibility for children's sex education, and at the minimum, families should focus on attention to gender differences, names for body parts, words for toileting, attention

---

TABLE 7-1   Coping with Overweight

- Increase exercise. Promoting physical activities, rather than changing food intake, is the most effective way to control a child's weight.
- Limit sedentary activities. Fascination with new media ensures low-level energy use. Encourage children to limit TV watching and Internet surfing.
- Monitor snacks. Use fruit or fat-free crackers for between-meal snacks.
- Ensure a planned meal schedule.
- Ensure that meals contain good amounts of food from all major food groups.
- Reduce the use of high-fat foods.
- Increase water intake between meals and reduce the use of soft drinks.
- Reduce fast-food use. Fast-food restaurants focus on high-fat foods. Home-cooked meals can provide a far greater balance in nutrition.
- Family adults must model good eating habits.

Source: Based on Leach (1996) and Marotz, Cross, and Rush (2005).

to privacy, and knowledge of "good touching" and "bad touching." Chrisman and Couchenour (2002) suggested that although there are different approaches to sex education among families, families who support healthy sexual development "include respectful interactions with one another, appropriate expressions of affection among family members, and a sensitive awareness of both expected behaviors and unacceptable behaviors" (p. 5).

Because sex education outside the home can be controversial, child-care centers and schools must be very clear about their procedures and maintain good communication with families on the content of their curriculum. Although some child-care programs have a planned curriculum for sexual education, most take a more informal approach. For example, when children ask questions or behave in certain ways, the adult provides accurate information and positive guidance. Child-care programs can also serve as a resource for families and support their role in children's sexual development. Readers may wish to consult Essa and Murray (1999) for a brief but helpful background on the sexual behavior of young children and how parents and teachers can cope with their concerns over identifying normal and deviant sexual play.

CHILD SEXUAL ABUSE   Most adults are deeply concerned about protecting children from any harm, but child sexual abuse is an individual and community problem that continues in our society. Child sexual abuse is any form of sexual activity (including obscene telephone or e-mail messages or taking pornographic photos) imposed on a child by an adult or another child in a position of power or influence. All of us in the helping professions must work to prevent this. And we know that appropriate sex education in homes and schools can greatly diminish the chances for sexual abuse and exploitation of children.

Perhaps the best way to prevent sexual abuse is for parents and other adults who have contact to communicate steadily and often with their children. But parents as well as other adults working with children should recognize the basic cues that signal abuse and be knowledgeable about ways to respond to abuse—including reporting it to authorities. Concerned adults should know the following information about the typical child victim:

- The victim may be a boy or a girl from any socioeconomic background.
- In most cases, the victim knows and trusts the abuser.
- The victim may be an infant, toddler, preschooler, or school-age child.
- The victim is usually reluctant to report the abuse for fear of punishment.
- The victim is rarely is abused by a stranger.

As we noted earlier, healthy education about our bodies provides a good base for discussion and education about abuse. Children must know that their bodies belong to them, and if someone wants to touch them in places that are not acceptable, they should refuse, leave, and tell someone. The best procedure for parents and child-care workers is to assure children that they will not be blamed for any abuse they sustain. Adults should take care not to frighten children when abuse is suspected, but rather to show support for the child. Also, children may be too frightened to talk about sexual molestation, but they may exhibit behavioral signs that suggest abuse. Adults should be alert to symptoms including:

- Changes in behavior, such as loss of appetite
- Fear of the dark or sleep disturbances
- Regression to more infantile behavior such as thumb sucking
- Excessive crying
- Expressing affection in ways inappropriate for a child of that age

- Interest in or precocious knowledge of sexual matters
- Fear or intense dislike of a particular person
- Fear of being left alone or in a particular place
- Change in school patterns—reduced attendance, excessive daydreaming, or inability to concentrate
- Aggressive or disruptive behavior, withdrawal, or delinquent behavior

As in other diagnoses, the above symptoms can be related to other difficulties in a child's life.

SUBSTANCE ABUSE   You will find extensive writings and resources relating to the effects of and remedies for substance abuse by youth in America. This is, of course, a significant issue, but with limited space we cannot address the problem in this book. It is important, however, that we point out the abuse of one particular class of drugs: inhalants. The abuse of inhalants is done primarily by children, and all too often it is not recognized by parents and teachers. If we are to emphasize wellness for our children, inhalant abuse in homes and schools requires our attention and action.

Inhalant Abuse.   The intentional inhaling of chemical vapors to achieve a mindaltering effect—much like intoxication—concerns many authorities. The greatest amount of abuse is by children, and the substances used are mostly inexpensive household products, such as cleaning fluids, nail polish remover, butane, hair spray, and a variety of glues. The statistics are startling: Some children as young as age 6 start this abuse, and the greatest amount of abuse is by 10- to 12-year-olds. The National Institute on Drug Abuse (2009) surveys find that over 10% of elementary school children have experimented with inhalants, and over 6% fall into the category of abusers.

The problem has social origins, and all too often it comes from peer group influences. Depression and other mental health issues are typically linked with inhalant abuse when individuals seek euphoric effects as reward or escape. But investigators inform us that frequent use of inhalants can be deadly when unconsciousness and suffocation result. Long-term physical effects include brain and nervous system damage, as well as kidney and liver damage.

Signs of Inhalant Abuse.   The following symptoms can relate to other mild and serious ailments, but if several of them are present, investigation is warranted by parents and child-care workers:

1. Stains on the body or clothing
2. Red and runny eyes
3. Slurred speech, dazed appearance
4. Balance problems
5. Nausea and loss of appetite
6. Anxiety, excitability, or depression
7. Chemical odors on the skin or clothes
8. Sores around the nose or mouth

Because young experimenters have minimal knowledge, they often can be persuaded to experiment with addictive substances that are cheap, available everywhere, and nonscheduled (unlike nicotine, alcohol, and barbiturates). Children all too often do not connect inhalant use with the harmful effects of scheduled drugs and substances, because the material is found in every family's cupboard or shop. Addictive habits are pleasurable, of course, and the child experimenter feels more confident and the senses "heightened," so it is easy to understand the appeal.

Careful and dedicated efforts by parents and teachers are required to educate children on the harmful effects of all dangerous substances and on inhalant abuse. All concerned adults, particularly parents and teachers, can develop strategies that will minimize the chances of a child developing a dangerous addiction. Some basic recommendations from the Canadian Pediatric Society (2009) for parents and teachers are the following:

1. Become educated and obtain current information about the products abused and the statistics on abuse.
2. Educate the child about the effects of inhalants and the risks of addiction.
3. Educate the child about mortality rates for abusers and the chances of death for first-time users.
4. Make it clear to the child that experiments and habits start with group experiments, challenges, and coaxing. But parents must be careful not to estrange their child by overreacting to experiments.
5. Be careful not to force the issue of peer group loyalty versus loyalty to the family.
6. Clarify and emphasize your own goals, beliefs, and concerns for the child.
7. Do not withdraw love, but be frank about the effects and consequences of habits.
8. Seek professional help (from a doctor or counselor) if problems escalate.

IMPLICATIONS FOR TEACHERS

Health and Safety

We have discussed several issues that focus on protection of children as they learn. And we have indicated in this section that although the main responsibility lies with parents, teachers and community members are involved too. Consider the following cooperative measures that you as a teacher can try as you plot out a year's activities focusing on health and safety.

1. *Health and safety concepts developed in school or day-care centers can be shared with parents. Most parents welcome additional information and ideas that they can use at home. For example, if your class is studying the food pyramid, invite parents to attend a session when the children present their food diagrams and then send the brochure home for discussion.*
2. *Parents can help present nutrition units at school. Some units will involve food displays and tasting sessions. This highlights the focus on the food pyramid and extends children's experience with new foods. Parents can supply favorite foods or different foods that other children can try. If you are fortunate enough to have a multiethnic neighborhood, the chance of obtaining ethnic foods is much greater.*
3. *When studying nutrition, many schools plan a trip to a working farm, an organic orchard, or a harvesting event. Involving parents in setting up, accompanying, and leading discussions of these experiences is a wonderful way to combine the learning at home with that at school. You are discussing the items that children have on their dinner plates.*
4. *Visits with parents to a fire station are a good way of accentuating the home safety issues that come up during firehouse demonstrations of extinguishers and flammable products common in the home. Have parents make a list of the most dangerous products, or have them show escape plans for fires at home to compare with fire drills at school.*

Parents' involvement in these school activities will engender more uniformity in the safety and health information that is promoted in the child's home and school. The discussions will bring out differences that can be analyzed for appropriateness.

Providing Organization and Management in the Home

As we discussed in Chapter 3, the United States contains numerous cultures, each of which represents a somewhat different pattern of child rearing. Across cultures, however, we find strands undergirding proficient homes and differentiating them from less effective ones. All homes are responsible for a basic organization of routines and procedures that acculturate youth.

Since the time of the classic studies by Bernstein (1972) and Baumrind (1966), social scientists have continued to recognize the several general management styles found in U.S. homes. The styles overlap and combinations exist, but most families tend toward one style or another. Baumrind (1966, 1968) defined three basic parenting styles: authoritarian, authoritative, and permissive. Family members managing according to the authoritative style are democratic and controlling but warm and receptive. These attributes contrast with the authoritarian's detached control and the noncontrolling and nondemanding approach of the permissive style. Readers may wish to review Chapter 4 for more discussion on parenting styles. In the present context, readers should know that all home management styles can be successful, but the wealth of anecdotal evidence points to the success of the authoritative mangagement style in many families.

Inadequate Home Nurturance

Some families provide minimal support for their children's education, either through lack of experience or uncertainty about how to help. Although they provide the basics of primary care—food, shelter, clothing, and safety—parents in impoverished homes may not fully appreciate the notion of educational practice, how learning comes about, or their effects on a child's life. **Parent education** (Moriarty & Fine, 2001) and family literacy programs (Paratore, 2001), when promoted by teachers and community agencies, can make a difference for minimally supportive families. When school programs are able to include marginalized family members in planning sessions and management teams, there is substantial evidence that these families' self-concept and level of achievement, as well as the motivations of their at-risk children, are raised (Maeroff, 1998).

In a few instances, parents are so remote and out of touch that the best teachers can do is to give constant support, believe in children, and hope that success unfolds in the classroom. Some hard-to-reach parents can be included through persistent communication and emphasis on their strengths and their successes with their children. Effective parent education involves seeking ways to support parents and encourage them to gradually accept responsibility for their children's overall education, and increasing parents' level of ability. It means trying out different approaches, such as listening to parents' responses, and building on what works.

REFLECTION

Think of young children you have worked with and reflect on the needs that their families support well. Also reflect on situations where support seems to be missing. Could you use this information if you were the assigned community worker or the child's teacher?

Some children need protection from themselves. Although the situation is uncommon, some children have disabilities that require special parental effort to ensure a safe home. Children with personality disorders, impaired mental functioning, and physical impairments require more supervision and monitoring by caregivers to ensure their safety.

Providing Consistent Social and Emotional Environments

Effective families develop environments that nurture children's social and emotional well-being, and the overriding dimension is one of care and interest. All of this translates into positive self-concepts for children, plus a good foundation for children's self-esteem. In addition, the child's **locus of control** is directly related to the parenting that a child receives (refer to Chapter 8). Whether children see themselves or others in control determines the way they look toward the future.

How can we encourage parents in guiding and nurturing their children and at the same time establish contacts outside the home? Workshops, information distribution, and discussions that parents attend are only part of the answer. Supporting families through family–school–community collaborations and involving parents in extended networks will do the most to enhance social and emotional health in homes. Support the community center programs, the local gardening projects, and the neighborhood summer camps that civic organizations establish in many districts. These are all wonderful extensions of our school programs. See the programs for Community Schools and Freedom Schools discussed in Chapter 11.

Parents' workplaces affect their perceptions of life and the way they interact with their children and other family members. In turn, these perceptions foster parenting styles that conform to parents' experiences and how they see themselves in the world. On the positive side, we have the effective-family investigations (Clark, 1983; Noddings, 2002), showing that the functioning family views itself as a problem-solving unit with a mutual support system and a spiritual life that is valued.

Child-rearing patterns certainly affect children's level of moral development. Children's attitudes form early, and parents and peers have a significant impact through instruction, modeling, rewards, and punishments (Bronfenbrenner, Moen, & Garbarino, 1984). Children's values tend to reflect those of their family, but other experiences also affect this development. Individuals exposed to many socializing agents (e.g., clergy members, family network friends, peers, and teachers) are more likely to achieve a higher level of moral reasoning than those exposed to only a few (Coles, 1997; Damon, 1988).

Many parents recognize the importance of providing their children with educational toys and experiences with other children.

DEVELOPING INTERACTIVE SKILLS Imparting basic wisdom about human relationships must begin in the home. It is the family's responsibility to develop children's initial interaction and negotiating skills, even though these are extended considerably in other groupings (i.e., peer group, child-care, and school situations). Teaching about sensitivity to others, the logic of cooperative action and taking turns, and the need to respect others and to share materials has a place in the social life of growing children.

Competent families demonstrate interactive skills that permit children to interact with the world with their values and moral notions in place. Modeling and discussions in the home will help, and when the family is an active part of the larger community, this extends children's social contacts so that they use more than one interactive style (Walker & Taylor, 1991). Children's growth will reflect their participation and experience.

Except in cases of severe neglect, parents and other family members automatically instill in children the basics of socialization. Children early and naturally learn to greet and respond to others, recognize acquaintances, play games with siblings, and mimic and follow one another. In addition, many parents recognize the importance of providing their children with educational toys and experiences with other children as part of the socialization process (Kieff & Casbergue, 2000). As noted in Chapter 5, more than 65% of American preschool children are in some form of child care, and this means that socialization skills are affected considerably by events and people outside the home.

NEGATIVE SOCIAL BEHAVIORS   In concert with expanded violence and aggression in the media, American schools and neighborhoods are experiencing negative social behaviors, such as hazing and bullying. **Bullying** is unprovoked verbal or physical aggression toward others and is traced to aggressive behaviors in homes and in media, to attachment problems, to child abuse, and even to genetic inheritance (Okagaki & Luster, 2005). Often linked with males in previous generations, bullying has become common among girls today (Prothrow-Stith & Spivak, 2003). Families as well as schools and communities are justly concerned about the increase in bullying, and plans are needed to modify this dangerous behavior. Socialization processes for youth need ongoing evaluation, and all families need to work with their schools to develop skills in anticipating **harassment** and bullying acts. Then they must use strategies to teach negotiation, compromise, and **conflict resolution**. Bullying is considered more fully below in the section Protecting Children in Schools.

Producing a Literacy Atmosphere

Babies are immersed in language from birth and begin to develop communication skills during the earliest months of life. Their skills expand rapidly because of planned and unplanned family interactions and experiences (Sparling, 2004). Parents echo their infant's vocalizations, name things, and direct the baby's attention to the objects, people, and events around them. Parents, other family members, and caregivers often explain to the baby what they and the baby are doing, demonstrating with real objects accompanied by language. Families often introduce babies to books during their first year: Talking about the pictures, turning the pages, and sharing the pleasure of snuggling together with a book will become the foundation for later reading development. Writing emerges in much the same way. Toddlers, given paper and crayons, will scribble, draw, and make lists in imitation of their parents' writing. All young children find it necessary to communicate with different adults and with their peers, and this develops language, which is the base for literacy.

Later literacy development in the home includes listening to, discussing, and making up stories; practicing reading and writing; and modeling more elaborate speech (Beaty, 2006; Jacobs, 2004). Research with children involved in a family literacy project (Paratore, 2001) indicates that "children who have parents who read to them, help with homework, monitor their performance in school by asking questions of them or their teacher, and who urged them to be on time and to behave courteously achieved success in school" (p. 67). Readers will find more information on home language development in Chapter 8.

IMPLICATIONS FOR TEACHERS

Partnering

In following up as a teacher, you will help children and their parents by partnering with the young families with whom you have contact. Make sure that you forward the early literacy information in your curriculum guide so that parents know what to expect. Then, when you have a chance, check to see if the following items are noticeable in the homes you visit or discuss. This is not a complete list, but it is a good indicator of home–school collaboration.

- *There is consistency in home management and family routines.*
- *Rules and codes of conduct are consistently enforced.*
- *Children have responsibilities in the home.*
- *Expectations are in keeping with children's stage of development.*
- *Family members show a sense of success and pride.*
- *Good nutrition practices are observed.*
- *Family members show warmth toward and acceptance of each other.*
- *The family has a social network of friends.*
- *Books and other intellectual stimuli are present.*
- *Health checkups are done regularly.*

Irrespective of culture, economic situation, and mode of parenting, almost all family units can be effective. All can be involved in partnering with schools and communities.

SCHOOLS NURTURE AND PROTECT CHILDREN

Schooling, whether at nursery school, a child-care center, or a public or private school, begins when the informal home curriculum starts to diminish. So, we expect that in all parts of the country, schools of all types will dominate a large amount of young children's time. The school is responsible for delivering many services to nurture children's learning and also fulfills a protective function. These programs are, on the whole, very helpful and effective. Numerous publications discuss the special programs and the character of effective schools, and we frequently see such items as "stellar student achievement," "dynamic inclusive programs," or special school values highlighted in the media. We also find that quality school programs have a proven record of collaborating with homes and communities in furthering their objectives.

Educating Children in Schools

The word *curriculum*, used constantly in most schools, serves as an organizer for all school programs. Different conceptions of curriculum do exist, and the philosophical orientation of a school's staff members will determine how and what children learn. In some schools, the curriculum will be an outline of content and skills presented in a tightly scripted sequence of lessons, whereas in others, it will be a constantly changing set of experiences that children and teachers decide to pursue in satisfying their interests. All gradations between these forms are found in schools in the United States. As a beginning professional, you should anticipate the definition of *curriculum* to be "the formal and informal content and processes used by and for learners in gaining skills, knowledge, and appreciation" (McNeil & Darby, 2005, p. 14). For now, think of preschool and primary-school teachers as responsible for extending and expanding the skills created in the home and the child-care center. The following are competencies that would normally be included in a typical teacher's objectives for a year:

1. *Language and literacy skills:*   reading, writing, speaking, and listening competencies.
2. *Math competencies:*   numeration skills, calculating, measuring, spatial relations, and problem solving.
3. *Physical and natural science competencies:*   observing phenomena, representing observations, drawing conclusions, experimenting with plant growth, animal care, and everyday chemical combinations.
4. *Social studies skills:*   those related to a variety of people in different circumstances—making friends, cooperating, respecting rules, and studying human relationships. These skills increase and intensify as children grow.
5. *Health education, nutrition, sex education, and recreation skills:*   extension of skills and habits learned in the home that address emerging concerns about obesity and inactivity.
6. *Aesthetic education:*   participation in and appreciation of music, dance, graphic arts, crafts, and other fine arts.
7. *Negotiating skills:*   procedures for planning activities, arranging teams, cooperative learning, and developing **assessments**.
8. *Attitudes and values:*   social, ethical, and moral judgment; respect for and cooperation with others.

Recognizing Student Achievement

Often we assume that standardized achievement test results are proof of what happens in schools. When related to aptitude test scores, program resources, or support, these tests may indicate statistically whether particular school programs have achieved expected gains. The federal NCLB requirements established in 2001 have intensified the urge for schools to measure learning results more vigorously. Caution is needed, however, because results from norm-referenced tests cannot be used in guiding individual children. Teachers must use observation-based diagnostic tools and inventories to guide selected children. If overall success rates are high, educators and citizens alike often assume that all is right at their school and that the programs must be appropriate. But group tests often hide areas of deficiency, and they often fail to assess the skills of specific children (Stiggins, 2005). Frequently, a test may be inappropriate for a particular subgroup in the school. For example, gifted children, although performing adequately in school, sometimes receive lower than anticipated scores on tests.

When problems appear in effective schools (e.g., if scores are well below an area norm), educators, parents, and other community citizens demand explanations. Are community problems or area demographics confounding parts of the program and the school curriculum? Are scores lower because schools are reserving time for nonacademic areas, such as developing esteem and readiness or expanding cultural backgrounds, before returning to achievement-tested basic skills? Again, standardized tests measure particular academic skill levels; they do not assess achievements in all the curriculum areas in which schools work today. Schools can, however, determine children's achievement using tools other than batteries of norm-referenced tests. In effective schools, you will find teachers using other assessment forms, such as diagnostic instruments, portfolios of children's work, or observation devices to diagnose needs for remediation or program changes. (For a thorough discussion of the relative strengths and weaknesses of the different types of assessment available to teachers, see Stiggins, 2005.)

REFLECTION

The next time you visit a classroom, take note of the way the teacher evaluates children; then consider how you were evaluated in your earlier years. Are the methods similar? What ways were most effective for you?

Fostering Values and Beliefs

With school comes the beginning of a child's community participation, and of course, there is much to wonder about and to learn about regarding the rights and wrongs of life. These experiences bring children to a point where skilled guidance and a protective attitude will help to steer the young learners.

Just as parents model values and beliefs, so do teachers and other school personnel (Coles, 1997). Getting along with others, sharing possessions, and helping others are areas that successful schools expand on after these basics (Evans, 1996) begin to be taught at home or in child-care centers. It is one thing to post rules for courtesy or sharing but another to inculcate these valuable features in an effective school. Teachers, like parents, must model these behaviors, and if the school has a record of partnering with parents, the values will expand. For example, primary-school teachers can develop units on social communication and ways of getting along with others and then share these plans with families to try at home. These communication challenges can be taken from the community life that the children know about or even from newspapers. And then students have an opportunity to analyze problems and discuss ways to work toward solutions.

Many teachers find that one of the best ways to address values is to use a story narrative. (The Appendix includes many suitable titles.) Others use film or video clips focusing on a challenging social situation, considering diverse cultures, or making positive connections with persons with special needs. Again, communities and homes are natural partners in extending this learning.

Providing for Individual Differences and Inclusion

Many American schools in the 21st century are administered under the principles of diversity, or inclusion. It has taken a generation to move to this point, but at present, all schools are required to provide educational experiences for children at all learning levels in the least restrictive environment. We discussed inclusion from a historical perspective in Chapter 2, and we presented a curriculum viewpoint in Chapter 6.

More than restructured buildings and more specialized personnel, what you will notice most in a school practicing inclusion is the attitude and demeanor toward the abilities of all children. Remember that typically developing children 50 years ago rarely encountered diversity in their classrooms. Through the 1960s, most schools were monolingual and monoracial and showed little evidence of special needs (Turnbull, Turnbull, & Wehmeyer, 2007). In effective schools today, the mix is truly comprehensive, and most educators agree that living with and learning about diversity makes all individuals more tolerant, accepting, and eager to use the skills and talents of persons they previously did not know or value.

Coping with Lobbyists and Policy Advocates

Volunteer groups often come together to be advocates and sources of support for schools. For example, a group formed to lobby for school building improvements can have a positive impact. However, some lobbying groups are formed, as shown in the following vignette, to counteract educational projects or to prevent curricula from being implemented.

⌒◡— A group of parents and two clergymen in one Texas community organized themselves as a self-appointed school review committee. When they reviewed the reproduction-of-creatures unit for the second-grade classes, the books and charts used became a highly charged topic. The group's complaints about the material became intense, and the committee's visits to the school caused confrontations and wild charges. One teacher resigned because of accusations, and negative publicity dragged on for weeks before the administration chose to abandon the unit. Even though the unit had been developed in previous years and had been accepted by the health education committee, a militant anti-sex-education group spread dissension and won their case in this community. Community–school working relations were set back considerably for several years. —◡⌒

Censorship of books is still a common occurrence in school districts throughout the United States (American Library Association, 2008). Too often, schools acquiesce to pressure from lobbying groups to abandon certain publications and other resources. When this happens, the scope and purpose of programs can suffer. All challenges are handled more effectively when schools have well-planned school objectives and an educational process that involves homes and communities in explaining the curriculum.

Here is where you can bring the power of your home and community partners to bear on a particular challenge. Anticipate pressure group action by developing an advisory committee of parents and representatives from your local churches and social groups. Prepare the group well by explaining the content of your projects and units. Invite them to help select materials. Talk about controversial topics and how to inform the committee about new literature or exhibits. Then if a challenge comes, you have a team working with you to interpret and help inform people who do not accept some features of your projects and units.

Protecting Children in Schools

CONFRONTING BIAS AND PREJUDICE   Our society still struggles to shed the problems associated with racism, ethnocentrism, elitism, sexism, homophobia, and discrimination against certain disabilities; regrettably, these qualities still affect some schools. When hints of bias and careless use of ethnocentric language appear in ethnically integrated schools, the problem has immediacy. When demeaning language and actions surface, minority persons are affronted, their aspirations suffer, and all children's growth in social competence is diminished (Sadker & Sadker, 2005). For all persons involved, bias is costly.

You will have a responsibility to confront bias and help young children move beyond it. Using multicultural materials in as many school projects as possible is a good start. Also, use and involve your parent group in presenting these materials. Planning regular units on diverse cultures and observing a variety of ethnic and religious holidays point students in positive directions. The materials by deRamirez (2006) and Banks and McGee-Banks (2005) contain excellent sources for strategies addressing this topic.

PROTECTING CHILDREN FROM BULLYING   Bullying behavior appears to be increasing in U.S. schools and neighborhoods, and this had led to serious study of its occurrences and implications. This cruel behavior used to be dismissed as "playground squabbling" or normal growing-up dander, but recent research (Rodkin & Hodges, 2003) shows long-term harmful effects on victims as well as perpetrators. The following vignette presents an episode from the 1950s.

Schoolyard bullying has long-term harmful effects on perpetrators as well as victims.

⌒ *A group of third graders is gathered at the corner of the school yard at recess time. Jamie, a robust and popular child, is surrounded by a group of friends, and all are joking and "horsing around." Ralphie, a small child with learning disabilities, stands on the sidelines, watching the others play jump rope.*

"Hey, Ralphie, want some gum? Look, I got some gum you can have." Jamie holds up a stick of gum toward Ralphie while pushing a wad of gum around in his mouth. Suddenly Ralphie and Jamie have the attention of all the children in the yard. Ralphie looks anxiously at Jamie for a moment but then begins to move forward. "Come on, Ralphie, you can have some, but you gotta come and get it! Right here! Come on! Come on! Jamie points to a spot just in front of him. Ralphie again moves forward as Jamie urges him to come closer and closer until both boys are almost nose to nose. Then Jamie suddenly pulls the wad of gum from his mouth and sticks it on Ralphie's nose. Most of the children on the playground burst out laughing as Ralphie runs back to his corner. ⌒

Christie (2005) informs us that 50% of schoolchildren are bullied at some point in their lives, and at least one-half of those children are victimized on a regular basis. This adds up to a huge number of children who, like Ralphie in the above vignette, lead anxious and hurtful lives every day. Bullying can occur anywhere, but most frequently it happens on school buses, on playgrounds, in school restrooms, in stairwells, and during after-school activities. Schools and communities have the resources to combat this behavior if responsible adults observe, investigate, and plan solutions. Changes do take time because interveners will need to reorient life patterns and habits of young people.

Defining Bullying. Bullying is present when a more powerful person hurts, frightens, or intimidates a weaker person on a continual and deliberate basis. A bully's actions are the unprovoked and repeated aggressive actions that cause fear, distress or harm to a victim. Bullying is not retaliatory anger; it is about contempt for someone considered inferior, as the above vignette demonstrates. Additionally, bullying often occurs in the presence of bystanders who can stimulate or encourage the assault or dampen the aggression when someone takes a stand against it. Figure 7-4 outlines the types of bullying.

Bullies come in all sizes and shapes: small or large, male or female, attractive or unattractive, popular or isolated, skillful or clumsy. Their common quality is that they all take pleasure in putting down and harassing their self-defined victims. Environmental factors, such as limited friendships, abusive homes, negative role models, or attachment problems, can contribute to bullying behaviors, and violent media effects seem to enhance these behaviors. Bullying is violence, and the behaviors often lead to more violence as the bully matures. Thus, intervention and redirection should be the goals of schools and communities when this problem comes to light.

Victims and Bystanders. Victims are frequently not assertive, but quiet, withdrawn, or timid children. They may have a disability or a minority background. The social skills of victims are often lacking, and they are easily upset or anxious about schoolwork or schedules. Of course, bullying extends the difficulties of a targeted child and

Physical Bullying

- Hitting, kicking, shoving, tripping

- Ruining or hiding someone's possessions

- Badgering or forcing a victim to do something he or she does not like or want to do

Verbal Bullying

- Teasing, taunting, or goading

- Insulting, making deriding remarks, or asking demeaning questions

- Expressing ethnic or racist slurs

Social or Relational Bullying

- Persuading others to exclude someone

- Manufacturing rumors or telling lies about someone

- Refusing to talk to or socialize with someone

- Coercing someone to do things he or she does not want to do

FIGURE 7-4 Types of Bullying *Source:* Based on Cole, Cornell, and Sheras (2006) and Rigby (2008).

may even bring about mental health issues. Bystanders are those who observe and at times participate in bullying. Rigby (2008) notes that bystanders are always for or against the victim, but they rarely take up the victim's cause.

All responsible educators and child-care workers must root out bullying behavior and work to redirect the lives of all concerned. Of course, all responsible adults should intervene when there is an obvious victim, but careful work needs to be done to defuse the behavior and to work toward a safer and happier school campus. This three-way dynamic in dealing with bullying behavior reveals situations, opportunities, and insights about methods that adults can use to reeducate perpetrators. Working with the bystanders is a good first step. Because of their sideline status, they can look more objectively at the problem and the reasons for it. And their participation will be valuable as a new regimen is instituted.

IMPLICATIONS FOR TEACHERS

Investigating a Bullying Problem

One way to start solving a bullying problem is to enlist the help of parents, other educators, and community helpers. Start with carefully selected parents, school specialists, or clergy members to interview children about the situations at their school. Questions could be:

- *Are you ever teased at school?*
- *Do you know if others are teased?*
- *How do you feel when you see others hurt or frustrated by teasing?*
- *Do you tell your teacher or anyone else about the teasing?*

The information gathered can be the basis of an intervention program. Getting a picture of the school program with its bullying scars is a base for deciding how to change it.

PROTECTING CHILDREN FROM DANGEROUS ADULTS Community violence can spill over into schools. Too often, weapons are carried to school by children who seek to protect themselves, prey on others, or maintain status in a peer group (Garbarino, 1999; Jenkins & Bell, 1997). In addition, although some schools are considered safe havens from distressful conditions in a neighborhood, too often these protected spaces are savaged by intrusions, bullets, and intimidation by gangs. Any talk about the use of weapons has an unsettling effect on the school climate, of course, but in the hands of secure teachers, the trauma resulting from witnessing violence can become a part of the school curriculum. One teacher, trying to resolve fears in a Baltimore neighborhood experiencing periodic violence, used story writing and sharing to deal with children's anxieties and to help the children understand precautions and safety measures.

In addition to hostile and aggressive outside groups, school personnel must be aware of predatory adults who sometimes focus on schools. Without causing alarm, educators must teach children the basics about being alert to possible dangers, how to move to safe places when they are concerned, and how to report suspicious adult behavior. All states now have Web sites that identify sex offenders living in a particular area. Although this content represents only a part of the predatory population, it can be an incentive to stimulate parent helpers to monitor the site and outline the defensive behaviors that young children need to know.

PROTECTING CHILDREN FROM HOME NEGLECT In addition to tending to children's educational needs, school personnel must be aware of children who may be mistreated by their families or other adults and step in to assist them. Many factors contribute to the maltreatment of children, and a discussion of this complex topic is beyond the scope of this book. It is essential, however, that educators and other community workers understand the types of abuse and neglect and recognize the signs and symptoms of children who may be mistreated (Aronson, 2002). They must also clearly understand the procedures for reporting their suspicions. Although the Child Abuse Prevention and Treatment Act of 1974 requires all states to establish some mandatory reporting of suspected abuse or neglect, the agencies involved, definitions of abuse, and reporting procedures vary from state to state. School professionals are obligated to know the regulations in their state. Figure 7-5 offers a summary of commonly accepted definitions, symptoms, and signs of child maltreatment, which include intentional physical injury, neglect, sexual molestation, and emotional abuse. The Resources section at the end of this chapter provides additional sources of information.

REFLECTION

This may be a good time to think back to your own primary-school years and reflect on how people at your school protected you. Can you identify some of their actions? Do you think those practices exist in the schools you see today?

By expanding and building on the protective strategies started in the home, partnerships between school and home assure protection for children and continuity of their learning. Whenever one enhances the objectives of the other, the result is enriched experience for children.

Maltreatment	Definition	Signs and Symptoms
Physical abuse	An intentional act affecting a child that produces tangible physical harm and can include shaking, beating, striking, or burning	Suspect physical abuse when a child has bruises, welts, burns, cuts, tears, scrapes or head injuries. The child may have repeated, unexplained injuries, complain of pain, report harsh treatment, show fear of adults, wear clothes to hide injuries, be frequently late or absent, or display withdrawn, anxious behavior or act out, especially if either is a change from usual behavior.
Emotional abuse	Psychologically damaging acts, such as verbal abuse, rejection, ignoring, terrorizing, isolating, or corrupting by parent or caregiver	Suspect emotional abuse when a child is generally unhappy, seldom smiles or laughs, is aggressive or disruptive or unusually shy and withdrawn, reacts without emotion to unpleasant situations, displays behaviors that are unusually adult or childish, exhibits delayed growth or delayed emotional and intellectual development, has low self-esteem, receives belittling or degrading comments from parents or guardians, or fears adults.
Sexual abuse	Any sexual act, such as rape, incest, fondling of the genitals, exhibitionism, or voyeurism, performed with a child by an adult who exerts control over the victim	Suspect sexual abuse when a child has physical indicators, such as difficulty walking or sitting; complaints of pain, itching, or swelling of genitals; pain when urinating; vaginal discharge; bruises or bleeding in external genitalia, vagina, anal areas, mouth, or throat. The child may also have behavioral indicators, such as unwillingness to have clothes changed or assistance with toileting, holding self, unwilling to participate in physical activities, withdrawn or infantile behaviors, unusual interest in or knowledge of sexual matters, or extremely aggressive or disruptive behavior.
Physical and emotional neglect	The failure to provide a child with the common necessities of food, shelter, a safe environment, education, and health care	Suspect when a child is unwashed and wears dirty clothes inadequate for the weather, is left unattended at a young age or left in the care of other children, lacks dental and medical care, is chronically absent, complains of hunger or rummages for food, or lacks safe housing.

FIGURE 7-5   Definitions, Signs, and Symptoms of Child Maltreatment   *Source:* Adapted from Aronson (2002), pp. 172–174.

IMPLICATIONS FOR TEACHERS

Safeguards

We do have measures to assess the effectiveness of particular school programs, and school effectiveness researchers have identified several characteristics that are observed consistently in schools demonstrating good achievement gains (Cruickshank, Jenkins, & Metcalf, 2002; Good & Brophy, 2007). The following are some questions that you can use when checking out the effectiveness of a particular school. The questions will reveal much about a school's adequacy and chances for success.

- *Are facilities adequate and is space used efficiently?*
- *Is the facility safe? Are discrimination and bullying absent?*
- *Are collaborations between home and school evident?*
- *Are teaching techniques varied for different children?*
- *Is time off task kept to a minimum?*
- *Is a pleasant climate for learning noticeable?*
- *Do teachers praise and encourage learners?*
- *Do all children succeed at something?*

The quality future school will emerge from secure connections among homes, schools, and communities as they become complementary and supplement all school objectives. Educational change and enhancement affect more than academic achievement, however. Also linked to school success are changes in health care, improved living conditions, improved interethnic relations, and diminished crime in neighborhoods. Liston and Zeichner (1996) remind us that "what goes on inside schools is greatly influenced by what occurs outside of schools" (p. xi).

COMMUNITY RESPONSIBILITY

Communities, large and small, are made up of individuals and what those people bring to their surroundings. The combination of persons and activities produces a community in which the ventures, endeavors, projects, and programs form a unique social setting. All communities have multiple facets, and the impact of different agencies and enterprises is pervasive in the lives of children. Although it is true that the youngest children have limited contacts beyond their home or child-care situation, primary-school children will experience, at some level, almost as much community conditioning, pressure, and influence as do adults.

The community as an institution is responsible for supporting its citizens, families, and schools and for furnishing a "curriculum" of experiences and opportunities. No laws or mandates require this involvement, and few would consider the particular services of a community to be features of a curriculum. In formal and informal ways, though, each community provides a way of life, bits of knowledge, chances for skill development, values and moral education, aesthetic validations, and an array of opportunities that will affect children's perceptions and promote particular attitudes.

Creating Cognitive Impact

Each community supplies news and information through publishing, television, radio, and **signage** that provide children with specific bits of knowledge. Religious centers have definite goals for developing understanding and practice. Recreation areas promote physical skills, exercise, and knowledge about sports and other activities. Libraries support literacy for even the youngest members of the community. Parks, zoos, museums, and theaters all provide information and aesthetic appreciation that benefit

	Home	School	Community
Age 1	Exploring nearby space		
Age 2	Rote counting, comparing objects for size		Sensing larger spaces
Age 3	Contrasting sizes More counting	Nursery rhymes of counting	Rote counting experiences
Age 4	Seriation, placing objects in sequence, acquiring number sense Grasp of time	Distinguishing geometric shapes Determining more and less, basics of addition and subtraction	Applying number sense to the larger world Counting games
Age 5	Ordering objects, grasp of money Sense of measurement in cooking and home projects	Making one-to-one correspondences Grasp of rational numbers Starting to understand time	Noting sizes of larger and smaller; noting geometric shapes
Age 6	Using knowledge of time; using the concept of number in the home to calculate	Addition algorithm, subtraction algorithm Measurement study Geometric study	Applying knowledge of money for purchases
Age 7	Application of measurement to projects and hobbies Estimating quantities, distances, etc.	Continuing practice of number facts Estimation problems	Figuring how far to throw a ball Sensing how long it takes to walk to friends' homes
Age 8		Multiplication algorithm	Using math concepts to solve problems in play, etc.

FIGURE 7-6   **Children's Math Development Interrelated in Three Social Settings**   *Source:* Adapted from Seefeldt and Barbour (1998).

the growing child. Community-service offices all have informational outlets to promote health, safety, and good parenting practices. These social organizations, religious institutions, and educational outlets interrelate with and expand the home and school curricula to promote skills, knowledge, and attitudes toward various subjects. Figure 7-6 illustrates how social settings interrelate to develop and reinforce one cognitive area—mathematic ability.

Recognizing Affective Impact

In the affective domain, communities and neighborhoods provide children with a sense of security, well-being, and identity. The kinds of protective services available and the attitudes and values modeled by citizens and leaders send children clear messages about community values and concerns. For example, citizens can demonstrate and support fair play in games and sports. By playing fairly and rewarding all players, rather than emphasizing and rewarding only winners, sports directors and spectators communicate pride in striving and participating instead of in winning at any cost.

Communities provide special events, and parents communicate pride in participating rather than winning.

Community services and functions do not, of course, fall easily into categories of formal and informal learning, but in differing ways they do show children the range of human responses—from sensitive and reasonable to greedy and malicious. Lessons emerge as children sense their community at work and at play, when celebrating, and when struggling economically and politically or with natural disasters.

Communities and Nurturance

In many communities, pride in and care for schools are evident to visitors and newcomers. A groundswell of support for promoting education does not just happen, however; such support indicates that committees, groups, and leaders have been active in establishing goals and lobbying for better conditions. We find that the electorate and the community decision makers are almost always motivated to strive hard to support increased educational opportunities—particularly for young children.

Regrettably, some communities do not facilitate and nurture children's education. Some references in this book portray conditions of despair and social crisis in too many U.S. communities (Coles, 2006; Garbarino, Dubrow, Kostelny, & Pardo, 1998). Extensive social remediation is needed in all those locations. The community context affects and controls family and school settings to a large extent, and when economic, social, and political crises arise, community problems always detract from school programs and other educational objectives. Controversy often minimizes nurturing, and too often it prevents the community from making changes that have been initiated in schools and the community at large.

Effective Communities

Because communities are made up of sets of subsystems, research on competent communities is problematic. It is difficult to determine cause-and-effect relationships within a community, especially those that affect children. The following factors, however, are closely related to community effectiveness.

HEALTH SERVICES   Children must remain healthy to develop properly, yet access to a health care system depends on the community in which children live and on the economic status of the family. It is well documented that poor families have greater health problems, including chronic health conditions, more infectious diseases, a higher incidence of low-birth-weight babies, and higher infant mortality rates (Children's Defense Fund, 2000).

The effective community will have comprehensive care systems that strive to serve citizens impartially. Many communities have both neighborhood health centers (such as those funded through the Office of Economic Opportunity) and a private health care system. By uniting family-care offices in one setting, officials diminish the expense, frustration, and transportation problems that poor families experience when seeking services.

In addition to offering health care, all medical facilities have an educational function. Health services also fulfill the important function of distributing materials about disease prevention and offering counseling by personnel who are positively oriented to their clients.

WELFARE AND SOCIAL SERVICES   Employment offices, legal aid offices, and counseling centers cut across socioeconomic levels and are needed to address concerns for most U.S. communities. Regrettably, welfare services in the United States have always carried a stigma, and only in recent years have programs such as Head Start led to changed attitudes on the part of middle-class citizens.

RELIGIOUS INSTITUTIONS   Churches, synagogues, and mosques are central facets of many communities. Although less so in recent decades, religious associations have dominated large portions of community life in the United States. In fact, they represented the largest part of out-of-home activity for pre-20th-century Americans.

National surveys reveal a drop in religious participation in recent years (Lindner, 2008), but still, more individuals belong to religious groups than to any other voluntary grouping. Religious institutions continue to influence many segments of U.S. communities, promoting ethnic as well as theological identity. With outreach programs and social action objectives, many places of worship now provide social, cultural, and other support for their communities, as well as spiritual nurturance for their membership groups. Food pantries, soup kitchens, and drug abuse and family counseling services are all operated by or through religious organizations in thousands of communities. Many care programs are not-for-profit arrangements developed and maintained by local religious organizations, even in the smallest communities. This service has received more attention since the Bush administration's proposals of 2002 and 2004 for **faith-based** group funding for community welfare. It is controversial in political as well as educational circles.

CIVIC SERVICES   All communities require fire departments, sanitation programs, and public safety offices. Supported by tax revenues, these services provide for the general stability and safety of the community.

Community services provide an educational function for children. What goes on in those departments, how the jobs are done, and the problems workers encounter are of interest to all children. Most offices publish materials and have personnel who head information programs for schools and other local groups. Elementary school children, when directed by their teachers, learn to understand the meaning of organized communities and the interdependence of community residents. They learn how community services affect their lives and perform for them as individuals.

BUSINESSES   Most communities include private commercial enterprises linked to daily life in those areas, such as the filling stations, newsstands, and grocery stores found in nonindustrialized suburbs. Other communities contain factories, wharves and piers, and large merchandise outlets, plus financial and information-processing establishments that employ residents and give flavor to a community. As children become acquainted with local businesses, they become knowledgeable about the economics of their town—where people work, what they produce, and where products go. They also learn of the need for many specialties as they become attuned to the world of work and the effects each institution has on community life and interaction.

In effective communities, commercial establishments cooperate with schools and families. Such cooperation demonstrates commitment to the interdependence of community settings and the need for mutual support. (Refer to Chapters 10 and 11 for discussions of techniques and models for such collaboration.)

MEDIA OUTLETS   With the explosion and transmission of knowledge in the information age, communities are engulfed by media of all kinds. From standard newspapers to television programs to the Internet, visual and aural messages descend on citizens across the United States at increasing levels. Whether in an isolated prairie town or an urban neighborhood, the impact of the media is all-encompassing.

Media affect all other institutions of a community. The type, quality, and amount of information an area receives produce responses from individuals, families, and schools. Effects can be positive or negative, but they are rarely neutral. Because most media are protected under First Amendment provisions, media outlets are largely self-policing, and public acceptance of the products determines the boundaries for individual distributors. Appropriateness of media products is a significant issue when we consider children's education. Many publications and recordings are adult oriented in topic, format, and relevance, but children are nonetheless exposed to large quantities of them. The V-chip for television, and Internet filters such as Net Nanny® and CYBERsitter®, block only a fraction of adult material. But criticizing media products that fall outside a community's standard invites thoughts of censorship, and problems always surface when that issue is raised. It is, therefore, desirable for communities, through public forums, to reach a consensus on acceptable quality and then to work for that standard through educational programs and lobbying efforts when required.

SPECIAL-INTEREST GROUPS In the late 20th century, the United States witnessed the formation of numerous special-interest groups, from the small group of citizens seeking to pressure schools to include or exclude something to the highly organized lobbying groups seeking changes in legislation. As we noted in Chapter 1, a special-interest group has a particular cause and stance (e.g., antinuclear energy, save the whales, antipornography, pro-choice or pro-life [regarding abortion]). Many groups disappear after accomplishing their mission; others become entrenched because their cause is ongoing.

Special-interest groups are grassroots associations that are very American in concept. Taking as their basis the constitutional amendment protecting association and assembly, citizens come together to work for or against some cause. In this way, altruistic groups have formed to gain privileges for disenfranchised persons (e.g., achieving passage of an education bill for persons with disabilities in the 1970s) or to highlight a public problem (such as cleaning up the Nashua River in Groton, Massachusetts; Cherry, 1982). Other groups form to oppose regulations or practices. A nonsmoking lobby is one example; a group censoring local library materials is another.

How do communities respond to special-interest groups? If partnerships are in good working order, we normally find that special-interest-group pressure can be accommodated and processed in a healthy fashion. All too often this is not the case, and part of the community bows to the pressure of the campaigning group. For example, one Pennsylvania library contained several volumes on cults and pagan rituals. When a member of a PTA subgroup saw these volumes, the group started a search through the library to identify and condemn all volumes containing information about the occult—even children's fantasy books featuring ghosts and goblins. Having no agency and little organization to counter the arguments of the group, library staff quickly acquiesced to the demands and removed all offending materials. This established a dangerous precedent for handling library materials in this community.

IMPLICATIONS FOR TEACHERS

Community Involvement

Our governing agencies assume that all professionals will do the best job of protecting and educating the nation's children. This means that you, as a developing professional, have an obligation to find the best opportunities for the children you encounter. In order to do this, you must be knowledgeable about the authority and responsibility for children's lives and know how to intervene if necessary.

So, think of yourself as filling a new niche in the home–school–community matrix and speculate about how it will unfold when you teach. As you approach the classroom, think of yourself as a type of "peace corps" worker who will analyze the classroom situation and then figure out how to best serve and protect the population of young people in front of you.

Ask yourself, "What should be happening for these children in language arts develop-ment, in science and math understanding, and in social and physical development?"

- *Speculate on how other responsible adults can be helpful as you produce a curriculum.*
- *Confer with home caregivers about reasonable objectives for the children and steps to take in meeting them.*
- *Consider how you can use community resources to enhance or illuminate a subject area or project. See the next paragraph for an example.*

The following scenario serves as an example of one simple collaboration on a social sci-ence project: Your chamber of commerce has invited your class to visit the local water treat-ment plant to learn about its operation and its effect on the community. Your small group of parent helpers will help plan the trip and study the site as a place for learning. After the visit, you can use in-class cooperative learning activities as well as coaching skills and re-source persons to help students list the particular benefits of the treatment plant for their city. Finally, you can guide children to use their literacy skills in describing the treatment plant in reports, drawings, and letters for their parents, other students, and community members who have worked with them.

Now try to identify one other community resource that will lend itself to this type of partnership work. How will community adults participate, and how will the children's care-givers be involved in processing the learning and follow-up work?

Social Networks

The informal, everyday contacts of relatives, neighbors, friends, and colleagues pro-duce social networks for adults and children in almost all neighborhoods. These group-ings, which can cross gender, age, and SES lines, provide enormous support for individuals. Werner (1999) showed in *Through the Eyes of Innocents* the strong impact of healthy behavior in a community on children caught up in war.

POSITIVE ADULT GROUPS   Social science research shows the importance of friends and relatives in providing psychological sup-port Werner and Smith (1992) and Cochran and Davila (1992) indicated that support groups are especially important for at-risk families when kin and col-leagues provide emotional support for child rearing, confronting adversity, or even integration into the community—the targeted family benefits. Healthier adult groups mean healthier environments for children. Information about social serv-ices, work opportunities, or new resources in a community is often delivered through the social networks of adults, and this benefits children.

CHILDREN'S PEER GROUPS   As we noted in Chapter 1, peer groups exert a strong influence in any community. **Peer groups**

Peer groups provide early experiences in social interaction and cooperation.

are social in nature and inculcate a curriculum of experience in those involved. Constructively, peer groups provide children's all-important coming-of-age experiences, where children encounter folklore and rituals, experience a sense of belonging, and begin to develop competitive skills (Ladd & Pettit, 2002). Peer groups also provide early experience in social interaction and cooperation. Destructively, peer groups may evolve into alienated gangs that commit acts of violence and hostility.

    Victoria and her mother walked next door to welcome to their southern California community the new family that had just arrived from Hawaii. The two new girls, Terry and Adrianne, came the next day to Victoria's yard to play. They taught Victoria a new version of hopscotch. But while the girls were playing, the neighborhood gang appeared and told Terry and Adrianne that they had to leave because "we don't play with Chinese kids." Victoria's mother, witnessing the scene, hurried out to the yard and asked the new neighbors to stay. "All children are welcome in this yard as long as you play well together. Now, I saw the fun you two had showing Victoria that new hopscotch. Perhaps you'll teach these other children how to play it, too?" The mother tended her shrubs and observed for a while, but as all the children got involved in play, she left them to negotiate on their own.

Victoria's mother warded off hostility toward the new children in the neighborhood by suggesting and guiding a constructive experience. Both teachers in schools and family members have a responsibility to monitor and guide children's peer interactions when conflict seems imminent.

REFLECTION

Consider children's interactions you have witnessed recently or observe a small group of children at play in your neighborhood. Now reflect on the social and educational value of that group's activities. Can you tie any of their planning, compromising, or maneuvering into the greater educational picture for development of the children's future skills?

Entertainment Facilities and Media

The entertainment industry is a part of the greater community and is probably the most pervasive force in children's lives today (Strasburger & Wilson, 2002). From earliest times, societies have recognized a need for activities that lift spirits and entertain, and a thriving community sanctions and supports entertainment for its citizens.

Communities have planned occasions and established recreational facilities that provide for entertainment—sports areas, natural areas, and parks. Parades, community fairs, and other celebrations are also typical. But in addition to the public venues, private industries have grown up in most communities for the purpose of delivering entertainment on command, day or night. The following are typical entertainment formats that children and young people now possess or have ready access to from family members:

- Radios, CD players, cell phones, play stations, iPods
- Cable and broadcast television
- Theaters, cinemas, malls, coffeehouses, arcades, and theme parks
- VCRs and DVD players
- Computer games and Internet linkages

Although many of the entertainment industry's offerings are consonant with typical community endeavors, the time and expense allotted to them can intrude on families' and children's schedules, personal objectives, creativity, schoolwork, and socializing (Gunter, Harrison, & Wykes, 2003; Singer & Singer, 2007). The challenge facing parents and schools is that entertainment may be overutilized in relation to other aspects of the home and school curriculum.

When is the community responsible for expanding or limiting its entertainment opportunities? Communities have legal responsibility to protect children from inappropriate situations, but they assume little responsibility for children's overexposure to sanctioned entertainment forms (Van Evra, 2004). The American Academy of Pediatrics officially recommended in 1999 that children under age 2 watch no television at all, but responsibility in guiding television viewing for children of all ages rests primarily with families and primary caregivers; some cannot manage this well. Technology, including filters for Internet surfing and the V-chip for TV programs, has been developed to help parents control what comes into and out of the home, and other devices can actually control the time when the television is on and off.

Some schools, communities, and families have successfully run programs in which children and their parents pledge to watch no television for a week. At the end of the week, sessions are planned to help the participants discuss the experience. The nonprofit organization TV-Turnoff Network provides an array of information and resources to encourage children and adults to watch less television in order to promote healthier lives and communities. See the Resources section at the end of this chapter for further information.

LINKING RESPONSIBILITIES

All communities have established schools within their boundaries to develop children's cognitive and affective skills. In recent years, however, increasingly heavy burdens have been placed on schools. In addition to normal monitoring activities, many schools provide two meals per day and pair with nonprofit (or for-profit) organizations for before- and after-school care. Schools are assuming a larger part of the parenting role, and this increase requires good communication, more understanding, and cooperation from families if the overload taking place in some schools is to be successfully managed.

Some skills and attitudes are best enhanced through projects and activities under community sponsorship. We as educators must be alert for opportunities for collaboration between community agencies and schools that promote children's education and welfare. The following vignette illustrates this point:

Life in the small coastal community was quiet, but Josh and his friends were restless after a month of summer vacation. Returning from the ball field one day, they pedaled their bikes toward home, throwing rubbish from their lunches at poles and fences. They seemed intent on marring their community's quiet roadside beauty. At one lovely spot near the ocean, however, they noticed a painter setting up his easel and stopped to watch. The painter paused, then asked the boys if they would help him clean up debris near the shoreline so that he could paint without distractions. The boys did, and then stayed to watch the man work. The boys became fascinated with the artist's rendering, and the painter became aware of how little experience these youngsters had in developing a sense of their surroundings.

A few days later, the artist and a colleague invited Josh, his friends, and their parents to their studio to talk about their art and its relationship to the world around them. This worked so well that the artists, with the help of a small group of parents, persuaded town officials to budget space and funds to open a modest gallery in the community. Classes in painting and art appreciation are now offered in the gallery, and the artists are helping teachers at the local elementary school integrate art into their curriculum.

No single agency—home, school, or community—felt a need or responsibility for developing the aesthetic senses of Josh and his friends, but an interested citizen was able to establish a link with this responsibility and provide a needed aspect of curriculum for the youth in that community.

REFLECTION

In the school you are visiting, ask the classroom teacher who decides what is to be taught to the children this week and how that content will be handled. Is it the teacher herself, a team, the administration, or someone else? Did your classmates find similar decision makers in their schools?

Summary and Review

It is important to understand who has overall responsibility of speaking and acting for children in our society. The three social settings have a shared responsibility for making certain that optimal conditions and arrangements are in place for protecting children and enhancing educational opportunities. A curriculum of experience accrues to every child, and this differs depending on the circumstances in the three social settings. Each child's curriculum is divided into two interactive parts: formal, or academic, and informal, or hidden. Tradition and law impose requirements on homes, schools, and communities to do their share in presenting the curriculum, but overlap, disagreements, and redundancies are not unusual as children move from one setting to another. Education is most productive when strong cooperation and alliances exist among homes, schools, and communities.

The objective observer can see the unique and vital position of the school in any cooperative endeavor. Parents and communities, of course, have a vested interest in the education of their children. Public schools are delegated the responsibility of accepting all entrants, organizing a curriculum, executing that curriculum, and generally steering children through the educational process. Because educators are trained professionals with daily contact with children, they are in a unique position to monitor them for bad health practices, undesirable social behaviors, and possible maltreatment. Educators can also identify the places where involvement by parents and the larger community will help. However, if the school as an institution neglects to urge and then support cooperative action among all social institutions, the interests and hopes of parents and communities are difficult to realize.

Suggested Activities and Questions

1. Because of your role as a child development services specialist, you must plan how to build support for two children whose families recently arrived in the United States. You know that the families are struggling economically, and they are also trying to learn a new language and culture. Even though all three social settings bear responsibility, how can you best enhance the educational opportunity for these youngsters?

2. Find a copy of your state's statutes regarding child maltreatment. Itemize the steps you are to take in reporting suspected abuse; then discuss with a teaching colleague your responsibility and its implications.

3. Construct a chart showing the areas of sex education you think children normally encounter between ages 3

and 8. Indicate home, school, and community responsibilities at each age level.

4. Imagine that you are designated as the leader of a new home–school–community collaboration effort based at your school. Outline for participants at the first meeting six particular ways that the three settings can support one another.

5. As a teacher, you are invited to a church preschool program to talk about "literacy atmospheres." Outline the points you wish to communicate to the mothers and fathers for creating a meaningful literary focus in their homes.

Resources

Organizations

Child Welfare League of America *http://www.cwla.org*

Child Welfare Information Gateway *http://www. childwelfare.gov*

National Network of Partnership Schools *http://www.csos. jhu.edu/p2000/*

TV-Turnoff Network *http://www.tvturnoff.org*

Centers for Disease Control and Prevention *http://www. cdc.gov*

Web Sites

http://www.childtrendsdatabank.org The Child Trends Data Bank provides a great deal of information on children's well-being.

http://www.futureofchildren.org The Future of Children promotes effective policies and programs for children by providing policymakers and service providers with timely, objective information based on best available research.

http://www.nea.org The National Education Association presents an overview of a major U.S. teacher association plus links to publications, reports, statistics on schools, and best practices.

http://www.commonsensemedia.org. Common Sense Media has extensive recommendations for parents on movies, books, and Internet material. It also has programs for school use.

http://www.cdc.gov The Centers for Disease Control and Prevention has a large variety of online sources and recommendations about diseases, healthy living, lifestyles, and demographics plus emergency measures.

http://www.kff.org. The Kaiser Family Foundation focuses on major health care issues in the United States and abroad. It serves as a source for facts and analysis as well as producing health policy analysis.

http://www.apha.org/ The American Public Health Association is the oldest professional health organization in the world. It serves as a public voice on health care and health care funding.

CHAPTER **8**

Curriculum of the Home

*They gave him afterward everyday . . . they and of them became part of him.
The family usages, the language, the company, the furniture . . . the
yearning and swelling heart.*

(WHITMAN, 1855, P. 91)

After reading this chapter, you will be able to do the following:

- Explain what families do that promotes children's literacy and cognitive development.
- Define **code switching** and state why adult involvement is important when children learn multiple languages and dialects.
- Point out what parents do to instill values and habits that produce a sense of purpose in their children's lives.
- Demonstrate how children's academic learning is enhanced by (a) daily routines in the home, (b) use of space, (c) family traditions, and (d) religious practices.
- Point out parents' uses of technology to lay a foundation for their children's emerging world view.
- Explain ways in which extended family members—particularly grandparents—affect features of the home curriculum.
- Discuss the pros and cons of home schooling and explain why some families embrace this trend.

A broad definition of *curriculum* signifies "all the experiences children have from the moment of waking to the moment of falling asleep" (Doll, 1995, p. 5). Because most of a child's waking hours are connected to family, this implies that the home must provide a great deal of children's learning experiences.

No single **home curriculum** is like any other, because America is one of the most diverse nations in the world, with a mix of cultures, races, old and new immigrants, and exceptionalities. This cascade of influence from external cultural factors, plus the internal family factors, becomes the home curriculum and leads children in developing their perceptions and interpretations of the world.

In this chapter, we provide examples of the many experiences children have at home, the implications of these experiences, and the resulting potential for expanded learning.

The educative processes of all homes are important ingredients for society in the United States, because, as social–cultural–context theorists indicate, how each person develops affects all who relate to that individual. In Chapters 3 and 4, we discussed the diversity and functions of U.S. families and defined a family unit as two or more persons living together and sharing common goals, resources, and a commitment to each other. Children in any family household will have at least one adult (referred to in this book as a *parent*) who is responsible for them. Siblings, who play an important role in any child's learning, also may be present.

Because of the diversity of U.S. families, we find not one single home curriculum but many variations. Too often, professional educators underestimate the power of the home curriculum and miscalculate the learning that children acquire outside of school. When there is disparity between children's home learning and the expectations of the school curriculum, children can be judged to be deficient rather than having different skills that may assist them in attaining skills at a higher level.

Research over time indicates that regardless of the ethnic or socioeconomic makeup of the family, a warm and responsive parenting style, a structured environment, and stimulating activities that include a variety of materials, plus parents' involvement as children use these materials, support children's growth toward a productive lifestyle (Bronfenbrenner, 2005). Conversely, in some family situations, parenting styles and habits can work against children's natural pursuit of knowledge and positive development.

All families have an organizational structure that defines family members and their roles. Many households have kinship networks of extended family members who may or may not be living in the home but who give added support and nurturance. Kinship influences on the family organizational structure are also supported by social networks that parents develop. This structure provides physical and emotional support as the child moves into the school and community. The reward system in the child's outside environment (Bronfenbrenner [1995] labeled it the *mesosystem*) is determined primarily by the predominant culture and may shift as the needs of the culture shift. In the 21st century, the rapid growth of technology is revolutionizing our society and presents us with new and altered perspectives. Just as young parents rely on technology and media for their outlook on child rearing, so, too, do different cultural values bombard families. The resulting worldview may therefore come in conflict with many traditional family values and perspectives (Long, 2004).

Still, whatever their environment, children first learn valuable information and life skills from their families. They learn who they are, how to communicate with others, what their role is in society, how to function in their environment, and the kind of world we live in. Regardless of their family structure, this learning is a consequence of family interactions and stimulations. The greater the variety of these influences, the richer the learning.

Early learning of appropriate or inappropriate communication behaviors, developing language, and acquiring literacy skills are the underpinnings of children's later cognitive development. Besides child–parent interactions, home learning is further supported by a family's use of time and space, the household routines, the sharing of interests and skills, and the family's rituals and religious practices. In all situations,

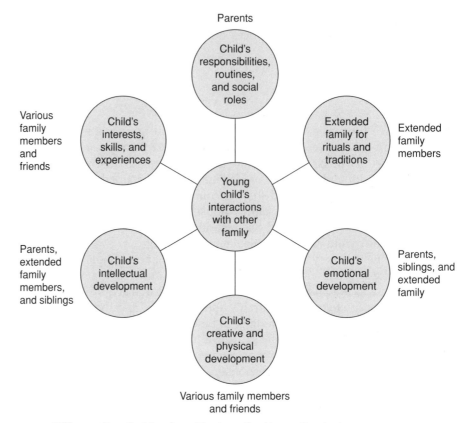

FIGURE 8-1 Different Family Members Nurture the Home Curriculum

Note: Foundational skills, concepts, attitudes, and experiences are developed in the child's home environment. Some areas are influenced more strongly by particular family members and the child's peers.

children's learning depends on their readiness for the tasks and experiences they encounter. Figure 8-1 shows the range of children's learning at home and the involvement of particular family members.

HOMES NURTURE COMMUNICATION AND COGNITIVE SKILLS

Language, literacy, communication skills, and cognitive development begin at birth. Parents and significant others talk to the baby, interpret the baby's responses, and establish communication patterns. They interpret the baby's movements, coos, laughs, cries, and other nonverbal behaviors. They enjoy interpreting, to babies and to the world at large, what these behaviors mean, as illustrated in the following vignette.

 During a family get-together, Christine is cuddling her 6-week-old niece, Lorelei, against her shoulder and neck. Murmurs and coos between the two seem to indicate contentment on both sides. Suddenly Lorelei begins sucking on Christine's neck.

"Oops, honey," Christine exclaims, "I guess you need your mommy!" Christine calls across the room, "Jenny, you're needed. Lorelei is hungry, and I sure can't provide for her." She passes Lorelei to Jenny, who snuggles Lorelei as she offers her breast, saying, "There! You're happy now." Gentle murmuring sounds can be heard from other family members in the room as they acknowledge that the important role of feeding the youngest member of this extended family is nicely met.

Although crying is one of the earliest forms of infant communication, other non-verbal behaviors also work, as we have just witnessed. Even though some of the interpretations may be incorrect, the fact that parents are responding provides the basis of child language development. Babies sense that their needs can be met if they somehow initiate the action. When certain actions get no response, they are likely to be stopped. The baby's skills expand rapidly because of planned and unplanned family interactions and experiences. Parents echo their infant's vocalizations, name things, and direct the baby's attention to nearby objects, people, and events. Parents, other family members, and caregivers explain to the baby what they and the baby are doing, demonstrating with real objects accompanied by language.

Families extend the communication process as children grow. In the first year, they will introduce babies to books. Adults read and reread the books; they talk about and ask questions about the pictures, such as "Where is the dog?" As they turn the pages, they ask, "Oh, what do you think is going to happen?" or they may point out where they are reading. They read books in a variety of settings, often snuggling with the child in a warm, pleasurable manner. The progressively more sophisticated manner of reading provides a foundation for later reading development as well as cognitive development. Writing emerges in a similar fashion. Children observe parents writing lists, notes, and letters and drawing pictures. Parents give paper and crayons to children, who then scribble, draw, and write sounds for letters or words, imitating their parents' writing.

Parents assist children's later literary development. They listen to what is said and agree with or correct the child's perceptions. While reading to children, parents use a variety of techniques. They modify the story to accommodate the child's language development or they use the more elaborate language of the text to arouse the child's interest—thus expanding the child's language. Parents almost unconsciously use other ways of involving the child in the story, such as taking part in the dialogue when reading familiar passages.

Literacy expands as extended family members, friends, and neighbors become a part of the communication process: engaging children in more and more extensive conversations, writing notes or letters, or providing materials and books. Children get the message that reading and writing are important to the entire family, and communication patterns vary from one family member to another.

Children learn vocabulary and grammatical patterns as important adults model language in the course of family interactions. In other words, children learn language from hearing it spoken. In a rich home curriculum, adults engage children in conversations beyond giving directions and correcting behavior—for example, teaching children **active listening skills** and involving them in give-and-take discussions. As parents broaden children's social contacts to the extended family, the neighborhood, and the larger community, children observe more than one way of communicating. It is in these different settings that children develop and expand their **interactive skills**.

In homes where multiple languages or dialects are used, children learn *code switching* to deal with different social venues (Tabors & Snow, 2001) as they observe adults using different language codes. Language expands and develops for all children as they are exposed through connections with extended family, family friends, neighbors, and playmates to various dialects or culture patterns.

REFLECTION

Who in your family read to you in your early years? Do you remember any special words or expressions from that early book sharing that you liked? Can you see how these preliteracy events connected with later schooling?

Parents' Knowledge of Child Development

In the homes of interested parents, instruction and expectations are adapted to account for their children's development. These adults rely on different sources to obtain this information, even though this knowledge appears in nonsequential ways and in an almost hit-or-miss fashion.

Over the years, young parents often looked to extended families and social networks established in their neighborhoods, schools, and communities for sources of information. They read books and articles published by authorities such as Dr. Spock or T. Berry Brazelton as guides for raising children. Many depended on neighborhood knowledge and interactions. Some attended parent education programs developed by such organizations as **Women, Infants, and Children (WIC)**, well-baby clinics, Head Start, and other social service programs. Some high schools provided basic courses on home management and child development for students even before they become parents.

Now, in addition to the sources just listed, technology is expanding to give parents access to child-rearing information far beyond what was available in the past. In the past, television offered entertainment programs, like *Leave it to Beaver*, that modeled positive middle-class White family interactions. Today's situation comedies portray culturally different family structures and unique forms of parent functioning. Parents, linked to Internet resources, have unlimited access to information from experts and agencies that can answer their questions. These parents also have the capacity to interact with other young parents as they visit **Weblogs** and exchange e-mails. In this manner, they can form close personal relationships and a sense of community without leaving their homes (Long, 2004). The advantages of such availability are a sense of unity with a larger group and a feeling of being in the mainstream. The disadvantages are that not all available information is based on sound practices or good research, and it suffers from the lack of a moderating environment provided by personal encounters. All linkage, of course, depends on a parent's interest and on having the time to investigate good sources of information. Often, these are problems not addressed in a busy world.

IMPLICATIONS FOR TEACHERS

Analyze a Child's Language Development

Think about one of your young nephews or nieces and what language skills he or she has brought from home to school. Can you detect any particular habits or skills in oral or written language that started at home? Is there an interest or an outlook that you realize stems from some member of the family? While you are recalling, consider any conflicting speech or verbal problems that have resulted from the child's home life. Basically, you are analyzing and assessing what home language this child is exposed to. It will have an impact on what develops in the child's school projects and routines.

LEARNING VALUES, ROLES, AND RESPONSIBILITIES

An important part of the home curriculum involves children learning family values and role expectations for themselves in relation to other members of the family or neighbors and friends. Children also learn the role expectations of family members toward each other and toward the extended family.

Parents Foster Beliefs and Value Structures

All families have commitments, values, and priorities. Some of these sentiments are explicit and well defined, but often many are only implied, and this is especially true for **marginalized families**. Some family values and goals are more immediate and are often expressed as wishes or as "what we are trying to do." Some families have both long-range and short-range goals, whereas other families are able to plan only from one day to the next.

Family members have a powerful effect on children's literary skills and language development.

A number of writers point out that children's attitudes, beliefs, and values resemble those of their parents, but all allow that schools, peers, and communities extend or modify these considerably. Educating children about stealing, lying, and disorderly conduct is normal for most families, although the instruction can take different forms. Some parents teach values and impose a moral code through intimidation and punishment, whereas others approach the challenge by explaining children's problems and discussing the impact of one's actions on others. The latter approach results in stronger development of conscience and internal control. Families who focus on values, morals, and attitudes by modeling behaviors, reasoning through solutions, and labeling the behavior when seen in public (see Figure 8-2) give children a much-needed sense of purpose and direction in their lives.

Whatever the organizational structure of the family, children absorb these values and goals and their role in accomplishing them. As children grow older and other events happen to families, such as the birth of a child with disabilities, what children

---

1. Allow children to accept the consequences of their actions; for example, they can manage cleanup after some water play.

2. Avoid performing tasks that children can do for themselves. Caregivers should encourage effort and experiments so that children learn to do these things themselves.

3. Give children responsibilities that fit their age and skill levels.

4. Praise children when they perform well; be encouraging and supportive when they make mistakes or fall short of expectations.

5. Model behaviors and attitudes that show you are proactive; for example, communicate to children that persons can make things happen.

6. Encourage and support children s particular interests and show respect for their accomplishments.

7. Be consistent in expectations by establishing reasonable standards of behavior.

8. Explain the reasons for needed rules and limits, as well as any deviations from normal expectations.

9. Allow children to make age-appropriate decisions (including rules and guidelines) as often as possible. Start with minor choices and graduate to consequence-bearing actions.

FIGURE 8-2 Helping Children Develop an Internal Locus of Control *Source:* Based on information in Berns (2006).

learn about themselves can be vastly different and can be quite contrary to school or societal expectations of families. The following vignette shows one family's approach—a strongly goal-oriented one defined by societal expectations. The second vignette demonstrates how this family modified its expectations after the birth of a child with Down syndrome.

Every morning before her children left for school, Mrs. Martinez wished each child a good day in Spanish. She reminded each child of strongly held family principles. She then asked each child to make a small commitment for the day. Studying hard, practicing the piano, or improving at shooting baskets were acceptable goals. At dinner one evening when the family shared accomplishments and worries, José told his family that he wasn't going to read with Louie (a child with a learning disability in his class) anymore because Louie was "just too hard to deal with." The older brothers and sisters sympathized with José but reminded him that they had read to him when he was little. Mrs. Martinez hugged José hard a few days later when he told her, "I'm going to read with Louie. I found out yesterday that he can read lots of words if you start them out and whisper the real hard ones."

In the Martinez family, the mother was a strong and dominant influence. She believed in goal setting and certain family values, and made them clear and explicit for her children.

Whether values and goals are stated each day, written, or merely implied, notions of having purpose and direction in one's life are modeled and communicated to children. Such strong purposes can help a family adjust and adapt to an unexpected event, such as the one the Martinez family experienced.

At the end of José's third-grade year, Manuela, a child with Down syndrome, was born to the Martinez family. José was thankful for his earlier school experiences with Louie, for they helped him and his family as they weathered the many and dramatic effects of this event. The strong sense of unity in the family allowed them to adjust their lives so that they all shared the responsibilities of raising this child. José always came home on Tuesdays to help his mother. The following vignette demonstrates how this strong family helped the school change its policies and also helped their child cope with conflicting expectations.

One Tuesday, José's teacher informed the class that they would all have to stay after school because of their rowdiness. José, greatly dismayed, tried to explain to her why he couldn't, and then walked out of school and went home. His mother was both pleased and dismayed, for she had received a phone call about the event. When José explained that he hadn't been rowdy and he couldn't let his mother down, the two of them began to work out plans for communicating their needs to the school personnel. Mrs. Martinez then called the school to make an early-morning appointment with the teacher and principal. At this meeting, many important changes between the school and this family began to take shape. Besides enabling the teacher and principal to reevaluate how they worked with families to meet their changing needs, Mrs. Martinez showed José how, by being proactive, parents can make things happen.

Most families expect their children to undertake responsibilities within the home. Some responsibilities may be explicit and others implicit. In some families, the responsibilities are fairly consistent with changes being negotiated, but in others they may be haphazard and even confusing to children. They may be communicated in dictatorial fashion, explained reasonably, or expected to be learned through observation. As with José in the vignettes just described, changing family circumstances and expectations can affect children's behavior in schools.

At times, home expectations can conflict with school expectations. Children can't always express or explain conflicting values. When conflict occurs, children become caught in the middle. In the preceding vignette, Mrs. Martinez was able to handle the situation and seek the school's support. In other families, negative attitudes can result in poor school–family relationships, with which both parents and schools must struggle. If you are to support the growth of all children in your community center or classroom, you must recognize that children and their families come with different skills, values, and circumstances.

Extended Family Fosters Roles and Rituals

In many families, parents garner emotional support from the extended family; in some cases, they receive economic support as well. Extended family members may live close by, or they may live at some distance but still have strong ties. In addition to teaching about role expectations and hierarchical structures, the extended family helps children absorb the traditions and rituals of the larger group. An interesting example of such learning is presented by Oladele (1999), who explains how her mother, during the daily routines, taught her academics and spirituality and also about her African heritage. Her grandparents also influenced and reinforced this learning, beginning with a ritual of listening to her Bible verse recitations.

Celebrations are often a time when children learn about who they are as extended family members share the rituals and customs of their particular culture. Children in bicultural homes often have very different experiences, especially when both sets of the extended family share holidays with the nuclear family. Sila, in the vignette that follows, is the child of a European American father, Dan, and a Turkish mother, Nara, whose own family members are practicing Muslims. Nara no longer observes religious practice, but Sila is introduced to the Muslim faith through visits from extended family members.

Seven-year-old Sila is excited about the upcoming holidays, because both Easter and Kurban Bayram are being celebrated close together. Greg, her father's brother, will be joining them for Easter week, and as he does every year, will help her dye eggs, take her shopping, and help her hunt for Easter eggs on the church lawn. Sila is only beginning to understand that Easter week is about Christ's crucifixion and has begun to ask questions such as "Why was Jesus killed? Did bad people kill him?" Although her father tries to explain, Sila is anxious for Uncle Greg's answer.

Then, at the end of the month, her mother's sister, Bilge, will join them to celebrate Kurban Bayram. Sila will not wear her new Easter hat or dress during this time, but instead will wear a special head scarf. The family will then go to the Muslim market to buy a lamb and have it killed in a special way, Sila believes, although she isn't quite sure how. Last year, her aunt explained that they kept only a small part of the lamb for cooking. She will need to ask about the lamb again this year. Although they have no relatives in the Muslim community in the city, Aunt Bilge and her mother will take her to visit the mosque. She does remember Aunt Bilge telling her that Mohammad was the great prophet in the Muslim faith, as Jesus was in the Christian faith. She wondered if they were friends. She will certainly ask her Aunt Bilge this time.

In some families, both sets of extended family members have equal access to the nuclear family. When this happens, the customs and habits children learn from these members are of equal importance. Because family structures differ, however, what children learn from the extended family depends on the influence these relatives have on the nuclear family (Berns, 2006). The extended family expands the home curriculum by sharing its own values and interaction patterns. When extended family members work out the cultural differences and values of the others, children like Sila will learn how to solve the problems or deal with confusions that arise because of these differences.

Older children help their younger siblings learn the ways of the world.

Siblings Aid in Role and Gender Identification

When children grow up with other children, they experience changing role patterns not dependent on age. A new baby in a home will alter the roles of other family members. A child with special needs, as in José's family, can affect children's school behavior. When parents see behavior change, they need to communicate with teachers and work to solve the problems. Hopefully, these parents will also be open to teachers' concerns and observations. José's mother contacted the school and received support in resolving the conflict. When a new baby is born or when older siblings start school or leave home, circumstances within the family change for all members, and a different curriculum emerges. An older sibling who has been a playmate may suddenly become bossy after starting school, and younger children must learn new ways of interacting. Older children teach younger siblings the ways of the world, but what is learned will depend on the younger children's interactions and emotional relationships with the older ones.

The siblings in the following vignette react differently to their older sister, and this difference could partially explain their different rate of learning certain concepts.

Much to her mother's surprise, Caitlin learned to spell some words when she was only 3 years old. Her older sister Jennifer, returning from second grade, often made Caitlin "her pupil" and insisted that she "write her letters," giving her words and then crackers as rewards. Brad, closer in age to Jennifer, didn't know letter names until he entered first grade, even though Jennifer at times tried to be his teacher as well. As a baby, Caitlin often called Jennifer her "other" mama and thus apparently was more receptive to her teaching, whereas Brad and Jennifer were closer in age and Brad resented Jennifer's bossiness.

Academic learning is only part of the curriculum children learn from siblings. For example, children learn physical skills faster and at an earlier age by competing with a more skilled family member. Children learn strategies for convincing others of their point of view as siblings squabble and handle their differences within the family unit. Even learning how to unite in family loyalty against the outside world gives children important social skills—although not always desirable ones.

Children tend to overcome adversity and adapt best to changing circumstances in environments of positive sibling relationships, low conflict, and supportive extended families (Hetherington & Stanley-Hagan, 2002). Harris (1998) maintains that this learning from siblings and peers is even more potent than learning from parents.

IMPLICATIONS FOR TEACHERS

Is a Sibling Helpful?

If a sibling contributes to the home curriculum, then that holds true for all of us who have brothers and sisters. Make a short list of things you feel you have learned from a sibling. It can involve any physical, social, or intellectual accomplishment. After you compare your list with those of teammates, discuss why there are considerable differences in the items you all marked down. Did your cultural situation come into play? Did age differences have anything to do with learning? Do you think your teachers had an inkling of those child-sharing skills that helped you?

You can relate this experience to your own teaching by encouraging children to reveal how older siblings help (or hinder) them. This will provide useful information as you look for cooperative family members to engage in projects and assignments.

LEARNING FROM THE PHYSICAL ENVIRONMENT OF THE HOME

Children's learning is greatly influenced by environmental factors. The amount of space, the kinds of materials in the space, and the ways in which families allow children to use the space all affect what children learn in the home. Children living in crowded conditions can be successful when the family is nurturing and supportive; if children are restricted in movements or ignored in their environment, regardless of the amount of space, learning is lessened. In his study of high and low achievers from poor families, Clark (1983) found that, among other nurturing qualities, high achievers' parents skillfully supervised their children's use of time and space.

Space Influences Emotional Growth

Great differences occur in the amount and kind of space that children have in their growing years, and space can be a factor in a family's ability to support children's physical and mental health. Of course, as family situations change, so can the amount of available space. Studies have shown that the greater the population density in a household, the more the family was subjected to stress and to unhealthy conditions affecting children's development.

Children learn different things about themselves, depending on the amount and quality of space they have. And the way parents respond to the family's living conditions and their children's needs will guide the outcomes. Resilient families overcome great adversity when sharing and mutual respect are evident in the family's use of available space.

Space Influences Intellectual Development

When rooms have different functions, children learn categorization skills in determining where household items belong and where people do different jobs. When families are crowded, rooms may have more than one function, and children learn that the same space is used differently. For example, in one crowded one-room apartment, an investigator found two people sleeping, another cooking, and two children playing on the floor most of the day. There appeared to be limited adult–child interaction. Across the hall, the same limited space for another family had distinct functions at different times of the day; the room was a living room during the daytime hours, a kitchen and dining room during early morning and evening, and a bedroom at night. During each part of the day, the second family appeared to use the space cooperatively, helping to prepare meals, making beds, and watching TV together. With the support of the entire family, household furniture was rearranged to fit the family's needs, although a lot of discussion (even argument) ensued about what belonged where. The processing skills of children in these two families appeared to be affected by these situations.

In their classroom, two children, one from each of the preceding homes, were asked to put household items into categories and place them in appropriate spaces. The child whose home space was haphazard did a random assignment of the items and could not explain why he organized the items that way. In fact, when asked to explain his strategy, he began to rearrange the items. The other child had a definite pattern to his selection of items for each category and a clear reason for putting each item in its chosen space.

Space Influences Problem-Solving Skills

Homes foster problem-solving skills through encouraging observation, exploration, and experimentation. When parents, both wittingly and unwittingly, allow children to explore their indoor and outdoor environments, children's problem-solving skills expand. In the early years, the sandbox or the dirt in the backyard offer countless experiences for curious children. One preschooler spent almost an hour observing an ant carry a large crumb to its nest in the sidewalk and try to poke it between the cracks. The boy ran to his mother for help, but she encouraged her son to watch and see what the ant might do to solve his problem. Later, after the ant had broken the crumb into small bits, he excitedly explained the process to his mother.

Three-year-old Jack discovered that the cookie jar could be reached by shoving a chair next to the cupboard and then climbing up. When his mother put the cookie jar on top of the refrigerator, out of his reach, he had a new problem to solve. He began some experimentation, first with a chair and then with different-sized boxes. Finally, he discovered that if he piled the boxes on top of each other, he could reach the forbidden cookies.

Such learning is usually not planned by parents. In the first instance, the mother was delighted with the child's interest and absorption. Jack's mother was none too pleased, however, with the child's cleverness at the moment she discovered him teetering on the piled-up boxes. Still, when homes are organized so that items for children's use are within easy grasp and other items are stored out of reach for various reasons, curious and determined children will try out their ideas if allowed enough freedom to explore safely.

By modeling problem-solving skills and exploring problems and solutions with children, parents steer their children toward competence. Homes where highly directive and punitive behaviors are the norm actually discourage interest and skill in analyzing tasks, and some even produce a sense of helplessness (Bronfenbrenner, 2005).

Space Influences Physical and Creative Development

Family space isn't necessarily limited to indoor space. Outdoor space and the freedom to explore it safely will assist children in developing physical skills and creative endeavors.

Kenisha shared a bedroom with her sisters wherever they lived, and as the family moved from farm to farm, they usually shared their meals in a crowded space. Kenisha's outdoor space, however, provided greater opportunities for physical and creative development. Many of the farms had large barns and fields where Kenisha and her siblings could play. There were trees nearby and beams in a barn where she and the others could climb when they were not expected in the fields. Cardboard boxes, old blankets, boards, nails, and hammers enabled them to create their own fantasy worlds. Kenisha and her siblings made creative use of the strong ropes that the family used to tie up their goods. They often tied the ropes to the barn beams or to strong tree limbs and then developed skill in climbing and swinging on ropes.

Psychological Space Needs

Space created by new technology is now a factor in every adult's life, and is becoming more and more a part of children's lives. This new domain of personal space, related to the digital tools society possesses, provides an atmosphere for learning and sensing as well as linking us with other places and people in our virtual communities. This amazing development of our digital age has the positive features of providing rapid communication and procuring images and information from any part of the world. The downside is that the virtual space maintained by computers, cell phones, and iphones is easily invaded by others at any time. In our virtual space, we have limited control of what comes to us and how often. Privacy is almost completely nonexistent for some people, and the nature and type of material thrown at us can have negative qualities.

With each new electronic gadget we use, we make a choice to integrate our own digital portraits with a world community. This holds a risk for all users and especially for children. Instantaneous communication and access accelerate knowledge gains, of course, but require the surrender of privacy and control of one's psychic energy.

IMPLICATIONS FOR TEACHERS

Experiment with Space

Study a few space situations to see the effects that the outside world is having on a child or a group. You can consider a playground, your classroom, a public space, or an area in a home. Try determining how the surroundings in these spaces control a child's play or other activity. Would the child's task or project be enhanced or modified if the space were changed?

As an experiment, set up a work project in more than one kind of space. For example, have a small group of 4-year-olds do a large brush painting outdoors and another one in your classroom. Is there a difference in the product or result?

In another experiment, have the group listen as you read a story. Try to do the reading outdoors on the ball field, then on the grass under a tree, and then on the floor in a corner of your classroom. Watch the children's faces to gauge their attentiveness and to see if there is a difference in perceptions of the story line. Did the location of the reading have a discernible effect?

Children thrive in whatever space they live in when adults provide consistent care, nurturing, and support while guiding their behavior and prizing their creations. Children learn important self-concepts when family members praise them for successes and help them overcome frustrations at times of failure. When children do not experience such nurturance, the home curriculum is more limited.

FAMILY PRACTICES AND HOME LEARNING

In Chapter 7, we defined the following areas of home responsibility for children's learning: early socialization skills; language learning; beginning experiments with natural phenomena; interaction and negotiation skills; values and attitudes, including aesthetic appreciation; and health and sex education. It should be clear that the home's responsibility is to develop basic skills—many taught through daily routines—that prepare children to function successfully in society, and parents fulfill these responsibilities to differing degrees.

Daily Routines

Although modern family lifestyles appear to be hurried because of job requirements, child care, children's sports, and other recreational activities, all families establish some sort of routine. It is during the routine events that children learn to assume certain roles and responsibilities within changing family structures.

When events happen in the home in a timed sequence, children develop a better sense of society's meaning of time. First is the process of getting up and getting ready for school or work. When mealtimes are regular, the second routine involves preparation and a specified mealtime. A further set of routines focuses on bathing and other toileting procedures. The family reuniting at the end of the day is often another routine event. Bedtime is the final routine as family members prepare for the night. During these daily events, parents support and encourage or negate and suppress children's physical, emotional, social, and intellectual development.

PREPARING FOR THE DAY   Children who arise, dress, eat breakfast, and then brush their teeth as routine morning activities establish a pattern whereby they learn through habit about a sequence of events. Parent–child discussion about these events reinforces parental values and attitudes toward the activities, assists in children's language development, assists children in learning a sense of time, and supports children's memory and recall. When parents can give explanations or answer children's questions when varying routines, they often lessen the stress and help children learn to reason, question, and adapt to new situations. Children develop a sense of well-being and security when limits are clear and deviations from routines are dealt with in a caring and supportive environment.

Even in **homeless families**, the risk factors diminish for children when their parents are able to maintain some daily routines and rituals and are able to strengthen their positive interaction patterns by playing with their children and caring for their emotional needs (Black, 2009).

MEALTIMES   Mealtime in families offers many educational opportunities. How events are handled determines the amount and types of learning that take place. Two examples will serve to support the idea and suggest the degree of variation in family habits.

In Bonita's family, mealtimes had established routines and consistent hours. There were expectations for shared responsibilities and behaviors. On one particular day, Bonita returned from her ballet lesson at 5:30 to find her father and brother starting dinner. They asked her to set the table and not watch TV, because Mum was late and Joe needed to leave for tae kwon do at 7:00 p.m. When Mum arrived at 6:00, the family sat down and, after a blessing, began to eat. When Bonita started to protest that she didn't like peas, her father quietly said, "Don't eat them, then, but don't fuss." Joe was going for his red belt that evening, so the family discussed how he was progressing. Then Bonita wanted to choose a word for her word bank. When her father said that the dinner was scrumptious, she wanted to use that word but didn't know how to spell it. Her mother suggested that she get the dictionary and the family would help her find the word and then practice it on the way to Joe's red-belt test. The entire family cleared the table and put the dishes in the sink for later washing.

Although Casey's family was equally supportive, their mealtimes reflected a different ambiance.

Casey's father picked her up at the child-care center and then got ready for an evening meeting. On his way home, he had picked up pizzas. He then engaged Casey in getting plates and helped her count the silverware for everyone. Casey read the instructions on the pizza package with her father as they warmed enough pizza for each of them. Casey then went to the den to watch TV while she ate, and her dad watched the news on the small kitchen TV. Her two older brothers arrived home and greeted their father and Casey. They got themselves pizza, milk, and ice cream and sat at the kitchen bar, discussing their soccer practice. Ready for his meeting, the children's father indicated that their mother would be home soon, so the boys were to help Casey if she needed something. When their mother arrived, she, too, had some pizza, watched some TV with Casey, and reminded the boys about homework.

When it was Casey's bedtime, the mother asked the boys to clean up the counter and then do their homework. Casey, with her mother supervising, followed her routine of getting undressed, brushing her teeth, kissing her brothers goodnight, reading a story with her mother, and then climbing into bed. The mother then went downstairs and supervised her sons' homework while preparing some materials for her own job.

In both families, mealtime is an end-of-the-day event with all family members sharing a meal. However, the purpose of the meal is very different in each family. In Bonita's family, mealtime is not only a time for feeding the family, but also one of sharing responsibilities and learning about each person's day. A special effort is made to keep the family a single unit during that time. Evening events are often shared by the entire family, but there is little freedom of choice, as adults make most of the decisions.

In Casey's home, mealtime is not that significant. The members eat as they come in. All members are united in greeting each other and assuming responsibilities. No attempt is made to keep the family as a unit. Although adults are definitely in charge, there are more choices and more freedom is allowed.

REFLECTION

After reading the two vignettes about mealtime, do you see any home teaching that occurs in the two families other than that mentioned? Do you think mealtime is a good time for teaching children, or can you think of other times that may be better?

The process of preparing food provides children with many learning opportunities, regardless of the circumstances and regardless of when and how family members share in the process:

- Fine motor skills are developed as children help in food preparation, such as cutting vegetables.
- Quantity measurement is learned as children help to bake cookies or a cake.
- Following along as the adult reads the recipe or the packaged directions develops sequencing skills and other prereading skills.
- Helping to make a grocery list supports writing and spelling skills and language development.
- Observing the change that takes place as liquid gelatin becomes solid in the refrigerator or as runny cake batter becomes solid in the oven provides basic scientific understanding of a change process.
- The kinds and varieties of food children eat during mealtime communicate the family's values regarding nutrition or the family's concern with obesity.
- Preparing or securing meals in a variety of settings extends children's knowledge of how foods are prepared (e.g., in the kitchen, with a microwave oven, while camping, or when ordering in a deli).

The different kinds of parental or sibling involvement in preparation and cleanup after meals teach children the family's attitude toward gender-role responsibilities. In some families, the mother is expected to prepare meals and clean up afterward, especially if she stays at home to care for the children. In other

Food preparation provides children with many learning opportunities.

families there is a sense of shared responsibility, particularly when the mother works outside the home. A growing sense of maturity and responsibility develops as children assume some of the tasks in the mealtime process.

FAMILY REUNITING AT THE END OF THE DAY   When the family's routine is such that each member goes off to work or to school, there is often a homecoming routine. The end of the day can be a stressful time, and both positive and negative lessons are learned.

Members of the family are usually tired, hungry, and anxious at day's end, particularly when both parents work or if a single parent must do more in meal preparation or if sleeping arrangements change frequently. Often this is a time when children begin to learn how to cope in difficult situations. When parents or partners argue and disagree, children are often frightened of the anger, and their sense of security is threatened. Nurturing parents and partners resolve their differences and provide models of negotiating behaviors. Those who lash out, demean each other, or even strike each other are modeling ways to diminish another person's self-concept. When parents or partners are able to resolve differences through discussion, apologizing, and coming to agreement, they provide lessons in how to negotiate a peaceful settlement.

Many end-of-the-day routines are pleasant experiences. In some families, children and adults at home share what happened to them during their absence from each other. In homeless situations, some parents are better able to cope if they can share their daily experiences with their children (Swick, 2004). In such sharing, children learn important **socialization skills**, such as how to listen, how to take turns talking, and how to explain so that someone else can understand; in some instances, they learn the skills of sticking to the topic being discussed. How much understanding and skill children develop in the routine situations of the home depends on a combination of factors, such as the age and gender of the children, **socioeconomic factors**, the children's interest, the level of previous understanding, and adult–children interactions.

BEDTIME   As children prepare for bed, there are many procedures that assist children's development. As in all routines, regularity and consistency help children develop a sense of time and order of events and a sense of security.

Four-year-old Kevin's parents went out for the evening, and Kevin had a new babysitter, whom he appeared to like very much. The sitter played games with him and read him his favorite stories. At his regular bedtime, she helped him get undressed and brush his teeth. After one last story, she tucked him in, turned out the light, and went downstairs. A little later, she heard Kevin crying and went up to see what was the matter. As she calmed Kevin down, she finally heard him whimper, "I want Mommy. She says my prayers, and you didn't."

Kevin derived a great deal of security from a series of routine bedtime activities. Although he apparently forgot part of the routine, he sensed that something was wrong, and when he remembered, he became upset. In addition to satisfying Kevin's sense of security, the episode demonstrates activities whereby Kevin's parents (or the babysitter in their absence) fulfill their educational responsibilities. As Kevin washes and brushes his teeth before retiring, he is learning good health habits. Saying prayers at night or at mealtime can be the beginning of religious training.

Rituals and Traditions

The established definition of *family ritual* is the formal procedure for defining routine patterns of behavior. These rituals and traditions are important to any society, for it is by such behaviors that individuals show respect for the value system within a family or clan. Certainly, children learn many social, cognitive, and affective skills that are also learned in other families. Perhaps the most important learnings children gain from rituals are the importance of family structure and the commitment that an individual makes to the solidarity of the group (Evans, 2004). In rituals and traditions, behavior patterns are neither questioned nor examined; the behavior is continued because it is important to the family. As children learn the expected behaviors of the rituals, they develop a sense of identity and a self-concept. In addition, religious ceremonies involve rituals whereby children extend their understanding about the world and their connection to their family (American Family Traditions, 2006).

Customs and folklore are often part of family traditions. Psychologists for years have stressed the importance of folklore to children's psychological and emotional development. They have demonstrated that as children hear old tales and rhymes, they sense deeper meanings and thus find emotional security and comfort (Fiese, 2006). Such stories serve as moral lessons as well. Oladele (1999) related how the rituals in her family of memorizing Bible verses, singing spirituals, and reading created a sense of connection to her heritage.

In addition to providing emotional or moral support, rituals create an intellectual stimulus. Traditional rhymes, chants, and incantations have a language pattern and a story structure that support literacy development. In many families, adults chant or read the rhymes they learned as children, often in the course of playing with children. "This Is the Way the Lady Rides," "One, Two, Buckle My Shoe," or "Shoe the Old Horse" provides rhythms and language patterns that form the foundation of children's developing language (Fiese, 2006). You have likely seen older children teaching younger ones special games, rituals, and the chants of childhood that parents do not attend to. Whether singing traditional songs, writing a letter to Santa Claus, helping count candles on the cake, or learning to read their part for the seder, parents and older siblings are engaging children in literacy events.

IMPLICATIONS FOR TEACHERS

Rituals and Learning

You have probably noticed that some of the rituals that come with your work habits and socializing affect what you do in your own work space. This is true for most people, so bring it into focus for your classroom group. First, take a few minutes to jot down some of the rituals that typify your family (usually at holiday time). Make sure that these are practices you will miss when you are separated from your family.

Now make this a project for classroom work. Have your class, in pairs or teams, make lists of the different rituals that they remember about their own holiday celebrations. Post the lists and then see if parents will come and share the practices with the class. It is a good time to share holiday decorations, special foods, and religious activities while forging cooperative links with your parent group.

Sharing Interests and Skills

The amount of knowledge that parents transmit to their children varies widely from family to family. The greatest differences in children's special knowledge occur between families who explore their interests together and those who ignore each other. For example, when computer enthusiasts involve their young children in learning rudimentary computer skills, the children often enter kindergarten very adept at using computers. Children's curiosity leads them to ask many questions. Parents respond differently, of course, depending on their own interests, knowledge, and style of interaction. But children's learning and continued interest depend greatly on the response they elicit.

Families may also share an interest in the arts, as the following vignette shows.

⌒ When Mrs. Jacobs placed a Seurat print in her third-grade classroom, Roberto explained to the class that Seurat used a special technique called pointillism. He and his artist father had experimented with the technique after a visit to their nearby museum. Roberto had been fascinated with the Seurat paintings, and his dad had extended that interest as the two explored the technique together through art books and in his father's studio. ⌒

Eager adults can destroy children's interest as well as expand it. For example, children may learn different things from the simple question "Where does the wind come from?" One parent may reply, "Gee, I don't know!" Given that answer too many times, children learn that their questions are not important or that they shouldn't bother trying to find answers. Another parent may respond, "From the east," and point in the direction from which the wind is now blowing. If that is the end of the conversation, children may learn where east is, that the wind's origin is east, and that adults know things and children can get information from them. Another parent may expand on this answer by pointing and then adding, "See, you can tell by how the trees are swaying." Children's knowledge is expanded to finding out something about how one determines the direction of the wind. Another parent, whose own knowledge about wind and directionality is limited, may answer, "I'm not sure exactly. Let's see if we can find out." When parents and children pursue an answer together, children learn about the importance of questioning and new ways of knowing.

Gardner (1993) discussed various intelligences that result from children's different learning styles. These styles may be innate, but parents also support, reinforce, or even squelch their children's natural learning style by the way they respond. Linguistically oriented parents tend to teach their children through explanations and expressive use of language. Parents with strong logical-mathematical orientations enjoy math and strategy games and encourage orderly and logical thinking in arriving at solutions. Spatially and kinesthetically oriented parents help their children move through space and use their bodies as they figure out how the world functions. Artistic parents expand their children's knowledge through imagining and creating. Naturalist-oriented parents discriminate among living things and are very sensitive to features of the natural world, such as cloud, rock, and land formations and configurations. These responses not only reflect the parents' orientations, they also communicate different ways of knowing.

Children whose parents reinforce their ways of knowing have greater success in school, but when the learning styles of the home and school are too disparate, children are at a disadvantage. Teachers who try to understand what and how children have learned at home, however, can create classroom opportunities for supporting and expanding children's skills and knowledge. Parents can help teachers understand how their children learn by discussing the particular methods used at home.

REFLECTION

Do you know of a child who seems to learn things differently than do others in the class? If so, watch him or her for a while, then try to relate the learning style to the notion of multiple intelligences.

As a teacher-researcher, Voss (1993) pointed out how she discovered a student's learning style by visiting his home and watching as his father taught him how to build. Eric could never explain in class how he did something other than by using his hands and saying, "I first did this and then this and then this." No amount of questioning and attempts at expanding his language worked. Expressing himself orally and in reading was painful for Eric. Eric enjoyed school only when the class worked on projects, and he spent hours figuring out how something went together. Upon visiting the home and getting to know the parents, Voss discovered that Eric had a special relationship with his father and was allowed to work on the projects his father did in business or around the house. Eric's father rarely explained what he was doing, but when asked by the child how he was doing something, he would slow down his activity to demonstrate. Realizing how kinesthetically oriented the child was, Voss was able to adjust the classroom learning to accommodate Eric's way of knowing and to expand his ability in other areas.

OTHER FAMILY ACTIVITIES THAT EDUCATE

The home curriculum is enriched or limited by the ways families engage in various activities in and out of the home. The amount of learning varies as a result of many factors, including economics and personal preferences. Even though parents living on a limited income can provide their children with many and varied learning opportunities, poverty does have a debilitating effect and reduces family choices and energy for pursuing these opportunities. Extreme poverty limits parents' ability and energy to interact with their children even more, often communicating a sense of hopelessness and cynicism.

Affluent parents have the means to provide an array of toys and reading materials in the home, and their children often have their own television sets and computers. These parents arrange trips for their children as well as a variety of entertainment events, cultural activities, and recreational opportunities. Other families can't afford as many opportunities, but the children learn important coping skills as their parents try to overcome economic deprivation. They learn to develop kinship relations with family members and neighbors as they all share material goods, share responsibility for children's safety, and help each other cope in a sometimes hostile environment. Although poverty is limiting, it does not mean that poor families are not committed to their children's education. We find that many do make wise choices, enriching their children's experiences with appropriate toys, books, family outings, and even scheduled home lessons.

Learning opportunities for children vary not only with parental involvement but also with the way parents interact with their children during these activities. The vignette in Chapter 1 about Steven's tae kwon do lessons demonstrated that the curriculum provided by structured lessons is not limited to the skills being taught. In that example, Steven, encouraged by suggestions from his mother, was also learning important skills regarding social interaction with adults. Other examples of the family outreach curriculum are recreational pursuits, toys and games, family use of technology, and travel.

Recreational Pursuits

Recreation, gaming sessions, and play with family members have great emotional, physical, social, and intellectual value for children, and few activities bond families better than recreational pursuits. Children normally select their own levels of participation in play, sports, and creative work, but parents and other family members can always encourage and support their interest. Children require time, space, and equipment to pursue recreation, and effective parents will plan for this, support it, and even participate. Children derive the following benefits from recreation and play:

- Working with others.
- Gaining small and large muscle exercise.
- Establishing an interest in fitness.
- Developing a lifelong interest in and a positive attitude toward recreation.
- Pursuing guided exploration of challenges and new ventures.

- Making sensible and accurate use of equipment.
- Achieving release from tension.
- Experiencing pleasure, gratification, and satisfaction.

Toys and Games

The types of toys parents provide reflect their value structure and extend children's development in different ways.

On the birth of her daughter Delaney, Mrs. Babbitt bought a set of unit blocks. When Delaney was old enough to sit and stack things, Mrs. Babbitt would take out a few blocks for the child to play with. The blocks were always stored according to their unit size, and gradually Delaney became involved in returning them to the shelf as she expanded her use of the blocks. Over time, other materials were added, such as play animals, toy trucks and cars, pieces of cloth, and paper and crayons for signs. At times, Delaney's father would join her in playing with the blocks, building towers and complicated structures.

Ashley's father, delighting in his new daughter, bought her a huge toy panda. He would sit on the floor beside the panda holding his infant as he fed her or played with her. As Ashley grew older, the panda became an important source of comfort and a wonderful companion to sit with while hearing a story or watching television. Ashley had many small toys that also entertained her, and she punched them and examined them when playing.

Zena, a staff member at the community-subsidized child-care center, often took home toys discarded by the center. One day she brought several sets of playing cards that were discarded because cards were missing. At home, using the numbers and pictures, she and her children made up several games of naming, sorting, matching, and trading, and these were shared by children in the apartment complex.

All children experience a curriculum provided by the toys they receive, and all three sets of parents described in the vignettes above played with their children as they used various types of materials. By selecting blocks as the most important toy for her daughter, Mrs. Babbitt established a highly cognitive curriculum, whereas Ashley's father's first gift reflected his wish to provide a warm, cozy support system. Zena provided her children with what she could find but recognized that these toys gave both nurturance and some academic support. All the children were prized and cherished, and their parents were teaching important self-concept and academic skills that would help them as they entered school.

Family Use of Technology

Although not the case with published materials, almost every home in the United States has one or more television sets. And children from 6 months to 6 years old spend as much time watching TV as they do playing. But among primary-school-age children, we find that computer use is now rapidly overtaking TV watching in many homes. How each family uses television is, of course, the salient factor. Sitcoms, game shows, and soap operas provide some stimulation, but unless parents and children both watch and discuss them, the shows appear to have little cognitive benefit (Van Evra, 2004). In fact, several studies (Christakis, Gilkerson, & Richard, 2009) show that TV watching by preschoolers actually impairs young children's language development.

TELEVISION WATCHING   Television shows' association with aggression and violence has been a concern for decades. Readers may recall the startling statistics on the number of violent acts viewed every hour by elementary-school children. These are sobering and seem not to be diminished in spite of parents' use of the V-chip for controlling access to particular programs and the increase in children's programming (Strasburger, Wilson, & Jordan, 2008). For example, wars around the globe are covered daily in the news media, and children of all ages view ethnic conflicts, terrorism, and the destructive effects of these wars on ordinary people.

Positive links to achievement have been found when children viewed television programs such as *Sesame Street* and *Blue's Clues*. These programs traditionally have focused on American values and cultures. However, in the era of globalization, there is great need for American children to expand their understanding of different world cultures. The Sesame Street Workshop is already having an impact, as its Global Grover travels around the world encountering children from many different cultures and showing cultural interactions. What is true for American children's TV is also true for children around the world.

Researchers have found greater benefits from TV viewing when parents watch television with their children and then discuss the programs (Lemish, 2006). Community and school programs can have a similar positive effect with "education via media" for at-risk children if advocates can influence home behaviors through parent education. As we noted, the Sesame Street Workshop works in other countries, and its creators are producing locally specific and socially relevant versions of *Sesame Street*. They also bring to the United States their international programs for parts of the K–8 curriculum. You will find some guidelines for management of family TV listed in Figure 8-3.

Children whose parents reinforce their ways of knowing have greater success in school.

INTERNET USE   Like TV, Internet access is available in virtually all schools and most homes in America. It is now a prominent part of young children's lives. In 2006, statistics showed that 57% of 5- to 7-year-olds used computers at home and nearly 80% used them at school (Smith, 2007).

Recommendations similar to those concerning TV apply to children's use and parents' supervision of the Internet. Parents can control children's access to Web sites through Internet filters such as Content Protect® or CYBERsitter® (more information on filters can be obtained at http://internet-filter-review.toptenreviews.com). Family agreements and sharing about positive Web sites is a far better method of control, however. Nationally, more concern about distasteful online material has appeared, and media manufacturers now distribute software to control children's online experiments.

There are a number of protected virtual communities for children. Two are http://www.juniornet.com and http://www.iknowthat, but they are not free and this limits participation. Smith (2007), a researcher in child use of the Internet, is not encouraging when he states that presently there is little stimulating and compelling material designed for children. However, he does provide a number of well-monitored sites that will interest children 3 to 10 years old.

REFLECTION

Most likely you are an experienced user of the Internet and have profited from its existence. How would you communicate to a group of parents three significant advantages of the Net for classroom learning?

Pediatricians, media specialists, and teachers advocate TV controls, as well as "media literacy" for children. Parents, however, are in the best position to shape any media effects into positive influences for their children.

1. Keep children under age 2 away from TV programs. Avoid using TV as an emergency babysitter.

2. Allow children 2 years and older only 2 hours of screen time daily (e.g., TV, computers, iPods).

3. Monitor what children watch and view the programs with them.

4. Encourage children to watch international programs such as *Sesame Street's* Global Grover that foster understanding of other cultures.

5. Encourage children's interaction with beneficial TV shows; then talk about the program after the TV set is off.

6. Place the TV set apart from family living areas so that it doesn't intrude on meals and other family times together.

7. Keep TV out of children's bedrooms. This leads to TV overdose.

8. Exploit the TV–book connection. Children's programming for shows such as *Arthur* and *Book of Pooh* comes from well-known books. After watching the programs, children are often enthused about reading the "real story."

9. Parents must watch their own TV behavior. Predetermine programs for everyone to watch, watch them, and then turn the set off. Surfing through programs encourages children to do the same.

FIGURE 8-3 Sensible Television Use: Controlling TV Use at Home *Source:* Based on information in Singer and Singer (2005) and Van Evra (2004).

In addition to monitoring children's use of the Internet, parents can use the Internet to connect their children and themselves to educational endeavors (Dowd, Singer, & Wilson, 2005). For example, parents can seek help or information about child development that enables them to respond more appropriately to their children at their level of development. Internet access means that parents can communicate more easily with their children's teachers and schools, especially when parents live in areas where it is difficult to attend their children's school programs. Parents can use the Internet to connect their children with school programs, pen pals, and, if monitored, childrens' **Weblogs** (Ray & Shelton, 2004). Figure 8-4 lists some general rules for families to follow when allowing children to use the Internet.

Economics and Money Issues for Children

The sobering financial climate of 2008–2010 demonstrates that many families are inadequately prepared for volatile economic pressures. Much financial pain

Parents now use the Internet to connect themselves and their children to many educational sources.

1. Adults must be familiar with the Children's Online Privacy Protection Act of 2002.

2. Adults must have a procedure for monitoring, and blocking if necessary, young children's use of the Internet. Software programs that perform this function are available from AOL and the Microsoft Network.

3. Caregivers should know their children's online visits and the amount of time spent online.

4. Adults must know the safe Web sites and how to steer children toward them. Parents should discuss with children the Web site content and their chat room participation.

5. All learners should agree that there will be no rudeness online and that they will not impersonate another person.

6. Adults and children should agree that learners need to be as wary of persons met online as they are of those met offline.

7. All learners should agree with their parents and instructors about not posting any personal data (including names, addresses, and phone numbers) to online diaries, to Weblogs, or in chat rooms.

8. Parents and instructors should know that online accounts, diaries, and chat rooms can all be password protected.

FIGURE 8-4   Internet Safety for Children   *Source:* Based on information in Common Sense Media (2009).

came about with the economic downturn; job losses, bankruptcies, and foreclosures were common. In analyzing the disruption, educators and economists realized that America had developed a generation of citizens who had an incomplete knowledge of basic budgeting and preparation for unfriendly economic times. Many of us realized that part of our education about money issues has been neglected.

Economists Blonigen and Harbaugh (2008) state that economic behavior begins at an early age and that much of a child's early learning about financial matters persists into adulthood. This suggests that parents and early childhood teachers should be working with children to help them understand the realities of money. The school curriculum and the home curriculum have not addressed the area of children's education where children earn, save, and spend money. In the adult world of natural concern for the physiological and emotional needs of children, we seemingly overlook the substantial amount of a child's time spent on economic matters. Children exchange and bargain among themselves, they share some of their resources, and they buy and consume. All of this is economic behavior, and its issues and needs fit naturally into the home curriculum.

A good place for parents and child-care workers to start is by introducing children to the world of goods and services plus buying and selling. One helpful way of introducing the concept is to show 5-, 6-, and 7-year-olds how everyone's finances can be viewed as three major domains or areas in the family budget: spending money, saving money, and gifting money.

If parents and educators simplify the concept with tangible objects, the young child will easily grasp the principles of money. For example, provide the child with "banks" of clear plastic jars or plastic sealable bags. Labels (that the child can make) show what the contents of each bank will be, and the child, with his or her parents, determines how much gift money and allowance money goes into each container. You can see that this setup is very close to the one each family should have for its own budgeting program. The important lessons come from learning how much to remove and for what purpose. With the simple viewable bank, practical and comfortable discussions can start with primary-school children about paying for our needs.

Parents can explain how the child's simple system is much the same as the one they use in operating the household. These beginning lessons create a pattern of behavior that shows young children that income and outgo must have a reasonable connection if the family is to stay within its financial abilities and limits. Parents need to point out that penalties arise if too much money is used for entertainment when there is need for school supplies or sport supplies for the child. Parents can relate the spending from the child's banks to the weekly or monthly obligations that each family must meet: for housing, utilities, food purchases, and transportation.

IMPLICATIONS FOR TEACHERS AND PARENTS

Go on a Shopping Trip

Every family needs to do grocery shopping and uses money to do so. Your local supermarket brings you and your children close to the stuff of everyday life, and every aisle in the market provides a chance for purchase decisions. During these trips, parents and others can teach children the basic financial lessons that all family members need to learn. So, take time to talk about the items to buy with your young shoppers. Get them to understand the factors that go into a purchase selection.

1. *Read the labels to check ingredients. Ingredients are listed according to amounts, so if the first listed ingredient is water, you may have an inferior brand. Compare the item with a competing brand to see if it is the same.*
2. *Quality is a factor in all decisions. If the item is being used for soup or a casserole, then brand X corn or beans may do. For a vegetable side dish, you'll probably want a higher-quality product. Purpose controls the need for value and quality in our purchases.*
3. *Check the figures. Do the supersized paper towels represent a bargain over two smaller rolls? Usually larger sizes offer savings, but not always if the quality differs. Math skills will come in handy here in checking to see which item represents a better economic purchase. But if your family is small, large quantities may not be used well.*
4. *Consider store brands versus name brands. Perhaps you will want to experiment and check out flavors and quality at home when you have a sample of each brand. How about doing a blind taste test of two competing brands of a vegetable? This can be a fun-filled lesson on getting our money's worth.*
5. *Plan your purchases. Having a list keeps you focused on what you need in a grocery store. Just looking and selecting is close to impulse buying, and that's not a good economic model for anyone.*

All this activity is designed to help children weigh as many factors as possible in making purchases. Make sure that they make some selections and then try to justify them. Set limits on the money spent, for all families have a budget for groceries and they try to stay within it. Make sure that children know that the purchases are coming from the "spending" part of the family's income allotments and not the savings or gifting parts.

Recycling and Conservation

Closely allied to budgeting and using good economic sense is the habit of recycling. Again, recessions and hard times prod many families to consider reusing or trading, thereby saving money, energy, or time. The label "living green" has become prominent in recent years among Americans who wish to make better use of natural resources and to create a cleaner planet. All these motivations point to recycling and making all household items serve as many purposes as possible. For example:

- Leftover foods can make tasty soups and casseroles.
- Worn cottons make good cleaning cloths.
- Food parts (shells, husks, skins) and spoiled food can be composted for fertilizing gardens.
- Clothing can be altered and reused (even hand-me-downs).
- Families can participate in sports equipment exchanges.

Figure 8-5 gives some interesting and artistic ideas on how families can use everyday objects to create household decorations and devices to use at home and in school. Readers may wish to find a copy of Bernice Arthur's (2008) small book on recycling of common everyday items in every home.

Recycling is a project that lends itself to opportunities for home–school partnerships. School projects for science and art often require materials (cans, bottles, paper, or boxes) that are found at home. Contributing material of this sort enhances home–school relations and promotes a civic duty. Young children quickly become excited about the ideas of recycling and helping with conservation efforts. In the following vignette, Ronnie shows that he is concerned about the recycling issue.

Ronnie encountered recycling on a personal level when his family decided that it was time to use hand-me-downs. So, the first grader sought his grandmother's view on the matter.

"Gramma, Daddy says it's important to recycle nowadays."

"Oh, Ronnie, why, did he tell you that?"

"Well, I wanted new pants for school. But Mom says I can wear Jud's old ones. They don't fit him any longer."

"So, how does he say recycling works with that?"

"Well, Daddy says we recycle lots of things, and clothes are just another thing. Do you recycle, Gramma?"

"Well, what do I have on?"

"An old shirt. Oh, I see. Is that one of Grampa's old shirts?"

"Makes a comfortable housecleaning outfit," Gramma noted as she twirled. "How do you like it, Ronnie?"

"Well, it's kinda b-i-g!"

"And there are other things, too. Look!" (Holds up a jar with pencils). "These are my drawing pencils. They were new. Does that mean every time I reuse them, I'm recycling?"

"Guess so. And they're in that old marmalade jar. Wow, we haven't had that kind of marmalade in a long time."

Gramma spotted a card on the window sill: "Remember, Ronnie, you sent me that birthday card this year. See the ribbons and buttons on the card? Where did they come from?"

Ronnie laughed. "Oh, those buttons are from an old shirt. When we made the card, Mom told me to go find an old shirt and said I could cut off the buttons for decorations! You really liked that card, Gramma!"

"Well, now do you think we recycle?"

"Oh, yeah, I see. When you recycle, it just means you are using something handy for something else."

Travel Experiences

Most families take trips together, some to the grocery store or to visit local relatives, others on lengthy vacations traveling throughout the United States or abroad. Local trips provide rich learning experiences when parents extend the experience with observations about the scenery and what has changed in the familiar environment or with

# 1 **CANDIED APPLE FANS**	# 4 **TAMBOURINE**
Cut apple 1/2 sheet of red construction paper ≈ glue on to tongue depressor with Elmer's glue	decorate a bright colored paper plate
back view	punch holes around edge ≈ tie bells on with wire twists
# 2 **LAUNDRY BAG**	# 5 **BOOKWORM BOOKMARK**
fold apron in half inside out ≈ stitch side and bottom ≈ leave top open = turn right side out	cut bookworm from foam sheet
stitch belt on to hang	WOODY sew beads on for eyes ≈ paint name with acrylics or sew letters cut from felt
# 3 **EASTER BASKET**	# 6 **BLUE RIBBON BOOKMARK**
styrofoam bowl ≈ punch holes for pipe cleaner handle ≈ line with fluted coffee filter	use blue construction paper for ribbon, double thickness ≈ put a dab of glue halfway up between ribbons
place on a bright doily ≈ line with green tissue strips	staple gold or silver sticker on top ≈ glue on decorative sticker 1 S T

FIGURE 8-5 The Art of Recycling *Source:* Arthur (2008). Used with permission.

discussions about what is to be bought, why, and where to find it. Such involvement helps children learn about their natural environment and become keen observers of change. Among other things, they learn the give-and-take of discussion, reasons for doing things, and classification skills. Parents provide valuable emotional support and express values as they demonstrate pleasure in sharing these times with their children.

Ricardo, living in a subsidized housing unit in a small community, was a town rubbish collector with responsibility for retrieving collectible bottles and cans. He was the caregiver for his two children and often took them on his rounds. The children counted the collectibles and sorted materials according to the size of the refund they would produce. Ricardo, a naturalist by interest and with some training, also enjoyed pointing out to his children features along the route, such as birds, new flowers in bloom, and interesting rock formations.

The following vignette illustrates some values learned during a camping trip.

Camping across the country, the Hi family discovered that temperatures varied considerably when they awoke in the morning. Mai Lin never seemed to dress right for the travel days. She was either too hot or too cold as they hiked or drove. Without saying anything to anyone, she began to solve her problem by sticking her hand out of the tent each morning to "test" the weather. As the trip progressed, she began to get better at sensing what the day's weather would be like and became a much happier traveler. She also learned how to dress by observing her parents and hearing their discussions on what they were going to wear that day. She discovered how to adapt to the abrupt changes in temperatures that sometimes occurred within a few hours as the family traveled through snowy mountains to a hot valley below. In addition to learning about geography and its effect on changes in climate, Mai Lin learned to figure out how to make herself comfortable.

All families educate their children to achieve some level of functioning in society. Although there are dysfunctional families in which children's learning is hampered or even distorted, most families provide varied educational opportunities for their children through daily routines and ongoing family activities. The best outcomes occur when families assume their share of responsibility for the education of their children and work with schools and communities to assist in the process. In Chapter 7, we discuss more aspects of family functioning and delineate the characteristics of competent families where positive learning takes place.

IMPLICATIONS FOR TEACHERS

Traveling Around Town

Get a large local map of your town or city (the chamber of commerce or the city planning office will have copies) and post it in your classroom. Then have the children identify the different places they visited last week. You will need to start them off with accounts of a few of your own trips (to the market, church, etc.).

With prompts (e.g., "Did anyone go to the movie last weekend?"), you will find children recalling much of their local traveling in a week. Put push pins or colored stars on the map for the spots named. You can then discuss with your group the value of the destinations for the families and the reasons for traveling. You may want to identify places in town that no one visited. And you may want to discuss the types of restrictions or the "freedom to roam" found in each of the places visited.

This project will heighten children's interest in the community and reveal the interconnectedness of our communities and neighborhoods. It will also provide a beginning study of the local geography and ecology.

GRANDPARENTS PROVIDE A CURRICULUM

In this section, we present some features of grandparents' influence on the home curriculum. The selections and examples are chosen from the authors' experiences working with grandparents from varying cultures and from several qualitative research studies (Barbour, Barbour, & Hildebrand, 2001).

Grandparents Influence Children's Development

As with other providers of the home curriculum, grandparents' influence on children is diverse. Although research on this question has existed for 50 years, the results of each study depend so much on ecological, historical, and cultural variability that generalizations are difficult to make (Tomlin, 1998). Age of grandparents, age of grandchildren, geographical differences, and relationships of grandparents with the nuclear family, plus family structure and processes, have an impact that ranges from minimal to substantial (Berns, 2006). Studies indicate four different categories of grandparents: the custodial grandparent, the nearby grandparent, the distant grandparent, and the emotionally remote grandparent.

The custodial grandparent influences the child's development in a manner very similar to that of a parent, so there is a significant influence. The emotionally remote grandparent has little contact with the child, so there is probably little influence. Caring and supporting grandparents, living nearby or in a distant area, who keep in close contact with their families, have considerable influence on the home curriculum.

Directly or indirectly, grandparents give their grandchildren a value system and a philosophy of how children are to be instructed, whether morally, religiously, culturally, or intellectually. Elizabeth, in the following vignette, is learning two ways of writing and expressing herself because of her grandmothers. Because both grandparents live at some distance, they keep in contact with her through letters, e-mail, and telephone calls.

Elizabeth was an active 6-year-old who had discovered the rhythms of language early. Her Grandmother Dailey, a former English teacher, firmly believed that children should learn to speak correctly and not use "silly phrases" or "special invented terms." Her Grandmother Denato, however, delighted in the "discovered" terms Elizabeth used and would often repeat them, thus reinforcing the idea that language can be created. At Christmas, Elizabeth received a collection of rocks from Grandmother Denato and books from Grandmother Dailey. Her thank-you letters to both grandmothers consisted of a drawing of the gift plus a statement. Before sending the letter to Grandmother Dailey, Elizabeth asked her mother about Babar, one of the book's characters and, with her mother's help, carefully copied on her drawing the words "I liked the elephant book best." On the picture she sent to Grandmother Denato, she wrote by herself, "Rnd redrks spkls lgblk rks wjshin ilvu Dne" ("Round red rocks with sparkles long black rocks which shine. I love you, Donny"— her pet name for this grandmother).

At age 6, Elizabeth has already learned what each grandmother values. In wanting to please each grandmother, she is learning valuable things. For the grandmother who is precise, she learns about story characters, and she has learned to

Nearby grandparents have shorter but more frequent contacts with their grandchildren.

copy a few short words with her mother's help. With her other grandmother, she has learned the fun of playing with words and sounds and is willing to experiment and try out her knowledge of letters and sounds. Elizabeth's mother supports the values of both grandparents by supporting Elizabeth's efforts without passing judgment.

In some situations, children receive mixed messages concerning their competence, their sense of safety, or the importance of taking risks. David, in the following vignette, receives two different messages about the same situation from his grandparents. Of course, other cultural and sociological factors will also determine how he interprets these messages, especially because he sees his Grandmother Hu, who lives nearby, more often. Visits to Grandmother Williams take place each summer for 3 or 4 weeks, plus other holidays.

David Hu, now 4 years old, was born with a partly developed left hand. He has only stubs for fingers, though his thumb appears to be well developed. His father is Chinese and his mother is European American. David, his mother, father, and Grandmother Hu, are visiting at the summer home of his maternal grandmother in a small seashore community. The grandmothers are supervising David at a summer playgroup program, and he has gone outside to play on the slide. Grandmother Hu immediately goes with him. Grandmother Williams finishes her reading with a group of 4-year-olds and follows later. When she arrives, David has begun climbing up the front of the slide, with his thumb firmly grasping the side of the slide. Occasionally he slips but catches himself. Grandmother Hu is trying to stop him from climbing, but David ignores her. Grandmother Williams speaks to Mrs. Hu rather sharply. "Oh, leave him alone, he's doing a great job."

Mrs. Hu says in a worried voice, "But he might get hurt," and then points to his left hand. Mrs. Williams replies, "We don't know that. Let's just watch and see how he handles it."

David continues to climb two or three times, sliding gleefully down the slide. On his last slide, he jerks back, loses his grip, hits his head on the slide, and begins to howl. Both grandmothers rush to him and try to comfort him. Suddenly, he breaks away from them both and begins climbing and sliding again. While the two grandmothers argue over his safety, he happily continues his activity until one of the helpers calls to tell him that the rest of the class is doing an art project. David rushes inside with the other children.

The two grandmothers have different views of how David should be treated. Mrs. Hu feels great responsibility and anxiety about his safety, but according to Mrs. Williams, she is overprotective. Mrs. Hu even hovers over him while he is doing his artwork. She is always ready to help him do the project "correctly." Mrs. Williams is satisfied with a cavalier approach, feeling that the art project is uniquely his.

David is developing his physical skills in a mixed-message environment. He already knows that he can do more around Mrs. Williams and less around Mrs. Hu. He knows Mrs. Hu will protect him more and make sure he doesn't overextend himself. Mrs. Williams will allow him to experiment more, but he is likely to hurt himself more.

Perhaps David will learn a middle course whereby he is willing to take risks but experiment more to test his skill level before plunging in.

Both nearby and distant grandparents can have a great influence on children. In general, the nearby grandparent has shorter but more frequent contacts, whereas the distant grandparent's contacts are longer but fewer in number. Grandparents tend to have more fun with their grandchildren than they had time for with their own children, and they tend to feel less responsible for the well-being of their grandchildren. Cultural differences become blurred when living in the United States, but we often find differences in how families view their kin relationships (Tomlin, 1998). European Americans, although often close geographically, believe in developing independence in their children and grandchildren. They encourage their children to move away, especially for college and work, and to become financially and socially independent. Grown children attend family gatherings, but their social network in European American families tends

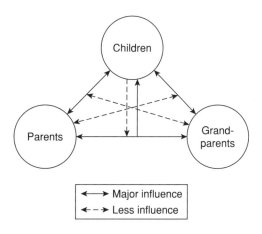

FIGURE 8-6   Grandparent Connection to Nuclear Family Members   *Source:* Barbour et al. (2001).

Note: For most families, there is substantial engagement between child and parents, between parents and grandparents, and between child and grandparents. The extent of engagement is related to living arrangements, marital situation and condition, and family history. The diagram assumes a typical nuclear family with grandparents living nearby and no estrangement. Note the lessened influence of grandparents on the parent–child connection and the similarly lessened influence of parents on the grandparent–child interaction. Children's influence on parent–grandparent interaction is different still.

to include their own age group. In other cultures, family relationships normally extend into their children's lives. In the families shown in this chapter's vignettes, the children experienced connections to their grandparents through the rituals of their heritage—Christmas gift giving and other holiday observations. Figure 8-6 gives cues to the different influence patterns found in extended families.

REFLECTION

Think back to the things you learned from your grandparents. What activities would you consider important enough to add to the list in Table 8-1?

IMPLICATIONS FOR TEACHERS

Grandparents or Parents?

Think for a moment about the different attitude your grandparents had, from those of your own parents, about schoolwork and the mastery of particular skills. If there are differences, make a two-column list for yourself: "Grammie believed this" and "Mum and Dad believed this." If the list you produce shows several differences (or even similarities), this will give you a good notion of some typical variations that most people encounter.

Now use a similar strategy with primary-school children with which you are comfortable. Start out with something like "When I visit Grammie for dinner, I usually have _____. At home, we usually have _____ for dinner." Then move to ways that grandparents help children that are different than those of one's parents. Perhaps prompts like "starting or learning a new game," "practicing dance steps," or "playing baseball" will bring out the different teaching methods and relational styles that grandparents have.

The result will be a greater appreciation of extended family members, but it will also give you insights into the family relationships of the children in the classroom.

Advantages of a Grandparent Curriculum

Although they have neither curriculum goals nor activities to achieve them, grandparents do realize that to establish a relationship with a grandchild, they need to make an effort to know them as they mature and change. An important aspect of grandparenthood

TABLE 8-1   Advantages of a Grandparent Curriculum

Goals	Activities
Sharing values and adapting to different value systems	Elizabeth's adaptation to cultural influences focused on her developing literacy skills, whereas David's focus was on developing physical skills.
Child gaining knowledge from grandparents	The Williamses are sailors, and at age 4, David was allowed to help steer the boat. Later, he learned to sail by himself.
Grandparents learning from grandchildren	Elizabeth's Grandmother Denato learned many computer skills from 6-year-old Elizabeth, including how to use e-mail. David's Grandmother Hu was timid when climbing, and 4-year-old David showed her where to put her feet and where to hold on as they climbed ledges together.
Learning the skills of interaction with older people and grandparents of different cultures	David learned to speak directly to his Grandfather Williams (who was a bit deaf) by looking him in the eye and "speaking up." With Grandpa Hu he spoke softly and was deferent. As he learned expressions of greeting, politeness, and questioning in both languages, he learned different inflections and different body language for each grandparent.
Understanding the geography and history of family members	Elizabeth's Grandmother Denato frequently traveled and sent postcards to Elizabeth. Later, Elizabeth and her grandmother played games; they found these places on maps and recalled who lived there.
Understanding the different household tasks and responsibilities	At one grandmother's house, Elizabeth learned that she was to make her bed, take her dishes off the table, and help with the sweeping before playing or watching TV. At Grandmother Denato's house, her responsibility was to get her grandmother up, and then the two of them would make plans for the day.
Building healthy self-esteem	Elizabeth and David's grandparents both helped build self-esteem, because they praised them, attended the grandchildren's sporting Events, and expressed pride in their art, music, and school papers. These grandparents attended to their grandchildren's successes and empathized with their struggles. Self-confidence was supported as the grandparents accepted help from the grandchildren, respected their opinions, and reinforced the parents' child-rearing practices.

is "having fun with them" or finding satisfaction in their encounters, whether one visits a zoo, reads a story, plays games, listens to them, or attends their activities. Some advantages of grandparent influence are shown in Table 8-1.

HOMESCHOOLING

Families that assume total responsibility for their children's education often opt to educate their children at home, at least for part of their schooling years. The term **homeschooling** is used to define academic learning that occurs as a result of activities provided in the home (or extensions of the home), with the parents acting as teacher-facilitators.

Homeschooling is not a new concept, but it has gained popularity in recent years, and enrollment estimates range up to 2 million. Homeschooling is a flexible and diverse system of teaching and learning with a variety of practices. Just as various philosophies guide curriculum in schools, parents also consider teaching and learning using a traditional approach as well as constructive methods. Because of their tutorlike environment, homeschool curriculum activities are more likely to be geared to children's interests. The definition of homeschooling is clarified by Kerman's (1990) description of a typical day of homeschooling, summarized as follows:

෨— *Their day starts with the family eating breakfast. Afterward, the 9-year-old daughter leaves with her father for the library, where she will do preplanned library study, then will carry out some errands for the family. At home, the mother provides unscheduled activities for the two preschoolers that relate to the children's interests, to household needs, and to events that happen in the neighborhood. They read several stories, wash dishes, make play dough, do "dress-up" and dramatic play, and then walk down the road to watch a fire truck putting out a fire.* —෨

History of Homeschooling

Homeschooling was the norm for most families during the early years of the republic. In the late 19th and early 20th centuries, with the advent of compulsory education, however, the practice of homeschooling diminished. In the late 1970s, many parents, disenchanted with their local schools, found support for their efforts in different writings, for example John Holt (1982). Since the 1980s, interest in homeschooling, driven by differing motivations, has increased dramatically. We now find specialized publishing houses, advocacy groups with legal departments, and national conferences supporting homeschooling programs.

Increased networking among homeschoolers and Internet access have provided parents with organizational support, publications, workshops, and legal support for those who have difficulty meeting state mandates. One prominent support agency, the Home School Legal Defense Association (HSLDA; http://www.hslda.org), maintains a large database of litigated cases on homeschooling.

An unstructured learning method in homeschooling allows children to follow particular interests.

The demand for information about homeschooling has become a sizable industry, and estimates show that Americans spend up to $1,200 per student per year for materials. Consolidation of support systems, plus easy access to a variety of resources, is now accompanied by greater public acceptance of homeschooling as a viable alternative to public education.

In some school districts, educators encourage homeschooling parents to use school services, attend some classes, and participate in extracurricular activities. In the past 10 years, some school systems have organized education centers, and other districts share their resources and allow homeschooled students to take special classes.

Motives for Homeschooling

Parents homeschool their children for a variety of reasons, but most parents fall into two distinct groups—the **ideologues** and the pedagogues. Both groups disagree with educators about what is happening in schools today. Ideologues disagree with the values presented by teachers or their children's peers; therefore, these parents choose to homeschool so that the family's religious and social values are the ones their children internalize.

The growing group of pedagogues feel that their children can receive a more personalized and better education if they are taught at home. Some parents choose to homeschool because they fear their children's exposure to problems such as violence, drugs, and disruptive behavior in the public school system. Others disagree with the instructional and managerial styles of teachers and school administrators. Some are concerned with the inability of teachers to handle all the individual needs, interests, and learning styles of their children, and they fear that school will discourage their children from learning. Still other parents decide to homeschool because their children experience difficulty in school, and they feel that school personnel are inadequate or punitive when addressing problems.

WHO HOMESCHOOLS?   If the reasons for homeschooling are varied, the largest number of homeschoolers is amazingly alike demographically. The typical homeschooling family has two parents, has an income near the U.S. median, and is Caucasian and Protestant. Parents tend to have some college education, are professional or skilled workers, and come mostly from rural areas, although some are suburban. Homeschoolers appear to be conservative and law abiding but also individualistic and very child centered (Stevens, 2001). Most authorities now agree that homeschooling has become a forceful social movement, with effective lobbies in state and national government circles (Reich, 2002).

Teaching Methods in Homeschooling

The curriculum and methods for homeschooling depend on the home, but most methods fall into three categories: **fixed curriculum**, **units of study**, and **unstructured learning events** (Wade, 2004). The fixed curriculum consists of published guides with specific lessons, suggestions on how to teach, and evaluation techniques. This curriculum satisfies parents who are unsure of what to teach and who find comfort in a fixed schedule and a prescribed curriculum. Some parents, especially those who view homeschooling as a temporary solution to their children's educational needs, use the same textbooks used in the local schools. Correspondence schools, in which some parents enroll their children, meet this need and provide a structure and routine for homeschooling. More and more homeschooling parents are using Internet resources to provide learning opportunities for their children.

Homeschool organizations, such as Oak Meadows (Brattleboro, Vermont) as well as regular publishing companies, have curriculum guides and suggestions for units of study (Oakmeadow Schools, 2009). In these materials, the teaching and learning are more flexible, and children move through specific units at their own pace and as their interests dictate. Homeschoolers themselves encourage others to use various teaching strategies that customize learning for a particular child (The Teaching Home, 2002).

The unstructured learning method deals with subjects in which the children are interested, and development of skills takes place as children experience various events in their family life. Each child's curriculum will be very different when parents follow this method. Parents using this method often write about the many ways they enable their children to be successfully schooled. Some read to their children a great deal and provide a range of quality materials. For these families, books of all sorts, including reference materials, are always available. In addition, computers provide these knowledgeable homeschooling families with many more learning opportunities: access to the Internet for searches on current events or other topics, use of e-mail for communicating with friends or relatives in distant places, and a multitude of computer games.

Children schooled at home are normally included in all family work activities, such as cooking, doing laundry, or construction projects. Family recreational and educational activities, such as visiting libraries and museums, are also done together. Math skills are developed as parents involve children in building, using money, and calculating family finances. Many children and parents explore their environment together, learning science concepts as they follow their interests.

Even within a single family, the routine and methods followed by homeschoolers will vary from year to year as children develop skills, new interests, and the ability to pursue their own learning. The common element is that children's interests are always paramount, and drill or practice is done at the pace the children set. Homeschooled children are less likely to become bored with learning tasks because they have greater access to their mentors. Also, parents are more likely to respond to a child's complaints about the material being too easy or too difficult (Fried, 2005).

Legal Aspects of Homeschooling

Laws concerning homeschooling vary, and as homeschooling has gained momentum, many states are changing their statutes. All 50 states have compulsory attendance laws and homeschoolers can encounter legal problems, depending on how state offices interpret these laws. Court and state offices use the following issues in deciding the legality of homeschooling:

1. Parents' right of choice regarding their children's welfare
2. Equivalency of education
3. Homeschools considered as private, religious, or charter schools
4. Issues of the qualifications of teachers

Specific state laws range from a most rigorous approach to parent-friendly support for homeschooling. The National Home Education Network (http://www.home-school-curriculum-and-support.com/) and the National Challenged Homeschoolers Associated Network (http://www.nathhan.com), an international association that helps in educating children with special needs, are both excellent sources for information on laws and regulations regarding homeschooling.

REFLECTION

Try to contact a parent who has homeschooled children, and list the advantages that person perceives. Then check with various school personnel to see if they share those views. Do any negative factors appear in your discussion with all parties?

Criticisms and Successes of Homeschools

As the homeschooling movement has grown, some states and school districts have registered concerns about truancy issues, appropriate curriculum, student achievement, and loss of matching funds.

Few data have been collected to support or to refute criticisms of homeschooling, but in those states requiring standardized tests, homeschoolers score on average 15% higher than their public school peers (National Center for Education Statistics, 2009). Studies also indicate that no significant relationship exists between homeschoolers' achievements and their parents' education level. This appears to counter the argument that parents lack the skills to teach a variety of subjects.

Examining the individual success stories of homeschooled children, we find evidence that many homeschoolers do well academically and socially when they return to public school, find jobs in the community, or gain acceptance to college. Communities and authorities do have an obligation to all children under their jurisdiction, however, and educators recognize that homeschooling is not for all parents or for all children. The reported successes are probably attributable to parents who wish to be an integral part of their children's learning and are willing to do the hard work and make the commitment it requires. Certainly not all parents have the time, inclination, patience, or ability to sustain such nourishment on a long-term basis. We must keep in mind that teachers are key personnel in many phases of children's education, including those children being homeschooled. Therefore, communication with homes where children are homeschooled is vital. As a teacher, you need to give support and keep communication lines open. The situation must be analogous to the home–school–community partnership.

Summary and Review

Children receive a great deal of education outside the classroom walls, and whether intentionally or accidentally, parents provide a rich and varied curriculum in the home. Although great differences appear in the quantity and quality of home curricula, all parents, as well as other family members, provide emotional, social, physical, and intellectual stimuli for children's development.

Parents begin the process of educating their young as they respond to the infant's vocalizations. These interactions nurture preliteracy and communication skills. Children learn role expectations and responsibilities as the family carries out routines and rituals. Parental interaction styles, the type of environment, and the space in which children are raised also affect children's learning.

Children's home curriculum is an accumulation of all the experiences they have in their homes. Thus, each child's curriculum is different, but similarities occur as a result of daily routines that exist for most families. Both skills and knowledge about the world are acquired as children participate in preparing for the day, meal preparation, and bedtime rituals. From family traditions and rituals, children gain an understanding of their ethnic and cultural identity and of their place in the world. As parents share

their own special interests and talents, children expand their concepts of the world around them. The expanding world of technology provides an extended curriculum, and the way parents monitor and interact with their children regarding new media determines the benefits or pitfalls of their use. The beginning steps of handling money are also necessary objectives in children's homes.

Extended family members will also provide stimulus for children's development. There is a "grandparent curriculum" that reinforces and supplements—or differs from—the nuclear family's practices. The amount of influence depends a great deal on the relationships between the nuclear and extended families and the caring and involvement of grandparents.

Although a small group has always believed in education at home, the homeschooling movement has grown rapidly since the 1960s. Numerous reasons are given for this increase, but most parents choose this route for religious and social reasons or because of philosophical differences with schools regarding education. Homeschooling is not for everybody, and all agree that this process requires a lot of hard work and a strong commitment to sustain positive outcomes.

Suggested Activities and Questions

1. Visit a suburban home and a city apartment and compare the amount of living space. What are some of the things you think children living in each space would learn about themselves?

2. Ask a child to share a story or event about home activities. Plan ways to extend the retelling or get additional information from the child. What skills do you need to listen well?

3. List the kinds of trips you took with your family when you were growing up. Include events such as shopping, visiting relatives, and recreational outings, as well as vacation trips. From your memory of the experiences, what do you think you learned (physically, emotionally, socially, and intellectually) from these trips?

4. Watch a news report that a child might watch with a parent and discuss with colleagues the violence that children would witness. Make a list of comments and questions that you believe will help children process any violence they might have viewed.

5. Check with your state's department of education to find out the regulations for homeschooling in your state. Discuss with classmates your feelings about the success of parents who choose this practice for their children.

6. Make a list of some childhood things you did with your grandparents; then share with classmates some valued learning that came from those interactions.

Resources

Organizations

Family Service Association of America   *http://www.family-service.org*

Children, Youth and Family Consortium   *http://www.cyfc.umm.edu*

Council on Economic Education   *http://www.cee.org*

Holt Associates/Growing Without Schooling   *http://www.holtgws.com*

National Homeschool Association   *http://www.N-H-A.org*

Web Sites

http://www.amazon.com   Lists the 100 top picks for home school curricula.

http://www.edexcellence.net   The Thomas B. Fordham Foundation sponsors the Education Excellence Network site to promote voucher programs, charter schools, and privatization.

http://www.ehow.com   Thousands of files offering step-by-step instructions for all sorts of home tasks and projects.

http://www.homeschoolreviews.com   Contains curriculum materials related to different philosophical views of curriculum, such as a Waldorf approach, an eclectic approach, a classical approach, and unit studies.

http://www.inspiration.com/   Inspiration K through 12 supports visual and thinking techniques to help children brainstorm, plan, organize, and create.

http://www.zerotothree.org   An excellent resource for parents and professionals working with infants and toddlers.

CHAPTER 9

Curriculum of the Community

*The child is an ever-attentive witness of grown-up morality—or lack thereof;
the child looks for cues as to how one ought to behave, and finds them galore
as we parents and teachers go about our lives, making choices, addressing
people, showing in action our rock-bottom assumptions, desires, values, and
thereby telling those young observers much more than we may realize.*

(COLES, 1997, P. 5)

After reading this chapter, you will be able to do the following:

- Describe how organizations and agencies within a community provide many and varied learning opportunities for children.
- Compare community education that is planned by members in organizations and agencies with the **incidental learning** that occurs informally.
- Specify how children's learning within the community is a result of their observations of how things work and how people interact with materials and other people.
- Discuss how the physical, emotional, and moral attributes of a community support and extend or hinder children's opportunities.
- Explain how social networks, involving both adults and peers, affect the amount and quality of learning that children derive from their community.
- Define mentoring and explain some guidelines that would be helpful in developing a mentor plan for young children.

The purpose of this chapter is to examine the rich but often overlooked features of the community for children's learning. Just as we have a curriculum of the school and of the home, we also have a curriculum of the community.

Most commonly associated with our dwelling places in neighborhoods and towns, the concept of *community* also includes the kinship community of extended family and close friends and communities of the mind, such as religious organizations and interest groups. Like the family curricula examined in Chapter 8, the community curriculum is affected by the location, cultural aspects, and physical makeup of the region, plus the social networks established by its inhabitants.

In the 21st century, the gap between the rich and poor grows wider, and many adults and agencies are trying new strategies to overcome the social, economic, and environmental barriers that hinder some children's learning. Most investigators agree that children growing up in affluent communities or with strong parental support have a greater chance of school success than those in poor communities with high crime rates, transient family life, and poverty where parents have trouble just providing shelter and food (Adelman & Taylor, 2002). Under poor and depressed conditions, the school is the social setting typically stretched to ensure that all students succeed. Community social agencies, entertainment outlets, and business organizations have an obligation to work with schools to find new solutions. We have evidence that this effort works.

Chapter 1 presented the many influences on children's learning, and we found that all curricula are affected by these influences. Although there are great differences among communities, there are also many commonalities that suggest similar educational experiences and opportunities.

Every community is composed of interconnected social systems, and the way the people of these systems relate to one another greatly affects children's learning and development (Bradley, 2002; Bronfenbrenner, 1979). Various organizations within the community offer different aspects of curriculum, and children learn just by being exposed to these organizations. In addition, the physical, moral, and emotional environments children encounter in their immediate neighborhoods enhance or hinder intellectual development. Whereas some communities deliberately plan additional opportunities for children's growth, others seem oblivious to the ways their organizational structure affects children's learning and, unfortunately, make no attempt to remove barriers.

In this chapter, we consider the wider community and its potential for helping children grow. We examine community organizational structure and suggest how some of the diverse agencies "educate" children. The physical and social-emotional environments in a community together constitute a basic support system for all families, one that enables parents and child-care staff to stimulate children in different ways. These situations are ready made for teachers to harness the surrounding learning opportunities.

In some communities, however, the physical and social-emotional environments are so destructive that children are placed at developmental and educational risk. There, the supportive interaction of community agencies with families and schools is a crucial key. Educators must ferret out the positives for children's benefit.

IMPLICATIONS FOR TEACHERS

Capitalize on Your Community

Take a ride through your school community to find what will be valuable for learning projects. These will be guesstimates if you are a new professional in the area, but many will turn out to be very helpful later on. Make a list of 10 things or places that could connect with your program; for example, there may be a new branch library, a recently built supermarket, or a renovated fishing pier.

Now, how do you approach these places? Will you visit the establishments and interview managers? Will you write to the directors? Perhaps you will get a few parents to go with you to analyze what will be useful in the community to enhance your school program.

All this scouting will require planning on your part, but start a list before you move on to the specifics described in this chapter and Chapter 10.

COMMUNITY CONFIGURATION AFFECTS CURRICULUM

Although every community varies in structure and the kinds of services available to its citizens, we find similar human, natural, and material resources. Figure 9-1 presents a partial list of these resources. A child's neighborhood may be in a city, small town, suburb,

---

NATURAL RESOURCES

Living Organisms: Plants, animals, insects, fish

Geographic: Minerals, bodies of water, beaches, parks, farmland

SERVICES

Educational: Zoos, museums, libraries, schools, parks

Communication: Telephones, radio and TV stations, post offices, newspaper offices, computer networks

Entertainment: Theaters, movies, fairs, festivals, circuses, restaurants, TV and radio stations

Recreation: Playgrounds, church or community clubs, athletic facilities, ballparks, tennis courts, parks

Transportation: Airports, train and bus stations, taxis, gas stations, car rental agencies

Commercial: Department stores, grocery stores, pharmacies, different types of farms (orchards, fish farms, dairy farms), special shops (toy stores, ice cream shops, salons, pet stores, craft shops), factories, other business enterprises

Professional: Offices of physicians, dentists, lawyers, and other professionals, fire and police departments, funeral homes, courts, clinics and hospitals, political offices, university campuses, school department headquarters

Service agencies: Employment offices, social services and public assistance offices, counseling centers, food coops, mayor's office

Living quarters: Children's and teachers' homes, apartment complexes, mobile homes, new home sites, real estate offices, retirement communities, nursing homes

MATERIALS AND MEDIA

Print: Books, pamphlets, brochures, magazines and newspapers, advertisements

Audiovisual: Films, TV, radio, audio and video cassettes, compact discs, DVDs, computer programs, Internet sites, exhibits

Recyclables: Fabric, wood or carpet samples, buttons, ribbon, wallpaper samples, bottles, cans, boxes, wire, spools, cartons, used paper

SOCIAL NETWORKS

Adult: Friends, neighbors, colleagues and coworkers, social clubs, religious groups, sports groups, family members, community theater groups

Peer: Young relatives, school and neighborhood friends, club and team partners

ETHNIC ASSOCIATIONS

Contacts: Various languages, cultural festivals, religious activities, artistic expressions

---

FIGURE 9-1   Community Resources That Educate Children

or rural area. The resources available in each of these settings will vary, but all provide the bases for a community curriculum. For example, whether in a rural area or in a city, children will observe aspects of nature. Trees, birds, animals, and stars at night are available to rural children, but city children also witness the warmth of the sun, wetness of rain, small plants pushing up between concrete slabs, and ants carrying away crumbs. Southern children know palm trees; northern children, fir trees; and southwestern children, juniper and cacti. Weather provides learning experiences as well. Some children experience tornado conditions and the haphazardness of destruction. Others may enjoy long spells of soothing hot weather but then learn the distress of drought.

Children constantly learn from persons in their neighborhoods. How much learning children gain from others besides kin in the home depends on how much association they have, how safe their neighborhood is, and how many community services and agencies their parents use. In safe neighborhoods, children have more freedom to move beyond their homes and to observe and interact with people involved in various activities and occupations. How people dress, what distinguishes young people from old, how adults treat each other and children in passing, and many other qualities and interactions teach children about life. In violent neighborhoods, children also learn important lessons from observation of community activities, but too often, out of fear, parents must confine their children or closely supervise them. This limits children's opportunities for physical exploration and thus limits their intellectual and social experimentation in favor of developing simple survival skills.

Children learn from various materials generated by people in society. Some materials, such as a brochure about good eating habits for primary-school-age children, are prepared with educational intentions. Toy companies induce adults to buy various items for children, and often advertisements will suggest a device's educational value. For example, the new Computer Cool School attachment for home computers shows a 4-year-old focusing on counting using the kid-friendly keyboard.

Children also learn from many other materials, including those that adults consider junk. From observing, touching, smelling, and manipulating wood scraps, earth and sand, Styrofoam, bottles, shells, cans, and the like, children learn variations in texture, size, shape, and smell. Without adult support, the learning may be minimal or the result could put children in harm's way. Even so, children left on their own do gain considerable knowledge about the materials around them.

Every community has **service agencies**, political establishments, **social agencies**, and business enterprises. Just as schools and homes provide a curriculum, so do community establishments and agencies. The efforts, products, and resources of all these agencies provide formal, informal, and hidden curricula similar to those of the school environment.

Children acquire knowledge, values, and social skills (positive as well as negative) from their experiences within their communities and interactions with community workers. We find, of course, no single established curriculum for a community, any more than we find a common

Children learn variations in texture, shape, and smell from touching and manipulating earth, sand, rocks, and shells.

curriculum for all families. Resources vary, and how these resources are made available, plus the family's and school's ability to make use of them, determine their learning potential.

REFLECTION

After you review Figure 9-1 on community resources, consider each area and try to recall one thing you learned specifically as a result of these resources. Share with classmates any dramatic memories of your own experiences.

Community Agencies

Service agencies provide families with health, transportation, protection, communication, and numerous professional services. These agencies provide experiences from which children gain knowledge through exhibits, demonstrations, and actual participation as well as in informal ways. Formal educational presentations from most agencies have been carefully thought through, and prepared materials are directed to parents or teachers to assist in instruction. Other materials or experiences are directed to children. A child's first experience with the family dentist is one example of a community professional "educating" a young client.

Since Rodrigo was 3 years old, he had accompanied his mother to the dentist for her semi-annual checkup. While his mother was in the chair, he would sit nearby with a few toys. One day, Dr. Garcelon asked him if he wouldn't like to sit in the big chair where his mother had sat. As Rodrigo climbed up, the dentist allowed him to touch the instruments and told him what they were for. He encouraged him to press the water tap and to rinse his mouth from the paper cup nearby. Gradually, over two or three visits, he introduced all the cleaning instruments and even turned on the polishing brush so that Rodrigo could see how it vibrated. At first, Rodrigo refused to have the brush placed in his mouth, but gradually he became so intrigued with the instruments that he wanted to see what would happen. One day a small squirrel came to the dentist's window and chattered away. Dr. Garcelon and the young child took a moment to feed the squirrel before the dentist gave Rodrigo a toothbrush and toothpaste with verbal and written pictorial instructions on how to use the brush at home.

This dentist had a planned program for introducing dental hygiene to young patients. At first, children observed parents' checkups—a rather informal learning experience. Parental comfort and the dentist's reassuring ways provided a safe and secure environment for the next phase. The formal instruction on what happens in a dentist's chair was designed to build children's trust as well as to start children on the road to good dental hygiene. The pamphlet Rodrigo received had simple instructions, with pictures, so that even at age 4, he could see how to brush his teeth. The squirrel's appearance was an accidental event during which Rodrigo observed an animal close-up, discovered something about feeding animals, and experienced an adult's gentle treatment of a particular animal.

Just as teachers and homes vary in how they instruct children, so do people in various agencies and professions. Some dentists are not as thorough as Dr. Garcelon in giving information to parents, whom they expect to instruct children. But many medical professionals work with schools, with child-care centers, and at health fairs to provide free initial health checkups. In some communities, free health clinics (many as mobile units) are regularly available for needy families. It is through these avenues that materials and curricula on health care are provided by medical professionals.

Most community agencies provide materials that schools and parents can use to feature the functions of those agencies. Police and fire departments, for example, provide speakers for schools and encourage field trips to their stations. Some police officers and firefighters get special training in how to work with young children, and children who visit are allowed to climb, under supervision, onto fire trucks or into police cars. Department representatives wear their uniforms and explain the equipment they carry and use. They also explain what children are to do when a police officer or firefighter is trying to assist them.

Transportation Services

In a mobile society, transportation is often necessary for children to participate in community events. Children who live in cities will experience various forms of public transportation, whereas those in suburbs may travel primarily in cars. Transportation in rural areas can be a limiting factor, as large distances may exist between homes and other facilities. Travel can also provide children with many enriching as well as hostile experiences, depending on the political, societal, or physical environment. A terminal in a small airport can be explored freely, but at large terminals, children must be under close supervision.

In times of tight national security, young children's needs are often disregarded because of the nervousness of officials. After 9/11, the authors witnessed a 3-year-old child being pulled from her father's protective arms and made to walk through the metal detector while in hysterics. Yet, at a less tense time, the official invited a child to watch what others did and then politely asked the child to remove her shoes, and together they watched them go through the scanner. She then skipped happily through the machine, smiled at the guard, and retrieved her shoes.

Transportation agencies provide many formal learning experiences for children as they collaborate with schools in planning trips to airports, train stations, or bus stops. Much of the learning about modes of travel comes from classes studying such a unit, from parents as children accompany them, or from materials (maps, brochures, schedules) that adults collect. Informal learning as children use different modes of travel is enormous. One 6-year-old's explanation of how she traveled from her home in Minnesota to visit her grandmother in Russia is a small example of the range of learning.

In answer to her grandmother's question about her trip, an eager Galina replied in one breath. "It took a l-o-o-ng time, Grandma, and I slept on the plane and I watched a movie. It was dark when Daddy put our luggage in the car and we drove to the airport. Daddy had to park our car—right, Daddy?—and Mommy and I took our luggage inside the station. I remember going through this machine, and the man asked me to take off my shoes. We were in lots of lines and there were s-o-o-o many people. There was a man with a gun, and I sat close to Mommy until he went, but Mommy said he was just making sure we were safe. On the plane, I fell asleep after we got some food on a little tray. Here in Moscow, we took a long escalator, and then I think some kind of train. Anyway, after we got our luggage, we had to wait in a long line until someone looked at the little book with our pictures in it. I think it's a passport. Right, Mommy? I am so glad to see you, Grandma! Just look at my red suitcase!! Uncle Vanya sent it to me—see, it has wheels, and it sure helped, 'cause Mommy said I had to carry my own luggage.

Galina's parents capitalized on her experiences and discovered that she was aware of many other aspects of transportation. Her cards to her friends, her journal writing, her drawings, and her conversations with her relatives not only revealed what she had assimilated, but also reinforced her understanding of new environments.

Political Agencies

All communities have government agencies, school boards, and task forces or committees empowered by the community government to provide different types of community curricula. The management decisions these agencies make will affect—directly and indirectly—the social, intellectual, and physical development of children in that community. Like social agencies, political agencies often provide written materials, films, or audiotapes designed to educate the public about their functions. Such agencies make use of newspapers, magazines, billboards, radio, television, and the Internet to carry their message to the public, and the assumption is that families and schools will then educate children.

In some communities, the formal curriculum on political organizations, usually handled through the schools, is more apparent, especially during election years. Mock elections are held in some schools, using local political campaign materials. Students sometimes visit local and state political offices, where teachers and political workers attempt to explain the functions and responsibilities of the resident officials. Children whose parents are active politically may begin to comprehend the functions, hierarchies, and decisions of an area's political agencies. The political implications of messages are usually beyond the comprehension of primary-school-age children, however. Children whose parents use social services managed by political officials can acquire confusing notions, especially when their parents have difficulty obtaining services. The political knowledge that children gain from such experiences tends to be serendipitous.

In the United States, national policies for children and their families began to be formulated only in the past 30 years (Bogenschneider & Corbett, 2004). Unlike other wealthy nations, the United States lacks supports for family life in areas such as adequate parental leave and child sick leave, universal health care coverage for children, a living minimum wage, and affordable, quality child care (Olfman, 2005). Consequently, available resources vary significantly from community to community.

Social policies established by community leaders affect the options and determine the resources of any family to establish networks and make use of available resources (Cochran, 2007). For instance, people living in wealthy communities often are able to negotiate with political figures for funding of well-equipped and well-maintained parks or recreational areas. They also make sure that libraries and museums have appropriate materials and outreach programs. Citizens in affluent areas have better access to child-care support services, community-based activities, and protective and health services. They tend to be better educated and so have developed better **networking** skills, which enable them to access these services (Cochran & Niegro, 2002). Children reared in poor communities, on the other hand, are often discriminated against and have fewer opportunities for learning. Parents in these neighborhoods appear to have less clout with governmental and management agencies, and with less education thus have fewer skills that enable them to access fully the benefits of community learning. The following vignette illustrates different potentials for social, intellectual, and physical learning as a result of two different policies for park maintenance.

In Wexton, the recreation department provided a park with grassy areas and paths. There are two swings, one piece of climbing equipment, and a basketball court. Maintenance of the park is poor. Swings are always in disrepair; garbage and debris litter the ground. Parents who bring children to the area will briefly exchange a smile or a word with the homeless man who frequents the park, and occasionally with adults rushing through it on their way to work or with those bringing dogs for an outing. Parents appear to allow their children to use the park for play, but they display little sense of coming here to meet other people. Parents are likely to discourage their children from interacting with others in the park.

In Overton, situated near a small shopping area, the community provided a small park with lots of climbing equipment, paths for tricycles, a basketball court, bicycle paths leading off into an open grove area, and benches where parents sit and supervise their children's play. The park is well maintained, with little debris. Paths are well cared for, as is all equipment. Park maintenance workers are seen frequently cleaning up the area and have been known to remind the older, unsupervised children to watch out for others as they play. In this park, parents chat with each other, watch their children interact with one another, and often begin to develop friendships. There is a sense that children are brought for outings, but also that parental contacts with others in the neighborhood are expanded. ⌒⌐

Children in these situations will learn many things in both parks, but the park in Overton, where more people, materials, and natural resources exist, has greater potential for positive learning opportunities. In both parks, one observes children gaining physical skills as they climb on equipment or play ball. Children use various strategies to engage other children in their play, and some appear to be skilled in interacting with other adults, such as when they crouch to pet a visitor's dog. There are differences, however.

In Wexton, there are fewer chances for personal interaction, because most parents discourage such interchanges, especially with disreputable-looking characters. Park maintenance is poor, so children receive different messages about the value of a clean environment. Some adults passing through the park are seen picking up trash and throwing it in available receptacles, but children witness others carelessly dropping litter. More potentially dangerous spots exist in Wexton, and children learn to be wary of their environment and aware of the danger signals.

In Overton, a different learning potential exists. Safe paths for children riding bicycles and tricycles from their homes to the park provide more opportunities for expanded physical development. Adults feel more comfortable with each other. The ambiance is welcoming, and the sense of trust among adults creates a stronger sense of trust in children. The park is kept free of debris, and maintenance personnel do not hesitate to remind children about respect for their environment. On the other hand, opportunities for learning danger signals may be more limited.

The community policy of providing and maintaining a park varies in these two communities. These policies are management choices, which in turn are influenced by the residents' pressure (or lack of such pressure) to maintain a safe environment. Adults' ability to use the resources available in the parks either enhance or limit what is learned in both situations.

It is not just with parks that communities provide options for adults to develop the social networks that enable them to use their community more advantageously. Governmental policy is inextricably interwoven with a community's social fabric. In some communities, policies regarding social service agencies make it much easier for adults to get the services they need (Cochran, 2007).

⌐⌐ *Darlene, a shy mother, had moved to a new community with her new baby and 4-year-old son. She needed help but dreaded applying for food stamps at the **Women, Infants, and Children (WIC)** program because of unpleasant experiences she had had before. When in desperation she finally went, however, she was pleasantly surprised at the quality of support. A community health organization had convinced the mayor's office to allow food stamp distribution at their **well-baby clinic**. Also, a group of volunteers had begun a program of reading with the babies and preschoolers at the clinic while their parents waited for appointments or discussed their children's health and nutritional needs. Darlene and the nurse discussed ways to entice children to develop good eating habits, and during her first visit, one of the volunteers invited Darlene to attend a parent support group for mothers with new babies. At these meetings, Darlene gained new confidence in herself, new skills in raising her children, and new friends.* ⌒⌐

Political decisions can affect the community curriculum presented to children. Not only is Darlene gaining help in feeding her children, but she is also learning how to educate them about good eating habits and learning to make social contacts with others.

Now she joins a group of mothers where children play together while the adults visit and exchange ideas on child rearing. In a more subtle way, parents at the WIC office and in the parent support group are exposed to models of adults reading to and interacting with children; thus, they may in turn provide expanded language experiences and positive social interactions for their own offspring.

IMPLICATIONS FOR TEACHERS

Using the System

Most persons know that the political offices in a community are power centers. You must know how to use these for your advantage in creating successful school support. Teachers, child-care workers, and specialists must be lobbyists as well as teachers at times.

When you have an assignment or a project to launch, determine how you can use city hall, your area representative to the legislature, candidates for political office, and so forth. No political figure will reject overtures from schools or teachers for help and support, because all of them are interested in education of the young. Use this base to enhance your work with children.

Start early and begin to provide information to political units and municipal officials before you make requests. All offices want up-to-date information on school practices, school programs, and particularly school success stories. You can start with the last item by mailing or calling the office with a success story about your class at school. For example:

> *I am a second-grade teacher at Bannock Elementary School, and I want to inform you that we are the regional chess champions for 2009.*

> *or*

> *I work with the primary team at Charleston Elementary School, and we are thrilled to inform you that five of our young students are featured in the Colorado Student Art Exhibit in Telluride.*

These positive notices can start a healthy communication line between you and your community power brokers. Follow your positive news with a brief message explaining the goals that you or your team has for your school. Invite representatives from their offices to visit your program, and ask for suggestions or reactions to the things they see. When you feel secure, ask the officials how they see their offices aiding your school programs.

Social and Cultural Agencies

The more skilled parents become at securing community services, the more opportunities they have to use other community resources, as illustrated in the following vignette.

Ginger's husband was a disabled veteran and had been moved twice for rehabilitation. Ginger and their two preschoolers moved to new states with him, but after the second move, she was left with few funds and no family support. After a few weeks, she swallowed her pride and went to a church soup kitchen so that her children could have one nutritious meal a day. A series of contacts with people at the center led her to the social agencies in her new community, where she learned how to tap resources for herself and her children. It wasn't always easy, for some of the policies seemed to hinder Ginger's progress. But the support systems she began to establish for herself did enable her to continue and adjust to her husband's long-term therapy. Ginger was able to finish her GED and find a part-time job. In the process, she expanded her network of friends in the service areas so that she could use community programs to enrich her children's experiences, of which museum programs and a 2-week summer recreational program were recent highlights.

Museums, aquariums, and zoos have hands-on and formal presentations for young children.

Religious groups, libraries, theaters, and recreational facilities as well as municipal human services departments are community agencies that supplement children's education. As with all situations, some children experience a richer curriculum than others. How well families are able to use available resources and how well agencies are able to reach all families in the community account for some of the disparity. These social and cultural agencies do not exist apart from one another, as the above vignette illustrates. A church agency providing physical and social nurturance helped Ginger access the governmental policies, which in turn helped her find other community resources for her children.

Governmental policies concerned with separation of church and state limit the resources that a religious organization can receive to support outreach programs for a community. Religious leaders, concerned with developing memberships, often wish to provide religious activities for young people within schools, but community policies normally exclude such events. However, under the recent NCLB legislation, such restrictions are beginning to change so that faith-based organizations, as well as nonprofit organizations, can receive funding to provide supplemental educational services, such as after-school programs and summer programs for economically deprived children (Center for Faith Based and Community Initiatives, 2007).

Librarians, theater personnel, and museum directors often try to develop programs with schools, whereby children are invited to cultural offerings at their centers. Too often, though, communities will not support such programs financially, or they believe that children will miss schoolwork and so must not be permitted to go. Those children whose parents have financial and social capital are able to profit by such community curriculum offerings, whereas other children are left out. Some cultural agencies locate financial sources other than political agencies to help community programs expand their curriculum to include more children and families. In one New Hampshire community, when schools eliminated art programs because of cutbacks in funding, the local artists' association provided art lessons to all children in the community with help from a local community foundation.

CULTURAL ORGANIZATIONS Many social and cultural agencies provide a rich formal curriculum to children. Such settings have a strong impact on children's information-processing skills, as well as on their physical, emotional, and moral development. Unless all families have equal access to these opportunities, a gap will remain between those who can afford to participate and those who cannot. The Walters Art Gallery in Baltimore, for example, has obtained grant funding to rescind their entry fee, so everyone in the community can visit the museum, regardless of ability to pay.

Art museums like the Walters offer both art instruction and art appreciation, as do opera companies and theaters. Often, theaters provide acting lessons, summer camp experiences, children's performances, and lectures about plays and playwrights. Not only do these groups want to enhance children's learning about the arts, they also want to develop future audiences. Science museums and zoos often offer hands-on experiences and formal presentations for young children. National and state parks provide various educational programs that emphasize education relating both to the park theme and to conservation and environmental protection.

Most libraries also seek to enhance children's appreciation of literature and learning through educational lectures, storytelling events, and book talks. Wilson (Wilson & Leslie, 2001) described a library program in which she uses guest speakers, media, Web sites, books, and hands-on experiences to enhance children's knowledge of the culture of Japan. The theme expands as children use reference books to find facts about Japanese food, celebrations, and cultural beliefs, as well as storybooks that describe everyday life in Japan. Children who participate in these **literacy events** expand their language, reading, writing, and computer skills, as well as their personal interaction skills and knowledge about where to find information.

Religious organizations offer summer day camp and religious education classes, and many integrate art, drama, and music in the instruction. Recreational facilities offer a wide array of courses in sports, such as gymnastics, basketball, or golf, as well as health-related classes in nutrition and physical fitness.

As with curriculum in any context, children acquire a great deal of knowledge through the informal and hidden curricula of these social and cultural agencies. For example, posters announcing coming events and programs inform adults, but in indirect ways, they inform children as well.

In a local theater while awaiting a performance, a 5-year-old observed an adult pointing to an announcement of the next production and commenting, "Oh, look, Bill Braunhof is appearing in Cats! *I wonder what the dates are?" Running her finger under the date, she exclaimed, "Oh, too bad. It's Wednesday the 22nd, and we won't be here."*

With no intention of teaching young children, theater personnel provided materials that could and did instruct. The adult, in seeking information for herself, unwittingly demonstrated to the child that such a poster offers information and that pieces of that information are found in different places on the poster. The child may even have discovered that "C-a-t-s" spells *cats*, and recognized it when seeing it again, or that "22" can mean 22nd.

Sometimes such informal teaching is intentional. In Overton, the community librarian discovered that children would look at and often take home books that were displayed attractively. He began to select more carefully for display outstanding books that had sat unused on the shelves. The quality of the books selected by young readers took a quantum leap. The librarian then began to coordinate his efforts with units of study done by local teachers. The teachers were pleased to find children bringing into class these extra resources from the local library for current topics.

SOCIAL AGENCIES Community clubs are another means of educating children. Scout organizations, trail clubs, outing clubs, ski and skimobile clubs, and others often sponsor projects in which students participate with adults. Some take trips into the community and surrounding areas, where children cook outdoors, practice trail maintenance, clean up litter on roadsides, observe different natural phenomena, and learn lessons in getting along with others. Some lessons are intentional, and some are unexpected. On one such trip, three 8-year-old boys came upon a family of skunks in a meadow. Wondering what the skunks would do if startled, the children gently tossed some pebbles toward the nest. To their and the other campers' dismay, the boys learned how startled skunks respond.

REFLECTION

Examine the picture on page 246 and speculate about what the child may be learning. Is it an intentional curriculum of the aquarium staff, or is it accidental and informal learning? Consider one museum experience that was meaningful in your life. Do you recall how the connection came about?

As Lareau (2003) pointed out in her book *Unequal Childhoods*, a family's social class determines how much children will participate in community opportunities, some of which are fee-based. Low-income and working-class families may not have the money, transportation, or time to avail themselves of these extras or may not be aware of the many free programs presented by the local library. Organizations and especially schools that reach out to this underserved group will help all children benefit from these experiences.

Business and Commercial Enterprises

All communities have business and commercial enterprises, many of which are located in large malls or along highways, although in some communities they still exist along main streets and are neighborhood shops. Wherever they are, these establishments have identifying marks to advertise what they sell or what service they perform. Intentionally and unintentionally, adults and older children help younger ones sort out information regarding such businesses. Drive or walk through any of these commercial areas and observe carefully what the buildings or shops look like. The signs advertising them, the types of vehicles in the parking areas, and the displays in the windows help children learn about their world. You can help them sort through this stimulating community curriculum.

Children hear comments from adults, note certain identifying characteristics of buildings, and learn without specific instruction where to buy ice cream, get stamps, find interesting books, or buy a desired toy. Children begin to recognize similar and different shapes. The stop sign is always red and octagonal. Children may question why their parents are stopping or may even figure out from adult conversations what *stop* means. They learn to recognize their own car and eventually are able to find it in a large parking area.

Business enterprises distribute advertising circulars and put signs in shop windows. Such materials provide information about prices and the kinds of items a store sells. Window signs, especially in smaller communities, may also present information about events in the community. Children who become adept at using such resources acquire many skills about how to get information. They may also become skilled in using adults as resources for achieving certain ends. As with other curricula, how and what children learn depend on many factors, including the kind of community in which they live, their developmental stage, and how significant adults share such information with them.

Parents are major influences, and how they perform and talk about their work affects children's perceptions.

Parents, of course, are major influences, and how much parents talk and interact with their children as they become involved in the community also influences children's learning. Sometimes an important community person compensates for parental neglect or disinterest. Comer (1988) described a shopkeeper in his community who taught a child, whom everyone believed to be mute, to talk. The shop was a candy store, and the child would only point to candy when he entered the shop. By refusing to acknowledge the child's pointing, the owner gradually got the child to tell her what he wanted and then eventually to talk to her. In large, impersonal malls, the lessons learned may not always be so positive, but many clerks will take the time to answer children's questions and assist parents as they support children's learning. Many business enterprises have special programs or relationships that support children's learning. Chapter 10 discusses several examples.

Media Outlets

Media, in the form of educational and commercial television, Internet sites, electronic and computer games, and print material, expose children to a world beyond their immediate neighborhoods and contribute to their learning. Some of this learning takes place serendipitously, but adults who extend and enhance children's media experiences through activities, conversation, and reflection help to maximize their learning potential.

Clearly, media provide education for children, but concerns about the amount of time children spend immersed in media are on the rise. Of particular concern are the sexual content (Levin, 2005) and violence (DeGaetano, 2005) that appear on television, Web sites, and video games and the marketing to children through these media. Some altruistic advertisements are aimed at providing drug or nutrition education, but most of them are designed to entice children to become lifelong consumers (Horgen, 2005). A study of programs will show that the media have their informal and hidden curricula.

Much of television, radio programming, and Internet sources are for adult consumption, but many children are exposed to programs that confuse, frighten, or misinform them when there is little or no adult guidance. The vast number of programs and the quantities of information that children can connect to makes it difficult, even with adult supervision, to ensure that children will not be exposed to inappropriate materials. This is a part of the community curriculum that educators must plan for and also help families to make good choices.

TELEVISION   The Public Broadcasting System has for years provided appropriate educational programs for young children. These include *Sesame Street, Mr. Rogers' Neighborhood, Barney,* and *Teletubbies,* which in spirited ways introduce children to the alphabet, new words and concepts, and interesting stories and facts about everyday events. Extensive research on *Sesame Street* over the past 30 years (Morrow, 2005) indicates that children who watched the program learned the alphabet, numbers, and vocabulary faster than those who did not. Further analysis found, however, that rather than being a boon to disadvantaged children, the show was more likely to be watched by middle-class children, and the gains children maintained were dependent on adult reinforcement of concepts. Other research on educational television (Fisch, 2004) confirmed the importance of parents viewing shows with their children and using the content of the programs for further learning and enriched experiences.

Positive Features of TV.   On both educational and commercial television stations, science and social studies programs, story reading, and reenactments of children's literature offer rich educational opportunities. In addition, network educational offices often provide teacher or parent guides for assisting children in gaining more from these programs. Some learning from these programs may have an unintentional and perhaps undesirable effect, however. Children become accustomed to fast-paced materials and do not develop longer attention spans or the ability to sustain interest in events that don't move rapidly. Gutrel (2003) discussed the vast changes in children's use of new media and highlighted new concerns about attention span and brain processing that were noted 30 years earlier.

Negative Effects of TV. The average American child or adolescent watches approximately 3.5 hours of television a day (Morrow, 2005). This takes time away from other pursuits, such as reading, indoor and outdoor play, and socialization with other children. Studies also indicate that other negative effects, such as an increase in aggressive and sexual behavior, obesity, and substance use, are associated with excessive television viewing of shows with violent and sexual content. Although parents are ultimately responsible for monitoring and limiting their children's television time, they can also use the television rating system and the V-chip to block inappropriate shows. The American Academy of Pediatrics also recommends that televisions be removed from children's bedrooms and that viewing be limited to 1 to 2 hours a day.

THE INTERNET The Internet is now a regular part of young children's learning environment. With access to the Internet, a child's world expands tremendously. Children have access to Web sites, chat groups, bulletin boards, and connections to individuals through e-mail, texting, instant messaging, and blogs. In some ways, this larger networking is very positive, but the openness of the World Wide Web and its lack of regulation present dangers to children. Adult-oriented material that many parents would find too sexual, violent, racist, or offensive is easily accessed and downloaded by young children (Federal Bureau of Investigation, 2009). In addition, children can become the target of unwanted attention from adults, other children, or advertisers. Some children become so involved with their cyber journeys that they become addicted and have difficulty reconnecting to their offline peers.

Parents can take steps to protect their children from dangers posed by the Internet by using blocking or filtering software. They also need to educate their children about Internet safety and establish rules about the kinds of family information that a child can divulge. With safeguards in place, the Internet can support children's schoolwork and enhance their interests, hobbies, and play. See Chapter 8 for guidelines on Internet use.

This is an area for good home–school discussions on how to manage a vast and growing cyber world for children and agree on best practices. As a teacher, you can get a PTA subcommittee to lead a discussion of the issues and secure input from homes and the community.

With parental guidance, children can use the Internet to support their schoolwork and enhance their interests and hobbies.

VIDEO GAMES The U.S. video game market gained nearly $10 billion in sales in 2006 (National Institute on Media and the Family, 2009), which indicates the popularity and pervasiveness of this form of entertainment in American homes. Children are being introduced to these games at younger and younger ages and are spending increasing amounts of time playing them. These games appeal to some children because they are perceived as enjoyable ways to feel in control. They also give children opportunities to follow directions, learn computer technology, and achieve a sense of mastery as they move through the various levels of the game. Unlike television and the Internet, however, these games are not educational. Their purpose is largely entertainment, and many children and adults use gaming for relaxation and enjoyment.

The amount of time that children spend playing video games can be problematic, however, because the games are often played alone and restrict children's interactions with others. The content of many games is also an issue; they have been characterized as violent and sexist. Fortunately for parents, video games are rated with a logo showing age recommendations. Games are marketed to children as young as 3 years of age with an "EC" rating for early childhood, an "E" for children over age 6, and an "E10+" for children ages 10 and over. Although theses guidelines are helpful for parents, monitoring the content, explaining why the content is objectionable, and limiting the time spent playing games will further protect children from the ill effects of excessive game playing.

REFLECTION

Think for a moment about the media's impact on today's children and how this impact has changed during your lifetime. Are there positive and negative implications for the current situation?

PRINT MEDIA   In nearly all families, we find printed materials in the form of books, magazines, and newspapers. Unlike the situation with electronic media, parents have much more control when it comes to the kinds of print media that enter their home. Children observe parents and older children looking at and reading these materials and soon begin to imitate these literate behaviors. Many parents also read to their children at a young age, and the youngsters learn to associate reading with pleasure and warm interactions with others.

Children's Books.   Printed materials educate children through pictures and printed words. Children learn early that pictures relate to real objects and have names. As stories are shared, children learn more about their world. For example, when children read Parnell's *Apple Tree*, their knowledge and concepts expand as they view the artist's interpretation and hear language describing the different ways the familiar features of apple trees are used. Children have experienced apples, if not apple trees, but may never have realized that ants and other insects feed from the trees, as do birds, who feed on the insects.

Children grow emotionally and intellectually when they can find, through books, security in loving and being loved, even while learning academic content. In Bang's *Ten, Nine, Eight*, a loving father hugs and tucks in his child as the two count the objects in the room. Such a book conveys, besides the knowledge of rational counting, many different messages to children. One child may have his understanding of a caring parent reaffirmed, whereas another child may realize that men as well as women can be nurturing. An Anglo child sees that African American children do things the same way she does.

Children feel secure when they see that book characters like themselves can be angry, frightened, frustrated, hateful, sad, or lonely. They see models for resolving conflict and learn valuable lessons from the book characters. In Zolotow's *The Hating Book*, children learn how misunderstandings come about when one listens to gossip and doesn't trust a friend.

Children's books appear regularly in all three of the social settings that we focus on in this book. And of course, their impact affects all parts of a child's life. These books can be used to support large parts of any school curriculum, so we urge readers to become acquainted with the extensive bibliography of children's books in the Appendix.

Newspapers for Education. Most newspapers have a special children's section, and some offer guidance to teachers on how to use the newspaper in classrooms. Comics have always been a way of nudging children toward reading. Comer (1988) reported that his mother always read the comics from three different newspapers to him and his siblings each Sunday. This undereducated mother instinctively realized the importance of rereading the parts of the newspaper that especially interested each child and understood how this would assist her children in learning to read.

In many newspapers, the Mini Page for Kids is a regular feature each week for children of primary-school age. The page contains puzzles, art activities, and frequently short essays on notable persons. Science topics and current news features are usually included as well. Unfortunately, newspapers all over the country are in decline today because of the growth of electronic media outlets. But this resource is important for local news and for the special stories about each locality. This aids children in understanding their own part of the world.

Newspapers have education writers and specialists who will visit schools and explain the arrangements of newspapers and how they are produced each day. They will discuss the various sections of a typical paper and show how and why items appeal to some people but not to others.

Cautions on Using Print Media. We must remember that the influence printed materials have on children is not necessarily positive. Some comic strips portray stereotyped characters and advocate violence as a way to solve problems. The excitement of Max chasing his dog with a fork in Sendak's *Where the Wild Things Are* may be so attractive to a 4-year-old that a mother can find her child imitating this action with another child. Stories and other printed materials, as well as television programs, also can reinforce prejudice when characters of a different ethnic origin are interpreted as having the stereotyped characteristics of a certain cultural group. Fairy tales have been cited as reinforcing stereotypes of men and women. It is possible to interpret such female characters as Snow White and Rapunzel as passive women in need of rescue by an active and handsome Prince Charming.

Cornell (1993) maintains that stereotyping may be especially true for children with particular cultural heritages. For example, many classic European tales present witches as old, ugly, mean, and to be feared, but in Asian cultures, the olds are wise, kind, and to be revered. The clash of cultures may be confusing, especially for new immigrants to the United States. In the 21st century, the globalization of technology is subsuming cultural and ethnic interests, priorities, and expectations across the planet in a way earlier media did not. This calls for increased understanding and more multicultural education.

Further, not all books and printed materials are well written, and the language in some of them is stilted and uninteresting. Children acquire language and richness of expression from books they read, so hackneyed, mundane expressions do nothing to enrich a child's vocabulary or imagination.

MEDIA VIGILANCE Some printed materials, television content, computer programs, and Internet information will not be comprehensible to or appropriate for children. Then, without support from an adult, that information could be harmful to a child's self-concept or to the child's emotional, social, or intellectual development. In order for children, and thus society, to benefit from this huge media curriculum, parents, schools, and community members must work together to help children make wise choices as they use the media tools and to learn important Internet behaviors when they use e-mail, chat rooms and **blogs**. Community members have a responsibility to engage schools and parents in forming healthy policies regarding the media available to children.

Readers will want to become familiar with http://www.commonsensemedia.org, a new Web site that promotes sensible use of media. This site contains guidelines and excellent references to help parents and teachers.

A rich curriculum can be provided through printed materials and electronic media when adults are sensitive to children's acceptance or confusion about these elements and help them interpret the information in light of their own experiences.

IMPLICATIONS FOR TEACHERS

Exploit Your Media Resources

We have shown that media are huge community resources that teachers can use to extend classroom learning. In the last few decades, these resources have exploded in scope and have changed the culture of life in many parts of the world. Now think carefully about how to take advantage of this major shift in our society's communication styles and its information gathering. Here are some things to start with:

1. *As a first step, expose children to healthy ways to access media in their community and discuss the values of print, film, and electronic media for all families.*
2. *Plan to go further with your primary-school-age class in extending the use of media that surround have them. (a) Could you establish e-mail contact with a primary-school-age group of children in New Zealand, Israel, or China? (b) Could you help children use various media to demonstrate their knowledge? For example, could children present a hobby via a digital camera slide show as well as by writing a story about it? (c) Could you invite community members who operate media establishments in your locality to demonstrate what they sell and how it links with other media in the community?*
3. *With more experience, children should be able to evaluate their work with media. Think about the following: (a) Which media are most useful to our school? (b) In how many different media formats could the story we wrote appear?*

SOCIAL AND EMOTIONAL ENVIRONMENTS IN A COMMUNITY

Children observe adults in their neighborhoods and often model their behavior on that of these adults. Usually, children look to parents as role models and identify with their positive qualities, such as caring, loving, and protecting. Depending on their age, children often find attractive models in their peer group, among young adults they know, and among media personalities. All of this interaction provides features of the community curriculum that impact much of children's development.

Children's chances of becoming healthy, confident, and competent adults are greater when they have both a safe home environment and a safe neighborhood in which they are able to play, explore, and form relationships. Regrettably, today many children are exposed to dangers within their family situations, in their communities, and from unhealthy media programs. When too many risk factors exist (see Chapter 4), children's total development is affected. Emergent intellectual capacity, motor development, coping strategies, social-emotional development of trust, autonomy, a sense of self-worth, and the ability to benefit from the environmental curriculum can be hampered (Hamilton, Hamilton, & Pittman, 2004) when risk is high. All professionals must be aware of these situations and work to achieve the best solutions.

Social Networks

Children's ability to benefit from their neighborhood is influenced greatly by the social networks their parents have established. As children mature, they develop additional social networks within their peer groups. In earlier generations, family structures tended to be stable, and community members formed bonds that enabled them to look after each other's children and to some degree control children's peer groups. Nowadays, however, children and their families need community support more than ever because parental supervision is far less constant in dual-income and single-parent homes (Adelman & Taylor, 2002; Bookman, 2004).

ADULT CONNECTIONS AND SUPPORT   In today's society, adults are likely to move often during children's growing years, and children's development is affected by adults' ability to adapt to change (Lichter & Crowley, 2002). Some parents establish new relationships easily, thus helping their children profit by participating in neighborhood activities, but in general, high mobility is a risk factor.

The ambiance of a particular neighborhood may be welcoming or threatening, making it easier or riskier to initiate social contact. For example, in one part of Eastern City, homes, streets, and sidewalks are well maintained. One residential street is a dead-end street with little traffic, so residents sit outside on doorsteps and watch their children play close to the street. Families moving into this community feel secure in reaching out to others. Children come to know the adults in the neighborhood easily and are able to interact with them.

In another part of Eastern City, broken bottles litter sidewalks, poorly maintained buildings discourage families from venturing out, and illicit activities are common. Adults and neighborhood gangs are in such conflict with each other that children feel unsafe, even in their own homes. The street violence causes such trauma for families that children have difficulty learning anything positive from any community source.

Rural and suburban neighborhoods also vary in providing physical and mental safety for inhabitants, and this influences children's learning. Poverty is perhaps the greatest deficit, as it limits families in making the diverse social ties that enable children to participate in a neighborhood's growth opportunities (Cochran, 2007). When children are able to move comfortably throughout their neighborhoods, healthy socialization becomes the norm and children benefit.

Janice and Peter lived on the same street in look-alike houses in a large suburban neighborhood. Although the yards were all fenced, children felt free to visit from one house to the other, stopping to watch and ask endless questions of kindly neighbors. One day, Janice and Peter roamed and stopped to watch while one neighbor trimmed roses in her front yard and another washed his car. They even got to spray some water on the soapy car, getting a bit wet themselves. After a while, they wandered to a muddy area in another neighbor's backyard. Making a few mud balls, they proceeded to toss the balls at the neighbor's garage. When Janice's mother caught up with them, she obtained buckets and water from the neighbors and insisted that the children clean up the mess they had made. With help from some of the older neighborhood children, Janice and Peter managed to get the garage quite clean.

That day, among other lessons, Janice and Peter learned a bit about the why and how of gardening, how cars are cleaned, and what makes water spray. They also discovered that they would be held accountable for any mess they created. They learned about helping others when they received help from the older children. Of course, children's everyday lessons from the neighborhood are not always the ones adults might wish. Still, Cochran and Niegro (2002) pointed out that when children have more adults and older children with whom they do a variety of activities, they tend to do better in school. Children who have caring adults beyond family members to assist them in mastering skills and attitudes in a gradual way have greater **metacognitive** and problem-solving strategies.

Not all children have extended support, and many can have regrettable experiences that create serious barriers to their cognitive accomplishments. Kumove (1966) found that when children under age 7 were able to move freely in their immediate environment, they became more independent than children whose parents found it necessary to keep them homebound. Children unable to move about in their community because of pervasive community violence often are unable to develop coping skills and thus are more likely to become aggressive or violent themselves (Swisher & Whitlock, 2004). If reforms are to take place in neighborhoods that are unsafe, these require help and support from schools. Some authorities contend that community-type schools are needed in this case. A neighborhood school would be a place "where people from the neighborhood come to learn and play together; share experiences and wisdom; nurture each other; and strengthen young people, families, and the fabric of community life. . . . It becomes a home away from home" (Adelman & Taylor, 2002, p. 263). Readers will want to check the Community School model presented in Chapter 11.

MENTORING Many schools now contain significant numbers of children from one-parent families, migrant and high-mobility families, and immigrant populations. As we noted in Chapters 3 and 4, children from these population subgroups are at higher risk for academic difficulty and social problems. Mentoring programs that use community adults have become increasingly popular to help address the problems that arise from frayed social networks in many communities. And recent studies show that mentoring programs do enhance positive development in youth (Jekielek, Moore, Hair, & Scarupa, 2002).

Mentoring programs have a significant history; the best-known of these are Big Brother/Big Sister and the Buddy System. Both programs have established offices in many states and curriculum and training procedures for volunteers to follow. However, any school and its community interested in helping youth grow in healthy ways can establish informal and helpful mentoring practices for children.

Basically, youth mentoring exists to provide positive role models and to help children develop socially and emotionally. Although academic support and tutoring are often features of a mentor plan, they have less importance, and research reveals that they are not very helpful (Herrara, Sipe, & McClanahan, 2000). The best results from mentoring come when the focus is on developing trusting relationships between a child and peers and the community adults. Many teachers are mentors for their students, and though this is not a defined assignment, teachers are in a position to recognize the need for mentoring and to refer children accordingly. If some community agencies have established a Big Brother or Big Sister program or any mentoring project in your district, this aspect of the community curriculum can support your partnering with others.

Strategies for mentoring programs vary from place to place, but the following are basic guidelines:

- Volunteers for mentoring plans need to be screened for appropriateness of background and to determine their interests and work styles.
- Volunteers need training and supervision by a community or school office with expertise in mentoring programs.
- The main focus of a mentoring program should be on social skills because this is the area that will benefit the child in other areas of school and community life.
- Mentors should be matched with youth on the basis of shared interests.
- Successful mentor relationships last at least a year. Short-term connections can be more harmful than helpful.

- Successful mentors see their role as that of trusted friend rather than instructor.
- Mentoring programs need structure and a weekly schedule.
- In healthy mentoring, the needs of the child take precedence over the expectations of the volunteer.
- Group mentoring, although far less common than one-on-one mentoring, can be successful with skilled leadership.

PEER GROUP SETTINGS Peers become strong socializing agents (Karcher, Brown, & Elliot, 2004). Both in school and in the community, children learn more about who they are and how to behave in society from their peers. And when the cultural milieu is diverse and inclusive, children can learn different interactions and expand their repertoire of social and language skills. Parents teach children moral and ethical values, but the peer group is powerful in setting the social tone and imposing behavioral patterns.

Even as early as 18 months of age, children learn how their actions affect others and thus begin the process of learning behavioral codes. A toddler who tries to take a desired toy away from another child soon learns the consequences of the behavior. It may be an indignant yell; it may be a slap; it may be acquiescence and the subsequent loss of a playmate. As children begin to form peer groups and play with one other, they begin to form rules of conduct so that they can continue to operate as a group. It is in peer groups that children learn to negotiate, solve problems, and compromise to continue to play and work together. Some children will be more dominant than others and will learn the rules for domination and acquiescence. Children are often rewarded by **significant others** in the group for conforming, or they are ostracized (Elkin & Handel, 1989).

Children experiment with various roles (leader, compromiser, follower, negotiator, etc.) and discover from their peers how to act to fulfill roles. They also see how their peers respond to them. Children learn about their own abilities from their peers. For example, they find out that they can run faster, jump higher, or read better at times as they compare their skills with those of others. However, the group dictates what skills are prized.

Although parents teach children about gender roles, by preschool, peers begin to segregate into boy and girl groups that dictate what roles each group is permitted to play. A physician's daughter, after beginning preschool, insisted that her doctor mother was really a nurse. At school, she had learned in her play group that doctors are boys and nurses are girls, even though her teacher and parents insisted differently. In addition, children learn cultural and social differences as they interact with their peers. They compare notes about their own family's customs, values, and ways of doing things. Peer group acceptance or rejection can influence how individual children change their own behaviors (Bigner, 2009).

Sexual understandings and misunderstandings are learned from family members, extensive media exposure, and peers. Many young children learn the physical difference between boys and girls by examining each other. They often learn about birth when some "wiser" child informs them of their knowledge or

Peers become socializing agents as children learn who they are and how to behave in society.

misunderstanding. It is through such discussions, along with other teachings, that children figure out for themselves the meaning of the confusing information they receive (Sadker & Sadker, 2005).

Cognitive information and development of numerous skills come from children's interactions with peers. Children have rituals and routines, just as adults do. Older peers teach younger ones the chants and rhymes of childhood. Memory skills and counting, as well as physical endurance, are enhanced as children jump rope to such rhymes as "One Potato, Two Potato" or "First Comes Love, Then Comes Marriage." As they play together, children learn from more skilled peers how to climb higher, catch a ball, read a story, or add up their money for ice cream. Learning may result from a desire to compete with a peer or because the peer has more information and passes it on. Learning may also come because a new idea has been introduced and children need to test out the new concept.

REFLECTION

What games did you play in your neighborhood when you were growing up? Think about positive things you learned as a result of these interactions. Were there some aspects of these games that may not have been healthy?

Billy was watching his friend Ahmed copy words from a book he was reading. "Whatcha doing?" asked Billy. "I'm making an "r" for red," replied Ahmed.

"Nunh, nunh, that's not an R. I'll show you how to make an R." And Billy wrote a capital R.

Ahmed retorted, "Oh! That's a big R, and I'm making a little r!" After much discussion, Ahmed, in disgust, turned to his book. "Look," he pointed, "that says 'Red' and that says 'red.' See, that's a big R and that's a little r."

Ahmed has challenged Billy's thinking, so now Billy will examine writing in a new way. New learning has been opened up to him by a friend. Ahmed's scorn for his not knowing seemed to spur Billy on, for later he got a book and paper, came to sit beside Ahmed, and tried to make the little *r*, asking his friend for help.

Not all learning from peer groups is positive. Gangs can be a destructive force in any society as children seek approval and find that they must develop antisocial codes of behavior to be accepted. Some children can be targets for peer victimization, but when these at-risk children have a best friend, this friendship acts as a strong buffer against such attacks (Orpinas & Horne, 2006). When a community provides opportunities for children to develop social networks among different adult and peer groups, children have more options. When this happens, the lure of destructive peer groups is lessened, and children are helped to find positive peer associations.

IMPLICATIONS FOR TEACHERS

Seniors as Correspondents

One very valuable resource for the community curriculum is the life and experience of the senior citizens in your area. Grandparents (see Chapter 8) can contribute much to the curriculum of the home, but other community elders are a gold mine for connecting schools with their communities. Children of all ages can connect with seniors for help with particular projects and even with regular classroom assignments.

Perhaps the best-known elder/student program is the FoxFire program developed in the 1970s by Eliot Wiggington in southern Appalachia. In this program, the entire school curriculum revolved around interviews that students did with community elders and the

*publication of the fascinating oral history captured by the area youth. Less ambitious proj-
ects can still be very useful for your classroom as you help children discover the rich talent
and stimulating stories stored in the minds of seniors.*

*Interviews and recordings can be done at the residence of the senior correspondent
who has expressed interest. Panel presentations by elders and exhibits of their collections
can be set up for your classroom to stimulate questions and open up discussions.*

*One way to start is to contact the administrator of a local retirement center or the sen-
ior circle of a local religious congregation about interviewing interested residents. Most will
be agreeable and excited about the connection of their facility with a school You should set
up careful guidelines for any child–senior conversations and begin with a brief first encounter that can be used to refine later visits. And make sure that you advise the local newspaper of your plans and the results.*

Ethnic Community Contributions

As we noted in Chapter 3, most American communities are becoming ethnically diverse. In recent decades, immigration to the United States (both sanctioned and illegal)
has intensified to such a degree that immigration has represented up to 50% of the population growth in selected counties each year since 2000 (U.S. Census Bureau News,
2008). In addition, ethnic minority groups are dispersing throughout the United States.
When observing the *American Demographics* minority population maps, we find only a
handful of areas showing no increases in integration for the last decade.

All of this means that our country is rapidly becoming a highly multiethnic nation, and schools need to take advantage of the dynamic aspects linked to ethnic differences in their communities. In almost all communities today, there is a rich mixture of
culture and races from which children learn about differences and how to accept and
learn about each other. Often, however, children do not understand their own culture,
and in order to be enriched by another culture, it is important that children first understand their own culture and its variations. This understanding should be the start of
multicultural education.

Schools can profit from the various ethnic cultures in learning about the richness of
community life, and students learn to be analytical thinkers as they discover the cultural
orientations of other persons in their school and community. In the past, schools focused
more on the outward manifestations of culture—clothing and celebrations—not recognizing variations of behavior. It is important to get beyond the stereotypic images that schools
often used in the past to present different cultures—Japanese women appearing with
kimono, obi, and parasol or a Hawaiian appearing barefoot with a grass skirt and leis.

Attainment in the arts, special festivals and entertainment performances, and the
business and commercial successes of ethnically different individuals in a community
are highly visible areas for enhancing a multicultural curriculum. Comparing similarities and differences in the daily events of children in one community offers insights into
another culture as well as variations within a culture. Becoming knowledgeable about
the history of a group of people is another way of learning about them, and civil rights
organizations like the Urban League, the Anti-Defamation League, and the National
Association for the Advancement of Colored People (NAACP) can provide some of this
information. Individual ethnic groups may also have organizations and societies that
can be useful in obtaining information about their culture.

We have to remember that the unique behaviors, language, learning patterns, and
values of different ethnic groups are acquired for a reason. The fact that they differ from
those of mainstream society means that they have a particular purpose in another cultural milieu, and when we seek to learn about the differences, we come closer to an appreciation of the rich cultural history we all have around us. If there are different

cultures in our community, we should want to understand and appreciate their talents and traditions. Everyone is proud of his or her culture and background and, if given a chance to share it, will do something that enriches our knowledge. Some teachers have used the following objectives in seeking to acknowledge a community's various cultural groups:

1. Research the stories behind the food choices that different ethnic groups make.
2. Uncover the history of the dances and music of each ethnic group.
3. Compare different family schedules, approaches to rearing children, and ways different families praise the successes of individual members.
4. Find out and record the stories behind the immigration journeys individuals in the community undertook to reach the place where they now live.

In one ethnically diverse classroom, a teacher extended the homework project designed for parent–child reading to promote different viewpoints. While reading "In Monet's Garden" to her class, Mrs. McCloud introduced a doll of Linnea, the story's main character, and talked about Linnea's interest in Monet's house and garden. From there, the children became intrigued with taking the Linnea doll home and introducing her to their families. With their parents' help, the children pretended to be Linnea and recorded in their journals the food they were eating that day, the games they played, the TV programs they watched, and the stories they read. At school they developed charts to list the experiences Linnea had in each child's home. The journal always went with Linnea so that the parents could read about the different adventures in other homes. Parents and children started to see commonalities they all shared, and they noted differences, too. This led to curiosity about the different ethnicities represented in their community and opened up an appreciation of the differences and the challenges of other's lives.

In extending the project, the teacher introduced stories with different ethnic protagonists, and the children took these books home to share them with their parents. The librarian noticed that the children were starting to select more books on different cultures, so she began displaying books describing different aspects of life in a single culture. Children's artwork and projects brought out diverse cultural elements. PTA meetings became quite lively, and Mrs. McCloud even introduced to parents Mary Pipher's (2002) The Middle of Everywhere: the World's Refugees Come to our Town. *Parents discussed the book and then began to share stories of their own family's arrival in the United States and how they adapted. Mrs. McCloud had each child develop a personal book titled* Who Am I and Where Did I Come From? *This meant that all children began to research their own family's history and arrival in this country.*

During this unit, the teachers, students, and families all witnessed the many cultural variations represented in the classroom. Thanks to the students' projects, parents and community members could appreciate differences in diets, clothing, living conditions, communication styles, celebrations, choice of music, literary interests, and skills in crafts, as well as everyday vocations.

The changing demographics in our society mean that our children must learn about and accept differences. No longer are schools a "melting pot" for immigrants in this country; rather, they are places where a **mosaic** of cultures exists and where we learn from each other's experiences (Futrell, Gomez, & Bedden, 2003). Many now refer to this cultural pluralism as a *tapestry* where individual cultures add their uniqueness to the continually expanding American fabric.

Multicultural Education

Multicultural education emerged in response to the concerns about educational equity in the United States. The term *multicultural education* is used in various ways to describe

Different cultures in our country add a unique quality to children's education.

programs and practices that schools have developed to ensure that all students—regardless of their gender, social class, abilities, or ethnic, racial, or cultural characteristics—have an equal opportunity to learn in school. Because schools are social systems with many inter-related parts and variables, multicultural education aims to help change the culture of the school. This may take the form of integrating content in the formal curriculum and in-cluding a variety of cultures and groups to illustrate key concepts. It may also include ac-knowledgment of negative attitudes toward different groups that children bring with them from home and become part of the hidden curriculum. Through prejudice reduction activities, students are guided in developing positive attitudes toward various racial, eth-nic, ability, and cultural groups.

Although curricular inclusion and prejudice reduction are important parts of multicultural education, the larger culture of the school must also be examined and restructured by teachers and other school staff to ensure that equity is being pro-moted for all. Teachers may need to modify their teaching to facilitate the learning of various groups; administrators may need to investigate interactions among groups and the differences in achievement and participation of different groups. School personnel and families need to come together to explore these issues and make the school a place that is welcoming to all. A large body of literature exists about multicultural education that can help guide you in understanding how to be more inclusive and fair to all children. (Derman-Sparks,1989; Ramsey, 2004; Sleeter & Grant, 2006).

PHYSICAL ENVIRONMENTS IN A COMMUNITY

Children's life space and the atmosphere around them, including the built structures, provide the physical portion of the community curriculum. This, of course, varies tremendously from one location to another. However, all ecological and physical struc-tures can provide learning opportunities, and skilled teachers find ways to maximize children's learning in the byways of their local area.

Natural Environments

As children move about their neighborhood, their surroundings offer a rich curriculum from which they gain understanding about their world. This curriculum is, of course, all of nature. Learning differs, depending on the combination of children's ability, social interactions regarding the environment, and children's freedom of movement to explore. Louv (2005) discovered that American children now spend less and less time outdoors. Although all children learn about nature in various ways, their understanding and appreciation of nature can be limited. This can be changed to positive interactions if teachers and parents pursue out-of-school learning.

CHILDREN'S PLAY   Studies on children's play activity indicate that the quality of children's outdoor and indoor play differs, and thus different learning opportunities emerge. Children engage in more dramatic and **constructive play** outdoors and in more **exploratory play** (Steglin, 2005) when they feel, examine, crunch, and test materials, such as learning the sounds different rocks make when dropped into the water. Balancing while walking on uneven rocks in a dry riverbed develops different skills than balancing on the surface of a gymnasium balance beam. Children may climb indoors, but viewing the world from a tree branch gives them broader perspectives. With increasing concerns about childhood obesity, the need for active play environments both indoors and out can hardly be overstated (Pica, 2006).

Good children's books capture the many wonders of nature and can extend children's appreciation of what they experience, but without experiencing the reality of the world, a child's knowledge is limited. In the following vignette, Davon has book knowledge about snow, but it is the real experience that enriches his understanding.

Davon lived all of his 5 years in Florida. He had heard a lot about snow and was especially fond of Ezra Jack Keats's The Snowy Day, *but he had never seen real snow. While visiting his cousin in Boston that winter, he awoke to white flakes floating down from the sky outside his window. He had never imagined that snow looked like that. As the week wore on and more snow fell, Davon learned much more about the feel of snow on his face and the taste of snow as he and his cousin held out their tongues to catch it. He learned how snow could limit and enhance activity and how it felt to walk through drifts.*

OBSERVING NATURE   Of course, not all of nature's lessons are pleasant. The first snow can be an exciting and beautiful event, but a blizzard followed by power outages and snarled traffic teaches a different lesson. Learning to observe the outdoor environment enhances children's cognitive learning as well as their social and emotional understanding. Joshua learned many things about his surroundings one late-winter day while watching the waterfront.

Joshua lived near the St. Lawrence River and with his mother loved to watch the seals bob up and down in the harbor. One winter day, a small, and undoubtedly ill, seal crawled out on the ice floe and collapsed. While watching and wondering about the seal, Joshua noted two eagles swoop down on the seal and begin tearing at the carcass. Alarmed, Joshua ran to get his mother, who tried to explain about the natural behavior of creatures in the wild. Then she remembered Cherie Mason's book Everybody's Somebody's Lunch. *Together they read how a young girl whose cat was devoured by a fox discovers that there are predators and prey in our world and that all are part of nature's food chain. Joshua then became quite fascinated with the eagles and their 3-day work of cleaning up the dead seal. He watched as several crows tried to claim their share but were chased away. A neighbor farther along the shore telephoned and asked Joshua's mother whether she knew what was agitating the crows. An excited Joshua took the phone to explain to the neighbor about the eagles.*

The environment and the formations around us show how our lives are changed by and through nature.

Joshua's nature lessons didn't all take place in one day, but he gradually became a more interested and astute student of the world around him.

Other Features of Nature

The typography, geography, and geology of our communities present other areas for children's study. Although not a living part of nature, the formations and terrain surrounding us do have an effect on our lives. The outdoors provides children with a wonderful area for investigation, observation, and experimentation to see how our environment impacts out lives.

Teachers on field trips to the community have an excellent opportunity to consolidate the science and social studies concepts and skills developed in the classroom. Learning opportunities abound when

1. children look at fields, forests, and pastures.
2. children looks at brooks, swamps, and rivers.
3. children see bays, harbors, lakes, and seas.
4. children see canyons, cliffs, hills, valleys, and mountains.
5. children understand how climate and weather change parts of the terrain.

If you are outdoors with children, consider having them do some of the following:

- Find and label as many land and water features as possible.
- Determine what uses the formations in the landscape have. Do they provide a place for other forms of life? Do we use any of their features in our daily living?
- Speculate on the land surfaces that make our lives easier, harder, or more interesting.

As a follow-up exercise, secure maps of your area and have the class study how the formations and the terrain are represented on the maps.

Human Creations and Structures

Young children are getting to know their immediate surroundings when they come to school. This includes their neighborhood and the places in the larger community that they visit often—the supermarket, the mall, their school, their house of worship, and recreational facilities. All of this is basically a built environment, and though overlapping with the natural one, it has a separate function that children will come to realize.

Human creations show what our society is capable of doing and completing. In the complex society where we live, children readily accept the towering buildings, roadways, and utilities as facts of life. No questions are raised about how these came to be, whereas in simpler societies, the assembling of homes and roads is often observed directly by the growing child. The comparison of structures is a key feature in any child's education.

All this means that young children do need to start looking at the built community they live in with respect and with the idea of examining it. In looking seriously at this part of our community curriculum, teachers will lead children to compare buildings in terms of function, type of construction, age, and design.

We should look at the function of a structure and consider how it differs from others. We also need to know why it came to be or why it was built. We need to see the type of material used to build it, and we should look at the design and see how well it works. Also, if it is an historical building, then why is it remaining if it is no longer used?

With roadways, bridges, piers, and utilities (to a lesser extent), we can apply the same evaluation. This leads us to develop respect for all of the labor required to erect this part of our community.

One popular and helpful project for primary-school children is to examine the building of homes in different parts of the world. This activity focuses on a familiar feature of the community that everyone knows about. Then, with some good photos, children can ascertain the functions and materials used to construct homes they have never seen. They will be drawn to a new appreciation for how the natural land features often determine and affect the types of homes people have.

INTERACTIONS AMONG COMMUNITY AGENCIES, FAMILIES, AND SCHOOLS

The learning that took place in the vignettes presented in this chapter did not happen in isolation within these communities, for the community curriculum was affected by how the families and schools linked children to community resources and agencies (see Figure 9-2). Stronger links heighten the potential for children's learning.

Many community agencies welcome children's visits, either with their families or with school teachers. Some agencies actively attempt to reach families with differing cultural and economic backgrounds. Other agencies limit their support to families who can afford their services or to families who reach out. Teachers and other community-service personnel can help families become aware of community organizations, events, and experiences that will enrich their children's lives. Ginger, in an earlier vignette, was able to use more community resources because church members described programs to assist her. As she became more confident of her ability to help her children, she more actively sought those recreational programs that provided richer learning experiences.

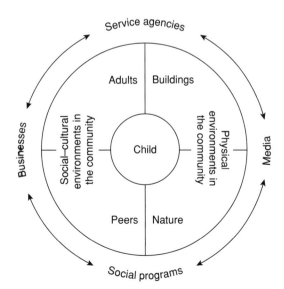

FIGURE 9-2   Community Impact on Children Through the Environment, Social Networks, and Cultural Events and from Interactions Among Agencies

REFLECTION

The next time you go shopping, observe the children in the store to see what is happening to them, their parents, and store personnel. Then speculate about what the children might be learning—emotionally, physically, and cognitively—on their shopping trip.

All families use the business enterprises of a community at some time, although many are increasingly using online resources to shop, pay bills, and obtain information. In today's society, many families also patronize large, impersonal organizations for purchasing, banking, and communicating. When this happens, the education those children receive is more limited than that in a small neighborhood, such as Joshua's, with supportive parents and neighbors.

Some community agencies that offer programs to children depend on family or Big Brother and Big Sister types of support. A scout-sponsored camping trip, for example, may include one or both parents or another adult accompanying the children. Trailblazing and fire-building lessons may be a planned part of the trip, but how the learning is extended depends on parental involvement with the organization. Some religious organizations sponsor family nights when leaders invite entire families to be involved in extended learning situations.

IMPLICATIONS FOR TEACHERS

Connecting to the Community

As you think about the community as a source of learning for children, remember that the concept of community includes the family and friends; the city, village, or neighborhood; and larger entities, such as the media and religious congregations; plus cultural, ethnic, and commercial organizations. Being part of a community means that one is recognized and can take part in the various opportunities for learning that it provides. As a future teacher or community-service professional, you are in a unique position to expand and enrich children's connections with the various communities with which they are connected.

- *From the list of community resources identified in Figure 9-1, identify those with which your family was connected as you grew up. Reflect on the things you think you learned from involvement with these resources, and think about how you could help the families with whom you will work become knowledgeable about such opportunities for their children.*
- *Consider your experiences with media as you were growing up and compare these to the media experiences available now. What do you recollect about the way media were monitored by adults in your family? How have the issues changed since you were a child?*
- *Become familiar with the cultural organizations in your community and participate in some of the activities they sponsor. Analyze how these will enrich the curriculum for the young children you will work with.*

Collaboration Needs to Grow

Communities and schools can collaborate to provide concrete experiences to extend children's learning, but this is not done as much as possible. Trips into the community are enriched when the agencies have materials, people, and specific events appropriate for the learning level of the children who visit. When teachers make visits and discuss the trip with community agencies beforehand, learning is more likely to be enhanced.

Some school trips within a community are not done collaboratively, however, and children's learning is thus limited and may even be negative.

⟋⟍   One child-care center decided to make a trip to McDonald's without checking first with the establishment. It was noon when they arrived, and the restaurant was crowded. When the children were let off the bus, they ran to the play area and began to play noisily. Teachers' attempts to find a place for the children to eat together and to give them experience in selecting and ordering food were disastrous. The bus driver had left, and the harassed teachers had to keep track of the children as they rushed to the playground, roamed the restaurant, and visited other children waiting for lunch. Another distraction was a family watching a miniature TV while eating their lunch, which attracted children from the child-care center. The teachers struggled to get the children to order their food. While in line, however, the children pushed and jostled the adults waiting to order. Some children finally received their food, but then the bus returned, and the teachers hurried everyone onto it. Some children carried uneaten food, and others protested that they hadn't gotten anything. The children, the teachers, and the McDonald's personnel were all unhappy with the experience. ⟋⟍

Many restaurants welcome children's visits and provide opportunities for children to visit the kitchen and to experience ordering and eating food in a relaxed manner. In the preceding episode, lack of planning resulted in an unpleasant experience for both adults and children. It would be wrong to assume that no learning took place during this trip; however, with more care, the trip could have been more valuable and pleasant for everyone.

REFLECTION

Consider with your classmates what the children on the trip described in the above vignette might have learned about nutrition. What might they have learned about themselves? About adults? Do you see any positive aspects of this questionable trip?

In community programs, where children interact with materials, observe events, or see animals acting in a natural environment, youngsters usually learn more than they do in programs where adults demonstrate and lecture, expecting children to be enraptured with what they say and do. The community, through natural phenomena and by the nature of its organization, offers a stimulating alternative for teachers who see the benefits for the children they work with.

Summary and Review

Most community curricula can be made rich and varied, depending on how adults in the society structure the environment and how they develop supportive educational policies in various service agencies. Political, social, cultural, and business agencies offer, both intentionally and unintentionally, a learning environment and materials aimed at educating the public about their services. What children learn from these environments depends largely on the use parents and teachers make of them.

The natural and manufactured resources found within communities provide learning experiences even when there is little adult intervention. Children see signs, notice buildings, observe nature, note adult actions, and learn something from all their encounters. Increasingly, children also interact with the larger world through their experiences with media. Print materials, television, video games, and the Internet expose children to ideas, concepts, and images in ways both positive and negative. The ways that important adults guide children's media encounters and use community resources by choosing wisely, explaining things, and interacting with them all enhance children's learning.

In the absence of a national policy on family support, political decisions in different communities can result in vastly different learning experiences. Children who live in communities providing safe physical and emotional environments have more educational opportunities, for in these areas families are better able to establish social networks that allow them to tap community resources. For children outside such safe environments, parents, schools, and other agencies must work especially hard to compensate and must strive to build a solid curriculum so that these children, too, will thrive in tomorrow's world.

Suggested Activities and Questions

1. Explore the area around a school neighborhood. List all the natural resources, human resources, and materials that you observe. Rate their learning potential for children living there and start a resource file from the information gathered. Compare your list to those of others in your group.
2. Expand your **resource file** using the categories in Figure 9-1 to organize the information you find that will support your work with children and families. Share your resources with others in the group.
3. Visit a business establishment in your community. Interview the owner or manager to learn whether the establishment has materials aimed at educating children and how they distribute such materials. While there, ask yourself what children might learn just from being in the building.
4. Select a children's television program, watch it, and note positive and negative examples of learning opportunities for children. Review the program to determine if you would recommend that children of various ages be encouraged or allowed to watch it.
5. Explore the Internet to locate five or more Web sites you would recommend for children under age 6.
6. Interview at least two community volunteers who have worked as mentors for elementary-school children. Ask them to identify their successes in improving the lives of the children and to point out the challenges of the mentoring role.

Resources

Organizations

The National Institute on Media and the Family   *http://www.mediafamily.org*

National Association for the Advancement of Colored People   *http://www.naacp.org*

Association for Childhood Education International (ACEI)   *http://www.acei.org*

Association for Supervision and Curriculum Development   *http://www.ascd.org*

National Association for Multicultural Education   *http://www.name.org*

Web Sites

http://www.aap.org   Web site for the American Academy of Pediatrics.

http://www.childrenssoftware.com   Web site for Children's Technology Review, a searchable online database and a print publication that help teachers and parents select appropriate interactive media for children.

http://www.fieldtripfactory.com   Web site that links teachers and community members with free field trips in their communities.

http://www.kidsnet.org   Web site that helps children, parents, and educators access the educational opportunities afforded by television, radio, and multimedia sources.

http://www.commonsensemedia.org   Web site that gives excellent advice on selecting and using media with children.

CHAPTER 10

Establishing and Maintaining Collaborative Relationships

To make sure that every one of our children meets high standards of achievement, all of us—teachers, parents, administrators, office holders, community members, students, family members, and local organizations— must work together to make it happen. This requires strong leadership, constant and open communication, and a passion for partnership.

(Henderson, Mapp, Johnson, & Davies, 2007, p. 3)

After reading this chapter, you will be able to do the following:

- Explain why it is essential to involve parents and community members in children's schooling.
- Describe a range of practices to develop rapport with parents, communicate with them about their children's progress, and encourage their involvement in the classroom and school.
- Devise options for parent involvement along a continuum that moves from basic to **participatory levels** to advocacy levels.
- Consider appropriate strategies for working with parents with diverse cultural backgrounds, economic situations, or family configurations.
- Recognize the characteristics of a welcoming school and be able to develop a welcoming classroom.
- Identify effective strategies to facilitate community involvement in schools.

Throughout the preceding chapters of this book, we have offered many strategies to help teachers work successfully with families and community members. In this chapter, we will take a broader and deeper look at additional ways to establish collaborative relationships. If partnerships are to flourish, teachers need a wide range of approaches to encourage increased involvement in children's learning by parents and the larger community. Someone must start collaborations, and the beginning steps may be small ones. Individual teachers can begin this process, but true collaboration works best when it also occurs at the school level. This chapter examines various practices for collaborative action and discusses things to consider when using these strategies.

Our changing society, even with the advantages of mass communication systems, has evolved to a point where, in the 21st century, school programs alone are not sufficient for the task of formally educating children. The collaboration of parents and community agencies is essential if schools are to succeed in educating young children for a rapidly evolving society. A review of the research on family and community involvement in schools (Henderson & Mapp, 2002) established that a strong collaboration between the three social settings led to higher achievement by children. The evidence also showed that children had improved grades, better attendance, more appropriate social skills and behavior, and a higher promotion rate than those in schools without strong partnerships. The same study also found that when community and parent groups organized to improve schools, their efforts led to upgraded school facilities, improved school leadership, higher-quality learning programs, and additional resources designed to improve teaching and family supports such as after-school programs.

Parental and community involvement have always been a part of U.S. education. As we discussed earlier, historically, most parents were in charge of their children's education, but beginning in the 1800s, schools accepted more responsibility for academic learning. Later, professional educators began to educate parents about children's growth and development, instructing them on ways to prepare their children for school and advising them on how to support their children's education once they began formal schooling.

By and large, parental cooperation in educational matters during the 20th century meant parental acquiescence to school suggestions, but this situation has begun to change. Parental and community involvement in some districts has moved gradually from teacher-dominated procedures to collaborations with parents and community agencies (Wohlstetter & Smith, 2006). We contend that to cope with increasing challenges in the educative process, successful schools need to become **embedded partners** with parents and community members. In this chapter, we discuss a wide array of strategies that schools and teachers use for building partnerships with parents and community agencies.

To establish such parternships, teachers need to consider ways of interacting with parents and community members that respect diverse communication and work styles. If children are to benefit, teachers must provide the impetus to break down communication barriers resulting from different cultural expectations and habits of interaction. For example, see Figure 10-1 for ways to increase your understanding of parents from various cultural groups. Of course, these characteristics are general and will not apply to all members of a particular group. Keep in mind, though, that it is the school's responsibility to lead, and teachers should be prepared to go more than halfway in reaching out to parents and the community.

Schools that develop more welcoming strategies help parents and other community members feel comfortable in visiting classrooms, becoming aides or volunteers, and contributing special expertise to children's learning. These individuals learn about the schools and about school culture, which enables them to help their children and to communicate their sense of the importance of school programs to others in their community.

The larger community is also an important educating force. Schools and families have always made excursions into their communities for educational purposes, and teachers have invited community members into the classroom. This involvement becomes even more important as schools include community and local social and environmental issues as part of the curriculum and as community agencies become partners with their neighborhood schools.

DEVELOPING WELCOMING SCHOOLS AND CLASSROOMS

Before families and community members can begin to establish collaborative relationships with schools, however, citizens must feel welcome. Schools have only one opportunity to make a great first impression, and a welcoming physical and social

Cultural Group	Potential Issues	Response
Hispanic American	Language barrier	Provide translators and translated school notices.
	There are differences between the various countries from which Hispanic Americans have come that teachers may be unaware of. The culture of Mexico may be the only one represented in school materials.	Provide books and materials about the cultures of many different Latin American countries, especially those represented in the school community. Ask parents to educate the school staff about their culture.
	Parent involvement in children's education may be more home-based.	Broaden the concept of involvement. Make special efforts to invite the whole family to school events.
African American	The family does not feel welcome or comfortable visiting the school, where they may be labeled a "minority."	Images of African American scientists, political leaders, and family groups should be displayed at school along with those from other diverse groups. Avoid labels.
	Extended family members and friends who are like family are very important.	Pair new families with a welcoming family who will introduce them to others and to the school culture.
		Celebrate important African American milestones throughout the year. Provide books and materials that represent African Americans.
Asian American	Language barrier	Provide translators and translate school notices.
	Lack of acknowledgment of the many different countries in Asia from which families have come. The culture of China may be the only one represented in school materials.	Provide books and materials about the cultures of many different Asian countries, especially those represented in the school community. Ask parents to educate the school staff about their culture.
	Stereotypic beliefs about all Asians being highly intelligent, hard-working, and good in math.	Avoid labels and assumptions. Focus on the strengths of the individual.
	Involvement in children's education often occurs in the home.	Make special efforts to invite families to school events but accept various levels of involvement.
Native American	There are differences between the various tribal groups that are unrecognized. Stereotypic depictions of native people	Ask parents to educate the school staff about their culture.
	Lack of awareness of Native American spiritual beliefs.	Evaluate classroom materials for signs of stereotyping.
		Make connections between Native American spiritual beliefs about the earth and the issues of global warming and pollution.
European American	Do not experience the culture as a core part of their identity and are a mix of many European ethnicities.	Provide opportunities to participate in workshops that address multiculturalism and diversity within the school.
	Have values and communication style that they view as normal, and other patterns may be considered strange or incorrect.	

FIGURE 10-1 **Understanding Families from Various Cultural Groups**

environment is the essential first step in creating a climate that encourages parent and community involvement. Sometimes a simple change in what visitors see when they enter a building makes a great difference. A clean, well-cared-for school with interesting displays of children's work will create a memorable impact on newcomers to the school, as will staff and faculty members who smile and greet them.

Friendly signs in English and other appropriate languages should welcome visitors and show the way to the main office, where they will be greeted pleasantly by the front office staff. A smile and a positive attitude from the office staff once a visitor arrives are essential. Space where parents can comfortably wait, perhaps with coffee and some interesting literature about schools, also makes visitors feel welcome.

Establishing good relationships with children's families early in the school year is important. Many schools have found that reaching out to children even before school begins can be a useful way to get to know families. A prekindergarten and/or kindergarten open house held the spring before the children are scheduled to begin school is a great way for teachers and parents to meet. This is also the time when parents can find out about the paperwork they will need to complete to enroll their children in school as well as in other services that their children may be eligible for, such as ESOL (English for Speakers of Other Languages) or free or reduced-price lunch. The teaching staff can spend time with the children and take their photographs with their parents. These photos will then be used to create a welcoming bulletin board when children arrive at school in the fall. By then, teachers will have learned the correct pronunciation of children's names, and a little about their heritage, and will have met their parents. All of this information will help teachers prepare for the coming year.

Tools for Early Contacts

As a follow-up to the spring open house, home visits, telephone calls, letters, post cards, or invitations to school for brief, informal meetings are tools teachers can use to set a welcoming tone and lay the foundation for an effective working relationship. Some schools also pair new families with a welcoming family, another family with a child in the school who has been there at least a year. The welcoming family helps the new family adjust to school and introduces them to some of the traditions and special events that they will be experiencing.

LETTERS, POST CARDS, AND E-MAIL   During the summer, some teachers send children a short note or post card to introduce themselves and to welcome the children to the class. The following vignette demonstrates how one kindergarten teacher created enthusiasm and excitement for a child and established a sense of security and trust with the parents even before school began.

Jack's eyes shone as he tore open the envelope that had come for him in the mail. Reaching inside, he found a small plastic dinosaur that he clutched eagerly as he handed the letter to his mother to read.

Dear Jack,

Welcome to kindergarten! I am so excited about your coming to my class. You can bring a favorite toy or book from home for your first day of school. I have lots of places ready for you to keep your things, and each place will have your name and a special sticker. Your sticker is a yellow star.

Our class mascot is the dinosaur, so I have sent you something special. You can bring it to school, too. I will see you at school on Tuesday, August, 26th!

Your teacher,
Ms. Howell

Jack's excitement over receiving mail and the family's satisfaction with this individual welcome to their child created an immediate bond between them and his new teacher. Carrying his dinosaur to school on the first day and knowing that there was a place waiting for him marked with some hearts eased Jack's transition to school.

REFLECTION

Consider the grade level you wish to teach and ways to welcome children of that age to your classroom. Now think about some ways you could communicate over the summer with children who will be placed in your class in the fall.

TELEPHONE CONTACT   In the past, parents and teachers telephoned each other only when concerned about a child's progress. Today, the telephone is a tool for collaborating on all aspects of a child's education. Teachers can begin this process with a brief telephone conversation before or soon after school begins for the year. In this first call, introduce yourself to the family and express pleasure in having their child in your class. Inform parents that unless they wish otherwise, you would like to call or e-mail them on a regular (once a week or month) basis just to keep in contact, inform them of their child's progress and of school events, and answer any questions or address any concerns they might have (Powers, 2005). Establishing positive communication early in the school year enables parents and teachers to be comfortable about contacting each other when later confusion or misunderstanding arises, as the following vignette demonstrates.

Melissa Jacobs was entering third grade in a new school. She knew no one and was terrified, especially because she "didn't read so good." Mrs. Jacobs was relieved when Ms. Thomas called to welcome Melissa to school and to invite the mother to visit. As the year wore on, Mrs. Jacobs was delighted with Melissa's successful adaptation to school. So, she called Ms. Thomas one November morning to see how Melissa's reading was going.

The next day, Melissa came home very angry, not wanting to go to school. "I don't see why I have to go to that dumb teacher and do **phonics***. I hate phonics!"*

Distressed, Mrs. Jacobs immediately called the teacher to ask what was happening. Before Mrs. Jacobs could say much more than "hello," Ms. Thomas said, "I am so glad you called. I was about to call you. You know, I really don't think it's a good idea for Melissa to go to the reading teacher. I know you are concerned about her reading, but she was just miserable today. Her reading is coming along well, and she doesn't need this extra pressure."

In the course of the conversation, it became clear that there had been a misunderstanding during the last telephone conversation. Mrs. Jacobs had only intended to maintain contact, and Ms. Thomas had interpreted it as concern. Because good communication had been established early, both teacher and parent could resolve the misunderstanding in good faith and do what was best for Melissa.

Formal and Informal Classroom Visits

In the past, parents were invited to children's classrooms only on special occasions, such as during American Education Week in November, or as an audience for special events. Increasingly, however, schools are establishing an open-door policy and welcome parents at any time. To initiate this approach, many schools invite parents and children to drop in during one of the days before school begins in the fall to meet the teacher and see the classroom. These short, 10- to 15-minute visits are especially helpful for younger children or children transferring to the school and can help ease some of the anxiety parents and children feel about entering a new classroom. As the following vignette illustrates, having a simple activity for the parent and child to participate in can set a welcoming tone.

> *After brief introductions, Ms. Bender gave Avi and his mother a pencil and a "Treasure Map" to locate various places in the classroom. As they explored the room, checking off the locations of the coat hooks, bathroom, and learning centers, and locating Avi's name on a bulletin board and on his desk, Ms. Bender chatted with other arriving families. Avi and his mother left the classroom, talking excitedly about the start of the new school year.*

A school in Maryland makes a point of inviting all parents to come to the first day of school each year. A celebratory atmosphere is created as families accompany their child to the classroom and stay for a while. The level of parent involvement has increased dramatically in this school since this policy was established several years ago.

Back-to-School Night gives parents a more formal introduction to their children's classroom. This event, held on an evening early in the school year and generally for adult family members only, gives teachers the opportunity to meet children's parents or caregivers. This is also a time for teachers to introduce themselves and help parents get to know them and understand why they became a teacher. Some schools hold Back-to-School Night or open house for one grade level per night so that families with several children can meet all the teachers without feeling rushed. Families also connect with other parents at Back-to-School Night and learn about the curriculum, classroom procedures, discipline policies, and ways the teacher plans to communicate with parents.

The following vignette demonstrates an innovation that one classroom teacher instituted in the way that invited parents were to participate in some of the classroom activities on Back-to-School Night. While parents participated, the teacher gave information about the value of the different activities and an overview of their child's day.

> *During the day before Back-to-School Night, Jack's teacher asked all children to tell what area of the classroom they thought their parent might want to explore. As a result, when Jack's mother arrived for the open house, she was instructed to start her evening at the snack table. Later, she had a chance to make something for him in the art area that he would find in his cubby when he arrived at school the next day.*

Home visits provide teachers with new insights into the social, cultural, and cognitive functioning of children with their parents.

Recognizing the needs of families, some schools are also offering child care during Back-to-School Night so that single parents or both parents can attend. Many schools use this event to introduce the many ways that families can contribute to the success of the classroom and to assist parents in getting to know one another. Because much important information is communicated at Back-to-School Night, teachers should prepare a written summary of key ideas; this will benefit the families who were able to attend as well as those who were not.

Home Visits

Visiting the homes of preschool-age children prior to the start of school has been common practice in some programs for many years. This is particularly true for Head Start, where such visits are required several times a year. Many public school prekindergarten classes, child-care programs, and private nursery schools also require or encourage teachers to visit children in their homes. Although these visits can be aimed at assisting parents in providing better health care, obtaining needed social services, and supporting their children's academic progress, they also help teachers become more knowledgeable about individual children and to get to know their families.

Such home visiting programs are designed to establish family–school relationships early by helping children become acquainted with the teacher and helping the teacher to understand the home situation (Morrison, 2006). The responsibility for such visits always rests with the classroom teacher, but most will have an assistant teacher or another adult accompany them on the home visit. This practice meets the need for safety and allows one visitor to talk to the parents while the other plays with the child.

Successful home visits depend on the teacher's ability to develop a trusting relationship with parents. Home visits can provide teachers with new insights into the social, cultural, and cognitive functioning of children and their parents. By working cooperatively, parents and teachers can more easily support children's development and learning. Keep in mind, however, that some parents may decline a home visit for various reasons, and their refusal must be respected and an alternate plan for meeting arranged.

Accepted practices for making the home visit comfortable for both teachers and parents abound in early childhood literature. Some basic recommendations for a productive home visit include the following:

1. Clarify the purpose of the visit with an initial telephone call.
2. Arrange a convenient time so that the children can be part of the process.
3. Set a specific time for the visit. Arrive and depart on time and leave earlier if events warrant it.
4. As a guest in the home, respect the cultural and ethnic values the family exhibits.
5. If other family members are present, include them in your conversation.
6. Be an attentive listener, but don't oversocialize or get drawn into family controversies.
7. Be prepared to suggest agencies and types of services that parents might pursue in getting help if the family asks.
8. Invite the parents to become active participants in the school program, suggesting several levels of involvement.
9. Follow up the visit with a thank-you note and indicate action for what was agreed on during the visit.

IMPLICATIONS FOR TEACHERS

Welcoming Parents and Children to School

After reading about some of the ways that teachers welcome parents and children to their class-rooms, you will want to think about those ideas that are most comfortable for you. An online search will reveal other activities that may appeal to you as well. It really comes down to your attitutde toward parents and how you can convey respect to them as the expert on their children. When teachers work to establish positive relationships with parents, the outcome can be a more equal partnership in developing good educational programs for children.

You will also have a lot of resources and information to share with parents at the beginning of the school year. You will be eager to share material that will help them understand how they can support their children's education, but don't try to present it all at once. Your main tasks at the beginning of the school year are to extend a warm welcome to parents and children and to begin to develop the rapport that will lead to a successful collaborative relationship. The most powerful way to build trust with families is by letting them know that you care about their child. Sending handwritten invitations to parents or making brief telephone calls to alert families about an upcoming school or classroom event will be powerful incentives for families to participate.

REFLECTION

Think about some of the reasons families might be hesitant to have a teacher make a home visit. What alternatives could you offer these parents that would still allow you to get to know the child's family life better?

ESTABLISHING ONGOING COMMUNICATION WITH PARENTS

Almost all parents are keenly interested in their children and what happens to them at school. Teachers, knowing of this concern, have developed various ways to communicate with parents about their children's school experiences. Parent–teacher conferences, newsletters, telephone contacts, e-mail, Web sites, and written notes inform parents about children's progress, school programs and curricula, and ways parents can help their children. Most of these techniques have proved to be very successful, and teachers have developed a number of ideas that are variations on these basic strategies.

Informal Contacts

Parents with children in preschool normally accompany their children to school, which gives both parents and teachers a chance to talk informally. Teachers can allow time at the beginning and end of the day for brief conversations with parents. Parents like to hear what their children have been doing, and a brief statement, such as "Phil climbed to the top of the jungle gym for the first time today; he'll be excited to tell you about it," communicates to parents that you are aware of what is happening with each child.

Parents also must share in the communication process. Parents who comment about how their child is at home or note their child's enjoyment of a school activity communicate their involvement in their child's learning. Teachers who post daily digital photos and a short synopsis of the day on the parent bulletin board labeled "Ask your child or me about . . ." help to foster communication between parent and child. By asking questions and being attentive, you can help parents feel more comfortable when talking with you.

Lengthy conversations, however, are a problem at the beginning or end of the day. Busy parents are anxious to go to work or home, and busy teachers need to prepare for the day or clean up after a long one. Brief statements at this time are important, and if a parent needs more time, you should suggest either a scheduled conference or a telephone call. When parents linger in the classroom at the beginning of the day, skilled teachers suggest that they observe something special or help their children in some constructive way.

Parents usually do not accompany their older children to school, but they are often present in welcoming schools where partnerships have been formed with parents and communities. These parents still anticipate brief words of welcome or an exchange about what is going on with their children. Such exchanges communicate to all parties, including children, that responsibility for educating the young is shared by the entire community.

All school personnel can assist or hinder parents' reactions to schools. School custodians, secretaries, and classroom aides are especially important members of the school team. They often live in the neighborhood and, when they are friendly and open, can offer a bridge to the school community. Principals and teachers who look up from their work and smile at, greet, or offer assistance to persons entering the school give parents the feeling that the school community cares about them.

Written Communication

Although face-to-face contact is ideal for establishing relationships between families and schools, by necessity, much communication must also occur in written form. School and classroom handbooks, questionnaires, newsletters, bulletin boards, Web pages, and informal notes are all used by teachers to gather information and to communicate with families about their children's school involvement.

QUESTIONNAIRES AND SURVEYS Well-designed questionnaires or surveys can help you learn more about children's families, but they are most useful when the questions are asked face-to-face. Some of this information can be gathered when the child is enrolled in school, during open house, and at parent conferences. See Table 10-1 for an example of a questionnaire that gathers information that will be helpful in welcoming families and planning activities that build on the children's home cultures.

TABLE 10-1   A Family Survey to Bring New Families Closer

Family Structure Questions

Who are the people who live in your home?

Beside yourself, who else cares for your child?

Would you describe the residence you live in?

Who is in your extended family?

Family Culture Questions

What is your family's ethnic or cultural background?

What languages are spoken in your home?

We all have family traditions. How do you celebrate birthdays and other family events?

What special activities do you do as a family?

What foods are important to your child and your family?

What is your religious affiliation?

School Involvement Questions

What are some ways you would like to be involved in your child's schooling?

What could our school do to help you be more involved?

What are the most convenient times for you to have meetings and activities at school?

Would you be willing to come and share some aspects of your home culture with your child's class?

Would you be willing to share information about your hobbies, talents, interests, and occupation with your child's class?

What is the best way and time for your child's teacher to communicate with you?

Source: Based on notations in Henderson et al. (2007) and York (2003).

HANDBOOKS   Every school and every early childhood program should have a family handbook that communicates policies and procedures. Handbooks can include such information as the school's philosophy; operating procedures, including the yearly calendar, daily schedule, discipline policy, and emergency plans; and parent involvement opportunities (Hiatt-Michael, 2001). Specialized classroom handbooks can supplement the general handbook and provide more detailed information on the curriculum of the particular student age or grade level.

HOMEWORK   Traditionally, teachers have given homework with the hope that parents would oversee the assignments and help their children as needed. Of course, homework provides children with practice on skills taught at school, and parents who review the work with their children certainly get information about what they are expected to learn. But these assignments are often seen by parents as a great nuisance.

All too often, traditional homework consists of worksheets to complete or drill work on specific skills. Changing the emphasis of homework, however, can help parents see that they are indeed contributing members of their child's classroom success. Assignments can be given that develop certain skills but can also be part of the family's life. For example, children and parents might cook something together to share in the classroom. One teacher had children and parents look at the moon each night and mark the time of observation and the place on the horizon where it was seen. Another teacher devised a Love Note Project in which children selected a book to read with a parent or another special person each evening. The parent or other person wrote a simple love note about the interaction, and the child (or teacher) read it to the class next morning. In all the preceding examples, the teacher created a follow-up system that informed parents of the success of their work with their children.

Parents also appreciate having advance notice of upcoming homework projects and adequate time to complete them during the busy school week. Some teachers provide a calendar for upcoming projects and a weekly homework packet that children and parents can work on at their own pace. Remember, too, that it might be an older sibling, babysitter, or after-school care provider helping with homework. Some schools have also established a homework hot line to help with the homework process. Community libraries are increasingly partnering with schools to support children and families with homework (Mediavilla, 2001).

BULLETIN BOARDS   All classrooms have bulletin boards, and most schools have boards in the halls. Teachers place children's work, information about special events, and material for a particular unit on these boards to inform parents of ongoing classroom activities. They also see their children's artwork, their written or retold stories, reports on books they have read, and information on units they have studied. They read the teacher's explanation of the work and what it shows about the children's learning. Photos with captions are especially appealing to parents, as they show children's involvement in classroom activities. Digital cameras allow teachers to easily share such photos with parents through e-mail as well. Some teachers also include family photos in the classroom so that children stay connected to their loved ones during the day and visiting parents are reminded of their importance in their children's lives.

Many schools also provide bulletin boards just for parents, and the interests of parents dictate what is posted. Parent volunteers often arrange the board or assist teachers in highlighting information, such as bibliographies of children's books, educational toy suggestions for birthdays or holidays, and recipes for nutritional snacks. Sometimes teachers photocopy materials and put them in a wall pocket for parents to take home. Information about school and community events, social services, and health and nutritional assistance may be provided, and if postings are changed regularly, parents will learn to consult the board for information. Parents are also invited to post materials of interest for other parents, and one school has even added a wipe board for parents to write notes to other parents.

NEWSLETTERS AND WEB SITES   Classroom and school newsletters, although varying in purpose, are useful ways for schools to communicate with parents. Most newsletters convey school news, including notices of school events, parent–teacher conferences, and other important meetings. Many newsletters also include tips for helping children at home and resources for parents. All information can go on a school Web site, too, with paper copies sent home to those families without a computer.

Increasingly, teachers are finding additional purposes for classroom newsletters or Web sites, supplementing them with a calendar of upcoming events and using them to recap what has been going on in the classroom. One teacher gives out the first newsletter on Back-to-School Night and uses it to communicate much of the information she shares verbally. Another teacher includes in her newsletters artwork by children, photos of classroom activities, thank-you notes for parental and community support, examples of how children use materials that parents contribute, and extracts of classroom discussions children had because of parental support. Such a complete newsletter provides parents with many examples of what and how children learn from various resources.

INFORMAL NOTES AND E-MAIL   Traditionally, teachers have used informal notes to alert parents to their concerns regarding students' work. Now more teachers recognize the value of notes that discuss students' special accomplishments in developing social, cognitive, or physical skills, thus giving both parents and children a sense of well-being. Of course, all notes can go to parents via e-mail in homes with a computer. Most notes don't require a response, but you may occasionally wish to query how parents see their child's skill development at home. You should also invite two-way communication through notes for parents who find this a helpful way to keep in touch. Some teachers provide a composition book, which is passed back and forth via the child's backpack, for both parent and teacher to write notes to each other.

Like the first telephone call to the child's home, the first note should be a positive communication designed to build a collaborative relationship. Some teachers like to send home some kind of weekly report for all children (see Figure 10-2) and ask parents to sign and return it. Informal notes or weekly reports can also express concern about a change in a child's behavior.

When notes are positive in tone, even if you have some concern, parents come to understand the importance of working cooperatively to provide the best for their children. Most teachers believe it is wise to let children know about communications with their parents and, in general, what the notes contain. Children's involvement is essential, for children need to know that parents and teachers are working together to help them learn. E-mail and telephone answering machines are other ways that teachers provide more information to parents. Some teachers update a Web site or an answering machine to record brief messages for parents concerning children's home assignments, events of the day, upcoming meetings, or things that children are asked to bring to school. Teachers have elicited the aid of bilingual parents in translating notes sent home to families who speak a language other than English. Web sites that translate notes into other languages are also available.

INTERACTIVE PORTFOLIOS   In many classrooms, teachers now have children assemble their work in a portfolio. Over time, the work accumulated there provides materials for children, teachers, and parents to assess the child's learning. Technology expands possibilities for communicating with parents via these portfolios. For example, digital

```
┌─────────────────────────────────────────────────────────────────────────┐
│                            WEEKLY REPORT                                  │
│                                                                           │
│  Dear Parent/Guardian,                                                    │
│                                                                           │
│  We will be sending home weekly reports this term for all children.       │
│  These will keep you aware of your child's progress in social skills.     │
│                                                                           │
│  NAME:_____ DATE: _____  │
│                                                                           │
│  In general, your child's behavior this week was:                         │
│                                                                           │
│  (G) GOOD              (F) FAIR            (N) IN NEED OF IMPROVEMENT      │
│                                                                           │
│  _____Listening skills              _____Behaves in specials         │
│                                                                           │
│  _____Works quietly                 _____Behaves in hallways         │
│                                                                           │
│  _____Stays on task                 _____Shows respect               │
│                                                                           │
│  _____Completes class work          _____Completes homework          │
│                                                                           │
│  _____Interacts appropriately with peers                               │
│                                                                           │
│  TEACHER COMMENTS:                                                        │
│                                                                           │
│                                                                           │
│  PARENT SIGNATURE AND COMMENTS:                                          │
│                                                                           │
└─────────────────────────────────────────────────────────────────────────┘
```

FIGURE 10-2   A Sample Weekly Progress Report

cameras allow teachers to record classroom events and share these photos with parents on a regular basis. Some teachers print the photos and include some of them in individual, **interactive portfolio** notebooks that are shared between the home and school. Periodically, the teacher will write a short entry about a special event, accomplishment, or issue in each child's portfolio and send it home with the child to share. Then the family is invited to write a response or to share information, photos, and news from home and add it to the portfolio.

REFLECTION

In your field-experience classroom, check to see how the teacher keeps in contact with parents. Has he or she used any of the suggested techniques discussed in this section? Does he or she view these ideas as realistic for a busy teacher?

IMPLICATIONS FOR TEACHERS

Written Communication

As you consider the many ways of communicating with parents in written form, think about how to make the flow of paper manageable for you and for busy families. At the start of the year, determine what day of the week you will send home newsletters, progress reports, and homework packs. Have a designated pocket folder labeled with "Return to School" and "Keep at Home" to help organize the material. Parents will learn to check for information on the designated day and will use the folder to send notes, permission slips, homework, and other types of information back to the school. Color coding materials so that the newsletter is always printed on yellow paper, progress reports on blue paper, and homework on white paper, for example, will also help families keep track of the materials. Ideally, all materials will also be available online for those families that prefer this method of communication.

Parent–Teacher Conferences

Conferences are one of the most frequently used methods of parent–teacher communication and are a successful way to discuss the child's progress. As schools begin to develop a sense of partnership, conferences, although not different on the surface, become forums for mutual exchange. Partnership conferences are those in which both partners share examples of children's development, show respect for each other's responsibility, and propose ideas for continuing a program or changing direction. In successful conferences, parents and teachers are able to communicate the child's strengths, progress, and possible areas for improvement in more detail than in any other format (Henniger, 2008).

Although initiating conferences has traditionally been the teacher's responsibility, schools are increasingly encouraging parents or other involved adults to suggest meetings and to come to conferences prepared to share their perspectives. Current strategies reflect changes in attitudes of teachers and parents as they see conferences as joint ventures that may even involve the participation of the student. Figure 10-3 presents a general scheme that you as a teacher may use to ensure that your parent–teacher conferences result in effective collaboration.

PARENTAL INVOLVEMENT   To enhance participation and involvement in conferences, teachers need to communicate the significant impact these meetings can have on children's learning. By anticipating the needs of individual families and sharing the following information in the classroom newsletter or in a note or e-mail home, teachers can help parents prepare for the conference more effectively.

- If children have more than one adult responsible for them, both adults should plan to attend, if possible. Other significant adults in the child's life are also welcome.
- Early morning, late afternoon, and evening appointments will be available for parents who need them. Because the conference is an important part of the child's education and evaluation, adults should make the appointment a priority and schedule it early.
- Children's understanding of the purpose of the conference is important,

Parents and teachers see conferences as joint ventures that may even include the child.

PREPARATION FOR THE CONFERENCE

1. Develop mutual respect by scheduling conferences at convenient times for both teachers and parents.

2. Establish a sense of equality with seating arrangements. Avoid physical barriers by sitting beside parents at a table where everyone can view all materials.

3. Prepare an agenda and send it to the parents. Include a statement of purpose and allow times for parent input, your input, and questions from both you and parents.

4. Assemble materials from areas of the curriculum that demonstrate children's classroom work over time.

5. To demonstrate the value placed on parent teaching, invite parents to bring items their children have produced at home, such as charts of children's home responsibilities, craft projects children have made, food they have prepared, letters they have written, any collections, or sets of favorite books.

THE CONFERENCE

1. Begin the conference on a positive note by sharing children's accomplishments at school with parents.

2. Invite parents to share their children's meaningful achievements at home.

3. Share your mutual academic and personal concerns.

4. Discuss ideas for resolving these concerns.

5. Allow time for parents' questions. If parents appear reluctant to ask questions, assist them by suggesting what other parents often focus on: codes of behavior for the classroom, academic questions not attended to in this particular conference, parent involvement in schools or in children's learning.

6. Keep the conference to the allotted time. If you need more time, schedule a new conference.

ENDING THE CONFERENCE

1. End the conference on a positive note; be complimentary to the children involved.

2. Review conference highlights.

3. Restate your understanding of any decisions mutually made.

4. Indicate how information or material parents have shared has helped you understand their children better.

5. Thank the parents for coming and inform them of the next conference period, next school event for parents, or next PTA meeting.

6. Indicate your anticipation at seeing the parents again.

CONFERENCE FOLLOW-UP

1. Write a brief summary for your records. Include any and all parental suggestions or questions.

2. Follow through on your promises and inform the parents of your efforts.

FIGURE 10-3 Making Parent–Teacher Conferences Work *Source:* Based on information in Seefeldt and Barbour (1998).

and parents or surrogates should talk with children about the conference and ask for their input about school and how they view their progress.

- Parents should bring to the conference any materials that they or their children want to share with the teacher.
- Adults attending the conference should make note of any questions or concerns that either they or their children wish to share with the teachers.
- Afterward, parents need to talk about the conference as positively as possible to help the children see the relationship of the home environment to school life.
- A follow-up letter or e-mail to the school clarifies for the teacher the parents' or surrogate's view of the conference.

STUDENT INVOLVEMENT Traditionally, students have had little say or involvement in parent–teacher conferences. Today, as parents assume more responsibility for conferences, both teachers and parents may seek input from children on questions they would like the adults to discuss. Another facet of innovative conferences is including students themselves. When students are included in the conferences, the following steps need to be taken to prepare them:

- Determine the reason for including the child; for example, the student's work has been collected in a portfolio, and evaluation of the work will be enhanced with his or her input.
- Review with the class the purpose of the conference, and help the children as a class to develop some possible questions and ideas to discuss in upcoming conferences. Students may want to consider their strengths as learners, how they have changed during this time period, any difficulties they may be having, and how they might improve (Weldin & Tumarkin, 1999).
- Help students gather materials they wish to bring to demonstrate their strengths and progress.
- During the conference, have students describe their materials and how they see their progress. Have them ask questions of both teachers and parents.
- Have parents discuss their observations and then discuss yours. Make sure that the children's are addressed, too.
- Review the conference highlights and recommendations made.
- Understand the importance for all parties to follow up conferences with notes to one another.

Although there are advantages to including children in a parent–teacher conference, there are drawbacks as well. Some information that the adults wish to share may not always be appropriate for the child to hear. If children are included, it is important that they understand that parents and teachers will also have some conferences without them.

IMPLICATIONS FOR TEACHERS

Keys to Effective Communication

Whether communication is verbal, written, or electronic, there are certain key elements to consider for effective communication and for avoiding misunderstandings:

- *Work at understanding the other's point of view. It is important to listen carefully to parents without interrupting. When responding to parents' messages, try to consider their perspective without becoming defensive. Repeat what you think you are hearing, seek clarification, and try to be empathetic in responding to parents' concerns.*

- *Language differences can cause misunderstandings when care is not taken. Avoid appearing to model or correct another person's speech pattern. When terms are used that either party is unfamiliar with, ask for or give an explanation in a nonjudgmental way.*
- *Traditionally, the teacher has been seen as the expert. Good collaboration requires a partnership in which teachers and parents acknowledge the contributions each makes to the child's development. Negative body language, such as pursed lips, folded arms, and hands on hips, can undermine positive communication by conveying a different message than the words express. Try to be aware of your own body language and respect the communication styles of various families.*
- *Voice pitch and tonal qualities are used to convey different meanings. Cultural and family differences exist, and they can cause misunderstandings. Learning about these differences in a reciprocal exchange can ease potential conflicts. In Chapter 4, Greg helps Philip learn "the school way." In the same way, it is incumbent on the teacher to lessen the gap by recognizing that parents may not know the school way. Being honest in discussing how you have been affected by differences will open communication and will help parents recognize and even accept differences.*

Thoughtful, ongoing communication with parents is an important component of parent–teacher cooperation. It involves parents at a basic level in their children's education. Table 10-2 summarizes the shift from a traditional teacher-centered approach to the collaborative communication strategies discussed in this section of the chapter.

As you consider the strategies presented here for building collaborative relationships with families and community members, think about how you would use what you have learned to foster involvement in your classroom. Remember, not all families or agencies can participate fully, nor is it even desirable for them to do so. What are some ways in which you will initiate communication with parents? How will you help them feel welcome in your classroom and understand their importance in their child's education? How will you use technology and other modes of communication to reach out to parents?

REFLECTION

Ask a fellow student to role-play a parent conference with you and ask another student to observe or videotape the role play. Then review your observer's comments and think about how you appear in working with parents.

PARENTS IN THE SCHOOLS

Many teachers invite parents to special events throughout the year, knowing that getting them into the classroom can be the first step toward further involvement. When parents are in classrooms, they see firsthand how their children respond to the school's learning environment. Although we find exceptions, involved parents usually become strong supporters of their children's schools. They come to appreciate what teachers are doing and what is involved in educating their children. In addition to basic participation as visitors or observers, some parents make a commitment to act as volunteers, classroom resource persons, or even paid aides. Teachers need to help parents understand that there are different levels of involvement (see Chapter 11, Figure 11-1) and encourage them to contribute where they can.

TABLE 10-2 Parent and Teacher Communication Strategies That Foster Collaboration

Conferences

Traditional	Collaborative
Conferences are scheduled only during the school day, and children are not permitted to attend.	Early morning, evening, and lunch-hour appointments are available, and child care is provided.
Teacher prepares materials, provides input, and directs the conference.	Parents, as well as teachers, prepare for the conference.
	Child contributes ideas to the conference or attends.

Home Visits

Traditional	Collaborative
Teacher, in the role of expert, attempts to understand the home, establish positive relations, and explain parental responsibility with regard to children's education.	Teacher assumes the role of facilitator and seeks to build a partership with the family.
	Parents are encouraged to plan visits and share ideas.
	Parent empowerment is sought.

Telephone Contact

Traditional	Collaborative
Teacher initiates telephone calls only when concerned.	Teacher establishes the relationship by initiating a friendly call early in the year.
Teacher uses the phone as a substitute for a conference.	Both parents and teachers call each other occasionally to communicate about the child.
	Leaving messages about schedules, homework, and other issues on answering machines permits exchange of information.

Informal Contact

Traditional	Collaborative
The beginning and end of the school day are times for brief exchanges between parent and teacher.	Schools establish an open-door policy and welcome parental visits during the school day.
Demonstrating interest is the goal.	Parents are encouraged to communicate regularly.

Written Communication

Traditional	Collaborative
Teachers develop bulletin boards.	Parent information bulletin boards are provided, and both school personnel and families provide materials.
Newsletters include school news, dates to remember, and tips for helping children at home.	Bulletin boards include family photos, photos of children in action, artwork, notes on parents' contributions, and what children have learned. Web sites highlight school news.
Informal notes are ways to keep in contact with and inform parents of difficulties.	Notes, e-mails, and program Web sites reflect children's special accomplishments and are designed to give both parents and children a sense of well-being.
	A program chat room encourages communication among families as well as between teachers and parents.

When parents volunteer in classrooms, they come to appreciate what is involved in educating their children.

School Visitation

As schools welcome parents with open-door policies that invite them to drop in on their child's classroom at any time, certain guidelines must be developed so that the visits are productive. Back-to-School Night and the follow-up newsletter provide two ways of introducing parents to routines of the day and how children are involved. Parents will know that when they visit, the teacher may suggest where they should sit to get the most from their observation. If there is activity that parents can observe better by moving about the room, the teacher suggests the best time to do so.

In some classrooms, children are accustomed to adults and are comfortable asking them for help. In such cases, parents are advised that children will approach them. If parents are visiting to observe general classroom activities and how children interact with one another, the teacher provides a list of things parents can watch for. If a parent is visiting for a particular reason, the parent and the teacher confer regarding what to look for and how.

In some families, grandparents, uncles, and aunts are closely involved in a child's life. Teachers should make it clear that these other important people are welcome in the school. At the Kensington/Forest Glen Children's Center (Silver Spring, Maryland), one of the classes has an "I Love You" dinner each February. The children cook and serve a simple meal to all their loved ones, including siblings, parents, extended family members, and other important people in their lives.

Most classrooms have special events to which teachers invite parents. (Some interesting examples are noted in Figure 10-4.) Such occasions give children experience in writing invitations, planning for the event, demonstrating some skill or talent, and even preparing special snacks. Increasingly, teachers are planning family breakfasts once a month or several times a year. Parents all bring some simple breakfast foods to share and join with their children, the teachers, and other families in an informal gathering that can fit easily into the daily routine. The list of events for such visits is almost endless, but when planning, teachers need to consider any family-related barriers that might inhibit involvement. See Figure 10-5 for items that some teachers found to be hurdles.

Children need to be prepared for adults visiting their classroom. Teachers usually have explained to their classes that parents and other adults enjoy coming in to see what they are doing. Traditionally, teachers introduce visitors, explaining to children the purpose of the visit. An innovative approach to these visits is to help children take responsibility for welcoming visitors.

Mrs. Horton has many visitors to her class at a school near Atlanta, and she established the role of greeter to be filled as one of the weekly classroom duties. Children practice the role so that they will feel comfortable with adults. When adults come into the room, the greeter quietly welcomes them, takes their coat, and suggests where to sit. The child points out the daily schedule, which is always posted, and tells the visitors what is currently happening.

1. **Stone Soup Day.** As part of their folktale study, a third-grade class invited their families to celebrate the end of the unit. Children performed their version of "Stone Soup" and then had their families join them in eating a nutritious meal of "stone" soup and corn muffins, which they had prepared the day before.

2. **Poetry Slam.** A fifth-grade poetry unit grew into a schoolwide celebration of books and poetry. Held in the evening in conjunction with the book fair, the poetry slam featured parents and children who recited or read poetry written by themselves or others. Some participants prepared ahead of time but others were spontaneous, using the large collection of poetry books and anthologies for inspiration. The audience snapped their fingers in response to each poem.

3. **Coffee Hour.** At one school, the principal, staff members, and teachers, on a rotating basis, were freed from responsibilities each Friday morning. Families were invited in to have coffee and chat with them about school in general and to get to know one another. As the year progressed, sharing "things that were working well" and "things that could work better" became part of the agenda. Gradually, the evolving good fellowship and trust led both parents and school personnel to take responsibility for seeking solutions for concerns.

4. **Literacy Night.** Parents were invited to bring their children to school one evening dressed in their pajamas. As children participated in storytelling sessions led by education students from the nearby college, parents attended short interactive workshops about how to encourage reading at home. The local library sent the bookmobile, and staff assisted parents in obtaining library cards. The evening ended with a bedtime snack and a story told to parents and children by a master storyteller.

5. **Heritage Night.** One school with a large multicultural population invited families to come to school on a spring Friday evening dressed in native clothing and with a special dish to share. Some families brought music to share and other items that were important in their culture. An informal fashion show was staged. The evening was so successful that the school decided to hold the event earlier in the year so that the involvement that was sparked could begin in the fall.

FIGURE 10-4   Special Events That Worked in Five Different Schools

Parents and Community Members as Volunteers

Most teachers realize that having parents who regularly assist children in the classroom pays off in a richer curriculum for students. Schools are also turning to grandparents, active retirees, high school students, and other community members as volunteers. Although some schools have money allotted to hire one or more parents to work as aides in classrooms, volunteers are increasingly needed to serve a variety of roles in schools.

To be most effective, classroom volunteers need orientation and training in order to participate in ongoing classroom activities. Teachers are legally responsible for the children in their classroom, and if volunteers don't understand the rules and procedures, conflicts can arise. Misunderstandings can result, and neither children, parents, nor teachers are well served. Back-to-School Night can provide a forum for teachers to acquaint parents with the volunteer opportunities in the classroom. At this point, some parents may be able to commit to a regular schedule of classroom participation, whereas others may only be able to contribute occasionally. A later meeting, sometimes, led by the reading specialist or guidance counselor together with the classroom teacher, introduces parents to the classroom routines and provides guidelines for their participation.

Barriers	Modifications
Time	❏ Breakfast meetings
	❏ Weekend events
	❏ One event scheduled over a number of days
	❏ Open invitations
Transportation	❏ School bus or van
	❏ Car pool arranged by teacher or parent volunteer
	❏ Buddy system among families
Child care	❏ School-provided child care
	❏ Child care provided by parent organization
	❏ Buddy system among families
Decorations/celebrations	❏ Artwork created by children in the art center
	❏ Artwork generated during a theme/project study
Curriculum	❏ Opportunities for children to make multiple gifts and cards and to pick their recipients
	❏ Family members share expertise and culture
	❏ Bias-free curriculum
Food	❏ Multiple menus available
	❏ Buffets
	❏ Picnics
Printed material	❏ Translate copies
	❏ Make audiotapes
	❏ Make telephone calls
	❏ Use voice mail or e-mail
Special guest	❏ Guest not specified by role
	❏ A pal or friend
	❏ Open invitations to extended family members or a noncustodial parent
Expense	❏ Support provided by community businesses underwriting the event or materials needed
Misunderstanding the role as parent volunteer in the classroom	❏ Volunteer training sessions
	❏ Specific routines created
	❏ Recorded or printed instructions
Misunderstanding the parental role in home-extension learning activities	❏ Specific routines created for home-extension learning activities
	❏ Parent workshops to explain activities
	❏ Demonstration tapes
	❏ Demonstrations during home visits
Discomfort in school situations	❏ Alternative home visits or neighborhood meetings
	❏ Buddy systems among families
	❏ Small-group meetings

FIGURE 10-5   Common Barriers and Possible Modifications Checklist   *Source:* Based on information in Kieff and Wellhousen (2000).

REGULARLY SCHEDULED VOLUNTEERS Schedules for regular classroom volunteers work more smoothly if teachers make a monthly calendar and send parents reminders of the volunteer days. Each morning before the children arrive, the teacher and volunteers spend a few minutes discussing the events of the day. At the end of the day, they meet again briefly to discuss how the day went. For the experience to be successful, both teachers and volunteers need to recognize that the teacher is the major decision maker and authority figure in the classroom. But teachers must respect the skills volunteers bring and explain the role of volunteers so that children do not receive mixed messages.

OCCASIONAL VOLUNTEERS Because many parents and community members are employed, teachers have become more flexible in their expectations of volunteers. Schools must also consider ways to involve parents who are home, caring for younger children. Facilitating a babysitting exchange or providing child care would allow such parents to volunteer.

To involve those who can only participate occasionally, one creative teacher has an open policy on volunteers and invites working parents to observe and help whenever they have time off. He keeps a list of special activities that need extra classroom help. When parent volunteers arrive, the teacher is then ready to use them productively to assist children. This policy has been especially helpful in securing more male volunteers.

When parents do not have time for regular classroom volunteer work, they can help with special activities, such as planning, organizing, or accompanying the class on field trips. Classrooms use materials that can be prepared or repaired at home. Parents can help by making play dough, sewing smocks, or cutting out items, and many parents are happy to participate in this way. Schools also hold functions in which parents can render support services; these include helping to organize for National Education Week, participating in fund-raising activities, or supporting the Read-a-Book Club.

PARENTS AS TUTORS Many programs use volunteers to help children with reading and provide special training sessions to help them develop skills for literacy tutoring. Volunteers agree to come regularly, take children to a quiet area, and read with and to them. The volunteers also help individual children with projects and assist them in practicing certain skills. This individual attention is especially helpful for children whose parents are unable to read to them at home or otherwise lack the time or ability to assist them with their developing reading skills.

PARENTS SHARING EXPERTISE Some educators have devised plans whereby volunteers offer an enriched program for children in their school. In one Maryland program, on Wednesday afternoons, community members present a variety of programs that reflect particular volunteers' skills and interests. An expert quilter provided quilting lessons for 6 weeks. A bird carver introduced the beginning steps of carving. There were flower-growing and -arranging classes, bird and rock identification classes, and discussions on topics from Caldecott and Newbery Award–winning children's books. At the beginning, volunteers wrote a brief description of their "course," indicating the number of lessons and the appropriate age range. Children then signed up, but as the program developed, some adults began to join their children in taking the classes. Both children and adults found that they enjoyed learning in such multiage groupings.

EXPRESSIONS OF APPRECIATION Volunteers receive rewards for their efforts in different ways. Seeing children's progress is very satisfying, and children have their unique ways of showing delight in having someone read to them or help them with a project. Reaching to take the adult's hand, offering a hug, saying, "I read this entire book to my mom after you helped me yesterday," or making a special drawing of "us reading together" expresses better than anything how much children benefit. Letters of appreciation can come from children, teachers, the parent coordinator, or the school principal. Many schools have special lunches or events to formally thank volunteers.

REFLECTION

Consider honestly your feelings about having classroom volunteers. Would you be apprehensive about inviting parents and others into your classroom when you are a beginning teacher? If so, resolve to talk with practicing teachers about how they coped with their anxieties about parent volunteers.

Parents and community members regularly involved in classrooms or school events find themselves at a committed level of involvement from which they gain knowledge about their schools. Children's education is further enhanced when the entire community recognizes the importance of this level of cooperation and participation.

Parents and Community Members as Advocates

In general, teachers expect parents to be involved with their children's education at the basic or **minimum level**. This means communicating with the school about the child's progress and participating in major events, such as conferences and special occasions. Some parents and community members become involved as more committed participants in the classroom by tutoring or volunteering in other ways. Teachers encourage this increased level of involvement because they find that it produces better results for their students. A third level of involvement concerns individuals who take on additional responsibilites at the school by assuming the role of advocates.

The National Parent–Teacher Association (PTA) is one advocacy organization that is well known for giving families a voice in education. It has been in existence for over 100 years and provides support, information, and resources for families to better the lives of children. The National PTA works with local and state PTAs to influence the formulation of laws, policies, and practices in schools. For many families, joining the school PTA is their first step toward becoming an educational advocate.

When parents or community members become advocates for children, they seek to influence school policy. Some parents in this role work within the framework of committees and the administrative structure. Besides joining the PTA, they may attend School Improvement Team (SIT) meetings or speak out at school board meetings. Parents who feel that a school policy is adversely affecting their children may initiate action. In such cases, they meet with teachers, principals, school board members, and even local and state legislators to advocate a change in policy. Recall that it was a single parent, and then a group of parents on a grassroots level, who eventually succeeded in securing appropriate education for children with disabilities through Public Law 94-142, the Individuals with Disabilities Education Act (IDEA).

Other parents become strong advocates for change within an entire school system. Parents may seek election to school board positions because they wish to see change and feel that this is a way for their voices to be heard. Federal legislation also has resulted in

A learning-literacy workshop assists parents in learning about skills and discussing ways to help their children develop literacy.

some parents having a policymaking role. Head Start Chapter I programs and programs under IDEA are required to have parents on their policy-level councils. These parents then have a voice in program development, hiring teachers, the kinds of training offered to teachers, and other policies that affect the programs.

Not all school systems or teachers embrace parent advocacy enthusiastically, nor can all parents operate at an oversight level of involvement. Such advocacy and involvement work well only when both parties—parents and teachers—have a voice in the decisions and work cooperatively together. Some parents have served on curriculum committees, steering committees, or school improvement teams and have advocated or demanded change, only to find that nothing happens. This creates frustration. Only when parents, teachers, and school administrators are able to recognize each other's expertise and are willing to assume responsibility for pulling together can change occur. Building coalitions of parents and teachers working for the best interests of their children is the most powerful advocacy role any person can undertake (Ferguson, 2005).

Parent Education

Chapter 2 discussed the trends in parent education in past centuries. As noted, in the early history of the United States, parents learned about educating their children from their own parents or relatives. Then, as psychology moved to the fore, professionals became the experts, and parent education regarding child development and wise parenting practices became a part of the school's responsibility.

Presently, we again find recognition of parents' skills and expertise. In some innovative programs, parent education means that teachers are learning new skills for interacting with parents. Teachers value parents' ideas, help parents understand their own skills, and more effectively integrate home and community knowledge with classroom learning. In addition, innovative practices in parent education reflect efforts to include parents from all economic and ethnic groups within a community.

Some schools attempt to involve their parent group in those education programs that parents themselves see as particularly needed. Seefeldt and Barbour (1998) described a program of outreach in which a principal succeeded in getting parents involved by allowing them to choose and plan their own topics. Many hard-to-reach parents became intrigued and began coming to these informal but educational sessions.

Some schools find that developing a **parent center** within the school gives parents a sense of belonging. Sessions in parent centers run the gamut from reviewing general child-rearing practices, to dealing with behavioral problems and drugs in the community, to providing language instruction for non-English speakers. The meetings often are un-structured, led by laypersons, and involve a great deal of discussion and idea exchange among the participants. Some schools provide a collection of materials, including books, videos, and articles related to child development, health and safety, managing behavior, and other topics of interest, in their parent centers and encourage parents to check them out. The center may also have listings of local resources and social services for parents.

Other programs have a more educational focus and are intended to help families help their children in academic ways. For example, Children's Resources International (Daniels, 2002), in partnership with Montgomery County, Maryland, Early Childhood Services, produced a unique series of workshops designed to assist parents in helping their children develop the skills needed to learn to read and write. Each *literacy-learning party*, as these workshops are called, introduces a specific literacy component and offers parents practical and useful activity suggestions for home use. Like most effective forms of parent education, these workshops include lectures and discussions, practical suggestions, and lots of opportunities for interaction among the participants. The Home Connections to Learning strategy (Mass & Cohan, 2006) incorporated videotaped class-room lessons that demonstrated how teachers were guiding and instructing children in literacy and math. Parents were encouraged to borrow the videos and use the suggested follow-up activities provided in a packet that accompanied the videos.

EDUCATION THROUGH MATERIALS   Learning packets and family theme bags are two practices that teachers have devised for helping parents of at-risk children. In these, parents receive information and ideas for how to interact in a way that increases chil-dren's early literacy development. This idea has been taken a step further with video-tapes and online (Narvaez, Feldman, & Theriot, 2006) modeling of strategies for teaching children at home with follow-up materials for parents to use.

In one Maine program, learning packets are sent to parents of newborns and each suc-ceeding year until age 5. The packet contains information about child development, ideas for fostering growth, and tips on good parenting. Ideas include ways to use books, simple games to play at each age level, and artworks or crafts to create using inexpensive materials.

Family theme bags are cloth bags sent home with preschoolers that contain a stuffed animal or puppet, a journal, a file-folder game, "What if . . . ?" cards, songs–finger plays, a storybook, and art supplies. An introductory letter outlines the purpose of the bag and the value of the activities suggested. The stuffed animal or puppet provides a theme, and games, songs, and activities relate to that theme. For example, the zoo bag contains ideas for making zoo sandwiches, a song about an elephant, and a simple board game with a zoo pattern. The journal is provided so that parents can write their comments on how children respond to the materials and games. When children return the bags, the teacher reads the journals to the class.

WORKING WITH SELECTED FAMILIES

The strategies used for collaborating with parents of all children in your classroom can be effective, no matter what the circumstances are. However, some groups need special consideration, especially when traditional methods are not working.

Members of ethnic minorities, **homeless** and migrant families, gay and lesbian parents, and certain individual families may be hard to reach. Yet, it is imperative that schools find ways to connect with all families. The first step is for teachers to examine their own feelings toward parents who are outside the mainstream and with whom it may be more difficult to establish contact. It is natural for teachers to feel angry, guilty, frustrated, exhausted, and even disapproving when no communication seems to work or when parents exhibit different priorities or a lifestyle different from their own. Being honest about your feelings and discussing them with others will help you to avoid using terms or making statements that hurt or anger parents who may have been rejected in other situations.

Culturally Diverse Families

When working with culturally diverse families, teachers must understand the differences that exist between the language of the school and that of the home (Neito, 2002). Keep in mind that more than 13 million residents of the United States do not speak English well, and another 4 million have almost no English-language facility. If parents speak limited English, it is essential to find someone who can translate written documents as well as oral communications during conferences and other face-to-face interactions. When teachers work with different linguistic groups, learning some words and expressions in the other language communicates to parents that the teacher values their language and accepts the two-way responsibility for communicating. Even when working with families whose native language is English, teachers must refrain from using educational jargon or other language patterns that may inhibit communication.

Teachers must also recognize that different cultural groups may have differing understandings about the roles of families and schools and may need to adjust to the heightened expectations of parents in American schools. In some cultures, one family member may have the power and authority to make decisions, and it is important that teachers know that this is the person with whom to establish communication. Remember, too, that the communication style that is characteristic of the European American culture may not work as well with other cultural groups. The brief, casual tone that you usually use might need to be more formal with certain families. Certain cultural groups also consider it the sole responsibility of the teacher to educate their children, and these parents would hesitate to intrude on the teacher's job (Joshi, 2005).

Maria, a recent immigrant from El Salvador, noted, "Once I put my kids on the bus for school in the morning, I felt like my parenting job was complete for the school day. I felt like they [the school] didn't want me there; only White people go in to help. It wasn't for me." Taking advantage of a parent-training program sponsored by a nonprofit community organization, Impact Silver Spring, Maria learned how to read a report card, press for the right class placements, and become more involved in her children's education. She went on to become a regular classroom volunteer and eventually was hired as an outreach coordinator for Hispanic parents.

Minority families who see pictures of diverse types of people on classroom walls, and in books and materials representing various racial and ethnic groups, as well as signs in their native language, will feel recognized and welcomed at the school. Educational activities designed to respect all cultures in the classroom also enhance communication between home and school. By making a special effort to involve families from ethnic minority groups, teachers can strengthen understanding. Most parents have special knowledge of their heritage and culture that they will share with a class when approached in a positive way. Invite families to share artifacts from their home culture such as traditional clothing or musical instruments, describe their customs or traditions, and/or explain some of their values and beliefs.

In one California school, parents of different ethnic backgrounds contributed in several ways. A Mexican American parent helped children prepare traditional foods for a holiday celebration, and a Japanese American mother showed children how to make origami birds. A Native American father told stories to a second-grade class that demonstrated some of the spiritual beliefs of his tribe. A recent German immigrant brought her collection of dolls to the school and explained the regional costumes the dolls wore. Inviting parents to add special items to the classroom, such as food containers and clothing to the dramatic play area, is another way to help the classroom environment reflect the lives and cultures of the children. Sending parents home-activity bags that include books from various minority groups, with related information and activity ideas, is another way to promote understanding across cultures. Children's literature is particularly useful in presenting abstract concepts about cultures in a simple yet meaningful way.

REFLECTION

Visit your local library to find children's literature about cultural groups you may encounter in your work with children and families. Consider how you can use these books to help families feel at home in your classroom, and add their titles to the collection in the Appendix.

Homeless and Migrant Families

Working with homeless and migrant families is one of the most challenging tasks a teacher faces. In spite of the McKinney Homeless Assistance Act of 1987 (Public Law 100-77) and subsequent amendments, which require states to guarantee access to education for homeless children, many homeless children are not in school. The requirements for registration, such as proof of residency, age, immunizations, and health records, are too much for many homeless families to cope with, and often these families find it easier to keep their children out of school (Ames & Farrell, 2005). Parents may also avoid putting their children in school because they are ashamed and embarrassed about their living situation. When children do have access to schooling, they often are not in the school for long before parents are forced to move again. Often homeless families are struggling with other problems as well, such as illness, spouse abuse, depression, and poverty.

Schools need to find services that enable migrant families to support their children's education.

Families who support themselves through migrant farm work also have many issues to deal with. Theirs is a dangerous occupation, and their children may be exposed to hazardous materials, motorized machinery, and lack of sanitation. Many migrant workers do not receive prenatal care, dental care, or other basic health care. Consequently, their children are at higher risk for disease and chronic illness than is the general population. These families need assistance in securing health and social services. If homeless and migrant parents are asked to help a school educate their children, the request may be beyond the skill of many of them. It is important to remember, however, that the lack of a permanent home and financial resources doesn't mean that parents don't love their children and want them to succeed. When homeless and migrant children are in a school, personnel need to unite their efforts to find services that will enable the parents to support their children's education. The following list contains several suggested ways that teachers and school counselors can assist migrant parents and parents in homeless situations:

1. Provide information about the availability of various services and funding options and how to qualify for mental health services, child care, after-school care, and transportation arrangements.

2. Suggest options for parent involvement in the school. Although a regular commitment to volunteering in classrooms is impossible for most homeless parents, it is wrong to assume that the parents are unable or unwilling to help. They may be able to spend a day tutoring or supervising recess. When they give comfort to another child, they receive the joy of assisting someone else.

3. Be sensitive to parents' ability to provide baked goods, pay for special class events, or have children bring materials for classroom projects. Children whose families cannot provide such materials are often discriminated against by other children and even by teachers. Consider asking homeless and migrant parents to assist in the classroom as their way of contributing.

4. Keep in mind that migrant and homeless parents, too, need parent workshops and opportunities to share their concerns and stories. It often takes special handling to get these parents to trust teachers enough to be a part of such sessions.

5. Coordinate efforts with local shelters. Some school programs or workshops can be started at shelters and temporary work sites. If parents develop confidence in shelter personnel, these parents often are willing to participate in school programs with support for transportation and even child care for younger children. We must try not to segregate the homeless and migrant populations, denying children and parents opportunities for interaction with diverse groups.

Gay, Lesbian, and Transgender Parents

Most teachers today are sensitive to different family structures and are trained to support children when families are in the process of change because of death, divorce, remarriage, or adoption. Less attention has been given to working with gay and lesbian parents or with families who have a parent who is transitioning to or living as a person of the opposite gender. Although relatively small in number, this group is becoming increasingly visible, and these parents need to be supported as partners in their children's education. Teachers may need workshops (Gelnaw, 2005) to enable them to deal with their feelings about alternative family configurations and to find ways to support children whose parents or other important family members are gay, lesbian, or transgender.

In a diverse society, parents expect that their family structure will be treated with dignity and respect in the classroom. Some educators, however, may fear being accused of promoting homosexuality when they are sensitive to the needs of children from gay and lesbian households. It may be helpful to recognize that this is an issue not of sexuality but of relationships. Children whose parents are gay, lesbian, or transgender feel the same sense of belonging and being taken care of by their parents as do all children. Using children's literature that includes various family configurations will reinforce this similarity and promote understanding of diverse types of families.

When children of gay and lesbian parents experience school difficulty related to their parents' gender or sexual orientation, teachers must approach the parents to discuss their problems. By developing a zero tolerance policy toward bullying and harassment, administrators, teachers, and parents can work together to promote respect and tolerance. In classrooms where some parents oppose books or discussions related to this topic, special handling is required. Sears and Williams (1997) provide many recommendations for working with families that include gay and lesbian members. Also, some communities have gay and lesbian groups specially trained to work with adults whose strong beliefs reject this lifestyle. Inviting parents to join you in one of these sessions can open the door for discussion and for better understanding of this controversial topic.

REFLECTION

Think back to your own childhood and the family configurations you encountered then. Compare these to the families you are reading about in this book and consider how you will welcome all kinds of families into your classroom.

Other Family Situations

Parents raising children with disabilities may need to be treated with sensitivity as well. It is also essential that educators and community workers be knowledgeable about disabilities and their implications for families. Some families may be working through the grief that can accompany the realization that a child is going to require special care and services. Others have developed extensive knowledge about their child's disabilities and have much information that will be helpful to the teaching staff (Hiatt-Michael, 2004). Effective communication between teachers and parents of children with special needs is key, as are clarity and precision in establishing procedures and objectives. See Chapter 6 for an in-depth exploration of ways parents and teachers can work together to share information, deal with everyday situations, and ensure the best outcome for children with disabilities.

Both typically developing children and those with special needs are being raised in foster families, by grandparents, by parents sharing custody, and by other adults in various family configurations. These parental figures may be difficult to reach, yet their participation in school is especially important to children who may have experienced much disruption in their short lives. Teachers need to reach out to these families in an especially inclusive and welcoming manner. Learning the names by which children call the adults who care for them is especially important. Many teachers are careful to avoid using gender-specific parental labels and instead urge children to bring important papers home to their "grown-up". Use inclusive language when defining family (see Figure 10-6) to send a message of welcome to gay and lesbian parents as well as to others whose family configuration is different than the one-mother/one-father model.

Families

We may be related by birth or adoption or invitation.

We may belong to the same race or we may be of different races.

We may look like each other or different from each other.

The important thing is, we belong to each other.

We care for each other.

We agree, disagree, love, fight, work together.

We belong to each other.

FIGURE 10-6   Inclusive Definition of Family   *Source:* Based on an exhibit in the Boston Children's Museum as quoted by Gelnaw (2005).

HANDLING COLLABORATIVE RELATIONSHIPS

As noted in earlier chapters, there is a long history of parental involvement in U.S. schools. Some relationships have been very positive for particular parents, teachers, and community members. Good relationships do not just happen, however. Both internal and external conditions and factors help establish better relationships.

Conditions for Positive Relationships

One important human factor in developing positive collaborations is mutual respect. Each party in a collaborative effort needs the concern of the others as well as the expertise, viewpoints, and experiences the others possess.

Recognizing and supporting the expertise of others is not always easy. Comer (1980), in developing his collaboration model, maintains that the project nearly failed several times. It took 3 years to develop the trust and respect necessary for the school to begin a change process that would offer equal access and opportunity for all students. Commenting on this, Comer stated, "In order to provide good learning experiences for students, trust and respect must exist so that behavior, teaching and learning issues can be addressed. Such a climate cannot be imposed: it must grow out of governance and management arrangements and ways of working based on knowledge of social conditions and human and system behaviors" (p. 230).

Developing such respect requires compassion, a willingness to listen to others' points of view, and a willingness to compromise. Often it is school personnel who must take the initiative in establishing a sense of respect. For the relationship between teachers and parents to develop to its fullest potential, however, both must consider each other as equals and share a commitment to open, two-way communication. No one right way exists to accomplish this, but concerned teachers and administrators devise ways that establish relationships with their students' parents through face-to-face, electronic, and written communication.

There are two very simple and immediate techniques that teachers can use to improve communication with parents. One is to *ask* instead of *tell.* The other is to *listen* instead of *talk.* A key component in establishing good partnerships is people's ability to really listen to each other. Regrettably, although professional adults are involved in communication activities about 70% of the time, less than half of that time is spent listening, and even then, the listening is not done well. When teachers listen well, they do not interrupt to move on to their own agenda. When they reply to parents, they reflect

A welcoming physical environment always helps to establish good relationships.

back what they have heard and seek to validate, empathize, and problem-solve with the parents. When both teachers and parents are willing to learn about and practice communication skills, student success increases (Gonzalez-Mena, 2006).

Beyond the willingness to establish respect and develop good communication, external factors help collaborative efforts to function. It is important to establish support systems such as workshops to assist people in developing better communication skills. Time must be provided for meetings to discuss needs and objectives. To accommodate parents', teachers', and community members' time constraints, schedules must remain as flexible as possible. Teachers may need to be released from classes or compensated for evening meetings. Businesses need to examine the possibility of flexible hours of operation or flexible working hours for their parent employees. Having options for parent and community member involvement establishes a good basis for collaborative efforts, allowing all who are or wish to be involved to select a comfortable participation level.

The process of collaboration is one of identifying, establishing, and cultivating positive factors to support interactions. Many ideas make sense for cooperative arrangements; the strategies of almost any helping profession can be adapted appropriately. If schools are to become engaged in true partnerships, everyone concerned must expand and refine their communication, negotiation, and cooperation skills.

Barriers to Good Relationships

No matter how well intentioned people are, some barriers surface that will result in breakdowns of communication and weakening of good relationships. One basic hurdle is the different philosophical positions and perspectives people have regarding how children learn and what they should be taught. For example, if a school attempts a constructivist approach to learning and parents do not understand how their children are being taught to read, write, and learn number facts, a barrier can develop. Parents could well become angry and accuse the school of ignoring discipline and not teaching the basics.

Different beliefs about how sex education should be taught, and by whom, can create misunderstandings. Another issue is that parents may consider discipline measures to be either too harsh or too lenient, and these different perceptions can cause friction among the home, school, and community. Issues such as these can spark problems, which will fester and add to existing subsurface distrust if no mechanism is present to address them.

Attitudes can also create barriers to good relationships. Parents and community members have feelings and attitudes about school that date back to their own childhood. Parents who had unpleasant school experiences are often reluctant to become involved with their children's schools. A diminished self-concept is often present in such cases, and the isolation breeds more fear. Such parents resist contact with schools out of fear of criticism of themselves and their children. This circumstance helps no one, least of all the children. Schools need to work gently but with determination to overcome negativism and encourage positive contact.

Nonverbal interactions often cause barriers to good relationships. Teachers or parents may say one thing, but their nonverbal stance communicates another. For example, during a conference, one parent crossed her arms, saying, in what seemed an annoyed tone, "I thought Janey did well on that project." The teacher interpreted this to mean "I don't agree with what you said." The teacher then paused, moved slightly away, and murmured, "Well, it was an interesting project." When both moved on to another topic, the real significance of Janey's effort was lost. Both left the situation feeling defensive because the nonverbal behavior of both parties cut off further communication.

Fear affects teachers as well as parents, and teachers may do little to encourage parental or community involvement. When teachers are uncertain or insecure about their own teaching skills, they fear criticism of how they do their job and discourage parent participation in their classrooms. When there is local criticism of schools, teachers become tired of being scapegoats for all the wrongs of society, and they often express a desire to be left alone to teach. When such attitudes permeate the school, parents are made to feel unwelcome in many different ways.

When wide socioeconomic and cultural differences exist between school personnel and local families, misunderstandings can cause friction and often anger. Barriers are created when value systems differ and neither party is willing or able to examine the differences and find common ground.

External features may also become barriers. Entering a new school for the first time can be daunting even for parents with numerous school encounters. In some schools, doors are locked for safety reasons, and one must ring to enter. Sometimes the first thing one sees on entering a school is the notice "All Visitors Must Report to the Principal's Office." Parents who were often sent to the principal's office during their school years will not feel very welcome. When the office is difficult to find and no one is around to assist, schools again communicate that visitors are unwelcome. Office personnel are sometimes too busy to assist or may appear annoyed at the interruption, or they may ask in an intimidating way, "Do you have an appointment?" Unwelcoming signals are easily discerned and too often found.

REFLECTION

Visit several schools to find out how it feels to go into a new school. Try to visit a library and a gym, as well as a classroom. Then imagine yourself as a parent and speculate about how you would feel in these settings.

Teachers and administrators are busy people struggling to maintain a productive environment for student learning. That is their most important task, and many think that the time and energy needed to add parental and community involvement to their workloads just isn't available. Such school personnel communicate the unimportance of parental involvement and miss out on the important contributions that involved families can make to the success of children in school.

COMMUNITY INVOLVEMENT

Like family involvement in schools, community involvement occurs at various levels, ranging from minimal contact to advocacy. Again, teachers and administrators have the greater responsibility for reaching out to the community to develop partnerships, but parents often play a role in getting individuals, agencies, and businesses involved with the local schools. Such involvement may entail a one-time contribution of goods and services, an ongoing site for field trips, or a continuing volunteer relationship.

Good ideas for collaboration aren't always between school and community agencies. The Chicago Public Library and the Chicago Police Department teamed up to provide a number of interactive programs. One program was a Mystery Beat Book Club where students read mysteries and met various police officers who explained how mysteries are solved in real life. Another was a Get Hooked on Fishing, Not on Drugs program. Police personnel spent time with youngsters, both in the library and at special fishing spots, examining the art of fishing. All agreed that the programs helped the police reach youngsters in positive ways, the library maximized its resources, and children had fun, associated with good role models, and became involved in interactive activities that enhanced their reading skills (Burnette, 1998).

Trips into the Community

All children have experience with their community and have learned many different concepts from these encounters. Building on this familiarity, preschool and primary school classes take field trips that focus on specific aspects of community life and provide children with new and extended insights. Carefully planned field trips enhance and make more meaningful the objectives of a unit of study. Students studying economics, for example, can set up a bank and a store in their classroom and practice using them in ways they have learned from their parents or from books they have read. A trip to an actual bank and a store, where they can ask specific questions, allows them to see how adults behave in such places. It gives students behind-the-scenes experience.

When children have particular questions to ask or things to see or do, they gain skills in observing, collecting information, making inferences, comparing information with others, and drawing conclusions. Also, trips produce new ideas, which children transfer to their dramatic play, reading, writing, and other classroom instruction. A trip provides motivation for further interests and learning, as it did for the first graders in the following vignette.

Nigel's class, accompanied by several parents, took a walking trip to the pet store to get food for the lizard they had found in the play yard and were now studying in class. While at the store, they were fascinated by a hermit crab and convinced their teacher to buy one for further study. Nigel became so interested that with his parents he visited the local aquarium. A naturalist there told him more about hermit crabs and where they lived. With this information, the family took a trip to the seashore, and all were able to observe hermit crabs in their natural habitat. Nigel's stepfather videotaped the family's excursion, and Nigel showed the tape to the class and described his experience to his classmates.

Trips into the community are not restricted to gaining understanding of the neighborhood. Children can make trips intended to contribute in some way to the community, such as enhancing the local environment. Trips around the school can focus on cleaning up the area or planting flowers or shrubs. Some organizations "adopt" a highway, assuming the responsibility to clean up litter along a specific section of the road. Classrooms can adopt a neighborhood park, a playground, or a street and keep it attractive.

A visit to a nursing home or hospital presents opportunities for children to show older or ill people their artwork, sing or play some special songs, or provide a dramatic presentation. When child-care centers are located in adult day-care centers or nursing homes, older persons often regularly read to children or engage in activities, such as cooking or making collages, with the children.

A related idea became a project for older children, who followed the Foxfire concept of visiting and interviewing older residents to hear their stories of the past. The class collected and published the stories in book form and sold the book at school functions. In this case, the intent was not to help other people but rather to help children interact, appreciate, and be involved with an older generation.

Bringing the Community into the School

Children can travel in their community for educational purposes, but it is also

Field trips enhance and make meaningful objectives for a unit of study.

possible to include community members in the classroom. Traditionally, teachers have invited doctors, firefighters, or police officers to describe their services to children, but imaginative teachers have found other ways to involve community members. One kindergarten teacher instituted a "Royal Reader" program and each week invited a person from the community to read aloud to the class. Using some regal music as background, the teacher introduced the reader, who entered the room wearing a crown and cape. Over the course of the year, employees of the power plant, water company, community college, retail stores, and various other local businesses and services came to the classroom to read and describe some of their work.

REFLECTION

Think about the resources available in your community and the kinds of activities that community members might be able to provide to the children in your class. What value do you see in such activities? How will you incorporate such experiences in your curriculum?

Teachers also invite specific community members to the classroom to extend or enhance a unit. One biology professor enjoyed taking part of his collection of rare butterflies to a second-grade classroom each year during their butterfly unit. In the spring, he walked in nearby fields with children searching for cocoons or newly hatched butterflies.

Increasingly, community agencies such as libraries and museums are offering *reverse field trips* by sending a member of their staff to schools with selected materials to present to children. At one nursery school, naturalists from a nonprofit foundation brought several rehabilitating owls to the school for the children to observe and then led an evening "owl prowl" in the woods surrounding the school. In a variation on this evening, fathers and other special adult males were invited on the owl prowl, offering them an opportunity to participate in a unique and appealing manner. Artists, musicians, and other performers can also be invited to schools to provide children with arts-based experiences.

As in planning for field trips, teachers need to plan for special guests. They should tell children about the guest, encourage them to think of things they want to know, and help them understand how they are expected to act during the visit. It is important that teachers remind visitors of children's interest level, attention span, and need for hands-on experience.

Some resources from the outdoor environment can be brought into the classroom for closer examination, but teachers must choose these resources carefully. Endangered plants must not be disturbed, and certain animals are unsafe to bring into classrooms. But colorful leaves, nuts, fruit, twigs fallen from trees, rocks and seashells, minerals embedded in bits of rock, insects in aerated jars, and pond creatures for classroom aquariums are specimens that children can examine and study in the classroom. See Figure 9-1 for a list of community resources.

Involving the Business Community

Businesses have provided support for schools in various ways for many years, most often in the form of contributions of goods or funds. Restaurants have contributed gift certificates but may also contribute a percentage of their profits on a particular night that has been designated a school fund-raiser. Parents are encouraged to patronize the restaurant on that evening. Other restaurants have established a "Dine Out for Charity" month and will donate a percentage of each order to the local school or agency. Still other businesses will contribute funds for a particular project or materials. Band uniforms or costumes for a school production are items that local businesspeople take pride in providing for community junior and senior high schools.

At a fund-raising carnival cosponsored by the PTAs of a middle school and an elementary school, local businesses participated in many ways. Some gave out free samples of ice cream. Others provided food at greatly reduced prices, and still others sponsored various rides and activities that were provided. All of the businesses were listed in a directory that was given out at the entrance, which provided them with advertising and community goodwill.

Other businesses have contributed classroom equipment, such as calculators and computers. Some businesses will sponsor special programs such as "Read to a Parent and Get a Pizza." A school-supplies store agreed to provide one enterprising kindergarten teacher with a year's supply of fingerpaints when her classroom budget was reduced. In return, children's work, demonstrating the creative potential of finger paint, was exhibited in the store.

IMPLICATIONS FOR TEACHERS

Fostering Community Involvement

Collaborating with businesses for better schools requires a spirit of mutual respect and reciprocity of benefit. But for any partnerships to be effective, teachers must visit the business establishment to determine its educational possibilities, and business personnel should visit the schools to become acquainted with their function, goals, and daily operation. Each partner needs to know the other's resources, ideas, and commitments. Remember, you can start small. A class walking trip in your school's neighborhood can begin the process, and it will lead to interesting ideas about community features. Children will have ideas about how they can work with neighbors and businesses for the good of the community.

Work with your school to set up a Business and School Committee consisting of local community businesspeople and school representatives. This group can start the dialog on collaboration. The first topic might be "Why good schools are important to a community." You will get lots of ideas in a few minutes of conversation. The next topic could be "How our community contributes to our schools' excellence."

Summary and Review

Forming special relationships with parents and communities to enhance the education of children is not a new concept in the United States. As educators have gained more responsibility and authority over children's education, they have realized that increasing family and community involvement enriches the experience for all. Although educators normally consider themselves experts in teaching children, they acknowledge that without parental and community support, their job is more difficult.

Frequent communication between home and school is important. Parent–teacher conferences, newsletters, phone calls, home visits, e-mail, and Web sites, as well as parents' participation in classroom and school activities, are more effective when teachers experiment with different strategies so that each family is reached at some level.

Many educators now recognize that when teachers, parents, and community members form a relationship of equality and shared responsibility, schools become strong and children acquire greater cognitive and social skills.

Suggested Activities and Questions

1. Ask your parents (or someone you know well) about parent–teacher conferences or home visits in which they were involved when you were a child. Determine how useful they felt such activity was. If you know a parent of a primary-school-age child, ask the same questions and compare strategies and parental reactions then and now.
2. Interview parents who volunteer in their children's classroom. Solicit their opinion of this involvement, asking how often they volunteer, how they became involved, why they think it is important, and what they are learning from the experience.
3. Locate a commercial establishment that displays children's work and ask how the school became involved.

Compare notes with classmates who have interviewed other establishments to determine what kinds of involvement your community appears to have with schools.
4. Obtain from a school administrator (or from parents of a school-age child) copies of newsletters sent home to parents. In your class, compare the kinds of information they contain. Discuss whether some are more "parent friendly" than others and why.
5. Locate a Web site designed for parents of children with special needs to determine some of the issues that are important to them. Develop a list of strategies that would help teachers build relationships with parents of children with disabilities.

Resources

Organizations

Community Action for Public Schools   *http://www.cleweb. org/caps.htm*

Learning First Alliance   *http://www.learningfirst.org*

National Coalition for Parent Involvement in Education   *http://www.ncpie.org*

Parent–Teacher Association   *http://www.pta.org/*

Web Sites

http://www.cec.sped.org   The Council for Exceptional Children is an organization for professionals and parents and provides multiple resources, such as training opportunities and legislation updates.

http://web.jhu.edu/csos   Center on School, Family, and Community Partnerships, a component of the Center for Social Organization of Schools, helps families, educators, and community members work together to improve schools.

http://www.naeyc.org/families/early_years   Early Years Are Learning Years,™ from the National Association for the Education of Young Children, offers short articles for teachers, parents, and community members that are suitable for newsletters.

CHAPTER | **11**

Building School Partnerships with Families and Community Groups

We are all the crew of Spaceship Earth. Like Apollo, the crew must work and learn together and manage the resources of this world with new imagination.

(JIM LOVELL, APOLLO 13 COMMANDER, IN *LOST MOON*, 1994, P. 4)

After reading this chapter, you will be able to do the following:

- Discuss the levels of involvement by community adults in true collaborative programs.
- Identify the conditions that enhance the growth of partnerships as well as factors that serve as barriers.
- State the criteria that demonstrate the status of partnerships.
- Discuss how thoughtful planning, careful implementation, straightforward accountability, and honest communication produce healthy partnerships.
- Explain the commonalities found in partnership models and how these remain constant in differing programs.

Much is right with U.S. educational experiences in spite of some well-publicized problems. Education planners and policymakers in most communities have a suitable base to build on, and they can draw from numerous models to bring about improvements and viable partnerships. Our final chapter presents the issues to be considered when working together, and it highlights several worthy collaborations found in American school districts today.

Although they seldom use the term *collaboration*, residents in rural and urban communities have always exercised ways of influencing the upbringing of their youngest citizens. In the following vignette, a retired teacher recalls her childhood years in a poor 1930s rural community and indicates some ideas that can serve us well in the 21st century.

⟨⟩—— *Our minister, the school principal, and our town fathers frequently discussed school problems in our little town and recommended solutions. Their efforts were supported by local parents, and our party-line telephone system, where most families could listen in, aided communication. For example, one child, returning late from school on a spring day, was easily found, reprimanded by a passerby, and sent on his way with the knowledge that his parents would follow through on the reprimand. Children who needed clothes were identified at school, and with the support of "town fathers," teachers and sometimes others visited their homes. Food, clothing, and other resources were found and delivered, and at times, negligent parents were counseled informally by other parents. Our teachers taught formal lessons in the schoolrooms, but they often walked home with us, continuing our education as they discussed the natural world around us. The community was our playground, and adults who were present supervised everyone's children. Older children educated younger ones in many skills and safety rules. One could feel that this was a cohesive community and one marked by caring. It was, of course, not an ideal system: A few children didn't reach their potential. An overarching support system enhanced our opportunities, though, and all 13 children in my first-grade class completed high school, and 7 went on to college in the 1940s. ——⟨⟩*

The narrator of the preceding vignette demonstrates how parents, schools, and community members all assumed responsibility for children's development. Times were simpler then, and many communities were closely knit, but the aura of communal caring and the need for shared expectations are still valid today. Author James Comer lived in a close-knit urban community during his childhood, and he tells of a similar collaboration of the social institutions that cared for him. In *Maggie's American Dream: The Life and Times of a Black Family,* Comer (1988) recalled his parents, neighbors, and teachers reinforcing each other's goals for children's engagement in learning. The process in Comer's case was also informal, but individuals in each social setting seemed to understand each other's roles. In both stories, these neighborhood children, whose parents were sympathetic to the school's and community's goals, were more successful than were children whose parents were out of touch.

Society at the beginning of the 21st century is different from that of several decades earlier. It is more difficult to establish common objectives toward which social institutions can work effectively together. Families have new pressures and heavier burdens, and children have fewer advocates. In many locations, schools have assumed more of the educative, counseling, and social oversight for children, but from many accounts, it is apparent that schools cannot effectively do the job alone (Meier, 2002).

In this chapter, we discuss eight program models that have shown success in improving schools and children's education through family–school–community collaborations. We examine the components that have led to the success of these models and remark on some of the changes made as a result of implementing them on a larger scale. First, though, we discuss some basic principles and distinctive features that characterize collaborative efforts.

LEVELS OF INVOLVEMENT IN COLLABORATIONS

Good collaborative efforts mean that the individuals in an evolving group endeavor will recognize that different levels of involvement exist in a partnership (Epstein et al., 2008; Rubin 2002). Some community participants will participate at a minimum level, others at an **associative level**, and still others at a **decision-making level**. Although educators are in the best position for encouraging and establishing partnerships in any area, parents and community members can and do work toward leadership roles in a collaborative effort.

Understanding Involvement

Laypeople interpret parental and community involvement in school affairs in different ways. Some citizens are proactive and feel naturally connected to their schools. A larger group views teachers as having total control of children's education, and they either do not seek involvement or feel shut out of the process. This latter group tends to view schools from afar, but its members are often critical when their children don't progress well. Therefore, all educators and involved community workers have a duty to work on attracting this part of the constituency.

So, how much involvement is productive? Different programs will call for differing amounts of involvement by parents and community members, and generally, participatory intensity varies with the level of involvement. The key to successful collaboration is for many community citizens to be involved at one level or another, with a few individuals contributing at all levels.

MINIMUM LEVEL For generations, school personnel have reached out to parents and community members in seeking basic support for school programs. For example, children have homework, which teachers request parents to supervise. Or a principal may request help from citizens to advertise some school events. Educators expect parents and other community members to respond to these requests and help with the projects.

The community at large is normally invited to school-sponsored events, and teachers often seek assistance. For example, parents and community members help make costumes for school plays or props for exhibits. Schools have various fund-raising events, such as bake sales and fairs. Again, school personnel seek cooperation from parents and others to attend, contribute items to, and help with the events.

The preceding are all examples of minimal involvement, and most readers will recognize and recall similar events from their own childhood. Such minimal involvement is commonplace; it serves a definite purpose, and it is a good foundation from which to start working for more complete community participation.

ASSOCIATIVE LEVEL Many teachers request parents and community members to become classroom volunteers on a regular basis. These volunteers assist teachers in various ways—from copying materials to reading with children and assisting them in activities. Still others become room mothers (or fathers), organizing other community members, helping to supervise children on school trips, or making calls to solicit classroom support. Some volunteers become involved in enrichment programs, offering their special expertise to children in a classroom. Another example is the advocacy work of parents of children with disabilities. These parents frequently become knowledgeable about their child's special needs and also about school processes, so they can go on to become local leaders and advocates for teachers working with children with disabilities. These are examples of associative-level participation.

At the associative level, community members also participate in local organizations that support schools. Parent–Teacher Association (PTA) chapters have traditionally supported schools, and through them, parents and teachers cooperate in school improvement ventures. At times, PTAs center on fund-raising events; at other times, they may become a political force in the community to improve conditions for children.

Children benefit from adult involvement at the associative level; because of their school experience and intensified role, the school's expectations are much clearer to these parents, and all communication is facilitated. Stronger ties mean stronger programs, and divisiveness is far less likely when schools and communities enjoy this level of interaction. At any point in time, fewer parents will be involved at the associative level than at the minimal level. Comer (1980) noted that if 5% to 10% of parents become actively involved at the associative level, that number constitutes an adequate group as long as it represents a cross section of the community.

DECISION-MAKING LEVEL   The third level of parent and community involvement in schools is the decision-making level. At this level, individual parents, businesspersons, professionals, and community leaders participate actively in decision making for the education of children.

Parent participation produces little controversy at the minimum and associative levels of involvement. Teachers and school administrators are still in charge of all educational decision making, and parents and community members assist and support the decisions. When parents and others become involved in decision making, however, friction can result (Rubin, 2002). Controversy that paralyzes is, of course, not in the best interests of children. Therefore, successful collaboration of parents, teachers, administrators, and community members at this level requires mutual respect and a new definition of shared responsibility and accountability (Comer, Ben-Avie, Haynes, & Joyner, 1999; Sanders, 2006). Acting at this level of involvement requires hard work.

Parents at the decision-making level move beyond being committed advocates for their children to sharing responsibility for providing quality (school) education for their own and other children. They serve on curriculum committees, identifying goals and objectives and deciding how to achieve them. At this level, parents are expected to serve on committees that hire school staff. They also may assist in forming advocacy groups to secure necessary local, state, or federal funding. Again, the parents of children with special needs are often able to take leadership roles because of their prior experience working with school personnel, making decisions for appropriate placement of their children, and developing their children's individualized education programs (IEPs).

Usually, parent and community involvement at this level requires only a small percentage of parents, but these persons must represent the different constituencies within the community. Such involvement dictates changes within the school hierarchy, and such changes can be detrimental unless teachers, administrators, parents, and community members work carefully and with genuine mutual respect to bring gradual change (Comer, Haynes, & Joyner, 1996). Figure 11-1 illustrates the collaborative relations of each level of involvement.

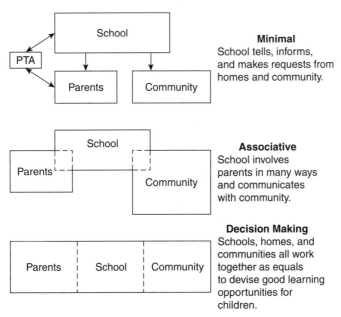

FIGURE 11-1   Three Levels of Involvement

Having community adults functioning at the decision-making level marks a true collaborative venture—and that is the goal. To get there, let's follow the ideas in the following section and then look at some examplary programs in the United States today.

IMPLICATIONS FOR TEACHERS

Checking Out Levels of Involvement

Now try to do some application. You have visited schools, and you know something about how much parent–teacher collaboration goes on. Now jot down three or four incidents you have witnessed this year that show parents (or community members) getting involved in a school situation. See if you can relate these incidents to the three levels of involvement we've been reading about here. For example, if your first incident involves the first-grade teacher calling three parents to help her with a field trip to the bakery, does that characterize the minimum level of involvement or the associative level?

COMPONENTS OF SUCCESSFUL CHANGE

Research (Epstein, 1999; U.S. Department of Education, 2006) shows that children improve academically when schools work for better family and community involvement. Because of this finding, and because of extensive federal interest in partnerships, a number of school districts are now caught up in the rhetoric of collaboration. Some have taken serious steps to establish links with other agencies to become full-service schools, where municipal services and social agency support are available at the school site. Others have struggled and had little success beyond goal statements and committee assignments (Sanders, 2006).

As more businesses and community agencies become involved with schools, there always exists the danger that leaders in these agencies will start to usurp the rights and responsibilities that classroom teachers owe to their students. In any collaboration, parents and teachers must assume the ethical responsibility for ensuring that everyone involved understands children's developmental levels and vulnerability. Most school personnel want parents and community members to share in the responsibility of educating children, and they seek outside support for solving nonacademic problems. In academic matters, however, educators are more hesitant to involve parents and community members. Nonetheless, successful partnerships mean shared responsibilities, and successful schools mean that parents, school personnel, and community groups share responsibilities for educational decision making.

We find that successful partnerships have different strategies for achieving collaboration, but all have certain elements in common. Collaboration will include three common elements: a planning process, an implementation process, and an accountability process. Equally important is that in

Children improve academically when schools include family and community members in establishing full-service schools.

each process, all involved pay constant attention to establishing good communication and nurturing trust.

Planning Process

Collaboration requires a communitywide team. Members of social agencies, businesses, and government agencies, plus teachers, administrators, and parents, come together, and all make a commitment to work for the benefit of the community's children. The community team needs a strong leader, and key people in the community are crucial for the project. All participants must be willing to work out differences when necessary, and trust and respect for other viewpoints are even more vital.

During planning, the team determines the needs of children in the community, develops goals, and designs procedures for accomplishing these goals. Communication, collaboration, and cooperation among the various team members mean that all agencies surrender some autonomy in seeking solutions, but in so doing, all recognize their mutual benefits.

Implementation Process

As the collaboration team develops procedures for implementing strategies, members ascertain which agencies can provide personnel and financial resources. Implementation is guaranteed greater success when a team provides orientation and training sessions, ensuring that parents, teachers, and community members have some basic collaborative skills.

A major step in beginning collaboration is providing workshops that reduce the social distance among participants and that also improve relationships among parents, community workers, school staff, and students. Another step involves understanding the interests and expertise of teachers, parents, and other volunteers so that all can contribute their best. Ideally, all participants gain an understanding of how their service contributes to the goals and objectives.

After the team sets the priorities for the community's needs, it begins to plan and collaborate on such activities as providing families with needed services, improving school and home discipline, adapting curriculum to particular community needs, establishing appropriate social activities, and developing program evaluation strategies.

Assessment Process

People working with collaborative programs must have ways to determine how well their goals are being met. Most projects review students' classroom work, and many programs develop questionnaires to get feedback from the community about the success of their activities. Data are collected and interpreted regularly; then strategies used in the school programs are altered or continued accordingly. At least once a year, parents, school staff, and community members will be informed about progress and the changes being made to improve conditions.

Communication

The success of all collaborative programs depends on good communication and careful monitoring of activities. Parents must feel welcome to visit schools and to participate, and teachers must feel that they are able to visit students' homes as needs arise. Community persons must also be part of the communication loop. All must feel welcome in schools and free to offer suggestions.

Good partnership teams will provide many avenues for parents and community members to get information about school activities and the status of the collaboration.

Routine notices, telephone messages, personal notes, newsletters, articles in local papers, a Web site, and the direct visiting approach, which volunteers employ in contacting hard-to-reach parents, are all used. Parents are encouraged to write notes, use e-mail, or call teachers when concerns arise; they are also encouraged to express appreciation. See Chapter 10 for a larger list of communication ideas.

IMPLICATIONS FOR TEACHERS

Starting Your Involvement with Parents

We trust we have persuaded you that family and community involvement in school life is a big benefit in achieving the goals of education. Now comes the task of starting this process when you become involved in a school.

If you had the power to implement your own program, think of two parents you have met this year and write down two ways you think they could be helpful in implementing the program. Write down the things you would say to these people you have considered for involvement. After making your notes, go back to Figure 11-1 and match what you would like these parents to do to the level of involvement. Is it minimal or is it a higher level?

PROGRAM MODELS

In this section, we examine the characteristics and the arrangements exhibited in eight program models. Although changes have been made in each, the underlying concepts remain the same as they were when they started. As you read about and compare these models, you should gain an understanding of how the partnership process unfolds.

Head Start

Head Start is one of the best-known educational programs in the United States; it enrolls approximately 1 million 4- and 5-year-olds each year (National Head Start Association, 2009). It precedes our current focus on family–school–community collaborations by many years, yet it fits the conditions of a true partnership.

When Project Head Start was conceived in 1965, authorities acknowledged that children were not only family members but also community members. Thus, if Head Start was to succeed in improving the lives of poor children, parental involvement and community commitment to the program's goals were paramount. Through this involvement and commitment, Head Start began to provide, in holistic rather than fragmented ways, comprehensive services in health, nutrition, and economic counseling for individuals, as well as school readiness for children and their low-income families.

OBJECTIVES AND GOALS   Communities were involved in Head Start to make their members aware of the importance of providing adequate health, educational, and nutritional services for children's development. Further, if skills developed in the Head Start programs were to be sustained, the developers knew that parents and communities had to reinforce the learning. Parent involvement reached even further, because the programs encouraged parents to gain skills for participating at different social levels and thereby gain greater confidence and self-esteem.

STRUCTURAL FEATURES   Parents assist at Head Start centers and classrooms in a variety of ways. The *Head Start Manual of Policies and Instruction*, still used today, outlines the primary types of parental involvement.

Parents as Partners.   Parents are partners with professionals in the decision-making process, and two levels are open to parents of Head Start children. At the informal level, parents work with center staff in determining program content and how their children will participate. At the formal level, parents serve on a parent policy committee or council. Council parents are involved in program improvements, recruiting volunteers, and planning and developing a budget for the parent activity fund. They are also involved in decisions about program goals, criteria for the selection of children, hiring of Head Start staff, and major changes in budget and work programs.

Parents as Observers.   Parents participate in Head Start classrooms as visitors, volunteers, and paid aides to see the different ways they can work with their children. They gain a better understanding of what their children are learning and what they can do to assist them at home. When parents become more involved as volunteers or as paid aides, they gain skills and confidence, which in turn help them qualify for employment elsewhere.

Parents as Learners.   Head Start parents enhance their own learning by planning and identifying opportunities that correspond to their own interests and aspirations. Workshops and other learning experiences for a center are often requested and designed by parents, who in this fashion increase their own education. Career ladders have been developed whereby parents are able to obtain their high school general equivalency diploma (GED), and some parents in Head Start have continued their education at technical schools and colleges.

Supporting Children's Learning.   Parents work at home with their children to support and reinforce children's Head Start experiences. Center personnel create and distribute ideas and suggestions for home activities and often visit homes to observe and suggest ways family members can support children's education. As parents become aware of their impact on children's learning, they become confident about helping their children grow and develop (Zigler & Styfco, 2004).

REFLECTION

In any of your field placements or observations, have there been any former Head Start children? If so, how does the teacher describe the parents' support for those children? Do these statements reflect what you have read here about Head Start?

RESEARCH AND ASSESSMENT   Since the inception of Project Head Start, the effects of early intervention on children's development have been a subject of much research and public concern. Initial studies by Westinghouse Learning Corporation–Ohio University (1969) indicated cognitive gains for Head Start children after the first year, but by the third year, these gains had nearly disappeared. Unfortunately, the study did not consider the wide variations in quality.

The study did alert the public that a basic assumption of the War on Poverty was unrealistic; that is, a single summer or 1-year program could not produce a rapid turnaround for economically disadvantaged children. This led to federally supported extensions and outgrowths of Head Start, for example, Even Start and Follow Through.

Long-term studies of the initial Head Start programs (Schweinhart & Weikart, 1997) reveal that the programs have been both cost effective and beneficial to society. For example, Head Start children did better in school, repeated fewer grades, had fewer emotional problems, and were less often placed in remedial classes. As adults, they were less likely to end up in jail and more likely to attend college, became more active volunteers in their communities, and were more likely to marry than peers who had not attended Head Start (Schweinhart & Weikart, 1997).

Studies (Administration for Children and Families, 2000) also revealed that Head Start children's social development improved to equal that of their middle-class peers. Children became more task oriented, sustained attention to tasks longer, and developed curiosity about learning. Children with disabilities appeared to benefit the most after involvement in Head Start programs. Collins's (1984) synthesis of more than 1,500 Head Start studies confirmed the positive impacts on children's cognitive, social, and health development, as well as improvements in parenting.

Communities that established and maintained Head Start programs have benefited as well. A number of poor and minority parents in these communities have moved into the workforce, and area public schools have changed programs because of the models that Head Start provided. Readers searching for current information on Head Start will want to check the Head Start Web site (http://www.headstartinfo.org) and Zigler and Styfco (2004) for good critiques.

Head Start has not fulfilled the dream of diminishing poverty in the United States or in eliminating all learning gaps, but its impact has been positive, and its benefits for helping poor and minority parents become partners in their children's education outweigh its costs. In addition, more recent collaborative efforts have profited from the procedures and experiences of this model program.

OUTGROWTHS OF HEAD START   Head Start evaluations in the late 1960s showed that poor children from birth to age 4 needed help earlier if they were to overcome the debilitating effects of poverty. This information led to ideas for developing home-based programs (e.g., the Ira Gordon and David Weikart models) in the late 1960s and 1970s that stimulated Head Start extensions.

Even Start.   Funded in 1988 and administered since 1992 by individual states, Even Start continues on a modest level as a pre–Head Start program centered in the child's home. A primary focus of Even Start is promoting family literacy with help from an educational social worker.

Early Head Start programs enhance children's total development while helping parents become better caregivers.

Early Head Start.   Several offshoots of Head Start programs are now grouped under the Early Head Start label, which was organized in 1994 when Head Start was reauthorized by Congress. The focus is on early intervention to enhance a child's physical, social, and cognitive development while helping parents become better caregivers and teachers.

Even Start and Early Head Start programs use the home as a beginning point in children's education, and the emphasis since the early 1990s has been on family literacy. This concept recognizes that parents are children's first teachers and that it is important to help parents become more effective teachers. The program was designed to provide

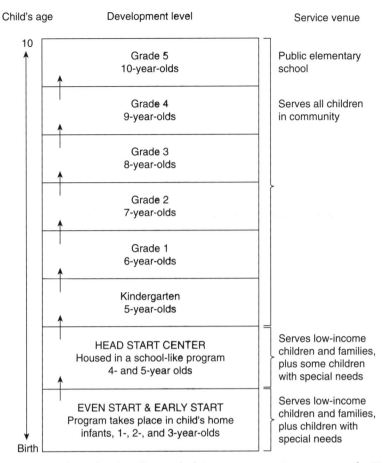

Child's age   Development level   Service venue

FIGURE 11-2 Relationship of Federally Funded Compensatory Programs to the Typical Elementary School (ages may vary at each level)

all-encompassing support to enlist parents as partners in their children's education, with the hope that they could then help their children reach their full potential as learners (Even Start, 2009). The parent educator, with help from local Head Start teachers, works directly with parents in the home. This person, a sort of educational social worker, plans home activities and arranges other social services needed by the family. Figure 11-2 presents the relationship of federally funded early education programs to typical elementary school programs.

Success in all the pre–Head Start programs depends on the quality of the individual venues. Still, we have some very encouraging results: When participation is high and many services are offered, children gain significantly in tests of school readiness and language development (Weikart, 2004).

Comer's School Development Program

In 1968, James Comer and his colleagues at the Yale Child Study Center began the School Development Program, a collaboration with two New Haven, Connecticut, elementary schools to increase parental involvement in children's education. Both schools were located in low-income areas, all children were African American, and parent participation in school activities had been very low. When the Comer team examined parents' interest, however, they discovered three patterns that revealed potential home–school linkages.

1. Most parents expressed interest in the activities in which their children participated at school.
2. Some parents were interested in volunteering for particular activities in the school.
3. A few parents were interested in the curriculum and how teachers instructed their children (Comer & Haynes, 1991).

With this knowledge, Comer and his team began a series of experiments and adjustments that used parents' interests to bring about collaboration. Now, more than two decades after the conclusion of the project, the experiment has become a highly touted model for involving parents.

GOALS AND OBJECTIVES　The initial School Development Program evolved over a 5-year period, and participants adjusted its structure as programs evolved and needs changed. A steering committee, consisting of administrators, teachers, parents, aides, professional and nonprofessional support staff, and the Yale Child Center mental health team, established the following major goals for the project (Comer, 1980):

- Modify the social and psychological climate of the school to facilitate greater student learning.
- Improve students' basic skills.
- Raise students' motivation for learning and their academic and occupational aspiration levels.
- Create a sense of shared responsibility and decision making among parents and staff.
- Connect child development and clinical services to the educational program of the schools.

STRUCTURAL FEATURES　The program consisted of three teams: the school planning and management team (SPMT), a Yale Child Study Center mental health team, and the pupil personnel team, plus four major features: a parent program, a focus program, workshops, and an extended-day program.

School Planning and Management Team.　The SPMT, composed of **stakeholders** in the school, developed and implemented academic and social programs, designed staff development, evaluated the program, and made necessary adjustments. After various experiments, three important guidelines evolved for the SPMT: (a) solving problems using a no-fault approach, (b) using principles of child development for decision making, and (c) ensuring that collaborative management did not paralyze the school principal (Comer & Haynes, 1991).

Mental Health Team.　The mental health team consisted of a child psychiatrist, two social workers, an educator with early childhood education training, an educator involved in teacher training, and a psychologist–program evaluator. Its main purpose was to assist school staff in understanding and applying principles of social and behavioral science to school problems and opportunities.

Pupil Personnel Team.　A pupil personnel team cooperated with the principal, community social-services personnel, and special teachers by giving services directly to students who needed such support. As conditions in the school changed and behavioral problems lessened, this service became more educational and less behavioral in nature.

Parent Program.   A parent program started, with a small group of parents receiving a stipend for assisting teachers. This core group formed the nucleus of the parent group and served on governing bodies and subcommittees that helped plan social and educational programs. Their function was to "bring the attitudes, values, and needs of the community to these committees and their activities" (Comer, 1980, p. 65). As the program changed to meet school and community needs, the parent program evolved to include parent involvement at three different levels.

At the first level, five or six parents were elected to serve on the school planning and management team, where decisions about programs and operations were made. These parents enlisted other community residents for other levels of participation and helped overcome the barriers inhibiting hard-to-reach parents.

At the second level, parents were involved in helping in classrooms or in sponsoring and supporting school programs. The strength of this involvement was that parents and teachers worked together to motivate students to achieve academically and socially.

At the modest third level, parents became involved in activities in which their children were engaged. They attended student performances and other teacher–parent activities, where "good news" was shared, and generally supported the program from a distance.

Focus Program.   At the start of the project, a focus program was established to help children 1 or more years behind their peers in reading and math skills. Three times a week, these children were taught in small groups to supplement classroom teaching of reading and mathematics. The focus groups changed as children's learning needs were identified.

Workshops for Adults.   From the onset, 2-week summer workshops allowed parents and teachers to get to know one another and share their perspective on the academic and social experiences they felt children needed. Workshops became ongoing and were offered when teachers or parents indicated a need.

Extended-Day Programs.   This program included workshops for teachers to learn more about child development and behavior, teaching and curriculum development, and the use of the arts in promoting academic skills. In addition, teachers developed skills in meeting with parents and planning parent participation projects.

Social Skills Curriculum.   In establishing community involvement, Comer's team found that many distinctions between low-income and middle-income children involved differences in social skills. As a result, the team devised a social skills curriculum for inner-city children consisting of four units: politics and government, business and economics, health and nutrition, and spiritual and leisure time. Field trips, visits by community members, and lots of hands-on activities—related to banking, musical productions, and local government organizations—enabled low-income children to enhance their interpersonal skills, writing skills, and ability to interact with adults.

SCHOOL DEVELOPMENT PROGRAM   Many aspects of the original implementation serve as guidance for schools associated with Comer's School Development Program. Figure 11-3 illustrates the current Comer process. To implement a model that offers respect to all and sustains learning, Comer et al. (1996) maintained that there are three guiding principles, three teams, and three operations:

- *Three principles: consensus*   (planning requires that all parties come to agreement on the plans), *collaboration* (all work in tandem with each other), and *no-fault* (no one party is at fault for any lack of success, but all share in the responsibility to improve).

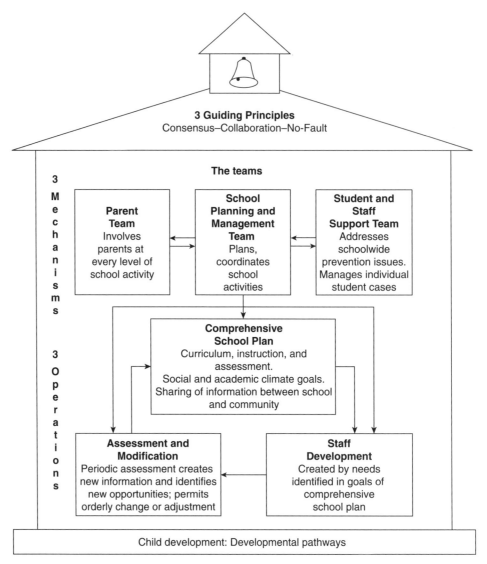

FIGURE 11-3   Comer's School Development Program   *Source:* From *Rallying the Whole Village: The Comer Process for Reforming Education* (p. 10), J. P. Comer et al. (Eds.), 1996. New York: Teachers College Press. Reprinted with permission.

- ***Three teams:***   the *school planning and management team,* which plans and coordinates all school activities; the *student and staff support team (SSST),* which addresses student and staff problems and manages individual situations; and the *parent team (PT),* which involves parents at all levels.
- ***Three operations:***   a *comprehensive school plan,* developed to meet academic and social goals; *assessment and modification,* for periodic assessments and provision for change when necessary; and *staff development,* as needed to achieve goals.

Comer et al. (1996) believed that this model permits communities to transform and change their programs by involving school personnel and families in a participatory approach.

REFLECTION

The Comer model is a comprehensive model of partnership. Has this been mentioned as a partnership model in schools with which you are acquainted? Reflect for a moment on how teachers you know might perceive this much involvement.

RESEARCH AND ASSESSMENT   After 5 years of working through problems and modifying procedures, rules, teaching strategies, and programs, the School Development Program showed remarkable success. Overall academic achievement went from third from the bottom to among the top schools in the city. Behavior problems were greatly reduced, and parent–teacher misunderstandings lessened as parental participation in school activities increased. The consensus is that home–school–community links growing from the School Development Program in New Haven have provided essential ingredients for children's healthy development (Comer & Haynes, 1991).

OUTGROWTHS OF THE MODEL   The Comer model has been replicated in more than 650 schools across the nation. In Washington, D.C., several neighborhoods have successfully changed their schools from places where violence, drugs, and crime were paramount to schools with "high expectations and where everyone working together . . . has become an attitude, a way of learning and an education for life" (Ramirez-Smith, 1995, p. 19). Further success of the Comer process is explicated in the publication by Comer et al. (1999), in which readers find firsthand accounts of communities working through the model. Comer et al.'s 1996 book, *Rallying the Whole Village,* is the publication that best describes the Comer process.

Reggio Emilia

The Reggio Emilia program was developed in northern Italy by a group of parents soon after World War II. The first school was staffed by parents and community members who held to a profound belief in and respect for children's natural learning. Under the leadership of Loris Malaguzzi, and with the parents' strong commitment to be decision makers for their children's education, the Reggio Emilia approach to education was born.

The curriculum in these 3-year preprimary schools evolved as teachers, children, and parents worked together, learned about each other, and valued each other's ways of processing information. The Reggio Emilia philosophical and educational precepts have also matured over the years, though never straying from the basic premises: Children are active participants in their own learning, and schooling should reflect community values and beliefs. In the past decade, American educators have attempted to emulate the practices of the Reggio Emilia approach, as it epitomizes a significant success for parent–school–community collaborations.

GOALS AND OBJECTIVES   The purpose of Reggio Emilia is to develop a school where children are at the center of the curriculum, where they develop a sense of belonging by participating in the school community. Leaders find that children's self-concepts are strengthened over their 3 years of belonging to the same group of children and adults. From the beginning, the founders recognized that parents, teachers, and community members were partners in planning and executing any curriculum, and they felt that a curriculum should reflect the community's values and distinct qualities, including all of nature. Young children in Reggio Emilia programs are viewed as informants to adults on their interests, unique learning styles, and prior knowledge. Therefore, the children are active participants and decision makers in what, when, and how to study. It is up to adults to follow and plan accordingly.

PHILOSOPHICAL PERSPECTIVE   One basic principle of Reggio Emilia is that a program for children must be dynamic, vibrant, and evolving. As new theories of children's development emerge and new social events unfold, the directors expect that the program's philosophical and psychological underpinnings will change and that programs will reflect these changes.

The ever-evolving philosophical views found in Reggio Emilia schools have reflected for some time the perspectives of Dewey, Piaget, Vygotsky, and other developmentalists. In recent years, New (2003) found substantial incorporation of Comer's partnership ideas and Gardner's views on multiple intelligences. Quite logically, decision makers in these schools also subscribe to Bronfenbrenner's social–cultural perspective. The expectation is that children, teachers, and other adults learn from each other and are both facilitators and constructors of new knowledge.

STRUCTURAL FEATURES   We do not find a set of procedures in Reggio Emilia schools, as we do in Montessori or Waldorf schools, because situation and context are considered first. We do find, however, common practices and modes that help describe the everyday school endeavors.

Organization.   A beginning objective for a Reggio Emilia school is to provide an amicable environment for children, families, and teachers. The classrooms are organized so that projects or themes are pursued according to children's and adults' interests. When people make arrangements, they need to consider that collaborative problem solving among children and between children and adults is important. Spaces for individual study (*ateliers*, "àtt'l yáy"), as well as small-group and total-group activities, are provided. Teachers and other adults are considered guides for children in exploring and investigating.

Children demonstrate their growth through many different "languages," or modes of communication: words, movement, artistic expression, play, music, and the like. Analysis of these communication activities by adults is the documentation of what is being learned. Because learning is viewed as spiral rather than linear, children continually examine their own development through this documentation. They observe what they have accomplished, consider what else they might learn, and then reconsider their objectives (Gandini, 1997).

Scheduling.   Because the philosophy of Reggio Emilia is that children learn by continual active involvement in their environment and by doing projects, the daily routine is related more to scheduling the staff's time than the children's time. Teachers spend most of their 36 hours per week observing children's activities, talking with them about what they are doing, and planning for children's additional study. Each week, staff members spend 4.5 hours in meetings, planning, and in-service training, plus 1.5 hours in documenting and analyzing children's work. They keep records (*diarios*) of the children's work, communications, and their own analyses for parental and administrator preview (Giovanni, 2001).

Implementation Is Evolving.   Society in Italy has changed since 1946, and the idea of schooling and who is responsible for schools has also changed. Validation for the process culminated in the 1970s as national laws in Italy were passed to formalize community-based management for schools similar to that advocated at Reggio Emilia. This is similar to the arrangement of many **charter school** programs in the United States today.

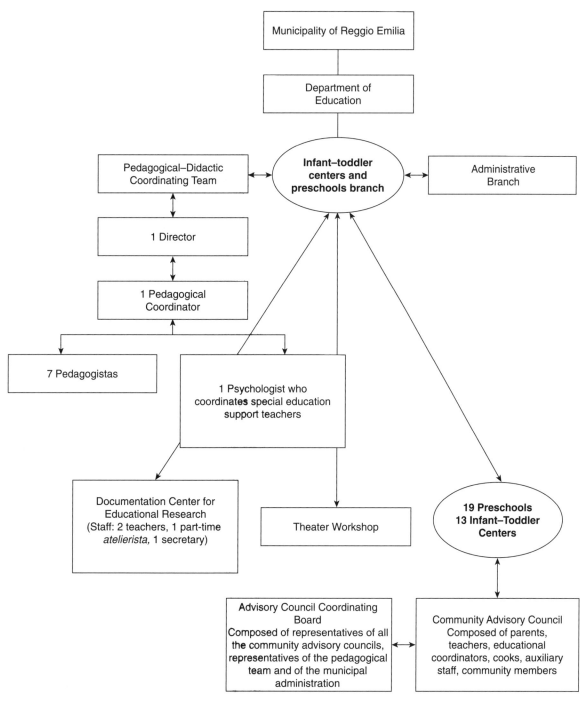

FIGURE 11-4   The Network of Educational Services of the Reggio Emilia Municipal Administration   *Source:* From *First Steps Toward Teaching the Reggio Way* (p. 12), J. Hendrick (Ed.), 1997. Upper Saddle River, NJ: Merrill/Prentice Hall. Reprinted by permission.

Parents and community members are also very important parts of the network. They serve on the community advisory councils, attend various school meetings for planning, and work in classrooms on specific tasks and projects.

The network of educational services has evolved over the years (see Figure 11-4). The line of authority proceeds upward, from the Community Advisory Council (parents,

Children demonstrate their growth through many different languages, or modes of communication: words, movement, artistic expression, play, and music.

all school staff, and townspeople) planning, making decisions, and supporting the educational process. Every 2 years, the community elects representatives to the Municipal Advisory Council Board. With members experienced in communicating and planning, this board forms strong subcommittees, each with specific objectives that focus on different concerns related to children. Because of such involvement, families learn that fully educating a child requires solidarity and support. Not only do children gain from such programs, but so do the families and municipalities (Spaggiari, 1998).

RESEARCH AND EVALUATION   Unlike our American penchant for assessment, there has been no attempt in Italy to validate by empirical research the practices of Reggio Emilia, nor has children's learning been measured by tests that compare their learning to predetermined scales. Children's learning is viewed as spiral, and the mode of evaluation used in Reggio Emilia programs is similar to that of qualitative research in the United States.

The components of evaluation in Reggio Emilia schools are the same for the children and for a program. The "researchers" are the teachers and other adults who record children's dialogues or monologues and reflect on children's other modes of expression. Children's work is collected, stored, and filed in *ateliers* to which everyone has access.

Adults working in the school record anecdotes and reflections on children's activity in a notebook for "two voices" (the child's and the adult's). When children first enter school, they receive a personal calendar that contains a record of each child's particular activities. From these materials, a diary reflecting the child's development from beginning to end is developed. These two sets of materials form the basis of information for any qualitative research.

REFLECTION

Reggio Emilia is a grassroots model of partnership. Think for a moment about how this model compares to Head Start and the Comer model. Does one have more appeal for your own work right now? Could Reggio Emilia be instituted in the United States?

OUTGROWTHS OF REGGIO EMILIA   The exchange of ideas and the traveling Hundred Languages Exhibit of children's work by Malaguzzi have created burgeoning interest in the **child-centered**, developmentally appropriate early childhood curricula of Reggio Emilia. A number of American teachers presently experiment with aspects of the Reggio Emilia philosophy by using projects that are suggested by children. Teachers then listen and document how children learn to read, write, count, and increase their language skills while they are learning science concepts.

The Grant Early Childhood Center in Cedar Rapids, Iowa (Edmiaston & Fitzgerald, 2000), with 350 children, is a designated site for inclusion of children with disabilities. Ten percent of the children attending the program have special needs, and the directors have combined the local and national requirements for special education with Reggio Emilia's approach of collaborative relationships. Children learn to develop a project working with a typically developing peer or a friend with disabilities who is also interested. Project groups learn how to be inclusive as they work with children with particular talents as well as children with disabilities.

Readers will find *The Hundred Languages of Children* (Edwards, Gandini, & Forman, 1998) to be the most useful reference on all aspects of Reggio Emilia. In addition, several volumes discussing American experiments with Reggio Emilia are valuable: *Bringing Reggio Emilia Home* (Cadwell, 1997) and *Next Steps Toward Teaching the Reggio Way* (Hendrick, 2004) give helpful examples of teachers working in American classrooms with this philosophy.

IMPLICATIONS FOR TEACHERS

Relating Reggio Emilia to Your School

You have just read about two successful partnership programs used in U.S. schools—Reggio Emilia and the Comer plan. Both have great appeal to different groups, but there are differences. Before going on to other partnership plans, take a moment to see how the parents you selected for your earlier "Implication" would fit into each.

List three things your potential parent volunteers would likely be doing if they were working as parent volunteers in a Reggio Emilia program.

_____ , _____ , _____

Now, look back at the Comer plan and see if those same tasks would likely appear for parent volunteers. Could they be altered or modified so that they could be used there? If not, would there be other tasks that the parents would more likely be doing? What are those?

_____ , _____

National Network of Partnership Schools

Joyce Epstein, with colleagues at Johns Hopkins University, has worked for more than 20 years conducting studies and establishing programs to enhance educational opportunities for children and to demonstrate the values of partnerships. In 1995, Epstein established the National Network of Partnership Schools at Johns Hopkins to demonstrate the important intersections of research, policy, and practice for school improvement. To date, more than 1,700 schools in 150 school districts across the United States have been involved to some degree in this network, which features partnerships.

As in other partnership models, the framework of Epstein's program centers on the idea of the shared responsibilities of parents, schools, and communities for children's learning and development. She referred to this idea as the "overlapping spheres of influence" in a student's schooling (see Figure 11-5), and she articulates it in her writings (Epstein, 2001; Epstein et al., 2008), which present the important structures and processes needed to develop effective partnership programs. We should note that Epstein places the school in the center of her paradigm and promotes the idea of school as a broker for starting and facilitating the partnership.

Epstein is confident that the education enterprise can work toward creating more "family-like" schools and more "school-like" families when the full power of partnership

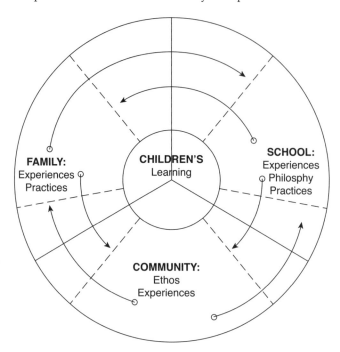

FIGURE 11-5 Overlapping Influences on Children's Learning *Source:* Based on Epstein et al. (2008) and Sanders (2006).

is employed. A family-like school makes each child feel special and included; a school-like family reinforces the importance of schooling and provides activities that build students' skills and a feeling of success. Communities also create family-like settings, services, and events to enable families to better support their children.

GOALS AND OBJECTIVES   The underpinnings and necessary ingredients, attitudes, and ways of working that maximize the endeavors of National Network programs are as follows:

1. "Caring for the children we share." Epstein feels that if this condition is present, then schools, parents, and communities recognize their shared interests in and their responsibilities for children.
2. Help children succeed in school and in life. Epstein points to the "overlapping spheres of influence" of the three social contexts as the key for harnessing their united power.
3. Students are central to a successful partnership and must be part of decision making. Epstein describes several items and qualities that we often overlook when planning programs: The student determines learning, and we should not think of him or her as something to do things for or to. In addition, the student interprets school activities to parents, interprets home activities to schools, and interprets the community to both teachers and parents.
4. The student is the stakeholder and has the most to gain or lose from schoolwork.
5. Effective partnerships have an accumulation of support. According to Epstein, whether the team is "raising a barn, playing tug of war, or building materials for learning units," the enthusiasm for and commitment to the group effort is far greater than anything individuals can accomplish singly.
6. Healthy partnerships tolerate changes, challenges, and disagreements because there is a base of trust and respect. Basic ground rules on communication and expression will develop the base of trust required for any cooperative endeavor. This

---

Keys to Successful School–Family–Community Partnerships

- **Focus on Parenting.** Work with families on child-rearing skills and understanding child development. Assist schools to understand families.

- **Focus on Communicating.** Devise strategies for school-to-home and home-to-school communication about school programs and student progress.

- **Focus on Volunteering.** Strengthen the recruitment and training of family members as volunteers and audiences at school and other locations.

- **Focus on Home Learning.** Produce helpful and interesting tactics to involve families in learning activities at home and in the community.

- **Focus on Decision Making.** Include families in school decisions, governance, and advocacy through action teams and parent organizations.

- **Focus on Community Collaboration.** Work with businesses and other groups to co-ordinate community resources and services to benefit students, families, schools and the community itself.

FIGURE 11-6   Epstein's Six Types of Involvement   *Source:* Based on Epstein et al. (2008) and Sanders (2006).

validates the reason to aim for a multiyear cycle of long-term improvement rather than a "fix-it" blitz of action for 1 year.

7. Partnerships will differ in size, focus, and arrangement but will have many common elements (see Figure 11-6).
8. Establishing an action team is key. All collaborations require some type of steering group if the program is to involve more than a handful of workers.
9. Collaboration focuses on curriculum areas. Participants must keep in mind that their work and energy are directed to enhanced educational opportunity. Public relations, community celebrations, and the like all have a cohesive quality but mean less if the student is not gaining in schooling.

Considerable research supports the need for these underlying qualities in programs using National Network designs.

STRUCTURAL FEATURES   In the National Network programs, six levels of involvement have evolved. These provide a basic structure for the National Network designs, and they help educators and other leaders develop a comprehensive schedule for any particular partnership. Each level of involvement (see Figure 11-6) will have many different practices from which schools can select to help them achieve a goal they have identified. Thus, any partnership will make a commitment to the six types of involvement as a framework; then each partnership will select practices that will produce results for their particular area of involvement. For example, if a partnership selects "Parenting" to focus on, they might select practices such as (a) set up parent education courses, (b) develop support groups on child rearing, or (c) develop home visiting teams to help needy families. All challenges must be addressed, and in many cases a redefinition is needed for the goal or practice that seemed promising. Epstein teams have provided a list of protocols that groups work through in settling their differences (Epstein et al., 2008).

Action Team.   The most essential component of the programs is decision making. For this, Epstein advises the establishment of an action team, or general steering committee, to guide the partnership effort and to act as the direction-setting team. The group membership is important and includes a reasonable arrangement of delegates from the following constituencies:

1. A few teachers from different grade levels
2. A few parents
3. The school principal
4. At least one community delegate
5. A student delegate if the school is a junior or senior high school

The job of the action team is to assess the partnership practices, arrange for the implementation of the agreed-on activities, and improve and coordinate all practices for the types of involvement. The action team leads in these responsibilities but is assisted by other teachers, parents, students, administrators, and community members.

Each year, the team updates its 3-year outline and develops a detailed 1-year action plan. In other words, the team continues to find out how it can improve its structure and practices to increase the role of families as partners.

RESEARCH AND ASSESSMENT   Research on the success rate of programs in the National Network is ongoing. Each year, a survey is returned to the headquarters from the numerous participating schools. These surveys are helpful in providing data about the successes, problems, and changes in the various programs. Research on individual experiments is also proceeding. These findings all result in new recommendations to practitioners who are in the Network programs.

Most of the current recommendations on levels of involvement, practices, and recommendations have resulted from the 20 years of research on particular parts of the Network's activities (see Epstein et al., 2008).

OUTGROWTHS OF THE NETWORK   As noted previously, the National Network has expanded over the years and is now located in 20 different states. Formal links with the League of Schools Reaching Out were established more than 10 years ago, and a number of partnership plans and collaborative efforts across the country have adopted parts of Epstein's recommendations. Readers wishing to examine detailed examples for the National Network programs will find Epstein et al. (2008) most helpful.

REFLECTION

Compare the features of the National Network of Partnership Schools with the other programs identified in this section. Again, consider how you would feel about being part of the team working with a National Network school, either as a parent or as a teacher.

Community Schools

The community school concept dates back to 1912, when Marie Turner Harvey, with help from John Dewey, established the Porter Rural School in Kirkville, Missouri. Harvey's focus was on a school curriculum that drew from the community and also worked to improve living conditions in the district served. Newer examples of community schools (often called *full-service schools*) have a mission similar to that of the Porter School. The community school concept relates to the writers' beliefs that children's education is best advanced when families, schools, and communities are involved in the day-to-day decisions concerning curriculum and instructional practice.

Community schools are public schools serving as sites that provide a range of services to children and their families. These services are provided because the schools partners with community agencies and organizations. The school building becomes a central site for a community, and typically the school facilities stay open after school hours and on weekends. The school offers after-school activities, adult education, health classes, recreation, and family support services of various types. Although the central aim is to improve education, this is achieved by improving the community around the children and using all resources fully.

Community schools tap community resources to enhance school projects.

GOALS AND OBJECTIVES A community school differs from other public schools in several ways. It offers a full-schedule school curriculum, but it also attempts to offer an array of health and social services typically handled by a city health department, welfare agencies, and adult education offices, as well as child-care and after-school programs (Dryfoos, 2003). By sharing facilities, and by overlapping and integrating the concerns of educators and community case workers, the objective of improving the whole community is served. Typical objectives include the following:

1. To have programs operating day and evening to serve the total community. This means that in addition to regular school hours, the community school will have before- and after-school programs, plus evening programs for parents and other community members.
2. To enrich life in the immediate community by using the community as a laboratory and a focus of study and to tap resources for school projects.
3. To eliminate logistical problems for families that need health and social services while they are involved with the school activities (a one-stop shopping feature that minimizes transportation problems).
4. To facilitate the delivery of appropriate services to children and their families.
5. To focus on educational improvement by bringing additional services to the school while building connections to the outside world for work opportunities and career planning.
6. To improve the life chances for a community's children by mobilizing community resources to head off social problems of delinquency, teenage pregnancy, and substance abuse.

STRUCTURAL FEATURES Community schools are built on the premise that "educators can't improve schools without paying attention to the children, their families, and the community around them" (Warren, 2005, p. 135). This basically sets the agenda for forming a "full-service" community school that blends and integrates a large number of services that young children (particularly in low-income areas) need to thrive as learners and as developing youth. It means thinking of a school as a campus containing not just regular and special classrooms but also health clinics, sports and recreation clubs, social support facilities, adult education facilities, and care programs that become the domain of community members and organizations in addition to teachers. Providing all services under one roof minimimizes communication and travel problems. The school becomes a hub for the community and in many ways strengthens all aspects of a community mission and pride in itself (Dryfoos, 1998). We have strong evidence (Warren, 2005) that community schools have turned communities around, and have enhanced the education of youngsters and the aspiration of parents and other community members as well.

The following is an outline of the features of a typical community school.

Extended School Day. The community school will be open all the time, that is, day hours and evening hours, plus weekend hours and hours for summer programs. Before-school hours and after-school hours are arranged for child-care service, and these are linked to homework help, academic enrichment, and other school-related projects. Sports and adult education programs are features associated with the extended school day.

School-Based Health Clinic. One valuable feature of community schools is an on-site clinic that works closely with teachers in assessing the health needs of children. The clinic provides state-mandated health screening and immunizations, as well as referrals for more complicated problems. School nurses and social workers, plus part-time pediatricians, dentists, and mental health workers, work with the clinic. The clinic is also available to adults on the school campus and to community members when large-scale screening and immunizations are needed.

Community Focus. Community schools develop a large and potent work force. Community projects such as development of parks, securing additional facilities for the campus, cleaning up the neighborhood, and improving transportation around the area are all projects that one of these schools has tried. Field trips into the larger community, so that children and adults can experience museums, nature preserves, and musical and dramatic productions, are frequent and common.

Parent Involvement. A community school becomes successful only when it brings in a large number of parents to work and advocate for the total school campus. Some parents work as classroom, cafeteria, or recreational aides. Others volunteer to mentor children or do clerical work. Many link the volunteer work with their own educational enhancement through the day and evening classes in adult education. The intense involvement of numbers of parents stimulates school pride and the desire to bring about total neighborhood improvement. Also, in this fashion, children see that the community works as a unit; they understand the relationship between community services and what they do as students.

RESEARCH AND ASSESSMENT   Test results show that academic achievement is improved in community schools (Dryfoos, 1998). In addition, improvements in behavior and socialization, as well as fewer problems in delinquency and truancy, occur. Surveys of parents, teachers, and community workers show significant positive changes in families and school staff members.

The success of programs does depend on several key factors: strong leaders (including school personnel), open communication, a full-time services coordinator, true integration of educational and support components, plus some initial funding to support planning and incentives to take the initial steps in cooperative work (Dryfoos, Quinn, & Barkin, 2005). Additional money is needed to support programs that have a longer school day and school year than traditional programs. The health and social services funding can be transferred from other municipal budgets, of course, but accessing these programs and getting started requires an additional investment of time and energy.

OUTGROWTHS OF THE PROGRAM   Community schools are growing in many areas in the United States and abroad. Their function in combining services makes for very practical procedures that reduce logistical requirements. The integration of school and community services also solves problems that seem to increase in some areas each year, such as youth alienation and the need for child-care services.

Note: Community schools will mesh with the objectives of all other models presented in this chapter. The notions of parent education, parent involvement in a child's work, and enhanced communication show all personnel that they are partners in efforts to help youth succeed. Readers will find a good description of the basics of community school arrangements in Joy Dryfoos's (1998) book, *Full-Service Schools: A Revolution in Health and Social Services for Children, Youth, and Families.*

Freedom Schools

The Children's Defense Fund (CDF) Freedom Schools program is a new endeavor by CDF to connect children and families to their cultural heritage and to their communities. It is primarily a summer program echoing the thrust of the 1964 Freedom Schools organized in the South to support civil rights initiatives. Although open to all applicants, the summer programs are aimed at African American children, focusing on literacy enhancement, cultural heritage, parent involvment, and neighborhood social action. In 2008, 90 summer school programs were operated throughout the United States; they enrolled 9000 children in 61 cities (Children's Defense Fund, 2009).

The CDF, a leading advocate for poor and minority children, has been for 30 years one of America's strongest voices in educating our nation about the needs of children. The CDF established Freedom Schools in 1993 and has set a course of objectives and schedules that individual sites in various states carry out with local leadership and sponsorship (Children's Defense Fund, 2006).

GOALS AND OBJECTIVES   The overall aim of a Freedom School summer session is to enhance the educational and social capabilities of young children while nurturing a group of **servant–leader interns** to advocate on behalf of children. The following objectives can be found in the 5- and 6-week summer programs:

1. Focus on high-quality educational enrichment for children and the promotion of cultural awareness.
2. Parents and caregivers are involved in children's daily activities and participation in workshops on child development, child advocacy, and child welfare.
3. Community adults volunteer time with children, explain their experiences, and serve as role models. This reunites generations and taps into the community traditions of self-help and mutual support.
4. Children focus on and learn about community problem solving.
5. Student interns focus on civic engagement with children, parents, and community partners to assess community needs, and then address these through rallies, town meetings, letter writing, voter registration, health projects, and other activities.
6. Servant–leader development: The college-age interns staffing the summer activities receive training on leadership and community-building skills.

STRUCTURAL FEATURES   The summer session Freedom Schools are generally a 5- or 6-week program set up to develop literacy skills, conflict resolution skills, and critical thinking skills, plus artistic and athletic competence (Children's Defense Fund, 2009). The central academic curriculum is contained in the Integrated Reading Curriculum (IRC). In addition to promoting literacy development, the program focuses on cooperative

8:00–8:30 A.M.	Breakfast with children and staff
8:30–9:00	*Harambee* (Swahili for "pulling together," informal sharing and celebration)
9:00–10:30	Integrated Reading Curriculum, conflict resolution and social action
10:30–10:45	Morning break
10:45–11:45	Integrated Reading Curriculum, continued
11:45–Noon	Drop Everything and Read (DEAR) time
Noon–1:00 P.M.	Lunch with children and staff
1:00–3:00	Afternoon activities: arts and crafts, dance, music, sports, computer lab, field trips, social action projects, and finale rehearsal
3:00	Dismissal
3:30	Daily staff debriefing

FIGURE 11-7 Sample Daily Schedule for a Freedom School Group   *Source:* Based on the CDF Freedom Schools program description.

learning, critical thinking, social action, and conflict resolution. Thus, the IRC becomes an activity-oriented phase intended to motivate, inspire, and rejuvenate young participants each day. The program uses a core of selected books, which interns and volunteers work with in creative ways to stimulate reading, presentation, discussion, and interpretion by all participants.

Most of the recommended books have lesson plans that guide the use of these works and serve as anchors for the work of the site coordinator and the interns. Field trips, presentations on the books' themes, and social activities are also worked into the daily schedule (see Figure 11-7).

Individual sites for the program are under local sponsorship and leadership. The national CDF office acts as coordinator and supplies materials and trainers to work with persons who wish to sponsor a program. The responsibility for operating a program is in the hands of a local sponsoring agency and its project director.

Sponsor.   The sponsoring agency can be a school district, college, community agency, or church. This agency has legal and fiscal responsibility for operating the particular Freedom School, and sponsors ensure that the program is in compliance with local, state, and federal regulations, including fire, health, safety, and civil rights laws. In addition, sponsors do the following:

1. Secure funds and space for a program.
2. Select a local advisory committe to promote community support.
3. Recruit a project director and a site coordinator to oversee and manage the program.
4. In conjunction with the director and the site coordinator, recruit and manage a staff of interns and volunteers.

Project Director.   This key person maintains communication with the national office, does staff recruitment, and supervises the program staff. Directors are trained at the CDF's national training site.

Site Coordinator. The site coordinator is in charge of day-to-day activities and ensures that the program and curriculum are implemented. He or she is key in maintaining a positive spirit and good communication among staff, parents, and community helpers. Coordinators are also trained at the CDF's national training site.

Servant–Leader Interns. The servant–leader interns are college-age staff members responsible for the front-line care and nurturing of children in the program. They facilitate in the classrooms and lead the community outreach activities. The interns, who receive a stipend for their work, come from the local community and are selected for their potential as future leaders in child advocacy. Maturity and ability to handle responsibility are required.

Volunteers. Other adults contribute to the program by demonstrating skills, sharing expertise, mentoring individuals, and helping with routine jobs. These are usually parents, extended family members, and community agents.

Servant–leader interns in the Freedom Schools are responsible for care and nurturing of the children.

REFLECTION

Try to get information on a Freedom School in your area. Would this program benefit young children that you know? What would attract you to that program? Would you consider being a servant–leader?

RESEARCH AND ASSESSMENT End-of-program evaluations for summer Freedom Schools are collected by site directors, but these are informal and focus on local priorities. The evaluations show enthusiam for and satisfaction with the individual programs, with notations about increased literacy skills for children, plus positive changes in social adjustment and the increased involvement of parents and community agents in the program. Only one city (Kansas City) has developed a statistical study of a Freedom School summer program. This study focused on the scholastic and social achievements of 2,033 students over a 3-year period (2005–2007). The results showed significant improvement in reading ability when measured against a comparison group. Data from parent surveys showed positive changes in children's attitudes toward learning, cultural appreciation, community involvement, and conflict resolution (Kauffman Foundation, 2008).

The Kansas City corps of 18 Freedom Schools has obtained a substantial Kauffman Foundation grant for evaluating the long-term effects of the Freedom School programs in that area. The evaluation started in 2005.

OUTGROWTHS OF THE PROGRAM Freedom Schools have been in operation for 15 consecutive years and have expanded from 2 to 90 sites (in 2006) in 24 states. The main extensions of the program are the weekend and after-school programs that are now sponsored in a similar fashion as the summer programs.

Readers can obtain information on the Freedom School programs from the CDF office (telephone: 202-628-8787) and can download materials and examples from their Web site: http://www.freedomschools.org.

IMPLICATIONS FOR TEACHERS

Comparing Models

Think about a community person that you know who does volunteer work in a school. Is this a retired person, a local artisan who works with schools, or a medical practitioner who takes part in "helping" programs at local schools? Now place that person in each of the last three model programs we have just considered and consider how she or he would be contributing.

1. In the Epstein National Network School, she or he would likely be _____
2. In the Community School, she or he would likely be working _____
3. In a Freedom School, she or he would probably be _____

Are the roles in the three model programs similar or are they quite different?

HABLA Program

HABLA, founded in 2001 by Virginia Mann, aims at improving the language skills of low-income preschool children in Santa Ana, California's, Hispanic families. The heart of HABLA, which means "speak" in Spanish, is, as its acronym notes, "Home-based Activities Building Language Acquisition." In the home visits, bilingual staff members, chosen for their cultural competence and language skills, work with the parents on reading, play, and verbal skills in their native language. The outreach workers plan twice-weekly visits to the homes for 2 years, bringing toys and books to share with the family (School of Social Science, University of California, Irvine, 2009).

Home visits focus on modeling verbal interaction skills and play strategies with the young children and encouraging parents—mothers typically—to replicate them. This weans children from TV watching and encourages them to engage adults in conversation, a neglected skill among poor adults with little education. All interactions—which range from toy characters to health and hygiene—focus on developing literacy and expressive language in children. The concept emphasizes parents as children's first teachers, and the higher-level Spanish that children acquire at home is the basis for the English that children learn later in public school.

GOALS AND OBJECTIVES The primary goal of HABLA is to expand communication and preliteracy skills in disadvantaged young children through parent–child talk and play (Taxim, 2008). Another goal is to convince parents that they are an important link in their child's education. Still another objective is to promote work and career opportunities for the home visitors (Latino community members) and the parents themselves.

STRUCTURAL FEATURES Selected home visitors who are bilingual are frequently college students and other community members. They are compensated in various ways (course credit or salary) for their involvement.

The biweekly visits are conducted in the children's homes, and the visitors promote the essentials of preschool social skills and language skills. While acting as role models for parents, they demonstrate the necessity for verbal interaction in the home and the community. Evaluations are consistent with the Inselberg and Larson (1988) studies, which show that low-SES families suffer from the limited amount of language they use and the limited vocabulary of their young children. The books and toys used in the visitors' interactions are left in the homes for continued use by family members.

RESEARCH AND ASSESSMENT   The HABLA program assesses children's language skills at the beginning of the program and at yearly intervals during the intervention period. The parental style of interaction is also measured.

Results to date show significant benefits for child and parent behaviors and in the growth of children's expressive and receptive language. The home visitors are convinced that they are reducing the deficits in primary language skills so typical of untreated children from economically disadvantaged families. HABLA children score within normal ranges on language development when they enter public school, whereas their untreated peers in the community score significantly below the norm. Local elementary school teachers note that HABLA is making a significant difference in children's interest, general literacy, and mastery of English.

In addition, parents are making gains. They are able to sustain verbal interaction with their children, and they grow in competence and in the quality of the attention given to their children. Whereas parents in the community at large tend to have a passive view of their roles in their child's education, HABLA parents are ready to form a responsive relationship with the educational system.

OUTGROWTHS OF THE PROGRAM   Although the outcomes are seen positively, the HABLA program has not yet been replicated in other areas. The assessment results seem destined to spark interest in other areas that will profit from home and community involvement to support schooling programs. HABLA has become accredited with the national Parent-Child-Home-Program (Brandt, 2008).

Charter Schools

Featuring charter schools as a positive model for family–school–community cooperation is risky, because in the 16 years of their existence, the philosphy direction of these programs has moved in many directions. For example, there are charter schools with traditional and highly directive programs that come nowhere close to the cooperative models espoused by the authors. At the same time, there are other schools with a structure so relaxed that they resemble an alternative school of the 1970s. In the mix, however, there are some charter schools that truly reflect the best practices of the partnerships highlighted in this book. In the Examples section below, we refer to several exemplary charter schools that are functioning in a collaborative manner. Web sites are provided with descriptions of these particular examples. See also the Web site for U.S. Charter Schools in the Resources section at the end of the chapter.

The charter school movement began in the early 1990s and grew rapidly. In 2008 we found 4,243 charter schools scattered over 41 states and serving 1,243,000 students (American Legislative Exchange Council, 2008). As noted before, though, the expectations for charter schools at present vary widely, and the proponents of these schools make strange bedfellows. For example, current legislation proposed in several states is supported by traditionalists seeking a return to classic study, by parents' rights advocates annoyed by school bureaucracy, and by progressives seeking a **project-oriented curriculum**.

GOALS AND OBJECTIVES   The basic concept of the charter school movement is to free individual public schools from large-district bureaucracy and grant them autonomy to make decisions regarding structure, personnel, curriculum, and educational emphasis while holding them accountable for academic achievement. This stems from the idea of *decentralization*, in which parents, teachers, and local citizens are the decision makers, as opposed to centralization and use of best practices, as determined at the state or district level (Wang & Walberg, 2001).

RESEARCH AND ASSESSMENT Vast differences exist in the effectiveness of charter schools, and there is minimal evidence that these schools, especially in urban systems, produce better academic results than does the larger system as a whole (Center for Education Reform, 2009). Yet, other studies have found that, especially after their second and third years of operation, parents and children are more satisfied with their new school experiences and support the new policies (Bulkley & Wohlstetter, 2004; Vanourek, 2005).

Findings show that almost all charter schools are smaller, friendlier, and more open than typical public schools. Students get more personal attention, and although the teachers are often less experienced and have minimal credentials, they show students that they care, are knowledgeable in content areas, and are excited about teaching. Most of these schools are places where parents have some decision-making power and develop a sense of community. Thus, teachers and students feel more comfortable in examining values, long-term goals, and a sense of morality (Naiskov, 2002; Schorr, 2002).

The charter schools are also effective in bringing changes to the professional culture; new ideas in teaching are integrated with other ideas and result in a more cohesive program (Murphy & Shiffman, 2002; US Charter Schools, 2009). In districts where there are enough charter schools to affect the traditional schools financially, investigators find that some public school personnel have started to make changes in their own schools. In addition, mainstream school administrators appear to reach out more to their communities, make schools more attractive, expect more of students, and offer more challenging courses (Center for Education Reform, 2009; Vanourek, 2005). These observations are satisfying to those proponents who expect the competitive effect of charter schools to enhance all education.

EXAMPLES OF CHARTER SCHOOLS The following are examples of successful charter schools that operate with a true collaborative system:

1. KIPP Explore Academy, Houston, Texas http://www.kipphouston.org
2. Fenton Avenue Charter School, Los Angeles http://www.fentoncharter.net
3. Community of Peace Academy, St. Paul, Minnesota http://www.cpa.charter.K12.mn.us
4. Oglethorpe Charter School, Savannah, Georgia http://www.oglethorpecharter.org
5. King Center Charter School, Buffalo, New York http://www.kingcentercharter-school.org
6. Ariel Community Academy, Chicago http://arielinvestments.com

OUTGROWTHS OF CHARTER SCHOOLS As we noted earlier, charter schools have proliferated in unprecedented fashion during the last decade, as most states have granted authority to establish them. Although a large literature exists to guide new schools, some have borrowed models from existing pilot schools in the Comer model, a National Network model, and even the Reggio Emilia plan. Comer (1997) comments on the degree of success found in school reform and experimental programs. He states that about one-third of experimental projects maintain the changes made, one-third achieve limited change until the initiators depart, and one-third have no success at all.

IMPLICATIONS FOR TEACHERS

Conventional or Charter Schools?

Charter schools are becoming more common in the United States every year. President Obama's children attended one in Chicago before moving to Washington, and now the president is an advocate for this school arrangement. This means that the model will expand.

Imagine yourself as a regular second-grade teacher in the school you are best acquainted with and think of the requirements that will come when it becomes a charter school. The new principal has elected to set up a plan based on the National Network of Partnership Schools. This means your program will be different than that of the conventional school. It means that you will doing some of the following (list three things):

_____
_____
_____

Can you see yourself fitting into this new structure? Compare it to what you have observed in schools during the past two years. Is it going to work for you?

FEATURES OF SUCCESSFUL COLLABORATIONS

New partnerships are emerging across the United States. The stimulus varies, but projects often begin in response to educational problems at the local and state levels. Irrespective of the motivation, we find that collaborative efforts do result in greater opportunities for students when the "whole child, whole community" concept is adopted. Frequently, each successful partnership is unique, but they all seem to include the following features (Comer, Haynes, Joyner, & Ben-Avie, 1996; Rubin, 2002):

- Programs integrate educational and social services for all children, and especially for needy families.
- Parents, school personnel, and community members are empowered to make decisions about, to plan for, and to implement changes for the community's children.
- School bureaucracy is reduced, and involvement of families and community members in school management increases.
- Schools become family centers to promote better interactions among teachers, children, parents, and community members.
- Programs include strong volunteer programs, with parents, grandparents, and community members contributing expertise to support children's learning and to assist in school operations.
- The community and the home are viewed as important child learning environments and are integrated into school learning.
- Programs have strong leadership and committed partners able to gain the support of **power brokers** in their setting.
- School faculty and staff develop skills needed to build and maintain relationships of trust and respect with children and families.
- Researchers, teachers, and parents work together in assessing the successes of school programs.

Researchers, teachers, and parents work together for the success of school programs.

REFLECTION

Think about the models described in this chapter and assess your reactions to being part of a team in partnership with homes and communities. Can you see yourself as a contributing member promoting the features of partnerships in one or more of these models? List some items that you feel confident about now.

ACHIEVING PARTNERSHIPS

In discussing program models, we have demonstrated that true collaboration does emerge when properly nurtured. These model collaborations take time to build, and as each continues, even more time is required to monitor and fine-tune it to ensure that it stays healthy. Successful models may be found in systems with schools of choice, such as charter schools, or in centralized-control systems where teachers can form a successful collaboration with parents and the community.

As such models show, the effort is worthwhile, and the reported educational benefits to children and communities are often inspirational. Anyone interested in achieving partnerships for their schools should carefully examine the literature on established programs. Information about the sustainability of these programs is helpful for beginners developing their own particular plans.

Individual Responsibility

Realizing the dream of partnerships requires more than the effort exhibited in most U.S. school districts today. A spirit for undertaking change has germinated in many areas, but it seems slow to blossom fully. We all know that change takes time. The recent surge of interest at state and federal levels for partnerships must be viewed positively, and publications, funding, and legislation all provide a fertile base for more collaboration.

When reading about model programs, we can certify that those programs including a research and assessment dimension have shown great strides in reaching a new level of participation. These model programs also demonstrate that exciting things happen when new ideas are introduced, nurtured carefully, and built as change mechanisms. The results certainly reinforce the desirability of bringing more collaborative work to our nation's schools.

IMPLICATIONS FOR TEACHERS

Getting Started

Partnerships can begin with a single teacher and a parent collaborating in a classroom. Then many possibilities exist for enthusiastic colleagues and parents to launch all sorts of desirable partnership programs in any school. When you affiliate with a program that is starting a collaborative venture, you will want to consider the following important steps.

When your team considers collaboration, first define your objectives and agree on what changes are necessary. It's also wise to find out how collaboration has worked for others. Your team will need to locate resources and decide how to assess the progress it makes. Bringing in new helpers and involving them in collaborative ventures always requires finesse. Communication is often a problem as more people become involved in collaborations. You and your teammates must be alert to how you are communicating and how your messages are being interpreted. Finally, you should first try out ideas on a small scale and then expand the experiment.

Summary and Review

When schools are brokers for new learning communities and when school personnel invest time and energy in forming links with parents and communities, exciting and productive results materialize. Much evidence proves that this is true. The work of James Comer in New Haven, Connecticut, and the expansion of Joyce Epstein's National Network of Schools, to name two successes, show that we have both a reason and a compelling need for communities to reach out further to achieve better-functioning school operations.

This chapter presents the levels of involvement that parents and community members can have in a collaboration with a school and describes the conditions that enhance partnerships. We have also seen the steps taken by people moving into collaborative ventures. The eight examples of existing collaborations show how those programs started and the reasons for their success. New collaborations demonstrate that similar goals and objectives can be reached by different routes and at different rates. Even implementing the principles of partnerships in part of a school district eventually enriches the experiences of all district students.

Schools are still the catalysts in most new educational endeavors. No other social institution in the United States has the oversight or the trained personnel to serve in this capacity. Partnership programs can start with a few small projects or may grow from a well-conceived and well-directed program. However it grows, a plan must call for teachers and administrators to be committed to the new practice. Being committed, gaining knowledge about other programs, devising a plan, establishing means for communicating the plan, and involving others are necessary to the success of any project.

Suggested Activities and Questions

1. Talk with three teachers about parent involvement in their programs. Have them describe the things parents do when they come to school. To determine the stage of collaboration, relate their statements to the three levels of involvement discussed in this chapter.
2. Interview three parents to learn how they have participated in their children's school programs within the past year. What levels of involvement do you find?
3. Examine a school district with which you are acquainted to ascertain its stage of evolution in collaborative efforts. How does your district compare to one or more of the programs featured in this chapter?
4. Select a school and start at the front door for a virtual tour of the facility. Make notes on the following as you walk: (a) your initial impressions, (b) classroom activities, (c) hallway activity, and (d) central office atmosphere. Now stop and reflect on what changes you might see in 4 years if this facility joined a collaborative program for that length of time.

Resources

Organizations

Center for Education Reform   *http://edreform.com*
Council of the Great City Schools   *http://www.cgcs.org*
National Head Start Association   *http://www.nhsa.org*
Phi Delta Kappa   *http://www.pdkintl.org*
US Charter Schools   *http://uscharterschools.org*

Web Sites

http://www.cgcs.org   Council of Great City Schools Online. It presents information on the nation's large public school systems and their interschool projects.

http://www.classroom.net   Classroom Connect has an online magazine for all levels of teachers and features online educational programs.

http://www.eric.ed.gov   The ERIC (Education Resources Information Center) Web site for information on Reggio Emilia.

http://www.ncpie.org   The National Coalition for Parent Involvement in Education Web site features a database for partnerships for family involvement in education and gives examples of successful collaborations.

APPENDIX

Bibliography of Children's Books

The following selected bibliography of children's books portrays a variety of American family structures where individuals are learning together in the home, the school, and the community. Codes used are as follows:

H Indicates that the book reveals children learning through the home environment.
S Indicates that children from different family structures are learning together at school.
C Indicates that different family members are sharing and learning from their community environment.

DIFFERENT CULTURES

Ada, A. (2002). *I love Saturdays and dominoes.* (S. Savadier, Illus.). New York: Atheneum. **S, C**

Allen, J. (2005). *Best little wingman.* (J. Postier, Illus.). Honesville, PA: Boyd's Mills. **H, S**

Anacona, G. (1998). *El barrio, Jose's neighborhood.* New York: Harcourt. **C**

Banks, L. R. (1992). *One more river.* New York: Morrow. **S, C**

Bartoletti, S. (1999). *Polish dancing with Dziadziu* (A. Nelson, Illus.). New York: Harcourt. **H**

Bloom, S. C. (1991). *A family for Jamie.* New York: Clarkson Potter. **H, S**

Breckler, R. K. (1992). *Hoang breaks the lucky teapot* (A. Frankel, Illus.). Boston: Houghton Mifflin. **H**

Bryan, A. (2003). *Beautiful blackbird.* New York: Atheneum. **H, S**

Bunting, E. (1996). *Going home* (D. Diaz, Illus.). New York: HarperCollins. **H, C**

Bunting, E. (1997). *Moonstick, the seasons of the Sioux* (J. Sanford, Paintings.). New York: HarperCollins. **C**

Calhoun, M. (1996). *Tonio's cat* (D. Stanley, Illus.). New York: Morrow Junior. **C**

Carling, A. L. (1998). *Mama and papa have a store.* New York: Dial. **H, C**

Crowley, J. (1998). *Big moon tortilla* (D. Strongbow, Illus.). Honesville, PA: Boyd's Mills. **H**

Curtis, J. L. (2006). *Is there really a human race?* New York: HarperCollins. **S, C**

Diouf, S. (2001). *Bintou's braids* (S. W. Evans, Illus.). San Francisco: Chronicle. **H, C**

Dooley, N. (1991). *Everybody cooks rice* (P. J. Thornton, Illus.). Minneapolis: Carolrhoda. **H, C**

Fazio, B. L. (1996). *Grandfather's story.* Seattle: Sasquatch. **H**

Franklin, K. L. (1994). *The shepherd boy* (J. Kastner, Illus.). New York: Atheneum. **C**

Germein, K. (2000). *Big rain coming* (B. Brancoft, Illus.). New York: Clarion. **H, S**

Good, M. (1993). *Reuben and the fire* (P. B. Moss, Illus.). Intercourse, PA: Good Books. **C**

Greenfield, L. (2003). *Honey, I love* (J. Gilchrist, Illus.). New York: Amistad. **H, S**

Hamilton, V. (2004). *The people could fly* (L. & D. Dillon, Illus.). New York: Knopf. **S, C**

Hartman, W. (1993). *All the magic in the world* (N. Daly, Illus.). New York: Dutton. **C**

Heide, F. P., & Gilliland, J. H. (1990). *The day of Ahmed's secret* (T. Lewin, Illus.). New York: Mulberry. **H, C**

Hooks, B. (1999). *Happy to be nappy* (C. Raschka, Illus.). New York: Jump at the Sun/Hyperion for Children. **H**

Hoyt-Goldsmith, D (1990). *Totem pole* (L. Migdale, Photos). New York: Holiday House. **H**

Joosse, B. (2005). *Papa, do you love me?* (B. Lavallee, Illus.). New York: Chronicle. **H**

Katz, K. (1999). *The color of us.* New York: Holt. **H, C**

Kendall, R. (1992). *Eskimo boy: Life in an Inupiaq Eskimo village.* New York: Scholastic. **C**

Knight, M. (1995). *Talking walls* (A. O'Brien, Illus.). Gardiner, ME: Tilbury House. **S, C**

Kroll, V. (1994). *Masai and I* (N. Carpenter, Illus.). New York: Four Winds. **C**

Kurtz, J. (1998). *The storyteller's beads.* New York: Gulliver. **S**

Kwelin, S. (1998). *How my family lives in America.* New York: Aladdin Picture Books. **S**

London, J. (1997). *Ali, child of the desert* (T. Lewin, Illus.). Shepard, NY: Lothrop, Lee & Shepard. **C**

MacDonald, S. (1995). *Nanta's lion: A search-and-find adventure.* New York: Morrow. **C**

Markhun, P. M. (1993). *The little painter of Sabana Grande* (R. Casilla, Illus.). New York: Bradbury. **C**

Mora, P. (2003). *The rainbow tulip.* New York: Puffin. **S**

Onyefulu, I. (1995). *E Meka's gift: An African counting book.* New York: Cobblehill. **C**

Partridge, E. (2003). *Oranges on Golden Mountain.* New York: Puffin. **H, C**

Pinkney, A. (2001). *Mim's Christmas jam* (B. Pinkney, Illus.). New York: Harcourt. **H, C**

Pinkney, B. (1994). *Max found two sticks.* New York: Simon & Schuster. **C**

Pinkney, S. (2002). *A rainbow all around me* (M. Pinkney, Photos). New York: Scholastic. **H, S**

Polacco, P. (1990). *Just plain fancy.* New York: Simon & Schuster. **C**

Pomeranc, M. (1998). *The American Wei* (A. Di Salvo-Ryan, Illus.). Morton Grove, IL: Whitman. **C**

Pryor, B. (1996). *The dream jar* (M. Graham, Illus.). New York: Morrow. **H**

St. James, S. (1996). *Sunday.* New York: Whitman. **H**

Say, A. (1991). *Tree of cranes.* New York: Scholastic. **H**

Smalls, I. (1994). *Dawn and the round to-it* (T. Geter, Illus.). New York: Simon & Schuster. **H**

Smith, D. J. (2002). *If the world were a village* (S. Armstrong, Illus.). Toronto: Kids Can Press. **S**

Soto, G. (1993). *Too many tamales* (E. Martinez, Illus.). New York: Putnam's. **H**

Steptoe, J. (1997). *Munfaro's beautiful daughters.* New York: Lothrop. **H, C**

Stroud, V. A. (1994). *Doesn't fall off his horse.* New York: Dial. **C**

Surat, M. M. (1993). *Angel child, dragon child* (V.D. Mai, Illus.). New York: Carnival. **S**

Villanueva, M. (1993). *Nene and the horrible math monster* (R. Unson, Illus.). Chicago: Polychrome. **S**

Waboose, J. (2000). *Sky sisters* (B. Deines, Illus.). Niagara Falls, NY: Kids Can Press. **C**

Watkins, S. (1994). *White bead ceremony* (K. Doner, Illus.). Tulsa, OK: Council Oak. **C**

White Deer of Autumn. (1992). *The great change* (C. Grigg, Illus.). Hillsboro, OR: Beyond Words. **C**

Williams, K. L. (1998). *Painted dreams* (C. Stock, Illus.). New York: Lothrop, Lee & Shepard. **H, C**

Woodson, J. (2001). *The other side.* New York: Putnam. **C**

Wright, C. C. (1994). *Jumping the broom* (G. Griffith, Illus.). New York: Holiday. **C**

Yamate, S. (1991). *Char Siu Bao boy.* Chicago: Polychrome. **S**

DIVORCED FAMILIES

Abercrombie, B. (1995, 1990). *Charlie Anderson.* Upper Saddle River, NJ: Simon & Schuster. **H**

Bernhard, D. (2001). *To & Fro, Fast & Slow.* London: Walker. **H**

Binch, C. (1998). *Since dad left.* Brookfield, CT: Millbrook. **H**

Bunting, E. (2001). *The days of summer* (W. Low, Illus.). New York: Harcourt. **H**

Masurel, C. (2003). *Two homes* (K. M. Denton, Illus.). Cambridge, MA: Candlewick.

Rodgers, F. (1998). *Let's talk about it: Divorce.* New York: Putnam. **H**

Rotner, S., & Sheila, K. (2002). *Something's different.* Brookfield, CT: Millbrook. **H**

Rush, K. (1994). *Friday's journey.* New York: Orchard. **C**

Schotter, R. (2003). *Room for rabbit* (C. Moore, Illus.). New York: Clarion. **H**

Weinger, B. (1995). *Good-bye, Daddy* (A. Mark, Illus.). New York: North–South. **H**

BLENDED FAMILIES

Bailey, M. (1990). *Stepfamilies.* New York: Crestwood House. **S**

Boyd, L. (1990). *Sam is my half-brother.* New York: Viking Penguin. **H**

Brooks, B. (1992). *What hearts.* New York: Dutton. **H, C**

Gibbons, F. (1996). *Mountain wedding* (T. Rand, Illus.). New York: Morrow Junior. **H, C**

Hines, A. G. (1996). *When we married Gary.* New York: Greenwillow. **H**

Hoffman, M. (1995). *Boundless grace* (C. Binch, Illus.). New York: Scholastic. **H, C**

Johnson, J. (1998). *How do I feel about my stepfamily?* Brookfield, CT: Copper Beach Press**. H**

Ransom, C. F. (1993). *We're growing together* (V. Frierson, Illus.). New York: Bradbury. **H, C**

Rodgers, F. (2001). *Let's talk about it: Stepfamilies.* New York: Putnam. **H**

Willner-Pardo, G. (1994). *What I'll remember when I am a grownup* (W. L. Krudop, Illus.). New York: Clarion. **H**

SINGLE-PARENT HOUSEHOLDS AND RELATIONSHIP WITH ONE PARENT OR GRANDPARENTS

Ackerman, K. (1994). *By the dawn's early light* (C. Stock, Illus.). New York: Atheneum. **H**

Atwell, D. (2003). *The Thanksgiving door*. Boston: Houghton Mifflin. **C**

Bunting, E. (1994). *Smoky night* (D. Diaz, Illus.). San Diego, CA: Harcourt Brace. **C**

Chaconas, D. (2003). *On a wintry morning* (S. T. Johnson, Illus.). New York: Puffin. **H, C**

Cleary, B. (2000). *Dear Mr. Henshaw.* New York: Morrow. **H, S**

Clifton, L. (2001). *One of the problems of Everett Anderson* (A. Grifalconi, Illus.). New York: Holt. **H, S**

Cohen, C. Lee. (2003). *Everything is different at Nonna's house* (H. Nakata, Illus.). New York: Clarion. **H**

Cooper, S. (1993). *Danny and the kings* (J. A. Smith, Illus.). New York: McElderry. **C**

Eager, E. (1999). *Half magic* (N. Bodecker, Illus.). New York: Harcourt. **H, C**

Haggerty, M. E. (1993). *A crack in the wall* (R. de Anda, Illus.). New York: Lee & Low. **H**

Harrison, T. (1994). *The long weekend.* New York: Harcourt Brace. **C**

Joosse, B. M. (1991). *Mama, do you love me?* (B. Lavallee, Illus.). New York: Scholastic. **H**

Juster, N. (2005). *The hello, goodbye window.* (C. Raschka, Illus.). New York: Hyperion. **H, C**

Lindsay, J. W. (1991). *Do I have a daddy? A story about a single-parent child* (C. Boeller, Illus). Buena Park, CA: Morning Glory. **H**

McKissack, P. (2000). *Ma dear's aprons.* (F. Cooper, Illus.). New York: Atheneum. **H**

Moon, N. (1994). *Lucy's picture* (A. Ayliffe, Illus.). New York: Scholastic. **S**

Parr, T. (2002). *The daddy book.* Boston: Little, Brown. **H**

Peterson, J. W. (1994). *My mama sings* (S. Speidel, Illus.). New York: HarperCollins. **H**

Plourde, L. (2003). *Thank you, Grandpa* (J. Cockcroft, Illus.). New York: Dutton. **H, C**

Rosenberg, L. (1997). *Monster Mama.* (S. Gammell, Illus.). New York: Putnam. **H**

Rosenberg, M. (1992). *Living with a single parent.* New York: Bradbury Press. **H, S**

Sharp, N. L. (1993). *Today I'm going fishing with my dad* (C. Demarest, Illus.). Honesville, PA: Boyd's Mills. **C**

Sisulu, E. B. (1996). *The day Gogo went to vote* (S. Wilson, Illus.). Boston: Little, Brown. **H, C**

Smalls, I. (1992). *Jonathan and his mommy* (M. Hays, Illus.). Boston: Little Brown. **C**

Smalls, I. (1999). *Kevin and his dad* (M. Hays, Illus.). Boston: Little Brown. **H, C**

Testa, M. (1996). *Nine candles* (A. Schaffer, Illus.). Minneapolis: Carolrhoda. **C**

Tran, K. L. (1994). *Tet: The new year* (M. Vo-Dinh, Illus.). New York: Simon & Schuster. **C**

Waddell, M. (1994). *The big, big sea* (J. Eachus, Illus.). Cambridge, MA: Candlewick. **C**

Woodson, J. (2002). *Visiting day.* New York: Scholastic. **H, S**

Ziefert, H. (2003). *Home for Navidad* (S. Cohen, Illus.). Boston: Houghton Mifflin. **H**

Ziefert, H. (2003). *31 Uses for a mom* (R. Doughty, Illus.). New York: Putnam. **C**

ADOPTIVE FAMILIES

Bloom, S. (1991). *A family for Jamie: An adoption story.* New York: Clarkson Potter. **H**

Brodzinsky, A. B. (1996). *The mulberry bird: An adoption story* (D. Stanley, Illus.). Indianapolis: Perspective. **H**

Cais, S. (1998). *Why so sad, Brown Rabbit?* New York: Dutton. **H**

Caseley, J. (2004). *Sisters.* New York: HarperCollins. **H, S**

Cole, J. (1995). *How I was adopted: Samantha's story* (M. Chambliss, Illus.). New York: Morrow. **H**

Curtis, J. L. (1996). *Tell me again about the night I was born* (L. Cornell, Illus.). New York: HarperCollins. **H, C**

D'Antonio, N. (1997). *Our baby from China: An adoption story.* Morton Grove, IL: Whitman. **H, C**

Kasza, K. (1992). *A mother for Choco.* New York: Putnam. **H**

Katz, K. (1997). *Over the moon: An adoption tale.* New York: Holt. **H, C**

Koehler, P. (1990, 1997). *The day we met you.* Old Tappen, NJ: Simon & Schuster. **H**

Krishnaswani, U. (2006). *Bringing Asha home* (J. Akib, Illus.). New York: Lee & Lowe. **H**

Lamperti, N. (1999). *Brown like me.* Johnstown, NY: New Victoria. **H, C**

Leman, K. (2007). *My adopted child. There's no one like you* (K. Lemon, Illus.). Grand Rapids, MI: Revell. **H**

Lewis, R. (2000). *I love you like crazy cakes* (J. Dyer, Illus.). New York: Little, Brown. **H**

Lewis, R. (2007). *Every year on your birthday* (J. Dyer, Illus). New York: Little, Brown. **H**

McCully, E. A. (1994). *My real family.* San Diego, CA: Harcourt. **H, C**

McCutcheon, J. (2001). *Happy adoption day* (J. Paschkis, Illus.). New York: Little, Brown. **H, S**

Miller, K. A. (1994). *Did my first mother love me? A story for an adopted child* (J. Moffett, Illus.). Buena Park, CA: Morning Glory. **H**

Okimoto, J. D., & Aoki, E. M. (2002). *White swan express* (M. So, Illus.). New York: Clarion. **C**

Park, T. (2007). *We belong together: A book about adoption.* New York: Little, Brown. **H**

Rogers, F. (1995, 1998). *Let's talk about it: Adoption* (J. Judkins, Illus.). New York: Putnam. **H**

Say, A. (2004). *Allison.* Boston: Houghton Mifflin. **H**

Turner, A. (1990). *Through moon and stars and night skies* (J. Graham Hale, Illus.). New York: Harper & Row. **H, C**

FOSTER CARE, ORPHANAGES, AND SHELTERS

Blomquist, G., & Blomquist, P. (1993, 1990). *Zachary's new home: A story for foster and adoptive children.* Milwaukee: Stevens. **H**

Bunting, E. (1996). *Train to somewhere* (R. Himler, Illus.). New York: Clarion. **C**

Cannon, J. (1994). *Stellaluna.* San Diego, CA: Harcourt. **H, C**

Chalofsky, M., Finland, G., & Wallace, J. (1992). *Changing places. A kid's view of shelter living.* Mt. Rainier, MD: Gryphon. **H, C**

Herbert, S. (1991). *I miss my foster parents.* Washington, DC: Child Welfare League of America. **H, C**

Jarrell, R. (1996). *The animal family.* New York: HarperCollins. **H, C**

MacLachlan, P. (1995). *Baby.* New York: Delacorte. **H**

Nixon, J. L. (2000). *The orphan train adventures.* New York: Bantam. **H, C**

MULTIGENERATIONAL HOUSEHOLDS AND EXTENDED FAMILIES

Bauer, M. D. (1995). *When I go camping with gramma* (A. Garns, Illus.). New York: Bridgewater. **C**

Burden-Patman, D., with Jones, K. D. (1992). *Carnival* (R. Ruffins, Illus.). New York: Simon & Schuster. **H, C**

Chiemruom, S. (1994). *Dara's Cambodian new year* (D. N. Pin, Illus.). New York: Simon & Schuster. **H**

Choi, S. N. (1993). *Halmoni and the picnic* (K. M. Dugan, Illus.). Boston: Houghton Mifflin. **S**

Coleman, E. (1996). *White socks only* (T. Geter, Illus.). Morton Grove, IL: Whitman. **H, C**

Crews, D. (1991). *Bigmama's.* New York: Greenwillow. **H, C**

Dorros, A. (1991). *Abuela* (E. Kleven, Illus.). New York: Dutton. **C**

Falwell, C. (1995). *Feast for 10.* New York: Clarion. **H, C**

Guback, G. (1994). *Luka's quilt.* New York: Greenwillow. **H**

Heide, F. P., & Pierce, R. H. (1998). *Tio Armolo.* New York: Lothrop & Shepard. **H**

Hoffman, M. (1991). *Amazing grace* (C. Binch, Illus.). New York: Dial. **H, S**

Howard, E. F. (1991). *Aunt Flossie's hats (and) crab cakes later.* New York: Clarion. **H, C**

Jones, R. (1995). *Great Aunt Martha.* New York: Dutton. **H**

Levine, A. (1995). *Bono and Nonno* (J. Lanfredi, Illus.). New York: Tambourine. **C**

Lewin, T. (1998). *The story tellers.* New York: Lothrop, Lee & Shepard. **C**

MacLachlan, P. (1993). *Journey.* New York: Delacorte. **H, C**

Matthews, M. (2000). *Magid fasts for Ramadan* (E. B. Lewis, Illus.). Boston: Houghton Mifflin. **H**

McCully, E. A. (1993). *Grandmas at bat.* New York: HarperCollins. **C**

McFarlane, S. (1991, 1993). *Waiting for the whales* (R. Lightburn, Illus.). New York: Philomel. **H, C**

Mills, C. (1999). *Gus and grandpa* (C. Stock, Illus.). New York: Farrar Strauss & Giroux. **H, C**

Moore, E. (1995). *Grandma's smile* (D. Andreasen, Illus.). New York: Lothrop, Lee & Shepard. **H**

Parr, T. (2006). *The grandpa book.* New York: Little, Brown. **H**

Polacco, P. (1992). *Mrs. Katz and Tush.* New York: Bantam (Little Rooster). **C**

Poydar, N. (1994). *Busy Bea.* New York: Macmillan. **H**

Reiser, L. (1998). *Cherry pies and lullabies.* New York: Greenwillow. **H**

Say, A. (1993). *Grandfather's journey.* Boston: Houghton Mifflin. **H, C**

Simon, F. (1998). *Where are you?* (D. Melling, Illus.). Atlanta, GA: Peachtree. **C**

Swartz, L. (1992, 1994). *A first Passover* (J. Chwast, Illus.). New York: Simon & Schuster. **H**

Swentzell, R. (1992). *Children of clay: A family of pueblo potters* (B. Steen, Photos). Minneapolis: Lerner. **C**

Wells, R. (1996). *The language of doves* (G. Shed, Illus.). New York: Dial. **H**

Wild, M. (1994). *Our granny* (J. Vivas, Illus.). New York: Ticknor & Fields. **H**

Wild, M. (1996). *Old pig.* New York: Ticknor & Fields. **H, C**

Williams, V. (1997). *Lucky song.* New York: Greenwillow. **H**

Woodruff, E. (1998). *Can you guess where we're going?* (C. Fisher, Illus.). New York: Holiday House. **C**

Zalben, J. B. (1996). *Papa's latkes.* New York: Holt. **H**

Zamorano, A. (1997). *Let's eat* (J. Vivas, Illus.). New York: Scholastic. **H**

GAY AND LESBIAN FAMILIES

Bosche, S. (1983). *Jenny lives with Eric and Martin.* London: Gay Men's Press. **H**

Brown, F. (1991). *Generous Jefferson Bartleby* (L. Trawin, Illus.). Boston: Alyson Wonderland. **H, C**

DeHaan, L., & Nigland, S. (2002). *King and king.* Berkeley, CA: Tricycle Press. **H, S**

Elwin, R., & Paulie, M. (1990). *Asha's mums* (D. Lee, Illus.). Toronto, Ontario, Canada: Women's Press. **S**

Greenberg, K. E. (1996). *Zack's story.* Minneapolis: Lerner. **H, S, C**

Heron, A., & Maran, M. (1991). *How would you feel if your dad was gay?* (K. Kovick, Illus.). Boston: Alyson Wonderland. **H**

Marcus, E. (2007). *What if someone I know is gay?* New York: Simon Pulse. **H, S, C**

Newman, L. (1991). *Belinda's bouquet* (M. Willhoite, Illus.). Boston: Alyson Wonderland. **H, C**

Newman, L. (1991). *Gloria goes to gay pride* (R. Crocker, Illus.). Boston: Alyson Wonderland. **H, C**

Newman, L. (1993). *Saturday is pattyday* (A. Hegel, Illus.). Norwich, CT: New Victoria. **C**

Newman, L. (2000). *Heather has two mommies, 10th anniversary* (D. Souza, Illus.). Boston: Alyson Wonderland. **H, S**

Quinlan, P. (1994). *Tiger flowers* (J. Wilson, Illus.). New York: Dial. **H**

Snow, J. (2004). *How it feels to have a gay or lesbian parent. A book by kids for kids.* New York: Harrington Park Press. **S, C**

Vigna, J. (1995). *My two uncles.* Morton Grove, IL: Whitman. **H**

Willhoite, M. (1990). *Daddy's roommate.* Boston: Alyson Wonderland. **H**

Willhoite, M. (1993). *Uncle what-is-it is coming to visit!* Boston: Alyson Wonderland. **H**

CHILDREN, FAMILY MEMBERS, AND FRIENDS WITH SPECIAL NEEDS

Bernstein, J., & Fireside, B. (1991). *Special parents, special children.* Morton Grove: IL: Whitman. **S, C**

Cohen, M. (1997). *See you tomorrow, Charles.* New York: Yearling. **S**

Cowen-Fletcher, J. (1993). *Mama zooms.* New York: Scholastic. **H**

Day, S. (1995). *Luna and the big blur: A story for children who wear glasses* (D. Morris, Illus.). New York: Brunner/Mazel. **H**

Dugan, B. (1992). *Loop the loop* (J. Stevenson, Illus.). New York: Greenwillow. **C**

Dwight, L. (1998). *We can do it.* New York: Starbright. **C**

Ely, L. (2004). *Looking after Louis* (P. Dunbar, Illus.). Morton Grove, IL: Whitman. **S**

Fleming, V. (1993). *Be good to Eddie Lee* (F. Cooper, Illus.). New York: Putnam. **S**

Gantos, J. (2000). *Joey Pigza swallowed the key.* New York: Farrar Strauss & Giroux. **S**

Hines, A. G. (1993). *Gramma's walk.* New York: Greenwillow. **C**

Karim, R. (1994). *Mandy Sue day.* New York: Clarion. **H, S**

Konigsburg, E. L. (1998). *A view from Saturday.* New York: Atheneum. **S, C**

Kroll, V. (1993). *Naomi knows it's springtime* (J. Kastner, Illus.). Honesville, PA: Boyd's Mills. **C**

Lakin, P. (1994). *Dad and me in the morning* (R. O. Steele, Illus.). Morton Grove, IL: Whitman. **C**

Lears, L. (1998). *Ian's walk: A story about autism* (K. Ritz, Illus.). Morton Grove, IL: Whitman. **S, C**

Lears, L. (2002). *Becky the brave: A story about epilepsy* (G. Piazza, Illus.). Morton Grove, IL: Whitman. **S, C**

Miller, M. B., & Ancona, G. (1991). *Handtalk school* (G. Ancona, Illus.). New York: Four Winds. **S**

Mills, J. (1992) *Little tree* (M. Chesworth, Illus.). New York: Magination Press. **C**

Mohr, N. (1995). *Old Lativia and the Mountain of Sorrows* (R. Gutierrez, Illus.). New York: Greenwillow. **H, C**

Osofsky, A. (1992). *My buddy* (T. Rand, Illus.). New York: Holt. **H, C**

Rabe, B. (1988). *Where's Chimpy?* (D. Schmidt, Photos). Morton Grove, IL: Whitman. **H**

Shriver, M. (2001). *What's wrong with Timmy?* (S. Speidel, Illus). New York: Warner Books. **H, S, C**

Stuve-Bodeen, S. (1998). *We'll paint the octopus red* (P. DeVito, Illus.). Bethesda, MD: Woodbine House. **H**

Thompson, M. (1992). *My brother Matthew.* Bethesda, MD: Woodbine House. **H**

Thompson, M. (1996). *Audy and his yellow frisbee.* New York: Woodbine House. **H, S**

Waddell, M. (1990). *My great grandpa* (D. Mansell, Illus.). New York: Putnam. **C**

Woloson, E. (2003). *My friend Isabelle* (B. Clough, Illus.). New York: Woodbine House. **H, S**

HOMELESS FAMILIES

Barbour, K. (1991). *Mr. Bowtie.* San Diego, CA: Harcourt. **C**

Berck, J. (1992). *No place to be: Voices of homeless children.* Boston: Houghton Mifflin. **S, C**

Bunting, E. (1991). *Fly away home* (R. Himler, Illus.). New York: Clarion. **C**

Bunting, E. (1999). *December* (D. Diaz, Illus.). New York: Harcourt. **H, C**

DiSalvo-Ryan, D. (1991). *Uncle Willie and the soup kitchen.* New York: Morrow Junior. **C**

Greenberg, K. (1992). *Eric is homeless* (C. Halebian, photos). Minneapolis: Lerner. **S, C**

Greenberg, K. (1995). *Runaways* (C. Halebian, photos). Minneapolis, MN: Lerner. **S, C**

Guthrie, D. (2000). *A rose for Abby.* Nashville, TN: Abington Press. **C**

Hathorn, L. (1994). *Way home* (G. Rogers, Illus.). New York: Crown. **C**

O'Neill, T. (1990). *The homeless: Distinguishing between fact and opinion.* San Diego, CA: Greenhaven Press. **S, C**

Park, L. S. (2003). *A single shard.* New York: Yearling. **H, S**

Paulsen, G. (2006). *The crossing.* New York: Scholastic. **H, S**

Sendak, M. (1993). *We are all down in the dumps with Jack and Guy.* New York: HarperCollins. **C**

Seymour-Jones, C. (1993). *Past and present: Homelessness.* New York: Heinemann Educational. **S, C**

Snyder, Z. (1996). *Cat running.* New York: Delacorte. **S, C**

Weninger, B. (1997). *Lumina* (A. Bell, Trans; J. Wintz-Litty, Illus.). New York: North–South. **C**

Wolf, B. (1995). *Homeless.* New York: Orchard. **H, C**

MIGRANT WORKERS AND IMMIGRANTS

Anacona, G. (2001). *Harvest.* New York: Cavendish. **S, C**

Bunting, E. (1994). *A day's work.* New York: Clarion. **H, C**

Cox, V. (1995). *The challenge of immigration.* Springfield, NJ: Enslow. **S**

Garland, S. (1997). *Lotus seed* (T. Kiuchi, Illus.). New York: Harcourt. **S, C**

Haerens, M. (2006). *Illegal immigration*. New York: Thomson Gale. **S, C**

Hassler, D. (2006). *Growing season: The life of a migrant community*. Kent, OH: Kent State University Press. **S, C**

Herrera, J. (2001). *Calling the doves* (E. Simmons, Illus.). New York: Children's Book Press. **H, S**

Holm, J. L. (2001). *Our only May Amelia*. New York: HarperCollins. **H, C**

Hopkinson, D. (2004). *Apples to Oregon* (H. Carpenter, Illus.). New York: Atheneum Books. **S**

Hoyt-Goldsmith, D. (1996). *Migrant worker: A boy from the Rio Grande Valley*. New York: Holiday House. **S, C**

Krall, K. (2003). *Harvesting hope* (Y. Morales, Illus.). New York: Harcourt. **H, C, S**

Levine, E. (1994). *If your name was changed at Ellis Island*. Berkeley, CA: Tricycle Press. **H, S**

Meltzer, M. (2002). *Bound for America: The story of the European immigrants*. New York: Benchmark Books. **S, C**

O'Connor, K. (1992). *Dan Thuy's new life in America*. Minneapolis: Lerner. **S**

Pak, S. (2002). *A place to grow* (M. Truono, Illus.). New York: Arthur Levine Books. **S, C**

Perez, L. (2002). *First day in grapes* (R. Casilla, Illus.). New York: Lee & Lowe. **S**

Roleff, T. (1998). *Immigration: Opposing viewpoints*. San Diego, CA: Greenhaven Press. **S, C**

Sandler, M. (1995). *Immigrants*. New York: HarperCollins. **S, C**

Sandler, M. (2004). *Island of hope: The story of Ellis Island and the journey to America*. New York: Scholastic. **S**

Williams, S. A. (1992). *Working cotton* (C. Byard, Illus.). San Diego, CA: Harcourt. **C**

Yin. (2001). *Coolies* (C. Soentpiet, Illus.). New York: Philomel. **S**

RELIGIOUS TRADITIONS

Brown, T. (2006). *A Muslim American boy's story* (K. Cardwell, photos). New York: Henry Holt. **S**

Buller, L. (2005). *A faith like mine: A celebration of the world's religions through the eyes of children*. New York: Dorling Kindersley. **H, S, C**

Demi. (1997). *Buddha stories*. New York: Henry Holt. **H, S**

Graham, R. B. (1995). *One wintry night* (R. Watson, Illus.). New York: Baker Books. **H**

Johnson, J. W. (1994). *The creation* (J. Ransome, Illus.). New York: Holiday House. **H, S**

Johnston, T. (2000). *Day of the dead* (J. Winter, Illus.). Orlando, FL: Harcourt. **H, C**

Macaulay, D. (2003). *Mosque*. Boston: Houghton Mifflin. **S**

Oberman, S. (1994). *The always prayer shawl*. New York: Puffin. **H, S**

Osborne, M. P. (1996). *One world, many religions: The ways we worship*. New York: Knopf. **H, C**

Palacco, P. (1998). *Chicken Sunday*. New York: Philomel. **C**

Pinkney, A. (1993). *Seven candles for Kwanza* (B. Pinkney, Illus.). Cambridge, MA: Candlewick. **H, C**

Shazi, S. H. (1996). *Ramadan* (O. Rayyan, Illus.). New York: Holiday House. **H, C**

Wildsmith, B. (1996). *Saint Francis*. Grand Rapids, MI: W. B. Eerdmans. **C, S**

Yolen, J. (1996). *Sacred places*. Fort Worth, TX: Harcourt. **S, C**

CHILD CARE

Antoine, H. (1996). *Curious kids go to preschool: Another big book of words*. Atlanta, GA: Peachtree. **H**

Gutman, A. (2004). *Gaspard and Lisa's ready for school words* (G. Hallensleben, Illus.). New York: Random House. **H**

Henkes, K. (2001). *Wemberley worried*. New York: HarperCollins. **H**

Johnston, T. (2007). *Off to kindergarten*. New York: Scholastic. **H**

McGhee, A. (2006). *Countdown to kindergarten* (H. Bliss, Illus.). Boston: Houghton Mifflin. **H**

Slate, J. (2001). *Miss Bindergarten gets ready for kindergarten* (A. Wolff, Illus.). New York: Penguin Group. **H**

Wilson, K. (2007). *Mama always comes home* (B. Dyer, Illus.). New York: HarperCollins. **H**

BULLYING AND INTOLERANCE

Caseley, J. (2001). *Bully*. New York: Greenwillow Books. **H, S**

Johnson, J. (1998). *Bullies and gangs*. Brookfield, CT: Copper Beach Books. **H, S, C**

Johnston, M. (1996). *Dealing with bullying*. New York: Powerkids Press. **H, S, C**

Lovell, P. (2001). *Stand tall Molly Lou Melon* (D. Catrow, Illus.). New York: Putnam. **C**

McCain, B. (2001). *Nobody knew what to do: A story about bullying*. Morton Grove, IL: Whitman. **H, S**

Mead, A. (1998). *Junebug and the Reverend*. New York: Farrar Strauss & Giroux. **H, S**

O"Neill, A. (2002). *The recess queen* (L. Huliska-Beith, Illus.). New York: Scholastic. **H, S**

Romain, T. (1997). *Bullies are a pain in the brain*. Minneapolis: Free Spirit. **H, S, C**

Shange, N. (1997). *Whitewash* (M. Sporn, Illus.). New York: Walker & Company. **C**

Slater, T. (1995). *Who's afraid of big bad bully?* (P. Parter, Illus.). New York: Scholastic. **S, C**

Tacang, B. (2006). *Bully be gone*. New York: HarperCollins. **H, S**

Webster-Doyle, T. (1998). *Why is everybody always picking on me? A guide to understanding bullies for young people* (R. Cameron, Illus.). Trunbull, CT: Weatherhill. **H, C**

SEXUALITY AND CHILD HEALTH

Avi. (1996). *The barn*. New York: Avon. **H, S, C**

Carle, E. (2007). *From head to toe*. New York: HarperCollins. **H, S**

Child, L. (2001). *I will never not ever eat a tomato*. Cambridge, MA: Candlewick. **H, S**

Falwell, C. (1994). *Feast for 10*. New York: Clarion Books. **H, S**

Harris, R. (2004). *It's so amazing: A book about eggs, sperm, birth, babies and families* (M. Emberley, Illus.). Cambridge, MA: Candlewick. **H, S**

Harris, R. (2004). *It's perfectly normal: Changing bodies, growing up, sex and sexual health*. Cambridge, MA: Candlewick. **H, S**

Harris, R. (2008). *It's not the stock* (M. Emberley, Illus.). Cambridge, MA: Candlewick. **H**

Jandl, E. (2003). *Next please* (N. Junge, Illus.). New York: Putnam. **H, S**

Kubler, A. (2002). *Head, shoulders, knees and toes*. New York: Child's Play International. **H, S**

Mayer, M. (2004). *Good for me and you (little critter)*. New York: HarperCollins. **H, S**

Mayle, P. (2000). *Where did I come from?* New York: Lyle Stuart. **H, C**

Nilsson, L. (1996). *How was I born? A child's journey through the miracle of birth* (L. Swanberg, Illus.). New York: Dell. **H, S, C**

Rockwell, L. (2004). *The busy body book*. New York: Random House. **H, S, C**

Ross, T. (2006). *Wash your hands!* New York: Kane Miller. **H, S, C**

Saltz, G. (2008). *Amazing you! Getting smart about your private parts* (L. Cravath, Illus.). New York: Dutton. **H, S**

Sirett, D. (2005). *Going to the dentist*. New York: Dorling Kindersley. **H, S**

Spelman, C. M., & Weidner, T. (2000). *Your body belongs to you*. Morton Grove, IL: Whitman. **H, S**

Verdick, E. (2006). *Germs are not for sharing* (M. Heinlen, Illus.). Minneapolis: Free Spirit. **H, S**

Yolan, J. (2003). *How do dinosaurs get well soon?* (M. Teague, Illus.). New York: Blue Sky. **H, S**

DEFINING FAMILIES

Abramchik, L. (1993). *Is your family like mine?* (A. Bradshaw, Illus.). New York: Open Heart, Open Mind. **H, S**

Adoff, A. (2002). *Black is brown is tan* (E. A. McCully, Illus.). New York: HarperCollins. **H**

East, K., & Thomas, R. (2007). *Across cultures: A guide to multicultural literature for children.* Westport, CT: Libraries Unlimited. **S**

Jenness, A. (1990). *Families: A celebration of diversity, commitment, and love.* Boston: Houghton Mifflin. **H**

Kroll, V. (1994). *Beginnings: How families come to be.* Morton Grove, IL: Whitman. **H**

Kuklin, S. (2006). *Families.* New York: Hyperion. **H, C**

Leedy, L. F. (1995, 1999). *Who's who in my family?* New York: Holiday House. **H**

Littlefield, G. (1993). *This land is my land.* Chicago: Children's Book. **S, C**

Morris, A. (1990). *Loving* (K. Heyman, Photos). New York: Mulberry. **H, C**

Morris, A. (2000). *Houses and homes* (K. Heyman, Illus.). New York: HarperCollins. **S**

Morris, A. (2000). *Families* (K. Heyman, Illus.). New York: HarperCollins. **S, C**

Skutch, R. (1995). *Who's in a family?* (L. Nienhaus, Illus.). Berkeley, CA: Tricycle. **H, C**

Strickland, D. S., & Strickland, M. S. (Eds.). (1994). *Families: Poems celebrating the African American experience* (J. Ward, Illus.). Honesville, PA: Boyd's Mills. **H**

Valentine, J. (1994). *One dad, two dads, brown dad, blue dads* (M. Sarecky, Illus.). Boston: Alyson Wonderland. **H**

GLOSSARY

academic curriculum The objectives, procedures, and materials schools use to ensure children's acquisition of the knowledge and skills affirmed by the community.

academic learning The acquisition of knowledge and skills relating to subject-matter disciplines and organized fields of study.

acculturation Modification of an individual's cultural behavior patterns by another cultural group (usually the dominant group).

active listening skills Ability to perceive and process what another person communicates (both verbally and nonverbally).

adaptive behaviors Ability to change one's behavior as the situation requires.

adoptive family A family unit with at least one legally adopted child.

advocacy The process of publicly supporting a group, person, or cause.

after-school care Care provided for working parents' children (usually 5–10 years of age) during after-school hours.

age-appropriate curriculum A course of study based on helping children develop and learn according to their age level. (See **gender-appropriate behavior**.)

alternative insemination A method of conception that consists of inserting gathered sperm into a woman's uterus to fertilize an egg. Also known as *artificial* or *donor insemination*.

assessment Evaluation or determination of the extent of learning or change in behavior.

assistive technology Both high-tech and low-tech devices that children with disabilities may need to accomplish practical tasks.

associative level When parents and community members accept some responsibility for helping in a school program. (See **participatory level**.)

at-risk children (families) Children or families in danger of experiencing developmental gaps and other problems because of poverty, abuse, illness, or social disturbance.

authoritarian parenting style Baumrind's term for an autocratic, controlling, and somewhat detached method of raising children.

authoritative parenting style Baumrind's term for a receptive and somewhat democratic, although firm and in-control, manner of raising children.

autonomy The ability of persons to regulate and determine their own behavior.

backup care Child care provided on an occasional basis when regular arrangements are not available (e.g., the school is closed) or inappropriate (e.g., the child is ill).

behaviorism The belief that learning occurs because of a system of rewards, punishments, and reinforcements.

biracial family Family in which the race of the parents is different. Some U.S. families claim multiracial makeup because of past generations' biracial marriages.

blended family Two basic family units with children that join together to form a single family unit; often a remarriage, although some partners choose to forego wedlock.

blogs Abbreviation of **Weblogs**—an interactive Web site.

bullying Intimidating another.

center-based care (See **child-care center**.)

charter school An authorized school designed to improve educational opportunities and supported but not regulated by a local or state authority.

child-care center A facility providing care and educational programs for children from infancy to 5 years of age.

child-care providers Adults who care for a group of children in family child care or a child-care center.

child-centered curriculum Teaching practices and materials focusing on children's interests, needs, and desires. Teachers respond to these by providing materials and guidance.

child find Process of locating children who are in need of special services. The term derives from a federally funded program called the Child Find Project.

code switching The ability to move easily from one language or dialect to another.

collaboration Two or more persons or groups working together on joint endeavors for mutually determined objectives.

conflict resolution Using peaceful discussions and interactions to reach agreement on differences in attitudes, feelings, and beliefs that have caused disharmony.

constructive play Stage of play whereby children begin to build and create things.

creationism A belief that the earth and all life developed according to God's plan as described in Genesis.

critical periods of development Erikson's label for periods of human development when positive aspects of behavior need to be achieved if development is to proceed in a positive manner.

cultural background The social behaviors and linguistic characteristics that distinguish societies and groups.

cultural deprivation   A term formerly used to describe the problems of certain families and groups. The notion that individuals lacked certain skills for productive school learning as a result of gaps in their cultural background.

cultural pluralism   The concept that all cultures have value and contribute to society.

custodial parent   The parent to whom a court assigns the primary responsibility of a child's care and upbringing.

decision-making level   Parents, community members, and educators sharing equally in making decisions regarding school policy.

drop-in child care   A place where parents may find child-care services for brief periods of time and with flexible schedules.

dual-income   A family in which both parents or resident adults earn an income.

Early Head Start   A component of the federal Head Start program that focuses on children younger than age 3 and assists parents in improving their nurturing skills.

early identification   Programmed assessment of the mental, social, and physical abilities of preschool children at the earliest opportunity.

early intervention service   Service provided in natural environments to infants and toddlers at risk for developmental delays.

elaborated language code   Syntactically complex speech that requires the persons with whom one communicates to use judgment, imagination, and reason to interpret ambiguities and abstractions.

embedded partners   Parents, teachers, and community persons who are an integral part of the education process for children in the community.

employer-sponsored child care   Child care provided for children of employees, generally at or near their workplace.

enculturation   The process by which one learns the mores and habits of a particular cultural group.

English Language Learner (ELL)   (See **Structured English Immersion**.)

ethnic orientation   Relating to the complex set of characteristics and values, including national origin and linguistic, physical, and religious traits, by which a social group identifies itself.

ethnocentrism   The process by which one concentrates on and specializes in the values of one's own cultural milieu.

Even Start   Federally funded home-based family literacy program requiring established links to the Head Start program.

evolution   A belief based on Darwinian theory that the earth and all living organisms developed by a gradual process of mutation and adaptation so that living creatures evolve to more complex forms.

exploratory play   A type of play whereby children begin to expand their horizons and experiment.

extended family   The kin of the basic family unit who are economically dependent on or emotionally attached to the household.

504 plan   A legal document under provisions of the 1973 Rehabilitation Act providing a program of services for students identified with special needs but placed in a regular education setting.

faith-based   Institutions and organizations affiliated with and normally supported by religious groups.

family   Two or more persons living together and linked for emotional and economic support.

family literacy program   Approach to helping children learn to read and write by assisting parents in improving their skills so that they can help their children and improve their own prospects.

fixed curriculum   The curriculum, often perceived to be mandated by local, state, and national education boards, that has been determined for a particular grade level.

formal community structure   The organizations and agencies within a community that support services for that community.

foster children   Children in the legal custody of a state office placed in an arranged living situation for a period of time.

free, appropriate education (FAPE)   A legal term used to indicate that a community must provide appropriate education, without cost to the family, for a 3- to 5-year-old child diagnosed with a disability.

full inclusion   Term used to indicate that children with disabilities are to be educated in a regular classroom full time but also are to receive from the trained specialist special services required as a result of their disability.

gay and lesbian   Persons with a sexual preference for a person of their own sex. *Gay* is a generic term; *lesbian* refers specifically to women.

gender-appropriate behavior   Qualities and behaviors a community or culture considers appropriate for female and male roles and actions.

global marketplace   An economy based on events and interactions that happen around the world.

group norm   Way in which most people in a group respond.

harassment   Incessant badgering or troubling of another person.

Head Start   Comprehensive federally funded program for poor preschool children and their families. It is designed to provide health, nutritional, social, and educational experiences to compensate for the negative effects of poverty.

home care   Care of children by someone other than the parents but provided in the child's home setting.

home curriculum   Learning that children acquire while under the influence of family members.

homeless family   A family that regularly has no permanent place of residence and thus constantly moves from one place to another.

homeschooling   The education of children undertaken completely by parents and done in the home environment.

ideologues   Advocates of ideas reflecting the social needs and beliefs of a particular group.

immersion and submersion   School plans to provide all instruction in English irrespective of the non-English-speaking child's background.

incidental learning   Learning as result of an event but happening without any adult planning.

inclusion   Instruction for each child provided, preferably in a regular classroom, with support services from personnel most appropriate at that moment in the child's schedule.

individualized education program (IEP)   A program, mandated by law, developed by those responsible for the education of a child with special needs.

individualized family service plan (IFSP)   A written plan, mandated by law, that provides appropriate services for at-risk infants and toddlers and their families.

individualized teaching   Teaching that requires the teacher to adjust materials and concepts to be learned and the type of instruction for each individual in the class.

Individuals with Disabilities Education Act (IDEA)   Reauthorization and amendment of the 1975 Education for All Handicapped Students Act, which governs how students with disabilities are to be educated in today's schools.

informal community structure   The personal relationships that families establish with members outside the home or extended family.

in-home care   (See **home care**.)

intact family   A married couple living with their biological, adopted, or foster children

intelligent design   A belief that the earth and living organisms developed according to a plan by a Superior Being.

interactive portfolio   A student's work and materials collected in a folder or portfolio, shared with and commented on by parents and teachers.

interactive skills   Ability to exchange thoughts, ideas, and actions both verbally and nonverbally.

interethnic   The combining of two or more ethnic qualities, characteristics, or backgrounds.

interracial   A relationship in which racial groups are combined; for example, interracial marriages.

involuntary refugees   Persons who have been forced to leave their homes and seek safety and sanctuary elsewhere.

itinerant family   A family unit that moves regularly, often following crop harvests, or is engaged in other temporary work.

kinship adoption   Child adopted into a family related by blood or marriage.

kinship care   Care of children provided by close relatives.

literacy development   The process of acquiring meaning from signs and symbols and of transferring meaning to signs and symbols.

literacy event   Activity related to reading and writing that supports literacy development.

locus of control   The perception one has of where responsibility for one's actions lies. It may be internal or external.

lower working class   The part of the population, usually consisting of unskilled laborers, that is less secure financially, at risk of unemployment, and at times receiving government assistance with basic living needs.

marginalized family (children)   Persons responsible for the welfare of families and children who are unable or unwilling to provide basic needs and nurturance. Also those whose needs are not met.

matriarchal   A form of family organization in which the mother or eldest female is recognized as head of the family.

mentor   Person serving as a guide or teacher to others on a one-to-one basis.

mesosystem   Bronfenbrenner's label for the area of secondary importance in a child's life space—usually the home and neighborhood.

metacognitive   The process used in understanding how one gains knowledge.

microsystem   Bronfenbrenner's label for the area of primary importance in a child's life space, such as the nuclear and extended family.

middle class   That part of the population whose income falls within the median range for the whole population. Professionals and businesspersons are often in this class.

migrant worker   (See **itinerant family**.)

minimum level   The minimal participation of parents and community members in school programs—for example, contributing cakes to a bake sale.

monocultural   Reflecting the beliefs, behavior patterns, and characteristics of a single cultural group.

mores   Those rituals, traditions, customs, and behavior patterns seen as essential for a social group's survival and well-being.

mosaic   A design made by laying small bits of colored stone, paper, or other material side by side. In educational terms, it means a variety of racial, cultural, and ethnic people that make up a society.

mother's-day-out programs   Programs that offer children a few hours of supervised care so that their mothers may take time for themselves.

multicultural education   Curriculum based on the inclusion and appreciation of the practices of different cultures, religions, and ethnic groups.

NAEYC Acronym for **National Association for the Education of Young Children**.

NAFCC Acronym for **National Association of Family Child Care**.

nature–nurture controversy The polarization of two opposing views of child growth and development—an innate plan of development versus development as a result of stimuli from the environment.

networking A system of making connections with individuals and groups that allows communication and involvement as a unit.

No Child Left Behind (NCLB) Act Congressional legislation adopted in 2001 to stimulate school performance.

nuclear family A family unit consisting of two parents and their biological and/or adopted children.

nursery school A program, usually private, designed for 2- to 5-year-olds. Often a half-day program, but may have a full-day schedule.

nurturing practice The process of raising and promoting the development of children.

obese Clinical definition—extremely overweight.

out-of-home care Regular care provided to young children outside the home setting.

overweight Having more body weight than is normal or healthy.

paradigm A pattern, example, or model.

parent center A specific location, usually within a school, where parents can work, socialize, and feel that they are a part of the school.

parent cooperative Private nursery school or preschool program where parents share both the teaching and administrative decision making.

parent education Courses, workshops, and reading materials designed to assist parents in improving their nurturing skills.

parent empowerment A process whereby parents become decision makers, often in collaboration with school personnel, for the education of their children.

participatory level The second level of involvement for parents in school partnerships whereby they cooperate and work as volunteers and helpers. (See **associative level**.)

patriarchal A form of family organization in which the father or eldest male is recognized as head of the family.

peer group People of similar race, ethnicity, age, social status, or other trait.

perceptual field The human range of recognition and organization of sensory input.

permissive parenting style Baumrind's term for a manner of raising children that is nondemanding and noncontrolling and that allows children to develop according to their natural instincts.

person-oriented family A family unit focused on the development of individual children.

phonics The letter–sound relationships of a language.

play-oriented curriculum Curriculum for children that emphasizes the belief that children learn as they play with materials and other children.

poor The condition of individuals or families lacking financial resources to move above the defined U.S. poverty level.

position-oriented family Manner of family functioning that is present- and object-oriented and that assigns roles according to position in the family.

postmodern family Family of today that views parenting as a shared responsibility of the father, mother, and care provider.

postnuclear family units Family units that vary from the traditional mother–father–child units.

power brokers Members of a community or group with enough influence and power to become major decision makers for that community or group.

predetermined curriculum A course of study, established by a person or a group, that determines what students should learn and how they should proceed in the learning process.

Project Follow Through U.S. government–sponsored program that supports students after Head Start programs through kindergarten and the primary grades. (See **Head Start**.)

project-oriented curriculum A curriculum of study that uses themes or projects as a means of presenting content and concepts.

resilient child (family) Child or family demonstrating the ability to cope and manage in spite of debilitating environmental circumstances.

resource file A professional's organized collection of plans, materials, and equipment to supplement units, projects, and daily activities.

resources and referral programs Community agencies that support the development and improvement of child care and assist parents in finding appropriate and affordable care for their children.

restricted language code A manner of speaking that is syntactically simple and direct and that has concrete meanings.

role expectation Behavioral expectation for an individual that depends on status or function within the family, peer group, school, or community.

Scholastic Aptitude Test (SAT) Norm-referenced exam for high school students. Often used by colleges and scholarship boards to determine the ability to pursue advanced study.

school-identified disability Learning difficulty or problem identified after a child enters school.

secular education Education in which there is no religious or spiritual training.

self-fulfilling prophecy The concept that expectations of others shape and reinforce one's behavior such that the expectations are eventually met. Also known as the *Pygmalion effect*.

servant–leader interns College-age students who pledge to serve and help in Freedom Schools (sponsored by the Children's Defense Fund) and learn the techniques of working with and advocating for children.

service agency Organization within a community that provides the health, education, transportation, protection, or communication services necessary to the community's citizens.

SES Acronym for **socioeconomic status**.

sexism Prejudice based on gender.

sexual energy Freudian concept that human behavior and energy are derived from the primal sex drive.

signage Public information signs.

significant other (adult) The person in a child's life who is particularly important to the child. This relationship exists independently of any biological or formal social relationship between child and adult.

single-parent family A family unit consisting of one parent, either a mother or father, and children, and no other adults.

skills ladder A careful ordering of the skills needed for a particular task.

social agencies Broad grouping of community offices and institutions that administer human services, governmental benefits, or counseling. (See **service agencies**.)

social capital The number of human connections and relationships that results in learning.

social climate The attitudes, feelings, and relationships that people within a community maintain toward one another.

socialization skills The verbal and nonverbal abilities to interact with and relate to a variety of other people.

socioeconomic factors The social relationships and financial developments that exist in a family or community.

socioeconomic status (SES) The economic and social level at which one belongs because of wealth, occupation, and educational background.

special-interest group Group with a narrow purpose or agenda organized to influence others to accept their point of view.

sponsored independence parenting style Clark's term, similar to Baumrind's *authoritative style*, describing a manner of raising children. Indicates a rational, receptive, and warm but demanding style.

stages of development Distinct steps in the growth process that individuals pass through from infancy through adulthood.

stakeholder Person who stands to gain or profit from selected activities and programs in a school or community.

standardized test Test with scientifically chosen items, given under similar conditions, that enables persons to be compared to a group standard. Tests may be either criterion referenced or norm referenced.

Structured English Immersion (SEI) Program in which bilingual children are taught all subjects in English, receiving special English-language assistance as needed and using their own language only to clarify concepts.

subfamily A family cluster living with other adults or families in which the parent in the cluster is not the central figure in the household.

subsidized child care Care supported by government funding for families with financial need.

technological intelligence Those parts of human intelligence related to literacy and numeracy skills.

theme-focused program A phase of the curriculum, based on a particular theme, wherein important objectives are identified and activities are prepared so that students acquire knowledge and skills relating to that theme.

Title I school School where students meet the poverty guidelines developed under Title I legislation.

transcultural Extending across cultures or involving more than one culture.

transracial Encompassing the physical features or interests of two or more races.

undocumented immigrants Persons who enter another country illegally to set up residency but lack any legal certification of their status.

unit of study Part of a curriculum based on a particular theme, around which learning activities are organized. Similar to **theme-focused program**.

unstructured learning events Incidental and self-selected experiences in which children become interested and involved, and learning results.

upper class The most economically advantaged group of a population; often its wealth is inherited.

upper working class The population group represented by skilled laborers who are financially able to cope but severely affected by economic depressions.

urban underclass Individuals and families living in cities with minimal resources for housing, nutrition, and health care.

voucher plan Plan whereby parents receive certificates indicating the financial support for their children's education. Parents have the right to select a school and use the certificate to pay the cost of education.

War on Poverty President Lyndon B. Johnson's War on Poverty became the byword for legislation aimed at helping disadvantaged populations overcome the effects of poverty.

Weblogs Internet programs on particular topics set up by individuals whereby others can contribute

welfare reform measures (See **welfare-to-work program**.)

welfare-to-work program Welfare Reform Act of 1996, requiring welfare parents to seek education and employment or lose benefits.

well-baby clinic Health clinic or hospital program where parents can, without cost, bring their children for regular checkups and discussions regarding ways to provide a healthy environment.

Women, Infants, and Children (WIC) A government program that provides health checkups, counseling, and food stamps for families below the poverty level.

working poor Individuals and families earning above the government-defined poverty level but still lacking adequate housing and health benefits.

zone of proximal development Vygotsky's label for the distance between a child's ability to perform a task independently and his or her ability to perform it under guidance.

REFERENCES

CHAPTER 1

Berk, L. E. (2005). Why parenting matters. In S. Olfman (Ed.), *Childhood lost: How American culture is failing our kids* (pp. 19–54). Westport, CT: Praeger.

Berns, R. M. (2009). *Child, family, school, community: Socialization and support.* Belmont, CA: Wadsworth.

Borkowski, J. G., Ramey, S. L., & Stile, C. (2002). Parenting research: Translating to parenting practices. In J. G. Borkowski, S. L. Ramey, & M. Bristol-Power (Eds.), *Parenting and the child's world* (pp. 365–386). Mahwah, NJ: Erlbaum.

Bornstein, M. H. (2002). Parenting infants. In M. H. Bornstein (Ed.), *Handbook of parenting: Vol 1, Children and parenting* (2nd ed., pp. 3–43). Mahwah, NJ: Erlbaum.

Bronfenbrenner, U. (1979). *The ecology of human development: Experiment by nature and design.* Cambridge, MA: Harvard University Press.

Bronfenbrenner, U. (1986). Ecology of the family as a context of human development: Research perspectives. *Developmental Psychology, 22,* 723–742.

Bronfenbrenner, U. (1993). The ecology of cognitive development: Research models and fugitive findings. In R. H. Wozniak & K. W. Fisher (Eds.), *Development in context: Activity and thinking in specific environments* (pp. 3–24). Hillsdale, NJ: Erlbaum.

Bruer, J. T. (2002, October). *A rational approach to education: Integrating behavioral, cognitive, and brain science.* Address presented at Oxford University, Oxford, U.K.

Byrnes, J. P. (2001). *Minds, brains and learning: Understanding the psychological and educational relevance of neuroscientific research.* New York: Guilford Press.

Carnegie Corporation. (1994). *Starting points: Meeting the needs of our youngest.* New York: Carnegie Corporation.

Chavkin, N. F. (2005). Strategies for preparing educators to enhance the involvement of diverse families in their children's education. *Multicultural Education, 13*(2), 16–20.

Coleman, J. S. (1991). *Policy perspectives: Parental involvement in education.* Washington, DC: Department of Education, Office of Educational Research and Development.

College Board. (2009). *2008 college-bound seniors: Total group profile report.* Retrieved July 31, 2009, from http://www.professionals.collegeboard.com.

Common Sense Media. (2008). *The impact of media on child and adolescent health: Executive summary of a systematic review.* Retrieved August 3, 2009, from http://www.commonsensemedia.org.

Desmond, R. (2001). Free reading. In D. G. Singer & J. L. Singer (Eds.), *Handbook of children and the media* (2nd ed., pp. 29–45). Thousand Oaks, CA: Sage.

Dilworth, M. E., & Brown, C. E. (2001). Consider the difference: Teaching and learning in culturally rich schools. In V. Richardson (Ed.), *Handbook of research on teaching* (4th ed., pp. 642–667). Washington, DC: American Educational Research Association.

Douville-Watson, L., & Watson, M. A. (2002). *Infants and toddlers: Curriculum and teaching* (5th ed.). Albany, NY: Delmar.

Durkin, D. D. (1966). *Children who read early.* New York: Teachers College Press.

Eccles, J., Wigfield, A., Harold, R., & Blumenfeld, P. (1993). Age and gender differences in children's self and task perceptions during elementary school. *Child Development, 64,* 830–847.

Erikson, E. (1963). *Childhood and society.* New York: Norton.

Gunter, B., Harrison, J., & Wykes, M. (2003). *Violence on television: Distribution, form, context and themes.* Mahwah, NJ: Erlbaum.

Harris, A. (2004). *All about the girls.* New York: Routledge.

Harris, J. (2002). Beyond the nurture assumption: Testing hypotheses about the child's environment. In J. G. Borkowski, S. L., Ramey, & M. Bristol-Power (Eds.), *Parenting and the child's world* (pp. 3–20). Mahwah, NJ: Erlbaum.

Harris, J. R. (1998). *The nuture assumption.* New York: Free Press.

Hatch, J. A. (2005). *Teaching in the new kindergarten.* Clifton Park, NY: Thomson Delmar Learning.

Heilman, E. (2008). Hegemonies and "transgressions" of family: Tales of pride and prejudice. In T. Turner-Vorbeck & M. M. Marsh (Eds.), *Other kinds of families: Embracing diversity in schools* (pp. 7–27). New York: Teachers College Press.

Horrigan, J. (2009). *Home broadband adoption 2009.* Retrieved August 3, 2009, from http://www.pewinternet.org.

Hrabowski, F. A., Maton, K. I., Greene, M., & Greif, G. L. (2002). *Overcoming the odds: Raising academically successful African American young women.* New York: Oxford University Press.

Kozol, J. (1991). *Savage inequalities: Children in America's schools.* New York: Crown.

Ladd, G. W., Herald, S. L., & Andrews, R. K. (2006). Young children's peer relations and social competence. In B. Spodek & O. N. Saracho (Eds.), *Handbook of research on the education of young children* (2nd ed., pp. 23–54). Mahwah, NJ: Erlbaum.

Long, S., Anderson, C., Clark, M., & McCraw, B. (2008). Going beyond our own worlds: A first step in envisioning equitable practice. In C. Genishi & A. L. Goodwin (Eds.), *Diversities in early childhood education: Rethinking and doing* (pp. 253–269). New York: Routledge.

Maeroff, G. I. (1998). Altered destinies: Making life better for school children in need. *Phi Delta Kappan, 79,* 424–432.

Maslow, A. H. (1970). *Motivation and personality* (Rev. ed.). New York: Norton.

Meringoff, L. K. (1980). Influence of the medium on children's story apprehension. *Journal of Educational Psychology, 72*(2), 240–249.

Neuman, S. B. (1997). Television as a learning environment: A theory of synergy. In J. Flood, S. B. Heath, & D. Lapp (Eds.), *Handbook of research on teaching literacy through the communicative and visual arts* (pp. 15–23). New York: Simon & Schuster.

Olfman, S. (2005). Where do the children play? In S. Olfman (Ed.), *Childhood lost: How American culture is failing our kids* (pp. 203–216). Westport, CT: Praeger.

Organization for Economic Co-Operation and Development. (2008). *The future of the Internet economy: A statistical profile.* Retrieved August 3, 2009, from http://www.oecde.org/datoecd.

Pecora, N. O., Murray, J. P., & Wartella, E. (Eds.). (2004). *Children and television: Fifty years of research.* Mahwah, NJ: Erlbaum.

Piaget, J. (1967). *Six psychological studies.* New York: Random House.

Pinker, S. (2002). *The blank slate: The modern denial of human nature.* New York: Viking.

Ramsey, P. G. (2004). *Teaching and learning in a diverse world* (3rd ed.). New York: Teachers College Press.

Rideout, V., & Hamel, E. (2006). *The media family:Electronic media in the lives of infants, toddlers, preschoolers, and their parents.* Menlo Park, CA: Kaiser Family Foundation.

Rose, L. C., & Gallup, A. M. (2008). *The 40th annual Phi Delta Kappa/Gallup poll of the public's attitude toward the public schools.* Retrieved July 31, 2009, from http://www.pdkmembers.org/members_online.

Rosenthal, R., & Jacobson, L. (1968). *Pygmalion in the classroom.* New York: Holt, Rinehart & Winston.

Rowe, D. C. (1994). *The limits of family influence: Genes, experience and behavior.* New York: Guilford Press.

Sacks, P. (2005). "No child left": What are schools for in a democratic society? In S. Olfman (Ed.), *Childhood lost: How American culture is failing our kids* (pp. 185–202). Westport, CT: Praeger.

Sadker, D., & Sadker, M. (2005). Gender bias: From colonial America to today's classrooms. In J. A. Banks & C. A. McGee-Banks (Eds.), *Multicultural education: Issues and perspectives* (pp. 135–163). Hoboken, NJ: Wiley.

Singer, D. G., & Singer, J. (2007). *Imagination and play in the electronic age.* Thousand Oaks, CA: Sage.

Strasburger, V. C., Wilson, B. J., & Jordan, A. B. (2008). *Children, adolescents, and the media* (2nd ed.). Thousand Oaks, CA: Sage.

Teacher Expectations and Student Achievement. (2004). *Teacher expectations and student achievement program evaluation.* Retrieved July 31, 2009, from http://www.lacoe./edu.

Van Evra, J. (2004). *Television and child development* (2nd ed.). Mahwah, NJ: Erlbaum.

Vygotsky, L. S. (1978). *Mind in society.* Cambridge, MA: Harvard University Press.

Weikart, D. P. (2004). Head Start and evidence-based educational models. In E. Zigler & S. Styfco (Eds.), *The Head Start debates* (pp. 143–159). Baltimore: Paul H. Brookes.

Woolfolk, A. E. (2009). *Educational psychology* (11th ed.). Upper Saddle River, NJ: Prentice-Hall.

Wynter, L. (2002). *American skin: Pop culture, big business, and the end of White America.* New York: Crown.

CHAPTER 2

Banks, J. A. (2007). *An introduction to multicultural education* (4th ed.). Boston: Allyn & Bacon.

Berlin, I. (1998). *Many thousands gone: The first two centuries of slavery in North America.* Cambridge, MA: Belknap/Harvard University Press.

Blank, H. (1997). Child care in the context of welfare reform. In S. B. Kamerman & A. J. Kahn (Eds.), *Child care in the context of welfare "reform"* (pp. 1–44). New York: Columbia University School of Social Work.

Boger, J. C., & Orfield, G. (2009). *School resegregation: Must the South turn back?* Chapel Hill: University of North Carolina Press.

Bowen, M. (1987). *Family therapy in clinical practice.* New York: Aronson.

Bronfenbrenner, U. (1979). *The ecology of human development: Experiment by nature and design.* Cambridge, MA: Harvard University Press.

Bruer, J. T. (1999). *The myth of the first three years: A new understanding of early brain development and life-long learning.* New York: Free Press.

Danzberger, J., & Gruskin, S. (1993). *Project abstracts: Educational partnerships program.* (Programs for the improvement of practice). Washington, DC: Office of Educational Research and Improvement.

Davis, T. J. (2006). *Race relations in America: A reference guide with primary documents.* Westport, CT: Greenwood Press.

Derman-Sparks, L. (1989). *Anti-bias curriculum: Tools for empowering young children.* Washington, DC: National Association for the Education of Young Children.

DeVita, C. J. (1995). The United States at mid-decade. *Population Bulletin, 50*(4), 2–42.

Dewey, J. (1910). *How we think.* New York: D. C. Heath.

Dewey, J. (1944). *Democracy and education.* New York: Macmillan. (Originally published in 1916.)

Dowling, T. E. (2004). *The great brain debate: Nature or nurture.* Washington, DC: National Academies Press.

Edwards, J. O., Derman-Sparks, L., & Ramsey. P. G. (2006). *What if all the kids are white? Anti-bias multicultural education with young children and families.* New York: Teachers College Press.

Eitzer, D. S., & Zinn, M. B. (2005). *Globalization: The transformation of social worlds.* Belmont, CA: Wadsworth.

Fass, P. S., & Mason, M. A. (Eds.). (2000). *Childhood in America.* New York: New York University Press.

Gandara, P., Maxwell, J. J., Garcia, E., Asato, J., Gutierez, K., & Stritikus, T. (1999). *The initial impact of Proposition 227.* Davis, CA: University of Linguistic Minority Institute.

Gardner, H. (1993). *Multiple intelligences: The theory in practice.* New York: Basic Books.

Gilbert, R. M. (2006). *The eight concepts of Bowen theory.* Falls Church, VA: Leading Systems Press.

Gollnick, D. M., & Chinn, P. (2006). *Multicultural education in a pluralistic society* (7th ed.). Upper Saddle River, NJ: Merrill/Prentice Hall.

Gutek, G. L. (2005). *Historical and philosophical foundations of education: A biographical introduction* (4th ed.). Upper Saddle River, NJ: Merrill/Prentice Hall.

Head Start Bureau. (2006). *U.S. Department of Health and Human Services, President Bush's proposal for Head Start, 2003.* Retrieved April 21, 2006, from http://www.acf.hhs.gov/programs/hbs.

Herrnstein, R. J., & Murray, G. (1994). *The bell curve.* New York: Free Press.

Jensen, A. R. (1998). *The g factor: The science of mental ability.* New York: Praeger.

Kamerman, S. B. (2005). Early childhood education and care in advanced industrialized countries: Current policy and program trends. *Phi Delta Kappan, 87*, 193–195.

Lichter, D. T., & Crowley, M. L. (2002). Poverty in America: Beyond welfare reform. *Population Bulletin, 57*(2), 3–34.

Mbugua, T., Wadas, J., Casey, M. A., & Finnerty, J. (2004). Authentic learning: Intercultural, international and intergenerational experience in the elementary classroom. *Childhood Education, 80*(5), 237–245.

McDevitt, T. M., & Ormrod , J. E. (2009). *Child development and education* (4th ed.). Upper Saddle River, NJ: Merrill/Prentice Hall.

Mitchell, C. J., & Spencer, L. M. (1997). *21st-century community learning centers program.* Washington, DC: U.S. Department of Education, Office of Educational Research and Improvement.

Nisbett, R. E. (2009). *Intelligence and how to get it: Why schools and culture count.* New York: Norton.

Orfield, G., & Yun, J. T. (1999). *Resegregation in America: Report from the Civil Rights Project, Harvard University.* Retrieved May 1, 2009, from http://www.law.harvard.edu/groups/civilrights/publications.

Pinker, S. (2002). *The blank slate: The modern denial of human nature.* New York: Viking.

Puckett, M. B., & Black, J. K. (2005). *The young child: Development from prebirth through age eight* (4th ed.). Upper Saddle River, NJ: Merrill/Prentice Hall.

Pulliam, J. D., & van Patten, J. (2007). *History of education in America* (9th ed.). Upper Saddle River, NJ: Merrill/Prentice Hall.

Reyna, V. F. (2005). The No Child Left Behind Act and scientific research: A view from Washington, DC. In J. S. Carlson & J. R. Levin (Eds.), *The No Child Left Behind legislation* (pp. 1–27). Greenwich, CT: Information Age.

Rich, J. M. (1997). *Foundations of education: Perspectives on American education.* Upper Saddle River, NJ: Prentice Hall.

Riley, R. W. (1995). Reflections on Goals 2000. *Teachers College Record, 96,* 380–389.

Sadker, D., & Sadker, M. (2005). Gender bias from colonial America to today's classrooms. In J. A. Banks and C. A. McGee-Banks (Eds.), *Multicultural education: Issues and perspectives* (pp. 135–163). Hoboken, NJ: Wiley.

Salend, S. J. (2001). *Creating inclusive classrooms: Effective and reflective practice* (4th ed.). Upper Saddle River, NJ: Merrill/Prentice Hall.

Schuman, D. (2004). *American schools, American teachers: Issues and perspectives.* Boston: Allyn & Bacon.

Sternberg, R. J. (1997). The concept of intelligence and its role in life-long learning and success. *American Psychologist, 52,* 1030–1037.

Stewart, V., & Kagan, S. L. (2005). A new world view: Education in a global era. *Phi Delta Kappan, 87,* 241–244.

Stille, A. (1998, June 11). The betrayal of history. *New York Review of Books, 45*(10), 8–11. Also retrieved May 4, 2003, from http://www.nybooks.com.

Swiniarski, L., & Breitborde, M. L. (2003). *Educating the global village: Including the child in the world* (2nd ed.). Upper Saddle River, NJ: Merrill/Prentice Hall.

Szaz, M. C. (1988). *Indian education in the American colonies, 1607–1783.* Albuquerque: University of New Mexico Press.

Taylor, K. W. (1981). *Parents and children learn together.* New York: Teachers College Press.

Trawick-Smith, J. (2009). *Early childhood development: A multicultural perspective* (5th ed.). Upper Saddle River, NJ: Merrill/Prentice Hall.

Turnbull, A., Turnbull, R., & Wehmeyer, M. (2007). *Exceptional lives: Special education in today's schools* (5th ed.). Upper Saddle River, NJ: Merrill/Prentice Hall.

U.S. Bureau of the Census. (2008). *Statistical abstract of the United States, 2008* (128th ed.). Washington, DC: Author.

U.S. Department of Education. (1993). *National education goals.* Gov. Doc. ED 1.2:G 53/5. Washington, DC: Author.

Vygotsky, L. S. (1978). *Mind in society.* Cambridge, MA: Harvard University Press.

Wartella, E., & Gray, G. E. (2004). Raising a world-wise child and the power of media: The impact of television on children in intercultural knowledge. *Phi Delta Kappan, 86,* 222–224.

Weinberg, M. (1977). *A chance to learn: A history of race and education in the United States.* New York: Cambridge University Press.

Withers, A. (2006). Personal communication from the Office of the Head Start Bureau, April 20, 2006.

CHAPTER 3

ACLU Lesbian and Gay Rights Project. (2002). *Too high a price: The case against restricting gay parenting.* New York: American Civil Liberties Union.

Alexander, B. (2003). The state of the nation's housing, 2003. Cambridge, MA: Joint Center for Housing Studies, Harvard University.

American Anthropological Association. (2002). *AAA statement on race.* Retrieved August 30, 2008, from http://www.aaanet.org/stmts.

Annie E. Casey Foundation. (2008). *Kids count data book: State profiles of child well- being.* Baltimore: Author.

Bianchi, S. M., & Casper, L. M. (2000). American families. *Population Bulletin, 55*(4), 3–43.

Bianchi, S. M., Robinson, J. P., & Milkie, M. A. (2006). *Changing rhythms of American family life.* New York: Russell Sage Foundation.

Bock, J. D. (2000), Doing the right thing?: Single mothers by choice and the struggle for legitimacy. *Gender and Society, 14,* 62–86.

Casper, L. M., & Bianchi, S. M. (2002). *Continuity and change in the American family.* Thousand Oaks, CA: Sage.

Child Trends Data Book. (2009). *Births to unmarried women in 2005.* Retrieved April 20, 2009, from http://www.childtrendsdatabank.org.

Child Welfare League of America. (2003). *Family foster care fact sheet.* Retrieved June 11, 2008, from http://www.cwla.org.

Cohler, B. J. (2006). Life-course social science perspectives on the GLBT family. In J. J. Bigner (Ed.), *An introduction to GLBT family studies* (pp. 23–49). New York: Haworth Press.

Coleman, J. S. (1966). *Equality of education opportunity.* Washington, DC: U.S. Government Printing Office.

Coleman, J. S. (1991). *Policy perspectives: Parental involvement in education.* Washington, DC: U.S. Department of Education, Office of Educational Research and Improvement.

Coles, R. L. (2006). *Race and family: A structural approach.* Thousand Oaks, CA: Sage.

Comer, J. P. (1997). *Waiting for a miracle: Why schools can't solve our problems and how we can.* New York: Penguin Putnam.

Coontz, S. (2005). *Marriage, a history: From obedience to intimacy, or how love conquered marriage.* New York: Viking.

DeVita, C. J., & Mosher-Williams, R. (2001). *Who speaks for America's children?* Washington, DC: Urban Institute.

Dimidijian, V. J. (2001). Helping vulnerable families give their children an even start toward school success. *Childhood Education, 27,* 379–395.

Erickson, F. (2005). Culture in society and in educational practices. In J. A. Banks & C. A. McGee-Banks (Eds.), *Multicultural education: Issues and perspectives* (5th ed., pp. 31–40). Hoboken, NJ: Wiley.

Gabe, T. (2003). *Trends in welfare, work and the economic well-being of female-headed households with children.* New York: Novinka Books.

Geen, R. (Ed.). (2005). *Kinship care: Making the most of a valuable resource.* Washington, DC: Urban Institute Press.

Goff, P. (2004). Diversity in religion. In P. Goff & P. Harvey (Eds.), *Themes in religion and American culture* (pp. 327–360). Chapel Hill: University of North Carolina Press.

Gollnick, D. M., & Chinn, P. (2006). *Multicultural education in a pluralistic society* (7th ed.). Upper Saddle River, NJ: Merrill/Prentice Hall.

Hansen, K. V. (2005). *Not-so-nuclear families: Class, gender, and networks of care.* New Brunswick, NJ: Rutgers University Press.

Hanson, M. J., & Lynch, E. W. (2004). *Understanding families: Approaches to diversity, disability and risk.* Baltimore: Paul H. Brookes.

Hayslip, B., & Patrick, J. H. (2006). *Custodial grandparenting: Individual, cultural and ethnic diversity.* New York: Springer.

Herman, E. (2007). Adoption statistics. *The adoption history project* (pp. 22–30). Eugene: University of Oregon Press.

Heward, W. L. (2006). *Exceptional children: An introduction to special education* (8th ed.). Upper Saddle River, NJ: Merrill/Prentice Hall.

Hoge, D. R. (1996). Religion in America: The demographics of belief and affiliation. In E. P. Shafranske (Ed.), *Religion and the clinical practice of psychology* (pp. 21– 41). Washington, DC: American Psychological Association.

Hrabowski, F. A., Maton, K. I., Greene, M., & Greif, G. L. (2002). *Overcoming the odds: Raising academically successful African American young women.* New York: Oxford University Press.

Ispa, J. M., Thornburg, K. R., & Find, M. A. (2006). *Keepin' on: The everyday struggles of young families in poverty.* Baltimore: Paul H. Brookes.

Kamerman, S. B. (2005). Early childhood education and care in advanced industrialized countries: Current policy and program trends. *Phi Delta Kappan, 87,* 193–195.

Lareau, A. (2003). *Unequal childhoods: Class, race, and family life.* Berkeley: University of California Press.

Lewin, E. (2006). Family values: Gay men and adoption in America. In K. Wegar (Ed.), *Adoptive families in a diverse society* (pp. 129–145). New Brunswick, NJ: Rutgers University Press.

Lichter, D. T., Qian, Z., & Crowley, M. L. (2007). Poverty and economic polarization among American minority and immigrant children. In R. Crane & T. Heaton (Eds.). *Handbook of families and poverty* (pp. 119–143). New York: Sage.

Lindner, E. (2009). *Yearbook of American and Canadian churches, 2009.* Nashville, TN: Abingdon.

Mayer, S. (1997). *What money can't buy: Family income and children's life chances.* Cambridge, MA: Harvard University Press.

Melton, J. G. (2009). *Melton's encyclopedia of American religions* (8th ed.). Detroit: Gale Cengage.

National Adoption Information Clearinghouse. (2004). *Adoption.* Retrieved August 29, 2008, from http://www.childwelfare.gov.

National Alliance to End Homelessness. (2006). *Family homelessness.* Retrieved June 20, 2008, from http://www.endhomelessness.org/back/familiesfacts.

National Center for Children in Poverty. (2006). *Basic facts on low income children.* Retrieved September 1, 2008, from http://www.nccp.org/preschool.

National Child Traumatic Stress Network. (2005). *Facts on trauma and homeless children.* Retrieved April 20, 2009, from http://www.nctsnet.org.

Orfield, G. (2004). *Dropouts in America: Confronting the graduation rate crisis.* Cambridge, MA: Harvard Education Press.

Ovando, C. J. (2005). Language diversity and education. In J. A. Banks & C. A. McGee-Banks (Eds.), *Multicultural education: Issues and perspectives* (5th ed., pp. 289–313). Hoboken, NJ: Wiley.

Penn, K. M., & Crosbie-Burnett, M. (2005). Remarriage and recoupling: A stress perspective. In P. C. McKenny & S. J. Price (Eds.), *Families and change: Coping with stressful events and transitions* (pp. 253–284). Thousand Oaks, CA: Sage.

Rainwater, L., & Smeeding, T. M. (2004). Single-parent poverty, inequality and the welfare state. In D. P. Moynihan, T. M. Smeeding, & L. Rainwater (Eds.), *The future of the family* (pp. 96–115). New York: Russell Sage Foundation.

Rieger, L. (2008). A welcoming tone in the classroom: Developing the potential of diverse students and their families. In T. Turner-Vorbeck & M. M. Marsh (Eds.), *Other kinds of families:Embracing diversity in schools* (pp. 64–80). New York: Teachers College Press.

Side, R. (2006). *Unsung heroines: Single mothers and the American dream.* Berkeley: University of California Press.

Thoennes, T. (2008). Emerging faces of homelessness: Young children, their families, and schooling. In T. Turner-Vorbeck & M. M. Marsh (Eds.), *Other kinds of families: Embracing diversity in schools* (pp. 162–175). New York: Teachers College Press.

Thompson, W., & Hickey, J. (2005). *Society in focus.* Boston: Allyn & Bacon.

Turnbull, A., Turnbull, R., & Wehmeyer, M. (2007). *Exceptional lives: Special education in today's schools* (5th ed.). Upper Saddle River, NJ: Merrill/Prentice Hall.

Turner-Vorbeck, T., & Marsh, M. M. (Eds.). (2008). *Other kinds of families: Embracing diversity in schools.* New York: Teachers College Press

Urban Institute. (2009). *Civil rights for the underclass.* Retrieved April 20, 2009, from http://www.urban.org.

U.S. Bureau of the Census. (2004). *U.S. interim projections by age, sex, race, and Hispanic origin.* Retrieved June 4, 2006, from http://www.census.gov/lpc/www/usinterproj.

U.S. Bureau of the Census. (2008). *Current population reports.* Retrieved October 5, 2008, from http://www.census.gov.

U.S. Bureau of the Census. (2009). *Current population survey 2008.* Washington, DC: Author.

U.S. Department of Education. (2004). *Individuals with Disabilities Education Act (IDEA) data,* Table AA3. Washington, DC: Author.

U.S. Department of Health and Human Services. (2008). *Foster child care and adoptions.* Retrieved September 8, 2008, from http://www.hhs.gov.

Waller, P. L., & Crawford, K. (2001). Education advocacy for the nation's invisible population—the migrant community. *Delta Kappa Gamma* Bulletin, *68*(1), 24–27.

Webb, L. D., Metha, A., & Jordan, K. F. (2007). *Foundations of American education* (5th ed.). Upper Saddle River, NJ: Merrill/Prentice Hall.

Wegar, K. (Ed.). (2006). *Adoptive families in a diverse society.* New Brunswick, NJ: Rutgers University Press.

Werts, M., Culatta, R., & Tompkins, J. (2007). *Fundamentals of education: What every teacher needs to know.* Upper Saddle River, NJ: Prentice Hall.

Wynter, L. (2002). *American skin: Pop culture, big business, and the end of White America.* New York: Crown.

CHAPTER 4

American Academy of Pediatrics. (2009). *Bedsharing/cosleeping: The data neither condemns nor endorses.* Retrieved May 22, 2009, from http://www.aap.org.

Anderson, C. (2003). The diversity, strength, and challenges of single-parent households. In F. Walsh (Ed.), *Normal family processes: Growing diversity and complexity* (3rd ed., pp. 121–152). New York: Guilford Press.

Banks, J. A. (2002). *Teaching strategies for ethnic studies* (7th ed.). Boston: Allyn & Bacon.

Banks, J. A., & McGee-Banks, C. A. (Eds.). (2005). *Multicultural education: Issues and perspectives* (5th ed.). Hoboken, NJ: Wiley.

Bardige, B. (2005). *At a loss for words: How America is failing our children and what we can do about it.* Philadelphia: Temple University Press.

Bartholomae, S., & Fox, J. (2005). Economic stress and families. In P. C. McKenry & S. J. Price (Eds.), *Families and change: Coping with stressful events and transitions* (pp. 205–225). Thousand Oaks, CA: Sage.

Baumrind, D. (1966). Effects of authoritative parental control on child behavior. *Child Development, 37,* 378–407.

Baumrind, D. (1968). Authoritarian vs. authoritative parental control. *Adolescence, 3,* 255–272.

Baumrind, D. (1995). *Child maltreatment and optimal caregiving in social contexts.* New York: Garland.

Clark, R. M. (1983). *Family life and school achievement: Why poor Black children succeed or fail.* Chicago: University of Chicago Press.

Berliner, D. (2009). *Poverty and potential: Out-of-school factors and school success.* Boulder and Tempe: Education and the Public Interest Center and Education Policy Research Unit. Retrieved August 24, 2009, from http://epicpolicy.org.

Bernstein, B. (1972). A social linguistic approach to socialization with some reference to educability. In J. Gumperz & D. Hymes (Eds.), *Directions in sociolinguistics* (pp. 465–497). New York: Holt, Rinehart & Winston.

Bianchi, S. M., Robinson, J. P., & Milkie, M. A. (2006). *Changing rhythms of American family life.* New York: Russell Sage Foundation.

Bookman, A. (2004). *Starting in our own backyards: How working families can build community and survive the new economy.* New York: Routledge.

Bowen, M. (1978). *Family therapy in clinical practice.* New York: Jason Aronson.

Brazelton, T. B., & Greenspan, S. I. (2000). *The irreducible needs of children:What every child must have to grow, learn, and flourish.* Cambridge, MA: Perseus.

Casper, L. M., & Bianchi, S. M. (2002). *Continuity and change in the American family.* Thousand Oaks, CA: Sage.

Center for Excellence to Prepare Teachers of Children of Poverty. (2009). *Report #3.* Retrieved June 20, 2009, from http://www.fmucenterofexcellence.org.

Children's Defense Fund. (2001). *The state of America's children: A report from the Children's Defense Fund.* Washington, DC: Author.

Children's Defense Fund (2005). *The state of America's children, 2005.* Washington, DC: Author.

Children's Defense Fund. (2008). *The state of America's children, 2008.* Washington, DC: Author.

Christian, L. G. (2006). Applying family systems theory to early childhood practice. *Young Children, 61*(2), 12–20.

Clark, R. M. (1983). *Family life and school achievement: Why poor Black children succeed or fail.* Chicago: University of Chicago Press.

Cotter, D., England, P., & Hermsen, J. (2008). Moms and jobs: Trends in mothers' employment and which mothers stay home. In S. Coontz, M. Parson, & G. Raley (Eds.), *American families: A multicultural reader* (2nd ed., pp. 379–388*).* New York: Routledge.

DeGaetano, G. (2005). The impact of media violence on developing minds and hearts. In S. Olfman (Ed.), *Childhood lost: How American culture is failing our kids* (pp. 137–153). Westport, CT: Praeger.

Dodson, L., & Bravo, E. (2005). When there is not time or money: Work, family and community lives of low-income families. In J. Heymann & C. Beem (Eds.), *Unfinished work: Building equality and democracy in an era of working families* (pp. 116–133). New York: New Press.

Fine, M. A., Ganong, H., & Demo, D. H. (2005). Divorce as a family stressor. In P. C. McKenry & S. J. Price (Eds.), *Families and change: Coping with stressful events and transitions* (pp. 227–252). Thousand Oaks, CA: Sage.

Giambo, D., & Szecsi, T. (2005). Parents can guide children through the world of two languages. *Childhood Education, 81,* 164–165.

Greenfield, P. M., & Suzuki, L. K. (2001). Culture and parenthood. In J. C. Westman (Ed.), *Parenthood in America: Undervalued, underpaid, under siege* (pp. 20–33). Madison: University of Wisconsin Press.

Haddock, S., Zimmerman, T., & Lyness, K. (2003). Changing gender norms: Transitional dilemmas. In F. Walsh (Ed.), *Normal family processes: Growing diversity and complexity* (3rd ed., pp. 301–336). New York: Guilford Press.

Harris, J. R. (1998). *The nurture assumption: Why children turn out the way they do.* New York: Free Press.

Hart, B., & Risley, T. R. (1995). *Meaningful differences in the everyday experience of young American children.* Baltimore: Paul H. Brookes.

Hart, B., & Risley, T. R. (1999). *The social world of children learning to talk.* Baltimore: Paul H. Brookes.

Heilman, E. (2008). Hegemonies and "transgressions" of family: Tales of pride and prejudice. In T. Turner-Vorbeck & M. Marsh (Eds.), *Other kinds of families: Embracing diversity in schools* (pp. 7–27). New York: Teachers College Press.

Helms, H. M., & Demo, D. (2005). Everyday hassles and family stress. In P. McKenry & J. Price (Eds.), *Families and change: Coping with stressful events and transitions* (3rd ed., pp. 405–435). Thousand Oaks, CA: Sage.

Hetherington, E. M., & Kelly, J. (2002). *For better or worse: Divorce reconsidered.* New York: Norton.

Karpowitz, D. H. (2001). American families in the 1990s and beyond. In M. J. Fine & S. W. Lee (Eds.), *Handbook of diversity of parent education* (pp. 3–14). San Diego, CA: Academic Press.

Lareau, A. (2003). *Unequal childhoods: Class, race and family life.* Berkeley: University of California Press.

Larzelere, R. E. (2001). Combining love and limits in authoritative parenting. In J. C. Westman (Ed.), *Parenthood in America:Undervalued, underpaid, under siege* (pp. 81–89). Madison: University of Wisconsin Press.

Levin, D. (2005). So sexy, so soon: The sexualization of childhood. In S. Olfman (Ed.), *Childhood lost: How American culture is failing our kids* (pp. 137–153). Westport, CT: Praeger.

Levine, S., & Ion, H. W. (2002). *Against terrible odds:Lessons in resilience from our children.* Boulder, CO: Bull.

Macauley, D. (1998). *The new how things work.* Boston: Houghton Mifflin.

Maccoby, E. C., & Martin, J. (1983). Socialization in the context of family: Parent and child interaction. In P. H. Mussen (Ed.), *Handbook of psychology: Socialization, personality and social development* (4th ed., pp. 1–102). New York: Wiley.

Mallett, D. (1995). *Inch by inch: The garden song.* New York: HarperCollins.

Maslow, A. H. (1968). *Toward a psychology of being.* Princeton, NJ: Van Nostrand.

McGoldrick, M. (2003). Culture: A challenge to concepts to normality. In F. Walsh (Ed.), *Normal family processes: Growing diversity and complexity* (3rd ed., pp. 235–259). New York: Guilford Press.

McKenry, P. C., & Price, S. J. (Eds.). (2005). *Families and change: Coping with stressful events and transitions.* Thousand Oaks, CA: Sage.

Monroe, L. (1997). *Nothing's impossible: Leadership lessons and stories from the front.* New York: Time Books.

National Center for Children in Poverty (NCCP). (2009). *Facts on poverty.* Retrieved April 20, 2009, from http://www.nccp.org/topics/childpoverty.html.

Noddings, N. (2005). *Happiness and education.* New York: Cambridge University Press.

Osofsky, J. D. (1998). Children as invisible victims of domestic and community violence. In G. Halden, R. Geffner, & E. Jouriles (Eds.), *Children exposed to marital violence* (pp. 95–120). Washington, DC: American Psychological Association.

Pann, K. M., & Crosbie-Burnett, M. (2005). Remarriage and recoupling: A stress perspective. In P. C. McKenry & S. J. Price (Eds.), *Families and change: Coping with stressful events and transitions* (pp. 253–284). Thousand Oaks, CA: Sage.

Piburn, D. E. (2006). Gender equality for a new generation: Expect male involvement in ECE. *Exchange, 168,* 18–22.

Ramsey, P. G. (2004). *Teaching and learning in a diverse world: Multicultural education for young children* (3rd ed.). New York: Teachers College Press.

Reppucci, N. D., Britner, P. A., & Woolard, J. L. (1997). *Preventing child abuse and neglect through parent education.* Baltimore: Paul H. Brookes.

Sameroff, A., Seifer, R., Barocas, R., Zax, M., & Greenspan, S. (1987). Intelligence quotient scores of four-year old children: Social environmental risk factors. *Pediatrics, 79,* 343–350.

Schwartz, L. L., & Kaslow, F. W. (1997). *Painful partings: Divorce and its aftermath.* New York: Wiley.

Sclafani, J. D. (2004). *The educated parent: Recent trends in child raising.* Westport, CT: Praeger.

Scully, P. (2003). Time out for tension: Teaching young children how to relax. *The Journal of Early Education and Family Review, 10*(4), 22–29.

Seefeldt, C., & Barbour, N. (1998). *Early childhood education: An introduction* (4th ed.). Upper Saddle River, NJ: Merrill/Prentice Hall.

Stanford, B. H., & Yamamoto, K. (Eds.). (2001). *Children and stress: Understanding and helping.* Olney, MD: Association for Childhood Education International.

Thoennes, T. (2008). Emerging faces of homelessness: Young children, their families, and schooling. In T. Turner-Vorbeck & M. Marsh (Eds.), *Other kinds of families: Embracing diversity in schools* (pp. 162–175). New York: Teachers College Press.

U.S. Bureau of the Census. (2009). *Population Division estimates in 2008.* Retrieved May 22, 2009, from http://www.census.gov.

U.S. Department of Labor, Bureau of Labor Statistics. (2008). *Women in the labor force: A data book.* Retrieved April 15, 2009, from http://www.bls.gov.

Van Evra, J. (2004). *Television and child development* (3rd ed.). Mahwah, NJ: Erlbaum.

Wallerstein, J., Lewis, J., & Blakeslee, S. (2000). *The unexpected legacy of divorce.* New York: Hyperion.

Westman, J. C. (2001). Growing together: Parenthood as a developmental experience. In J. C. Westman (Ed.), *Parenthood in America: Undervalued, underpaid, under siege* (pp. 34–46). Madison: University of Wisconsin Press.

Wright, M. A. (1998). *I'm chocolate, you're vanilla: Raising healthy Black and biracial children in a race conscious world.* San Francisco: Jossey-Bass.

CHAPTER 5

Afterschool Alliance. (2009). *Afterschool programs benefit youth, families, and communities.* Retrieved June 8, 2009, from http://afterschoolalliance.com.

Bardige, B. (2005). *At a loss for words: How America is failing our children and what we can do about it.* Philadelphia: Temple University Press

Casper, L. M., & Bianchi, S. M. (2002). *Continuity and change in the American family.* Thousand Oaks, CA: Sage.

Children's Defense Fund. (2001). *The state of America's children: A report from the Children's Defense Fund.* Washington, DC: Author.

Children's Defense Fund. (2009). *The state of America's children 2008.* Washington, DC: Author.

Children's Initiative. (2009). *After school.* Retrieved June 8, 2009, from http://www.thechildreninitiative.org/afterschool.htm.

Cohen, S. (2001). *Championing child care.* New York: Columbia University Press.

Connell, L. H. (2005). *The childcare answer book.* Naperville, IL: Sphinx.

Copple, C., & Bredekamp, S. (2005). *Basics of developmentally appropriate practice.* Washington, DC: National Association for the Education of Young Children.

Council on Accreditation. (2009). *After school program standards.* Retrieved June 8, 2009, from http://www.COAafterschool.org/standards.

Cryer, D., & Clifford, R. M. (Eds.). (2003). *Early childhood education and care in the USA.* Baltimore: Paul H. Brookes.

Greenman, J. (2005). *Caring spaces, learning places: Children's environments that work.* Redmond, WA: Exchange Press.

Greenman, J., Stonehouse, A., & Schweikert, G. (2009). *Prime times: A handbook for excellence in infant and toddler programs* (2nd ed.). St. Paul, MN: Redleaf Press.

Greenspan, I., & Salmon, J. (2001). *The four thirds solution: Solving the child care crisis in America.* Cambridge, MA: Persus Press.

Harrington, M. (2000). *Care and equality: Inventing a new family politics.* New York: Routledge.

Hartman, A. (2003). Family policy: Dilemmas, controversies and opportunities. In F. Walsh (Ed.), *Normal family processes: Growing diversity and complexity* (3rd ed., pp. 635–662). New York: Guilford Press.

Helburn, S., & Bergmann, B. (2002). *America's child care problem: The way out.* New York: Palgrave/St. Martin's.

Kinch, A. F., & Schweinhart, L. J. (1999). Making child care work for everyone. *Young Children, 54*(1), 68–73.

Koralek, D. (2002). Professionalism leads to quality in family care. *Young Children, 52*(1), 8.

Lawrence, S., & Kreader, J. L. (2006). *School-age child care arrangements.* New York: National Center for Children in Poverty.

Mardell, B. (2002). *Growing up in child care: A case for quality early childhood education.* Portsmouth, NH: Heineman.

National Association for Family Child Care. (2009). *Parents.* Retrieved May 20, 2009, from http://www.nafcc.org.

National Association for Regulatory Administration (2009). *The 2007 child care licensing study.* Retrieved June 3, 2009, from http://naralicensing.org.

National Association for the Education of Young Children. (2009). *Position statement on developmentally appropriate practice.* Washington, DC: Author.

National Association of Child Care Professionals (2009). *National Accreditation Commission for Early Care and Education Programs: An accreditation program committed to excellence.* Retrieved June 8, 2009, from http://www.naccp.org.

National Association of Child Care Resource and Referral Agencies (NACCRRA). (2009). *Child care in America: 2008 State Fact Sheets.* Retrieved May 27, 2009, from http://naccrra.org/policy.

National Early Childhood Program Accreditation (2009). *About our accreditation.* Retrieved June 8, 2009, from http://necpa.net.

Neugebauer, R. (2005). The U.S. military child care system: A model worth replicating. *Exchange, 161,* 31–32.

Presser, H. B. (2003). *Working in a 24/7 economy: Challenges for American families.* New York: Russell Sage Foundation.

Singer, D. G., Golinkoff, R., & Hirsh-Pasek, K. (Eds.). (2007). *Play = learning: How play motivates and enhances children's cognitive and social-emotional growth.* New York: Oxford University Press.

Urban Institute. (2007). *Child-care expenses of America's families.* Retrieved January 30, 2009, from http://www.urban.org.

U.S. Bureau of Labor Statistics (2009). *Occupational outlook handbook, 2008–2009 edition.* Retrieved June 4, 2009, from http://ww.bls.gov/oco.

Vandell, D. L., & Pierce, K. M. (2003). Child care quality and children's success at school. In A. J. Reynolds, M. C. Wang, & H. J. Walberg (Eds.), *Early childhood programs for a new century* (pp. 115–139). Washington, DC: CWLA Press.

Wortham, S. (2006). *Early childhood curriculum: Developmental bases for learning and teaching* (4th ed.). Upper Saddle River, NJ: Prentice Hall.

CHAPTER 6

Anderson, W., Chitwood, S., & Hayden, D. (2004). *Negotiating the special education maze: A guide for parents and teachers* (3rd ed.). Bethesda, MD: Woodbine House.

Anstine-Templeton, R., & Johnston, M. A. (2004). Helping children with learning disabilities succeed. In D. B. Hiatt-Michael (Ed.), *Promising practices connecting schools to families of children with special needs* (pp. 57–78). Greenwich, CT: Information Age.

Falvey, M. A. (2005). *Believe in my child with special needs: Helping children achieve their potential in schools.* Baltimore: Paul H. Brookes.

Gorman, J. C. (2004). *Working with challenging parents of students with special needs.* Thousand Oaks, CA: Corwin.

Hanson, M. J., & Lynch, E. W. (2004). *Understanding families: Approaches to diversity, disability, and risk.* Baltimore: Paul H. Brookes.

Hayden, D., Takemoto, C., Anderson, W., & Chitwood, S. (2008). *Negotiating the special education maze: A guide for parents and teachers* (4th ed.). Bethesda, MD: Woodbine House.

Heward, W. L. (2006). *Exceptional children's introduction to special education* (8th ed.). Upper Saddle River, NJ: Merrill/Prentice Hall.

Heward, W. L., Cavanaugh, R. A., & Ernsbarger, S. C. (2005). Educational equality for students with disabilities. In J. A. Banks & C. A. Banks (Eds.), *Multicultural education: Issues and perspectives* (pp. 317–349). Hoboken, NJ: Wiley.

Hiatt-Michael, D. B. (2004). Connecting schools to families with special needs. In D. B. Hiatt-Michael (Ed.), *Promising practices connecting schools to families of children with special needs* (pp. 1–14). Greenwich, CT: Information Age.

Lee, H., & Ostrowsky, M. (2004). Toward successful collaboration: Voices from families of children with developmental delays and disabilities. In D. B. Hiatt-Michael (Ed.), *Promising practices connecting schools to families with special needs* (pp. 101–128). Greenwich, CT: Information Age.

Lerner, J. W., Lowenthal, B., & Egan, R. W. (2003). *Preschool children with special needs: Children at risk and children with disabilities.* Boston: Allyn & Bacon.

Lewis, R. B., & Doorlag, D. (2006). *Teaching special students in general education classrooms* (7th ed.). Upper Saddle River, NJ: Merrill/Prentice Hall.

McCormick, L., Wong, M., & Yagi, L. (2003). Individualization in the inclusive preschool: A planning process. *Childhood Education, 79,* 212–217.

Merz, M. (2009, March 15). Strategies workshop on special needs at Montgomery County (MD) schools.

National Research Council. (2002). *Minority students in special and gifted education.* Washington, DC: National Academy Press.

Newman, L. A. (2004). A national study of parent involvement in education of youth and disabilities. In D. B. Hiatt-Michael (Ed.), *Promising practices connecting schools to families with special needs* (pp. 25–40). Greenwich, CT: Information Age.

Schweinhart, L. J. (2004). *The High/Scope Perry preschool study through age 40: Summary, conclusions and frequently asked questions.* Ypsilanti, MI: High/Scope Press.

Schweinhart, L. J., & Weikart, D. P. (1997). *Lasting differences: The High-Scope preschool curriculum study through age 23* (Monographs of the High/Scope Educational Research Foundation, 12). Ypsilanti, MI: High/Scope Press.

Simmons, L. L. (2004). Historical antecedents, legal issues, and government policies related to family involvement for children with special needs. In D. B. Hiatt-Michael (Ed.), *Promising practices connecting schools to families with special needs* (pp. 15–24). Greenwich, CT: Information Age.

Turnbull, A., Turnbull, R., & Wehmeyer, M. (2007). *Exceptional lives: Special education in today's schools* (5th ed.). Upper Saddle River, NJ: Merrill/Prentice Hall.

U.S. Department of Education. (2002*). Twenty fourth annual report to Congress on the implementation of the Individuals with Disabilities Education Act.* Washington, DC: Author.

U.S. Department of Education. (2007). *IDEA data.* Retrieved April 2, 2009, from http://www.ideadata.org/PartBReport.asp.

Wood , J. (2002). *Adapting instruction to accommodate students in inclusive settings* (4th ed.). Upper Saddle River, NJ: Merrill/Prentice Hall.

CHAPTER 7

American Library Association. (2008). *Censorship and challenges.* Retrieved November 26, 2008, from http://www.ala.org.

Apple, M. W. (1995). *Education and power.* New York: Routledge.

Arce, E. (1999). Family-centered communities benefit young children. In E. Arce (Ed.), *Perspectives: Early childhood education* (pp. 136–137). Boulder, CO: Coursewise.

Aronson, S. (2002). *Healthy young children: A manual for programs.* Washington, DC: National Association for the Education of Young Children.

Banks, J. A., & McGee-Banks, C. A. (Eds.). (2005). *Multicultural education: Issues and perspectives* (5th ed.). Hoboken, NJ: Wiley.

Baumrind, D. (1966). Effects of authoritative control on child behavior. *Child Development, 37,* 387–407.

Baumrind, D. (1968). Authoritarian vs. authoritative parental control. *Adolescence, 3,* 255–272.

Beaty, J. J. (2006). *Observing development of the young child* (6th ed.). Upper Saddle River: NJ: Merrill/Prentice Hall.

Bernstein, B. (1972). A sociolinguistic approach to socialization with some reference to educability. In J. Gumperz & D. Hymes (Eds.), *Directions in sociolinguistics* (pp. 465–497). New York: Holt, Rinehart & Winston.

Bronfenbrenner, U., Moen, P., & Garbarino, J. (1984). Child, family, and community. In P. D. Parke (Ed.), *Review of child development research: Vol 7. The family* (pp. 283–328). Chicago: University of Chicago Press.

Canadian Pediatric Society. (2009). *Keeping kids safe.* Retrieved June 30, 2009, from http://www.caringforkids.cps.ca.

Centers for Disease Control and Prevention. (2009). *Overweight and obesity.* Retrieved January 5, 2009, from www.cdc.gov.

Cherry, L. (1982). *A river ran wild.* San Diego, CA: Harcourt Brace.

Child Welfare Information Gateway. (2009). *Child protection: Child abuse.* Retrieved January 30, 2009, from http://www.childwelfare.gov.

Children's Defense Fund. (2000). *The state of America's children, 2000: A report from the Children's Defense Fund.* Boston: Beacon Press.

Chrisman, K., & Couchenour, D. (2002). *Healthy sexuality development: A guide for early childhood educators and families.* Washington, DC: National Association for the Education of Young Children.

Christie, K. (2005). Chasing the bullies away. *Phi Delta Kappan, 86,* 725–726.

Clark, R. M. (1983). *Family life and school achievement: Why poor Black children succeed or fail.* Chicago: University of Chicago Press.

Cochran, M., & Davila, V. (1992). Societal influences on children's peer relationships. In R. D. Parke & G. W. Ladd (Eds.), *Family–peer relationships: Modes of linkage* (pp. 191–214). Hillsdale, NJ: Erlbaum.

Cole, J., Cornell, D., & Sheras, P. (2006). Identification of school bullies by survey methods. *Professional School Counseling, 9,* 305–313.

Coles, R. (1997). *The moral intelligence of children.* New York: Random House.

Coles, R. L. (2006). *Race and family: A structural approach.* Thousand Oaks, CA: Sage.

Cruickshank, D., Jenkins, D., & Metcalf, K. (2002). *The act of teaching* (3rd ed.). New York: McGraw-Hill.

Damon, W. (1988). *The moral child: Nurturing children's moral growth.* New York: Free Press.

deRamirez, L. L. (2006). *Voices of diversity: Stories, activities and resources for the multicultural classroom.* Upper Saddle River, NJ: Prentice Hall.

Essa, E. L., & Murray, C. I. (1999). Sexual play: When should you be concerned? *Childhood Education, 75*(4), 231–234.

Evans, R. (1996). *The human side of school change.* San Francisco: Jossey-Bass.

Garbarino, J. (1999). *Lost boys: Why our sons turn violent and how we can save them.* New York: Free Press.

Garbarino, J., Dubrow, N., Kostelny, K., & Pardo, C. (1998). *Children in danger: Coping with the consequences of community violence* (2nd ed.). San Francisco: Jossey-Bass.

Good, T. L., & Brophy, J. E. (2007). *Looking in classrooms* (10th ed.). Boston: Allyn & Bacon.

Gunter, B., Harrison, J., & Wykes, M. (2003). *Violence on television: Distribution form, context and themes.* Mahwah, NJ: Erlbaum.

Institute of Medicine. (2006). *Child obesity in the United States: Facts and figures, 2006.* Washington, DC: Author.

Jacobs, K. (2004). Parent and child together time. In B. H.Wasik (Ed.), *Handbook on family literacy* (pp. 193–221). Mahwah, NJ: Erlbaum.

Jenkins, E. J., & Bell, C. C. (1997). Exposure and response to community violence among children and adolescents. In J. Osofsky (Ed.), *Children in a violent society* (pp. 9–31). New York: Guilford Press.

Kieff, J. E., & Casbergue, R. M. (2000). *Playful learning and teaching: Integrating play into preschool and primary programs.* Boston: Allyn & Bacon.

Ladd, G. W., & Pettit, G. S. (2002). Parents and children's peer relationships. In M. Bornstein (Ed.), *Handbook of parenting: Vol 4. Applied and practical parenting* (pp. 377–409). Mahwah, NJ: Erlbaum.

Leach, P. (1996). *Your growing child.* New York: Knopf.

Lindner, E. (2008). *Yearbook of American and Canadian churches, 2008.* Nashville, TN: Abingdon.

Liston, D. P., & Zeichner, K. (1996). *Reflective teaching: An introduction.* Mahwah, NJ: Erlbaum.

Liverman, C. T., Kraak, V. I., & Koplan, J. (2005). *Preventing childhood obesity: Health in the balance.* Washington, DC: National Academies Press.

Maeroff, G. I. (1998). Altered destinies: Making life better for schoolchildren in need. *Phi Delta Kappan, 79,* 424–432.

Marotz, L., Cross, M., & Rush, J. (2005). *Health, safety and nutrition for the young child* (6th ed.). Clifton Park, NY: Thomson Delmar Learning.

McNeil, J. D., & Darby, J. (2005). *Curriculum: A comprehensive introduction* (6th ed.). New York: Wiley.

Moriarty, M. L., & Fine, M. J. (2001). Educating parents to be advocates for their children. In M. Fine & S. W. Lee (Eds.), *Handbook of diversity in parent education: The changing faces of parenting and parent education* (pp. 315–336). San Diego, CA: Academic Press.

National Center for Missing and Exploited Children. (2009). *Child safety.* Retrieved January 5, 2009, from www.missingkids.com.

National Institute on Drug Abuse. (2009). *The science of addiction.* Retrieved May 4, 2009, from http://www.nida.nih.gov.

Noddings, N. (2002). *Educating moral people: A caring alternative to character education.* New York: Teachers College Press.

Okagaki, L., & Luster, T. (2005). Research on parental socialization of child outcomes. In T. Luster & L. Okagaki (Eds.), *Parenting: An ecological perspective* (pp. 377–401). Mahwah, NJ: Erlbaum.

Paratore, J. R. (2001). *Opening doors, opening opportunities: Family literacy in an urban community.* Boston: Allyn & Bacon.

Prothrow-Stith, D., & Spivak, H. (2003). *Murder is no accident: Understanding and preventing youth violence in America.* Hoboken, NJ: Wiley.

Rigby, K. (2008). *Children and bullying: How parents and educators can reduce bullying at school.* Malden, MA: Blackwell.

Rodkin, P. C., & Hodges, E. V. (2003). Bullies and victims in the peer ecology. *School Psychology Review, 32,* 384–400.

Sadker, D., & Sadker, M. (2005). Gender bias from colonial America to today's classrooms. In J. A. Banks & C. A. McGee-Banks (Eds.), *Multicultural education: Issues and perspectives* (pp. 135–163). Hoboken, NJ: Wiley.

Seefeldt, C., & Barbour, N. (1998). *Early childhood education: An introduction* (4th ed.). Upper Saddle River, NJ: Merrill/Prentice Hall.

Singer, D. G., & Singer, J. L. (2007). *Imagination and play in the electronic age.* Cambridge, MA: Harvard University Press.

Sparling, J. (2004). Earliest literacy: From birth to age three. In B. H. Wasik (Ed.), *Handbook of family literacy* (pp. 45–56). Mahwah, NJ: Erlbaum.

Stiggins, R. J. (2005). *Student-involved classroom assessment* (4th ed.). Upper Saddle River, NJ: Merrill/Prentice Hall.

Strasburger, V. C., & Wilson, B. J. (2002). *Children, adolescents and the media.* Thousand Oaks, CA: Sage.

Turnbull, A., Turnbull, R., & Wehmeyer, M. (2007). *Exceptional lives: Special education in today's schools* (5th ed.). Upper Saddle River, NJ: Merrill/Prentice Hall.

U.S. Department of Agriculture (USDA). (2009). *My Pyramid, Center for Nutrition Policy and Promotion.* Retrieved March 4, 2009, from http://www.mypyramid.gov.

Van Evra, J. (2004). *Television and child development* (3rd ed.). Mahwah, NJ: Erlbaum.

Walker, L. J., & Taylor, J. H. (1991). Family interaction and the development of moral reasoning. *Child Development, 62,* 264–283.

Werner, E. E. (1999). *Through the eyes of innocents: Children witness World War II.* Boulder, CO: Westview Press.

Werner, E. E., & Smith, R. S. (1992). *Overcoming the odds: High-risk children from birth to adulthood.* Ithaca, NY: Cornell University Press.

CHAPTER 8

American Family Traditions. (2006). *Statistics for 2005.* Retrieved February 8, 2006, from http://www.americanfamilytraditions.com.

Arthur, B. (2008). *The art of recycle.* Belfast, ME: Bernice Arthur.

Barbour, C., Barbour, N., & Hildebrand, J. (2001, April 16). *Building a grandparent curriculum.* Paper presented at the conference for Childhood Education International, Toronto, Canada.

Berns, R. M. (2006). *Child, family, school, community: Socialization and support* (6th ed.). Belmont, CA: Wadsworth.

Black, J. (2009). *Homelessness in America.* Retrieved June 1, 2009, from http://articlet.com.

Blonigen, B. A., & Harbaugh, W. (2008). Application of economic analysis to school-wide positive behavior support programs. *Journal of Positive Behavior Interventions, 10*(1), 5–15.

Bronfenbrenner, U. (1995). Developmental ecology through space and time: A future perspective. In P. Moen, G. Elder, & K. Luecher (Eds.), *Examining lives in context* (pp. 619–648). Washington, DC: American Psychological Association.

Bronfenbrenner, U. (2005). The social ecology of human development. In U. Bronfenbrenner (Ed.), *Making human beings human: Bioecological perspectives on human development* (pp. 27–40). Thousand Oaks, CA: Sage.

Christakis, D., Gilkerson, J., & Richard, J. (2009). Audible television and decreased adult words, infant vocalizations and conversational turns. *Archives of Pediatrics & Adolescent Medicine, 163*(6), 554–558.

Clark, R. M. (1983). *Family life and school achievement: Why poor Black children succeed or fail.* Chicago: University of Chicago Press.

Common Sense Media. (2009). *Internet guide for parents.* Retrieved June 1, 2009, from http://www.commonsense.com.

Doll, R. C. (1995). *Curriculum improvement: Decision making and process* (7th ed.). Boston: Allyn & Bacon.

Dowd, N. E., Singer, D. G., & Wilson, R. F. (Eds.). (2005). *Handbook of children, culture and violence.* Thousand Oaks, CA: Sage.

Evans, R. (2004). *Family matters: How schools can cope with the crisis in child raising.* San Francisco: Jossey-Bass.

Fiese, B. H. (2006). *Family routines and rituals.* New Haven, CT: Yale University Press.

Fried, R. L. (2005). *The game of school: Why we play it, how it hurts kids, and what it will take to change it.* San Francisco: Jossey-Bass.

Gardner, H. (1993). *Multiple intelligences: The theory in practice.* New York: Basic Books.

Harris, J. R. (1998). *The nuture assumption.* New York: Free Press.

Hetherington, E. M., & Stanley-Hagan, M. H. (2002). *Parenting in divorced and remarried families.* In M. Bornstein (Ed.), *Handbook of parenting: Vol 3. Being and becoming a parent* (pp. 287–316). Mahwah, NJ: Erlbaum.

Holt, J. (1982). *How children fail* (Rev. ed.). New York: Delta/Seymour Lawrence.

Kerman, K. (1990). Homeschooling day by day. In A. Pederson & P. O'Mara (Eds.), *Schooling at home: Parents, kids, and learning* (pp. 175–182). Santa Fe, NM: Muir.

Lemish, D. (2006). *Children and television: A global perspective.* New York: Wiley-Blackwell.

Long, N. (2004). e-Parenting. In M. S. Hoghughi & N. Long (Eds.), *Handbook on parenting: Theory and research for practice* (pp. 369–380). Thousand Oaks, CA: Sage.

National Center for Education Statistics. (2009). *Home school statistics.* Retrieved June 1, 2009, from http://www.nces.ed.gov.

Oakmeadow Schools. (2009). *Homeschool organization.* Retrieved June 1, 2009, from http://www.oakmeadow.com.

Oladele, F. (1999). Passing the spirit. *Educational Leadership, 56*(4), 62–65.

Ray, J. A., & Shelton, D. (2004). E-pals: Connecting with families through technology. *Young Children, 59*(3), 30–34.

Reich, R. (2002).The civic perils of homeschooling. *Educational Leadership, 59*(7), 56–59.

Sadker, M. P., & Sadker, D. (2005). *Teachers, schools and society* (7th ed.). New York: McGraw-Hill.

Singer, D. G., & Singer, J. L. (2005). *Imagination and play in the electronic age.* Thousand Oaks, CA: Sage.

Smith, G. S. (2007). *How to protect your children on the Internet.* New York: Praeger.

Stevens, M. L. (2001). *The kingdom of children: Culture and controversy in the homeschooling movement.* Princeton, NJ: Princeton University Press.

Strasburger, V. C., Wilson, B. J., & Jordan, A. (2008). *Children, adolescents and the media* (2nd ed.). Thousand Oaks, CA: Sage.

Swick, K. J. (2004). The dynamics of families who are homeless: Implications for early childhood education. *Childhood Education, 80*(3), 116–120.

Tabors, P. O., & Snow, C. E. (2001). Young children and early literacy development. In S. Neuman & D. K. Dickinson (Eds.), *Handbook of early literacy research* (pp. 159–178). New York: Guilford Press.

The Teaching Home. (2002). *Educational approaches and methods.* Retrieved May 3, 2009, from http://www.teachinghome.com.

Tomlin, A. M. (1998). Grandparents' influences on grand-children. In M. E. Szinovacz (Ed.), *Handbook on grand-parenthood* (pp. 161–171). Westport, CT: Greenwood.

Van Evra, J. (2004). *Television and child development* (3rd ed.). Mahwah, NJ: Erlbaum.

Voss, M. M. (1993). "I just watched": Family influences on one child's learning. *Language Arts, 70*, 632–641.

Wade, S. M. (2004). Parenting influences on intellectual and educational achievement. In M. A. Hoghughi & N. Long (Eds.), *Handbook of parenting: Theory and research for practice* (pp. 198–212). Thousand Oaks, CA: Corwin Press.

Whitman, W. (1855). *Leaves of grass.* New York: Andrew & James Rome.

CHAPTER 9

Adelman, H. S., & Taylor, L. (2002). Building comprehensive multifaceted and integrated approaches to address barriers to student learning. *Childhood Education, 78*, 261–273.

Bigner, J. J. (2009). *Parent–child relations: An introduction to parenting* (8th ed.). Upper Saddle River, NJ: Merrill/Prentice Hall.

Bogenschneider, K., & Corbett, T. (2004). Building enduring family policies in the 21st century: The past as prologue. In M. Coleman & L. H. Ganong (Eds.), *Handbook of contemporary families: Considering the past, contemplating our future* (pp. 451–468). Thousand Oaks, CA: Sage.

Bookman, A. (2004). *Starting in our own backyards: How working families can build community and survive the new economy.* New York: Routledge.

Bradley, R. H. (2002). Environment and parenting. In M. H. Bornstein (Ed.), *Handbook of parenting: Vol. 2, Biology and ecology of parenting* (2nd ed., pp. 281–314). Mahwah, NJ: Erlbaum.

Bronfenbrenner, U. (1979). *The ecology of human development: Experiment by nature and design.* Cambridge, MA: Harvard University Press.

Center for Faith-Based and Community Initiatives. (2007). *Initiatives: U.S. Department of Education.* Retrieved October 1, 2008, from http://www.ed.gov/about/inits/list.

Cochran, M. (2007). *Finding our way: The future of early care and education.* Washington, DC: Zero to Three Press.

Cochran, M., & Niegro, S. (2002). Parenting and social networks. In M. H. Bornstein (Ed.), *Handbook of Parenting: Vol 4, Social conditions and applied parenting* (2nd ed., pp. 123–148). Mahwah, NJ: Erlbaum.

Coles, R. (1997). *The moral intelligence of children.* New York: Random House.

Comer, J. P. (1988). *Maggie's American dream: The life and times of a Black family.* New York: American Library.

Cornell, C. E. (1993). Language and culture monsters that lurk in our traditional rhymes and folktales. *Young Children, 48*(6), 40–46.

DeGaetano, G. (2005). The impact of media violence on developing minds and hearts. In S. Olfman (Ed.), *Childhood lost: How American culture is failing our kids* (pp. 89–106). Westport, CT: Praeger.

Derman-Sparks, L. (1989). *Anti-bias curriculum: Tools for empowering children.* Washington, DC: National Association for the Education of Young Children.

Derman-Sparks, L., Ramsey, P., Edwards, J., & Day, C. B. (2006). *What if all the kids are White? Anti-bias multicultural education with young children and families.* New York: Teachers College Press.

Elkin, F., & Handel, G. (1989). *The child and society* (5th ed.). New York: Random House.

Federal Bureau of Investigation. (2009). *Parents' guide to Internet safety.* Retrieved February 3, 2009, from http://www.fbi.gov/publications.

Fisch, S. M. (2004). *Children's learning from educational television: Sesame Street and beyond.* Mahwah, NJ: Erlbaum.

Futrell, M. H., Gomez, J., & Bedden, D. (2003). Teaching the children of a new America: The challenge of diversity. *Phi Delta Kappan, 84*, 381–385.

Gutrel, F. (2003, September 8). Overloaded: Today's kids are tech addicts. *Newsweek, 162*(10), E4–E8.

Hamilton, S. F., Hamilton, M. A., & Pittman, K. (2004). Principles for youth development. In S. F. Hamilton & M. A. Hamilton (Eds.), *The youth development handbook: Coming of age in American communities* (pp. 3–22*).* Thousand Oaks, CA: Sage.

Herrara, C., Sipe, C. L., & McClanahan, W. S. (2000). *Mentoring school-age children.* Philadelphia: Public/Private Ventures.

Horgan, K. B. (2005). Big food, big money, big children. In S. Olfman (Ed.), *Childhood lost: How American culture is failing our kids* (pp. 123–135). Westport, CT: Praeger.

Jekielek, S. M., Moore, K., Hair, E. C., & Scarupa, H. (2002). *Mentoring: A promising strategy for youth development.* Washington, DC: Child Trends.

Karcher, M. J., Brown, R. B., & Elliot, D. W. (2004). Enlisting peers in developmental interventions: Principles and practices. In S. F. Hamilton & M. A. Hamilton (Eds.), *The youth development handbook: Coming of age in American communities* (pp. 193–214). Thousand Oaks, CA: Sage.

Kumove, L. (1966). *A preliminary study of the social implications of high-density living conditions.* Toronto, Canada: Social Planning Council of Metropolitan Toronto.

Lareau, A. (2003). *Unequal childhoods: Class, race and family life.* Berkeley: University of California Press.

Levin, D. (2005). So sexy, so soon: The sexualization of childhood. In S. Olfman (Ed.), *Childhood lost: How American culture is failing our kids* (pp. 89–106). Westport, CT: Praeger.

Lichter, D. T., & Crowley, M. L. (2002). Parenting and social networks. In M. H. Bornstein (Ed.), *Handbook of parenting: Vol 4, Social conditions and applied parenting* (2nd ed., pp. 123–148). Mahwah, NJ: Erlbaum.

Louv, R. (2005). *Last child in the woods: Saving our children from nature-deficit disorder.* Chapel Hill, NC: Algonquin Books.

Morrow, R. W. (2005). *Sesame Street and the reform of children's television.* Baltimore: Johns Hopkins University Press.

National Institute on Media and the family. (2009). *Focus on families.* Retrieved March 2, 2009, from http://www.mediafamily.org.

Olfman, S. (2005). Introduction. In S. Olfman (Ed.), *Childhood lost: How American culture is failing our kids* (pp. i–xiv). Westport, CT: Praeger.

Orpinas, P., & Horne, A. M. (2006). *Bullying prevention: Creating a positive school climate and developing social competence.* Washington, DC: American Psychological Association.

Pica, R. (2006). Physical fitness and the early childhood curriculum. *Young Children, 61*(3), 12–19.

Pipher, M. (2002). *The middle of everywhere: The world's refugees come to our town.* New York: Harcourt.

Ramsey, P. G. (2004). *Teaching and learning in a diverse world: Multicultural education for young children* (3rd ed.). New York: Teachers College Press.

Sadker, M. P., & Sadker, D. M. (2005). *Teachers, schools and society* (7th ed.). New York: McGraw-Hill.

Sleeter, C. E., & Grant, C. A. (2006). *Making choices for multicultural education: Five approaches to race, class and gender* (5th ed.). New York: Wiley.

Steglin, D. A. (2005). Making the case for play policy: Research based reasons to support play based environments. *Young Children, 60*(2), 76–85.

Swisher, R., & Whitlock, J. (2004). How neighborhoods matter for youth development. In S. F. Hamilton & M. A. Hamilton (Eds.), *The youth development handbook: Coming of age in American communities* (pp. 216–237). Thousand Oaks, CA: Sage.

U.S. Census Bureau News. (2008). *Census Bureau releases population estimates for states and counties, August 4, 2008.* Washington, DC: U.S. Bureau of the Census, U.S. Department of Commerce.

Wilson, P. P., & Leslie, R. (2001). *Premier events: Library programs that inspire elementary school patrons.* Englewood, CO: Libraries Unlimited.

CHAPTER 10

Ames, B. D., & Farrell, P. (2005). An ecological approach: A community school strategy for health promotion. *Journal of Family and Consumer Sciences, 97*(2), 29–36.

Burnette, S. (1998). Book 'em! Cops and librarians working together. *American Libraries, 29*(2), 48–50.

Comer, J. P. (1980). *School power: Implication for an intervention project.* New York: Free Press.

Daniels, E. (2002). *Family literacy parties.* Washington, DC: Children's Resources International.

Ferguson, C. (2005). *Developing a collaborative team approach to support family and community connections with schools: What can school leaders do?* Boulder, CO: Westview Press.

Gelnaw, A. (2005). Belonging: Including children of gay and lesbian parents and all children in your program. *Child Care Information Exchange, 163,* 42–45.

Gonzalez-Mena, J. (2006). *The young child in the family and the community* (4th ed.). Upper Saddle River, NJ: Merrill/Prentice Hall.

Henderson, A. T., & Mapp, K. L. (2002). *A new wave of evidence: The impact of school, family and community connections on student achievement.* Austin, TX: Southwest Educational Development Laboratory.

Henderson, A. T., Mapp, K. L., Johnson, V. R., & Davies, D. (2007). *Beyond the bake sale: The essential guide to family school partnerships.* New York: New Press.

Henniger, M. L. (2008). *Teaching young children: An introduction* (2nd ed.). Upper Saddle River, NJ: Merrill/Prentice Hall.

Hiatt-Michael, D. (2001). *Promising practices for family involvement in schools.* Greenwich, CT: Information Age.

Hiatt-Michael, D. B. (2004). Connecting schools to families of children with special needs. In D. B. Hiatt-Michael (Ed.), *Promising practices connecting schools to families of children with special needs* (pp. 1–14). Greenwich, CT: Information Age.

Joshi, A. (2005). Understanding Asian Indian families: Facilitating meaningful home–school relations. *Young Children, 60*(3), 75–78.

Kieff, J., & Wellhousen, K. (2000). Planning family involvement in early childhood programs. *Young Children, 55*(3), 18–25.

Mass, Y., & Cohan, K. A. (2006). Home connections to learning: Supporting parents as teachers. *Young Children, 61*(1), 54–55.

Mediavilla, C. (2001). *Creating a full-service home center in your library.* Chicago: American Library Association.

Morrison, G. S. (2006). *Fundamentals of early childhood education* (4th ed.). Upper Saddle River, NJ: Merrill/Prentice Hall.

Narvaez, A., Feldman, J., & Theriot, C. (2006). Virtual pre-K: Connecting home, school and community. *Young Children, 49*(4), 48–52.

Neito, S. (2002). *Language culture and teaching: Critical perspectives for a new century.* Mahwah, NJ: Erlbaum.

Powers, J. (2005). *Parent friendly early learning: Tips and strategies for working well with families.* St. Paul, MN: Redleaf Press.

Sears, J. T., & Williams, W. (1997). *Overcoming heterosexism and homophobia.* New York: Columbia University Press.

Seefeldt, C., & Barbour, N. (1998). *Early childhood education: An introduction* (4th ed.). Upper Saddle River, NJ: Merrill/Prentice Hall.

Weldin, D. J., & Tumarkin, S. R. (1999). Parent involvement: More power in the portfolio process. *Childhood Education, 75*(2), 90–95.

Wohlstetter, P., & Smith, J. (2006). Improving schools through partnerships. *Phi Delta Kappan, 86,* 464–467.

York, S. (2003). *Roots and wings: Affirming culture in early childhood program* (2nd ed.). St. Paul, MN: Redleaf Press.

CHAPTER 11

Administration for Children and Families. (2000). *Head Start Bulletin, Issue # 69.* Washington, DC: U.S. Department of Health and Human Services. Also available at http://www.headstartinfo.org.

American Legislative Exchange Council. (2008). *Report card on American education.* Washington, DC: Author. Retrieved February 20, 2009, from http://www.alec.org.

Brandt, L. (2008). HABLA program. *Today at UCI,* July 18, 2008. Retrieved February 17, 2009, from http://today.uce.edu/features.

Bulkley, K. E., & Wohlstetter, P. (2004). *Taking account of charter schools: What's happened and what's next?* New York: Teachers College Press.

Cadwell, L. B. (1997). *Bringing Reggio Emilia home: An innovative approach to early childhood education.* New York: Teachers College Press.

Center for Education Reform. (2009). *Charter schools.* Retrieved February 20, 2009, from http://www.edreform.com.

Children's Defense Fund. (2006). *CDF Freedom Schools.* Retrieved May 21, 2006, from http://www.freedomschools.org/programs.

Children's Defense Fund. (2009). *About the CDF Freedom Schools program.* Retrieved February 11, 2009, from http://www.childrensdefense.org/helping-Americas-children/cdf-freedom-schools-program.

Collins, R. C. (1984, April 8). *Head Start: A review of research with implications for practice in early childhood education.* Paper presented at the annual meeting of the American Educational Research Association, New Orleans. [ERIC Document Reproduction Service, #ED245-833.]

Comer, J. P. (1980). *School power: Implications of an intervention project.* New York: Free Press.

Comer, J. P. (1988). *Maggie's American dream: The life and times of a Black family.* New York: New American Library.

Comer, J. P. (1997). *Waiting for a miracle: Why schools can't solve our problems and how we can.* New York: Penguin/Putnam.

Comer, J. P., Ben-Avie, M., Haynes, N., & Joyner, E. T. (Eds.). (1999). *Child by child: The Comer process for change in education.* New York: Teachers College Press.

Comer, J. P., & Haynes, N. M. (1991). Parent involvement in schools: An ecological approach. *Elementary School Journal, 91,* 271–277.

Comer, J. P., Haynes, N. M., & Joyner, E. T. (1996). The school development program. In J. P. Comer, N. M. Haynes, E. T. Joyner, & M. Ben-Avie (Eds.), *Rallying the whole village: The Comer process for reforming education* (pp. 1–27). New York: Teachers College Press.

Comer, J. P., Haynes, N., Joyner, E. T., & Ben-Avie, M. (1996). *Rallying the whole village: The Comer process for reforming education.* New York: Teachers College Press.

Dryfoos, J. D. (1998). *Full service schools: A revolution in health and social services for children, youth and families.* San Francisco: Jossey-Bass.

Dryfoos, J. D. (2003). A community school in action. *Reclaiming Children & Youth, 11*(4), 203–205.

Dryfoos, J. D., Quinn, J., & Barkin, C. (2005). *Community schools in action.* New York: Oxford University Press.

Edmiaston, R. K., & Fitzgerald, L. (2000). How Reggio Emilia encourages inclusion. *Educational Leadership, 58*(1), 66–69.

Edwards, C. P., Gandini, L., & Forman, G. (1998). *The hundred languages of children: The Reggio Emilia approach* (2nd ed.). Greenwich, CT: Ablex.

Epstein, J. L. (1999). *School and family partnerships: Preparing educators and improving schools.* Boulder, CO: Westview Press.

Epstein, J. L. (2001). *School, family and community partnership: Preparing educators and improving schools.* Boulder, CO: Westview Press.

Epstein, J. L., Sanders, M. G., Simon, B., Salinas, K., Jansorn, N., & vanVoorhis, F. (2002). *School, family, and community partnerships: Your handbook for action* (2nd ed.). Thousand Oaks, CA: Corwin Press.

Epstein, J. L., Sanders, M., Sheldon, S., Salinas, K., Jansorn, N., vanVoorhis, F., et al. (2008). *School, family, and community partnerships: Your handbook for action* (3rd ed.). Thousand Oaks, CA: Corwin Press.

Even Start (2009). *Even Start :Program description.* Retrieved January 30, 2009, from http://www.ed.gov/programs/evenstartformula/index.html.

Gandini, L. (1997). Foundations of the Reggio Emilia approach. In J. Hendrick (Ed.), *First steps toward teaching the Reggio way* (pp. 14–25). Upper Saddle River, NJ: Merrill/Prentice Hall.

Giovanni, D. (2001). Traces of childhood: A child's diary. In L. Gandini & C. Edwards (Eds.), *The Italian approach to infant/toddler care* (pp. 146–152). New York: Teachers College Press.

Hendrick, J. (Ed.). (1997). *First steps toward teaching the Reggio way.* Upper Saddle River, NJ: Merrill/Prentice Hall.

Hendrick, J. (Ed.). (2004). *Next steps toward teaching the Reggio way: Accepting the challenge to change.* Upper Saddle River: NJ: Merrill/Prentice Hall.

Inselberg, R., & Larson, D. (1988). Maternal language and children's receptive language. *Home Economics Research Journal, 16*(3), 205–214.

Kauffman Foundation. (2008). *New Kauffman study shows success of CDF Freedom Schools program.* Retrieved February 2, 2009, from http://www.kauffman.org.

Lovell, J., & Kluger, J. (1994). *Lost moon: The perilous voyage of Apollo 13.* Boston: Houghton Mifflin.

Meier, D. (2002). *In schools we trust: Creating communities of learning in an era of testing and standardization.* Boston: Beacon Press.

Murphy, J., & Shiffman, C. D. (2002). *Understanding and assessing the charter school movement.* New York: Teachers College Press.

Naiskov, A. (2002, June 16). Charter schools share ideas. *Boston Globe*, p. E6.

National Head Start Association. (2009). *Head Start fact sheets.* Retrieved January 30, 2009, from http://www.nhsa.org.

New, R. S. (2003). Reggio Emilia: New ways to think about schooling. *Educational Leadership, 60*(7), 34–39.

Ramirez-Smith, C. (1995). Stopping the cycle of failure: The Comer model. *Educational Leadership, 52*(5), 14–19.

Rubin, H. (2002). *Collaborative leadership: Developing effective partnerships in communities and schools.* Thousand Oaks, CA: Corwin Press.

Sanders, M. G. (2006). *Building school–community relationships: Collaborations for school success.* Thousand Oaks, CA: Corwin Press.

School of Social Sciences, University of California, Irvine. (2009). *HABLA: A preschool intervention program.* Retrieved February 17, 2009, from http://www.socsci.uci.edu/habla.

Schorr, J. (2002). *Hard lessons: The promises of an inner city charter school.* New York: Ballantine Books.

Schweinhart, L. J., & Weikart, D. P. (1997). *Lasting differences: The High/Scope preschool curriculum comparison study through age 3* (Monographs of the High/Scope Educational Research Foundation, 12). Ypsilanti, MI: High/Scope.

Spaggiari, S. (1998). The community–teacher partnership and its expansion in the governance of the schools. In C. Edwards, L. Gandini, & G. Forman (Eds.), *The hundred languages of children: The Reggio Emilia approach—Advanced reflections* (pp. 99–113). Greenwich, CT: Ablex.

Taxim, A. (2008). HABLA program builds on the idea: More words make better readers. *Orange County Register* (July 2, 2008, pp. 1, 3). Retrieved February 17, 2009, from http://today.uci.edu/features.

U.S. Charter Schools. (2009). *New research and reports.* Retrieved February 17, 2009, from http://www.uscharterschools.org.

U.S. Department of Education. (2006). *National Coalition for Parent Involvement in Education (NCPIE) reports.* Retrieved February 20, 2009, from http://www.ncpie.org.

Vanourek, G. (2005). *State of the charter movement, 2005: Trends, issues and indicators.* Washington, DC: National Alliance for Public Charter Schools.

Wang, M. C., & Walberg, H. J. (2001). Epilogue. In M. C. Wang & H. J. Walberg (Eds.), *School choices or best systems: What improves education?* (pp. 396–399). Mahwah, NJ: Erlbaum.

Warren, M. R. (2005). Communities and schools: A new view of urban education reform. *Harvard Educational Review, 75*(2), 133–173.

Weikart, D. P. (2004). Head Start and evidence-based educational models. In E. Zigler & S. Styfco (Eds.), *The Head Start debates* (pp. 143–159). Baltimore: Paul H. Brookes.

Westinghouse Learning Corporation–Ohio University. (1969). *The impact of Head Start.* Springfield, VA: U.S. Department of Commerce, Clearinghouse for Federal Scientific and Technical Information.

Zigler, E., & Styfco, S. J. (Eds.). (2004). *The Head Start debates.* Baltimore: Paul H. Brookes.

NAME INDEX

A

Adelman, H. S., 238, 254–255
American Anthropological Association, 67
American Association of University Women, 39
Ames, B. D., 292
Anderson, W., 111–112
Andrews, R. K., 9
Anstine-Templeton, R., 155
Apple, M. W., 171
Asato, J., 51
Association for Childhood Education International (ACEI), 19

B

Banks, L. R., 54, 96, 98, 187
Barbour, N., 104, 193, 280, 289
Bardige, B., 104–105
Barkin, C., 324
Bartholomae, S., 110
Beaty, J. J., 183
Bedden, D., 259
Bell, C. C., 192
Ben-Avie, M., 305, 331
Bergmann, B., 127
Berk, L. E., 9
Berlin, I., 48, 50
Berns, R. M., 207, 209
Bianchi, S. M., 57–58, 62, 75, 91, 93, 111–113, 122
Bigner, J. J., 256
Blakeslee, S., 111
Blank, H., 45
Bock, J. D., 61
Bogenschneider, K., 243
Boger, J. C., 50
Bookman, A., 95, 97, 254
Borkowski, J. G., 7
Bornstein, M. H., 9
Bowen, M., 26, 90
Brandt, L., 329
Bravo, E., 113
Bredekamp, S., 133
Breitborde, M. L., 42
Britner, P. A., 117
Bronfenbrenner, U., 8, 26, 30, 182, 203, 212, 238

Brophy, J. E., 192
Brown, H., 7, 256
Bruer, J. T., 15, 38
Bulkley, K. E., 330
Burnette, S., 298

C

Cadwell, L. B., 319
Casbergue, R. M., 183
Casey, A. E., 61
Casey, M. A., 53
Casper, L. M., 57–58, 62, 93, 111–112, 122
Cavanaugh, R. A., 154
Chavkin, N. F., 7
Chinn, P., 47, 49, 52, 54, 79–80, 82
Christakis, D., 220
Christian, L. G., 90
Clark, R. M., 103, 106, 182, 211
Clifford, R. M., 125, 144
Cochran, M., 197, 243–244, 254
Cohan, K. A., 290
Cohen, C., 143
Cohler, B. J., 65
Coleman, E., 5, 16
Coleman, J. S., 23, 78
Coleman, M., 83
Coles, R., 182, 186
Coles, R. L., 70, 194
Collins, R. C., 310
Comer, J. P., 295, 303–305, 311–316
Coontz, S., 60
Copple, C., 133
Corbett, T., 243
Crawford, K., 77
Crosbie-Burnett, M., 62, 111
Crowley, M. L., 48, 73, 254
Cruickshank, D., 192
Cryer, D., 125, 144
Culatta, R., 77

D

Damon, W., 182
Daniels, E., 290
Danzberger, J., 44
Darby, J., 184
Davis, T. J., 35, 37, 47–48, 50, 52
DeGaetano, G., 94, 249
deRamirez, L. L., 187

Derman-Sparks, L., 38, 53, 260
Desmond, R., 10–11
DeVita, C. J., 47, 83
Dewey, J., 27
Dilworth, M. E., 7
Dimidijian, V. J., 77
Dodson, L., 113
Doll, R. C., 202
Doorlag, D., 147
Dowd, N. E., 222
Dowling, T. E., 38
Dryfoos, J. D., 323–325
Dubrow, N., 194
Durkin, D. D., 5

E

Eccles, J., 6
Edmiaston, R. K., 319
Edwards, C., 316, 319
Edwards, J. O., 38, 42, 46, 52, 319
Egan, R. W., 152
Eitzer, D. S., 34, 38
Elkin, F., 256
Elliot, D. W., 256
Epstein, J. L., 303, 306, 319–322, 328, 333
Erickson, F., 67
Ernsbarger, S. C., 154

F

Falvey, M. A., 168
Farrell, P., 292
Fass, P. S., 38–39
Feldman, J., 290
Ferguson, C., 289
Fiese, B. H., 217
Fine, M. A., 76, 111, 181
Finnerty, J., 53
Fisch, S. M., 249
Fitzgerald, L., 319
Forman, G., 319
Fox, J., 110
Fried, R. L., 234
Futrell, M. H., 259

G

Gabe, T., 64
Gallup, A. M., 4
Gandara, P., 51

SUBJECT INDEX